CASEBOOK ON
LAND LAW

CASEBOOK ON

LAND LAW

Meryl Thomas BA, LLM

Lecturer in Law, University of Wales College of Cardiff

BLACKSTONE PRESS LIMITED

First published in Great Britain 1992 by Blackstone Press Limited,
9-15 Aldine Street, London W12 8AW. Telephone 081-740 1173

© M. Thomas, 1992

ISBN: 1 85431 193 X

British Library Cataloguing in Publication Data
A CIP catalogue record for this book is available from the British Library

Typeset by Style Photosetting, Mayfield, East Sussex
Printed by Redwood Press Limited, Melksham, Wiltshire

All rights reserved. No part of this book may be reproduced or transmitted in any form or by any means, electronic or mechanical, including photocopying, recording, or any information storage or retrieval system without prior permission from the publisher.

CONTENTS

Preface ix

Acknowledgments x

Table of Cases xi

Table of Statutes xxv

Table of Statutory Instruments xxx

1 Introduction 1
Section 1: the classification of property 1
Section 2: the meaning of land 2
Section 3: development of equity 2
Section 4: the contributions of equity to land law 2
Section 5: the doctrine of notice 3

2 The 1925 Legislation 14
Section 1: the doctrine of tenures and estates 14
Section 2: outline of the 1925 legislation and its effects 14
Section 3: protection of equitable interests 23
Section 4: effect of registration of land charges 41

3 Registration of Title 53
Section 1: introduction 53
Section 2: relationship between the Land Registration Act 1925 and the Land Charges Act 1925 (now Land Charges Act 1972) 53
Section 3: the register 54
Section 4: categories of interests in registered land 55
Section 5: rectification of title 95
Section 6: indemnity 98
Section 7: priorities 99

4 Acquisition of Land: Contract and Conveyance   102
Section 1: pre-contract procedure   102
Section 2: the contract   103
Section 3: the conveyance or transfer   113
Section 4: conveyance to self   116
Section 5: transfer of equitable interests   117
Section 6: incomplete transfers or creations   117
Section 7: options to purchase land   119

5 Acquisition of Land: Adverse Possession   126
Section 1: introduction   126
Section 2: the running of time   127
Section 3: the nature of the interest acquired   142
Section 4: successive squatters   147
Section 5: adverse possession and registered land   148

6 Leasehold Interests and Covenants   154
Section 1: essentials for a valid lease   154
Section 2: distinction between a lease and a licence   170
Section 3: form of a lease   183
Section 4: types of leases and tenancies   185
Section 5: termination of leases and tenancies   189
Section 6: remedies for breach of covenants   193
Section 7: enforceability of leasehold covenants   198
Section 8: enforcement of leasehold covenants in an agreement for a lease   209
Section 9: commonholds   215

7 Licences   216
Section 1: the nature of a licence   216
Section 2: categories of licences   216

8 Strict Settlements and Trusts for Sale   248
Section 1: introduction   248
Section 2: strict settlements   249
Section 3: trusts for sale   271
Section 4: overreaching — strict settlements and trusts for sale   282
Section 5: nature of a beneficiary's interest under a trust for sale   286

9 Co-ownership of Land   294
Section 1: introduction   294
Section 2: position in law and equity   297
Section 3: creation of a joint tenancy   300
Section 4: severance of a joint tenancy   302
Section 5: termination of co-ownership   310
Section 6: Law of Property Act 1925, s. 30   311
Section 7: matrimonial and quasi matrimonial property   332

10 Easements and Profits à Prendre   342
Section 1: the nature of an easement   342
Section 2: characteristics of a valid easement   342
Section 3: factors which negate an easement   349

Section 4: valid legal easements 354
Section 5: acquisition of easements 354
Section 6: extinguishment of easements 390
Section 7: profits à prendre 391

11 Freehold Covenants 392

Section 1: general 392
Section 2: enforceability between the original parties 392
Section 3: enforcement of covenants at common law 394
Section 4: enforceability of covenants in equity 401
Section 5: discharge of restrictive covenants 421
Section 6: registered land 423

12 Mortgages 424

Section 1: introduction 424
Section 2: creation of a mortgage 424
Section 3: the rights of the mortgagor 428
Section 4: the rights of the legal mortgagee 447
Section 5: rights of an equitable mortgagee 464
Section 6: discharge of mortgages 468
Section 7: priority of mortgages 469
Section 8: mortgages of registered land 481

Index 485

PREFACE

This book has been written for students of land law at undergraduate level or those studying land law for professional examinations. The materials contained in it cover the traditional university land law course and the object of the book is to provide the student with a comprehensive selection of cases and extracts of judgments referred to in such courses.

Land law is a subject where a thorough knowledge and insight into the case law is essential for an understanding of the areas but, in my experience, students are reluctant to spend hours in a library sifting through the judgments of cases in order to understand the principles of land law. The aim of this book is to shortcut the 'sifting' process, by selecting the most relevant extracts of the cases and, where appropriate, adding explanatory or further notes for the student.

All cases are supplemented by linking text, notes and questions aimed to stimulate the student's thoughts and ideas on land law, and references for further reading. Extracts from statutes are included where appropriate. The cases that have been selected are those I regard as the standard cases in land law, but particular emphasis has been placed on the more recent decisions in the courts.

The book is designed to be used in conjunction with lecture and tutorial notes and a standard textbook, although it is possible to use it without the latter.

It is not possible to mention everyone who has assisted in the preparation of this work, but the following deserve particular mention. First, my research assistant, Brian Dowrick, for the substantial assistance which he gave me in writing this book; my husband Bruce who greatly helped at the proof reading stage and finally the ever-patient Kathryn Bates for typing the manuscript and performing other secretarial duties for me.

The law is as stated on 2 October 1992.

Meryl Thomas

ACKNOWLEDGMENTS

The publishers and author would like to thank the following for permission to reproduce extracts from the publications listed below:

The Incorporated Council of Law Reporting for England and Wales — *Weekly Law Reports* and *The Law Reports*.
The Estates Gazette — *The Estates Gazette Law Reports*.
Blackwell Publishers — *Modern Law Review*.
Butterworth Law Publishers Ltd — *All England Law Reports, Law Times Reports, New Law Journal* reports, LEXIS and extracts from the following textbooks: Underhill and Hayton, *Law of Trusts and Trustees*; Gray, *Elements of Land Law*; and Cheshire and Burn, *Modern Law of Real Property*.
Sweet & Maxwell Ltd — *Property and Compensation Reports, English Reports* and an extract from Megarry and Wade, *The Law of Real Property*.

TABLE OF CASES

Page numbers relating to extracts from cases reproduced or relating to references in the notes are printed in bold type.

Abbey National Building Society v Cann [1990] 1 All ER 1085	**76, 81,** 99
Abbeyfield (Harpenden) Society Ltd v Woods [1968] 1 WLR 374	167
Ackroyd v Smith (1850) 10 CB 164	343, 345, 346
Addiscombe Garden Estates Ltd v Crabbe [1958] 1 QB 513	166, 174
Adler v Blackman [1953] 1 QB 146	**185**
AG Securities v Vaughan [1988] 3 All ER 1058; [1988] 3 WLR 1205	**174,** 177, 180
AG v Balliol College, Oxford (1744) 9 Mod Rep 407	243
Alan Estates v W.G. Stores [1982] Ch 511	116
Aldin v Latimer Clark, Muirhead & Co. [1894] 2 Ch 437	347
Aldred's Case (1610) 9 Co. Rep 57b	347, 351
Aldridge v Wright [1929] 2 KB 117	365
Aldrington Garages Ltd v Fielder (1978) 37 P & CR 461	168
Alefounder's WT, Re, [1927] 1 Ch 360	254
Allan v Liverpool Overseers (1874) LR 9 QB 180	163
Allen v Greenwood [1980] Ch 119	**385**
Allen v Roughley (1955) 94 CLR 98; [1956] 29	142
Angus v Dalton (1877) 3 QBD 85; (1878) 4 QBD 162; (1881) 6 App Cas 740	377, 378, 380
Anns v Merton London Borough Council [1978] AC 728	460
Antoniades v Villiers [1988] 3 WLR 1205; [1988] 3 All ER 1058	175, 180
Applegate v Moss [1971] 1 QB 406	141
Argyle Building Society v Hammond (1985) 49 P & CR 148	**96**
Arlesford Trading Co. Ltd v Servansingh [1971] 3 All ER 113	**205**
Ashburn Anstalt v Arnold [1989] Ch 1; [1988] 2 WLR 706	71, 157, 179, **230,** 231, **234**
Asher v Whitlock (1865) LR 1 QB 1	**147**
Attorney-General to the Prince of Wales v Collom [1916] 2 KB 193	240
Attorney-General v Antrobus [1905] 2 Ch 188	345
Attorney-General v Jacobs Smith [1895] 2 QB 341	4
Austerberry v Oldham Corp (1885) 29 ChD 750	396, **397,** 401
Austin-Fell v Austin-Fell [1990] 2 All ER 455	**318**
Bailey v Barnes [1894] 1 Ch 25	5, 6, 7, 459
Bailey v Stephens (1862) 12 CB(NS) 91	343, 346
Bailey, Re, [1977] 2 All ER 26	326, 330
Ballard's Conveyance, Re, [1937] Ch 473	**406**
Bank Negara Indonesia v Hoalim [1973] 2 MLJ 3	240
Bannister v Bannister [1948] 2 All ER 133	94, 95, 229, 230, **232,** 233, 234, 235, 250

Barclays Bank plc v Tennet [1984] CA Transcript	448
Barclays Bank v Bird [1954] Ch 274	465
Barclays Bank v Taylor [1974] Ch 137	**100**
Barker v Richardson (1821) 4 B & A 579	380
Barnes v Barratt [1970] 2 QB 657	162
Barnett v Hassett [1981] 1 WLR 1385	**36**
Barnhart v Greenshields (1853) 9 Moo PCC 18	72, 79
Barrow's Case (1880) 14 ChD 432	13
Barry v Hasseldine [1952] Ch 835	**363**
Barton v Morris [1985] 2 All ER 1032	301, **310**
Bassett v Nosworthy (1673) Rep temp Finch 102	4
Baxter v Four Oaks Properties Ltd [1965] Ch 816	420
Bayley v GWR Co. (1884) 26 ChD 434	368
Beatty v Guggenheim Exploration Co. (1919) 225 NY 380	229
Bedson v Bedson [1965] 2 QB 666	287, 304, 306, 316
Beesly v Hallwood Estates Ltd [1961] Ch 105, [1960] 1 WLR 549	116, 119, 123
Beggan v McDonald 2 LR Ir 560	375
Berkley Road, 88, Re, London, NW9 [1971] Ch 648	**302**
Bernard v Josephs [1982] 3 All ER 162	**332**
Berwick & Co. v Price [1905] 1 Ch 632	45, 470
Beswick v Beswick [1968] AC 58	229, 393
Bibby J. & Sons Ltd v Wawrszkowicz (unreported) 28 October 1957	291
Bickford v Parson (1848) 5 CB 920	212
Biddle v Bond (1865) 6 B & S 225	189
Biggs v Hoddinott [1898] 2 Ch 307	435, 437
Billson v Residential Apartments Ltd [1992] 2 WLR 15	197
Binions v Evans [1972] Ch 359	39, 94, 95, **227**, 230, 233, 235, 236, 250
Bird v Syme-Thomson [1979] 1 WLR 440	73
Bird, Re, [1927] 1 Ch 210	250
Birmingham and District Land Co. v London and North Western Railway Co. (1888) 40 ChD 268	240
Blacklocks v J B Developments (Godalming) Ltd [1981] 3 All ER 392	67
Bland v Moseley (1587) cited in 9 Co. Rep 58a	350
Bolton v Bolton (1879) 11 ChD 968	362
Booker v Palmer [1942] 2 All ER 674	164, 225
Booth v Turle (1873) LR 16 Eq 182	232
Borman v Griffith [1930] 1 Ch 493	360, 369
Boydell v Gillespie (1970) 216 EG 1505	325, 330
Boyer v Warbey [1953] 1 QB 234	**211**
Boyer's Settled Estates [1916] 2 Ch 404	228
Brace v Duchess of Marlborough (1728) 2 P Wms 491	6
Bradburn v Lindsay [1983] 2 All ER 408	352
Bradley v Carritt [1903] AC 253	437, 441
Bridges v Mees [1957] Ch 475	**65**, 67
Bridgett & Hayes' Contract, Re, [1928] Ch 163	263
Bridle v Ruby [1988] 3 All ER 64	381
Bright v Walker (1834) 1 CM & R 211	375
Brinnard v Ewens [1987] 2 EGLR 67	238
Bristol & West Building Society v Henning [1985] 1 WLR 778	99
British Railways Board v Glass [1965] Ch 538	**386**
Brown v Gould [1972] 1 Ch 53	162
Browne v Flower [1911] 1 Ch 219	347
Browne v Ryan [1901] 2 IR 653	438
Browne v Warner (1808) 14 Ves 409	228
Brunner v Greenslade [1971] Ch 993	418, **420**
Bryant v Foot (1867) LR 2 QB 161	**376**
Bryant v Lefever (1879) 4 CPD 172	**348**

Table of Cases

Buchanan-Wollaston's Conveyance, Re, [1939] 2 All ER 302; [1939] Ch 738
    278, 287, 299, 312, 313, 314, 315, 324
Buckinghamshire County Council v Moran [1989] 3 WLR 152; [1989] 2 All ER 225
    128, 131, 132
Bull v Bull [1955] 1 QB 234   279, **298**, 299, 301
Burgess v Rawnsley [1975] 1 Ch 429   **307**, 309
Burke v Burke [1974] 2 All ER 944   314, 321, 326, 327
Burnett (Marjorie) Ltd v Barclay (1981) 258 EG 642   **160**
Burns v Burns [1984] 1 All ER 244; [1984] Ch 317   **336, 337**
Burrows v Lang [1901] 2 Ch 502   358
Button's Lease, Re, [1964] Ch 263   200

Cable v Bryant [1908] 1 Ch 259   347
Calgary & Edmonton Land Co. Ltd v Dobinson [1974] 1 All ER 484   27, 29
Campbell v Holyland (1877) 7 ChD 166   **463**
Canadian Imperial Bank of Commerce v Bello, *The Times*, 18 November 1991   157
Cargill v Gotts [1981] 1 WLR 441   370
Carne's Settled Estates, Re, [1899] 1 Ch 324   228, 255
Carr v Foster (1842) 3 QB 581   383
Carr v London & North Western Railway Co. (1875) LR 10 CP 307   214
Carter v Carter (1857) 3 K & J 617   6
Casborne v Scarfe (1738) 1 Atk 603   **429**
Catling, Re, [1931] 2 Ch 359   255
Caton v Caton (1867) LR 2 HL 127   110
Caunce v Caunce [1969] 1 WLR 286   11, 34, 37, 39, 73, 285
Cave v Cave (1880) 15 ChD 639   4, 5
Cedar Holdings Ltd v Green [1981] Ch 129   **292**, 293
Celsteel Ltd v Alton House Holdings [1985] 1 WLR 204   **63, 64, 65, 389**
Central Estates (Belgravia) Ltd v Woolgar (No. 2) [1972] 3 All ER 610   196
Central London Property Trust Ltd v High Trees House Ltd [1947] KB 130   240
Centrax Trustees Ltd v Ross [1979] 2 All ER 952   452
Chandler v Kerley [1978] 2 All ER 942   221
Chaprionière v Lambert [1917] 2 Ch 356   108
Charles Rickards Ltd v Oppenhaim [1950] 1 KB 616   240
Chasemore v Richards (1859) 7 HL Cas 349   380
Chatsworth Estates Co. v Fewell [1931] 1 Ch 224   421
Chattock v Muller (1878) 8 ChDiv 177   232
Cheah Theam Swee v Equiticorp Finance Group Ltd [1991] 4 All ER 989   480
Cheapside Land Development Co. Ltd v Messels Service Co. [1977] 2 All ER 62   123
Cheshire Lines Committee v Lewis & Co. 50 LJQB 121   156
Chhokar v Chhokar [1984] FLR 313   77
Chowood Ltd v Lyall (No. 2) [1930] 2 Ch 156   **96**, 99
Chowood's Registered Land, Re, [1933] Ch 574   99
Church of England Building Society v Piskor [1954] Ch 553   **186**, 446
Citibank Trust Ltd v Ayivor [1987] 3 All ER 241   **448, 450**
Citro, Re, [1990] 3 All ER 952   **323**, 331
City of London Building Society v Flegg [1987] 2 WLR 1266; [1988] AC 54
    66, 74, **85**, 285
City Permanent Building Society v Miller [1952] Ch 840   65
Cityland & Property (Holdings) Ltd v Dabrah [1968] Ch 166   **441**
Clancy v Byrne (1877) IR 11 CL 355   375
Clark v Wright (1737) 1 Atk 12   105
Clayton v Illingworth (1853) 10 Hare 451   213
Clifford v Hoare (1874) LR 9 CP 362   389
Clore v Theatrical Properties Ltd v Westby & Co. Ltd [1936] 3 All ER 483
    224, 227, 229, 230, 231
Coatsworth v Johnson (1886) 55 LJ QB 220   119, **184**

Table of Cases

Cobb v Lane [1952] 1 TLR 1037	71, 165
Cochrane v Verner (1895) 29 ILT 571	351
Colchester Borough Council v Smith [1991] 2 All ER 29 (first instance)	131, 179
Colchester Borough Council v Smith [1992] 2 All ER 561 (CA)	132, 182
Coldunell Ltd v Gallon [1986] 1 All ER 429	443
Congleton Corp v Pattison (1808) 10 East 130	395, 403
Cooper v Critchley [1955] Ch 431	110, 287, 289, 290, 291, 293
Copeland v Greenhalf [1952] 1 Ch 488	344, **352**, 353, 354
Cornish v Midland Bank plc [1985] 3 All ER 513	**430**
Corporation of London v Riggs (1880) 13 ChD 798	**363**
Cottage Holiday Associates v Customs and Excise Commissioners [1983] 1 QB 735	155
Cowper v Cowper (1734) 2 P Wms 753	298
Crabb v Arun District Council [1976] Ch 179	**239**, 337
Crago v Julian [1992] 1 All ER 744	114
Cross v Lewis (1823) 2 B & C 686	379, 380
Crossley & Sons Ltd v Lightowler (1867) LR 2 Ch 478	364, 366
Crow v Wood [1971] 1 QB 77	**349, 400**
Cuckmere Brick Co. Ltd v Mutual Finance Ltd [1971] Ch 949	**460**
Cummins v Fletcher (1879) 14 ChD 699	**466**
Dalton v Angus & Co. (1881) 6 App Cas 740	347, 350, 351, **370**, 372, 373
Daly v Edwardes (1900) 83 LT 548	231
Darwin v Upton 2 Will Saund 506	379
Davenport's Case (1608) 8 Co. Rep 144 b	145
David v Sabin [1893] 1 Ch 523	145
Davies v Du Paver [1953] 1 QB 184	372, 384
Davies v Marshall (1861) 10 CB(NS) 697	390
Davies v Sweet [1962] 2 QB 300	104
Davis v Whitby [1973] 1 WLR 629	374
Davy doe dem v Oxenham 7 M & W 131	144
Dearle v Hall (1823-8) 3 Russ 1	5, 16, **473**, 475, 476
Dennis v McDonald [1981] 2 All ER 632	296
Dennis, Re, (a Bankrupt) [1992] 3 WLR 204	307
Densham (a bankrupt), Re, [1975] 3 All ER 726; [1975] 1 WLR 1519	320, 326, 330
DHN Food Distributors Ltd v Tower Hamlets BC [1976] 1 WLR 852	235
Diligent Finance Co. Ltd v Alleyne (1972) 23 P & CR 346	48
Dillwyn v Llewelyn (1862) 4 De GF & J 517	238, 242, 243
Diment v NH Foot Ltd [1974] 2 All ER 785	372, 374
Dodsworth v Dodsworth (1973) 228 EG 115	243
Dolphin's Conveyance, Re, [1970] Ch 654	420
Donoghue v Stevenson [1932] AC 562	460
Dorset Yacht Co. Ltd v Home Office [1970] AC 1004	460
Dougal v McCarthy [1893] 1 QB 736	**185**
Downes v Grazebrook 3 Mer 200	461
Draper's Conveyance, Re, Niham v Porter [1967] 3 All ER 853; [1969] 1 Ch 486	303, 307, 308, 309
Dresden Estates v Collinson [1987] 1 EGLR 45	**181**
Dudley (Lord) and Ward v Lady Dudley (1705) Prec Ch 241	2
Duke of Marlborough, Re, [1894] 2 Ch 133	232
Duke v Robson [1973] 1 WLR 267	**458**
Duncan v Louch (1845) 6 QB 904	345
Dundee Harbour Trustees v Dougall (1852) 1 Macq 317	127
Dyce v Lady James Hay (1852) 1 Macq 305	348
E & GC Ltd v Bate (1935) 79 Law J News 203	398
Eaton v Swansea Waterworks Co. (1851) 17 QBD 267	372
Ecclesiastical Commissioners for England's Conveyance, Re, [1936] Ch 430	393

Table of Cases

Case	Pages
Ecclesiastical Commissioners of England and Wales v Rowe (1880) 5 App Cas 736	145, 146
Ecclesiastical Commissioners' for England v Treemer [1893] 1 Ch 166	146
Eden Park Estates Ltd v Longman, Unreported, 19 May 1980	72
Edwards v Barrington (1901) 85 LT 650	231
Elias v Mitchell [1972] Ch 652	**288**, 293
Ellenborough Park, Re, [1956] Ch 131	**342**, 348
Elliott v Johnson (1868) LR 2 QB 120	211
Elliston v Reacher [1908] 2 Ch 374	400, 418, **419**
Epps v Esso Petroleum Co. Ltd [1973] 1 WLR 1071	**80, 81, 97**
Equity and Law Home Loans Ltd v Prestidge [1992] 1 All ER 909	74, 76, 99
Errington v Errington and Woods [1952] 1 KB 290	164, 165, 166, 167, **225**, 226, 227, 228, 229, 230, 231
Esso Petroleum Co. Ltd v Harper's Garage (Stourport) Ltd [1968] AC 269	**444**
Evans v Bicknell (1801) 6 Ves 174	475
Evers's Trust, Re [1980] 3 All ER 399	**312**, 315, 317
Eves v Eves [1975] 1 WLR 1338; [1975] 3 All ER 768	336, 337, 339, 340
Facchini v Bryson [1952] 1 TLR 1386	165, 166, 171
Fairclough v Swan Brewery Co. Ltd [1912] AC 565	434, **435**
Fairweather v St Marylebone Property Co. Ltd [1963] AC 510	143, 144, 147, 153
Farrand v Yorkshire Banking Co. (1888) 40 ChD 182	473
Farrar v Farrars Ltd (1888) 40 ChD 395	**461**
Farrell v Green (1974) 232 EG 587	109, 111
Federated Homes v Mill Lodge Properties Ltd [1980] 1 All ER 371	396, 401, **409**, 413, 414, 415, 417
First National Securities Ltd v Hegerty [1984] 3 All ER 641 aff'd [1985] 1 QB 850	317, 427
Fleetwood v Hull (1889) 23 QBD 35	199, 395
Flight v Thomas (1841) 8 Cl & Fin 231	383
Formby v Barker [1903] 2 Ch 539	404, 408
Forsey and Hollebone's Contract, Re, [1927] 2 Ch 379	49
Foster v Reeves [1892] 2 QB 255	213
Foster v Robinson [1951] 1 KB 149	71, **191**, 226, 228, 230
Four-Maids Ltd v Dudley Marshall (Properties) Ltd [1957] 1 Ch 317	447
Fox, Re, [1913] 2 Ch 75	288
Frank Warr & Co. v London CC [1904] 1 KB 713	231
Freer v Unwins Ltd [1976] Ch 288	**98**, 99
Frewen, Re, [1926] Ch 580	256
Friary, Holroyd and Healey's Breweries v Singleton [1899] 1 Ch 86	214
Gadd's Land Transfer, Re, [1966] Ch 56	404
Gallenga WT, Re, [1938] 1 All ER 106	256
Gardner v Hodgson's Kingston Brewery Co. Ltd [1903] AC 229	**370**, 372
Gayford v Moffatt LR 4 Ch 133	375
Giles v County Buildings Constructors (Hertford) Ltd [1971] 22 P & CR 978	387
Gissing v Gissing [1970] 2 All ER 780; [1971] AC 886	229, 231, 234, 334, 335, 336, 337, 339
Goddard's Case (1584) 2 Co. Rep 4b	115
Goldberg v Edwards [1950] Ch 247	**359**
Goodall's Settlement, Re, [1909] 1 Ch 440	275
Goodman v Gallant [1986] Fam 106	**332**
Gorman (a bankrupt), Re, [1990] 1 WLR 616	307
Grace Rymer Investments v Waite [1958] Ch 831	184, 482
Graham v Philcox [1984] QB 747	**388**
Grand Junction Co. Ltd v Bates [1954] 2 QB 160	426
Grant v Edwards [1986] Ch 638	**334**, 339, 340, 341
Greasley v Cooke [1980] 3 All ER 710; [1980] 1 WLR 1306	223, **239**, 242
Greater London Council v Connolly [1970] 2 QB 100	**162**
Greaves v Tofield (1880) 14 ChD 563	46

Table of Cases

Greenhi Builders v Allen [1979] 1 WLR 156	28
Grey v Inland Revenue Commissioners [1960] AC 1	45
Grierson v National Provincial Bank of England Ltd [1913] 2 Ch 18	471
Griffith v Pelton [1958] Ch 205	119, 120, 122
Griffiths v Williams (1977) 248 EG 947	242
Grigsby v Melville [1974] 1 WLR 80	**353**
Gurasz v Gurasz [1970] P 11	36
Habib Bank Ltd v Tailor [1982] 1 WLR 1218	**451**
Hadjiloucas v Crean [1987] 3 All ER 1008	**174**, 176
Hall v Lichfield Brewery Co. 49 LJ (Ch) 655	347
Halsall v Brizell [1957] Ch 169	94, 245, **399**
Hamilton v Geraghty (1901) 1 SR NSW Eq 81	246
Hammersmith & Fulham London Borough Council v Monk (1991) *The Times*, 6 December	185
Hammond v Mitchell [1991] 1 WLR 1127	340
Hardwick v Johnson [1978] 2 All ER 935	222
Hardy's Trust, Re, Sutherst v Sutherst (1970) 114 SJ 864	325
Harman v Glencross [1986] Fam 81; [1986] 1 All ER 545	**318**, 319, 329
Harris v De Pinna (1886) 33 ChD 238	**347**
Harris v Goddard [1983] 3 All ER 242	**305**, 307
Harter v Colman (1882) 19 ChD 360	468
Haselmere Estates Ltd v Baker [1982] 1 WLR 1109	28
Hastings (Lord) v Saddler (1898) 79 LT 355	137
Hawkesley v May [1956] 1 QB 304	303, 308, 309
Hayward v Chaloner [1968] 1 QB 107	137
Haywood v The Brunswick Permanent Benefit Building Society (1881) 8 QBD 403	403
Healey v Hawkins [1968] 1 WLR 1967	373
Heathe v Heathe (1740) 2 Atk 121	301
Helby v Matthews [1895] AC 471	119, 120, 121
Herklots' WT, Re, [1964] 1 WLR 583	**273**, 279
Heslop v Burns [1974] 1 WLR 1241	167, 171
Hewitt v Loosemore (1851) 9 Hare 449	471
Heywood v Mallalieu (1883) 25 Ch 357	353
High Street, 139, Deptford, Re, [1951] 1 Ch 884	97
Hill v Tupper (1863) 2 H & C 121	346
Hilton, Re, [1909] 2 Ch 548	278
Hodgson v Marks [1971] Ch 892	11, 67, 73, 74, 80, 87, 229
Hoggett v Hoggett (1980) 39 P & CR 121	190
Holliday (a bankrupt), Re, [1980] 3 All ER 385; [1981] Ch 405	315, 317, 326, 328, 329, 330, 331
Hollington Bros v Rhodes [1951] 2 TLR 691	**42**, 184
Hollins v Verney (1884) 13 QBD 304	373, 374
Hopgood v Brown [1955] 1 WLR 213	245
Horrocks v Forray [1976] 1 All ER 737	222
Horsey Estate Ltd v Steiger [1899] 2 QB 79	200
Hounslow London Borough Council v Twickenham Garden Developments Ltd [1971] 1 Ch 233	**219**
Hoyle, Re, [1893] 1 Ch 84	104
Hughes v Metropolitan Railway Co. (1877) 2 App Cas 439	239
Humphry v Damion (1612) 3 Cro Jac 300	145
Hunt v Elmes (1860) 2 DF & J 578	471
Hunt v Luck [1902] 1 Ch 428	9, 38, 39, 66, 76, 84
Hurst v Picture Theatres Ltd [1915] 1 KB 1	**218**, 219, 220
Hussey v Palmer [1972] 1 WLR 1286; [1972] 3 All ER 744	234, 243
Hyde's Conveyance, Re, (1952) LJN 58	287, 299
Hyman v Van Den Bergh [1907] 2 Ch 516; aff'd [1908] 1 Ch 167	385

Table of Cases   xvii

Industrial Properties (Barton Hill) Ltd v Associated Electrical Industries Ltd
   [1977] 2 WLR 726   118, **188**
International Tea Stores Co. v Hobbs [1903] 2 Ch 165   345, 358
Inwards v Baker [1965] 2 QB 29   237, 240, **241**, 242, 245, 246
Irani Finance Ltd v Singh [1971] Ch 59   286, **289**, 293
Ives (E R) Investment Ltd v High [1967] 2 QB 379   33, **40**, 240, **245, 246**

J T Developments Ltd v Quinn [1991] 2 EGLR 257   244
Jackson v Jackson (1804) 9 Ves 591   309
Jacobs v Seward (1872) LR 5 HL 464   298
Javad v Aqil [1991] 1 All ER 243   **186**
Jeff's Transfer, Re, Rogers v Astley (No. 2) [1960] 1 All ER 937   414
Jefferys, Re, [1939] Ch 205   255, 256
Jelbert v Davis [1968] 1 WLR 589   **388**
Jessamine Investment Co. v Schwartz [1978] QB 264   151, 152
Jones (AE) v Jones (FW) [1977] 2 All ER 231   238, 242
Jones v Challenger [1960] 1 All ER 785   313, 314, 324, 325, 327, 330
Jones v Earl of Tankerville [1909] 2 Ch 440   218, 220
Jones v Price (1836) 3 Bing NC 52   384
Jones v Price [1965] 2 QB 618   349
Jones v Pritchard [1908] 1 Ch 630   364
Joyce v Barker Bros (Builders) Ltd (1980) 40 P & C R 512   301

K, re F, Re, [1988] 1 All ER 358   121
Kaur v Gill [1988] 2 All ER 288   70
Keefe v Amor [1965] 1 QB 334   **387**, 389
Keller (Samuel) Holdings Ltd v Martins Bank Ltd [1970] 3 All ER 950   449
Kempthorne, Re, [1930] 1 Ch 268   287
Kerrison v Smith [1897] 2 QB 445   218, 220
Ketley (A.) Ltd v Scott [1981] ICR 241   443
Kilgour v Gaddes [1904] 1 KB 457   **374**
King v David Allen and Sons, Billposting Ltd [1916] 2 AC 54   223, 227, 229, 230, 231
King v South Nottinghamshire DC (1991) *The Times*, 3 December   350
King's Leasehold Estates, Re, (1873) LR 16 Eq 521   228
King's Motors (Oxford) Ltd v Lax [1970] 1 WLR 426   162
King's Trusts, Re, (1892) 29 LR Ir 401   20
King, Re, [1963] Ch 459   **206**
Kings North Trust Ltd v Bell [1986] 1 WLR 119   **430**
Kingsmill v Millard (1855) 11 Exch 313   136, 137
Kingsnorth Finance Co. Ltd v Tizard [1986] 1 WLR 783   **10**
Kingswood Estate Co. Ltd v Anderson [1963] 2 QB 169   107
Kinnaird v Trollope (1888) 389 ChD 636   453
Kling v Keston (1983) 49 P & CR 212   124
Knight's Case (1588) 5 Co. Rep 54b   162
Knightsbridge Estates Trust Ltd v Byrne [1939] Ch 441   **433**
Kreglinger v New Patagonia Meat & Cold Storage Co. Ltd [1914] AC 25   **439**, 441
Kumar v Dunning [1987] 2 All ER 801   199
Kushner v Law Society [1952] 1 KB 264   183

Lace v Chantler [1944] KB 368   **155**, 156
Lashbrook v Cock (1816) 2 Mer 70   301
Law v Jones [1974] Ch 112   109
Lazarus Estates Ltd v Beasley [1956] 1 QB 702   48
Le Neve v Le Neve (1748) 3 Atk 646   46
Leach, Re, [1912] 2 Ch 422   **19**
Lee v Lee [1952] 2 QB 489   305
Lee-Parker v Izzet [1971] 1 WLR 1688   198

Leech v Schweder (1874) 9 Ch App 463	351
Leicester (Earl of) v Wells-next-the-sea Urban District Council [1973] Ch 110	406
Leigh v Jack (1879) 5 Ex D 264	128, 130, 131, 138
Leigh's SE, Re, (No. 1) [1926] Ch 852	273, 274, 275
Leighton's Conveyance [1936] 1 All ER 667	96, **97**
Lester v Foxcroft (1701) Colles 108	112
Lewen v Dodd (1595) Cro Eliz 443	301
Lewis v Frank Love Ltd [1961] 1 WLR 261	**431**
Lewisham Borough Council v Maloney [1948] 1 KB 50	40
Liddiard v Waldron [1934] 1 KB 435	365
Lim Teng Huan v Ang Swee Chuan [1992] 1 WLR 113	**243**
Littledale v Liverpool College [1900] 1 Ch 19	130
Liverpool City Council v Irwin [1977] AC 239	**349**
Liverpool Corp v H Coghill & Son Ltd [1918] 1 Ch 307	372
Lloyds Bank v Bundy [1975] QB 326	429
Lloyds Bank Plc v Rosset [1988] 3 All ER 915; revsd [1990] 1 All ER 1111	78, 80, **338**, 341
Lobb (Alec) (Garages) Ltd v Total Oil (Great Britain) Ltd [1985] 1 WLR 173	**444**
London and County (A & D) Ltd v Wilfred Sportsman Ltd [1971] Ch 764	**204**, 205
London & South Western Railway Co. v Gomm (1882) 20 ChD 562	30, 121
London and Cheshire Insurance Co. Ltd v Laplargrene Property Co. Ltd & Another [1971] 1 All ER 766, [1971] 1 Ch 499	67, 85
London County Council v Allen [1914] 3 KB 642	236, **403**, 362
Long v Gowlett [1923] 2 Ch 177	**360**
Lowe v Adams [1901] 2 Ch 598	218
Lowrie (a bankrupt), Re, [1981] 3 All ER 353	328, 330
Lowther v Heaver (1889) 41 ChD 248	183, 213
Lynes v Snaith [1899] 1 QB 486	170, 225
Lysaght v Edwards [1876] 2 ChD 499	**112**
Lyttletone Times Co. Ltd v Warners Ltd [1907] AC 476	364
Lyus v Prowsa Developments [1982] 1 WLR 1044	93, 95, 234, 235, 236
Maddison v Alderson (1883) 8 App Cas 467	105
Malayan Credit Ltd v Jack Chia MPH Ltd [1986] AC 549	**301**
Manchester Brewery v Coombs [1901] 2 Ch 608	119, **211**
Mander v Falcke [1891] 2 Ch 554	**404**
Mann v Stephens (1846) 15 Sim 377	395
Marchant v Charters [1977] 1 WLR 1181	167
Marcroft Wagons Ltd v Smith [1951] 2 KB 496	164, 166, **172**
Markou v Da Silvaesa (1986) 52 P & CR 204	**172**
Marsden v Miller (1992) LEXIS, 16 January	131
Marshall v Taylor [1895] 1 Ch 641	129
Marten v Flight Refuelling Ltd [1962] Ch 115	**407**
Martin v Martin (1987) 54 P & CR 238	301
Martin v Smith (1874) LR 9 Exch 50	184
Martinson v Clowes (1882) 21 ChD 857	462
Matthews v Goodday (1861) 31 LJ Ch 282	**428**
May v Belleville [1905] 2 Ch 605	245, **355**, 356
Mayhew v Suttle (1854) 4 EL & BL 347	164
Mayo, Re, [1943] Ch 302	**278**, 279, 287, 312, 313, 324
Mayor of Congleton v Pattison (1808) 10 East 130	200
McBlain v Cross (1871) 25 LT 804	104
McCarthy & Stone Ltd v Julian S. Hodge & Co. Ltd [1971] 1 WLR 1547	6, 8, 480
McFarlane v McFarlane [1972] NI 59	339
McManus v Cooke (1887) 35 ChD 681	118, **355**, 356
Mellor v Watkins (1874) LR 9 QB 400	146
Mercer v Denne [1905] 2 Ch 538	346
Mercier v Mercier [1903] 2 Ch 98	334

Table of Cases

Meux v Smith 11 Sim 410	187
Middlemass v Stevens [1901] 1 Ch 574	**262**
Midland Bank Ltd v Farmpride Hatcheries Ltd (1980) 260 EG 493	**9**
Midland Bank plc v Dobson [1986] 1 FLR 171	336
Midland Bank Trust Co. Ltd v Green [1981] AC 513	12, 44, 48, 94, 95
Midland Railway Co.'s Agreement, Re, [1971] Ch 725	156, 157
Miles v Bull (No. 2) [1969] 3 All ER 1585	**89**, 94
Miles v Easter; Re Union of London and Smith's Bank Ltd Conveyance [1933] Ch 611	407
Miller v Emcer Products Ltd [1956] Ch 304	352
Mills v Silver [1991] Ch 271	**374**
Minister of Health v Bellotti [1944] KB 298	71
Mobil Oil Co. Ltd v Rawlinson [1981] Lexis 31 July; 261 Est Gaz 260	449
Mogridge v Clapp [1892] 3 Ch 382	269
Monolithic Building Co., Re, [1915] 1 Ch 643	46
Moore v Rawson (1824) 3 B & C 332	390
Moore, Re, (1888) 39 ChD 116	**20**
Moorgate Mercantile Co. Ltd v Twitchings [1976] QB 225	240, 242
Morgan v Fear [1907] AC 425	**385**
Morgan's Lease, Re, [1972] Ch 1	**268**, 270
Morphett v Jones (1818) 1 Swans 172	356
Mortgage Corporation Ltd v The Nationwide Credit Corporation Ltd, *The Times*, 27 July 1992	101, 483
Moses v Lovegrove [1952] 2 QB 533	138
Moule v Garrett (1872) LR 7 Ex 101	202
Mounsey v Ismay (1865) 3 H & C 486	345
Mount Carmel Investments Ltd v Peter Thurlow Ltd [1988] 3 All ER 129	148
Mountford v Scott [1975] Ch 258	119
Mountnoy v Collier (1853) 1 E & B 630	189
Mulholland's Will Trusts, Re, Bryan v Westminster Bank Ltd [1949] 1 All ER 460	124
Multiservice Bookbinding Ltd v Marden [1979] Ch 84	**442**
Mumford v Stohwasser (1874) Law Rep 18 Eq 556	6
Murray, Bull & Co. Ltd v Murray [1953] 1 QB 211	166
National Carriers Ltd v Panalpina (Northern) Ltd [1981] AC 675	**193**
National Provincial Bank Ltd v Hastings Car Mart Ltd [1964] Ch 665 revsd sub nom National Provincial Bank v Ainsworth [1965] AC 1175	**8**, 33, 39, **68**, 71, 226, 227, 229, 230, 231
National Westminster Bank v Hart [1983] 1 QB 773	189
National Westminster Bank v Morgan [1985] AC 686	429, 430
Nationwide Building Society v Registry of Friendly Societies [1983] 3 All ER 296	442
New Hart Builders Ltd v Brindley [1975] 1 Ch 342	105
Newman, Re, [1930] 2 Ch 409	287
Newsome v Graham (1829) 10 B&C 234	189
Newton Abbot Co-operative Society Ltd v Willamson & Treadgold Ltd [1952] Ch 286	407, 408, **416**
Nicholson v England [1926] 2 KB 93	138
Nielson-Jones v Fedden [1974] 3 All ER 38; [1975] Ch 222	307
Nisbet and Pott's Contract, Re [1905] 1 Ch 391 aff'd [1906] 1 Ch 386	143, 209, **404**
Noakes & Co. Ltd v Rice [1902] AC 24	**436**, 438, 441
Norris v Checksfield [1991] 1 WLR 1241	179
Northbourne (Lord) v Johnston & Son [1922] 2 Ch 309	408
Northern Counties of England Fire Insurance Co. v Whipp (1884) 26 ChD 482	472
Norton, Re, [1929] 1 Ch 84	275
Oak Co-operative Building Society v Blackburn [1968] Ch 730	**48**
Official Custodian for Charities v Mackey [1985] Ch 168	197
Oliver v Hinton [1899] 2 Ch 264	45, 470

Paddington Building Society v Mendelsohn (1985) 50 P & CR 244	74, 247
Parker v Taswell (1858) 2 De G & J 559	118
Parker's Settled Estates, Re, [1928] Ch 247	**274, 276**
Parker-Tweedale v Dunbar Bank plc (No. 1) [1990] 2 All ER 577	**461**
Pascoe v Turner [1979] 1 WLR 431	**239, 242, 243**
Payne v Cardiff RDC [1932] 1 KB 241	456
Payne v Webb (1874) LR 19 Eq 26	301
Peat v Chapman (1750) 1 Ves Sen 542	301
Peffer v Rigg [1977] 1 WLR 285	**90,** 92, 93
Perez-Adamson v Perez-Rivas [1987] 3 All ER 20	**26**
Perrot J.F. & Co. Ltd v Cohen [1951] 1 KB 705	137
Perry Herrick v Attwood (1857) 2 De G & J 21	**472**
Perry v Phoenix Assurance plc [1988] 3 All ER 60	**41**
Pettey v Parsons [1914] 2 Ch 653	389
Pettitt v Pettitt [1970] AC 777	333, 334, **339**
Pettiward Estates v Shepherd [1986] 6 CL 1186	208
Phillips v Mobil Oil Co. Ltd [1989] 3 All ER 97	31
Phillips v Phillips (1862) 4 De G F & J 208	8
Phillips-Higgins v Harper [1954] 1 QB 411	141
Phipps v Pears [1965] 1 QB 76	**350,** 351
Pilcher v Rawlins (1872) 7 Ch App 259	3, 6, 12, 45
Pinewood Estate, Re, Farnborough [1958] Ch 280	416
Pleasant (Lessee of Hayton) v Benson (1811) 14 East 234	146
Pledge v White [1890] AC 187	466, 467, 468
Plimmer v Mayor Councillors and Citizens of the City of Wellington (1884) 9 App Cas 699	
	240, 242, **245**
Poster v Slough Estates Ltd [1968] 1 WLR 1515	37
Powell v McFarlane (1977) 38 P&CR 452	128, 129, 131
Price v Strange [1978] Ch 337	94
Prior's Case (1368) YB 42 Edw 3	395
Pritchard v Briggs [1980] 1 Ch 338	**29,** 125
Property & Bloodstock Ltd v Emerton [1968] Ch 94	458
Prudential Assurance Co. Ltd v London Residuary Body & Others [1992] 3 WLR 279	
	155, 157, 161
Pugh v Savage [1970] 2 QB 373	373, **375**
Purchase v Lichfield Brewery Co. [1915] 1 KB 184	**210**
Pwllbach Colliery Co. Ltd v Woodman [1915] AC 634	364, 366
Pyer v Carter (1857) 1 H & N 916	368
Quennell v Maltby [1979] 1 WLR 318	**452**
Radaich v Smith (1959) 101 CLR 209	169
Radnor's WT (Earl of), Re, (1890) 45 ChD 402	**261**
Rains v Baxton (1880) 14 ChD 537	127
Ramsden v Dyson (1866) LR 1 HL 129	237, 240, **241**
Rankin v M'Murtry (1889) 24 LR Ir 290	144
Ratcliffe v Barnard LR 6 Ch 652	471
Rawlings v Rawlings [1964] 2 All ER 804; [1964] P 398	287, 314, 325, 327
Rawlinson v Ames [1925] Ch 96	105
Record v Bell [1991] 4 All ER 471	111
Reeve v Lisle [1902] AC 461	**431,** 432
Refuge Assurance Co. Ltd v Pearlberg [1938] Ch 687	455
Regan and Blackburn Ltd v Rogers [1985] 1 WLR 870	28
Regent Oil Co. Ltd v J. A. Gregory (Hatch End) Ltd [1966] Ch 402	404, **426**
Regis Property Co. Ltd v Redman [1956] 2 QB 612	349
Reid v Bickerstaff [1909] 2 Ch 305	420
Reilly v Orange [1955] 2 QB 112	**383**

Table of Cases

Renals v Cowlishaw (1878) 9 ChD 125; aff'd Renals v Cowlishaw (1879) 11 ChD 866
    405, 408, 416, 419
Richards v Creighton Griffiths (Investments) Ltd (1972) 225 EG 2104   122
Richards v Rose (1853) 9 Ex 218   363
Richardson, Re, [1904] 2 Ch 777   250
Rickett v Green [1910] 1 KB 253   209
Rignall Developments Ltd v Halil [1987] 3 All ER 170   50
Roake v Chadha [1984] 1 WLR 40   **413**, 415, **417**
Robertson v Norris 1 Giff 421   462
Rochefoucauld v Boustead [1897] 1 Ch 196   94, 95, 232
Rodenhurst Estates Ltd v W H Barnes Ltd [1936] 2 All ER 3   214
Roe v Siddons (1888) 22 QBD 224   346
Rogers v Hosegood [1900] 2 Ch 388   395, **403,** 405, 406, 407, 410, 413, 416, 417
Rooke, Re, [1953] Ch 716   277
Roth, Re, (1896) 74 LT 50   278
Royal Trust Co. of Canada v Markham [1975] 3 All ER 433   451
Russel v Russel (1783) 1 Bro CC 269   427
Ryall v Rowles 1 Ves Sen 348   475
Ryder and Steadman's Contract, Re, [1927] 2 Ch 62   275
Rye v Rye [1962] AC 496   117, 360

Sainsbury J. plc v O'Connor (Inspector of Taxes) [1990] STC 516   121
Sainsbury J. plc v Enfield London Borough Council [1989] 2 All ER 817   415
Samuel v Jarrah Timber & Wood Paving Corporation Ltd [1904] AC 323   **430,** 432
Santley v Wilde [1899] 2 Ch 474   424, **435,** 437, 441
Saunders v Dehew (1692) 2 Vern 271   6
Saunders v Vautier (1841) 4 Beav 115   287
Say v Smith (1563) 1 Plowd 269   156
Schebsman, Re, decd [1944] Ch 83   235
Seddon v Smith (1877) 36 LT 168   130
Sedgwick Forbes Bland Payne Group Ltd v Regional Properties (1981) 257 EG 64   351
Selwyn's Conveyance, Re, [1967] Ch 674   **407,** 409
Sharpe, Re, (a Bankrupt) [1980] 1 WLR 219   **233,** 234, 235, 236, 246
Shaw v Applegate [1978] 1 All ER 123   421
Shaw v Foster (1872) LR 5 HL 321   113
Shell-Mex & B.P. Ltd v Manchester Garages Ltd [1971] 1 WLR 612   167, 228
Shiloh Spinners Ltd v Harding [1973] AC 691   **31,** 37, 400
Sichel v Mosenthal (1862) 30 Beav 371   427
Siew Soon Wah v Yong Tan Hong [1973] AC 836   235, 240
Simpson v Weber (1925) 133 LT 46   365
Smirk v Lyndale Developments Ltd [1975] 1 Ch 317   **135**
Smith and Snipes Hall Farm Ltd v River Douglas Catchment Board [1949] 2 KB 500;
    [1949] 2 All ER 179   209, **394,** 411
Smith v Seghill Overseas (1875) LR 10 QB 422   164
Smith v Smith (1833) 2 C & M 231   476
Smith v Smith and Smith (1976) 120 SJ 100   315
Soloman v Vintners' Co. (1859) 4 H & N 585   345
Solomon, Re, [1967] Ch 573; [1966] 3 All ER 255   229, 230, 325, 330
Somerset Coal Canal Co. v Harcourt (1858) 2 De G & J 596   242
Somma v Hazelhurst [1978] 1 WLR 1014   168, 174, 175, 176
Southampton (Lord) v Brown (1827) 6 B & C 718   392
Sovmots Investments Ltd v Secretary of State for the Environment [1979] AC 144   **361**
Spectrum Investment v Holmes [1981] 1 WLR 221   **149,** 153
Spencer's Case (1583) 5 Co. Rep 16a   **201,** 210, 395, 396
Spicer v Martin (1888) 14 App Cas 12   418, 419, 420
Spiro v Glencrown Properties [1991] 1 All ER 600   **120**
Springette v Defoe, *The Independent*, 24 March 1992   333

St Edmundsbury & Ipswich Diocesan Board of Finance v Clarke (No. 2) [1975] 1 All ER 772	**387**
St Marylebone Property Co. v Fairweather [1963] AC 510	149, 150, 151, 152
Standard Chartered Bank Ltd v Walker [1982] 1 WLR 1410	**460**
Standen v Chrismas 10 QB 135	212
Steadman v Steadman [1976] AC 536	105, **106,** 108, 110
Steed v Whitaker (1740) Barn Ch 220	242
Stevens v Hutchinson [1953] Ch 299	277, 291
Strand & Savoy Properties Ltd, Re, v Cumbrae Properties Ltd [1960] 1 Ch 582	158
Strand Securities Ltd v Caswell [1965] 1 Ch 958, [1965] 1 All ER 820	71, **77,** 78, 79
Street v Mountford [1985] AC 809	**163,** 170, 171, 173, 175, 177, 179, 180, 181, 182
Stribling v Wickham (1989) 27 EG 81	178
Sturolson & Co. v Weniz (1984) 272 EG 326	168
Sudbrook Trading Estates Ltd v Eggleton [1983] 1 AC 444	162
Suffield v Brown (1864) 4 De GJ & S 185	364, 366, 368
Sutton v Sutton [1984] 1 All ER 168	111
Swain v Ayres (1888) 21 QBD 289	213
Sweet v Southcote (1786) 2 Bro CC 66	13
Tabor v Godfrey (1895) 64 LJQB 245	136
Tanner v Tanner [1975] 3 All ER 776	**221,** 222, 223
Taylor v London and County Banking Co. [1901] 2 Ch 231	8, 45
Taylor v Stibbert (1794) 2 Ves Jun 437	72
Taylor v Taylor [1968] 1 WLR 378	29
Taylor v Twinberrow [1930] 2 KB 16	143, 145, 147
Taylors Fashions Ltd v Liverpool Victoria Trustees Co. Ltd [1982] 1 QB 133; [1981] 1 All ER 897	31, 237, 242, **244**
Tebb v Hodge (1869) LR 5 CP 73	427
Tehidy Minerals Ltd v Norman [1971] 2 QB 528	**377**
Texaco Antilles Ltd v Dorothy Kernochan [1973] AC 609	421
Thames Guaranty Ltd v Campbell [1984] 2 All ER 585	427
Thomas v Cross (1865) 2 Dr & Sm 423	291
Thomas v Hayward (1869) LR 4 Exch 311	**199**
Thomas v Owen (1887) 20 QBD 225	365
Thomas v Sorrell (1693) Vaugh 330	216, 231
Thomson doe dem v Amey (1840) 12 Ad & El 476	118
Thompson v Park [1944] KB 408	225
Thornhill Road, 90, Tolworth, Surrey, Re, [1970] Ch 261	287
Thornhill's Settlement, Re, [1941] 1 Ch 24	**261**
Thursby v Plant (1670) 1 Wms Saund 230	198
Tichborne v Weir (1892) 67 LT 735	143, 209, **405**
Tickner v Buzzacott [1965] Ch 426	147
Tiltwood, Re, Sussex [1978] Ch 269	421
Timmins v Moreland St Property Co. Ltd [1958] Ch 110	109
Timmons v Hewitt (1888) 22 LR Ir 627	375
Tinker v Tinker [1970] P 136	333
Tiverton Estates v Wearwell Ltd [1975] Ch 146	109, 110
Todrick v Western National Omnibus Co. Ltd [1934] Ch 561	346
Tootal Clothing Ltd v Guinea Properties Management Ltd, *The Independent*, 8 June 1992	110
Tophams Ltd v Earl of Sefton [1966] 1 All ER 1039	**401,** 412, 414
Tottenham Hotspur Football & Athletic Co. v Princegrove Publishers [1974] 1 WLR 113	118
Tower Hamlets LBC v Miah, *The Times*, 17 December 1991	181
Tse Kwong Lam v Wong Chit Sen [1983] 1 WLR 1349	462
Tulk v Moxhay (1848) 2 Ph 774	208, 209, 227, 398, **402,** 403, 404
Turner (a bankrupt), Re, ex p the trustee of a bankrupt v Turner [1975] 1 All ER 5; [1974] 1 WLR 1556	321, 322, 325, 330
Twyne's Case (1602) 3 Rep 80	475

Table of Cases   xxiii

Case	Pages
Ungurian v Lesnoff [1989] 3 WLR 840	**233**, 340
Union Lighterage Co. v London Graving Dock Co. [1902] 2 Ch 557	**362**, 372
Union of London & Smith's Bank Ltd's Conveyance, Re, [1933] Ch 611	412, 416
United Scientific Holdings Ltd v Burnley BC [1977] 2 All ER 62	123
University of Reading v Johnson-Houghton (1985) 276 EG 1353	**173**, 174
Varty (Inspector of Taxes) v British South Africa Co. [1964] 2 All ER 975	121
Verrall v Great Yarmouth Borough Council [1981] 1 QB 202	**223**
Vincent v Premo Enterprises [1969] 2 QB 609	115
Vyvyan v Arthur (1823) 1 B & C 410	199, **395**
Wakeham v Wood (1981) 43 P & CR 40	347
Wakeham v Mackenzie [1968] 1 WLR 1175	**105**
Wakeman, Re, [1945] 1 Ch 177	**281**
Waldron v Sloper (1852) 1 Drew 193	473
Walker v Linom [1907] 2 Ch 104	**470**
Walmsley v Foxhall (1870) 40 LJ Ch 28	303
Walsh v Lonsdale (1882) 21 ChD 9	**118**, 119, 183, 210, 213, 214, 217, 355, 360, 427
Walter v Yalden [1902] 2 KB 304	145, 147
Ward v Byham [1956] 2 All ER 318	222, 223
Ward v Kirkland [1967] Ch 194; [1966] 1 WLR 601	245, **368**, **384**
Waring (Lord) v London and Manchester Assurance Co. Ltd [1935] 1 Ch 310	457
Warner doe d. v Browne 8 East 165	156, 228
Warren, Re, [1932] 1 Ch 32	287, 299
Watson v Lane (1856) 11 Exch 769	189
Webb v Bird (1861) 10 CBNS 268 aff'd Webb v Bird (1862) 13 CBNS 841	348, 351, 380
Webb v Paternoster (1619) Poph 151	228
Webb v Pollmount Ltd [1966] Ch 584	66
Webb v Russell (1789) 3 Term Rep 393	146, 212, 394
Webb's Lease, Re, [1951] Ch 808	**364**
Weeding v Weeding (1861) 1 John & H 424	122
Weg Motors Ltd v Hales [1962] 1 Ch 49	**158**, 208, 210
Wellsted's WT, Re, [1949] Ch 296	**281**
Western Bank Ltd v Schindler [1976] 2 All ER 393	448, 450
Western Fish Products Ltd v Penwith District Council [1981] 2 All ER 204	**238**, 242
Westminster Bank Ltd v Lee [1956] Ch 7	8
Westminster CC v Clark [1992] 1 All ER 695	179
Weston v Henshaw [1950] Ch 510	**268**, 269, 270
Wheaton v Maple & Co. [1893] 3 Ch 48	375
Wheeldon v Burrows (1879) 12 ChD 31	361, 363, 364, 365, **367**, 368, 369
Wheeler v Mercer [1957] AC 416	186
Wheelwright v Walker (No. 1) (1883) 23 ChD 752	**262**
Whitcomb v Minchin (1820) 5 Madd 91	462
White Rose Cottage, Re, [1965] Ch 940	**464**, 482
White v Bijou Mansions Ltd [1937] Ch 610	**393**
White v City of London Brewery Company (1889) 42 ChD 237	448
White v Grand Hotel Eastbourne Ltd [1913] 1 Ch 113	388
White v Southend Hotel Co. [1897] 1 Ch 767	395
Witham, Re, [1992] 2 Ch 413	288
Whitmore v Humphries (1871) LR 7 CP 1	136
Whittingham v Whittingham (National Westminster Bank Ltd Intervening) [1978] 3 All ER 805, [1979] Fam 9	27, 36
Wilkes v Spooner [1911] 2 KB 473	**13**
Wilks, Re, Child v Bulmer [1891] 3 Ch 59	307, 308, 309
Williams & Glyn's Bank v Boland [1980] 3 WLR 138, [1981] AC 487	11, 39, 67, **72**, 74, 76, 78, 79, 80, 83, 84, 85, 86, 87, 151, 285, 289
Williams Bros Direct Supply Ltd v Raftery [1958] 1 QB 159	138

Williams v Bosanquet 1 Brod & Bing 238	210
Williams v Hensman (1861) 1 J & H 546	303, 306, 308, 310
Williams v Unit Construction Co. Ltd (1951) 19 Conv NS 262	412
Williams v Williams [1977] 1 All ER 28	314
Willmott v Barber (1880) 15 ChD 96	236
Wilson v Anderton (1830) 1 B & Ad 450	189
Wilson v Bell (1843) 5 Ir Eq R 501	309
Wilson v Tavener [1901] 1 Ch 578	224
Wimpey (George) & Co. Ltd v Sohn [1967] Ch 487	130
Winter Garden Theatre (London) Ltd v Millennium Productions [1948] AC 173	
	218, 219, 223, 226
Witham, Re, [1922] 2 Ch 413	288
Wong v Beaumont Property Trust Ltd [1965] 1 QB 173	**366**
Wood v Leadbitter (1845) 13 M & W 838	217, 218, 225, 226, 354
Woodall v Clifton [1905] 2 Ch 257	200
Woodhouse Co. Ltd v Kirkland (Derby) Ltd [1970] 1 WLR 1185	**386**
Woodstead Finance Ltd v Petrou [1986] NLJ Rep 188	**443**
Woolwich Equitable BS v Marshall [1952] Ch 1	187
Wright v Dean [1948] 64 TLR 467, [1948] Ch 686	43
Wright v Macadam [1949] 2 KB 744	352, 353, 357, 360, **388**
Wroth v Tyler [1974] 1 Ch 30	**34**
Zetland (Marquess of) v Driver [1939] Ch 1	**407**, 414
Zimbler v Abraham [1903] 1 KB 577	228

TABLE OF STATUTES

Administration of Estates Act 1925   15
   s. 1   264
   s. 22(1)–(2)   **263**, 264
   ss. 23–24   264
   s. 33(1)   **276–7**
   s. 34(3)   16
   s. 37   264
   s. 45–46   16
   s. 55(1)(xi)   264
   s. 55(1)(xviii)   45, 264
   s. 83   264
   sch. 1   16
Administration of Justice Act 1956
   s. 35   291
Administration of Justice Act 1970
   s. 8   452
   s. 8(1)   **449–50**
   s. 36   450, 451
   s. 36(1)   **449**
   s. 36(1)(b)   **449**, 450
   s. 36(2)–(4)   **449**
   s. 36(5)   **449**, 450
   s. 38A   **449**

Bankruptcy Act 1914
   s. 42   319, 320
Building Societies Act 1986
   sch. 4, para.1(1)–(2)   **461**

Charging Orders Act 1979   41
   s. 1(1)   **316**
   s. 1(5)   **316**
   s. 2   317
   s. 2(1)   **316–17**
   s. 2(2)–(3)   **317**
Common Law Procedure Act 1852   194
   s. 210   **194**
Commons Registration Act 1965   103

Companies Act 1929
   s. 380   433
Companies (Consolidation) Act 1908
   s. 93   46
Consumer Credit Act 1974
   s. 137(1)   **442**
   s. 137(2)   **442–3**
   s. 138(1)–(2)   **443**
   s. 138(5)   **443**
Conveyancing Act 1881   15
   s. 6   358, 418
   s. 10   209, 210
   s. 58   209, 414
Conveyancing Act 1882
   s. 3   45
Conveyancing and Law of Property Act 1881
   s. 58(1)   411
County Courts Act 1888
   s. 139   209
Criminal Law Act 1977
   ss. 6–7   193

Factors Act 1889   121
Family Law Reform Act 1969
   Part II   314
Finance Act 1963   23

Housing Act 1988   170
   s. 32   162

Inheritance Tax Act 1984   25
Insolvency Act 1986   191, 319
   s. 336   331
   s. 336(1)–(4)   **322**
   s. 336(5)   **322**, 331
   s. 337(1)–(6)   **323**
   s. 423(1)   **319**
   s. 423(2)–(3)   **320**

Judicature Act 1873 2, 211, 212
Judicature Act 1875 2

Land Charges Act 1925 6, 11, 15, 27, 50,
  51, 53–4, 125, 283, 291, 311
  s. 2(4) 477
  s. 2(4)(iv) 32
  s. 2(5)(iii) 32
  s. 3(1) 46
  s. 4(5) 477
  s. 7(1) 46
  s. 10 34, 43
  s. 10(1) 123
  s. 13 40, 43, 44
  s. 13(2) 43, 44, 45, 46, 47
  s. 17(1) 477
  s. 17(3) 48
  s. 20(8) 44
  s. 29(8) 47
  s. 72(2)–(3) 283
  s. 97 478
  s. 205(1)(xxi) 47
Land Charges Act 1972 15, 23, 24, 30, 37,
  41, 50, 51, 53–4, 115, 125, 283, 286, 291,
  311, 404
  s. 1(1) 26
  s. 1(1)(a) 26
  s. 2 **24–6**
  s. 2(4) 118
  s. 2(4)(iv) 29
  s. 4 **42**, 43
  s. 4(5) 477, 479
  s. 5 26
  s. 5(7) 27
  s. 11 **51–2**
  s. 11(5)(b) 49
  s. 17 27, **42**
  s. 17(1) 26, 36
Land Charges Registration and Searches Act
  1888 45
  s. 4 46
Land Clauses Acts 21
Land Registration Act 1925 15, 24, 49,
  53–4
  s. 1 **54**
  s. 1(2) 58
  s. 2 **55–6**, 208
  s. 3 91
  s. 3(xv) **87**, 289
  s. 3(xvi) **61**, 82, 83
  s. 3(xxi) 45, 92
  s. 3(2)–(5) **99**
  s. 3(11) **99**
  s. 5 57
  s. 6 **57–8**
  s. 7(1)–(2) **58**
  s. 8(1)(b)(i) 59

Land Registration Act 1925 – *continued*
  s. 9 **58–9**, 150
  s. 10 **59**
  s. 11 **59**, 150
  s. 12 **59–60**
  s. 18(5) 91
  s. 19(1) **61**
  s. 19(2) 63
  s. 20 82, 83, 89–90, 91, 93, 94
  s. 20(1) 67, 82, 83, **88**, 89, 92, 98
  s. 20(1)(b) 82
  s. 20(2)–(3) **88**
  s. 20(4) **88**, 90, 91
  ss. 21–22 150
  s. 22(1) **61**
  s. 22(2) 63
  s. 23 83
  s. 23(1) 82, 83
  s. 23(1)(a) 208
  s. 23(1)(c) 82
  s. 25(1)–(2) **481**
  s. 25(3) **481**–2
  s. 26(1)–(3) **482**
  s. 27(1)–(4) **482**
  s. 29 **483**
  s. 30(1)–(3) **483**
  s. 34 482
  s. 34(4) 93, 94
  s. 37 82
  s. 40(1)–(3) **423**
  s. 49(2) **271**
  s. 50(1)–(4) **423**
  s. 54 100, 289
  s. 54(1) 288, 289
  s. 55 100
  s. 56(2) 100
  s. 59 90, 91
  s. 59(6) **88**, 92
  ss. 63–64 55
  s. 66 **483**–4
  s. 69 82, 83, 150
  s. 69(1) 83, 150
  s. 69(4) 150
  s. 70 60, 70, 83, 86
  s. 70(1) **61**–2, 67, 82, 83, 85
  s. 70(1)(a) **63**–5, 65
  s. 70(1)(f) 65, 97, 148
  s. 70(1)(g) **65**–87, 289
  s. 70(1)(k) 62, 65
  s. 70(3) 63
  s. 74 **271**
  s. 75 142, 145, 148, 149
  s. 75(1) 147, **149**, 151
  s. 75(2) **149**, 150, 151, 152
  s. 75(3) **149**, 150, 151–2
  s. 75(5) **149**
  s. 77 59

Table of Statutes   xxvii

Land Registration Act 1925 – *continued*
  s. 77(1)   60
  s. 77(2)   **58**
  s. 77(3)–(4)   **60**
  s. 77(6)   **60**
  s. 82   **95–6**, 98
  s. 82(1)   97
  s. 83   99
  s. 83(1)   **98**
  s. 86   **68**
  s. 86(1)   **271**
  s. 86(3)   **271**
  s. 86(5)   **271**
  s. 94(1)–(3)   **281**
  s. 95   **281**
  s. 102(2)   100
  s. 106   100
  s. 123   **56–7**
  s. 123(1)   **56–7**
  s. 144   64
  s. 144(2)   64
Land Registration Act 1986   60, 62
  s. 1   **60**
  s. 5   476
Land Registry Act 1862   53
Land Transfer Act 1875   53
Law of Property Act 1922   45, 49, 292
  sch. 7   45
Law of Property Act 1925   14, 87, 103, 248, 275, 296, 299, 424
  s. 1   33
  s. 1(1)   **16–17**, 21, 56, 154, 156
  s. 1(2)   56, 353
  s. 1(2)(a)   33, 40, 354
  s. 1(2)(e)   33
  s. 1(3)   40
  s. 1(4)   **18**
  s. 1(5)   154
  s. 1(6)   250, 298
  s. 1(8)   33
  s. 2(1)   **283**
  s. 2(2)–(5)   **284**
  s. 2(3)(iii)   40
  s. 4   **17**
  s. 4(1)   40
  s. 7(1)   **21**
  s. 13   **478**, 479
  s. 14   86, 299
  s. 24   **49–50**
  s. 25   **50–1**
  s. 25(1)–(2)   **277**
  s. 25(4)   **272**
  s. 26   287
  s. 26(1)–(2)   **279**
  s. 26(3)   **279**, 299
  s. 26(4)   **279**
  s. 27   86, 285

Law of Property Act 1925 – *continued*
  s. 27(1)   **284**
  s. 27(2)   **284–5**
  s. 28(1)   **279–80**
  s. 28(2)   **280**
  s. 28(3)   287, 310
  s. 29(1)–(3)   **280**
  s. 29(4)   **280–1**
  s. 30   277, **278**, 297, 299, 311–16, 318, 321, 322, 324, 327
  s. 30(1)(i)   272
  s. 31(1)   277
  s. 34(1)   **294**, 297
  s. 34(2)–(3)   **294**, 300
  s. 34(4)   **295**
  s. 35   292, **295**, 299
  s. 36   **295**
  s. 36(2)   302, 304, 309, 311
  s. 37(2)–(3)   **476**
  s. 40   **104**, 106, 107, 108, 109, 110, 111, 112, 119, 122, 287, 288, 291
  s. 40(1)   109
  s. 40(2)   **104**
  s. 42   300
  s. 42(6)   **300**
  s. 44(1)   24
  s. 51   338
  s. 52   113, 117, **190**
  s. 52(1)   **113**, 183, 354
  s. 52(2)   **113–14**
  s. 52(2)(g)   183
  s. 53   233
  s. 53(1)   **117**, 338
  s. 53(1)(c)   **428**
  s. 54   113, **114**, 233
  s. 54(2)   109, **114**
  s. 56(1)–(2)   **393**
  s. 60   **15**
  s. 62   183, 349, 357–62, 417–18
  s. 62(1)   **357**, 417
  s. 62(2)   417
  s. 63   292
  s. 63(1)   292–3
  s. 65(1)–(3)   **357**
  s. 72   311
  s. 72(1)   **116–17**
  s. 72(2)–(4)   **117**
  s. 77(1)   **203**
  s. 78   208, 396, 401, 409, 410–15
  s. 78(1)   209, 394, 396, 409
  s. 78(2)   **209**
  s. 79   208, 401, 404, 411, 412, 414, 415
  s. 79(1)–(4)   **202**
  s. 80(1)   **459**
  s. 81(6)   297
  s. 84(1)   **421–2**
  s. 84(1B)   **422**

Law of Property Act 1925 – *continued*
  s. 84(1C) 422
  s. 84(2)–(3) 422
  s. 84(3A) 422
  s. 84(5) 422–3
  s. 85–87 16
  s. 85(1) 425, 455
  s. 85(2)–(4) 425
  s. 86(1) 425, 455
  s. 86(2) 425–6
  s. 86(3)–(4) 426
  s. 87(1) 426
  s. 88(2) 462
  s. 89(2) 463
  s. 93(1) 467
  s. 93(1)(d) 467
  s. 94 483
  s. 94(1)–(4) 480
  s. 97 477, 479
  s. 98(1)–(3) 447
  s. 99(1) 187, 445, 454
  s. 99(2)–(3) 445
  s. 99(5)–(8) 445
  s. 99(11)–(14) 445
  s. 99(15) 445–6
  s. 100(1) 446
  s. 100(2) 446, 454
  s. 100(5) 446
  s. 100(7) 446
  s. 101 457
  s. 101(1)(i) 456
  s. 101(1)(ii) 454
  s. 101(1)(iii) 455
  s. 101(2) 456–7
  s. 103(i)–(iii) 456
  s. 104(1) 458
  s. 104(2) 458–9
  s. 104(3) 459
  s. 105 459
  s. 108(1)–(4) 455
  s. 109 272
  s. 115(1) 468–9
  s. 115(2)–(10) 469
  s. 130 15, 16
  s. 136(1) 397
  s. 137 16, 317, 475
  s. 137(1) 428, 473
  s. 139 146
  s. 141 200, 204, 205, 206
  s. 141(1) 204, 210
  s. 141(2)–(4) 204
  s. 142 200
  s. 142(1) 207, 210
  s. 142(2) 207
  s. 146 415
  s. 146(1) 195
  s. 146(2) 195, 197

Law of Property Act 1925 – *continued*
  s. 146(4) 195
  s. 146(5) 195–6
  s. 146(8)–(12) 196
  s. 146(10) 197
  s. 149(3) 158
  s. 149(6) 158–9, 183, 255–6
  s. 150 146
  s. 153 399
  s. 153(1) 191–2
  s. 153(2)–(8) 192
  s. 153(9) 192–3
  s. 153(10) 193
  s. 162(1)(d) 33
  s. 172(1)–(3) 319
  s. 196(4) 302
  s. 198 26–7, 41, 49, 51, 479
  s. 198(1) 7, 477, 481
  s. 199 34, 38, 43
  s. 199(1) 7, 10, 37, 479
  s. 199(1)(i) 47
  s. 199(1)(ii)(a)–(b) 11
  s. 199(2) 38, 479
  s. 199(3)–(4) 479
  s. 200(4) 43
  s. 204 264
  s. 205 18, 288
  s. 205(ii) 360
  s. 205(xxvii) 18–19
  s. 205(xxix) 271–2
  s. 205(1) 11
  s. 205(1)(ii) 110
  s. 205(1)(ix) 2, 288
  s. 205(1)(xxi) 45
  s. 205(1)(xxvii) 154, 156, 158
  s. 205(1)(xxix) 281, 286
  sch. 1
    para.3 of Part II 275
  sch. 2
    Part IX 203
  sch. 15
    para.1 159
    para.2 159–60
    para.5 160
Law of Property Act 1969
  s. 23 24
Law of Property (Amendment) Act 1924 45
Law of Property (Amendment) Act 1926
    21, 274, 287
  s. 1 251, 254
Law of Property (Joint Tenants) Act 1964
  s. 1(1)–(2) 311
Law of Property (Miscellaneous Provisions)
    Act 1989 104, 119, 427
  s. 1 110, 117, 354
  s. 1(1) 114
  s. 1(2)–(3) 110, 114

Table of Statutes

Law of Property (Miscellaneous Provisons) Act 1989 – *continued*
  s. 1(4) **114**
  s. 1(5) **114–15**, 116
  s. 1(6)–(7) **115**
  s. 1(10)–(11) **115**
  s. 2 110, 111–12, 119, 120, 123, 124, 355, 427
  s. 2(1) **108**, 119
  s. 2(2)–(5) **109**
  s. 2(6) **109**, 110
  s. 2(7) **109**
  s. 2(8) **109**, 112
Leasehold Reform Act 1967 71
  s. 5(5) 31
Limitation Act 1833
  s. 34 143, 405
Limitation Act 1939 138, 149, 152
  s. 4(3) 144
  s. 6(1) 144, 146
  s. 16 145
Limitation Act 1980 99
  s. 10 **127**
  s. 15(1) **126**
  s. 15(2)–(3) **132**
  s. 15(4)–(6) **133**
  s. 16 **138**
  s. 17 **142**
  s. 18 **133–4**, 142
  s. 19 **137**
  s. 20(1) **454**
  s. 20(5)–(7) **454**
  s. 21 **134**
  s. 28(1) **139**
  s. 28(2)–(4) **140**
  s. 29(1)–(7) **139**
  s. 30(1) **141**
  s. 31(1)–(3) **141**
  s. 31(4) **141–2**
  s. 31(5)–(9) **142**
  s. 32(1)–(3) **140**
  s. 38(2)–(3) **140**
  s. 38(4) **140–1**
  s. 38(7) **137**
  sch. 1
    para. 1 **127**
    para. 2 **128**
    para. 3 **128**
    para. 4 **133**
    para. 7 **133**
    para. 7(2) **137**
    para. 8 **128**
    para. 8(2) **148**
    para. 9 **135**
Local Land Charges Act 1975 102
  s. 17 385
  sch. 1 385

Married Women's Property Act 1882 316
  s. 17 29, 303, 304, 315
  s. 36(1) 304
  s. 36(2) 305, 306
  s. 36(3) 304
Matrimonial Causes Act 1973 315, 333
  Part II 318
  s. 24 26, 27, 28, 306, 312, 314
  s. 24(1)(a)–(b) 306
  s. 37 27–8
Matrimonial and Family Proceedings Act 1984 315
Matrimonial Homes Act 1967 34, 36, 39, 69, 89, 90
  s. 1(1) 35
  s. 1(1)(b) 36
  s. 1(3) 35
  s. 2(1) 35
  s. 3 36
Matrimonial Homes Act 1983
  s. 1 **69–70**
  s. 1(11) 34
  s. 2(1) **71**
  s. 2(8) **71**
  s. 2(8)(b) 70
Matrimonial Proceedings and Property Act 1970
  s. 37 **333**
  s. 38 34
Middlesex Deeds Registration Act 45

Prescription Act 1832 369, 372, 375, 377
  s. 1 **381**
  s. 2 370, 378, **382**, 383, 384
  s. 3 **382**
  s. 4 **382**, 383, 384
  s. 5 370
  s. 7 **382**, **384–5**
  s. 8 **382**, 384, 385
  s. 62 389
Protection from Eviction Act 1977
  s. 5 **190**

Real Property Act 1845
  s. 3 209
  s. 5 393
Rent Act 1977 170
  s. 5(1) 162
  s. 98(1) 193
Rent Restriction Acts 187
Rentcharges Act 1977
  s. 1(1)(v) 23
  s. 2 **22–3**
  s. 2(1) 22, 23
  s. 2(3)(c) 400
  s. 2(4)–(5) 400
Rights of Light Act 1959 385

School Sites Acts 21
Settled Land Act 1882 250, 258
Settled Land Act 1925 15, 22, 68, 86, 87,
    228, 230, 233, 235, 248, 264, 275, 280,
    282, 423
  s. 1 275
  s. 1(1) **249**
  s. 1(1)(i) 250
  s. 1(1)(iii) 250–1
  s. 1(1)(v) 22, 251
  s. 1(2) **249–50**
  s. 1(4) **250**
  s. 1(5) 250, 276
  s. 1(6) **250**
  s. 1(7) 250, 274, 276
  s. 3 270, 276
  ss. 4–5 **252**
  s. 6 **253**
  s. 7(1)–(2) **262**
  s. 7(3) **262–3**
  s. 7(4)–(5) **263**
  s. 9 **253**
  s. 13 253–4, 265
  s. 18 268
  s. 18(1) **265–6**
  s. 18(2) **266**
  s. 19 **254**
  s. 19(2) 298
  s. 20 **255**
  s. 20(1)(iv) 255
  s. 20(1)(viii) 274
  s. 23(1) **256**
  s. 24(1)–(2) **260**
  s. 24(3) **260–1**
  s. 26(1) **256**
  s. 27(1) 250
  s. 30(1)(i) **256**
  s. 30(1)(ii)–(v) **257**
  s. 31(1) **257**
  s. 34(1)–(2) **257**
  s. 36 **278**
  s. 36(1) **295–6**
  s. 36(2)–(3) **296**
  s. 36(4) 296, 298
  s. 36(5)–(6) **296**
  ss. 38–42 259
  s. 46 259
  s. 51 259
  s. 54 269
  s. 58(1)–(2) 259
  ss. 64–67 259
  s. 71 259

Settled Land Act 1925 – *continued*
  s. 72(1) **282**
  s. 72(2) **282–3**
  s. 75 259
  s. 81(7) 275
  ss. 83–84 259
  s. 95 **266**
  s. 101 259, 266
  s. 102 258
  s. 104(1) 260
  s. 104(4)(a)–(b) 260
  s. 105(1) **261**
  s. 106 258
  s. 107(1) **261**
  s. 108(1)–(3) **272**
  s. 109 258
  s. 110 268, 270
  s. 110(1) **266**, 268, 269, 270
  s. 110(2) **266–7**, 271
  s. 110(3)–(5) **267**
  s. 117(xxviii) **255**
  s. 117(1)(ix) 275
  s. 117(1)(xxi) 45
Statute of Frauds 1677 112, 355
  s. 4 106
Statute of Limitations 1677 143, 144
Statute of Westminster 1275 376
Supreme Court Act 1981
  s. 38(1)–(2) **194**

Town and Country Planning Act 1971
  s. 118 390
  s. 127 390
Trustee Act 1925 15, 397
  s. 14 299
  s. 34(2) **300**
  s. 36(6) 299

Water Resources Act 1963 370
Wills Act 1837
  s. 9 354
  s. 28 16

Yorkshire Deeds Registration Act 45

Table of Statutory Instruments

Land Registration (Official Searches) Rules
    1981 (SI No.1135) 82
Land Registration Rules 1925
    r.258 64

1 INTRODUCTION

SECTION 1: THE CLASSIFICATION OF PROPERTY

English law makes a distinction between real property and personal property. The former category covers interests in land, whereas the latter generally covers interests in property other than land. The term 'real property' derives from the fact that land was the only type of property that could be the subject matter of a real action, i.e. an action to recover the actual thing (or *res*), in the common-law courts. The term 'personal property' derives from the fact that this type of property could only be the subject of a personal action, i.e. an action for compensation for loss. This division into real property (realty) and personal property (personalty or chattels) roughly corresponds to the division into immovables and movables in civil law jurisdictions.

Personal property can be subdivided into two categories, chattels real and chattels personal. Chattels real include leases. Historically leases were regarded as personal property, not rights in the land, since they were originally personal contracts between the parties under which one party allowed the other to use his land in return for the payment of rent. Chattels personal in turn can be subdivided into choses in possession and choses in action. The former category comprises choses that can be enjoyed by taking possession of them, for example a car or a book, whereas the latter category of choses can be enjoyed only by bringing an action for them, for example, the right to a debt or the proceeds of a cheque.

Real property can be divided into corporeal hereditaments and incorporeal hereditaments. 'Corporeal [hereditaments] consist of such as affect the senses such as may be seen and handled by the body; incorporeal are not the object of sensation, can neither be seen nor handled, are creatures of the mind and exist only in contemplation. Corporeal hereditaments consist of substantial and permanent objects.' (Blackstone, *Commentaries*, vol. ii, p. 17) Corporeal hereditaments are inheritable rights which are capable of possession, i.e. the land and buildings on the land, whereas incorporeal hereditaments are inheritable rights in land which are not capable of being possessed, for example, easements, profits and rentcharges.

SECTION 2: THE MEANING OF LAND

The Concise Oxford Dictionary defines land as the 'solid part of [the] earth's surface'. Section 205(1)(ix) of the Law of Property Act 1925 provides:

> (ix) 'Land' includes land of any tenure, and mines and minerals, whether or not held apart from the surface, buildings or parts of buildings (whether the division is horizontal, vertical or made in any other way) and other corporeal hereditaments; also a manor, an advowson, and a rent and other incorporeal hereditaments, and an easement, right, privilege, or benefit in, over, or derived from land; but not an undivided share in land; and 'mines and minerals' include any strata or seam of minerals or substances in or under any land, and powers of working and getting the same but not an undivided share thereof; and 'manor' includes a lordship, and reputed manor or lordship; and 'hereditament' means any real property which on an intestacy occurring before the commencement of this Act might have devolved upon an heir; . . .

SECTION 3: DEVELOPMENT OF EQUITY

(For a detailed discussion, see *Snell's Principles of Equity*, 29th edn, chapter 1 or *Keeton and Sheridan's Equity*, 3rd edn, chapters 1 and 2.)

Equity developed because of the deficiencies of the common law. Such deficiencies included delay, complicated procedures in the writ system and inadequate remedies. The classic statement defining equity can be found in *Lord Dudley and Ward* v *Lady Dudley* (1705) Prec Ch 241, at p. 244 per Nathan Wright LK.

> Equity is not part of the law, but a moral virtue, which qualifies, moderates and reforms the rigour, hardness and edge of the law, and is a universal truth; it does also assist the law where it is defective and weak in constitution (which is the life of the law) and defends the law from crafty evasions, delusions and new subtleties, invented and contrived to evade and delude the common law, whereby such as have undoubted right are made remediless; and this is the office of equity, to support and protect the common law from shifts and crafty contrivances against the justice of the law. Equity therefore does not destroy the law, nor create it, but assists it.

The rules of equity were developed and originally enforced in the Court of Chancery. Until the Judicature Acts 1873–75 there were two separate court systems operating in England and Wales, the Court of Chancery and the common-law courts. Each had its own set of rules and procedures. The two systems then became 'fused', and they are now administered by the same court and by the same process.

SECTION 4: THE CONTRIBUTIONS OF EQUITY TO LAND LAW

(a) One of the most important contributions of equity to land law is the development of the trust. In Underhill and Hayton, *Law of Trusts and*

Introduction

Trustees, 14th edn, a trust is defined as 'an equitable obligation binding a person (who is called a trustee) to deal with property over which he has control (which is called the trust property), for the benefit of persons (who are called the beneficiaries or *cestuis que trust*) of whom he may himself be one, and any one of whom may enforce the obligation'.

Historically the common law courts would not recognise the beneficiaries' rights, only those of the trustee in whom the legal estate was vested. Equity, however, looked at the object and purpose of the arrangement, which was to give the trustee merely the management of the property for the benefit of the beneficiaries. Equity therefore gave effect to the beneficiaries' rights which were equitable in nature. Thus a unique form of duality of ownership evolved.

(b) Equity also developed the equity of redemption. (See chapter 12.)

(c) The common-law rules governing restrictive covenants were narrow and equity developed its own set of rules. (See chapter 11.)

(d) Equity developed the doctrine of proprietary estoppel. (See chapter 7.)

(e) Equity developed its own set of rules relating to agreements for leases or estate contracts. (See chapters 4 and 6.)

SECTION 5: THE DOCTRINE OF NOTICE

The difference between a right that is recognised only in equity and one that is recognised at law is of considerable importance for two reasons:

(a) Rights in equity are enforceable only at the discretion of the court, the court being governed by equitable maxims such as 'He who comes to equity must come with clean hands' and 'He who seeks equity must do equity'. Legal rights are enforceable *as of right*. Once the legal right has been established the court cannot examine the merits of the case before awarding a remedy.

(b) The second significant distinction between rights in equity and rights at law is in relation to the enforceability of those rights against third parties. A legal right is said to be a right in the thing itself — a right *in res* or *in rem* — and can therefore be enforced against any person who subsequently acquires the land. An equitable right is not so extensive in its nature and is said to be a right *in personam*, in that it is enforceable only against certain categories of person. Such an interest is enforceable against all except a bona fide purchaser for valuable consideration of the legal estate (which is subject to the equitable interest) where that purchaser has acquired the legal estate without notice of the equitable interest affecting it. This is commonly called the doctrine of notice.

Pilcher v Rawlins
(1872) 7 Ch App 259 (Court of Appeal in Chancery)

Pilcher lent money, which he held on trust for A and his children, to Rawlins by way of a legal mortgage. Rawlins wished to mortgage the property to Stockwell and Lamb for £10,000. He thus conspired with Pilcher to produce a document which showed Rawlins as holding the fee simple, but the document excluded the mortgage. Rawlins was to repay only £3,500 of the mortgage (which was of £8,373), whilst Pilcher reconveyed the property to him. Thus Stockwell and Lamb received the title deeds to the fee simple. The beneficiaries then discovered the fraud and brought an action, claiming they were entitled to the property as against Stockwell and Lamb. Held: Stockwell and Lamb were bona fide purchasers for value of the legal estate without notice, and thus took free from the equitable interests of the beneficiaries under the trust.

JAMES LJ: I propose simply to apply myself to the case of a purchaser for valuable consideration, without notice, obtaining, upon the occasion of his purchase, and by means of his purchase deed, some legal estate, some legal right, some legal advantage; and, according to my view of the established law of this Court, such a purchaser's plea of a purchase for valuable consideration without notice is an absolute, unqualified, unanswerable defence, and an unanswerable plea to the jurisdiction of this Court. Such a purchaser, when he has once put in that plea, may be interrogated and tested to any extent as to the valuable consideration which he has given in order to shew the *bona fides* or *mala fides* of his purchase, and also the presence or the absence of notice; but when once he has gone through that ordeal, and has satisfied the terms of the plea of purchase for valuable consideration without notice, then, according to my judgment, this Court has no jurisdiction whatever to do anything more than to let him depart in possession of that legal estate, that legal right, that legal advantage which he has obtained, whatever it may be. In such a case a purchaser is entitled to hold that which, without breach of duty, he has had conveyed to him.

A: PURCHASER FOR VALUE

The purchaser must provide consideration in money or money's worth or by means of marriage consideration. The term 'money's worth' includes non-monetary consideration such as the exchange of stocks and shares and even other land. Marriage consideration is limited to future marriages, and a promise in consideration of a future marriage is deemed to be made for value (*Attorney-General* v *Jacobs Smith* [1895] 2 QB 341).

The consideration need not be adequate and can be nominal (*Bassett* v *Nosworthy* (1673) Rep temp Finch 102).

A purchaser can include any person who takes the property by means of sale, mortgage, lease etc., but excludes the acquisition of property by operation of law.

B: LEGAL ESTATE

The purchaser must show that he has acquired the legal estate in land in order to invoke the bona fide purchaser doctrine. The purchaser of an equitable interest in land is in general bound by all prior equitable interests whether he has notice of them or not.

(a) Priority of competing interests

The general rule is that where there are competing equitable interests affecting a legal estate in land, the first in time prevails (*Cave* v *Cave* (1880) 15 ChD

Introduction

639). The rule may be modified, however, in cases of misconduct when the priority of the owner of a legal interest may be postponed to a subsequent equitable interest. Misconduct includes fraud on the part of the legal owner or negligence. The interest may also be postponed by the operation of the doctrine of estoppel.

The rule in *Cave* v *Cave* has no application, however, in successive dealings with an equitable interest in land, for example, if a beneficiary with an equitable interest under a trust mortgages his interest first to bank A, then to bank B. Since the beneficiary's interest is equitable and does not affect the legal estate, both mortgages are necessarily equitable. In such a case the priority of the mortgages is governed by the rule in *Dearle* v *Hall* (1828) 3 Russ 1 (see also chapter 12).

(b) Subsequent acquisition of legal estate

Bailey v Barnes
[1894] 1 Ch 25 (CA)

J mortgaged four freehold houses of which he was the owner for £1,500 each. The mortgagees transferred their mortgages to B in return for payment of the principal and interest due. B then sold the houses to H for the same sum he paid for the transfer to himself. He conveyed them to H, in exercise of the power for sale in the mortgages, free from the equity of redemption. H then mortgaged the houses for £6,000. H died and M, her successor in title, sold the equity of redemption to L for £2,500 subject to the prior mortgage of £6,000. J's creditors succeeded in getting the sale to H set aside as a fraudulent exercise of the power of sale. L on hearing of this paid the £6,000 mortgage and took a reconveyance from the mortgagees. L had no actual notice of any impropriety in the sale to H at the time he purchased the equity of redemption. The mortgagor claimed to be entitled as against L to redeem the mortgaged property on owning the prior equity of redemption. Held: (the Court of Appeal affirming the decision of Stirling J) L did not have constructive notice of the impropriety in the sale, and the acquisition of the legal estate by him protected him against the prior equitable interest of the plaintiff.

LINDLEY LJ: The question is whether he [L] can now hold the property free from the Plaintiff's judgment.

We are of opinion that he can. The maxim *Qui prior est tempore potior est jure* is in the Plaintiffs' favour, and it seems strange that they should, without any default of their own, lose a security which they once possessed. But the above maxim is, in our law, subject to an important qualification, that, where equities are equal, the legal title prevails. Equality, here, does not mean or refer to priority in point of time, as is shewn by the cases on tacking. Equality means the non-existence of any circumstance which affects the conduct of one of the rival claimants, and makes it less meritorious than that of the other. Equtiable owners who are upon an equality in this respect may struggle for the legal estate, and he who obtains it, having both law and equity on his side, is in a better situation than he who has equity only. The reasoning is technical and not satisfactory; but, as long ago as 1728, the law was judicially declared to be well settled and only alterable by Act of Parliament: see *Brace* v *Duchess of Marlborough* 2 P Wms 491.

It was contended that this doctrine was confined to tacking mortgages. But this is not so. The doctrine applies in favour of all equitable owners or incumbrancers for value without notice of prior equitable interests, who get in the legal estate from persons who commit no breach of trust in parting with it to them: see *Saunders* v *Dehew* 2 Vern 271, and *Pilcher* v *Rawlins* Law Rep 7 Ch 259. It is true that the doctrine does not apply to an equitable owner or incumbrancer who gets in the legal estate from a trustee who commits a breach of trust in conveying it to him — at all events, if such breach of trust is known to the person who gets in the estate, and, perhaps, even if he does not know of it: see *Carter* v *Carter* 3 K & J 617; *Mumford* v *Stohwasser* Law Rep 18 Eq 556. But the present case does not fall within this exception to or qualification of the general principle; for *Lilley* obtained the legal estate from a mortgagee whom he paid off, and who committed no breach of trust in conveying the legal estate to him.

But see the following case.

McCarthy & Stone Ltd v *Julian S. Hodge & Co. Ltd*
[1971] 1 WLR 1547 (Ch D)

C negotiated first with B to build dwellings on their land, and secondly with a bank to provide finance. The bank was aware of the fact that B was carrying out the development. An agreement was signed in February 1964 whereby B said they would purchase the land for £56,100 and that the agreement could be completed at any time after March 1964. In March 1964 the bank agreed to provide £39,270 of the £56,100 by way of overdraft, and a memorandum of deposit of title deeds with the intent to create an equitable mortgage on the land was executed. The bank was also appointed as attorney to C to perfect any legal charge on the land, and C declared itself possessed of the property as trustee for the bank.

In April 1964 the bank registered the equitable mortgage, and in September 1965 B registered the agreement as a class C(iv) land charge under the Land Charges Act 1925.

In June 1967 the bank appointed a nominee to perfect a legal charge on the property. In October 1967 C was wound up and B sought a declaration that the bank was not entitled to any charge or other interest adverse to their interest in the property. Held: *inter alia*, the builders' unregistered interest under the agreement was not affected by the bank's subsequent legal charge. The bank must show that at the time of the equitable mortgage it had no knowledge of the terms of the agreement such as would put it on inquiry. It had failed to do so.

FOSTER J: Is McStone's interest affected by the bank obtaining a legal mortgage on June 21, 1967? The bank relied on the equitable doctrine that a subsequent equitable incumbrancer who gets in the legal estate takes precedence over the prior incumbrancer. It is enshrined in *Bailey* v *Barnes* [1894] 1 Ch 25. It is a doctrine which qualifies the rule: *Qui prior est tempore potior est jure* and can be shortly stated as follows: 'Where the equities are equal, the legal title prevails.' . . .

Introduction

[Foster J then refers to Lindley LJ's judgment in *Bailey* v *Barnes*.] In order for the bank to succeed, however, it must show that it had no notice actual or constructive of McStone's equitable interest under the agreement. As a result of the provisions of section 198(1) of the Law of Property Act 1925, it is clear that the bank is deemed to have had actual notice of the estate contract when it was registered on September 27, 1965, and therefore before it got in the legal interest. But did the bank have notice of the agreement when it acquired its equitable mortgage on March 14, 1964? The evidence on this point is as follows. Mr McCarthy, in his affidavit sworn on May 14, 1969, states that 48 cleft oak piles and 4 range lines were collected on February 26, 1964, and for several days following were used by him and his co-director Mr Stone for the initial laying out of the site for development. He then refers to various time sheets of workmen and the delivery on site of 14,000 bricks on March 13, 1964. In paragraph 5, he states:

> My co-director, Mr Stone, and I continued to take a very keen interest in the work on the site and I attended to progress the work almost daily for some weeks after February 26, 1964. I can recollect that the work of laying out the roads and the situation of the first of the proposed houses and bungalows, the grading of the roads, the digging for foundations and drainage pipes and the removal of top soil had progressed to such a point prior to March 14, 1964, that any observer could not have failed to notice on and prior to that date that building works had commenced, that earth moving machinery was at work and further that bulky and obvious building materials had been delivered to the site. The 14,000 bricks alone would be stacked in a pile approximately 30 feet long and 6 feet high and 3 feet deep.

There is no evidence that the bank had actual notice of the agreement of February 17, 1964, before the equitable mortgage on March 14, 1964. Did the bank have constructive notice? By section 199(1) of the Law of Property Act 1925, it is provided:

> A purchaser shall not be prejudicially affected by notice of — . . . (ii) any other instrument or matter or any fact or thing unless — (a) it is within his own knowledge, or would have come to his knowledge if such inquiries and inspections had been made as ought reasonably to have been made by him;

For the bank, it was submitted that the only occupation which imputes notice is occupation inconsistent with Cityfield remaining in occupation and the bank had no reason to suppose that Cityfield was out of occupation. It was said that McStone's activities were consistent with McStone being merely licensees of Cityfield. It is, however, clear that the bank knew that the building was to be done by McStone not as builders for Cityfield but as purchasers of the land from Cityfield, because the amount of the initial overdraft of £39,720 was 70 per cent of the purchase price of £56,100, of which price the bank must have known. In my judgment, the activities carried out on the land prior to March 14, 1964, were sufficient to put the bank on inquiry whether they were being carried out by McStone under a contract, or as licensee pending a contract, and the bank having failed to make that inquiry must be taken on March 14, 1964, to have had constructive notice of McStone's position.

Note

1. The effect of *Bailey* v *Barnes* would seem to be that a purchaser of an equitable interest *who at the time of the purchase of the equitable interest has no notice* of a prior equitable interest and who subsequently obtains the legal estate obtains priority over the prior equitable interest, *even* if at the time of acquisition of the legal estate he has notice of the prior equitable interest. Notice can be actual or constructive.

2. If the purchaser of an estate has the equitable interest conveyed to himself, but the legal estate is, for example, conveyed to a trustee on trust, both he and the trustee will take free of any prior equitable interests affecting the land, provided that neither had notice of the prior interest, since he has a better right to the legal estate (see *Taylor* v *London & County Banking Co.* [1901] 2 Ch 231, at p. 262). There is an obiter statement in *McCarthy & Stone* that this doctrine may apply where there is a declaration of trust of the legal estate by the vendor for the purchaser.

(c) Equitable interests and mere equities

An equitable interest in property must be distinguished from a mere equity. The former gives the owner of the interest a right in the land, whereas the latter does not bestow on its owner any right in the property. It is a right, usually but not always, of a procedural nature, which is ancillary to some right of property, such as a right to have a transaction set aside for fraud or undue influence. The importance of the distinction between the concepts lies in the fact that a purchaser for value of an equitable interest without notice takes free of a mere equity (see *Phillips* v *Phillips* (1862) 4 De G F & J 208, at p. 217-18). See Ann Everton, '"Equitable Interests" and "Equities" — in Search of a Pattern' (1976) 40 Conv 209.

In ***National Provincial Bank Ltd* v *Hastings Car Mart Ltd*** [1965] AC 1175, Lord Upjohn said (at p. 1238):

As Professor Crane has pointed out in an interesting article in The Conveyancer and Property Lawyer, Vol. 19 (N.S.), p. 343 at p. 346: 'Beneficial interests under trusts, equitable mortgages, vendors' liens, restrictive covenants and estate contracts are all equitable interests.' No lesser interests have been held to be sufficient. A mere 'equity' used in contradistinction to an 'equitable interest' but as a phrase denoting a right which in some circumstances may bind successors is a word of limited application and, like the learned editors of Snell, 25th edition, at p. 18, I shall attempt no definition of that phrase. It was illustrated in the case before me of *Westminster Bank Ltd* v *Lee*, where I was constrained in the then state of the authorities to assume that a mere equity might bind successors, yet being at most a mere equity, even subsequent equitable encumbrancers, contrary to the usual rule, could plead purchaser for value without notice. But, my Lords, freed from the fetters which there bound me, I myself cannot see how it is possible for a 'mere equity' to bind a purchaser unless such an equity is ancillary to or dependent upon an equitable estate or interest in the land. As Mr Megarry has pointed out in the Law Quarterly Review, Vol. 71, at p. 482, the reason why a mere equity can be defeated by a subsequent purchaser of an *equitable* estate for value without notice is that the entire equitable estate passes and it is not encumbered or burdened by a mere equity of which he has no notice. For example, a purchaser takes subject to the rights of a tenant in possession whatever they may be. If he sees a document under which the tenant holds, that is sufficient unless he knows, or possibly in some circumstances is put on inquiry to discover, that the tenant has in addition a mere equity, e.g., a right to rectify the document. If the purchaser knows that, he knows that the document does not correctly describe the estate or interest of the tenant in the land and he takes subject to that estate or interest, whatever it may be. But a mere 'equity' naked and alone is, in my opinion, incapable of binding successors in title even with notice; it is personal to the parties.

C: WITHOUT NOTICE

(a) Actual notice
A purchaser of a legal estate is not bound by any equitable interests affecting the land if he had no notice of them at the time of purchase.

(b) Constructive notice
A purchaser cannot deliberately omit to investigate the vendor's title properly and 'shut his eyes' to the matters that come to light, for a purchaser is always deemed to have notice of things of which a prudent, careful and reasonable man would have inquired when purchasing the property. What inquiries are to be made, however, depend upon the facts of the case.

Midland Bank Ltd v *Farmpride Hatcheries Ltd*
(1980) 260 EG 493 (CA)

A bank lent money to a company of which the appellant (W) and his wife were sole directors and shareholders. The company owned land and mortgaged it to the bank as security for the loan. Under a service agreement with the company made prior to the mortgage, W and his family had been given a licence to live in the premises for a period of 20 years. W claimed that this right of occupation under the licence overrode the rights of the bank under the mortgage because the bank had constructive notice of his right to occupy the premises. W had not disclosed his interest to the bank during negotiations for the mortgage. Held: the bank was entitled to possession.

OLIVER LJ: Now of course, an agent who negotiates a sale or mortgage on his principal's behalf does not thereby make any representation that his principal has an indefeasible title to the property offered for sale or as security. As to that the purchaser or mortgagee must satisfy himself by making the usual enquiries before he completes. But in negotiating on his principal's behalf he does, in my judgment, at least represent that he has his principal's authority to offer the property free from any undisclosed adverse interest of his own. I would therefore be prepared to hold that the purchaser or mortgagee dealing with such an agent can reasonably assume that if the agent with whom he is dealing has himself an interest adverse to the title which he offers on his principal's behalf, he will disclose it. It was in my judgment reasonable for Mr Timbers not to make enquiry about an adverse interest of the negotiating agent which that agent's own reticence entitled him to assume did not exist and he did not, therefore, have constructive notice of it. . . .

Notes
1. A purchaser should make inquiries of any person in occupation of the land, since such occupation is deemed to be constructive notice to the purchaser of any rights the occupier may have in the land. A tenant's occupation of the land affects the purchaser of the land with constructive notice of all the tenant's rights, but not with notice of his landlord's title or rights (*Hunt* v *Luck* [1902] 1 Ch 428).

2. If the person in occupation of the land intentionally withholds information relating to his interest in the land from the purchaser, then he cannot later claim the purchaser had constructive notice of his interest. He is estopped from so doing.

Question
Have the courts exhibited a willingness to extend the doctrine of constructive notice?

(c)   Imputed notice
Where a purchaser employs an agent to conduct the purchase for him, then any actual or constructive notice the agent receives in the course of that transaction is imputed to the purchaser.

Kingsnorth Finance Co. Ltd v *Tizard*
[1986] 1 WLR 783 (ChD)

In 1979, the proceeds of sale of a matrimonial home were used to purchase land upon which a new matrimonial home was built. Both properties had been vested in the name of the husband. The marriage broke down in 1982 and an agreement was reached between the husband and wife that the house and land should be sold and the net proceeds divided equally between them. The wife only slept in the house when the husband was away, but returned for some time each day to look after the children. In March 1983, the husband took out a loan with the plaintiffs who sent a surveyor to the property as their agent. The surveyor saw only the husband on the property and the husband told him that he and his wife had separated and she was living elsewhere. The agent's report, which was sent to the plaintiff, listed the occupants as husband, son and daughter but gave no more information. The question arose as to whether the plaintiffs' legal mortgage was subject to the wife's equitable interests in the house. Held: the bank was bound by the wife's equitable rights.

JUDGE FINLAY QC: Section 199(1) of the Law of Property Act 1925 provides:

A purchaser shall not be prejudicially affected by notice of — (i) any instrument or matter capable of registration under the provisions of the Land Charges Act 1925, or any enactment which it replaces, which is void or not enforceable as against him under that Act or enactment, by reason of the non-registration thereof; (ii) any other instrument or matter or any fact or thing unless — (a) it is within his own knowledge, or would have come to his knowledge if such inquiries and inspections had been made as ought reasonably to have been made by him; or (b) in the same transaction with respect to which a question of notice to the purchaser arises, it has come to the knowledge of his counsel, as such, or of his solicitor or other agent, as such, or would have come to the knowledge of his solicitor or other agent, as such, if such inquiries and inspections had been made as ought reasonably to have been made by the solicitor or other agent.

'Purchaser' in that provision, includes a mortgagee: see section 205(1) of the Act.

Although a spouse's statutory rights of occupation under section 1 of the Matrimonial Homes Act 1983, and the statutory provisions replaced by that Act are capable of protection by registration as a Class F land charge, by virtue of the Land Charges Act 1972, the equitable interest of such a spouse in the matrimonial home is not capable of being so protected. The plaintiffs were prejudicially affected by the knowledge of their agent, Mr Marshall, that Mr Tizard, contrary to what he had said in his application, was married: see section 199(1)(ii)(b). That put them on notice that further inquiries were necessary; the inquiries which in these circumstances ought reasonably to have been made by the plaintiffs would, in my judgment, have been such as to have apprised them of the fact that Mrs Tizard claimed a beneficial interest in the property; and accordingly, they would have had notice of such equitable rights as she had and the mortgage in these circumstances takes effect subject to these rights: see section 199(1)(ii)(a).

I arrive at that conclusion without having considered the question: does the occupation of Mrs Tizard affect the mortgagees with notice of her rights, or are they only so affected if, as Mr Wigmore submits, they are aware of her occupation, that is, if they find her in occupation?

On the balance of probabilities, I find that the reason Mr Marshall did not find Mrs Tizard in the house was that Mr Tizard had arranged matters to achieve that result. He told Mrs Tizard that on a particular Sunday, and I find in fact that it was the Sunday that Mr Marshall did inspect, he was going to entertain friends to lunch and would she take the children out for the day. She did; and having regard to the manner in which I find that the signs of her occupation were temporarily eliminated by Mr Tizard, the reasonable inference is that he made this request so that Mr Marshall could inspect and find no evidence of Mrs Tizard's occupation.

In *Caunce* v *Caunce* [1969] 1 WLR 286 Stamp J held that where a wife who had an equitable interest in a property being mortgaged to the bank by her husband was resident with him in the property, that circumstance did not result in the bank taking the property fixed with notice of her rights because, finding her in occupation, the bank made no inquiry of her. Stamp J said, at p. 293:

> Here it is said that the plaintiff was in possession or occupation. No inquiry was made of her and therefore the bank is fixed with notice of her equitable interest. In my judgment, it is here that the fallacy arises, for the plaintiff, unlike the deserted wife, was not in apparent occupation or possession. She was there, ostensibly, because she was the wife, and her presence was wholly consistent with the title offered by the husband to the bank.

In *Williams & Glyn's Bank Ltd* v *Boland* [1981] AC 487, 505, Lord Wilberforce said in the passage I have already read: 'But the presence of the vendor, with occupation, does not exclude the possibility of occupation of others.' He went on to say there were observations suggesting the contrary in *Caunce* v *Caunce* [1969] 1 WLR 286 but he agreed with the disapproval of those and with the assertion expressed by Russell LJ in *Hodgson* v *Marks* [1971] Ch 892, 934. Russell LJ there stated:

> I would only add that I do not consider it necessary to this decision to pronounce on the decision in *Caunce* v *Caunce* [1969] 1 WLR 286. In that case the occupation of the wife may have been rightly taken to be not her occupation but that of her husband. In so far, however, as some phrases in the judgment might appear to lay down a general proposition that inquiry need not be made of any person on the

premises if the proposed vendor himself appears to be in occupation, I would not accept them.

I have already stated my finding that the wife was in occupation. In the circumstances in which she was, I find that her occupation was not that of her husband. . . . I conclude that had Mrs Tizard been found to be in occupation by the plaintiffs or their agent and so found in the context of what had been said by Mr Tizard to Mr Marshall and stated or implied in the forms he had signed, they, the plaintiffs, would clearly either have learned of her rights by inquiry of her or been fixed with notice of those rights had not inquiry of her been made.

In the light of my finding that Mr Marshall's information about Mr Tizard's wife is to be imputed to the plaintiffs and my conclusion that further inquiries should have been made by the plaintiffs because of that imputed knowledge, do I ask myself whether such an inspection as would have disclosed that Mrs Tizard was in the premises is one which ought reasonably to have been made by them, or is the proper question: can the plaintiffs show that no such inspection was reasonably necessary? The latter appears to me to be the proper way to put it. The plaintiffs did not make any further inquiries or inspections; had they done so it would have been open to them to contend that they had done all that was reasonably required and if they still had no knowledge of Mrs Tizard's rights or claims, that they were not fixed with notice of them. But in the absence of further inquiries or inspections, I do not think that it is open to the plaintiffs to say that if they had made a further inspection they would still not have found Mrs Tizard in occupation.

Note
See M. P. Thompson [1986] Conv 283.

D: BONA FIDE

Lord Wilberforce in *Midland Bank Trust Co. Ltd* v *Green* [1981] AC 513, said (at p. 528):

My Lords, the character in the law known as the bona fide (good faith) purchaser for value without notice was the creation of equity. In order to affect a purchaser for value of a legal estate with some equity or equitable interest, equity fastened upon his conscience and the composite expression was used to epitomise the circumstances in which equity would or rather would not do so. I think that it would generally be true to say that the words 'in good faith' related to the existence of notice. Equity, in other words, required not only absence of notice, but genuine and honest absence of notice. As the law developed, this requirement became crystallised in the doctrine of constructive notice which assumed a statutory form in the Conveyancing Act 1882, section 3. But, and so far I would be willing to accompany the respondents, it would be a mistake to suppose that the requirement of good faith extended only to the matter of notice, or that when notice came to be regulated by statute, the requirement of good faith became obsolete. Equity still retained its interest in and power over the purchaser's conscience. The classic judgment of James LJ in *Pilcher* v *Rawlins* (1872) LR 7 Ch App 259, 269 is clear authority that it did: good faith there is stated as a separate test which may have to be passed even though absence of notice is proved. And there are references in cases subsequent to 1882 which confirm the proposition that honesty or bona fides remained something which might be inquired into . . .

Purchaser with notice from purchaser without notice

Wilkes v *Spooner*
[1911] 2 KB 473 (CA)

The lease of premises contained a covenant that the lessee was not to carry on any noisy or offensive trade other than that of a pork butcher. The lessee sold and assigned his interest to the plaintiff and he covenanted that he, his executors, administrators and assigns would not 'cut, sell or deal in fresh hind quarter beef, mutton, veal, lamb or poultry' at the premises or 'in connection with the business of a pork butcher now carried on there by him'. He later gave up the business and surrendered the lease to the landlord. A new lease was granted to his son by the landlord. The new lease contained a covenant that the lessee would not carry on upon the premises any noisy or offensive trade other than (not that of a pork butcher as in the old lease) that of a butcher. At the time the landlord accepted the surrender he did not have notice of the restrictive covenant entered into by the father with the plaintiff, but the son knew of the existence of the covenant when the lease was granted to him. Held: in the circumstances of the case the landlord was not affected with constructive notice of the father's covenant, and could therefore grant to the son a lease which was free from the restriction of the covenant.

VAUGHAN WILLIAMS LJ: It cannot seriously be disputed that the proposition which I quoted from Ashburner's Principles of Equity, p. 75, is good law. It is as follows: 'A purchaser for valuable consideration without notice can give a good title to a purchaser from him with notice. The only exception is that a trustee who has sold property in breach of trust, or a person who has acquired property by fraud, cannot protect himself by purchasing it from a bona fide purchaser for value without notice.' The learned author cites as authorities for that proposition the cases of *Sweet* v *Southcote* 2 Bro CC 66 and *Barrow's Case* 14 ChD 432.

2 THE 1925 LEGISLATION

SECTION 1: THE DOCTRINE OF TENURES AND ESTATES

A detailed discussion of the historical nature of land law is beyond the scope of this book. For further reading on this point, see *Megarry & Wade*, 5th edn, chapters 2 and 3.

At common law, in theory at least, all land is held by the Crown, as the supreme feudal lord. Only the Crown can have absolute ownership of the land. All other persons may only have rights in or over the land. Historically every person held their land either from the King directly (such persons were called tenants in chief) or from some superior feudal lord. These tenants owed feudal services to the superior lord. Only one common-law tenure still remains in English law, that of freehold tenure, but it no longer carries with it the old feudal incidents that it once did.

Since a tenant was not regarded as owning the land itself, the question is what did he own? What was the extent of his proprietary interest? The nature of his estate in land would determine this issue. Estates are classified according to the time for which they can endure, and it should be noted that several persons can at the same time own distinct and separate estates in the same piece of land. See page 17 *et seq.* for a discussion of the types of estates in land.

SECTION 2: OUTLINE OF THE 1925 LEGISLATION AND ITS EFFECTS

A radical reform of land law was undertaken in 1925. Comprehensive reform was needed because conveying property had become a cumbersome process and many out of date rules had never been abolished. The legislation introduced in 1925 was a series of Acts, most of which were passed in 1925 and came into operation on 1 January 1926, namely:

— The Law of Property Act 1925

— The Settled Land Act 1925
— The Land Charges Act 1925 (now the Land Charges Act 1972)
— The Land Registration Act 1925
— The Trustee Act 1925
— The Administration of Estates Act 1925.

The main purposes of the legislation were two-fold. The first was to achieve a closer assimilation of the rules relating to realty with the rules relating to personalty. This was achieved by the following provisions:

(a)   Law of Property Act 1925, s. 130.

Law of Property Act 1925

130. Creation of entailed interests in real and personal property
(1)   An interest in tail or in tail male or in tail female or in tail special (in this Act referred to as 'an entailed interest') may be created by way of trust in any property, real or personal, but only by the like expressions as those by which before the commencement of this Act a similar estate tail could have been created by deed (not being an executory instrument) in freehold land, and with the like results, including the right to bar the entail either absolutely or so as to create an interest equivalent to a base fee, and accordingly all statutory provisions relating to estates tail in real property shall apply to entailed interests in personal property.

Personal estate so entailed (not being chattels settled as heirlooms) may be invested, applied, and otherwise dealt with as if the same were capital money or securities representing capital money arising under the Settled Land Act, 1925, from land settled on the like trusts.

(b)   Law of Property Act 1925, s. 60.

Law of Property Act 1925

60. Abolition of technicalities in regard to conveyances and deeds
(1)   A conveyance of freehold land to any person without words of limitation, or any equivalent expression, shall pass to the grantee the fee simple or other the whole interest which the grantor had power to convey in such land, unless a contrary intention appears in the conveyance.

Note
Words of limitation are words that are necessary to transfer or create a particular interest in land, such as a fee simple or a fee tail. Before 1926, in order to transfer a fee simple estate the grant had to be made to A 'and his heirs' or 'in fee simple' (the latter phrase being first allowed by the Conveyancing Act 1881). No other words would suffice to pass an estate in fee simple. Before 1926, in order to create a fee tail the grant had to be made to A 'and the heirs of his body' or 'in tail' (the latter phrase being first allowed by the Conveyancing Act 1881). The rule relating to the transfer of a fee tail, however, is still the same and has not been modified by the 1925 legislation.

The Wills Act 1837, s. 28 provided that a testator's whole estate in land passed to a devisee unless the will showed a contrary intention. Before 1926, a fee tail could be created by the use of any words in a will which sufficiently evinced an intention to create one. Section 130 of the Law of Property Act 1925, however, says that in the case of the death of a testator dying after 1925, in order to create an interest in tail the same strict common law or statutory expressions must be used in a will as would be required to create one by deed.

(c) Changes were made in the way in which legal mortgages were created (Law of Property Act 1925, ss. 85–87: see chapter 12).

(d) The rule in *Dearle* v *Hall* (see chapter 12) governing the priority of competing equitable interests in certain situations is now applicable to realty and personalty (Law of Property Act 1925, s. 137).

(e) The Administration of Estates Act 1925, ss. 45 and 46, now provide that both realty and personalty pass in the same manner where the deceased dies intestate. This was not the case before 1925.

(f) Prior to 1925 only personalty was available to pay the deceased's debts. Now both realty and personalty are available (Administration of Estates Act 1925, s. 34(3) and First Schedule).

(g) Any form of property, whether realty or personalty, may be limited in tail (Law of Property Act 1925, s. 130). Before 1925, only realty could be so limited.

Secondly, the legislation sought to reduce the number of legal estates and interests in land. Prior to 1925 there were four freehold estates in land: the fee simple, the fee tail, the life estate and an estate per autre vie.

Law of Property Act 1925

1. Legal estates and equitable interests

(1) The only estates in land which are capable of subsisting or of being conveyed or created at law are—

    (a) An estate in fee simple absolute in possession;

    (b) A term of years absolute.

(2) The only interests or charges in or over land which are capable of subsisting or of being conveyed or created at law are—

    (a) An easement, right, or privilege in or over land for an interest equivalent to an estate in fee simple absolute in possession or a term of years absolute;

    (b) A rentcharge in possession issuing out of or charged on land being either perpetual or for a term of years absolute;

    (c) A charge by way of legal mortgage;

    (d) . . . and any other similar charge on land which is not created by an instrument;

    (e) Rights of entry exercisable over or in respect of a legal term of years absolute, or annexed, for any purpose, to a legal rentcharge.

(3) All other estates, interests, and charges in or over land take effect as equitable interests.

Note
The effect of s. 1(1) is that all interests such as entailed interests and life estates which could previously have been held at law, can now only exist behind a trust in equity. A fee tail is an estate that resembles a fee simple in that on the death of the tenant in tail the property devolves upon the heir, but the heir has to be found amongst the descendants of the original tenant in tail and the land cannot be inherited by a collateral relation of the original tenant in tail. Thus a fee tail comes to an end if no descendants of the original tenant in tail can be found. The life estate is self-explanatory in that land is given to a person for the period of his life and the estate determines on his death. It is not an inheritable estate. Another form of life estate, the estate per autre vie, exists whenever a tenant is entitled to land during the life of another. The estate in such a case determines not on the death of the tenant but on the death of the other party.

Law of Property Act 1925

4. Creation and disposition of equitable interests
(1) Interests in land validly created or arising after the commencement of this Act, which are not capable of subsisting as legal estates, shall take effect as equitable interests, and, save as otherwise expressly provided by statute, interests in land which under the Statute of Uses or otherwise could before the commencement of this Act have been created as legal interests, shall be capable of being created as equitable interests:

Provided that, after the commencement of this Act (and save as hereinafter expressly enacted), an equitable interest in land shall only be capable of being validly created in any case in which an equivalent equitable interest in property real or personal could have been validly created before such commencement.

(2) All rights and interests in land may be disposed of, including—
   (a) a contingent, executory or future equitable interest in any land, or a possibility coupled with an interest in any land, whether or not the object of the gift or limitation of such interest or possibility be ascertained;
   (b) a right of entry, into or upon land whether immediate or future, and whether vested or contingent.

(3) All rights of entry affecting a legal estate which are exercisable on condition broken or for any other reason may after the commencement of this Act, be made exercisable by any person and the persons deriving title under him, but, in regard to an estate in fee simple (not being a rentcharge held for a legal estate) only within the period authorised by the rule relating to perpetuities.

A: LEGAL ESTATES (SECTION 1(1))

(a) The fee simple absolute in possession

This is the best estate in land that can exist in English law. As Megarry and Wade say, 'Although strictly speaking it is still held in tenure and therefore falls short of absolute ownership, in practice it is absolute ownership, for nearly all traces of the old feudal burdens have disappeared. A tenant in fee simple enjoys all the advantages of absolute ownership, except the form' (*Law of Real Property*, 5th edn, p. 59). It may be helpful to analyse the meaning of the constituent parts of the expression.

(i) *Fee simple* This really has lost its significance post 1925. The word 'fee' means that the estate was one that, before 1925, was inheritable, and the term 'simple' denotes that the estate could be inherited by the 'general heirs' (as opposed, for example, to male heirs only). As long as there were general heirs to inherit, then the estate would endure. The 1925 legislation abolished the importance of the 'heir'.

(ii) *Absolute* The term 'absolute' 'qualifies the character of a fee simple estate in such a way as to distinguish it from various forms of modified fee(s)' (Gray, 'Elements of Land Law', p. 71). Modified fees are fees that are limited in some way, such as a determinable fee simple and conditional fee simple (see pages 19–22). A fee simple will still be absolute, however, if it is encumbered in some way, for example by a mortgage.

(iii) *Possession*

Law of Property Act 1925

205. General definitions
(xix) 'Possession' includes receipt of rents and profits or the right to receive the same, if any; and 'income' includes rents and profits; . . .

Notes
1. The term 'in possession' is used to distinguish a present enjoyment in the property from a future enjoyment.
2. A fee simple owner who grants a lease of his property is nevertheless a legal owner of a fee simple even though he does not have possession of the property.

Law of Property Act 1925

1. Legal estates and equitable interests
(5) A legal estate may subsist concurrently with or subject to any other legal estate in the same land in like manner as it could have done before the commencement of this Act.

(b) Terms of years absolute (commonly called a lease)

Law of Property Act 1925

205. General definitions
(xxvii) 'Term of years absolute' means a term of years (taking effect either in possession or in reversion whether or not at a rent) with or without impeachment for waste, subject or not to another legal estate, and either certain or liable to determination by notice, re-entry, operation of law, or by a provision for cesser on redemption, or in any other event (other than the dropping of a life, or the determination of a determinable life interest); but does not include any term of years determinable with life or lives or with the cesser of a determinable life interest, nor, if created after the

commencement of this Act, a term of years which is not expressed to take effect in possession within twenty-one years after the creation thereof where required by this Act to take effect within that period; and in this definition the expression 'terms of years' includes a term for less than a year, or for a year or years and a fraction of a year or from year to year; . . .

Notes
1. The term of years is inferior to the fee simple absolute, since it is of limited duration.
2. The word 'absolute' in the phrase 'term of years absolute' is apparently meaningless, because a term of years will not cease merely because of the occurrence of some event, for example, re-entry.

B: MODIFIED FEES

Fees that are subject to a limitation or provision are known as modified fees. There are two kinds of modified fees:

(a) determinable fees;
(b) conditional fees.

(a) Determinable fee
This is a fee simple which will automatically determine on the occurrence of some specified event which may never occur. If the event is bound to occur, then there is no determinable fee.

Re Leach
[1912] 2 Ch 422 (ChD)

A brother devised certain real property upon trust to pay the annual income from it to the plaintiff, until he should assign, charge or otherwise dispose of the same or become bankrupt. If the estate should determine in the plaintiff's lifetime, the trustees were to accumulate the interest for the male heir of the plaintiff's body until he was 21. If the plaintiff were to die without leaving a male heir, then the income was to go to the plaintiff's brothers and their respective male heirs with remainder to the plaintiff's sisters as tenants in common. Held: the plaintiff took an equitable estate in fee simple determinable on the happening of any of the specified events.

JOYCE J: In other words, I think that what Robert takes is an equitable estate in fee simple, determinable in the event of his assigning, charging, or becoming bankrupt, &c., which estate, if he dies without assigning, charging, or becoming bankrupt, &c., becomes an ordinary estate in fee simple, but subject to the executory limitation over to the testator's nephews in the event of Robert dying without leaving any male heir of his body at the time of his decease. I will make a declaration to that effect, but it must be without prejudice to any claim which after Robert's death his male heir or the male heir of his body living at his death may make.

(b) Conditional fee

This is a fee simple which has a condition attached to it, by which the estate given to the grantee may be cut short, for example a gift of Blackacre to Harry on condition that he does not marry Mary.

(c) Difference between conditional and determinable fees

Re Moore
(1888) 39 ChD 116 (CA)

By his will, T directed his trustees to pay to his sister M 'during such time as she may live apart from her husband, before my son attains the age of 21 years, the sum of £2 10s per week for her maintenance whilst so living apart from her husband'. After the testator's death M and her husband lived apart and T's son was living and an infant. Held: The gift was not one *upon a condition* that she and her husband should live apart, but the words relating to living apart were *part of the limitation or gift*. The gift was therefore a limited gift of weekly payments to be made during a period, the commencement and duration of which the law did not allow, and thus was void.

COTTON LJ: Are the words relating to living separate a condition? In my opinion they are not a condition, but a part of the limitation, and although in some respects a condition and a limitation may have the same effect, yet in English law there is a great distinction between them. Here if you give effect to the Appellant's contention, you give her what the testator never intended to give her, an annuity during the whole of her life if the son is so long under age. It is wrong to give to an expression a forced construction in order to prevent a particular result that follows from the natural construction. . . . Many authorities have been cited, but it has not been laid down in any of them that a gift in this form is to be treated as a gift upon condition.

Note

This case illustrates the difficulty that exists in determining the difference between a determinable and conditional fee. It would seem that in a determinable fee the determining event itself sets the limit for the estate granted. In a conditional fee the condition is an independent clause added to a limitation of a fee simple absolute which, if it comes into operation, defeats it. Therefore, words such as 'while', 'during' and 'so long as' are apt to create a determinable fee, whereas words which form a separate clause of defeasance such as 'provided that', or 'on condition that' are apt to create a conditional fee. This distinction has been described in the following way by Porter MR in *Re King's Trusts* (1892) 29 LR Ir 401, at p. 410.

> It is little short of disgraceful to our jurisprudence that in reference to a rule professedly founded on considerations of public policy, a gift of an annuity to AB for life, coupled with a proviso that if he married the annuity should cease, whether there be a gift over or not, gives AB a life estate, whether he marries or not; while a gift to CD until he marries or dies, with a gift over, is at an end if CD should marry. The distinction is intelligible to a lawyer;

but no testator except a lawyer could be expected to understand it, much less to have regard to it in framing his will.

Although the dividing line between a conditional fee and determinable fee is not always clear, the consequences of the distinction are important for the following reasons:

(a) In a determinable fee, if the determining event occurs, the estate automatically determines and reverts back to the grantor — a right of reverter. The grantee ceases to have any interest in the property. In a fee simple upon a condition, if the condition occurs there is no automatic right of reverter. The grantor merely has a right of entry arising from the breach of condition when the event occurs. The fee simple continues unless and until the grantor enters the land.

(b) Neither the conditional fee nor the determinable fee comes within s. 1(1) of the Law of Property Act 1925. This has led to problems since many estates in certain areas of the country were granted subject to a condition or a rentcharge which would allow the owner of the rentcharge to enter the land if the rentcharge was not paid. Such interests could take effect only as equitable interests after 1925. The Law of Property (Amendment) Act 1926 was therefore passed (amending s. 7(1) of the Law of Property Act 1925) to deal with the problem.

Law of Property Act 1925

7. Saving of certain legal estates and statutory powers

(1) A fee simple which, by virtue of the Lands Clauses Acts, the School Sites Acts, or any similar statute, is liable to be divested, is for the purposes of this Act a fee simple absolute, and remains liable to be divested as if this Act had not been passed [and a fee simple subject to a legal or equitable right of entry or re-entry is for the purposes of this Act a fee simple absolute.]

Note
The effect of this provision was that all fee simples subject to a right of re-entry became legal estates. The Act did not affect determinable fees, however, which are still equitable.

(c) Certain types of conditions are repugnant to the courts. Conditions in this category include those that curtail a person's power of alienation, since this is one of the incidents of ownership of property; conditions directed against a course of devolution prescribed by the law, for example the rendering of a fee simple to be defeated if the tenant dies intestate; and conditions that are against public policy such as those in restraint of marriage.

If a conditional fee is subject to such conditions, then the conditions are more readily held to be void than in a determinable fee. If the courts decide the condition is void as being repugnant, the fee simple becomes absolute since the fee is properly limited even though the condition fails.

Repugnant clauses in determinable fee are less likely to be held to be contrary to public policy. If they are, however, the whole gift fails for there is no proper limitation.

(d) Enlargement of modified fees

The owner of a modified fee has the same rights over the land as a fee simple absolute owner, but at common law the owner of a modified fee could not convey a fee simple absolute, but merely a fee liable to determination. These interests now fall within the Settled Land Act 1925 and therefore are subject to the powers contained in that Act (see chapter 9). A modified fee may also become enlarged into a fee simple absolute where the determining event becomes impossible.

C: LEGAL INTERESTS (SECTION 1(2))

(a) Legal easements

(See chapter 10.) These can only be legal if held for an equivalent of either of the two legal estates.

(b) Rentcharges

A rentcharge is a right to be paid, a periodical sum of money secured on the land. If the money is not paid, the person with the benefit of the rentcharge can enter upon the land in order to enforce payment. The importance of rentcharges lies in the way in which they can be used to provide a solution to the problem that the burden of a positive covenant does not run with the land (see chapter 11).

Rent Charges Act 1977

2. Creation of rentcharges prohibited

(1) Subject to this section, no rentcharge may be created whether at law or in equity after the coming into force of this section.

(2) Any instrument made after the coming into force of this section shall, to the extent that it purports to create a rentcharge the creation of which is prohibited by this section, be void.

(3) This section does not prohibit the creation of a rentcharge—
  (a) which has the effect of making the land on which the rent is charged settled land by virtue of section 1(1)(v) of the Settled Land Act 1925;
  (b) which would have that effect but for the fact that the land on which the rent is charged is already settled land or is held on trust for sale;
  (c) which is an estate rentcharge;
  (d) under any Act of Parliament providing for the creation of rentcharges in connection with the execution of works on land (whether by way of improvements, repairs or otherwise) or the commutation of any obligation to do any such work; or
  (e) by, or in accordance with the requirements of, any order of a court.

(4) For the purposes of this section 'estate rentcharge' means (subject to subsection (5) below) a rentcharge created for the purpose—

(a) of making covenants to be performed by the owner of the land affected by the rentcharge enforceable by the rent owner against the owner for the time being of the land; or

(b) of meeting, or contributing towards, the cost of the performance by the rent owner of covenants for the provision of services, the carrying out of maintenance or repairs, the effecting of insurance or the making of any payment by him for the benefit of the land affected by the rentcharge or for the benefit of that and other land.

(5) A rentcharge of more than a nominal amount shall not be treated as an estate rentcharge for the purposes of this section unless it represents a payment for the performance by the rent owner of any such covenant as is mentioned in subsection (4)(b) above which is reasonable in relation to that covenant.

Notes
1. Section 2(1) came into effect on 22 August 1977.
2. Property can be left to a person, subject to an obligation to provide a periodical payment for another person, in order to maintain such a person. Such a rentcharge comes within the Settled Land Act 1925, s. 1(1)(v).
3. Estate rentcharges can still be created, and these are used to enforce positive covenants.

(c) Charge by way of legal mortgage
See chapter 12.

(d) A charge on land not created by an instrument
These are created by statute and are rarely encountered, for example land tax which was abolished by the Finance Act 1963.

(e) Rights of entry
These are rights that are reserved in a lease or annexed to a rentcharge to enable the landlord, for example, to recover the property if the tenant breaches any of the obligations under his lease.

SECTION 3: PROTECTION OF EQUITABLE INTERESTS

The estate and interests listed in Section 2 are legal in nature and are therefore enforceable against the whole world. We have said previously that equitable interests are enforceable against anyone except a bona fide purchaser. The object of the 1925 legislation was to make registrable all equitable interests affecting the land if such interests were not overreachable, and to thereby abolish the doctrine of notice in all but a few cases. Basically 'commercial' interests were given the benefit of registration, whereas 'family' interests were protected by means of overreaching.

The system of registration of land charges should not be confused with the system of registration of the title to the land. In the former case the title to the land is traced through the title deeds to the property, and only interests affecting the land and not the title can be registered. The law governing the area is the Land Charges Act 1972. In the latter case the title to the land is traced by means of registration; interests affecting the land are also registered and the law governing the area is the Land Registration Act 1925 (see chapter 3).

In unregistered land, title is evidenced by the title deeds and the purchaser is given details of the more recent title deeds, starting with the root of title and tracing the chain of ownership to the vendor. The question is, however, how far back should we go to find the root of title. The Law of Property Act 1925, s. 44(1) as amended by the Law of Property Act 1969, s. 23, provides that the purchaser can require the title to be deduced for at least the last 15 years. Thus the root of the title must be at least 15 years at the date of the contract.

Not only must there be a 15-year root of title but generally there must be a good root. This means that the instrument which deals with or shows title to all the legal and equitable interest to be sold, must contain an adequate description of the property and not in any way cast doubt on the title. Once a good root of title is shown, the vendor must produce every deed after the root of title. These deeds include conveyances, wills and trust deeds. If the vendor cannot do this, then the purchaser can rescind the contract. The vendor usually proves his title by sending an 'abstract of title', i.e. summaries or copies of the documents, to the purchaser which is checked against the originals before completion.

As well as checking that the vendor has title to the property, the purchaser will also want to check that there are no third-party rights affecting the land which he is purchasing. Third-party rights are of two kinds:

(a) those charges and interests registered under the Land Charges Act 1972;

(b) those legal and equitable interests that are not registered under the Land Charges Act 1972.

A: REGISTRABLE INTERESTS

Land Charges Act 1972

2. The register of land charges

(1) If a charge on or obligation affecting land falls into one of the classes described in this section, it may be registered in the register of land charges as a land charge of that class.

(2) A Class A land charge is—

(a) a rent or annuity or principal money payable by instalments or otherwise, with or without interest, which is not a charge created by deed but is a charge upon land (other than a rate) created pursuant to the application of some person under the provisions of any Act of Parliament, for securing to any person either the money spent by him or the costs, charges and expenses incurred by him under such Act, or the money advanced by him for repaying the money spent or the costs, charges and expenses incurred by another person under the authority of an Act of Parliament; or

(b) a rent or annuity or principal money payable as mentioned in paragraph (a) above which is not a charge created by deed but is a charge upon land (other than a rate) created pursuant to the application of some person under any of the enactments mentioned in Schedule 2 to this Act.

(3) A Class B land charge is a charge on land (not being a local land charge) . . . of any of the kinds described in paragraph (a) of subsection (2) above, created otherwise than pursuant to the application of any person.

(4) A Class C land charge is any of the following, [(not being a local land charge)], namely—

(i) a puisne mortgage;
(ii) a limited owner's charge;
(iii) a general equitable charge;
(iv) an estate contract;

and for this purpose—

(i) a puisne mortgage is a legal mortgage which is not protected by a deposit of documents relating to the legal estate affected;

(ii) a limited owner's charge is an equitable charge acquired by a tenant for life or statutory owner under [[the Inheritance Tax Act 1984] or under] any other statute by reason of the discharge by him of any [inheritance tax] or other liabilities and to which special priority is given by the statute;

(iii) a general equitable charge is any equitable charge which—

(a) is not secured by a deposit of documents relating to the legal estate affected; and

(b) does not arise or affect an interest arising under a trust for sale or a settlement; and

(c) is not a charge given by way of indemnity against rents equitably apportioned or charged exclusively on land in exoneration of other land and against the breach or non-observance of covenants or conditions; and

(d) is not included in any other class of land charge;

(iv) an estate contract is a contract by an estate owner or by a person entitled at the date of the contract to have a legal estate conveyed to him to convey or create a legal estate, including a contract conferring either expressly or by statutory implication a valid option to purchase, a right of pre-emption or any other like right.

(5) A Class D land charge is any of the following, [(not being a local land charge)], namely—

(i) an Inland Revenue charge;
(ii) a restrictive covenant;
(iii) an equitable easement;

and for this purpose—

(i) an Inland Revenue charge is a charge on land, being a charge acquired by the Board under [the Inheritance Tax Act 1984];

(ii) a restrictive covenant is a covenant or agreement (other than a covenant or agreement between a lessor and a lessee) restrictive of the user of land and entered into on or after 1st January 1926;

(iii) an equitable easement is an easement, right or privilege over or affecting land created or arising on or after 1st January 1926, and being merely an equitable interest.

(6) A Class E land charge is an annuity created before 1st January 1926 and not registered in the register of annuities.

(7) A Class F land charge is a charge affecting any land by virtue of the [Matrimonial Homes Act 1983].

(8) A charge or obligation created before 1st January 1926 can only be registered as a Class B land charge or a Class C land charge if it is acquired under a conveyance made on or after that date.

Notes
1. Only interests that appear in this section are land charges capable of being registered as such under s. 1(1)(a) of the Act at the Land Charges Registry at Plymouth.
2. Section 1(1) lists the five registers that are kept there:

   (a) a register of land charges;
   (b) a register of pending actions;
   (c) a register of writs and orders affecting land;
   (d) a register of deeds of arrangement affecting land;
   (e) a register of annuities.

(a) Pending actions

Pending actions relate to 'any action or proceeding pending in court relating to land or any interest in or charge on land' (Land Charges Act 1972, s. 17(1)). Thus the section is widely worded.

The following case involves a spouse's claim to a property adjustment order.

Perez-Adamson v Perez-Rivas
[1987] 3 All ER 20 (CA)

W left the matrimonial home, which was in H's sole name. On 4 June 1985, she presented a petition for divorce and sought a property adjustment order. On 7 June, she registered her claim for a property adjustment order as a pending action under s. 5 of the Land Charges Act 1972. On 21 June, H asked his bank for a bridging loan for the purpose of purchasing a house to be secured by a first charge on the matrimonial home. The bank manager agreed to the loan and H executed a legal charge over the property on 4 July 1985. The bank advanced the money without searching the land charges register, and thus had no actual knowledge of W's registration of a pending action. The bank subsequently discovered H had acted dishonestly. W applied for the property adjustment order and for an order to set aside the bank's legal charge. Held: a wife's application for a property adjustment order (under Matrimonial Causes Act 1973, s. 24) is a claim which, if registered against the matrimonial home under s. 5 of the 1972 Act, constitutes a pending land action and amounts to notice to the parties to any subsequent mortgage or conveyance and would therefore have priority.

DILLON LJ: Then comes the question: what is the effect of a registration under s. 5 of the 1972 Act? It is referred to as a registration in the register of pending actions, and it seems that registration of pending actions by the term lis pendens goes back as far as the Judgments Act 1839. Section 5(7) of the 1972 Act provides:

> A pending land action [that is the description of what is to be registered] shall not bind a purchaser without express notice of it unless it is for the time being registered under this section.

Section 198 of the Law of Property Act 1925 provides:

(1) The registration of any instrument or matter under the provisions of the Land Charges Act, 1925, or any enactment which it replaces, in any register kept at the land registry or elsewhere, shall be deemed to constitute actual notice of such instrument or matter, and of the fact of such registration, to all persons and for all purposes connected with the land affected, as from the date of registration or other prescribed date and so long as the registration continues in force...

The clear implication, as it seems to me, from s. 5(7) of the 1972 Act is that a pending land action does bind a purchaser, even if he has no express notice of it, if it is for the time being registered under the section. The term 'pending land action' is defined in s. 17 of the 1972 Act as meaning 'any action or proceeding pending in court relating to land or any interest in or charge on land'. 'Land' is widely defined, but does not include an undivided share in land. That definition was considered by Megarry J in *Calgary & Edmonton Land Co. Ltd* v *Dobinson* [1974] 1 All ER 484 at 489, [1974] Ch 102 at 107. He said:

... The rights made registrable under the Land Charges Act 1972, as under the Land Charges Act 1925, are in general substantive rights in the land. Those with specified rights or *claims* to the land or any interest in it must register those rights or claims (and so give warning to purchasers) or else suffer the consequences of failure to register. What is protected is some substantive right adverse to the owner, rather than a mere fetter on the owner's rights of disposition ... What is registrable as a pending land action is an action or proceeding which claims some proprietary right in the land and not an action merely claiming that the owner should be restrained from exercising his powers of disposition. (My emphasis.)

The effect of that, because otherwise there is no point in having registration to give warning to purchasers, seems to me to be that the claim, if it be a claim rather than a present right which is being protected, will bind the purchaser once registration has been effected, so long as the registration subsists.

The position of registration of claims for ancillary relief was considered by the courts in *Whittingham* v *Whittingham (National Westminster Bank Ltd intervening)* [1978] 3 All ER 805, [1979] Fam 9. What that case actually decided was that, where a wife had applied in divorce proceedings for an order that a certain property be transferred to her but she had not effected any registration of the claim as a pending action and her husband subsequently charged the property in favour of a bank, the wife could not apply to set aside the charge because her claim under s. 24 of the 1973 Act for the transfer of the property was not binding on the bank. Of course registration of such a claim for a property adjustment order could only arise after a divorce petition has been presented, and there may well be cases in which the avoidance transaction, or, as it is put in s. 37, 'the reviewable disposition', has been made before the petition was presented. In those cases all that will have to be considerd where a third party is concerned is whether the third party gave valuable consideration and at the time of the disposition acted in relation to it in good faith and without notice of any intention on the part of the other party to defeat the applicant's claim for financial relief. Where, however, there has been a registration, the position is not quite the same. Balcombe J, having given his reasons in *Whittingham* v *Whittingham* at first instance for concluding that on the facts of that case the wife's claim for ancillary relief was not binding on the bank, said at the end of his judgment ([1978] 3 All ER 805 at 812, [1979] Fam 9 at 18):

I do not believe that the practical effect of this judgment will be seriously to prejudice the ability of a spouse, usually a wife, to set aside a reviewable disposition of land under s. 37 of the 1973 Act. Where a party has applied for a transfer of property order, registration of that application as a pending land action should afford an effective protection against any future disposition.

When that case came to this court the decision of Balcombe J was affirmed. Stamp LJ said in giving the leading judgment of this court ([1978] 3 All ER 805 at 813–814, [1979] Fam 9 at 21):

> I am bound to say that considering the matter without the aid of authority I would not feel much hesitation in holding that a summons to obtain the transfer of a specified property under s. 24 does relate to that property. Furthermore it appears to me desirable that a wife who has issued such a summons should be able to safeguard the property, pending hearing of the application, by registering a lis. If this is not so, she is placed in the unenviable position of having to establish that a transaction which subsequently takes place by way of sale or mortgage is a reviewable disposition within s. 37, involving litigation in which the good faith of the purchaser [or] mortgagee and the question whether he had notice of the wife's intention fall to be considered. Such questions are not usually at all easy to decide; in fact it was because of the difficulties involved in establishing whether a purchaser or mortgagor had or had not constructive notice of a particular dealing with land that the policy of registration of interests in land was brought into force by the effect of the Land Charges Acts. The right of a wife or husband to apply for a transfer of property under s. 24 is of recent origin, and I can see no good reason for not regarding a summons to obtain a transfer of a particular property as one which does relate to that property.

Orr LJ agreed.

The position therefore is that the long-established procedure for the registration of a lis pendens has to be married with the code under the 1973 Act for property adjustment as between spouses. The 1972 Act also includes provisions for the registration of various other property rights or interests which have in some cases been previously the subject of registrations under quite different statutes.

Taking the whole together, I would accept the view of Stamp LJ that the code, as we now have it, has the effect that the registration of the lis pendens in respect of the wife's claim for property adjustment gives her priority over any subsequent conveyance or mortgage of the property executed by the husband. . . . I would dismiss the appeal because the wife's claim for a property adjustment order has priority to the bank's charge and the wife has obtained, from the order of the judge now under appeal, an order for the transfer of the proceeds of the property to her.

Notes

1. A pending land action has been held to cover:

   (a) an action in which the issue was whether an easement existed over certain land (*Greenhi Builders* v *Allen* [1979] 1 WLR 156);

   (b) an action asserting rights based on estoppel (*Haselmere Estates Ltd* v *Baker* [1982] 1 WLR 1109).

2. The following have been held not to be pending land actions:

   (a) an action for damages for breach of a landlord's repairing covenant, since the lessees were not claiming any interest in the land (*Regan and Blackburn Ltd* v *Rogers* [1985] 1 WLR 870);

(b) an action seeking to restrain a liquidator from disposing of land (*Calgary & Edmonton Land Co. Ltd* v *Dobinson* [1974] 1 All ER 484);

(c) an action under s. 17 of the Married Women's Property Act 1882.

Section 17 was purely procedural in its nature, 'enabling disputes with regard to the matrimonial property to be brought before the court in a summary and cheap manner; it is not intended to alter the rights of the parties in the property in question' (per Danckwerts LJ in *Taylor* v *Taylor* [1968] 1 WLR 378, at p. 383). The wife's interest was to a share in the proceeds in the sale of the house and not an interest in the land under the Land Charges Act 1925.

3. The registration of a pending land action remains effective for five years and can be renewed for successive periods of five years.

See H. W. Wilkinson, 'Pending Land Actions' (1986) 136 NLJ 157.

(b) Writs and orders affecting land

Writs and orders affecting land would include writs and orders enforcing judgment, orders of the court and any receiving order in bankruptcy which has been made after 1925.

(c) Deeds of arrangement

A deed of arrangement is a document in which control over a debtor's property is given for the benefit of his creditors.

(d) Register of annuities

The register of annuities deals only with annuities created after 25 April 1855 and before 1 January 1926.

(e) Section 2 explained

(i) *A puisne mortgage* This is a legal mortgage of the legal estate which is not protected by the deposit of the title deeds. It is an example of a non-equitable interest that requires registration.

(ii) *A general equitable charge* This covers an equitable mortgage of a legal estate unprotected by the deposit of title deeds and an unpaid vendor's lien.

(iii) *An estate contract* This is a contract that is made by the owner of a legal estate to convey or create a legal estate. It covers contracts for the sale, lease or mortgage of land; leases that arise in equity (because the lease lacks the necessary formalities (see chapter 4)) and options to purchase (see chapter 4). A right of pre-emption, i.e. a right of first refusal, is expressly included in the category by s. 2(4)(iv) of the Land Charges Act 1972.

Pritchard v *Briggs*
[1980] 1 Ch 338 (CA)

The owners of a piece of land granted the defendants' predecessor in title a right of first refusal at a fixed price. The owners then granted the plaintiff a lease, and the lease contained an option giving the plaintiff the right to purchase the land on three months' notice after the death of the owners, again at a fixed price. The right of pre-emption and the option were registered as estate contracts under the Land Charges Act 1972. Held:

(1) the grantee of a right of pre-emption has no right to call for a conveyance of the land unless the grantor chooses to fulfil the conditions on which the right may be exercised;

(2) (Templeman and Stephenson LJJ) if the conditions upon which the grantee could exercise the right of pre-emption were fulfilled by the grantor, then the grantee had a right to call for a conveyance;

(3) (Goff LJ) the right of pre-emption must be from the start and throughout either an interest in land capable of binding a successor in title or a mere personal contract which is not so capable. A right of pre-emption is not an interest in land and the property legislation of 1925 proceeded on the mistaken assumption that it was.

GOFF LJ: . . . [A] right of pre-emption gives no present right, even contingent, to call for a conveyance of the legal estate. So far as the parties are concerned, whatever economic or other pressures may come to affect the grantor, he is still absolutely free to sell or not. The grantee cannot require him to do so, or demand that an offer be made to him. Moreover, even if the grantor decides to sell and makes an offer it seems to me that so long as he does not sell to anyone else he can withdraw that offer at any time before acceptance.

The judge said, . . .

. . . there would appear to be no essential difference, from the point of view of creating an interest in land, between an option on the one hand and a right of pre-emption on the other. In the well known option case, *London and South Western Railway Co.* v *Gomm*, 20 Ch D 562, 573, Kay J in the court of first instance put it happily thus: '. . . a present right to an interest in property which may arise at a period beyond the legal limit is void . . .' and thus the option in that case was in any event void as infringing the rule against perpetuities. But the point of his remark is that it is, so far as I can see, equally applicable to a right of pre-emption: it is a present right to an interest in property which may arise in the future. . . . It is, however, difficult to see why in theory the fact that the condition is one whch may be controllable by the owner of the land should make any difference.

With respect I find myself unable to accept this reasoning. The condition being one which leaves the grantee's interest subject to the volition of the grantor is different in kind from other conditions; does prevent a present interest from arising; and takes the case out of the principle enunciated by Sir George Jessel MR in *Gomm's* case, 20 ChD 562.

TEMPLEMAN LJ: Rights of option and rights of pre-emption share one feature in common; each prescribes circumstances in which the relationship between the owner of the property which is the subject of the right and the holder of the right will become the relationship of vendor and purchaser. In the case of an option, the evolution of the relationship of vendor and purchaser may depend on the fulfilment of certain specified conditions and will depend on the volition of the option holder. If the option applies to land, the grant of the the option creates a contingent equitable interest which, if registered as an estate contract, is binding on successors in title of the grantor and takes priority from the date of its registration. In the case of a right of pre-emption, the evolution of the relationship of vendor and purchaser depends on the grantor, of his own volition, choosing to fulfil certain specified conditions and thus converting the pre-emption into an option. The grant of the right of pre-emption creates a mere spes which the grantor of the right may either frustrate by choosing not to fulfil the necessary conditions or may convert into an option and thus into equitable interest by fulfilling the conditions. An equitable interest thus created is protected by prior registration of the right of pre-emption as an estate contract but takes its priority from the date when the right of pre-emption becomes exercisable and the right is converted into an option and the equitable interest is then created. The holder of a right of pre-emption is in much the same position as a beneficiary under a will of a testator who is still alive, save that the holder of the right of pre-emption must hope for some future positive action by the grantor which will elevate his hope into an interest. It does not seem to me that the property legislation of 1925 was intended to create, or operated to create an equitable interest in land where none existed.

Notes
1. See also *Taylors Fashions Ltd.* v *Liverpool Victoria Trustees Co. Ltd* [1982] 1 QB 133 (chapter 7), where there was expenditure by the tenants of premises on improvements to the premises in reliance on an option.
2. An estate contract includes a lessee's option to renew a lease which is contained in that lease even when the option runs with the reversion (see *Phillips* v *Mobil Oil Co. Ltd* [1989] 3 All ER 97).
3. A notice to treat served under a compulsory purchase order does not give rise to a contract to sell, and it is thus not registrable as an estate contract. It is merely a preliminary step.
4. A notice given by a tenant of his wish to acquire the freehold is an estate contract (see s. 5(5) of the Leasehold Reform Act 1967).

(iv)   *Class D land charges*   Class D is divided into three categories:

(i)   A charge for unpaid inheritance tax in favour of the Inland Revenue.
(ii)   A restrictive covenant made after 1925. Restrictive covenants which are made between a lessor and a lessee are expressly excluded.
(iii)   An equitable easement.

Shiloh Spinners Ltd v Harding
[1973] AC 691 (HL)

The plaintiffs assigned their leasehold interest to T in 1961. T covenanted on its own behalf and that of its successors to perform certain fencing obligations and obligations of support for buildings retained by the plaintiff. The plaintiffs had a right to re-enter and retake the premises in the event of any breach of the covenants. The right was not registered as a land charge. In 1965, T sold its interest to the defendant. Under the terms of the 1961 assignment T was thereby freed from further liability. In 1969, the plaintiffs, relying on the right of re-entry, sued the defendant for possession alleging a failure to perform the various obligations. Held: *inter alia*, that the right of entry which was not registered under the Land Charges Act 1925 was nevertheless exercisable against the defendant. The right of entry was equitable and *did not* come within either class C(iv) or class D(iii).

LORD WILBERFORCE: The next question is of a substantial character. The right of entry, it is said, is unenforceable against the respondent, although he took with actual notice of it, because it was not registered as a charge under the Land Charges Act 1925. There is no doubt that if it was capable of registration under that Act, it is unenforceable if not registered: the appellants deny that it was so capable either (i) because it was a legal right, not an equitable right, or (ii) because, if equitable, it does not fall within any of the classes or descriptions of charges registration of which is required. . . .

So I pass, as did the Court of Appeal, to the Land Charges Act 1925. The original contention of the respondents was that the equitable right of entry was capable of registration under Class D(iii) of the Act. In the Court of Appeal an alternative contention was raised, apparently at the court's suggestion, that it might come within Class C(iv). In my opinion this is unmaintainable. [Lord Wilberforce outlines s. 2(4)(iv) LCA 1925.]

The only words capable of including a right of entry are 'any other like right,' but, in my opinion, no relevant likeness can be found. An option or right of pre-emption eventuates in a contract for sale at a price; this is inherent in 'purchase' and 'pre-emption'; the right of entry is penal in character and involves the revesting of the lease, in the event of default, in a previous owner. There is no similarity in law or fact between these situations.

[Lord Wilberforce outlines s. 2(5)(iii).]

The argument for inclusion in this class falls into two parts. First it is said that a right of entry falls fairly within the description, or at least that, if the words do not appear to include it, they are sufficiently open in meaning to admit it. Secondly it is said that the provisions of the Law of Property Act as to 'overreaching' compel the conclusion that a right of entry must fall under some class or sub-class of the Land Charges Act, and since this is the only one whose words can admit it, they should be so interpreted as to do so. Thus the argument depends for its success upon a combination of ambiguity, or openness of Class D(iii) with compelling consideration brought about in the overreaching provisions. In my opinion it fails under both limbs: Class D(iii) cannot be interpreted so as to admit equitable rights of entry, and no conclusive, compelling, or even clear conclusions can be drawn from the overreaching provisions which can influence the interpretation of Class D(iii).

Dealing with Class D(iii), I reject at once the suggestion that any help (by way of enlarging the content of this class) can be derived either from the introductory words, for they limit themselves to the 'following kinds,' or from the words 'and being merely an equitable interest,' for these are limiting, not enlarging, words. I leave out of account the label at the end — though I should think it surprising if so expert a draftsman had attached that particular label if the class included a right of entry. To include a right of entry in the description of 'equitable easement' offends a sense both of elegance and accuracy. That leaves 'easement right or privilege over or affecting land.' If this were the only place where the expression occurred in this legislation, I should find it difficult to attribute to 'right' a meaning so different in quality from easement and privilege as to include a right of entry. The difference between a right to use or draw profit from another man's land, and a right to take his land altogether away, is one of quality, not of degree. But the words are plentifully used both in the Law of Property Act and elsewhere in the 1925 legislation, so are the words 'rights of entry,' and I find it impossible to believe that in this one context the one includes the other. The two expressions are even used by way of what seems deliberate contrast in two contexts: first in section 1 of the Law of Property Act, where subsection (2)(a) mentions 'An easement, right, or privilege in or over land' and paragraph (e) of the same subsection 'Rights of entry': secondly, in section 162(1)(d) which mentions both. An argument, unattractive but perhaps just palatable, can be devised why it might have been necessary in section 1 of the Law of Property Act to mention both easements, rights or privileges and the particular rights of entry described in subsection (2)(e), but no explanation can be given why, if the latter are capable of being included in the former, they should be mentioned with such a degree of separation. I do not further elaborate this point because a reading of their judgments leaves little doubt that the Lords Justices would themselves have read Class D(iii) as I can only read it but for the influence of the overreaching argument.

So I turn to the latter. This, in my opinion, only becomes compellng if one first accepts the conclusion that all equitable claims relating to land are either registrable under the Land Charges Act, or capable of being overreached under section 2 of the Law of Property Act; i.e., are capable by use of the appropriate mechanism of being transferred to the proceeds of sale of the land they affect. If this dilemma could be made good, then there could be an argument for forcing, within the limits of the possible, an equitable right of entry into one of the registrable classes since it is obviously not suitable for overreaching. But the dilemma cannot be made good. What may be overreached is 'any equitable interest or power affecting that estate': yet 'equitable interest' (for powers do not enter into the debate) is a word of most uncertain content. The searcher after a definition has to be satisfied with section 1(8) 'Estates, interests, and charges in or over land which are not legal estates are in this Act referred to as "equitable interests"' — a tautology rather than a definition. There is certainly nothing exhaustive about the expression 'equitable interests' — just as certainly it has no clear boundaries. The debate whether such rights as equity, over the centuries, has conferred against the holder of the legal estate are truly proprietary in character, or merely rights in personam, or a hybrid between the two, may have lost some of its vitality in the statutory context but the question inevitably rises to mind whether the 'curtain' or 'overreaching' provisions of the 1925 legislation extend to what are still conveniently called 'equities' or 'mere equities,' such as rights to rectification, or to set aside a conveyance. There is good authority, which I do not presume to doubt, for a sharp distinction between the two — I instance Lord Upjohn in *National Provincial Bank Ltd v Hastings Car Mart Ltd* [1965] AC 1175, 1238 and *Snell's Principles of Equity*, 25th edn. (1960) p. 38. I am impressed by the decision in *E. R. Ives Investment Ltd v High* [1967] 2 QB 379 in which the Court of Appeal held that a right by estoppel — producing an effect similar to an easement — was not registrable under Class D(iii). Lord Denning MR referred to the right as subsisting only in equity. Danckwerts LJ thought it was an equity created by estoppel or a proprietary estoppel: plainly this was not an equitable interest capable of being overreached, yet no member of the court considered that the right — so like an easement — could be brought within Class D(iii). The conclusion followed, and the court accepted it, that whether it was binding on a purchaser depended on notice. All this seems to show that there may well be rights, of an equitable character, outside the provisions as to registration and which are incapable of being overreached.

That equitable rights of entry should be among them is not in principle unacceptable. First, rights of entry, before 1925, were not considered to confer an interest in the land. They were described as bare possibilities (*Challis's Real Property*, 3rd edn.

(1911), p. 76) so that it is not anomalous that equitable rights of entry should not be treated as equitable interests. Secondly, it is important that section 10 of the Land Charges Act 1925 should be given a plain and ordinary interpretation. It is a section which involves day to day operation by solicitors doing conveyancing work: they should be able to take decisions and advise their clients upon a straight-forward interpretation of the registration classes, not upon one depending upon a sophisticated, not to say disputable, analysis of other statutes. Thirdly, the consequence of equitable rights of entry not being registrable is that they are subject to the doctrine of notice, preserved by section 199 of the Law of Property Act. This may not give complete protection, but neither is it demonstrable that it is likely to be less effective than the present system of registration against names. I am therefore of opinion that Class D(iii) should be given its plain prima facie meaning and that so read it does not comprise equitable rights of entry. It follows that non-registration does not make the appellants' right unenforceable in this case.

Note
See Paul Fairest, '*Shiloh*: The Skein Unravelled?' [1973] CLJ 218.

(v) *Class F land charges* The Matrimonial Homes Act 1967 was implemented to provide machinery whereby a spouse could effectively protect her rights of occupation in the matrimonial home against third parties. The Act was originally designed to protect a spouse (X) who was as risk because the other spouse (Y) had sole legal ownership of the property, and could therefore deal with it without X's knowledge and consent. The Act was never designed to protect spouses who had the legal estate vested in both of them, since the property could not be effectively dealt with in such a situation without the consent and knowledge of both parties. A problem occurred, however, if the legal estate was vested in one spouse (Y) on trust for himself and the other spouse (X and Y) (see *Caunce* v *Caunce*, at page 37). The Act was therefore amended by s. 38 of the Matrimonial Proceedings and Property Act 1970, now the Matrimonial Homes Act 1983, s. 1(11), so that X in the above example, could protect his or her right of occupation without prejudicing his or her claim to any proprietary interest.

A class F land charge is one that arises from the Matrimonial Homes Act 1983.

Megarry J described the nature of the right (in relation to the 1967 Act) in the following case.

Wroth* v *Tyler
[1974] 1 Ch 30 (ChD)

MEGARRY J: I can now say something about the nature of the charge and the mode of operation of the Act. First, for a spouse in occupation, the right seems to be a mere statutory right for the spouse not to be evicted. There appears to be nothing to stay the eviction of others. For example, if a wife is living in her husband's house with their children and her parents, her charge, even if registered, appears to give no protection against eviction to the children or parents. (I shall return to this point.) Nor if the wife takes in lodgers does there seem to be anything to prevent the husband from evicting them. If, for example, the husband is himself living in the house, it would be remarkable if the Act gives the wife the right to insist upon having other occupants in the home against his will. The statutory right appears in essence to be a purely personal right for the wife not to be evicted; and it seems wholly inconsistent with the Act that this right should be assignable or otherwise disposable. I may add that there is nothing to require the wife to make any payment to the husband for her occupation, unless ordered by the court under section 1(3), though if she is in occupation against his will and by virtue of her statutory rights, it may be that she will be in rateable occupation.

Second, although the right given to an occupying wife by section 1(1) is merely a right not to be evicted or excluded 'by the other spouse,' and so at first sight does not appear to be effective against anyone except that other spouse, section 2(1) makes the right 'a charge' on the husband's estate or interest; and it is this, rather than the provisions for registration, which makes the right binding on successors in title. The operation of the provision for registration seems to be essentially negative; the right is a charge which, if not duly protected by registration, will become void against subsequent purchasers, or fail to bind them. In this, the right seems not to differ from other registrable charges, such as general equitable charges or puisne mortgages. Yet there is this difference. For other charges, the expectation of the statute is plainly that they will all be protected by registration, whereas under the Act of 1967 there does not seem to be the same expectation.

The case of multiple matrimonial homes illustrates this point. If a husband owns three houses that either are or have been a matrimonial home for him and his wife, under section 3 she can only have one of her charges protected by registration at any one time. For the unregistered two, the Act plainly contemplates that although each is subject to a charge under the Act in favour of the wife, if the husband sells them her charges, for want of registration, will not bind the purchaser. Furthermore, it may well be doubted whether in the ordinary case of single matrimonial homes the Act contemplated that there would be mass registrations in respect of all matrimonial homes, however happy and stable the marriage. In such cases, it may well be that the expectation was that there would be no registration, and so no need for any release of the statutory rights or cancellation of the registration when the home was sold; for although the wife held a charge on the husband's estate in the house, that charge would be void against the purchaser. There is no evidence before me on what has in fact happened, but it would not be surprising if in fact the Act in the main has been operating on a basis of the mass invalidation of the statutory charges for want of registration, with registration being effected only in cases of actual or impending disputes.

Third, the Act has put into the hands of all spouses with statutory rights of occupation a weapon of great power and flexibility. Registration is a relatively simple, speedy and secret process, as compared with the necessarily more complex, protracted and less private process of selling a house and carrying through the contract to completion. As this case illustrates, Parliament has made it possible for the protected spouse to go far towards having his or her way as to not moving from the matrimonial home, at the expense of the other spouse and innocent purchasers. No doubt, too, the protected spouse may, by registering the statutory charge, and particularly by registering it at an inconvenient moment, require the owning spouse to buy off the charge. In some cases this may be very proper; in others it may be less so: but the power to do it is a unilateral power, free from any restraints. . . .

At this stage I may summarise my conclusions as to the essentials of the right given by the Act to an occupying spouse as follows. The right is in essence a personal and non-assignable statutory right not to be evicted from the matrimonial home in question during marriage or until the court otherwise orders; and this right constitutes a charge on the estate or interest of the owning spouse which requires protection against third parties by registration. For various reasons, the right may be said to be one which readily fits into no category known to conveyancers before 1967; the phrase sui generis seems apt, but of little help.

Barnett v Hassett
[1981] 1 WLR 1385 (Fam Div)

Prior to their marriage, H exchanged contracts for the purchase of a house in Barnet and paid a deposit. In March 1980, after their marriage, H moved into W's house and sold his former house. In May H told the vendors of the house in Barnet that he could not complete the purchase, and H therefore forfeited the deposit. H moved out of W's house, and on 17 July W exchanged contracts for the sale of her house. H assured the purchaser in writing that he would not register a charge against the property under the Matrimonial Homes Act 1967. In November 1980, H registered a class F land charge against W's home on the basis that W had originally agreed that the Barnet house would be purchased in joint names with W paying half. Therefore H had suffered loss when W repudiated that agreement. Held: the charge was an improper use of the procedure under the Act and was set aside.

WOOD J: [S]ection 1 of the Act protects a spouse who has no rights to remain in the matrimonial home. It does not protect a spouse who has proprietary, contractual or statutory rights of occupation: see *Gurasz v Gurasz* [1970] P 11. If not in occupation the right of a spouse is 'with the leave of the court so given to enter into and occupy the dwelling house': section 1(1)(b). The whole emphasis of the Act is to create and protect the right to occupation of a spouse not in occupation or a spouse already in occupation. This is made clear throughout the Act. The right to occupation must relate to a matrimonial home, and only continues during the existence of the marriage. A Class F charge is intended to protect that right.

One thing is abundantly clear, namely that this husband does not seek 'to enter into and occupy' the whole or any part of the matrimonial home. Is he entitled to ask the court to freeze any part of the proceeds of sale? I do not think so. Mr Price did not draw my attention to any specific parts of the Act itself, but quite apart from the points to which I have already referred, section 3 of the Act seems to me to emphasise that any interest other than a right to occupy is to be excluded or disregarded. By that section a charge can only be registered on one matrimonial home at a time. If the intention of the Act had been to allow a spouse to place his or her hands upon proceeds of sale or to allow the prevention of such a sale then I would have thought that a charge on a matrimonial home not in occupation and when a sale was likely would be an obvious source for funds.

When a spouse is applying for a transfer of property order involving the matrimonial home or other land, then it will fall within the definition of 'pending land action' in section 17(1) of the Land Charges Act 1972 and is registerable as such; see *Whittingham v Whittingham (National Westminster Bank Ltd, intervener)* [1979] Fam 9.

I was informed that the present point is as yet undecided but for the reasons which I have given above and each of them, in my judgment, the registration of this Class F charge in the circumstances of the present case was not a proper use of the process set up by the Act of 1967 and the charge will be set aside. No further order will be made in respect of the proceeds of sale.

B: UNREGISTRABLE INTERESTS

There are certain interests that do not come within the provisions of the Land Charges Act 1972, nor do they come within the provisions of the overreaching machinery (see pages 282–6 and chapter 8). The interests that come within the category of unregistrable interests are either unregistrable because the Land Charges Act 1972 expressly makes them so, or because the courts have declared them to be so. In either situation their enforceability is governed by the old doctrine of notice. Such interests include:

(a) Restrictive covenants created before 1926.
(b) Equitable easements created before 1926.
(c) Beneficial interests under a bare trust.
(d) Pre-1926 equitable mortgages where there was a deposit of title deeds or there has been no transfer since 1925.
(e) Equitable rights of entry (see *Shiloh Spinners* v *Harding, supra*) and also *Poster* v *Slough Estates Ltd* [1968] 1 WLR 1515 where it was said that a right of entry to remove fixtures on the termination of the term of the lease was not governed by the LCA, but by the doctrine of notice.
(f) Beneficial interests under resulting or implied trusts.
(g) Contractual licences.
(h) Equitable interests based on estoppel.
(i) A charging order on an undivided share of land.

Interests (f) to (i) above are considered below.

Beneficial interests under resulting or implied trusts

Caunce v *Caunce*
[1969] 1 WLR 286 (ChD)

H and W intended to purchase property as their matrimonial home, and contributed the purchase moneys unequally. They agreed that the property should be conveyed to them as joint tenants but H, in breach of the agreement, procured a conveyance into his sole name. H therefore held the property on an implied or resulting trust for himself and W. Without W's knowledge H raised three mortgages on the property and subsequently became bankrupt. W claimed the bank had constructive notice of her equitable interest as it should have inquired whether she had an interest. Held: unless the bank had constructive notice of W's equitable interest it took free from it. The inquiries were not of a type the bank ought reasonably to have made under s. 199(1) of the Law of Property Act 1925.

STAMP LJ: [Discusses the doctrine of constructive notice under the bona fide doctrine.] In this connection I would borrow two passages in the judgment of Farwell

J in *Hunt* v *Luck* [1901] 1 Ch 45, to which I have already referred. The first is on p. 48 of the report, and runs as follows:

> This doctrine of constructive notice, imputing as it does knowledge which the person affected does not actually possess, is one which the courts of late years have been unwilling to extend. I am not referring to cases where a man wilfully shuts his eyes so as to avoid notice, but to cases like the present, where honest men are to be affected by knowledge which every one admits they did not in fact possess. So far as regards the merits of the case, even assuming both parties to the action to be equally innocent, the man who has been swindled by too great confidence in his own agent has surely less claim to the assistance of a court of equity than a purchaser for value who gets the legal estate, and pays his money without notice. Granted that the vendor has every reason to believe his agent an honest man, still, if he is mistaken and trusts a rogue, he, rather than the purchaser for value without notice who is misled by his having so trusted, ought to bear the burden.

And so it appears to me, as between a wife who has trusted her husband to have the property vested in his sole name, or who has not taken steps to get it vested in joint names, on the one hand and a mortgagee bank on the other.

The second passage of Farwell J's judgment is at p. 52 of the report, and runs as follows:

> Constructive notice is the knowledge which the courts impute to a person upon a presumption so strong of the existence of the knowledge that it cannot be allowed to be rebutted, either from his knowing something which ought to have put him to further inquiry or from his wilfully abstaining from inquiry, to avoid notice. How can I hold that the mortgagees here wilfully neglected to make some inquiry which is usual in cases of mortgages or sales of real estate in order to avoid acquiring some knowledge which they would thereby have obtained.

The last sentence of that passage appears to be applicable to the facts of the present case.... Nor do I find the suggestion that a bank mortgagee should at its peril be bound to conduct an inquiry into the financial relations between husband and wife, before it can advance money on security of property vested in the husband, at all an attractive one, and in my view in this day and age husbands and wives ought to be able to bank at the same bank without having their accounts analysed by the bank in order to find out if one of them is deceiving the other....

I can, perhaps, most conveniently summarise my judgment on this part of the case by referring to section 199 of the Law of Property Act, 1925, and saying that at the times of the several advances to the husband an inquiry into the details of the plaintiff's bank account, with a view to ascertaining whether she had provided a part of the purchase price, was not an inquiry which ought reasonably to have been made within the meaning of subsection (2) of that section.

I must now consider a further argument advanced on behalf of the plaintiff. It is contended that an inquiry ought to have been made on the property and that if such an inquiry had been made the plaintiff would have asserted her equitable interest, ergo — so the argument runs — the bank had constructive notice of that interest. Before going on to consider this contention it is, perhaps, convenient that I should remark by way of warning, that section 199 is a section designed not to extend but to limit the doctrine of constructive notice. The section does not operate so as to fix a purchaser with constructive notice of a matter of which he would not have had constructive notice prior to the coming into force of the Law of Property Act. The law, as I understand it, is this:

The 1925 Legislation

if there be in possession or occupation of the property, contracted to be sold or mortgaged, a person other than the vendor, or, as in this case, other than the mortgagor, and the purchaser makes no inquiry of that person, he takes the property fixed with notice of that person's rights and interests, however that may be. (See the judgment in the Court of Appeal of Vaughan-Williams LJ in *Hunt v Luck* [1902] 1 Ch 428, 432.) Here it is said that the plaintiff was in possession or occupation. No inquiry was made of her and therefore the bank is fixed with notice of her equitable interest. In my judgment, it is here that the fallacy arises, for the plaintiff, unlike the deserted wife, was not in apparent occupation or possession. She was there, ostensibly, because she was the wife, and her presence there was wholly consistent with the title offered by the husband to the bank.

A similar point was touched upon by Lord Wilberforce in *National Provincial Bank Ltd v Hastings Car Mart Ltd* [1965] AC 1175, 1248, when he said:

> For to hold that the wife acquires on marriage a right valid against third parties to remain in the house where she lives with her husband would not only fly in the face of the reality of the marriage relationship which requires the spouses to live together, as they can agree, wherever circumstances may prescribe, but would create impossible difficulties for those dealing with the property of a married man. It would mean that the concurrence of the wife would be necessary for all dealings.

In my judgment, where the vendor or mortgagor is himself in possession and occupation of the property, the purchaser or the mortgagee is not affected with notice of the equitable interests of any other person who may be resident there, and whose presence is wholly consistent with the title offered. If you buy with vacant possession on completion and you know, or find out, that the vendor is himself in possession and occupation of the property, you are, in my judgment, by reason of your failure to make further inquiries on the premises, no more fixed with notice of the equitable interest of the vendor's wife who is living there with him than you would be affected with notice of the equitable interest of any other person who might also be resident on the premises, e.g., the vendor's father, his 'Uncle Harry' or his 'Aunt Matilda,' any of whom, be it observed, might have contributed towards the purchase of the property. The reason is that the vendor being in possession, the presence of his wife or guest or lodger implies nothing to negative the title offered. It is otherwise if the vendor is not in occupation and you find another party whose presence demands an explanation and whose presence you ignore at your peril. . . .

Note
W did not register her 'right of occupation' under the Matrimonial Homes Act 1967 because at the time the Act did not cover the position of beneficial owners.

Question
Would the position be different if there had been an express trust for sale in *Caunce v Caunce*?

See *Williams & Glyn's Bank v Boland* [1980] 2 All ER 408 (chapter 3) in relation to registered land.

Contractual licences
See chapter 7 and in particular *Binions v Evans* [1972] Ch 359.

Equitable interests based on estoppel

E. R. Ives Investments Ltd v High
[1967] 2 QB 379 (CA)

The defendant bought a building site and started to build a house on it. W bought an adjoining site and started to build a block of flats there. The foundations of the flats encroached on the defendant's land and the defendant complained of the trespass. The parties agreed that W be allowed to keep the foundations of the flats on the defendant's land and the defendant was to have a right of way across W's land. X bought W's land, aware of the agreement. The defendant used the right of way and, relying on the right of way, built a garage which could only be reached by means of the right of way. X raised no objection. X sold the property to the plaintiffs, the sale and conveyance making reference to the right of way. The right of way was never registered as a land charge and the plaintiffs claimed that as such it was void against them under s. 13 of the Land Charges Act 1925. Held: (per Lord Denning MR) the defendant's right was not a right that could have been created or conveyed at law. It subsisted only in equity, and still subsists in equity without being registered.

LORD DENNING MR: The next question is this: was that right a land charge such as to need registration under the Land Charges Act, 1925? For if it was a land charge, it was never registered and would be void as against any purchaser: see section 13 of the Act. It would, therefore, be void against the plaintiffs, even though they took with the most express knowledge and notice of the right.

It was suggested that the agreement of November 2, 1949, was 'an estate contract' within Class C(iv). I do not think so. There was no contract by Mr Westgate to convey a legal estate of any kind.

It was next suggested that the right was an equitable easement' within Class D(iii). This class is defined as 'any easement right or privilege over or affecting land created or arising after the commencement of this Act, and being merely an equitable interest.' Those words are almost identical with section 2(3)(iii) of the Law of Property Act, 1925, and should be given the same meaning. They must be read in conjunction with sections 1(2)(a), 1(3) and 4(1) of the Law of Property Act, 1925. It then appears that an 'equitable easement' is a proprietary interest in land such as would before 1926 have been recognised as capable of being conveyed or created *at law*, but which since 1926 only takes effect as an equitable interest. An instance of such a proprietary interest is a profit à prendre for life. It does not include a right to possession by a requisitioning authority: see *Lewisham Borough Council* v *Maloney* [1948] 1 KB 50; 63 TLR 330; [1947] All ER 36, CA. Nor does it include a right, liberty or privilege arising in equity by reason of 'mutual benefit and burden,' or arising out of 'acquiescence,' or by reason of a contractual licence: because none of those before 1926 were proprietary interests such as were capable of being conveyed or created *at law*. They only subsisted *in equity*. They do not need to be registered as land charges, so as to bind successors, but take effect in equity without registration: see an article by Mr C. V. Davidge on 'Equitable Easements' in (1937) 59 Law Quarterly Review, p. 259 and by Professor H. W. R. Wade in [1956] Cambridge Law Journal, pp. 225–226.

The right of Mr High to cross this yard was not a right such as could ever have been created or conveyed at law. It subsisted only in equity. It therefore still subsists in equity without being registered. Any other view would enable the owners of the flats to perpetrate the grossest injustice. They could block up Mr High's access to the garage, whilst keeping their foundations in his land. That cannot be right.

I am confirmed in this construction of the statute when I remember that there are many houses adjoining one another which have drainage systems in common, with mutual benefits and burdens. The statute cannot have required all these to be registered as land charges.

I know that this greatly restricts the scope of Class D(iii) but this is not disturbing. A special committee has already suggested that Class D(iii) should be abolished altogether: see the report of the Committee on Land Charges ((1956) Command Paper 9825, para. 16).

A charging order on an undivided share of land

Perry v *Phoenix Assurance plc* [1988] 3 All ER 60 (ChD)

H and W were debtors and owners of a house, which they held as joint tenants on a trust for sale. P obtained judgment against H and W on 4 September 1985. The order remained unpaid and P applied for a charging order under the Charging Orders Act 1979, s. 2 with respect to the house. On 4 November, a *nisi* order was made against H alone and it was registered on 14 November. On 20 November, the charging order was made absolute against H and W and was registered on 2 December. On 26 November, D searched the land charges register and obtained a certificate disclosing only the charge against H. As a result of this they advanced money to H and W secured by a charge by way of a legal mortgage. The registration of the *nisi* order against H was cancelled. H and W failed to pay the mortgage instalments and on 19 December 1986 D sold the property as mortgagee. P claimed that he was entitled to be paid his judgment debt from the husband's share of the proceeds of sale of the property in priority to the defendants' right to satisfy their debts, because of the registration of the order prior to 26 November. Held: though a charging order could be made on an undivided share in land, it was incapable of being registered under the Land Charges Act 1972.

C: OVERREACHING

For a detailed discussion of this point, see chapter 8, section 4.

The 1925 legislation expressly preserves the overreaching machinery in relation to equitable interests that arise under a trust for sale or strict settlement. Such interests do not come within the classes of interests that are registrable under the Land Charges Act, and the purchaser of property subject to these interests can take free of them if certain conditions are fulfilled.

SECTION 4: EFFECT OF REGISTRATION OF LAND CHARGES

See Law of Property Act 1925, s. 198, page 27.

A: EFFECT OF NON-REGISTRATION OF LAND CHARGES

Land Charges Act 1972

4. Effect of land charges and protection of purchasers

(1) A land charge of Class A (other than a land improvement charge registered after 31st December 1969) or of Class B shall, when registered, take effect as if it had been created by a deed of charge by way of legal mortgage, but without prejudice to the priority of the charge.

(2) A land charge of Class A created after 31st December 1888 shall be void as against a purchaser of the land charged with it or of any interest in such land, unless the land charge is registered in the register of land charges before the completion of the purchase.

(3) After the expiration of one year from the first conveyance occurring on or after 1st January 1889 of a land charge of Class A created before that date the person entitled to the land charge shall not be able to recover the land charge or any part of it as against a purchaser of the land charged with it or of any interest in the land, unless the land charge is registered in the register of land charges before the completion of the purchase.

(4) If a land improvement charge was registered as a land charge of Class A before 1st January 1970, any body corporate which, but for the charge, would have power to advance money on the security of the estate or interest affected by it shall have that power notwithstanding the charge.

(5) A land charge of Class B and a land charge of Class C (other than an estate contract) created or arising on or after 1st January 1926 shall be void as against a purchaser of the land charged with it, or of any interest in such land, unless the land charge is registered in the appropriate register before the completion of the purchase.

(6) An estate contract and a land charge of Class D created or entered into on or after 1st January 1926 shall be void as against a purchaser for money or money's worth (or in the case of an Inland Revenue charge, a purchaser within the meaning of the Inheritance Tax Act 1984) of a legal estate in the land charged with it, unless the land charge is registered in the appropriate register before the completion of the purchase.

(7) After the expiration of one year from the first conveyance occurring on or after 1st January 1926 of a land charge of Class B or Class C created before that date the person entitled to the land charge shall not be able to enforce or recover the land charge or any part of it as against a purchaser of the land charged with it, or of any interest in the land, unless the land charge is registered in the appropriate register before the completion of the purchase.

(8) A land charge of Class F shall be void as against a purchaser of the land charged with it, or of any interest in such land, unless the land charge is registered in the appropriate register before the completion of the purchase.

17. Interpretation

'purchaser' means any person (including a mortgagee or lessee) who, for valuable consideration, takes any interest in land or in a charge on land, and 'purchase' has a corresponding meaning; . . .

Hollington Brothers Ltd v *Rhodes*
[1951] 2 TLR 691 (ChD)

The defendants were tenants of a block of offices. In 1945, they agreed to grant an underlease of part to the plaintiffs. The lease and counterpart-lease were never exchanged and so the underlease was never granted; neither was the agreement registered as an estate contract. Nevertheless, the plaintiffs went into possession. The defendants assigned the head lease to D 'subject to and with the benefit of such tenancies as may affect the premises'. D gave the plaintiffs notice to quit, claiming they were annual tenants. The plaintiffs negotiated with D who granted them an underlease on payment of a premium of £2,000 and an increased rent. Held: the arrangement between the plaintiffs and defendants was void for non-registration under s. 13 of the Land Charges Act 1925 (now Land Charges Act 1972, s. 4), even though at common law D would have had constructive notice of the plaintiffs' rights by virtue of their occupation.

HARMAN J: After 1925, however, by virtue of secion 10 of the Land Charges Act, 1925, this contract came within Class C(4) as a charge on or obligation affecting land, and therefore might be registered as a land charge in the Registry of Land Charges. Accordingly, by virtue of section 13(2), this being a land charge of Class C is void 'against a purchaser of the land charged therewith, or of any interest in such land, unless the land charge is registered in the appropriate register before the completion of the purchase.' Moreover, by section 199 of The Law of Property Act, 1925, a purchaser is not to be prejudicially affected by notice of any instrument or matter capable of registration under the Land Charges Act, 1925, which is void against him by reason of non-registration. This land charge was not registered, and accordingly it is said that it was void against Daymar Estates, Limited, notwithstanding their notice or knowledge, and, moreover, that there was no duty lying on the plaintiffs to register the contract in order to prevent this result. This has been held to be so by Mr Justice Wynn Parry in *Wright* v *Dean* ([1948] 64 *The Times* LR 467; [1948] Ch 686) where he said that it could not be urged that there was any such duty on the plaintiff. I propose to follow that decision, although I may observe in passing that there is in section 200(4) of the Law of Property Act, 1925, a reference to 'the obligation to register a land charge in respect of . . . any estate contract.'

The defendants' answer to this point was that in fact Daymar Estates, Limited, did not contract to obtain, and did not by the assignment get, any estate in the land expressed to override the plaintiffs' rights, and that consequently they took subject to those rights which are expressly mentioned, and that the land which they purchased was in fact only an interest in the land subject to the right of the plaintiffs in it. This argument seemed to be attractive because it appears at first glance wrong that a purchaser, who knows perfectly well of rights subject to which he is expressed to take, should be able to ignore them. It was, moreover, pointed out that *Wright* v *Dean* (*supra*) was distinguishable in this respect because there the option which was overridden by the conveyance was not mentioned in it, nor did the purchaser take expressly subject to it. It seems to me, however, that this argument cannot prevail having regard to the words in section 13(2) of the Land Charges Act, 1925, which I have quoted, coupled with the definition of 'land' in the Act. The fact is that it was the policy of the framers of the 1925 legislation to get rid of equitable rights of this sort unless registered. . . .

Finally, as under section 13 of The Land Charges Act to which I have referred, an unregistered estate contract is void, and under section 199 of The Law of Property Act, 1925, the purchaser is not to be prejudicially affected by it, I do not see how that which is void and which is not to prejudice the purchaser can be validated by some equitable doctrine. There is after all, no great hardship in this. The plaintiffs could at any time right up to the completion of the assignment to Daymar Estates, Limited, have preserved their rights by registration just as the defendants could have fulfilled their obligations by completing the lease of which Daymar Estates, Limited, could not have complained as they knew all about it.

Midland Bank Trust Co. v *Green*
[1981] AC 513 (HL)

A father granted his son a 10-year option to purchase a farm of which the son was a tenant. The son failed to register the option as a land charge. Within the option period the father conveyed the farm to his wife for £500, although the true value was about £40,000. The son, on discovering this, gave notice exercising his option to purchase. Held: the mother was 'a purchaser of a legal estate for money or money's worth' within the Land Charges Act 1925. The option was void as against her.

LORD WILBERFORCE: An appeal was brought to the Court of Appeal which ... declared the option specifically enforceable. The ground of this decision appears to have been that the sale in 1967 was not for 'money or money's worth,' within the meaning of section 13 of the Land Charges Act 1925. In addition Lord Denning MR was prepared to hold that the protection of the Act was not available in a case of fraud meaning thereby 'any dishonest dealing done so as to deprive unwary innocents of their rightful dues.' The respondents, however, did not seek to support this except to the extent that they relied upon lack of good faith on the part of Evelyne.

My Lords, section 13(2) of the Land Charges Act 1925 reads as follows:

A land charge of class B, class C or class D, created or arising after the commencement of this Act, shall (except as hereinafter provided) be void as against a purchaser of the land charged therewith ... unless the land charge is registered in the appropriate register before the completion of the purchase: Provided that, as respects a land charge of class D and an estate contract created or entered into after the commencement of this Act, this subsection only applies in favour of a purchaser of a legal estate for money or money's worth.

As regards the word 'purchaser' section 20(8) of the same Act reads: '"Purchaser" means any person ... who, for valuable consideration, takes any interest in land ...'

Thus the case appears to be a plain one. The 'estate contract,' which by definition (section 11) includes an option of purchase, was entered into after January 1, 1926; Evelyne took an interest (in fee simple) in the land 'for valuable consideration' — so was a 'purchaser'; she was a purchaser for money — namely £500: the option was not registered before the completion of the purchase. It is therefore void as against her.

In my opinion this appearance is also the reality. The case is plain: the Act is clear and definite. Intended as it was to provide a simple and understandable system for the protection of title to land, it should not be read down or glossed: to do so would destroy the usefulness of the Act. Any temptation to remould the Act to meet the facts of the present case, on the supposition that it is a hard one and that justice requires it, is, for me at least, removed by the consideration that the Act itself provides a simple and effective protection for persons in Geoffrey's position — viz. — by registration.

The respondents submitted two arguments as to the interpretation of section 13(2): the one sought to introduce into it a requirement that the purchaser should be 'in good faith'; the other related to the words 'in money or money's worth.'

The argument as to good faith fell into three parts: first, that 'good faith' was something required of a 'purchaser' before 1926; secondly, that this requirement was

The 1925 Legislation

preserved by the 1925 legislation and in particular by section 13(2) of the Land Charges Act 1925. If these points could be made good, it would then have to be decided whether the purchaser (Evelyne) was in 'good faith' on the facts of the case.

My Lords, the character in the law known as the bona fide (good faith) purchaser for value without notice was the creation of equity. In order to affect a purchaser for value of a legal estate with some equity or equitable interest, equity fastened upon his conscience and the composite expression was used to epitomise the circumstances in which equity would or rather would not do so. I think that it would generally be true to say that the words 'in good faith' related to the existence of notice. Equity, in other words, required not only absence of notice, but genuine and honest absence of notice. As the law developed, this requirement became crystallised in the doctrine of constructive notice which assumed a statutory form in the Conveyancing Act 1882, section 3. But, and so far I would be willing to accompany the respondents, it would be a mistake to suppose that the requirement of good faith extended only to the matter of notice, or that when notice came to be regulated by statute, the requirement of good faith became obsolete. Equity still retained its interest in and power over the purchaser's conscience. The classic judgment of James LJ in *Pilcher* v *Rawlins* (1872) LR 7 Ch App 259, 269 is clear authority that it did: good faith there is stated as a separate test which may have to be passed even though absence of notice is proved. And there are references in cases subsequent to 1882 which confirm the proposition that honesty or bona fides remained something which might be inquired into (see *Berwick & Co.* v *Price* [1905] 1 Ch 632, 639; *Taylor* v *London and County Banking Co.* [1901] 2 Ch 231, 256; *Oliver* v *Hinton* [1899] 2 Ch 264, 273).

But did this requirement, or test, pass into the property legislation of 1925?

My Lords, I do not think it safe to seek the answer to this question by means of a general assertion that the property legislation of 1922–25 was not intended to alter the law, or not intended to alter it in a particular field, such as that relating to purchases of legal estates. All the Acts of 1925, and their precursors, were drafted with the utmost care, and their wording, certainly where this is apparently clear, has to be accorded firm respect. As was pointed out in *Grey* v *Inland Revenue Commissioners* [1960] AC 1, the Acts of 1922–4 effected massive changes in the law affecting property and the House, in consequence, was persuaded to give to a plain word ('disposition') its plain meaning, and not to narrow it by reference to its antecedents. Certainly that case should firmly discourage us from muddying clear waters. I accept that there is merit in looking at the corpus as a whole in order to produce if possible a consistent scheme. But there are limits to the possibilities of this process: for example it cannot eliminate the difference between registered and unregistered land, or the respective charges on them.

As to the requirement of 'good faith' we are faced with a situation of some perplexity. The expression 'good faith,' appears in the Law of Property Act 1925 definition of 'purchaser' ('a purchaser in good faith for valuable consideration'), section 205(1)(xxi); in the Settled Land Act 1925, section 117(1)(xxi) (ditto); in the Administration of Estates Act 1925, section 55(1)(xviii) ('"Purchaser" means a lessee, mortgagee or other person who in good faith acquires an interest in property for valuable consideration') and in the Land Registration Act 1925, section 3(xxi) which does not however, as the other Acts do, include a reference to nominal consideration. So there is certainly some indication of an intention to carry the concept of 'good faith' into much of the 1925 code. What then do we find in the Land Charges Act 1925? We were taken along a scholarly peregrination through the numerous Acts antecedent to the final codification and consolidation in 1925 — the Land Charges Registration and Searches Act 1888, the Law of Property Act 1922, particularly Schedule 7, the Law of Property (Amendment) Act 1924 as well as the Yorkshire and Middlesex Deeds Registration Acts. But I think, with genuine respect for an interesting argument, that such solution as there is of the problem under consideration must be sought in the terms of the various Acts of 1925 themselves. So far as concerns the Land Charges Act 1925, the definition of 'purchaser' quoted above does not mention 'good faith' at all. 'Good faith' did not appear in the original Act of 1888, nor in the extension made to that Act by the Act of 1922, Schedule 7, nor in the Act of 1924, Schedule 6. It should be a secure assumption that the definition of 'purchaser for value' which is found in section 4 of the Act of 1888 (. . . 'person who for valuable consideration takes any interest in land') together with the limitation which is now the proviso to section 13(2) of the Act of 1925, introduced in 1922, was intended to be carried forward into the Act of 1925. The expression 'good faith' appears nowhere in the antecedents. To write the word in, from the examples of contemporaneous Acts, would be bold. It becomes impossible when it is seen that the words appear in section 3(1) and in section 7(1), in each case in a proviso very similar, in structure, to the relevant proviso in section 13(2). If canons of constructions have any validity at all, they must lead to the conclusion that the omission in section 13(2) was deliberate. . . .

Before leaving this part of the case, I must comment on *In re Monolithic Building Co.* [1915] 1 Ch 643, which was discussed in the Court of Appeal. That was a case arising under section 93 of the Companies (Consolidation) Act 1908 which made an unregistered mortgage void against any creditor of the company. The defendant Jenkins was a managing director of the company, and clearly had notice of the first unregistered mortgage: he himself subsequently took and registered a mortgage debenture and claimed priority over the unregistered mortgage. It was held by the Court of Appeal, first that this was not a case of fraud: 'it is not fraud to take advantage of legal rights, the existence of which may be taken to be known to both parties' (*per* Lord Cozens-Hardy MR, p. 663), secondly that section 93 of the Act was clear in its terms, should be applied according to its plain meaning, and should not be weakened by infusion of equitable doctrines applied by the courts during the 19th century. The judgment of Lord Cozens-Hardy MR contains a valuable critique of the well known cases of *Le Neve* v *Le Neve* (1748) 3 Atk 646 and *Greaves* v *Tofield* (1880) 14 ChD 563 which, arising under the Middlesex Registry Act 1708 and other enactments, had led the judges to import equitable doctrines into cases of priority arising under those Acts and establishes that the principles of those cases should not be applied to modern Acts of Parliament.

My Lords, I fail to see how this authority can be invoked in support of the respondents' argument, or of the judgments of the majority of the Court of Appeal. So far from supporting them, it is strongly the other way. It disposes, for the future, of the old arguments based, ultimately, upon *Le Neve* v *Le Neve*, 3 Atk 643 for reading equitable doctrines (as to notice, etc.) into modern Acts of Parliament: it makes it clear that it is not 'fraud' to rely on legal rights conferred by Act of Parliament: it confirms the validity of interpreting clear enactments as to registration and priority according to their tenor.

The judgment of Phillimore LJ in *In re Monolithic Building Co.* [1915] 1 Ch 643, 669, 670 does indeed contain a passage which appears to favour application of the principle of *Le Neve* v *Le Neve*, 3 Atk 646 and to make a distinction between a transaction designed to obtain an advantage, and one designed to defeat a prior (unregistered) interest. But, as I have explained, this distinction is unreal and unworkable: this whole passage is impossible to reconcile with the views of the other members of the Court of Appeal in the case, and I respectfully consider that it is not good law.

My Lords, I can deal more shortly with the respondents' second argument. It relates to the consideration for the purchase. The argument is that the protection of section

13(2) of the Land Charges Act 1925 does not extend to a purchaser who has provided only a nominal consideration and that £500 is nominal. A variation of this was the argument accepted by the Court of Appeal that the consideration must be 'adequate' — an expression of transparent difficulty. The answer to both contentions lies in the language of the subsection. The word 'purchaser,' by definition (section 20(8)), means one who provides valuable consideration — a term of art which precludes any inquiry as to adequacy. This definition is, of course, subject to the context. Section 13(2), proviso, requires money or money's worth to be provided: the purpose of this being to exclude the consideration of marriage. There is nothing here which suggests, or admits of, the introduction of a further requirement that the money must not be nominal.

The argument for this requirement is based upon the Law of Property Act 1925 which, in section 205(1)(xxi) defining 'purchaser' provides that 'valuable consideration' includes marriage but does not include a 'nominal consideration in money.' The Land Charges Act 1925 contains no definition of 'valuable consideration,' so it is said to be necessary to have resort to the Law of Property Act definition: thus 'nominal consideration in money' is excluded. An indication that this is intended is said to be provided by section 199(1)(i). I cannot accept this. The fallacy lies in supposing that the Acts — either of them — set out to define 'valuable consideration'; they do not: they define 'purchaser,' and they define the word differently (see the first part of the argument). 'Valuable consideration' requires no definition: it is an expression denoting an advantage conferred or detriment suffered. What each Act does is, for its own purposes, to exclude some things from this general expression: the Law of Property Act includes marriage but not a nominal sum in money; the Land Charges Act excludes marriage but allows 'money or money's worth.' There is no coincidence between these two; no link by reference or necessary logic between them. Section 199(1)(i) by referring to the Land Charges Act 1925, necessarily incorporates — for the purposes of this provision — the definition of 'purchaser' in the latter Act, for it is only against such a 'purchaser' that an instrument is void under that Act. It cannot be read as incorporating the Law of Property Act definition into the Land Charges Act. As I have pointed out the land charges legislation has contained its own definition since 1888, carried through, with the addition of the reference to 'money or money's worth' into 1925. To exclude a nominal sum of money from section 13(2) of the Land Charges Act would be to rewrite the section.

This conclusion makes it unnecessary to determine whether £500 is a nominal sum of money or not. But I must say that for my part I should have great difficulty in so holding. 'Nominal consideration' and a 'nominal sum' in the law appear to me, as terms of art, to refer to a sum or consideration which can be mentioned as consideration but is not necessarily paid. To equate 'nominal' with inadequate' or even 'grossly inadequate' would embark the law upon inquiries which I cannot think were contemplated by Parliament.

Note

Failure to register a land charge does not affect the original parties to the transactions. The land charge remains valid and enforceable between them whether it is registered or not. See R. J. Smith, 'Land Charges and Actual Notice: Justice More or Less Fanciful?' (1980) 96 LQR 8; Charles Harpum, 'Purchasers with Notice of Unregistered Land Charges' (1981) CLJ 213; Brian Green, 'Void Land Charges — Literalism Triumphs in the House of Lords' (1981) 97 LQR 518.

Questions
1. 'No court in the land will allow a person to keep an advantage which he has obtained by fraud' (per Denning LJ in *Lazarus Estates Ltd* v *Beasley* [1956] 1 QB 702, at p. 712). How accurate is such a statement in the light of the decision of the House of Lords in *Midland Bank* v *Green*?
2. How does the Court of Appeal's decision and the House of Lord's decision in *Midland Bank* v *Green* reflect the differing views taken by the judiciary as to the purpose and role of English property law in the latter part of the twentieth century?
3. If the facts of *Midland Bank* v *Green* had occurred before 1925, would the result have been the same?
4. What would be the outcome of *Midland Bank* v *Green* if the area had been one where the title to the land was registered?

B: ENTRY ON THE REGISTER

A person wishing to protect his interest in the land must register it against the name of the present land owner. This has caused problems.

Oak Co-operative Building Society v *Blackburn* [1968] Ch 730 (CA)

In January 1958, C agreed purchase property from Francis David Blackburn. C went into possession. In 1959, Blackburn mortgaged the property and it was registered under the name of Francis David Blackburn as estate owner. An application was made on C's behalf to the Land Registry for registration of the agreement as an estate contract under the Land Charges Act 1925, s. 10. The application stated the name of the owner as Frank David Blackburn. In 1962, Blackburn asked a building society for a mortgage advance on the property and the building society applied for an official search in the name of Francis *Davis* Blackburn. The official certificate of search showed no entries under the name searched, but drew attention to the mortgage in 1959 under the name of Francis David Blackburn. The building society, relying on the certificate, made an advance to Blackburn, who subsequently became bankrupt. Held: registration of an estate contract in a name that might be described as a version of the proper name of an estate owner was not a nullity. It was ineffective under s. 17(3) of the Land Charges Act 1925 against a purchaser who applied for an official search in the correct name of the estate owner and obtained a nil certificate, but it was effective against any person who failed to apply for an official search and applied in the wrong name. Therefore, C's registration in the name of Frank, a well recognised abbreviation of Francis, was an effective registration against the building society who had received a nil certificate because of their application in the wrong name of the estate owner.
See also *Diligent Finance Co. Ltd* v *Alleyne* (1972) 23 P & CR 346.

C: SEARCHES

Once the purchaser and vendor have exchanged contracts, before the conveyance takes place, the purchaser will need to know whether there are any land charges that have been registered which affect the land. He will then make a search of the Land Charges Registry. If there are any entries which affect the land, details of such will be entered onto a Search Certificate for the purchaser. If there are no such entries, the certificate will be returned to the purchaser telling him this. If a charge is registered by a person between the time the certificate is issued and the time of completion by the certificate holder, the registration does not affect the certificate holder, provided that completion takes place within 15 days of the issue of the certificate (Land Charges Act 1972, s. 11(5)(b)).

If an official search certificate fails to reveal a properly registered charge, the purchaser will take free of it and the owner of the interest is deprived of it. An action for negligence will then lie against the public authority responsible, but no statutory compensation is available in such a situation.

See Theodore Ruoff, 'The Land Charges Computer' 118 SJ 692.

(a) Land charge discovered after contracts have been exchanged

Re Forsey and Hollebone's Contract [1927] 2 Ch 379 (CA)

Clause 1 of a contract said that the purchaser agreed to purchase property 'for an estate in fee simple absolute free from incumbrances', except as thereinafter mentioned. Clause 2 said the property was sold subject to restrictive and other covenants contained in or referred to in a conveyance dated 28 September 1925. The purchaser paid a deposit on 10 December 1926, the same day as the contract was signed. Before completion the purchaser discovered the property was in an area proposed to be dealt with by a local authority resolution of 26 October 1925 for town planning purposes. The resolution had been registered as a land charge under the Land Charges Registration Act 1925, in January 1926. Neither the vendor nor the purchaser knew of the resolution at the date of the contract. Held:

(1) The passing and registration of the resolution by the local authority did not operate to impose on the land any subsisting incumbrance within the meaning of Clause 1 of the contract. The sections of the 1925 Act showed that the purpose of the registered resolution was not so much to impose restrictions on the land, as to prevent unreasonable claims being made by persons who bought land.

(2) Even if the registered resolution were an incumbrance, it was an incumbrance of such nature that a purchaser (by means of s. 198 of the Law of Property Act 1925) must be deemed to have contracted with actual notice of its existence and therefore be precluded from refusing to complete the contract.

Law of Property Act 1969

24. Contracts for purchase of land affected by land charge, etc.
(1) Where under a contract for the sale or other disposition of any estate or interest in land the title to which is not registered under the Land Registration Act 1925 or any

enactment replaced by it any question arises whether the purchaser had knowledge, at the time of entering into the contract, of a registered land charge, that question shall be determined by reference to his actual knowledge and without regard to the provisions of section 198 of the Law of Property Act 1925 (under which registration under the Land Charges Act 1925 [now the Land Charges Act 1972] or any enactment replaced by it is deemed to constitute actual notice).

(2) Where any estate or interest with which such a contract is concerned is affected by a registered land charge and the purchaser, at the time of entering into the contract, had not received notice and did not otherwise actually know that the estate or interest was affected by the charge, any provision of the contract shall be void so far as it purports to exclude the operation of subsection (1) above or to exclude or restrict any right or remedy that might otherwise be exercisable by the purchaser on the ground that the estate or interest is affected by the charge.

(3) In this section—
'purchaser' includes a lessee, mortgagee or other person acquiring or intending to acquire an estate or interest in land; and
'registered land charge' means any instrument or matter registered, otherwise than in a register of local land charges, under the Land Charges Act 1925 [now the Land Charges Act 1972] or any Act replaced by it.

(4) For the purposes of this section any knowledge acquired in the course of a transaction by a person who is acting therein as counsel, or as solicitor or other agent, for another shall be treated as the knowledge of that other.

(5) This section does not apply to contracts made before the commencement of this Act.

Note
This section affects contracts for the sale of land entered into after 1 January 1970. The effect of the section is that where a search reveals a registered land charge which was unknown to a purchaser at the date of the contract, a purchaser can now refuse to complete the contract, stating his ignorance as a ground for non-completion. See also *Rignall Developments Ltd* v *Halil* [1987] 3 All ER 170.

(b) Land charge discovered after completion
A purchaser who has carried out a thorough investigation of title may nevertheless discover after completion that he is bound by a land charge that had been registered *before the vendor's title commenced*. A purchaser can ask for a complete list of all estate owners since 1 January 1926, when buying the property, but this may prove to be impracticable.

Law of Property Act 1969

25. Compensation in certain cases for loss due to undisclosed land charges
(1) Where a purchaser of any estate or interest in land under a disposition to which this section applies has suffered loss by reason that the estate or interest is affected by a registered land charge, then if—
    (a) the date of completion was after the commencement of this Act; and
    (b) on that date the purchaser had no actual knowledge of the charge; and

(c) the charge was registered against the name of an owner of an estate in the land who was not as owner of any such estate a party to any transaction, or concerned in any event, comprised in the relevant title;
the purchaser shall be entitled to compensation for the loss.

(2) For the purposes of subsection (1)(b) above, the question whether any person had actual knowledge of a charge shall be determined without regard to the provisions of section 198 of the Law of Property Act 1925 (under which registration under the Land Charges Act 1925 [now the Land Charges Act 1972] or any enactment replaced by it is deemed to constitute actual notice).

Note
Relevant title means the statutory period of 15 years in an open contract, or the period of title in fact contracted for, whichever is the larger.

(c) Land charge discovered after grant of lease
In an open contract for the grant or assignment of a lease, the lessee or assignee is not at liberty to investigate the reversionary titles. Nevertheless, he may still be bound by land charges that have been registered which affect those titles.

D: PRIORITY NOTICES

In the sale of land it is often the case that a series of operations take place simultaneously at completion, for example the granting of a mortgage and the taking out of restrictive covenants. Since a charge or mortgage cannot be registered until it has been created this can cause some difficulty. In the above example, the creation of the restrictive covenant would occur a few moments before the creation of the mortgage, and therefore the restrictive covenant would be void as against the mortgagee.

See Phillip Freedman, 'Priority Notices' (1977) 74 LSG 136.

Land Charges Act 1972

11. Date of effective registration and priority notices
(1) Any person intending to make an application for the registration of any contemplated charge, instrument or other matter in pursuance of this Act or any rule made under this Act may give a priority notice in the prescribed form at least the relevant number of days before the registration is to take effect.

(2) Where a notice is given under subsection (1) above, it shall be entered in the register to which the intended application when made will relate.

(3) If the application is presented within the relevant number of days thereafter and refers in the prescribed manner to the notice, the registration shall take effect as if the registration had been made at the time when the charge, instrument or matter was created, entered into, made or arose, and the date at which the registration so takes effect shall be deemed to be the date of registration.

(4) Where—
  (a) any two charges, instruments or matters are contemporaneous; and
  (b) one of them (whether or not protected by a priority notice) is subject to or dependent on the other; and
  (c) the latter is protected by a priority notice,

the subsequent or dependent charge, instrument or matter shall be deemed to have been created, entered into or made, or to have arisen, after the registration of the other.

(5) Where a purchaser has obtained a certificate under section 10 above, any entry which is made in the register after the date of the certificate and before the completion of the purchase, and is not made pursuant to a priority notice entered on the register on or before the date of the certificate, shall not affect the purchaser if the purchase is completed before the expiration of the relevant number of days after the date of the certificate.

(6) The relevant number of days is—
    (a)   for the purposes of subsection (1) and (5) above, fifteen;
    (b)   for the purposes of subsection (3) above, thirty,
or such other number as may be prescribed; but in reckoning the relevant number of days for any of the purposes of this section any days when the registry is not open to the public shall be excluded.

3 REGISTRATION OF TITLE

SECTION 1: INTRODUCTION

Registration of title in England and Wales was originally introduced by the Land Registry Act 1862, which was followed by the Land Transfer Act 1875. The current legislation is contained in the Land Registration Act 1925 and the Land Registration Rules 1925.

The aims of land registration are two-fold:

(a) To provide a simplified and quicker method of proving title when land is conveyed. This is achieved as the full root of title need only be investigated once — by the Chief Land Registrar — and, once approved, a certificate of title (the land certificate) may be relied upon.

(b) To provide better protection for purchasers and the owners of equitable interests in land.

SECTION 2: RELATIONSHIP BETWEEN THE LAND REGISTRATION ACT 1925 AND THE LAND CHARGES ACT 1925 (NOW LAND CHARGES ACT 1972)

It is intended that the whole of England and Wales ultimately be governed by a registered conveyancing system, although the system has been introduced in a piecemeal fashion starting in urban areas. Certain areas have been designated areas of compulsory registration (see *post*) and these areas have been gradually increased so as to now cover the whole country. Most dealings with unregistered land in an area of compulsory registration will give rise to an obligation to make an application for first registration, although certain transactions, such as mortgages, may not. The land in these compulsory areas will remain unregistered, however, until the first dealing with the land after the area has been designated an area of compulsory registration. The Land

Charges Act 1925 was introduced to act as a stop-gap measure to protect equitable interests until all land was covered by the Land Registration Act.

SECTION 3: THE REGISTER

The land register is controlled by the Chief Land Registrar. It is maintained in London at the Land Registry and at regional registries. It is the role of the Chief Land Registrar to keep a register of title to land.

Land Registration Act 1925

1. Registers to be continued
   (1) The Chief Land Registrar shall continue to keep a register of title to freehold land and leasehold land.
   (2) The register need not be kept in documentary form.

Note
Each title is identified by a title number which is given to each piece of land. The register of each individual title is divided into three parts, namely:

(a) the property register;
(b) the proprietorship register;
(c) the charges register.

(a) The property register
This contains a description of the property and a reference to a filed plan of the land. It also shows the title number which has been given to the property. Each estate in the property is given a different entry and a different title number.

The property register also contains details of rights, easements, privileges and covenants of which the registered land has the benefit.

(b) The proprietorship register
This details the name and address of the registered owner of the land and may also contain details of any limitation on his power to deal with the land.

(c) The charges register
This records all encumbrances that are registered against the land, for example mortgages and financial charges, restrictive covenants and rights of occupation under the Matrimonial Homes Act 1983.

Once a purchaser becomes the registered proprietor of the land, he is issued with a land certificate which provides evidence of title and is equivalent to the title deeds in unregistered conveyancing. The certificate is divided into the same three sections as the register and contains the same things as are in the register. Where the property is subject to a mortgage which has been registered, the proprietor is issued with a Charge Certificate as opposed to a Land Certificate.

Land Registration Act 1925

63. Issue of land and charge certificates

(1) On the first registration of a freehold or leasehold interest in land, and on the registration of a charge, a land certificate, or charge certificate, as the case may be, shall be prepared in the prescribed form: it shall state whether the title is absolute, good leasehold, qualified or possessory, and it shall be either delivered to the proprietor or deposited in the registry as the proprietor may prefer.

64. Certificates to be produced and noted on dealings

(1) So long as a land certificate or charge certificate is outstanding, it shall be produced to the registrar—
   (a) on every entry in the register of a disposition by the proprietor of the registered land or charge to which it relates; and
   (b) on every registered transmission; and
   (c) in every case (except as hereinafter mentioned) where under this Act or otherwise notice of any estate right or claim or a restriction is entered or placed on the register, adversely affecting the title of the proprietor of the registered land or charge, but not in the case of the lodgment of a caution or of an inhibition or of a creditors' notice, or of the entry of a notice of a lease at a rent without taking a fine [or a notice of a charge for [inheritance tax]].

(2) A note of every such entry or transmission shall be officially entered on the certificate . . .

SECTION 4: CATEGORIES OF INTERESTS IN REGISTERED LAND

Under the Land Registration Act 1925, interests and estates in land are divided into four categories:

(a) registered interests;
(b) overriding interests;
(c) minor interests;
(d) registered charges (see chapter 12).

This list is not exhaustive, and does not cover, for example, the liability which arises in tort in relation to the land and the consequences of planning laws. Nor do the classes represent 'Watertight Compartments' (Law Comm No. 108), for an interest can move from one category to another or belong in two categories simultaneously.

A: REGISTERED INTERESTS

Land Registration Act 1925

2. What estates may be registered

(1) After the commencement of this Act, estates capable of subsisting as legal estates shall be the only interests in land in respect of which a proprietor can be registered and all other interests in registered land (except overriding interests and

interests entered on the register at or before such commencement) shall take effect in equity as minor interests, but all interests (except undivided shares in land) entered on the register at such commencement which are not legal estates shall be capable of being dealt with under this Act:

Provided that, on the occasion of the first dealing with any such interest, the register shall be rectified in such manner as may be provided by rules made to secure that the entries therein shall be similar to those which would have been made if the title to the land had been registered after the commencement of this Act.

Notes
1. Only those legal estates and interests set out in s. 1(1) and (2) of the Law of Property Act 1925 are registrable, namely the fee simple absolute in possession, legal leases (exceeding 21 years), legal rentcharges, legal easements and legal mortgages.
2. Interests and estates covered by the Land Registration Act 1925, s. 2, are capable of being registered in their own right under their own number, i.e. they are capable of 'substantive' registration.

(a) First registration of a registered interest

In areas that have been designated areas of compulsory registration, the requirement for entry in the land register only takes effect on the first 'dealing' with the land, for example when the fee simple is sold or when a lease for over 21 years or more is created or assigned, after the date of designation.

The Land Registration Act 1986 reduced the term of a registrable lease from 40 years to in excess of 21 years.

In all other cases voluntary registration is permitted only in exceptional circumstances and in cases of building estates of at least 20 houses.

Failure to register in an area of compulsory registration is governed by the Land Registration Act 1925, s. 123(1).

Land Registration Act 1925

123. Effect of Act in areas where registration is compulsory

(1) In any area in which an Order in Council declaring that registration of title to land within that area is to be compulsory on sale is for the time being in force, every conveyance on sale of freehold land and every grant of [a term of years absolute of more than twenty-one years from the date of delivery of the grant,] and every assignment on sale of leasehold land held for a term of years absolute [having more than twenty-one years to run from the date of delivery of the assignment], shall (save as hereinafter provided), on the expiration of two months from the date thereof or of any authorised extension of that period, become void so far as regards the grant or conveyance of the legal estate in the freehold or leasehold land comprised in the conveyance, grant, or assignment, or so much of such land as is situated within the area affected, unless the grantee (that is to say, the person who is entitled to be registered as proprietor of the freehold or leasehold land) or his successor in title or assign has in the meantime applied to be registered as proprietor of such land:

Provided that the registrar, or the court on appeal from the registrar, may, on the application of any persons interested in any particular case in which the registrar or the court is satisfied that the application for first registration cannot be made within the said period, or can only be made within that period by incurring unreasonable expense, or that the application has not been made within the said period by reason of some accident or other sufficient cause, make an order extending the said period; and if such order be made, then, upon the registration of the grantee or his successor or assign, a note of the order shall be endorsed on the conveyance, grant or assignment:

In the case of land in an area where, at the date of the commencement of this Act, registration of title is already compulsory on sale, this subsection shall apply to every such conveyance, grant, or assignment, executed on or after that date.

(b) Grades of title

When land is first registered, the grade of title which is attributed to the proprietor will depend upon the title which the estate owner can prove.

(i) *Absolute freehold title* This is the highest grade of title in the registered land system. It is granted where the Registrar is satisfied that the title cannot be successfully challenged.

Land Registration Act 1925

5. Effect of first registration with absolute title
Where the registered land is a freehold estate, the registration of any person as first proprietor thereof with an absolute title shall vest in the person so registered an estate in fee simple in possession in the land, together with all rights, privileges, and appurtenances belonging or appurtenant thereto, subject to the following rights and interests, that is to say,—

(a) Subject to the incumbrances, and other entries, if any, appearing on the register; and

(b) Unless the contrary is expressed on the register, subject to such overriding interests, if any, as affect the registered land; and

(c) Where the first proprietor is not entitled for his own benefit to the registered land subject, as between himself and the persons entitled to minor interests, to any minor interests of such persons of which he has notice,

but free from all other estates and interests whatsoever, including estates and interests of His Majesty.

(ii) *Possessory freehold title* This is granted where the applicant cannot prove his title to the land by documentary evidence and the ownership of the land is proved merely by the fact that the applicant is in occupation of the land or in receipt of rent and profits from the land. Clearly this will be the case in situations where the applicant is claiming his title by means of adverse possession.

Land Registration Act 1925

6. Effect of first registration with possessory title
Where the registered land is a freehold estate, the registration of any person as first proprietor thereof with a possessory title only shall not affect or prejudice the enforcement of any estate, right or interest adverse to or in derogation of the title of the first proprietor, and subsisting or capable of arising at the time of registration of that

proprietor; but save as aforesaid, shall have the same effect as registration of a person with an absolute title.

77. Conversion of title
(2) Where land is registered with a possessory title, the registrar may, and on application by the proprietor shall—
    (a) if he is satisfied as to the title, or
    (b) if the land has been so registered for at least twelve years and he is satisfied that the proprietor is in possession,
enter the title in the case of freehold land as absolute and in the case of leasehold land as good leasehold.

Note
The 12-year period was introduced by the Land Registration Act 1986, s. 1(2). Previously the period was 15 years.

(iii) *Qualified freehold title* These are rarely granted and occur, for example, where the owner cannot prove a good root of title.

Land Registration Act 1925

7. Qualified title
(1) Where an absolute title is required, and on the examination of the title it appears to the registrar that the title can be established only for a limited period, or only subject to certain reservations, the registrar may, on the application of the party applying to be registered, by an entry made in the register, except from the effect of registration any estate, right, or interest—
    (a) arising before a specified date, or
    (b) arising under a specified instrument or otherwise particularly described in the register,
and a title registered subject to such excepted estate, right, or interest shall be called a qualified title.
(2) Where the registered land is a freehold estate, the registration of a person as first proprietor thereof with a qualified title shall have the same effect as the registration of such person with an absolute title, save that registration with a qualified title shall not affect or prejudice the enforcement of any estate, right or interest appearing by the register to be excepted.

(iv) *Absolute leasehold title* This is the leasehold equivalent of absolute freehold title.

Land Registration Act 1925

9. Effect of first registration with absolute title
Where the registered land is a leasehold interest, the registration under this Act of any person as first proprietor thereof with an absolute title shall be deemed to vest in such person the possession of the leasehold interest described, with all implied or expressed rights, privileges, and appurtenances attached to such interest, subject to the following obligations, rights, and interests, that is to say,—
    (a) Subject to all implied and express covenants, obligations, and liabilities incident to the registered land; and

(b) Subject to the incumbrances and other entries (if any) appearing on the register; and
(c) Unless the contrary is expressed on the register, subject to such overriding interests, if any, as affect the registered land; and
(d) Where such first proprietor is not entitled for his own benefit to the registered land subject, as between himself and the persons entitled to minor interests, to any minor interests of such persons of which he has notice;
but free from all other estates and interests whatsoever, including estates and interests of His Majesty.

8. Application for registration of leasehold land
(1)(b)(i) Where an absolute title is required, the applicant or his nominee shall not be registered as proprietor until and unless the title both to the leasehold and to the freehold, and to any intermediate leasehold that may exist, is approved by the registrar;

(v) *Good leasehold title* This is granted where there is some doubt about the quality of the superior title, or where proof of that superior title is not provided to the Registry, but the title to the leasehold interest being registered is satisfactory.

Land Registration Act 1925

10. Effect of first registration with good leasehold title
Where the registered land is a leasehold interest, the registration of a person as first proprietor thereof with a good leasehold title shall not affect or prejudice the enforcement of any estate, right or interest affecting or in derogation of the title of the lessor to grant the lease, but, save as aforesaid, shall have the same effect as registration with an absolute title.

(vi) *Possessory leasehold title* This is granted to a lessee who can prove his title, for example, by means of occupation of the land but who has no documentary proof.

Land Registration Act 1925

11. Effect of first registration with possessory title
Where the registered land is a leasehold interest, the registration of a person as first proprietor thereof with a possessory title shall not affect or prejudice the enforcement of any estate, right, or interest (whether in respect of the lessor's title or otherwise) adverse to or in derogation of the title of such first registered proprietor, and subsisting or capable or arising at the time of the registration of such proprietor; but, save as aforesaid, shall have the same effect as registration with an absolute title.

Note
For conversion of title see Land Registration Act 1925, s. 77.

(vii) *Qualified leasehold title* This is similar to a qualified freehold title.

Land Registration Act 1925

12. Qualified title
(1) Where on examination it appears to the registrar that the title, either of the lessor to the reversion or of the lessee to the leasehold interest, can be established only

for a limited period, or subject to certain reservations, the registrar may, upon the request in writing of the person applying to be registered, by an entry made in the register, except from the effect of registration any estate, right or interest—
    (a)   arising before a specified date, or
    (b)   arising under a specified instrument, or otherwise particularly described in the register,
and a title registered subject to any such exception shall be called a qualified title.

(2) Where the registered land is a leasehold interest, the registration of a person as first proprietor thereof with a qualified title shall not affect or prejudice the enforcement of any estate, right, or interest appearing by the register to be excepted, but, save as aforesaid, shall have the same effect as registration with a good leasehold title or an absolute title, as the case may be.

(c) Upgrading of titles

Land Registration Act 1925

77. Conversion of title

(1) Where land is registered with a good leasehold title, or satisfies the conditions for each registration under this section, the registrar may, and on application by the proprietor shall, if he is satisfied as to the title to the freehold and the title to any intermediate leasehold, enter the title as absolute.

(2) [See page 58.]

(3) Where land is registered with a qualified title, the registrar may, and on application by the proprietor shall, if he is satisfied as to the title, enter it in the case of freehold land as good leasehold.

(4) If any claim adverse to the title of the proprietor has been made, an entry shall not be made in the register under this section unless and until the claim has been disposed of.

(6) Any person, other than the proprietor, who suffers loss by reason of any entry on the register made by virtue of this section shall be entitled to be indemnified under this Act as if a mistake had been made in the register.

Note
The above provisions were substituted by the Land Registration Act 1986, s. 1.

(d) Registration of leaseholds
The new law on the registration of leasehold interests was introduced in the Land Registration Act 1986, and can be summarised as follows:

(a) The registration of a lease is forbidden even though it is a legal estate in land if the lease is one that is for a period of 21 years or less, or the lease contains an absolute prohibition against assignment, or the lease is a mortgage term subject to a right of redemption.

(b) The registration of a lease is compulsory if it is a legal lease for a period of more than 21 years, and this covers both the creation of a new lease for 21 years or more and the assignment of an old lease with over 21 years left to run.

(c) Legal leases for 21 years or less are now dealt with under the Land Registration Act 1925, s. 70.

(e) Subsequent transfers of registered land

After the first registration of a registered interest, all transfers or assignments of the registered estate have to be recorded in the register and the transfer is only complete once this has been done.

Land Registration Act 1925

19. Registration of disposition of freeholds

(1) The transfer of the registered estate in the land or part thereof shall be completed by the registrar entering on the register the transferee as the proprietor of the estate transferred, but until such entry is made the transferor shall be deemed to remain proprietor of the registered estate; and, where part only of the land is transferred, notice thereof shall also be noted on the register.

22. Registration of dispositions of leaseholds

(1) A transfer of the registered estate in the land or part thereof shall be completed by the registrar entering on the register the transferee as proprietor of the estate transferred, but until such entry is made the transferor shall be deemed to remain the proprietor of the registered estate; and where part only of the land is transferred, notice thereof shall also be noted on the register.

B: OVERRIDING INTERESTS

See Law Commission Report, *Third Report on Land Registration* (Law Com No. 158).

Certain interests, such as overriding interests in land, cannot be registered with separate titles. These interests bind a purchaser whether they are registered or not. Their existence is somewhat of an anomaly since one of the principles on which the registered land system is based is that the register should contain all the information about the estate — the 'mirror principle' — so that the purchaser need only examine the register to find all the encumbrances affecting the land. The justification for such an anomaly is that there are some third-party rights which are so important in their nature that they should bind a purchaser whether or not they are entered onto the register.

Land Registration Act 1925

3. Interpretation

(xvi) 'Overriding interests' mean all the incumbrances, interests, rights, and powers not entered on the register but subject to which registered dispositions are by this Act to take effect, and in regard to land registered at the commencement of this Act include the matters which are by any enactment repealed by this Act declared not to be incumbrances. . .

70. Liability of registered land to overriding interests

(1) All registered land shall, unless under the provisions of this Act the contrary is expressed on the register, be deemed to be subject to such of the following overriding interests as may be for the time being subsisting in reference thereto, and such interests shall not be treated as incumbrances within the meaning of this Act, (that is to say):—

(a) Rights of common, drainage rights, customary rights (until extinguished), public rights, profits à prendre, rights of sheepwalk, rights of way, watercourses, rights of user, and other easements not being equitable easements required to be protected by notice on the register;

(b) Liability to repair highways by reason of tenure, quit-rents, crown rents, heriots and other rents and charges (until extinguished) having their origin in tenure;

(c) Liability to repair the chancel of any church;

(d) Liability in respect of embankments, and sea and river walls;

(e) . . . payments in lieu of tithe, and charges or annuities payable for the redemption of tithe rentcharges;

(f) Subject to the provisions of this Act, rights acquired or in course of being acquired under the Limitation Acts;

(g) The rights of every person in actual occupation of the land or in receipt of the rents and profits thereof, save where enquiry is made of such person and the rights are not disclosed;

(h) In the case of a possessory, qualified, or good leasehold title, all estates, rights, interests, and powers excepted from the effect of registration;

(i) Rights under local land charges unless and until registered or protected on the register in the prescribed manner;

(j) Rights of fishing and sporting, seignorial and manorial rights of all descriptions (until extinguished), and franchises;

(k) Leases granted for a term not exceeding twenty-one years;

(l) In respect of land registered before the commencement of this Act, rights to mines and minerals, and rights of entry, search, and user, and other rights and reservations incidental to or required for the purpose of giving full effect to the enjoyment of rights to mines and minerals or of property in mines or minerals, being rights which, where the title was first registered before the first day of January, eighteen hundred and ninety-eight, were created before that date, and where the title was first registered after the thirty-first day of December, eighteen hundred and ninety-seven, were created before the date of first registration:

Provided that, where it is proved to the satisfaction of the registrar that any land registered or about to be registered is exempt from land tax, or tithe rentcharge or payments in lieu of tithe, or from charges or annuities payable for the redemption of tithe rentcharge, the registrar may notify the fact on the register in the prescribed manner.

(2) Where at the time of first registration any easement, right, privilege, or benefit created by an instrument and appearing on the title adversely affects the land, the registrar shall enter a note thereof on the register.

(3) Where the existence of any overriding interest mentioned in this section is proved to the satisfaction of the registar or admitted, he may (subject to any prescribed exceptions) enter notice of the same or of a claim thereto on the register, but no claim to an easement, right, or privilege not created by an instrument shall be noted against the title to the servient land if the proprietor of such land (after the prescribed notice is given to him) shows sufficient cause to the contrary.

Note

Section 70(1)(k) applies only in relation to dispositions made after the commencement of the Land Registration Act 1986. Where a lease granted before the commencement of this Act was not an overriding interest because it was not granted at a rent without taking a fine, the amendment applies in relation to it only if the land was subject to it immediately before that commencement.

Questions
1. What is the effect of entering on the register an overriding interest? (See T. Ruoff, 'Protection of the purchaser of land' (1969) 32 MLR 121.)
2. What is the effect of the Land Registration Act 1925, s. 70(3)?

(a) Section 70(1)(a)
This subsection is intended to cover a selection of incorporeal hereditaments. There are, however, two problems which are inherent in the section.

First, where a legal easement or profit à prendre is expressly granted for a term of not less than 21 years *at a rent without taking a fine* (the words in italics were removed by the Land Registration Act 1986), then such a creation must be 'completed by registration' (Land Registration Act 1925, ss. 19(2) and 22(2)). This would involve the entry of a notice against the servient title, and if the dominant title were registered the easement or profit would be included in the registration as appurtenant. However, s. 70(1)(a) provides that easements and profits are overriding interests, not needing registration. The Law Commission has said:

> We consider that it is reasonable to expect and sensible to require such express grantees to protect their interests against subsequent purchases on the register. Pending 'completion by registration', such express easements and profits should be treated as minor interests only — para 2.26.

Easements and profits can arise other than by means of express creation (see chapter 11). They can arise by means of implied grant or reservation, by estoppel or by prescription. As these easements are not expressly granted they are not subject to ss. 19(2) and 22(2) of the Land Registration Act 1925. It is to these easements that the overriding interest status should apply, although specific entry of any established right can be requested. This can lead to problems since it should be noted that easements that arise by means of s. 62 of the Law of Property Act 1925 are incorporated by express reference where registered titles are concerned since they are express grants to be imported by statute but to be construed in the context of the deed.

The second problem with s. 70(1)(a) is whether or not equitable easements are within its scope. The problem arises because there are two alternative interpretations that can be placed upon the final 16 words of the subsection. Should the section be read, 'easements (not being equitable easements) required to be protected by notice on the register', or 'easements (not being equitable easements required to be protected by notice on the register)'. It would seem since the case of *Celsteel Ltd* v *Alton House Holdings* [1985] 1 WLR 204 (approved in the Court of Appeal), that the second interpretation has been adopted.

Celsteel Ltd v *Alton House Holdings*
[1985] 1 WLR 204 (ChD)

An agreement was made in writing for the lease of a garage and the agreement contained a right of way. The premium was paid, but neither the lease, which was subsequently granted but incorrectly so, nor the agreement for the lease was registered and the leasehold estate and easement therefore took effect only in equity. The lessee was in occupation and the easement was used openly, but was not protected by registration.

SCOTT J: Section 144 of the Land Registration Act 1925 contains power for rules to be made for a number of specified purposes. The Land Registration Rules 1925, SR & O 1925/1093, were accordingly made and r. 258 provides as follows:

> Rights, privileges, and appurtenances appertaining or reputed to appertain to land or demised, occupied, or enjoyed therewith or reputed or known as part or parcel of or appurtenant thereto, which adversely affect registered land, are overriding interests within Section 70 of the Act, and shall not be deemed incumbrances for the pupposes of the Act.

The third plaintiff's equitable right of way over the rear driveway was, in my view, at the time when Mobil acquired its registered leasehold title, a right enjoyed with land for the purposes of this rule. It was plainly a right which adversely affected registered land, including the part of the rear driveway comprised in Mobil's lease. Rule 258 of the 1925 rules categorises such a right as an overriding interest. Section 144(2) of the 1925 Act provides: 'Any rules made in pursuance of this section shall be of the same force as if enacted in this Act.' Accordingly, in my judgment, the third plaintiff's right ranks as an overriding interest, does not need to be protected by entry of notice on the register and is binding on Mobil.

Note
It should be noted that *Celsteel* v *Alton House Holdings* does not bring all equitable easements within the scope of its provision, only those that are 'not ... required to be protected'. Scott J said of this:

> In my opinion, the words 'required to be protected' in para (a) should be read in the sense 'need to be protected'. The exception in the paragraph was, in my view, intended to cover all equitable easements other than such as, by reason of some other statutory provision or applicable principle of law, could obtain protection otherwise than by notice on the register. The most obvious example would be equitable easements which qualified for protection under para (g) as part of the rights of a person in actual occupation. In my view I must examine the easement claimed by the third plaintiff and consider whether there is any statutory provision or principle of law which entitles it to protection otherwise than by entry of notice on the register.

Also, only equitable easements that were openly enjoyed could be overriding interests. This is because of the wording of rule 258 of the Land Registration Rules. It was an overriding interest because at the time the defendant acquired the registered leasehold interest, the plaintiff exercised a right of way, i.e. exercised the right at the time the servient land was transferred.

The Law Commission recommended that equitable easements and profits should be protected by entry on the register as minor interests, not as overriding interests (para 2.33). Legal easements and profits granted or arising before first registration of any title should continue to be overriding interests.

See A. M. Prichard, 'Easements and profits as overriding interests' [1987] Conv 328; M. P. Thompson, 'Equitable easements in registered land' [1986] Conv 31.

(b) Section 70(1)(f)
This subsection includes 'rights acquired or in course of being acquired under the Limitation Acts'.

Bridges v *Mees* [1957] Ch 475 (ChD)

In 1939, the purchaser orally contracted to purchase a fee simple estate from the vendor. He paid the full purchase price and went into possession. The vendor, however, never transferred the land to the purchaser, and the purchaser never protected his right by entering a caution against first registration. In 1955, the vendor conveyed the land to the defendant who was duly registered as proprietor of it. Harman J held that the purchaser's contractual rights were protected under s. 70(1)(f) by reason of his adverse possession (and also by s. 70(1)(g), see *post*). The defendant was the trustee of the land for the purchaser and the vendor was a bare trustee of the legal estate for the purchaser after the purchase money was paid to him.

(c) Section 70(1)(k)
Leases which are granted for a term not exceeding 21 years cannot be registered, but are protected as overriding interests. Even though the Land Registration Act 1925 defines a lease as including an agreement for a lease, the use of the word 'granted' imports the actual creation of a term of years, whereas agreements for leases do not create a term of years but give a right in a court of equity to specific performance of the contract (see *City Permanent Building Society* v *Miller* [1952] Ch 840). Nevertheless, agreements for leases may be overriding interests within s. 70(1)(g) if coupled with actual occupation (see *post*).

Section 70(1)(k) no longer excludes leases which were granted on payment of a fine or premium (i.e., a capital sum). Prior to the Land Registration Act 1986, such leases were minor interests while leases granted at a rent were overriding interests.

(d) Section 70(1)(g)

(i) *Object of section 70(1)(g)* The object of the 1925 Act was to preserve the old doctrine that legal interests are good against the whole world, but to make equitable interests registrable as minor interests. We have already seen that there is an exception to this in s. 70(1)(a) (as interpreted in *Celsteel* v *Alton House Holdings*). Section 70(1)(g) distorts the framework of the Act even further, since it allows purchasers of a legal estate who have acted in good faith to be bound by unregistered equitable interests of which they had no notice. So why have the courts interpreted the section in this way?

Strand Securities v Caswell
[1965] Ch 958 (CA)

DENNING MR:... Section 70(1)(g) is an important provision. Fundamentally its object is to protect a person in actual occupation of land from having his rights lost in the welter of registration. He can stay there and do nothing. Yet he will be protected. No one can buy the land over his head and thereby take away or diminish his rights. It is up to every purchaser before he buys to make inquiry on the premises. If he fails to do so, it is at his own risk. He must take subject to whatever rights the occupier may have. Such is the doctrine of *Hunt* v *Luck* [1901] 1 Ch 45 for unregistered land. Section 70(1)(g) carries the same doctrine forward into registered land but with this difference. Not only is the actual occupier protected, but also the person from whom he holds. It is up to the purchaser to inquire of the occupier, not only about the occupier's own rights, but also about the rights of his immediate superior. The purchaser must ask the occupier: 'To whom do you pay your rent?' And the purchaser must inquire what the rights of that person are. If he fails to do so, it is at his own risk for he takes subject to 'the rights of every person in actual occupation of the land or in receipt of the rents and profits thereof.'

Note
The rule in *Hunt* v *Luck* (see chapters 1 and 2) basically says that a purchaser has constructive notice of anything reasonably detectable from an inspection of the property, and in particular anything which might be discovered by a reasonable inquiry of any occupier.

Question
Can the protection of occupiers' rights in registered land be justified by reference to the rule in *Hunt* v *Luck* in unregistered land? (See Law Commission Report, No. 158, paras 2.61–2.67.)

(ii) *Conditions for section 70(1)(g) to apply*   Section 70(1)(g) applies where:

(a) There is a right 'subsisting' in relation to the land.
(b) The owner of the right is in actual occupation of the land, or in receipt of rent and profits from it.
(c) But not where the purchaser has made inquiry of the holder of the right, and has not been told of the right.

See F. R. Crane, 'Equitable interests in registered land' (1958) 22 Conv 14.

Section 70(1)(g) does not create new rights in land but protects *existing rights* in land if they can be brought within the section. The section does not protect a person merely because he or she is in occupation of the land: he or she must have a right in the land before s. 70(1)(g) can apply. 'Actual occupation is not an interest in itself' (per Lord Templeman in *City of London Building Society* v *Flegg* [1987] 2 WLR 1266, at p. 1272).

(iii) *Rights that come within s. 70(1)(g)*

(a) An option to purchase — *Webb* v *Pollmount Ltd* [1966] Ch 584.

Registration of Title

(b) The rights of a beneficiary under a resulting trust — *Hodgson v Marks* [1971] Ch 892.

(c) The equitable interests of co-owners under a statutory trust for sale — *Williams and Glyn's Bank v Boland and Another* [1980] 2 All ER 408; [1981] AC 487 (HC).

(d) An unpaid vendor's lien over the land sold — *London and Cheshire Insurance Co. Ltd v Laplargrene Property Co. Ltd and Another* [1971] 1 All ER 766. See F. R. Crane, '*London & Cheshire Ins Co. v Laplagrene*' (1971) 35 Conv 188.

(e) A right to rectify — *Blacklocks v JB Developments (Godalming) Ltd* [1981] 3 All ER 392. See J. T. Farrand, 'Misreading reports', [1983] Conv 169; D. G. Barnsley, 'Rectification, trusts and overriding interests' [1983] Conv 361.

(f) The right to specific performance of an estate contract — *Bridges v Mees* [1957] Ch 475.

(iv) *Rights that do not come within s. 70(1)(g)*

Land Registration Act 1925

20. Effect of registration of dispositions of freeholds

(1) In the case of a freehold estate registered with an absolute title, a disposition of the registered land or of a legal estate therein, including a lease thereof, for valuable consideration shall, when registered, confer on the transferee or grantee an estate in fee simple or the term of years absolute or other legal estate expressed to be created in the land dealt with, together with all rights, privileges, and appurtenances belonging or appurtenant thereto, including (subject to any entry to the contrary in the register) the appropriate rights and interests which would, under the Law of Property Act 1925, have been transferred if the land had not been registered, subject—

(a) to the incumbrances and other entries, if any, appearing on the register and any charge for inheritance tax subject to which the disposition takes effect under section 73 of this Act; and

(b) unless the contrary is expressed on the register, to the overriding interests, if any, affecting the estate transferred or created,

but free from all other estates and interests whatsoever, including estates and interests of His Majesty, and the disposition shall operate in like manner as if the registered transferor or grantor were (subject to any entry to the contrary in the register) entitled to the registered land in fee simple in possession for his own benefit.

Note

The effect of ss. 70(1) and 20(1) would seem to indicate that s. 70(1)(g) relates only to proprietary interests in the land as determined by the general principles of land law. The sections do not include pure personal rights in or over the land, or mere contractual rights that do not give rise to something more. (This is consistent with the principles of unregistered conveyancing.)

Five categories of rights call for particular attention:

(A) The rights of a beneficiary under the Settled Land Act 1925.

Land Registration Act 1925

86. Registration of settled land
(2) The successive or other interests created by or arising under a settlement shall (save as regards any legal estate which cannot be overridden under the powers of the Settled Land Act 1925, or any other statute) take effect as minor interests and not otherwise; and effect shall be given thereto by the proprietor of the settled land as provided by statute with respect to the estate owner, with such adaptations, if any, as may be prescribed in the case of registered land by rules made under this Act.

(B) Rights of a spouse to occupation of the matrimonial home.

National Provincial Bank v *Ainsworth*
[1965] AC 1175 (HL)

H was the sole registered proprietor of a matrimonial home. He deserted W and their four children in August 1957 and they were left in occupation. By November 1959 H owed £6,000 to a bank, secured by a charge. W commenced divorce proceedings. H formed a company and transferred his properties to the company. The company charged the properties to the bank and the money H owed personally was repaid and that mortgage discharged.

The bank only then discovered that H had deserted W. H's company fell into arrears on the loan repayments and eventually the bank sought possession. W claimed a deserted wife's equity to remain in the property. Held: The rights of a deserted wife were of a personal nature and, as such, a deserted wife could not resist a claim from a genuine purchaser whether this purchase occurred before or after desertion. A deserted wife is not a licensee of her husband.

LORD UPJOHN: My Lords, I think a great deal of the trouble that has arisen in this branch of the law is by reason of attaching to the wife the label of 'licensee.' But a wife does not remain lawfully in the matrimonial home by leave or licence of her husband as the owner of the property. She remains there because as a result of the status of marriage it is her right and duty so to do and if her husband fails in his duty to remain there that cannot affect her right to do so. She is not a trespasser, she is not a licensee of her husband, she is lawfully there as a wife, the situation is one sui generis. She may be described as a licensee if that word means no more than one who is lawfully present, but it is objectionable for the description of anyone, as a licensee at once conjures up the notion of a licensor, which her deserting husband most emphatically is not.

But apart from authority, what is the extent and ambit of her right to continue in occupation? I have already pointed out that before desertion she has no special rights in the particular house where the spouses are living and I cannot see why on principle any better rights should arise on desertion. . . .

Now such being the general nature of the rights of the wife against the husband after desertion, how do they affect third parties dealing with the husband at a date after the desertion who I will assume (though it is certainly not conceded in this case) have full notice of the desertion. The right of the wife to remain in occupation even as against her deserting husband is incapable of precise definition, it depends so much on all the circumstances of the case, on the exercise of purely discretionary remedies, and the right to remain may change overnight by the act or behaviour of either spouse. So as a matter of broad principle I am of opinion that the rights of husband and wife must be regarded as purely personal inter se and that these rights as a matter of law do not affect third parties.

The whole question is whether the right of the wife as against her husband to remain in actual occupation of the matrimonial home is an overriding interest for the purposes of section 70(1)(g).... it seems to me clear that such a right cannot possibly be elevated to the status of an overriding interest for the purposes of the section.

Note

Following this decision, a new statutory right was created in 1967 in the Matrimonial Homes Act. The Act provided machinery whereby either spouse could protect rights of occupation in the matrimonial home against third parties (see chapter 2). The right is now embodied in the Matrimonial Homes Act 1983.

Matrimonial Homes Act 1983

1. Rights concerning matrimonial home where one spouse has no estate, etc.

(1) Where one spouse is entitled to occupy a dwelling house by virtue of a beneficial estate or interest or contract or by virtue of any enactment giving him or her the right to remain in occupation, and the other spouse is not so entitled, then, subject to the provisions of this Act, the spouse not so entitled shall have the following rights (in this Act referred to as 'rights of occupation')—

(a) if in occupation, a right not to be evicted or excluded from the dwelling house or any part thereof by the other spouse except with the leave of the court given by an order under this section;

(b) if not in occupation, a right with the leave of the court so given to enter into and occupy the dwelling house.

(2) so long as one spouse has rights of occupation, either of the spouses may apply to the court for an order—

(a) declaring, enforcing, restricting or terminating those rights, or

(b) prohibiting, suspending or restricting the exercise by either spouse of the right to occupy the dwelling house, or

(c) requiring either spouse to permit the exercise by the other of that right.

(3) On an application for an order under this section, the court may make such order as it thinks just and reasonable having regard to the conduct of the spouses in relation to each other and otherwise, to their respective needs and financial resources, to the needs of any children and to all the circumstances of the case, and, without prejudice to the generality of the foregoing provision—

(a) may except part of the dwelling house from a spouse's rights of occupation (and in particular a part used wholly or mainly for or in connection with the trade, business or profession of the other spouse),

(b) may order a spouse occupying the dwelling house or any part thereof by virtue of this section to make periodical payments to the other in respect of the occupation,

(c) may impose on either spouse obligations as to the repair and maintenance of the dwelling house or the discharge of any liabilities in respect of the dwelling house.

(4) Orders under this section may, in so far as they have a continuing effect, be limited so as to have effect for a period specified in the order or until further order.

(5) Where a spouse is entitled under this section to occupy a dwelling house or any part thereof, any payment or tender made or other thing done by that spouse in or towards satisfaction of any liability of the other spouse in respect of rent, rates, mortgage payments or other outgoings affecting the dwelling house shall, whether or not it is made or done in pursuance of an order under this section, be as good as if made or done by the other spouse.

(6) A spouse's occupation by virtue of this section shall for the purposes of the Rent (Agriculture) Act 1976, and of the Rent Act 1977 (other than Part V and sections 103 to 106), be treated as possession by the other spouse and for the purposes of Part IV of the Housing Act 1985 [and Part I of the Housing Act 1988 (secure tenancies)] be treated as occupation by the other spouse.

(7) Where a spouse is entitled under this section to occupy a dwelling house or any part thereof and makes any payment in or towards satisfaction of any liability of the other spouse in respect of mortgage payments affecting the dwelling house, the person to whom the payment is made may treat it as having been made by that other spouse, but the fact that that person has treated any such payment as having been so made shall not affect any claim of the first-mentioned spouse against the other to an interest in the dwelling house by virtue of the payment.

(8) Where a spouse is entitled under this section to occupy a dwelling house or part thereof by reason of an interest of the other spouse under a trust, all the provisions of subsections (5) to (7) above shall apply in relation to the trustees as they apply in relation to the other spouse.

(10) This Act shall not apply to a dwelling house which has at no time been a matrimonial home of the spouses in question; and a spouse's rights of occupation shall continue only so long as the marriage subsists and the other spouse is entitled as mentioned in subsection (1) above to occupy the dwelling house, except where provision is made by section 2 of this Act for those rights to be a charge on an estate or interest in the dwelling house.

(11) It is hereby declared that a spouse who has an equitable interest in a dwelling house or in the proceeds of sale thereof, not being a spouse in whom is vested (whether solely or as a joint tenant) a legal estate in fee simple or a legal term of years absolute in the dwelling house, is to be treated for the purpose only of determining whether he or she has rights of occupation under this section as not being entitled to occupy the dwelling house by virtue of that interest.

Notes

1. Section 70 of the Land Registration Act 1925 in all of its parts deals with rights in reference to land and therefore does not cover rights that arise under the Matrimonial Homes Act 1983. The Matrimonial Homes Act 1983, s. 2(8)(b), says 'a spouse's right of occupation shall not be an overriding interest within the meaning of [the Land Registration Act 1925] affecting the dwelling house notwithstanding that the spouse is in actual occupation of the dwelling house'.

2. A spouse's right of occupation can be protected by entry of a notice on the register.

3. Section 1(3) says that 'all the circumstances of the case' should be looked at and therefore the court is at liberty to consider the purchaser's circumstances as well as those of the husband and wife — see *Kashmir Kaur* v *Gill* [1988] 2 All ER 288.

Matrimonial Homes Act 1983

2. Effect of rights of occupation as charge on dwelling house
(1) Where, at any time during the subsistence of a marriage, one spouse is entitled to occupy a dwelling house by virtue of a beneficial estate or interest, then the other spouse's rights of occupation shall be a charge on that estate or interest, having the like priority as if it were an equitable interest created at whichever is the latest of the following dates, that is to say—
    (a) the date when the spouse so entitled acquires the estate or interest,
    (b) the date of the marriage, and
    (c) the 1st January 1968 (which is the date of commencement of the Act of 1967).
(8) Where the title to the legal estate by virtue of which a spouse is entitled to occupy a dwelling house (including any legal estate held by trustees for that spouse) is registered under the Land Registration Act 1925 or any enactment replaced by that Act—
    (b) a spouse's rights of occupation shall not be an overriding interest within the meaning of that Act affecting the dwelling house notwithstanding that the spouse is in actual occupation of the dwelling house.

Note
The effect of s. 2(1) is that the interest created by s. 1 operates as a charge on the estate of the other spouse.

(C) The rights of a tenant arising from a notice under the Leasehold Reform Act 1967 of his intention to purchase the freehold or a long leasehold in the property occupied by him.
Such rights do not come within s. 70(1)(g).

(D) The right to occupy land under a licence.
There appears to be a degree of uncertainty regarding the status of a contractual licence in English law (see chapter 8). In *National Provincial Bank Ltd* v *Hastings Car Mart Ltd* [1965] AC 1175 (CA), Lord Denning MR seemed to think that it was a right that could come within s. 70(1)(g). The issue came up for discussion in *Ashburn Anstalt* v *Arnold* [1988] 2 WLR 706 (see pages 230–1). Fox LJ said, *per curiam*, that a mere contractual licence is not, without more, an interest in land binding on a purchaser even with notice. The position of a bare licensee was also discussed in the following case.

Strand Securities Ltd v *Caswell* [1965] 1 Ch 958 (CA)

LORD DENNING MR: In this case it is clear that the second defendant was in actual occupation of the flat. The plaintiffs, therefore, took subject to her rights, whatever they were; see *National Provincial Bank Ltd* v *Hastings Car Mart Ltd*. She was not a tenant but only a licensee; see *Foster* v *Robinson* [1951] 1 KB 149; *Cobb* v *Lane* [1952] 1 TLR 1037. She had no contractual right to stay there. Her licence could be determined at any time and she would have to go in a reasonable time thereafter; see *Minister of Health* v *Bellotti* [1944] KB 298. So the plaintiffs could get her out, provided always that they could get rid of the first defendant's sublease.

(E) Collateral contractual rights cannot rank as overriding interests within s. 70(1)(g).

Eden Park Estates Ltd v *Longman*, Unreported, 19 May 1980

L rented property from B for a term of five years at a rent of £1,200, payable monthly in advance. L agreed to pay T a substantial deposit as security against non-payment of rent or breach of covenants in the lease. Eventually the plaintiff became the reversioner of the registered land through a series of assignments. The plaintiff sued L for arrears of rent. Held: that the collateral agreement did nothing more than create rights *in personam* between B and L.

See P. Kenny, '*Eden Park Estates* v *Longman*' [1982] Conv 239.

(v) *Actual occupation or in receipt of rents and profits* The meaning of the term 'actual occupation' was discussed in *Williams & Glyn's Bank* v *Boland*.

Williams & Glyn's Bank v *Boland*
[1981] AC 487 (HL)

A matrimonial home was purchased by contributions from both husband and wife but the property was registered solely in the husband's (H) name. H then arranged a legal mortgage of the matrimonial home. The bank involved made no investigation of any possible interest in the property held by the wife, who remained ignorant of the mortgage until her husband ceased mortgage repayments. The plaintiffs sought possession as mortgagees. Held: the wife had an equitable interest in the property under a statutory trust for sale and this was a sufficient 'right' to give her protection under s. 70(1)(g).

LORD WILBERFORCE: I now deal with the first question. Were the wives here in 'actual occupation'? These words are ordinary words of plain English, and should, in my opinion, be interpreted as such. Historically they appear to have emerged in the judgment of Lord Loughborough LC in *Taylor* v *Stibbert* (1794) 2 Ves Jun 437, 439–440, in a passage which repays quotation:

> ... whoever purchases an estate from the owner, knowing it to be in possession of tenants, is bound to inquire into the estates, those tenants have. It has been determined, that a purchaser being told, particular parts of the estate were in possession of a tenant, without any information as to his interest, and taking it for granted it was only from year to year, was bound by a lease, that tenant had, which was a surprise upon him. That was rightly determined; for it was sufficient to put the purchaser upon inquiry, that he was informed, the estate was not in the *actual possession* of the person, with whom he contracted; that he could not transfer the ownership and possession at the same time; that there were interests, as to the extent and terms of which it was his duty to inquire.

They were taken up in the judgment of the Privy Council in *Barnhart* v *Greenshields* (1853) 9 Moo PCC 18. The purpose for which they were used, in that case, was evidently to distinguish the case of a person who was in some kind of legal possession, as by receipt of the rents and profits, from that of a person actually in occupation as tenant. Given occupation, i.e., presence on the land, I do not think that the word 'actual' was intended to introduce any additional qualification, certainly not to suggest that possession must be 'adverse': it merely emphasises that what is required is physical presence, not some entitlement in law. So even if it were necessary to look behind these plain words into history, I would find no reason for denying them their plain meaning.

Then, were the wives in actual occupation? I ask: why not? There was physical presence, with all the rights that occupiers have, including the right to exclude all others except those having similar rights. The house was a matrimonial home, intended to be occupied, and in fact occupied by both spouses, both of whom have an interest in it: it would require some special doctrine of law to avoid the result that each is in occupation. Three arguments were used for a contrary conclusion. First, it was said that if the vendor (I use this word to include a mortgagor) is in occupation, that is enough to prevent the application of the paragraph. This seems to be a proposition of general application, not limited to the case of husbands, and no doubt, if correct, would be very convenient for purchasers and intending mortgagees. But the presence of the vendor, with occupation, does not exclude the possibility of occupation of others. There are observations which suggest the contrary in the unregistered land case of *Caunce* v *Caune* [1969] 1 WLR 286, but I agree with the disapproval of these, and with the assertion of the proposition I have just stated by Russell LJ in *Hodgson* v *Marks* [1971] Ch 892, 924. Then it was suggested that the wife's occupation was nothing but the shadow of the husband's — a version I suppose of the doctrine of unity of husband and wife. This expression and the argument flowing from it was used by Templeman J in *Bird* v *Syme-Thomson* [1979] 1 WLR 440, 444, a decision preceding and which he followed in the present case. The argument was also inherent in the judgment in *Caunce* v *Caunce* [1969] 1 WLR 286 which influenced the decisions of Templeman J. It somewhat faded from the arguments in the present case and appears to me to be heavily obsolete. The appellant's main and final position became in the end this: that, to come within the paragraph, the occupation in question must be apparently inconsistent with the title of the vendor. This, it was suggested, would exclude the wife of a husband-vendor because her apparent occupation would be satisfactorily accounted for by his. But, apart from the rewriting of the paragraph which this would involve, the suggestion is unacceptable. . . . A wife may, and everyone knows this, have rights of her own; particularly, many wives have a share in a matrimonial home. How can it be said that the presence of a wife in the house, as occupier, is consistent or inconsistent with the husband's rights until one knows what rights she has? And if she has rights, why, just because she is a wife (or in the converse case, just because an occupier is the husband), should these rights be denied protection under the paragraph? If one looks beyond the case of husband and wife, the difficulty of all these arguments stands out if one considers the case of a man living with a mistress, or of a man and a woman — or for that matter two persons of the same sex — living in a house in separate or partially shared rooms. Are these cases of apparently consistent occupation, so that the rights of the other person (other than the vendor) can be disregarded? The only solution which is consistent with the Act (section 70(1)(g)) and with common sense is to read the paragraph for what it says. Occupation, existing as a fact, may protect rights if the person in occupation has rights. On this part of the case I have no difficulty in concluding that a spouse, living in a house, has an actual occupation capable of conferring protection, as an overriding interest, upon rights of that spouse.

Notes

1. The fact that the person seeking to rely on s. 70(1)(g) is in 'actual occupation' with the registered proprietor does not affect his position. This had first been decided in *Hodgson* v *Marks* [1971] 1 Ch 893, where it was said that the rights of a person who was in occupation of land were not overridden merely because the vendor was or appeared to be in occupation also. *Williams & Glyn's Bank* v *Boland* applied this principle to a situation where the parties were husband and wife, whereas in *Hodgson* v *Marks* the parties were not husband and wife.

2. Both *Williams & Glyn's Bank* v *Boland* and *City of London Building Society* v *Flegg* (see *post*) should be viewed in the light of *Bristol & West Building Society* v *Henning* [1985] 1 WLR 778 and *Paddington Building Society* v *Mendelsohn* (1985) 50 P & CR 244, the latter case illustrating the same principle in unregistered land. From these cases it would appear that if the occupant knows the property is being acquired by the purchaser with the aid of a mortgage, and derives a benefit in the sense that he is living in the property, then the occupant's interest may not bind the mortgagee and gain priority to it because there is an imputed intention that the occupier's interest is subject to the mortgagee's right or on the basis of estoppel. In *Paddington Building Society* v *Mendelsohn* property was registered in S's name, although the purchase money had been provided partly by S, partly by his mother, M, and partly by an advance from P. M moved into the property with S and his girlfriend after the conveyance but before the charge had been registered by P. M claimed she had an overriding interest under s. 70(1)(g) which was binding on P. The court said that since she knew and intended at the date the property was purchased that there was to be a mortgage in P's favour, there was to be imputed to the parties an intention that M's rights were subject to P's. This approach has been followed in the recent decision below.

Equity and Law Home Loans Ltd v Prestidge
[1992] 1 All ER 909 (CA)

B and P bought a house together which was conveyed into P's sole name. B contributed approximately £10,000 to the purchase price, the remaining £30,000 being raised by means of a mortgage from the Britannia Building Society who knew P was the sole mortgagor. P subsequently and without B's knowledge mortgaged the property to Equity and Law for the sum of over £42,000. P redeemed the first mortgage and kept the balance of £12,000 for himself. P subsequently left B and made no mortgage repayments. B was unable to make any repayments herself. Equity and Law sought possession against B. They claimed that B's interest was subject to their mortgage to the extent of the original loan. B claimed that if the original mortgage were still in existence she would have no answer to a claim for possession, but the change of mortgage changed the situation and she was entitled to remain in occupation as against Equity and Law. Held: Equity and Law could enforce the sale and were entitled to £30,000 of the proceeds of sale.

MUSTILL LJ: So it seems to me that one must ask the question: what intention must one impute to the parties as regards the position which would exist if the mortgage which had been obtained in order to enable the purchase of the house, and which the parties intended to have priority over Mrs Brown's beneficial interest, should be replaced by another mortgage on no less favourable terms?

In my judgment, this question need only to be posed for it to be answered in favour of the new mortgagees. Any other answer would be absurd, for it would mean that, if Mr Prestidge had in good faith and without the knowledge of the appellant transferred the mortgage to another society in order (say) to obtain a more favourable rate of interest, Mrs Brown would suddenly receive a windfall in the shape of the removal of the encumbrance which she had intended should be created in consequence of a transaction which could not do her any harm and of which she was entirely ignorant.

If this answer is correct, it disposes of two objections to the judgment of the learned recorder which were canvassed in argument. First, it is said that the appellant's interest could not be encumbered by a mortgage of which she was unaware, especially in circumstances where there was ample on the documents to put the society on notice of that interest. Well, this would have been right if the mortgage to Equity and Law had been the first and only transaction. But it was not. The new mortgage was made against the background of a consent by the appellant to the creation of an encumbrance so that the transaction could proceed. This imputed consent must, in common sense, apply to the creation of a new encumbrance in replacement of the old, whether the appellant knew about it or not, provided that it did not change her position for the worse.

The second objection receives the same answer. It presupposes that there was a scintilla temporis between the discharge of the first mortgage and the attachment of the second when the property was entirely unencumbered and the appellant's interest therein was also unencumbered. It could be said that this interest could not effectively be re-encumbered by a transaction of which she was unaware. I doubt whether this argument is even technically correct, for it may very well be that if the position in law were closely examined (which very sensibly it was not in the argument before us) it would be found that the transactions were simultaneous. But, apart from this, to give effect to such a technicality would go against the grain of the broad equity expounded in *Henning's* case. If it was just to enforce the first mortgage, it must inevitably be just to enforce the second by virtue of an imputed consent which applied to the creation of both.

This leaves the fourth question: what is the position where the replacement mortgage creates a greater encumbrance than before? If Equity and Law had sought to argue that they could enforce their charge in full the judgment in *Henning's* case would have provided a conclusive answer, for no intention to prefer a mortgage in any amount greater than £30,000 plus interest could properly be imputed to the appellant. But the judge has not made any order to this effect, nor have Equity and Law sought by cross-appeal to obtain one. The issue is therefore not whether the new mortgage has made the appellant's position worse, but whether, as she contends, it has made it very much better. This would be a strange result if it were so, and I do not think that it is so. I repeat that the purchase could not have taken place at all without some encumbrance, and in my view it is a natural development of *Henning's* case to hold that in justice to both parties the original or substituted encumbrance should rank ahead of the beneficial interest as far as, but no further than, the consent which is to be imputed to the appellant. I therefore conclude that the judge's order was right. . . .

I am quite unable to see how Equity and Law could be regarded as owing towards her [the applicant] any duty of care which could alter the consequences of her initial imputed consent to the encumbering of the property.

This leads to the second observation. After the conclusion of the argument I had begun to wonder whether the combination of Equity and Law's means of knowledge with the fact that the appellant's interest was in the nature of an equity might mean that they could not claim to be bona fide purchasers without notice whose title defeated the equity. This point was not raised on the argument of the appeal, and we have not sought to open it up by further argument because on reflection it appears unsound. The rights of the mortgagees are preferred, not because they override the equity, but because the appellant's beneficial interest was of a very special kind, which from the outset had carved out of it by anticipation a recognition of the rights of the mortgagees whose finance was intended to bring the purchase into being. In my view once this is recognised the problem disappears.

Notes
1. The effect of such decisions is to shift the onus from the purchaser to investigate title and rights affecting the land to the equitable owner to make known his rights to the purchaser.
2. The effect of *Abbey National Building Society* v *Cann* (see *post*) should also be noted, in that a mortgage executed by a sole legal owner contemporaneously with the completion of the purchase takes priority over a mere equitable interest in the property.

Questions
1. In the light of this decision, do you think that the decision in *Williams & Glyn's Bank* v *Boland* would have been different:

    (a)   if the wife had known of the second mortgage?
    (b)   if the wife had not known of it, but that she derived a benefit of some kind from it?

2. Is *Equity and Law Home Loans Ltd* v *Prestidge* a just decision?
3. What would have been the result of *Williams & Glyn's Bank* v *Boland* if the land had been unregistered land?
4. Section 70(1)(g) would appear to enshrine the doctrine of *Hunt* v *Luck* into registered land. Are there any ways in which s. 70(1)(g) differs from the rule in *Hunt* v *Luck*?

Act of 'actual occupation'

Abbey National Building Society v Cann
[1990] 1 All ER 1085 (HL)

The facts of this case appear at page 81. The House of Lords had to consider whether a vendor allowing a prospective purchaser or tenant into the property prior to completion (for example, to measure for furnishings or plan decorations) constituted acts of 'actual occupation'.

LORD OLIVER: It is, perhaps, dangerous to suggest any test for what is essentially a question of fact, for 'occupation' is a concept which may have different connotations according to the nature and purpose of the property which is claimed to be occupied. It does not necessarily, I think, involve the personal presence of the person claiming to occupy. A caretaker or the representative of a company can occupy, I should have thought, on behalf of his employer. On the other hand, it does, in my judgment, involve some degree of permanence and continuity which would rule out mere fleeting presence. A prospective tenant or purchaser who is allowed, as a matter of indulgence, to go into property in order to plan decorations or measure for furnishings would not, in ordinary parlance, be said to be occupying it, even though he might be there for hours at a time. Of course, in the instant case, there was, no doubt, on the part of the persons involved in moving Mrs Cann's belongings, an intention that they would remain there and would render the premises suitable for her ultimate use as a residential occupier. Like the trial judge, however, I am unable to accept that acts of this preparatory character carried out by courtesy of the vendor prior to completion can constitute 'actual occupation' for the purposes of s. 70(1)(g). Accordingly, all other considerations apart, Mrs Cann fails, in my judgment, to establish the necessary condition for the assertion of an overriding interest.

Notes
1. The presence of the wife's furniture in the property has been held to be relevant in a situation where the wife was taken to hospital and the husband, during this period, sold the house to X, deliberately intending to be rid of his wife and obtain as much money as possible from the sale. See *Chhokar* v *Chhokar* [1984] FLR 313. See Simon Baughen, 'Some lessons of *Cann*' [1991] Conv 116; P. T. Evans [1991] Conv 155.
2. A person who has rights in the property cannot have the benefit of s. 70(1)(g) if there is no actual occupation.

Strand Securities v *Caswell*
[1965] Ch 958 (CA)

The first defendant was a sub-lessee of a flat. The headlease was for a term of 42 years and the proprietor registered the head lease. The sub-lease was for a term of 39 and a quarter years less three days and was not at the material time entered on the register. The sub-lessee used the flat as his London home, but lived in the country. He allowed his step-daughter (the second defendant) to use the flat rent free. The question was whether the first defendant had an overriding interest under s. 70(1)(g). Held: C did not have the benefit of s. 70(1)(g).

LORD DENNING MR: I, would like to hold that the first defendant was sharing the occupation of the flat with the second defendant. But I cannot bring myself to this conclusion. The truth is that he allowed her to be in actual occupation, and that is all there is to it. She was a licensee rent free and I fear that it does not give him protection. It seems to be a very rare case — a case which the legislature did not think of. For it is quite clear that if the second defendant had paid a token sum as rent, or for use and occupation, to the first defendant, he would be 'in receipt of the rents and profits' and his rights would be protected under section 70(1)(g). Again if the first defendant put his servant or caretaker into the flat, rent free, he would be protected because his agent would have actual occupation on his behalf. It is odd that the first defendant is not protected simply because he let his stepdaughter in rent free. Odd as it is, however, I fear the words of the statute do not cover this case and the first defendant does not succeed on this point. But he does on the other. And on that ground I would allow this appeal.

Occupation through an agent

Lloyds Bank v Rosset
[1988] 3 All ER 915 (CA)

H and W negotiated to buy a semi-derelict property using money given to H by the trustees of a family trust. H and W intended to renovate the building jointly as a family home, but the house was registered in H's sole name. It was the common intention that W should acquire some sort of beneficial interest in the property. H and W were allowed into the property before completion and they employed builders. W also helped doing building work. H obtained an overdraft of £15,000 to help pay for the purchase and renovations. W knew nothing of that overdraft. On completion, which took place on 17 December, H executed a charge in favour of the bank. W spent some nights in the property but the family did not move in until the middle of February 1983. The transfer and charge were not registered until 7 February. The bank demanded repayment of the outstanding amount on H's overdraft, then £23,000. No repayment was made and the bank commenced proceedings for possession and an order for sale. W claimed she had an overriding interest under s. 70(1)(g) of the Land Registration Act 1925 because she had been in actual occupation of the land on the date the bank's charge was registered. Held: (Mustill LJ dissenting) H and W had taken over the property prior to completion by means of a licence granted by the vendor and were in actual occupation by the presence of their builder on the property at the time the charge was executed. The wife therefore was in 'actual occupation' at that date.

NICHOLLS LJ: ... What constitutes occupation will depend on the nature and state of the property in question. I can see no reason, in principle or in practice, why a semi-derelict house such as Vincent Farmhouse should not be capable of actual occupation while the works proceed and before anyone has started to live in the building.

... I can detect nothing in the context in which the expression 'actual occupation' is used in para (g) to suggest that the physical presence of an employee or agent cannot be regarded as the presence of the employer or principal when determining whether the employer or principal is in actual occupation. Whether the presence of an employee or agent is to be so regarded will depend on the function which the employee or agent is discharging in the premises in the particular case. I am fortified in this approach by noting that it accords with the view, espoused in passing by Ormrod LJ in the *Boland* case in the Court of Appeal, that a person may be in occupation through another (see [1979] 2 All ER 697 at 710–711, [1979] Ch 312 at 338), and with the views expressed in *Strand Securities Ltd* v *Caswell* [1965] 1 All ER 820 at 827, 829, [1965] Ch 958 at 981, 984. In the latter case both Lord Denning MR and Russell LJ accepted that, if a tenant puts a resident caretaker into a residential flat to look after it, that would be actual occupation by the tenant. Russell LJ observed that the caretaker, by her occupation for which she was employed, would be the representative of the tenant and her occupation might therefore be regarded as his. Likewise, in my view, the presence of a builder engaged by a householder to do work for him in a house is to be regarded as the presence of the owner when considering whether or not the owner is in actual occupation.

Registration of Title

In the *Boland* case [1980] 2 All ER 408 at 413, [1981] AC 487 at 505 Lord Wilberforce explained the significance of the word 'actual' in the phrase 'actual occupation' as merely emphasising that what is required is physical presence, not some entitlement in law. He referred to the origin of the phrase 'actual possession', and commented that in the judgment of the Privy Council in *Barnhart* v *Greenshields* (1853) 9 Moo PCC 18 at 34, 14 ER 204 at 210 the expression was used to distinguish the case of a person who was in some kind of legal possession, as by receipt of the rents and profits, from that of a person actually in occupation as tenant. I can see nothing in that exposition inconsistent with the views expressed in *Strand Securities Ltd* v *Caswell* or with those I have sought to state.

I turn to the facts of the present case, which I have already summarised. The vendors had ceased to be in actual occupation long before 17 December. The house was empty and semi-derelict. They permitted the husband to go on to the property before completion. From 7 November until after Christmas the builder and his men were there every working day. One of them slept in the property on most nights. The wife spent almost every weekday at the property, from 10 am to 4 pm. Thus there was physical presence on the property throughout the period leading up to completion on 17 December, and that physical presence was to the extent that one would expect of an occupier, having regard to the then state of the property.

Thus far I am in agreement with the judge. Where I feel obliged to part company from him is his conclusion that, although (as I read his judgment) the husband, through the presence of the builder and his men, was in actual occupation of the property on 17 December, the wife was not. As appears from the second extract from his judgment that I have quoted above, in reaching that conclusion the judge attached importance to the answer which Mr Griffin would have given to the question 'Who occupies the building?' With all respect to the judge, I do not think that was the right question to pose. What mattered was not the builder's views on who occupied the building, but on whose behalf the builder was in the building. The judge himself had observed earlier that that was the vital question. As to that, the facts seem reasonably clear. Mr Griffin regarded himself as being employed by both the husband and the wife. There was no clear evidence that in this he was mistaken. Mr Griffin addressed his invoices to both Mr and Mrs Rosset. He looked to both of them for payment. In those circumstances, even though the husband alone was the contracting purchaser of the property, it seems to me that the presence of the builder and his men on the property was as much on behalf of the wife as it was on behalf of the husband. Mr Griffin was working there under a contract made with both of them, renovating the property for both of them. He was there on behalf of both of them. There was no sound basis for distinguishing between the two of them. If the builder's presence was sufficient to constitute occupation by the husband, it was equally sufficient to constitute occupation by the wife. This was so even after the incident mentioned by the judge. A stage was reached when the workmen complained that both the husband and the wife were giving them instructions. The husband then 'laid it down' that the workmen should take their instructions from him alone.

So the position was that the builder and his men were in the building, carrying out a contract made with the husband and the wife. Additionally, the wife herself was there almost every weekday. In my view, those facts amounted to actual occupation of the property by the wife on 17 December 1982. There was, I repeat, physical presence on the property by the wife and her agent of the nature, and to the extent, that one would expect of an occupier having regard to the then state of the property, namely the presence involved in actively carrying out the renovation necessary to make the house fit for residential use.

In my view, therefore, the judge erred in the inference he drew from the primary facts which he found. The reality was that before completion the husband and the wife had already taken over this semi-derelict house, under a revocable licence granted to the husband by the vendors. By 17 December renovation was well under way. Completion took place on 17 December, but no physical change then took place in their use of the property, save that the wife slept there more frequently. Eventually in February the family began to live there.

This conclusion has the attraction that it gives effect to the purpose of para. (g). Had a representative of the bank inspected the property before 17 December to check if anyone was in actual occupation, he would have seen that, indeed, someone was there. Builders were working there, day after day, plainly on behalf of someone. Had he gone up to the door, he would probably have found the wife in the house. In such circumstances the bank really has only itself to blame if it lends money without looking into the position further. In particular, I find it surprising that the bank, knowing that this was to be the matrimonial home, did not seek the wife's written consent to the grant of the charge. This was in December 1982. *Williams & Glyn's Bank Ltd* v *Boland* [1980] 2 All ER 408, [1981] AC 487 was decided by the House of Lords over two years earlier, in June 1980.

Note
In the House of Lords, the court held that the wife did not acquire a beneficial interest in the land because her work, expressed as a contribution to the cost of acquiring the property, was almost *de minimis*. Therefore the question of 'actual occupation' was not relevant since she had not acquired an interest in the property. See M. P. Thompson, 'Priorities in registered land, *Lloyd's Bank* v *Rosset*' [1988] Conv 453.

Extent of occupation

Epps v *Esso Petroleum Co. Ltd*
[1973] 1 WLR 1071 (ChD)

J leased a house and a garage for 20 years and parked his car on a strip of land which separated the two. In 1955, the house and strip were conveyed to his wife and J took out a new lease on the garage. This lease inadvertently and incorrectly included the strip of land. The fee simple to the garage was then conveyed to B and the mistake perpetuated in the Land Registry plan. When the lease expired, the fee simple was conveyed to the defendants under the same mistake. J's wife died and the plaintiffs acquired the title to the house and strip, but the Land Registry plans showed the strip as belonging to the garage, not the house. The plaintiffs sought rectification of the register. Held: The fact that J parked his car on the strip was insufficient to constitute actual occupation under s. 70(1)(g) of the Land Registration Act 1925.

TEMPLEMAN J: In *Hodgson* v *Marks* [1971] Ch 892, 931, Russell LJ said, on actual occupation as an ingredient of an overriding interest, that he was prepared for the purpose of that case to assume, without necessarily accepting, that section 70(1)(g) of the Land Registration Act 1925 is designed only to apply to a case in which the occupation is such in point of fact as would in the case of unregistered land affect a purchaser with constructive notice of the rights of the occupier. Then Russell LJ said, at p. 932:

> I do not think it desirable to attempt to lay down a code or catalogue of situations in which a person other than the vendor should be held to be in occupation of unregistered land for the purpose of constructive notice of his rights, or in actual occupation of registered land for the purposes of section 70(1)(g). It must depend on the circumstances, and a wise purchaser or vendor will take no risks. Indeed, however wise he may be he may have no ready opportunity of finding out; but, nevertheless, the law will protect the occupier.

In my judgment Mr Jones was not in actual occupation of the disputed strip when the defendants completed their purchase of Darland Garage and was not thereafter in actual occupation.

Mr Jones gave evidence that every night he parked his car on the disputed strip, and sometimes the car was there during the day. Mr Jones's recollection, not unnaturally, was not very reliable, and I find that he sometimes parked his car on the disputed strip, but how often and when no one can now determine with any certainty. But even if Mr Jones regularly parked his car on the disputed strip I do not consider that this constituted actual occupation of the disputed strip in the circumstances of the present case. I reach this conclusion for the following reasons: first, the parking of a car on a strip 11 feet wide by 80 feet long does not actually occupy the whole, or a substantial, or any defined part of that disputed strip for the whole or any defined time. Secondly, the parking of a car on an unidentified piece of land, apparently comprised in garage premises, is not an assertion of actual occupation of anything.

Note
See F. R. Crane, *Epps* v *Esso Petroluem* [1973] 2 All ER 465, (1973) 37 Conv 284.

Date at which actual occupation must occur

Abbey National Building Society v Cann
[1990] 1 All ER 1085 (HL)

The defendants lived in a leasehold property purchased for them by their son in his own name for the sum of £34,000 with the aid of a £25,000 mortgage from the plaintiff. The balance of the purchase money came from the sale of another house purchased by the son for the defendants. The sale of the old property and purchase of the new property took place on 13 August 1984, and a simultaneous registration of the son's title to the property and the building society's charge took place a month later. The son subsequently defaulted in paying the mortgage instalments and the plaintiff brought proceedings against the son and the defendants. The first defendant said that by reason of her contribution to the previous house she had an equitable interest in the new property either on or immediately prior to completion, and this was an overriding interest which by reason of her occupation at the date of registration took priority over the plaintiff's charge. Held: actual occupation must be shown at the date the charge was created not the date it was registered.

LORD OLIVER: First in logical order is the question of the appropriate date for ascertaining the existence of overriding interests under the Land Registration Acts. . . . The question arose directly in *Rosset's* case, in which the Court of Appeal decided unanimously that the relevant date was the date of completion of the purchase and not that of registration. Your Lordships are now invited to overrule that decision.

My Lords, the conclusion at which the Court of Appeal arrived makes good conveyancing sense and, speaking for myself, I should be extremely reluctant to overrule it unless compulsively driven to do so, the more so because it produces a result which is just, convenient and certain, as opposed to one which is capable of leading to manifest injustice and absurdity. It has, I think, to be acknowledged that the interrelation between the provisions of ss. 3(xvi), 20 and 23, 37, 69 and 70(1) is not altogether easy to understand, particularly in relation to the position of a chargee whose charge is created by a purchaser of land who is not yet himself the registered proprietor. The solution propounded by the trial judge and by counsel for the bank in *Rosset's* case depends on the words 'affecting the estate transferred or created' in ss. 20(1)(b) and 23(1)(c) and construes them as if there were added the words 'at the time at which it was transferred or created', thus excluding from the category of interests affecting the estate the rights of a person entering into occupation after the transfer or creation of the estate effected by completion of the transaction. It will be convenient to refer to this as 'the judge's construction'.

This is an attractive solution because it is, as Nicholls LJ observed in the course of his judgment in *Rosset's* case [1988] 3 All ER 915 at 922, [1989] Ch 350 at 373, a conveyancing absurdity that, for instance, a mortgagee should, after completion and after having made all possible inquiries and parted with his money, be bound by the interest asserted by a newly-arrived occupant coming in between completion and the registration of his charge. So far as registered interests are concerned the chargee can protect himself by an official search which will preserve his priority over any further registered entries during a priority period well sufficient to enable him to have his charge stamped and lodged for registration: see rr. 3 and 5 of the Land Registration (Official Searches) Rules 1981, SI 1981/1135. There is, however, no similar protection against overriding interests which are not recorded on the register and whose existence can be ascertained only by inquiry and there is, accordingly, good sense in so construing ss. 20(1) and 23(1) as to preserve the priority of the purchaser or chargee as from the date of completion, when both are irrevocably committed to the transaction, which only awaits the formal step of registration in order to vest the legal estate.

In *Rosset's* case, however, the Court of Appeal found some difficulty in accepting that the solution could be found simply in construing ss. 20(1) and 23(1) in the manner suggested. Nicholls LJ pointed out that it was common ground that para. (a) of s. 20(1) (para. (b) of s. 23(1)), which subjects the land transferred to entries appearing on the register, undoubtedly refers to entries so appearing at the date of registration (see [1988] 3 All ER 915 at 921, [1989] Ch 350 at 371). This appears to me to be beyond doubt. One would, therefore, expect that the paragraph subjecting the land to overriding interests would be related to the same date. Nicholls LJ reached, in relation to overriding interests within s. 70(1)(g), the same result as that produced by the judge's construction but by reference to the words 'for the time being subsisting' in s. 70(1) and by holding that, in relation to para. (g) specifically, an interest was not a subsisting interest except in a case in which the claimant was in occupation of the land prior to and at the date of completion of the purchase.

I share the difficulty that Nicholls LJ felt in accepting the attractive solution of the judge's construction and I agree with him that the key to the problem lies in the words of s. 70(1) rather than in the reference to the interests affecting the estate transferred or created in ss. 20(1) and 23(1). The 1925 Act displays a degree of circularity in its general

Registration of Title

definition of what an overriding interest is. Section 3(xvi) defines it as an unregistered encumbrance 'subject to which registered dispositions . . . take effect', but when one turns to inquire to what unregistered encumbrances a disposition is subject, ss. 20(1) and 23(1) merely specify that they are 'overriding interests, if any, affecting the estate transferred or created'. As a definition, therefore, this is a little less than satisfactory, for it simply means 'overriding interests' are 'overriding interests'. It does, however, involve this consequence, that if the judge's construction is correct no interest which does not affect the estate or interest at the time when a relevant disposition is effected by transfer, grant or charge can be an overriding interest. That, of course, does not demonstrate that the judge's construction is erroneous, but it might be thought to be a surprising result when consideration is given to the remaining words in ss. 20 and 23 and to the terms of ss. 69 and 70.

I turn to those sections, because the circularity of the definition so far compels a reference to other provisions of the 1925 Act in order to ascertain the nature of the interests which are to override. They are, to begin with, not 'minor interests' (s. 3(xv)), that is to say interests not capable of being disposed of or created by registered dispositions and interests created by unregistered dealings and subsisting only in equity. Unless protected by notice, caution, inhibition or restriction entered on the register, these will be overriden by registered dispositions for valuable consideration. Specifying what overriding interests are not does not, however, assist in determining what they are and, moreover, it is clear from *Williams & Glyn's Bank Ltd v Boland* [1980] 2 All ER 408, [1981] AC 487 that a minor interest may become an overriding interest if the claimant is in actual occupation. Section 69 is of some assistance in that it demonstrates that the list of miscellaneous overriding interests contained in s. 70(1) is not exhaustive, since the legal estate is vested in the registered proprietor under this section subject to—

> The overriding interests . . . including any . . . charge by way of legal mortgage created . . . under . . . this Act or otherwise which has priority to the registered estate.

(See s. 69(1).) Section 70(1) contains no reference to a mortgage or charge as an overriding interest, but s. 69(1) necessarily implies that it is one so long as it has priority to the registered estate.

When regard is had to the list of overriding interests in s. 70(1) it is apparent that all of them are interests which can come into being at any time, and some of them may arise without any volition on the part of the registered proprietor or anyone else seised of an estate in the land. . . . Yet, on the judge's construction, a purchaser would, on registration, take free from any such interests arising after completion of his purchase (in the sense of payment of the price against delivery of the executed transfer) even though, if the land were unregistered land, he would clearly be subjected to them. This necessarily follows, if the judge's construction is right, from the words which immediately follow para. (b) of s. 20(1) (para. (c) of s. 23(1)): 'But free from all other estates and interests whatsoever . . .' It also involves, I think, a conflict between ss. 20(1) and 23(1) on the one hand and ss. 69(1) and 70(1) on the other. Section 69, as it seems to me, is looking at the continuous position of the registered proprietor and providing that the legal estate is deemed to be vested in him subject to such overriding interests as shall from time to time subsist during his proprietorship, whereas, if the judge's construction is correct, it is indeed subject to all such interests but with the exception of those which come into being between the date when he took his transfer and the date when he became registered. Moreover it would also follow that the effect of registration of the transferee would be to free him even from overriding interests which he himself had created in the interval between completion and registration. . . .

I conclude, therefore, like Nicholls LJ, that the relevant date for determining the existence of overriding interests which will 'affect the estate transferred or created' is the date of registration. This does, of course, give rise to the theoretical difficulty that, since a transferor remains the registered proprietor until registration of the transfer, it would be possible for him in breach of trust, to create overriding interests, for instance by grant of an easement or of a lease, which would be binding on the transferee and against which the transferee would not be protected by an official search. That would, of course, equally be the case in a purchase of unregistered land where the purchaser pays the price in advance of receiving a conveyance. I cannot, however, find in the theoretical possibility of so improbable event a context for preferring the judge's construction.

The question remains, however, whether the date of registration is also the relevant date for determining whether a claimant to a right is in actual occupation. It is to be noted that it is not the actual occupation which gives rise to the right or determines its existence. Actual occupation merely operates as the trigger, as it were, for the treatment of the right, whatever it may be, as an overriding interest. Nor does the additional quality of the right as an overriding interest alter the nature or quality of the right itself. If it is an equitable right it remains an equitable right. As was observed in *Williams & Glyn's Bank Ltd* v *Boland* [1980] 2 All ER 408 at 412, [1981] AC 487 at 504, the purpose of s. 70(1)(g) was to make applicable to registered land the same rule for the protection of persons in actual occupation as had been applied in the case of unregistered land in, for instance, *Hunt* v *Luck* [1902] 1 Ch 428, [1900–3] All ER Rep 295. In relation to legal rights it does nothing, for it is not easy to conceive of a legal right in the land which would not already be an overriding interest under some other head, as, for instance, para. (a) or (k). Again, as regards equitable rights in an occupier which arise before completion and are supported by occupation at that date there is no difficulty. A chargee who advances money and so acquires an equitable charge prior to the creation of the occupier's right does not lose his priority because the occupier's right becomes an overriding interest. That interest remains what it always was, an interest subject to the prior equity of the chargee which, on registration, is fortified by the legal estate. Equally, a chargee advancing his money after the creation of the occupier's equitable right is, as one would expect, subject to such right.

The case which does give rise to difficulty if the date of registration is the relevant date for determining whether there is a claimant in actual occupation is one in which the sequence of events is that the right, unaccompanied by occupation, is created before completion and before the chargee has advanced his money and then subsequently the claimant enters into actual occupation after completion and remains in occupation up to the date when the registration of the charge is effected. The chargee in that event would have no possibility of discovering the existence of the claimant's interest before advancing his money and taking his charge, but would nevertheless be subject, on registration, to the claimant's prior equitable interest which, ex hypothesi, would not have been subject to the charge at its creation.

This does indeed produce a conveyancing absurdity and there is, as Nicholls LJ observed, an internal context for supposing that the legislature, in enacting para. (g), must have been contemplating an occupation which preceded and existed at completion of a transfer or disposition. Not only was the paragraph clearly intended to reflect the rule discussed in *Hunt* v *Luck* with regard to unregistered conveyancing, but the reference to inquiry and failure to disclose cannot make any sense unless it is related to a period in which such inquiry could be other than otiose. That absurdity can, I think, be avoided only by the route which the Court of Appeal adopted and by referring the 'actual occupation' in para. (g) to the date of completion of the transaction by transfer and payment of the purchase money. Section 70(1) refers to such interests 'as may be for the time being subsisting' and in order to affect 'the estate transferred or created' on registration such interests would no doubt require to be subsisting on that date. But I see no insuperable difficulty in holding that the actual occupation required to support such an interest as a subsisting interest must exist at the date of completion of the transaction giving rise to the right to be registered, for that is the only date at which the inquiry referred to in para. (g) could, in practice, be made and be relevant.

Note
Once one has established actual occupation on the relevant date, the overriding status of the holder's right is not lost by the holder subsequently going out of occupation (*London and Cheshire Insurance Company* v *Laplargrene Property Co.* [1971] 1 Ch 499). See P. G. McHugh, 'Overriding interests, registration gaps and actual "Occupation"' [1989] CLJ 180; R. J. Smith, 'Land registration and conveyancing absurdity' (1988) 104 LQR 507.

(vi)   *Overreaching and s. 70(1)(g)*   See chapter 8 for a detailed discussion of the doctrine of overreaching.

In *Williams & Glyn's Bank* v *Boland*, the legal title to the land was vested in a sole trustee and therefore the doctrine of overreaching did not apply. This caused a great deal of concern amongst banks and building societies because it resulted in a mortgagee being bound by a prior equitable interest which had arisen through co-ownership. For a full discussion of this issue, see James Russell, '*Williams & Glyn's Bank Ltd* v *Boland and Brown*: the practical implication' (1981) 32 NILQ 3; R. J. Smith, 'Overriding interests and wives' (1979) 95 LQR 501; R. J. Smith, 'Overriding interests, wives and the House of Lords' (1981) 97 LQR 12; Jill Martin, 'Section 70(1)(g) and the vendor's spouse' [1980] Conv 361; Jill Martin, 'Overreaching and s. 70(1)(g), the wide view versus the narrow' [1981] Conv 219; W. J. Swadling, '*City of London Building Society* v *Flegg*' [1987] Conv 451.

Nevertheless, the decision in *Williams & Glyn's Bank* v *Boland* must now be looked at in the light of *City of London Building Society* v *Flegg* [1988] AC 54.

City of London Building Society v Flegg
[1988] AC 54 (HL)

In 1977, Bleak House was acquired by Mr and Mrs B as beneficial joint tenants, and was occupied by them and Mrs B's parents, the Fleggs. £18,000 of the purchase price of £34,000 had been provided by the Fleggs, the remainder by means of a mortgage, which was registered in the names of Mr and Mrs B only. The Fleggs were unaware of two subsequent mortgages taken out by Mr and Mrs B, or of the final, consolidating mortgage of £37,500 with the City of London Building Society, who had made no inquiries regarding the Fleggs' occupation or interest in the property prior to granting the mortgage. When Mr and Mrs B defaulted on the mortgage repayments, the Building Society sought possession and the Fleggs claimed to have an overriding interest under s. 70(1)(g) of the Land Registration Act 1925. Held: the property was held on trust for sale, and the mortgage money had been paid to the two trustees (Mr and Mrs B), overreaching the Fleggs' equitable interest by way of s. 27 of the Law of Property Act 1925. The Fleggs' occupation arose only by way of their equitable interest under the trust for sale. Their interest in the property would have to be recovered from Mr and Mrs B, who as trustees had received the £37,500 from the mortgage.

LORD WILBERFORCE: In my view the object of s. 70 was to reproduce for registered land the same limitations as s. 14 of the Law of Property Act 1925 produced for land whether registered or unregistered. The respondents claim to be entitled to overriding interests because they were in actual occupation of Bleak House on the date of the legal charge. But the interests of the respondents cannot at one and the same time be overreached and overridden and at the same time be overriding interests. The appellants cannot at one and the same time take free from all the interests of the respondents yet at the same time be subject to some of those interests. The right of the respondents to be and remain in actual occupation of Bleak House ceased when the respondents' interests were overreached by the legal charge save in so far as their rights were transferred to the equity of redemption. As persons interested under the trust for sale the respondents had no right to possession as against the appellants and the fact that the respondents were in actual occupation at the date of the legal charge did not create a new right or transfer an old right so as to make the right enforceable against the appellants.

One of the main objects of the legislation of 1925 was to effect a compromise between, on the one hand, the interests of the public in securing that land held in trust is freely marketable and, on the other hand, the interests of the beneficiaries in preserving their rights under the trusts. By the Settled Land Act 1925 a tenant for life may convey the settled land discharged from all the trusts, powers and provisions of the settlement. By the Law of Property Act 1925 trustees for sale may convey land held on trust for sale discharged from the trusts affecting the proceeds of sale and rents and profits until sale. Under both forms of trust the protection and the only protection of the beneficiaries is that capital money must be paid to at least two trustees or a trust corporation. Section 14 of the Law of Property Act 1925 and s. 70 of the Land Registration Act 1925 cannot have been intended to frustrate this compromise and to subject the purchaser to some beneficial interests but not others depending on the waywardness of actual occupation. The Court of Appeal took a different view, largely in reliance on the decision of this House in *Williams & Glyn's Bank Ltd* v *Boland* [1980] 2 All ER 408, [1981] AC 487. In that case the sole proprietor of registered land held the land as sole trustee on trust for sale and to stand possessed of the net proceeds of sale and rents and profits until sale on trust for himself and his wife as tenants in common. This House held that the wife's beneficial interest coupled with actual possession by her constituted an overriding interest and that a mortgagee from the husband, despite the concluding words of s. 20(1), took subject to the wife's overriding interest. But in that case the interest of the wife was not overreached or overridden because the mortgagee advanced capital moneys to a sole trustee. If the wife's interest had been overreached by the mortgagee advancing capital moneys to two trustees there would have been nothing to justify the wife in remaining in occupation as against the mortgagee. There must be a combination of an interest which justifies continuing occupation plus actual occupation to constitute an overriding interest. Actual occupation is not an interest in itself.

For these reasons and for the reasons to be given by my noble and learned friend Lord Oliver, I would allow this appeal and restore the order of his Honour Judge Thomas, who ordered the respondents to deliver up Bleak House to the appellants.

Registration of Title

Question
Could the Fleggs have protected their interest by registering it as a caution?

(vii) *Inquiry* It is important to note that inquiry must be made of the holder of the right; inquiry of the vendor alone is not sufficient to save a purchaser from the effect of s. 70(1)(g) (*Hodgson* v *Marks* [1971] 1 Ch 892, at p. 932). This is particularly important since according to *Williams & Glyn's Bank Ltd* v *Boland,* the person's actual occupation does not necessarily give constructive notice to a purchaser. See Jill Martin, 'Section 70(1)(g) and the vendor's spouse' [1980] Conv 361.

Question
Does this third condition for an overriding interest under s. 70(1)(g) introduce the doctrine of notice into overriding interests?

C: MINOR INTERESTS

(a) What is a minor interest?

Land Registration Act 1925

3. Interpretation
(xv) 'Minor interests' mean the interests not capable of being disposed of or created by registered dispositions and capable of being overridden (whether or not a purchaser has notice thereof, by the proprietors unless protected as provided by this Act, and all rights and interests which are not registered or protected on the register and are not overriding interests, and include—
(a) in the case of land held on trust for sale, all interests and powers which are under the Law of Property Act 1925, capable of being overridden by the trustees for sale, whether or not such interests and powers are so protected; and
(b) in the case of settled land, all interests and powers which are under the Settled Land Act 1925, and the Law of Property Act 1925, or either of them, capable of being overridden by the tenant for life or statutory owner, whether or not such interests and powers are so protected as aforesaid; . . .

(b) Protection of minor interests

Minor interests are interests that need protection by entry on the register. The entry may take one of four forms, which to some extent depends on the nature of the interest to be protected. Certain minor interests cannot bind a purchaser even if they are protected by entry. Entry in such a case merely affects the way that the land can be disposed of.

(i) *Notice* Certain interests can be protected by notice entered on the charges register, and such entry ensures that any future dealings with the land can only take place subject to the interest that has been protected by notice. Notice can be entered on the register only if the land certificate is produced, and therefore generally needs the consent of the registererd proprietor. Entry by notice is available to a range of interests such as estate contracts, options and certain kinds of charges.

(ii) *Restriction* This type of entry prevents any dealings with the land unless certain conditions are fulfilled. It is used most commonly in cases where land is held on trust for sale or is settled land. The restriction in such a case will stipulate that no further transaction with the title can be registered until the beneficiaries' interests have been overreached.

(iii) *Caution* This gives the person entering the caution the right to be informed of any proposed dealing with the land and gives him time to object to it. A caution is used when a notice cannot be, because the land certificate cannot be obtained.

(iv) *Inhibition* This is an order from the court or the Registrar preventing all dealings with the land until the occurence of a specified event or for a period of time. It is mainly used in cases of emergency or in bankruptcy matters.

See T. B. F. Ruoff, 'Rights of third parties in registered property' (1932) 17 Conv 105.

(c) Failure to enter a minor interest on the register

Land Registration Act 1925

20. Effect of registration of dispositions of freeholds
(1) [See page 67.]
(2) In the case of a freehold estate registered with a qualified title a disposition of the registered land or of a legal estate therein, including a lease thereof, for valuable consideration shall, when registered, have the same effect as it would have had if the land had been registered with an absolute title, save that such disposition shall not affect or prejudice the enforcement of any right or interest appearing by the register to be excepted.
(3) In the case of a freehold estate registered with a possessory title, a disposition of the registered land or of a legal estate therein, including a lease thereof, for valuable consideration shall not affect or prejudice the enforcement of any right or interest adverse to or in derogation of the title of the first registered proprietor, and subsisting or capable of arising at the time of the registration of such proprietor; but, save as aforesaid, shall when registered have the same effect as it would have had if the land had been registered with an absolute title.
(4) Where any such disposition is made without valuable consideration, it shall, so far as the transferee or grantee is concerned, be subject to any minor interests subject to which the transferor or grantor held the same, but, save as aforesaid, shall, when registered, in all respects, and in particular as respects any registered dealings on the part of the transferee or grantee, have the same effect as if the disposition had been made for valuable consideration.

59. Writs, orders, deeds of arrangement, pending actions, etc.
(6) Subject to the provisions of this Act relating to fraud and to the title of a trustee in bankruptcy, a purchaser acquiring title under a registered disposition, shall not be concerned with any pending action, writ, order, deed of arrangement, or other document, matter, or claim (not being an overriding interest or a charge for inheritance tax subject to which the disposition takes effect under section 73 of this Act) which is not protected by a caution or other entry on the register, whether he has or has not notice thereof, express, implied, or constructive.

Notes

1. A purchaser will take free from minor interests if they are not entered on the register. This occurs even if the purchaser has actual notice of their existence.
2. A donee is bound by minor interests even if they are not protected by entry on the register.

Traditional view of s. 20

Miles v Bull (No. 2)
[1969] 3 All ER 1585 (QBD)

The defendant occupied a house which formed part of a farm. The farm was sold by the defendant's husband and brother-in-law to the plaintiff. The sale was made subject to any existing rights of occupation which the defendant might enjoy, provided that should not be deemed to imply that she had or would have any such rights against the plaintiff. The defendant had not protected her occupation by registration under the Land Registration Act 1925. The defendant, after the date of completion, remained in the property. Held: this was a genuine and legitimate sale. The Matrimonial Homes Act 1967 made clear provision for the way in which a spouse could protect her rights of occupation against third parties. This superseded the equitable doctrine of notice. Therefore, under s. 20(1) of the Land Registration Act 1925, the plaintiff took the property free from all other estates and interests.

BRIDGE J: It is I think in the end conceded by counsel for the defendant that on their face the very wide words of s. 20 of the Land Registration Act 1925 which I have already read, namely, the phrase 'free from all other estates and interests whatsoever' embrace prima facie not only all kinds of legal interests but all kinds of equitable interests. It is conceded again that the provisions of the Land Registration Act 1925 and the corresponding provisions of the Law of Property Act 1925 and Land Charges Act 1925, which substitute registration and non-registration as the touchstone on which the enforceability of equitable interests against purchasers depends for the old equitable doctrine of constructive notice, in general are effective and that in the ordinary way actual or constructive notice on the part of the purchaser of an unregistered interest will not have the effect of imposing a constructive trust on him. But counsel for the defendant says nevertheless that the interest created in favour of a spouse by the Matrimonial Homes Act 1967 is sui generis, and that I should hold that in the case of this one exceptional interest where the purchaser has purchased from vendors who were in any event (because there happened to be two of them) trustees for sale in circumstances which suggest that completion was hastened against the contingency that the hitherto unregistered interest of the defendant might be registered any day, this was a fraudulent transaction in the Chancery sense and was a transaction which did give rise to a constructive trust binding the property in the hands of the plaintiff.

Of course in a case of this kind one feels every sympathy for the position of the defendant, which is a very unenviable one, but it seems to me that the right approach to the question which I have to determine is to bear in mind that the Matrimonial Homes Act 1967 is an Act which, however socially desirable, creates new rights in favour of certain spouses and correspondingly takes away — provided the statutory machinery is operated according to its terms — certain common law rights which, apart from the Act, would be exercisable by property owners. When such an Act, particularly in that aspect of its operations which deprives a property owner of his common law rights, contains, as this statute and its effective incorporation of the provisions of the Land Registration Act 1925 does, provisions which make it perfectly clear what steps are to be taken in order that the spouse's right of occupation shall be appropriately protected if the property which the spouse is entitled to occupy comes into the hands of third parties, it does not seem to me that it is for the court to say that Parliament really did not mean what it said, that Parliament has not provided adequate or effective protection, or that the old equitable doctrines of the court can be introduced for the purpose in effect of widening the protection to extend it to those who have not protected themselves by taking the appropriate statutory steps.

In the end I would be content to rest my judgment on this short ground — and if I have expressed myself at greater length it has really been in deference to the argument of counsel for the defendant — that by the plain operation of s. 20 of the Land Registration Act 1925 the plaintiff has acquired an absolute title to Cranham Place Farm in circumstances in which he is entitled to take that property free from all other estates and interests whatsoever, including the right of occupation of that property vested in the defendant by the Matrimonial Homes Act 1967. It follows in those circumstances that there must be judgment for the plaintiff for possession.

Knowledge of unprotected minor interests

Peffer v Rigg
[1977] 1 WLR 285 (ChD)

A house was purchased by the plaintiff and first defendant. It was registered in the first defendant's name only, but it was agreed that both parties were to pay all outgoings in equal shares and the property was to be held by them as tenants in common in equal shares. The purpose of the purchase was twofold: (a) to provide permanent accommodation for their mother-in-law and (b) an investment. The arrangements between the plaintiff and first defendant were embodied in a formal trust deed. The second defendant moved in with the mother-in-law. His interest was not registered. The first and second defendants subsequently divorced. The financial settlement involved the first defendant conveying the house to the second defendant for a nominal consideration of £1. The second defendant was to receive rents from the property and to repay the mortgage. Both parties knew, however, that the plaintiff held a beneficial interest in half the property. The plaintiff claimed the house was held half on trust for himself. Held:

(1) When the house was transferred to the second defendant the first defendant knew the property was subject to a trust for the plaintiff and first defendant, and therefore, because the transfer was for nominal consideration, the second defendant (under s. 20(4) of Land Registration Act 1925) took subject to the plaintiff's unregistered interest. Even if the transfer had been for valuable consideration, being part of the divorce settlement, it was still necessary under the Land Registration Act 1925, ss. 20 and 59 for the second defendant to have been a purchaser in good faith.

(2) Since the second defendant knew when the property was transferred to her that it was trust property, she took it on constructive trust.

GRAHAM J: ... It was argued by Mr Banks, for the second defendant, that the property was transferred to her for valuable consideration as part of the divorce agreement and that, therefore, the combined effect of sections 20 and 59 of the Land Registration Act 1925 protected the second defendant against any claim or interest of the plaintiff because there is no entry on the register in his favour prior to the transfer to the second defendant. This argument would be convincing if it were not for my finding that the second defendant at the time knew perfectly well that the first defendant could not transfer to her more than a half share of the property. It is this knowledge which seems to me to cause great difficulty to her and prevents her argument succeeding for a number of different reasons put forward by Mr Poulton for the plaintiff at the second hearing. He argues first that the purported transfer from the first defendant to the second defendant of the beneficial interest of the whole of the property of 103, Leighton Road was expressed to be for the consideration of £1. This is a nominal consideration and not valuable consideration and it follows that the second defendant is not protected by section 20 of the Land Registration Act 1925. In accordance with the provisions of section 20(4) she can only take subject to any minor interests subject to which the first defendant held the same. He was party to the trust deed of May 30, 1968, and clearly had notice of the plaintiff's half interest in the property. The second defendant can therefore only take subject to the minor interest of the plaintiff in the property subject to which the first defendant held it.

The argument to the contrary is that the transfer was only part of the whole agreement entered into by the first and second defendants on the occasion of the divorce and it is not therefore right to limit the consideration for the transfer to the £1 expressed to be therefor. The consideration, there, was a great deal more and included all the obligations undertaken by the second defendant. Such consideration was therefore not nominal but valuable within section 20 and the second defendant received the protection of the section. I do not see why, when the parties have chosen to express a transfer as being for a nominal consideration, the court should seek to hold that the consideration was in fact otherwise than as agreed and stated. If, however, the proper view is that there was valuable consideration for the transfer here, then it is argued as follows. There is a contrast between sections 20 and 59 of the Act. Section 20(1) protects any 'transferee' for valuable consideration. By section 18(5) 'transfer' and 'transferee' in relation to freehold land have very wide meanings but are not specifically defined in section 3. It is to be noted, however, that section 20, though it mentions valuable consideration, does not mention 'good faith' as being necessary on the part of the transferee, nor does it mention notice. It can be argued therefore that the section seems to be saying that a transferee whether he has good faith or not, and whether he has notice or not, takes free of all interests (other than overriding interests) provided he has given valuable consideration.

This at first sight seems a remarkable proposition and though undoubtedly the property legislation of 1925 was intended to simplify such matters of title as far as possible, I find it difficult to think that section 20 of this Act can have been intended to be as broad in scope as this. Similar doubt is expressed in *Brickdale & Stewart-Wallace's Land Registration Act 1925*, 4th edn. (1939), p. 107, note (1). The provisions for rectification in section 82 as against a proprietor in possession who has been a party to a fraud, mistake or an omission in consequence of which rectification of the register is sought also seems to me to show that section 20 must be read with some limitations: see also *Ruoff & Roper, Registered Conveyancing*, 3rd edn. (1972), p. 417. Section 59(6) on the other hand speaks of a 'purchaser' not being affected by matters which are not protected by a caution or other entry on the register. By definition, however (see section 3(xxi), 'purchaser' means a purchaser in good faith for valuable consideration. It seems clear therefore that as a matter of construction a purchaser who is not in fact one 'in good faith' *will* be concerned with matters not protected by a caution or other entry on the register, at any rate, as I hold, if he has notice thereof. If these sections 20 and 59 are read together in the context of the Act they can be reconciled by holding that if the 'transferee' spoken of in section 20 is in fact a 'purchaser' he will only be protected if he has given valuable consideration and is in good faith. He cannot in my judgment be in good faith if he has in fact notice of something which affects his title as in the present case. Of course if he and, a fortiori, if a purchaser from him has given valuable consideration and in fact has no notice he is under no obligation to go behind the register, and will in such a case be fully protected. This view of the matter seems to me to enable the two sections to be construed consistently together without producing the unreasonable result of permitting a transferee purchaser to take advantage of the Act, and divest himself of knowldge of defects in his own title, and secure to himself a flawless title which he ought not in justice to be allowed to obtain. This view of the Act produces a result which is also produced by applying the principles applicable in the case of a constructive trust, which I will now consider.

On the evidence in this case I have found that the second defendant knew quite well that the first defendant held the property on trust for himself and the plaintiff in equal shares. The second defendant knew this was so and that the property was trust property when the transfer was made to her, and therefore she took the property on a constructive trust in accordance with general equitable principles: see *Snell's Principles of Equity*, 27th edn. (1973), pp. 98–99. This is a new trust imposed by equity and is distinct from the trust which bound the first defendant. Even if, therefore, I am wrong as to the proper construction of sections 20 and 59, when read together, and even if section 20 strikes off the shackles of the express trust which bound the first defendant, this cannot invalidate the new trust imposed on the second defendant.

Notes

1. Section 20(1) of the Act provides that a registered diposition made for *valuable consideration* confers the legal estate on the transferee subject to any minor interests that have been protected by entry on the Register, but free from unprotected minor interests. Graham J said that the transfer had been for nominal consideration only and that s. 20(1) requires a transfer to be for valuable consideration. Therefore the parties in this case did not come within the conditions necessary for s. 20(1) to apply.

2. Section 59(6) provides that a *purchaser* is not to be concerned with any matter (not being an overriding interest) which is not protected by entry on the register, whether or not he has notice of the issue. Graham J said that a purchaser within s. 59(6) must act in good faith because of the definition given to purchaser in the Land Registration Act 1925, s. 3(xxi).

3. There is a general principle in trust law that a stranger to a trust who knowingly receives or deals with the trust property in breach of trust is held to be a constructive trustee of the property for the original beneficiaries. In *Peffer v Rigg* the two brothers-in-law (X and Y) purchased the property with joint moneys. The property was registered in X's sole name with the effect that, although X had legal title to the property vested in him he held it as trustee, on

trust for X and Y beneficially in proportion to the money contributed. X's ex-wife took the legal title knowing of the prior trust, and therefore the above principle can be applied and X's ex-wife holds the property on trust for the original beneficiaries.

For a commentary and discussion of the merits of these arguments, see Jill Martin, 'Constructive trusts of registered land' [1978] Conv 52; Stuart Anderson, 'Notice of unprotected trusts' (1977) 40 MLR 602; David Hayton, 'Purchasers of registered land' [1977] CLJ 227; D. C. Jackson, 'Security of title in registered land' [1978] 94 LQR 239; Roger J. Smith, 'Registered land: purchasers with actual notice' (1977) 93 LQR 341; F. R. Crane, *'Peffer v Rigg'* (1977) 41 Conv 207.

Questions
1. Has the decision in *Peffer* v *Rigg* introduced the doctrine of notice into registered land?
2. Do you think that Graham's J judgment is good law?

Lyus v *Prowsa Developments*
[1982] 1 WLR 1044 (ChD)

The plaintiffs exchanged contracts for the purchase of land from a developer. The land was registered and formed part of an estate under construction. The land was not to be transferred until a house had been built upon it. The company developing the land became insolvent before the house was completed. The company's bank held a legal charge over the building estate which pre-dated the plaintiffs' contract. The bank was not bound to complete the sale to the plaintiffs and sold the land to the first defendant. The sale was made subject to the plaintiffs' contract. The first defendant contracted to sell to the second defendant. The contract contained a special condition that the land was sold subject to the plaintiffs' contract so far as it may be enforceable against the first defendant. The sale was completed but the transfer contained no reference to the plaintiffs' contract. Both sales were registered, but the undertaking regarding the plaintiffs' contract was not. The plaintiffs claimed the condition in the contract between the bank and the first defendant gave rise to a constructive trust, and that they were entitled to specific performance of the contract. The defendants claimed the plaintiffs could not enforce their interest since it was not registered. Held: the first defendant, having accepted the land under the agreement with the bank, held the plot upon a constructive trust in favour of the plaintiffs. Similarly the special condition in the contract between the first defendant and the second defendant gave rise to a constructive trust in favour of the plaintiffs. It would be a fraud by the first defendant to renege on the stipulation in favour of the plaintiffs and for the second defendants to rely upon the transfer of land to them as giving them absolute title free of any encumbrance. Since the Land Registration Act 1925 could not be used as an instrument of fraud, the defendants could not rely on ss. 20 and 34(4).

DILLON J: ... it would follow, in my judgment, from the judgment of Scott LJ in *Bannister* v *Bannister* [1948] 2 All ER 133 and from the judgment in *Binions* v *Evans* [1972] Ch 359 of Lord Denning MR at p. 368, unless the Land Registration Act 1925 requires a different conclusion, that the first defendant, having accepted the land under the agreement of October 18, 1979, and the consequent transfer, holds Plot 29 on a constructive trust in favour of the plaintiffs to give effect to the plaintiffs' contract. That trust is also imposed on the second defendants by virtue of condition (b) of their agreement with the first defendant.

It has been submitted for the defendants that such a conclusion would involve a want of mutuality which is offensive to the traditional approach of the courts of equity, in that it would involve that the plaintiffs acquire rights against the first defendant by virtue of the agreement to which they are not parties, while the first defendant, for want of privity of contract, has no corresponding right to sue the plaintiffs for specific performance or damages. I do not think that that submission is valid. Want of mutuality is merely a factor which a court of equity may have to consider in deciding whether or not to grant a decree of specific performance. It is not an absolute bar to specific performance: see *Price* v *Strange* [1978] Ch. 337. Moreover, there are well established authorities, such as *Halsall* v *Brizell* [1957] Ch 169, to the effect that any person who takes the benefit of a contract must assume the burden. In so far, therefore, as the plaintiffs have sought to assert the benefits of their contract with the vendor company of January 30, 1978, they must submit to the burden of that contract.

This does not, however, conclude the matter since I also have to consider the effect of the provisions of the Land Registration Act 1925, Plot 29 having at all material times, as I have mentioned, been registered land. In the course of the argument, emphasis was laid on the effect of section 34(4) of the Land Registration Act 1925, which is concerned with the effect on subsequent interests of a transfer of registered land by a mortgagee. Section 34 has, however, to be read with section 20, which is concerned with the effect of the registration of a transfer of registered land by the registered proprietor. The protection conferred by section 34 on a transfer by a mortgagee is thus additional to the protection which is conferred by section 20 on registration of a transfer by a registered proprietor.

It has been pointed out by Lord Wilberforce in *Midland Bank Trust Co. Ltd* v *Green* [1981] AC 513, 531, that it is not fraud to rely on legal rights conferred by Act of Parliament. Under section 20, the effect of the registration of the transferee of a freehold title is to confer an absolute title subject to entries on the register and overriding interests, but, 'free from all other estates and interests whatsoever, including estates and interests of His Majesty . . .' In *Miles* v *Bull (No. 2)* [1969] 3 All ER 1585, Bridge J expressed the view that the words which I have quoted embraced, prima facie, not only all kinds of legal interests, but all kinds of equitable interests: see p. 1589. He therefore held, at p. 1590, as I read his judgment, that actual or constructive notice on the part of a purchaser of an unregistered interest would not have the effect of imposing a constructive trust on him. [*Miles* v *Bull (No. 2)* was considered and distinguished.]

...

It seems to me that the fraud on the part of the defendants in the present case lies not just in relying on the legal rights conferred by an Act of Parliament, but in the first defendant reneging on a positive stipulation in favour of the plaintiffs in the bargain under which the first defendant acquired the land. That makes, as it seems to me, all the difference. It has long since been held, for instance, in *Rochefoucauld* v *Boustead* [1897] 1 Ch 196, that the provisions of the Statute of Frauds 1677 (29 Car 2 c.3). now incorporated in certain sections of the Law of Property Act 1925, cannot be used as an instrument of fraud, and that it is fraud for a person to whom land is agreed to be conveyed as trustee for another to deny the trust and relying on the terms of the statute to claim the land for himself. *Rochefoucauld* v *Boustead* was one of the authorities on which the judgment in *Bannister* v *Bannister* [1948] 2 All ER 133 was founded.

It seems to me that the same considerations are applicable in relation to the Land Registration Act 1925. If, for instance, the agreement of October 18, 1979, between the bank and the first defendant had expressly stated that the first defendant would hold Plot 29 upon trust to give effect for the benefit of the plaintiffs to the plaintiffs' agreement with the vendor company, it would be difficult to say that that express trust was overreached and rendered nugatory by the Land Registration Act 1925. The Land Registration Act 1925 does not, therefore, affect the conclusion which I would otherwise have reached in reliance on *Bannister* v *Bannister* and the judgment of Lord Denning MR in *Binions* v *Evans* [1972] Ch 359 had Plot 29 been unregistered land.

Questions
1. Does *Lyus* v *Prowsa Developments* represent an extension of *Binions* v *Evans*?
2. Do the courts view fraud differently in registered and unregistered land (see *Midland Bank* v *Green*)?
3. What is meant by the term 'fraud' in property law?

See P. H. Kenny, 'Constructive trusts of registered land' (1983) 46 MLR 96; Charles Harpum, 'Constructive trusts and registered land' [1983] CLJ 54; Paul Jackson, 'Estate contracts, trusts and registered land' [1983] Conv 64.

SECTION 5: RECTIFICATION OF TITLE

The registration of title is not an infallible system and mistakes are sometimes made. Therefore, the Land Registration Act 1925 provides the court with a power of rectification in certain circumstances.

Land Registration Act 1925

82. Rectification of the register

(1) The register may be rectified pursuant to an order of the court or by the registrar, subject to an appeal to the court, in any of the following cases, but subject to the provisions of this section:—

(a) Subject to any express provisions of this Act to the contrary, where a court of competent jurisdiction has decided that any person is entitled to any estate right or interest in or to any registered land or charge, and as a consequence of such decision such court is of opinion that a rectification of the register is required, and makes an order to that effect;

(b) Subject to any express provision of this Act to the contrary, where the court, on the application in the prescribed manner of any person who is aggrieved by any entry made in, or by the omission of any entry from, the register, or by any default being made, or unnecessary delay taking place, in the making of any entry in the register, makes an order for the rectification of the register;

(c) In any case and at any time with the consent of all persons interested;

(d) Where the court or the registrar is satisfied that any entry in the register has been obtained by fraud;

(e) Where two or more persons are, by mistake, registered as proprietors of the same registered estate or of the same charge;

(f) Where a mortgagee has been registered as proprietor of the land instead of as proprietor of a charge and a right of redemption is subsisting;

(g) Where a legal estate has been registered in the name of a person who if the land had not been registered would not have been the estate owner; and

(h) In any other case where, by reason of any error or omission in the register, or by reason of any entry made under a mistake, it may be deemed just to rectify the register.

(2) The register may be rectified under this section, notwithstanding that the rectification may affect any estates, rights, charges, or interests acquired or protected by registration, or by any entry on the register, or otherwise.

(3) The register shall not be rectified, except for the purpose of giving effect to an overriding interest [or an order of the court], so as to affect the title of the proprietor who is in possession —

[(a) unless the proprietor has caused or substantially contributed to the error or omission by fraud or lack of proper care; or]

(b) [. . .]

(c) unless for any other reason, in any particular case, it is considered that it would be unjust not to rectify the register against him.

Argyle Building Society v *Hammond* (1985) 49 P & CR 148 (CA)

The appellant was the registered proprietor of a freehold property. The appellant emigrated to the USA but his mother, sister and brother-in-law continued to reside at the property. Later he was persuaded by his sister and brother-in-law to sign a power of attorney to enable the house to be sold on his behalf. A transfer of the house took place by way of a forged deed, and as a result the sister and brother-in-law were registered as joint owners. The plaintiffs in good faith granted the sister and her husband £15,000 by way of a legal charge on the property. The charge was registered. When the couple failed to make repayments, the plaintiffs sought possession. The appellant was subsequently allowed to become a party to the action and sought rectification of the register because of the forgery. Held: the court had power to rectify. The court has a 'theoretical discretion to rectify any part of the register', as soon as the statutory specified circumstances exist (per Slade LJ).

See also *Leighton's Conveyance* [1936] 1 All ER 667.

See A. Sydendam '*Argyle Building Society* v *Hammond and Others*' [1985] Conv 135; R. J. Smith, 'Forgeries and land registration' (1985) 101 LQR 79.

A: STATUTORY SPECIFIED CIRCUMSTANCES

(a) The rectification will give effect to an overriding interest or order of the court

Chowood Ltd v *Lyall (No. 2)* [1930] 2 Ch 156 (CA)

The plaintiffs were entered at the Land Registry as having absolute title to the freehold land they had purchased. This land comprised, *inter alia*, two narrow areas of woodland which were occupied by a neighbouring land owner who, by way of adverse possession, had attained a good title to the land prior to registration. Held: at first instance it was held that the register should be rectified. The two areas of woodland should not have been included in the plaintiffs' title and should be deleted. On appeal it was held that this decision was in accordance with s. 82(1) of the Land Registration Act 1925 and was therefore valid. The effect of rectification was to give effect to the neighbour's overriding interest under s. 70(1)(f).

(b) The registered proprietor has caused or substantially contributed to the error or omission by fraud or lack of care

In re 139 High Street, Deptford [1951] 1 Ch 884 (ChD)

The description in a conveyance (with no plan) mistakenly included some land which was in fact owned by the British Transport Commission. Both the vendor and purchaser believed the description was correct. The purchaser was registered with absolute freehold title. The purchaser had supplied the Land Registry with the conveyance to himself for the purpose of registration. A plan was later drawn up and annexed to the land certificate and it was apparent that a parcel of land belonged to BTC. Held: BTC were entitled to rectification. The purchaser had given a misleading description of the property for registration purposes and had thereby substantially contributed to the mistake, although he had done so innocently.

(c) It would be unjust not to rectify the register

Epps v Esso Petroleum Co. Ltd [1973] 1 WLR 1071 (ChD)

The facts of this case appear at page 80.

Held:
(1) The plaintiffs should have made sufficient investigation and have appreciated the potential conflict regarding the land since ownership had not been clearly established earlier — there had been no reason for the defendants to query ownership, nor would any investigations have necessarily revealed the true position. Therefore it would not be unjust to refuse to rectify the register.
(2) Although the plaintiffs would have received no compensation for a refusal to rectify, the fact that the defendants would have been indemnified was an insufficient reason to rectify the register, the indemnity not being comparable in value to the commercial purposes for which the garage and land had been bought.

B: EFFECT OF RECTIFICATION

Re Leighton's Conveyance [1936] 1 All ER 667 (ChD)

A daughter tricked her mother into signing a transfer of certain registered land to herself. The daughter then created charges upon the property, the chargees knowing nothing of the fraud. Held: the mother was entitled to rectification of the proprietorship register under s. 82 of the Land Registration Act 1925 but not to rectification of the charges register.

C: EFFECTIVE DATE

Freer v *Unwins Ltd* [1976] Ch 288 (ChD)

The plaintiffs purchased a shop and enjoyed the benefit of a restrictive covenant which prevented the remaining shops from selling tobacco. The covenant was registered according to the land charges register, but when titles to the other shops were registered one shop's title did not show that it was subject to this covenant. The second shop was leased in December 1969. The defendants acquired the lease in December 1974, having made careful inquiry to ensure they could trade unhindered and sell tobacco. The covenant was entered as a burden on the second shop in April 1975. The plaintiff sought and obtained rectification of the register from the Chief Land Registrar, and then sought an injunction to prevent the sale of tobacco by the defendants in breach of that covenant. Held: the lease was deemed to have taken effect as if it were a registered disposition immediately on its grant. The lease was, by s. 20(1), subject to any entries on the register at that date and any overriding interests. It was not subject to any other estates and interests. Therefore the defendants were not affected by notice of restrictive covenants entered by virtue of rectification after the lease had been granted.

Questions
1. Do you agree with the Law Commission's (Report No. 158) criticism of the decision in *Freer* v *Unwins Ltd*?
2. Are the compensation provisions which exist when the register is rectified adequate?

SECTION 6: INDEMNITY

An intending purchaser will search the register in order to ascertain that the vendor has the right to sell the property and to see whether there are any minor interests entered on the register. If he does this he will acquire a 30-day priority period during which time he can apply to have the title in the land transferred to him, safe in the knowledge that his title will have priority over the minor interests.

If the official search mistakenly reveals that there are no minor interests affecting the land, then the purchaser must take subject to them, but in such a case he is entitled to an indemnity.

Land Registration Act 1925

83. Right to indemnity in certain cases
(1) Subject to the provisions of this Act to the contrary, any persons suffering loss by reason of any rectification of the register under this Act shall be entitled to be indemnified.

(2) Where an error or omission has occurred in the register, but the register is not rectified, any person suffering loss by reason of such error or omission, shall, subject to the provisions of this Act, be entitled to be indemnified.

(3) Where any person suffers loss by reason of the loss or destruction of any document lodged at the registry for inspection or safe custody or by reason of an error in any official search, he shall be entitled to be indemnified under this Act.

(4) Subject as hereinafter provided, a proprietor of any registered land or charge claiming in good faith under a forged disposition shall, where the register is rectified, be deemed to have suffered loss by reason of such rectification and shall be entitled to be indemnified under this Act.

(5) No indemnity shall be payable under this Act in any of the following cases:—

(a) Where the applicant or a person from whom he derives title (otherwise than under a disposition for valuable consideration which is registered or protected on the register) has caused or substantially contributed to the loss by fraud or lack of proper care; ...

(11) A liability to pay indemnity under this Act shall be deemed a simple contract debt, and for the purposes of the Limitation Act 1980, the cause of action shall be deemed to arise at the time when the claimant knows, or but for his own default might have known, of the existence of his claim:

Provided that, when a claim to indemnity arises in consequence of the registration of an estate in land with an absolute or good leasehold title, the claim shall be enforceable only if made within six years from the date of such registration.

Note
There are certain limitations to s. 83:

(a) *Re Chowood's Registered Land* [1933] Ch 574 (ChD)   See page 96 for facts and decision of *Chowood Ltd v Lyall (No. 2)* in which the register was rectified to remove land for the title to give effect to Lyall's rights under the Limitation Acts. Chowood now claimed that it should be indemnified under s. 83 of the Land Registration Act 1925 in respect of losses alleged to have been suffered by reason of the rectification. Held: when the rectification was made, Lyall had already acquired an overriding interest by way of limitation of action. Chowood suffered no deterioration in his position as a consequence of the rectification, and as a result was not entitled to any indemnity under s. 83.

(b) *Freer v Unwins Ltd* [1976] Ch 288   Where the claimant successfully claims rectification there is no right to compensation even if loss is suffered.

See R. J. Smith, 'Forgeries and land registration' (1985) 101 LQR 79; Stephen Cretney and Gerald Dworkin, 'Rectification and indemnity: illusion and reality' (1968) 84 LQR 528; T. Ruoff, 'Land registration: the recent act' (1971) 35 Conv 390.

SECTION 7: PRIORITIES

A registered proprietor or a person who acquires a registered interest in land takes the land subject to any overriding interests (but see *Equity and Law Home Loans Ltd v Prestidge*; *Bristol & West Building Society v Henning* and *Abbey*

National Builing Society v *Cann*) and those minor interests entered on the register. Overriding interests usually bind a person who later acquires an overriding interest or a protected minor interest, and a protected minor interest similarly binds a person who later acquires a protected minor interest or an overriding interest.

Barclays Bank v Taylor
[1974] Ch 137 (CA)

R, the registered proprietors of some land, were indebted to a bank on two bank accounts. In 1961 they deposited the land certificate with the bank and the bank caused a notice of deposit to be registered against the title. R signed a memorandum acknowledging the land certificate was deposited as security for their liabilities and undertook to execute a legal mortgage when called upon to do so. They did so in August 1962, at the bank's request. The bank's charge was not registered. In 1968, the defendants entered into a contract for the purchase of the land and paid the purchase price but never obtained a transfer of the land. They lodged a caution pursuant to s. 54 of the Land Registration Act 1925. The bank later took one year to register their charge and the defendants were given notice. They claimed priority over the bank's charge. The caution lodged pursuant to s. 54, Land Registration Act 1925 did not affect priority. The defendants' contract and the bank's unregistered charge were minor interests and applying the normal rules, the bank's mortgage being first in time should be registered in priority to the defendants' contract.

RUSSELL LJ: Now, quite apart from the question of deposit of the land certificate, and on the footing that the mortgage of August 29, 1962, until registration cannot take effect save in equity, we ask ourselves what provision is there in the Act which reverses the ordinary rule that as between equities — for the Taylors have only an interest in equity under their contract of purchase — priority is governed by the time sequence?

Goulding J based his decision upon the language of section 106 relating to a mortgage made by deed which is not registered, which provides that it may be protected by a caution in specially prescribed form 'and in no other way.' The section also provides that until the mortgage is protected on the register under that section it shall be capable of taking effect only in equity and of being overridden as a minor interest. The judge, simply on the ground that this mortgage was 'made under' section 106 (which we will assume without deciding) and had not been made the subject of a caution in special form, held that it must be postponed to the estate contract presumably because it was not 'protected' against it. But the estate contract was itself only a similar minor interest: see section 101. The caution lodged on behalf of the purchasers had no effect whatever by itself on priorities: it simply conferred on the cautioners the right to be given notice of any dealing proposed to be registered (see sections 54 and 55) so that they might have the opportunity of contending that it would be a dealing which would infringe their rights and to which the applicants for the registration were not as against them entitled. The limited function of such a caution is stressed by section 56(2), which enacts that a caution lodged in pursuance of this Act shall not prejudice the claim or title of any person and shall have no effect whatever except as in this Act mentioned. See also section 102(2), which provides that save in a limited field of minor interests 'priorities as between persons interested in minor interests shall not be affected by the lodgement of cautions.'

In truth the bank in respect of its mortgage, albeit taking effect as a minor interest only in equity, did not need any protection against the subsequent equitable interest of the Taylors: it only needed protection against a registration of the Taylors as proprietors (and, for this, possession of the land certificate was at least de facto protection), or against a subsequent mortgagee whose charge was registered or perhaps who lodged a caution in special form (though again here there would, we apprehend, be the same de facto protection).

Consequently, in our view, and quite apart from the fact that the land certificate was in the possession of the bank, (a) failure by the bank to lodge a caution in special form is irrelevant, (b) the Taylors' caution did not and could not confer on their equitable entitlement or interest any priority over the bank's equitable charge, (c) the ordinary rules of priority between persons equitably interested in the land must apply, there being nothing in the conduct of the bank (which was sitting on the land certificate, notice of deposit of which remained on the register) to justify postponement of its equity, and (d) consequently the bank is entitled to be registered in respect of the mortgage without being subject to the contract of the Taylors.

Notes
1. As between two unregistered interests the entry of a notice or a caution protecting the later interest against all subsequent interests does not give the later interest priority over the earlier unprotected one — see *The Mortgage Corporation Ltd* v *Nationwide Credit Corporation Ltd*, (1992) *The Times*, 27 July.
2. See R. J. Smith, 'The priority of competing minor interests in registered land' (1977) 93 LQR 541.

For priority of mortgages, see chapter 12.

4 ACQUISITION OF LAND: CONTRACT AND CONVEYANCE

Most conveyances of land in England and Wales take place in two stages:

(a) a contract; and
(b) a conveyance (in the case of unregistered land) or a transfer (in the case of registered land).

Before examining these two stages in detail, it may be helpful to consider what happens before a contract for the sale of land is executed.

SECTION 1: PRE-CONTRACT PROCEDURE

Before contracts are exchanged the purchaser will want to make a number of searches and inquiries in order to collect as much information as possible about the property.

(a) Local authority searches
A local land charges search should be carried out by the purchaser whether he is buying registered or unregistered land. Local land charges are overriding interests in relation to registered land (see chapter 3). Matters capable of being protected as local land charges are set out in the Local Land Charges Act 1975. They are essentially 'local' in nature and include, *inter alia*, tree preservation orders and enforcement notices.

In addition to the local land charges search, the purchaser should also make 'additional inquiries' of the District Council. These inquiries relate to matters which may affect the property but which are not local land charges. Such a search could reveal, for example, any proposed new trunk roads and motorways and whether the roads and sewers servicing the property are maintained publicly or privately.

In the past the purchaser of property always performed the local search (the name given to the combined search and inquiries). However, this led to conveyancing delays, especially in a booming property market. Where the parties decide to use the newly introduced National Conveyancing Protocol (a set of procedures designed to 'streamline conveyancing procedures' in domestic conveyancing transactions), the seller performs these preliminary searches on the purchaser's behalf, often before a purchaser has been found, thus minimising delay.

(b) Inquiries of the vendor
A purchaser may elicit further information by raising 'preliminary inquiries' of the vendor. Under the National Conveyancing Protocol, the seller supplies the buyer with a standard 'property information form', together with a list of fixtures and fittings included in the sale. The inquiries attempt to elicit information about various matters such as disputes relating to the property, services, restrictive covenants, easements, adverse rights and any alterations carried out to the property within the four years preceding the sale. The property information form deals with the same matters.

(c) Survey of the property
The purchaser will usually wish to commission a structural survey of the property.

(d) Other searches
Such searches can include:

(a) a search of the Public Index Map, which will reveal whether the land is in an area of compulsory registration of title, whether the title is freehold or leasehold in all or any parts which are already registered, and whether there are any cautions against first registration;
(b) a search in the register kept under the Commons Registration Act 1965, in order to ascertain whether all or any part of the land is registered as a common, or town or village green;
(c) inquiries of British Coal if the land is in an area of past, present or potential mining, in order to ascertain whether there has been or may be mining underneath the property.

SECTION 2: THE CONTRACT

Having satisfactorily discovered as much as possible about the property and arranged suitable finance to cover the transaction, the parties will be in a position to exchange contracts. Until this is done the vendor is not legally bound to sell and the purchaser not legally bound to buy the property. The contract may take any form provided that it complies with the general rules of contract law and the evidential requirements imposed by statute. For contracts made before 27 September 1989 these evidential requirements were contained in the Law of Property Act 1925, s. 40, and for contracts made on or after 27

September 1989 the provisions of s. 2 of the Law of Property (Miscellaneous Provisions) Act 1989 apply. In practice, however, a standard form contract is used which contains standard terms.

A: CONTRACTS MADE BEFORE 27 SEPTEMBER 1989

Law of Property Act 1925

40. Contracts for sale of land to be in writing etc.
(1) No action may be brought upon any contract for the sale or other disposition of land or any interest in land, unless the agreement upon which such action is brought, or some memorandum or note thereof, is in writing, and signed by the party to be charged or by some other person thereunto by him lawfully authorised.
(2) This section applies to contracts whether made before or after the commencement of this Act and does not affect the law relating to part performance, or sales by the court.

Notes
1. The effect of this section is to make an oral contract for the sale of land unenforceable unless there is a written memorandum or note reflecting the oral contract. An agreement in writing for the sale of land is sufficient in itself and need not be evidenced by a written note or memorandum.
2. The document (i.e. the memorandum or the agreement) must contain all the material terms of the contract, namely a description of the parties, the property and the price to be paid for the property.
3. Various kinds of documents have been accepted as amounting to a memorandum for the purpose of s. 40, for example a telegram (*McBlain* v *Cross* (1871) 25 LT 804); a receipt (*Davies* v *Sweet* [1962] 2 QB 300); and a clause in a will (*In re Hoyle* [1893] 1 Ch 84).
4. It is also possible to link a number of related documents to form a complete memorandum if the doctrine of joinder of documents can be employed (see page 109).
5. The court will enforce a contract, despite the absence of writing required by s. 40, if the plaintiff has been put in a situation which would make it unconscionable for the defendant to insist on the want of writing as a bar to relief.

The doctrine of part performance
In the absence of a note or memorandum complying with the Law of Property Act 1925, s. 40, equity would intervene and order a decree of specific performance if there were sufficient acts of part performance by the plaintiff. The doctrine of part performance is based on the equitable maxim that equity will not allow a statute to be used as an instrument of fraud. This doctrine was expressly recognised by the Law of Property Act 1925, s. 40(2).

Under the traditional view of the doctrine, in order for acts of part performance to be sufficient they 'must be unequivocally, and in their own nature, referable to some such agreement as that alleged' (*Maddison* v *Alderson* (1883) 8 App Cas 467, per Lord Selborne LC at p. 479).

Rawlinson v *Ames*
[1925] Ch 96 (ChD)

The plaintiff and defendant orally agreed that the defendant would lease a flat. It was agreed that the plaintiff would carry out some alterations before the defendant went into occupation. The defendant oversaw the alterations and made further suggestions for alterations which the plaintiff complied with. The defendant repudiated the contract. The plaintiff sought and was granted specific performance.

ROMER J: Now the mere fact that the plaintiff converted part of her premises into the flat and expended money thereon is not *only* referable to a contract such as that alleged. It is equally referable to her ownership of the premises. Nor would this improvement by the plaintiff of her own property be such an act as to render it a fraud in the defendant to take advantage of the contract not being in writing. It is, however, to be observed that in the present case the plaintiff in altering her premises and expending money in the alterations was doing so in accordance with requests and suggestions made to her or her employees from time to time by the defendant. It appears to me that this fact necessarily suggests the existence of some such contract as alleged. . . .

Wakeham v *Mackenzie* [1968] 1 WLR 1175 (ChD)

In this case the defendant orally agreed with the plaintiff that if she moved out of her flat and moved into his house in order to look after him for the rest of his life, she would be given both the house and the contents when he died. The plaintiff received no wage or salary for her services and contributed to the food and fuel bills. The defendant died without making any provision for her. It was held that the plaintiff's acts of giving up her home and moving in with the defendant were acts which referred to the alleged oral agreement so that a decree of specific performance would be granted.

Notes
1. This case has to be contrasted with the case of *Maddison* v *Alderson* (1883) 8 App Cas 467, in which a housekeeper initially received wages but later worked for nothing because her employer had promised to leave her his property. The House of Lords took the view that the housekeeper's actions were not solely referable to the alleged contract, but could be explained in a number of different ways.
2. The acts that are relied on must be acts of part performance and not merely perfunctory in nature, such as applying for planning permission (*New Hart Builders Ltd* v *Brindley* [1975] 1 Ch 342) or viewing the land and making valuations and surveys (*Clark* v *Wright* (1737) 1 Atk 12).
3. The decision in *Steadman* v *Steadman* below, led to uncertainty in the area of part performance.

Steadman v *Steadman*
[1976] AC 536 (HL)

The parties had been married and the marriage dissolved. The parties met outside the magistrates' court (before an application by the former husband was due to be heard for variation of maintenance and remittance of arrears). An agreement was reached to settle the wife's claims whereby it was agreed that the wife would surrender her interest in the house for £1,500; that the maintenance order for the wife should be discharged; and that the maintenance for the child should be remitted except for £100 to be paid by 30 March. The husband did not proceed with his application but advised the magistrate of the terms of the settlement. The husband paid the £100 but the wife refused to transfer the house to him, claiming that there was no enforceable contract. Held: (Lord Morris of Borth-y-Gest dissenting) that there were sufficient acts of part performance by the husband.

LORD REID: Section 40 replaced a part of section 4 of the Statute of Frauds 1677 (29 Car 2, c. 3), and very soon after the passing of that Act authorities on this matter began to accumulate. It is now very difficult to find from them any clear guidance of general application. But it is not difficult to see at least one principle behind them. If one party to an agreement stands by and lets the other party incur expense or prejudice his position on the faith of the agreement being valid he will not then be allowed to run round and assert that the agreement is unenforceable. Using fraud in its older and less precise sense, that would be fraudulent on his part and it has become proverbial that courts of equity will not permit the statute to be made an instrument of fraud....

So it is in keeping with equitable principles that in proper circumstances a person will not be allowed 'fraudulently' to take advantage of a defence of this kind. There is nothing about part performance in the Statute of Frauds. It is an invention of the Court of Chancery and in deciding any case not clearly covered by authority I think that the equitable nature of the remedy must be kept in mind.

A large number of the authorities are cases where a purchaser under an oral agreement has been permitted to take possession of or to do things on the land which he has agreed to buy. But sometimes rules appropriate to that situation have been sought to be applied to other cases of part performance where they are not appropriate. Indeed the courts have sometimes seemed disinclined to apply the principle at all to such other cases.

Normally the consideration for the purchase of land is a sum of money and there are statements that a sum of money can never be treated as part performance. Such statements would be reasonable if the person pleading the statute tendered repayment of any part of the price which he had received and was able thus to make restitutio in integrum. That would remove any 'fraud' or any equity on which the purchaser could properly rely. But to make a general rule that payment of money can never be part performance would seem to me to defeat the whole purpose of the doctrine and I do not think that we are compelled by authority to do that.

The argument for the wife, for which there is a good deal of authority, is that no act can be relied on as an act of part performance unless it relates to the land to be acquired and can only be explained by the existence of a contract relating to the land. But let me suppose a case of an oral contract where the consideration for the transfer of the land was not money but the transfer of some personal property or the performance of some obligation. The personal property is then transferred or the obligation is performed to the knowledge of the owner of the land in circumstances where there can be no restitutio in integrum. On what rational principle could it be said that the doctrine of part performance is not to apply? And we were not referred to any case of that kind where the court had refused to apply it. The transfer of the personal property or the performance of the obligation would indicate the existence of a contract but it would not indicate that that contract related to that or any other land.

I think that there has been some confusion between this supposed rule and another perfectly good rule. You would not first look at the oral contract and then see whether the alleged acts of part performance are consistent with it. You must first look at the alleged acts of part performance to see whether they prove that there must have been a contract and it is only if they do so prove that you can bring in the oral contract. . . .

In my view, unless the law is to be divorced from reason and principle, the rule must be that you take the whole circumstances, leaving aside evidence about the oral contract, to see whether it is proved that the acts relied on were done in reliance on a contract: that will be proved if it is shown to be more probable than not.

Authorities which seem to require more than that appear to be based on an idea, never clearly defined, to the effect that the law of part performance is a rule of evidence rather than an application of an equitable principle. I do not know on what ground any court could say that, although you cannot produce the evidence required by the Statute of Frauds, some other kind of evidence will do instead. But I can see that if part performance is simply regarded as evidence, then it would be reasonable to hold not only that the acts of part performance must relate to the land but that they must indicate the nature of the oral contract with regard to the land. But that appears to me to be a fundamental departure from the true doctrine of part performance, and it is not supported by recent authorities such as *Kingswood Estate Co. Ltd* v *Anderson* [1963] 2 QB 169.

LORD MORRIS OF BORTH-Y-GEST: I turn then to the question whether the payment of £100 by the husband can be regarded as an act of part performance. In my view, it cannot possibly be. The money was paid by the husband to the petty sessional court in Bromley. It was paid after that court had made the order of March 2, 1972, in the terms which I have set out. The payment into court by a husband of a sum of money to be sent by the court to his wife does not, in my view, prove that there had been some contract between them: even more emphatically it does not prove that there had been any contract concerning land. The only inference that would be drawn from the payment of £100 into court by a husband in matrimonial proceedings would be that he was in arrears in regard to some payments that he had been ordered to make. Without a connection established by parol testimony the payment of the money would not begin to suggest or to establish either the existence of a contract or of a contract in relation to land.

The other suggested acts relied upon on behalf of the husband do not, in my view, possess any greater merit. Nor, in my view, if they fail to qualify as acts of part performance do they have an accrual of merit by being linked with other suggested acts which also fail to qualify. It was submitted that the fact of mentioning the agreed terms to the magistrates and inviting them to make orders can be regarded as an act of part performance. But in agreement with Edmund Davies LJ I consider that an act of part performance, in order to be such, must be an act in relation to that term of a contract (in a case where there are other terms) which alone is required to be in writing if it is to be enforceable as satisfying section 40. In the present litigation what is being considered is whether an oral and prima facie unenforceable contract in relation to land has been made enforceable by reason of there being some act of part performance which shows that there must have been a contract in relation to land. An oral statement (or concurrence in an oral statement) that there was such an oral contract cannot, in my view, suffice.

Nor do I consider that any abandonment on the part of the husband of any attempt to ask the magistrates to remit the whole amount of the arrears of maintenance he owed to his wife can qualify as an act of part performance in relation to land. The fact that he incurred legal costs and then caused a draft conveyance to be sent to his wife's solicitors (which she ignored after receiving it – indicating to her solicitors that she was very reluctant to agree the terms) could certainly indicate a belief on his part that there had been an oral contract or it could indicate a hope or expectation that agreement would in the future be reached. Without more I do not think that an act of part performance was established.

This is most unfortunate litigation. Having regard to the findings of fact which must be accepted, I much regret that I am reaching a different conclusion from that of your Lordships. The case is a very special one, but even so I consider that the decision of the majority in the Court of Appeal involves extending the law relating to part performance in a way which I do not consider to be warranted.

I would allow the appeal.

Note
See '*Steadman* v *Steadman*' (1974) 38 Conv 354; H. W. R. Wade, 'Part performance back to square one' (1974) 90 LQR 433; C. T. Emery, 'Part performance — no judicial development after all?' [1974] CLJ 205; M. P. Thompson, 'The role of evidence in part performance' [1979] Conv 402; M. P. Thompson, 'Do it yourself divorce' [1984] Conv 152.

B: CONTRACTS MADE ON OR AFTER 27 SEPTEMBER 1989

Section 40 of the Law of Property Act 1925 is repealed for contracts made on or after the above date. The chief reasons for its repeal are as follows:

(a) Section 40 was one-sided. A person who had not signed any document constituting written evidence could choose to sue the one who had, even though he could not be sued. This lack of mutuality could lead to unfairness.

(b) The House of Lords decision in the case of *Steadman* v *Steadman*, had exacerbated the uncertainties surrounding the doctrine of part performance, and in particular whether the payment of money could amount to an act of part performance (see *Chaprionière* v *Lambert* [1917] 2 Ch 356, where it was said that the payment of rent in advance in respect of an oral agreement for a lease, where the lessees had not taken possession, was not a sufficient act of part performance).

See Law Commission No. 163 (1987), *The Transfer of Land: Formalities for Contracts for the Sale etc. of Land.*

Law of Property (Miscellaneous Provisions) Act 1989

2. Contracts for sale etc. of land to be made by signed writing

(1) A contract for the sale or other disposition of an interest in land can only be made in writing and only by incorporating all the terms which the parties have expressly agreed in one document or, where contracts are exchanged, in each.

Acquisition of Land: Contract and Conveyance

(2) The terms may be incorporated in a document either by being set out in it or by reference to some other document.

(3) The document incorporating the terms or, where contracts are exchanged, one of the documents incorporating them (but not necessarily the same one) must be signed by or on behalf of each party to the contract.

(4) Where a contract for the sale or other disposition of an interest in land satisfies the conditions of this section by reason only of the rectification of one or more documents in pursuance of an order of a court, the contract shall come into being, or be deemed to have come into being, at such time as may be specified in the order.

(5) This section does not apply in relation to—
   (a) a contract to grant such a lease as is mentioned in section 54(2) of the Law of Property Act 1926 (short leases);
   (b) a contract made in the course of a public auction; or
   (c) a contract regulated under the Financial Services Act 1986;
and nothing in this section affects the creation or operation of resulting, implied or constructive trusts.

(6) In this section—
'disposition' has the same meaning as in the Law of Property Act 1925;
'interest in land' means any estate, interest or charge in or over land or in or over the proceeds of sale of land.

(7) Nothing in this section shall apply in relation to contracts made before this section comes into force.

(8) Section 40 of the Law of Property Act 1925 (which is superseded by this section) shall cease to have effect.

Notes

1. Section 2(2) gives statutory effect to the joinder of documents doctrine (the rule in *Timmins* v *Moreland Street Property Co. Ltd* [1958] Ch 110) which says that if there is no single document complying with s. 40, then, in certain circumstances, two or more documents may be read together, to provide the memorandum, provided that there is some express or implied reference in the document signed by the party to be charged to some other document. In such a case parol evidence may be admitted to identify the document referred to. Section 2(3) overcomes the one-sidedness of s. 40. Pennycuick V-C said in *Farrell* v *Green* (1974) 232 EG 587, at p. 589, 'there was something distasteful to one's idea of fairness in a transaction under which one party to an intended purchase took from another a memorandum signed by that other only, with the confidence that the other party would be bound and he himself would not be bound, having regard to section 40 of the Law of Property Act.'

2. The new provisions also seem to settle the controversy surrounding *Law* v *Jones* [1974] Ch 112 and *Tiverton Estates* v *Wearwell* [1975] Ch 146. In the former case the Court of Appeal appeared to think that a 'subject to contract' letter might constitute a sufficient memorandum to come within s. 40(1) of the Law of Property Act 1925, provided it recorded the agreed terms. It was generally considered to be unnecessary that the memorandum should acknowledge the existence of a contract. In *Tiverton Estates* v *Wearwell*, the Court of Appeal refused to follow *Law* v *Jones* and said that for the purposes of s. 40 of the 1925 Act, the memorandum or note had not only to state the terms of the contract, but had also to contain an acknowledgement or recognition by the signatory to the document that a contract had been entered into. See J. F. Farrand, 'Magic Words' [1981] Conv 165; *Tiverton Estates* v *Wearwell* (1974) 38 Conv 127; R. W. Clark, "'Subject to Contract" — I English Problems' [1984] Conv 173. Now the writing must embody the actual agreement as well as its terms. 'Subject to contract' letters therefore cannot constitute a valid contract for the sale of land.

3. The term 'signature' under the old s. 40 was widely interpreted by the courts. Signature in the usual sense of the word was not necessary — initials or a facsimile signature made by the impression of a rubber stamp were sufficient. Nor did the signature need to be at any particular place in the document. See, for example, *Caton* v *Caton* (1867) LR 2 HL 127. It is thought that the same construction can be applied to s. 2. Section 1 of the 1989 Act says that 'signs' includes making one's mark on an instrument and 'signature' is to be construed accordingly. This definition expressly applies only to s. 1(2) and (3) and it would seem to have no application to s. 2.

4. Section 2 applies to any 'contract for the sale or other disposition of an interest in land'. Section 2(6) says that 'disposition' has the same meaning as in the Law of Property Act 1925. Section 205(1)(ii) of the 1925 Act defines 'disposition' by reference to 'conveyance'.

Law of Property Act 1925

205. Interpretation

(1)(ii) A 'conveyance' includes a mortgage, charge, lease, assent, vesting declaration, vesting instrument, disclaimer, release and every other assurance of property or of an interest therein by an instrument, except a will; 'convey' has a corresponding meaning and 'disposition' includes a conveyance and also a devise, bequest or an appointment of property contained in a will; and 'dispose of' has a corresponding meaning'.

Note

'Interest in land' is given a new definition and means 'any estate, interest or charge in or over land or in or over the proceeds of sale of land'. Therefore the new requirement for signed writing will now apply to a contract to create or dispose of an equitable interest in land or the proceeds of sale and to a charge of land or interest in the proceeds of sale of land (see chapter 13).

5. The section is applicable only to executory contracts and has no application to contracts already completed — *Tootal Clothing Ltd* v *Guinea Properties Management Ltd* (1992) *The Independent*, 8 June.

Questions

1. Section 40 referred to 'land or any interest in land'; section 2 refers to 'an interest in land'. Is there a significant difference between the two terms?
2. Why did Parliament decide to alter the wording of section 2? (See *Cooper* v *Critchley* [1955] Ch 431, page 287 *et seq.*, *Steadman* v *Steadman* [1974] QB 161, affirmed [1976] AC 536.)

Acquisition of Land: Contract and Conveyance

Note

Section 40 has been interpreted strictly so that an action would fail where the written document omitted any of the agreed terms, and it was open to the defendant to adduce extrinsic evidence of any such omitted term (see, for example, *Sutton* v *Sutton* [1984] 1 All ER 168). It is thought that the same principle will apply to s. 2. There are, however, several specific problems relating to the terms of the contract:

(a) It has been suggested that where a term is expressly agreed between the parties and the term would be the same as that which the law would imply in the absence of the agreement, such a term need not be included in the memorandum (see Pennycuick V-C in *Farrell* v *Green* (1974) 232 EG 587). Will this be so under s. 2?

(b) It is thought that because s. 2 requires the contract for the sale or other disposition of an interest in land to be made in writing, parol variations will not be allowed. These were allowed in cases under s. 40.

(c) The courts have allowed the doctrine of waiver to operate in cases under s. 40. A plaintiff could succeed by showing that an omitted term was wholly for his benefit *and* that he was willing to waive it, although this was not possible if the omitted term was an essential part of the contract. Even if the omitted term was for the defendant's benefit, the court may have been willing to grant a decree of specific performance if the plaintiff was prepared to fulfil the contract. The decisions in which waiver of an omitted term were permitted derived from an application of the maxim that equity will not permit a statute to be used as an instrument of fraud. How will the courts decide such an issue now?

(d) Collateral contracts.

Record v *Bell* [1991] 4 All ER 471 (ChD)

In May 1990, V and P entered into an agreement in writing for the sale of property to be completed on 31 July 1990. As V's solicitor did not have up to date office copy entries immediately prior to exchange of contracts a conditional exchange was agreed. P's solicitor wrote to V's solicitor stating that the contract for the sale was conditional on the office copies showing V as registered owner and that the letter setting out that condition was to be attached to the contract for sale. The office copies duly showed V to be registered proprietor, but P failed to complete on 31 July. P claimed that the contract for the sale of the house did not comply with the Law of Property (Miscellaneous Provisions) Act 1989, s. 2. Held: a letter of variation or a letter of additional terms signed by both parties but which was not itself a contract for sale, could be a variation of the original contract but it could not be part of the original contract unless it was referred to in the contract for sale.

Where there is more than one contract the terms must be expressly incorporated in each contract. In this case the contract for sale did not refer to the supplementary term regarding office copies, and thus the letters did not satisfy s. 2. V's letter, however, was an offer of a warranty by V's solicitor to P's solicitor as to the state of title which would induce him to exchange. That offer had been accepted by exchanging contracts. Therefore there was a *collateral contract* in existence of which specific performance could be granted.

Note
See Michael Harwood, 'Law of Property (Miscellaneous Provisions) Act 1989, s. 2–s. 40 Reincarnate?' [1991] Conv 147.

The equitable doctrine of part performance and s. 2
Section 40 replaced the provisions originally enacted in the Statute of Frauds 1677 which were introduced to prevent unfairness and possible fraud arising from oral evidence being admitted to court. Thus, when interpreting a statute, the Court of Chancery would depart from a strict interpretation if the words as written tended to encourage rather than to prevent fraud. From this the doctrine of part performance developed (see *Lester* v *Foxcroft* (1701) Colles 108.

The Law Commission was adamant that the rules relating to part performance should be abolished, and many believe that s. 2(8) has the effect of abolishing the doctrine of part performance. The Law Commission thought that the doctrine of estoppel should be preserved and used if necessary.

See Bently and Coughlan 'Informal dealings with land after section 2' [1990] 10 *Legal Studies* 325; Jean Howell, 'Informal conveyances and section 2 of Law of Property (Miscellaneous Provisions) Act 1989' [1990] Conv 441; H. W. Wilkinson, 'Sign & deliver leases without contracts' [1990] Conv 1; P. H. Pettit, 'Farewell section 40' [1989] Conv 431; Gregory Hill, 'Law of Property (Miscellaneous Provisions) Act 1989, section 2' (1990) 106 LQR 396.

Questions
1. What did the Law Commission find so abhorrent in the doctrine of part performance?
2. Do you think that the Law of Property (Miscellaneous Provisions) Act 1989, s. 2 has in fact abolished the equitable doctrine of part performance?

C: THE EFFECT OF THE CONTRACT

Lysaght* v *Edwards
[1876] 2 ChD 499 (CA)

The plaintiffs entered into a contract to purchase some property. After the contract had been signed in 1874 and before completion the vendor died. In his will made in 1873 the vendor devised all his real estate to H and M upon trust for sale, and the vendor devised to H alone the property comprised in the purported sale to the plaintiff.

JESSEL MR: What is the effect of the contract? . . . It is that the moment you have a valid contract for sale the vendor becomes in equity a trustee for the purchaser of the

Acquisition of Land: Contract and Conveyance

estate sold, and the beneficial ownership passes to the purchaser, the vendor having a right to the purchase-money, a charge or lien on the estate for the security of that purchase-money, and a right to retain possession of the estate until the purchase-money is paid, in the absence of express contract as to the time of delivering possession. . . . [The vendor] has a right to say to the purchaser, 'Either pay me the purchase-money, or lose the estate.' . . . If anything happens to the estate between the time of sale and the time of completion of the purchase it is at the risk of the purchaser. If it is a house that is sold, and the house is burnt down, the purchaser loses the house. He must insure it himself if he wants to provide against such an accident. . . . In the same way there is a correlative liability on the part of the vendor in possession. He is not entitled to treat the estate as his own. If he wilfully damages or injures it, he is liable to the purchaser; and more than that, he is liable if he does not take reasonable care of it. So far he is treated in all respects as a trustee, subject of course to his right to being paid the purchase-money and his right to enforce his security against the estate. With those exceptions, and his right to rents till the day for completion, he appears to me to have no other rights. . . .

[Jessel MR then examines *Shaw* v *Foster* (1872) LR 5 HL 321, where Lord O'Hagan says:] 'By the contract of sale the vendor, in the view of the Court of Equity, disposes of his right over the estate, and on the execution of the contract he becomes constructively a trustee for the vendee, who is thereupon on the other side bound by a trust for the payment of the purchase-money' — that is, perhaps, not quite accurate — it is not 'a trust for the payment of the purchase-money,' but it is a charge or lien — however, he meant the same thing. . .

Note
The vendor remains the legal owner at law until a deed complying with the Law of Property Act 1925, s. 52 (see *post*), is executed. See M. P. Thompson, 'Must a purchaser buy a charred ruin?' [1984] Conv 43.

SECTION 3: THE CONVEYANCE OR TRANSFER

Before the transaction is completed, i.e. concluded, both the vendor's and purchaser's solicitors should take all the necessary steps in deducing and investigating the title. Once this has been done the vendor must convey or transfer the land to the purchaser.

In order for the conveyance or transfer to be valid, it must be executed in the form of a deed described in the Law of Property Act 1925, s. 52. The purchaser's solicitor generally prepares the necessary deed. After this has been carried out, in the case of unregistered land there are no further formalities required, whereas in the case of registered land the transfer has to be registered at the Land Registry. It should be noted, however, that s. 54 of the Act provides for the situation where interests in land can be created orally.

Law of Property Act 1925

52. Conveyances to be by deed
(1) All conveyances of land or of any interest therein are void for the purpose of conveying or creating a legal estate unless made by deed.
(2) This section does not apply to—

(a) assents by a personal representative;
(b) disclaimers made in accordance with sections 178 to 180 or sections 315 to 319 of the Insolvency Act 1986 or not required to be evidenced in writing;
(c) surrenders by operation of law, including surrenders which may, by law, be effected without writing;
(d) leases or tenancies or other assurances not required by law to be made in writing;
(e) receipts other than those falling within section 115 below;
(f) vesting orders of the court or other competent authority;
(g) conveyances taking effect by operation of law.

54. Creation of interests in land by parol
(2) Nothing in the foregoing provisions of this Part of this Act shall affect the creation by parol of leases taking effect in possession for a term not exceeding three years (whether or not the lessee is given power to extend the term) at the best rent which can be reasonably obtained without taking a fine.

Note
Section 54(2) applies only to the *creation* of certain kinds of leases and tenancies. It does not extend to their subsequent assignment which must be made by means of a deed. Therefore, periodic tenancies, for example, while they can be effectively created orally, must be assigned by deed if the assignee is to receive the legal estate in the land (*Crago* v *Julian* [1992] 1 All ER 744).

Law of Property (Miscellaneous Provisions) Act 1989

1. Deeds and their execution
(1) Any rule of law which—
(a) restricts the substances on which a deed may be written;
(b) requires a seal for the valid execution of an instrument as a deed by an individual; or
(c) requires authority by one person to another to deliver an instrument as a deed on his behalf to be given by deed, is abolished.
(2) An instrument shall not be a deed unless—
(a) it makes it clear on its face that it is intended to be a deed by the person making it or, as the case may be, by the parties to it (whether describing itself as a deed or expressing itself to be executed or signed as a deed or otherwise); and
(b) it is validly executed as a deed by that person or, as the case may be, one or more of those parties,
(3) An instrument is validly executed as a deed by an individual if, and only if—
(a) it is signed—
(i) by him in the presence of a witness who attests the signature; or
(ii) at his direction and in his presence and the presence of two witnesses who each attest the signature; and
(b) it is delivered as a deed by him or a person authorised to do so on his behalf.
(4) In subsection (2) and (3) above 'sign', in relation to an instrument, includes making one's mark on the instrument and 'signature' is to be construed accordingly.
(5) Where a solicitor or licensed conveyancer, or an agent or employee of a solicitor or licensed conveyancer, in the course of or in connection with a transaction involving the disposition or creation of an interest in land, purports to deliver an instrument as a

deed on behalf of a party to the instrument, it shall be conclusively presumed in favour of a purchaser that he is authorised so to deliver the instrument.

(6) In subsection (5) above—
'disposition' and 'purchaser' have the same meaning as in the Law of Property Act 1925; and
'interest in land' means any estate, interest or charge in or over land or in or over the proceeds of sale of land.

(7) Where an instrument under seal that constitutes a deed is required for the purposes of an Act passed before this section comes into force, this section shall have effect as to signing, sealing or delivery of an instrument by an individual in place of any provision of that Act as to signing, sealing or delivery.

(8)–(9) ...

(10) The references in this section to the execution of a deed by an individual do not include execution by a corporation sole and the reference in subsection (7) above to signing, sealing or delivery by an individual does not include signing, sealing or delivery by such a corporation.

(11) Nothing in this section applies in relation to instruments delivered as deeds before this section comes into force.

Notes

1. The 1989 Act has no effect on when deeds are required but s. 1 introduces new formalities for their execution. All deeds must now comply with the new formalities, not only those relating to land.

2. In *Goddard's Case* (1584) 2 Co Rep 4b, 5a, it was said 'There are but three things of the essence and substance of a deed, that is to say, writing on paper or parchment, sealing and delivery'. Since s. 1 came into force on 31 July 1990, deeds need no longer be sealed except and where a party to the deed is a corporation, either sole or aggregate. Now however every deed must show clearly on its face that it is intended to be a deed. No prescribed manner is specified.

Section 1 now makes the witnessing and attestation of a deed mandatory, although it was the norm in practice anyway. The Law Commission suggested that failure to have a signature witnessed and attested should not necessarily be fatal, and that the signatory should be bound by a deed if he takes the benefit of it. Similarly, estoppel will prevent a signatory from escaping the effect of a deed if another acts on the strength of it. These recommendations were not, however, incorporated into the Act.

A deed which is not properly witnessed will almost certainly take effect in equity, for example as an agreement to convey a fee simple or to grant a lease. In unregistered land the purchaser should register an estate contract under the Land Charges Act 1972 in those circumstances. The deed will also be subject to rectification so as to give effect to the true intention of the parties.

A deed still must be delivered to be enforceable, despite the report of the Working Paper (No. 93). The meaning of 'delivery' has caused great difficulty: its legal meaning differs from the ordinary accepted meaning of the word.

The notion of delivery developed from a physical fact into a question of the deliverer's intention to be bound — see Lord Denning MR in *Vincent* v *Premo Enterprises* [1969] 2 QB 609, where he said:

Delivery does not mean 'handed over' to the other side. It means delivered in the old legal sense, namely, an act done so as to evidence an intention to be bound. Even though the deed remains in the possession of the maker, or of his solicitor, he is bound by it if he has done some act evidencing an intention to be bound.

The act of delivery by a party to a deed in the usual transaction will often be the handing over of the signed and sealed deed by a client to his own solicitor, in readiness for completion. Delivery is the final formality of execution, and the deed once delivered becomes fully effective; thus the date of the deed is the date of delivery. However, delivery may be conditional — for example, delivery of a deed by a vendor to his solicitor may be conditional upon that solicitor's receiving the purchase price from the purchaser. Thus, the absurdity of a deed becoming effective in favour of a purchaser before payment of the purchase price is effectively avoided. Where delivery is conditional, not absolute, the deed is said to be a deed in escrow. Conditions will often be implied upon delivery, as would be the case in the example. The condition in that case would be satisfied on completion when the purchase money is paid, and the deed then would become effective to pass the legal estate to the purchaser at that time.

Delivery is irrevocable, even if conditional. Provided the condition is satisfied the deed becomes effective (see *Beesly* v *Hallwood Estates Ltd* [1961] Ch 105). Even if the condition is not satisfied at the time a vendor wants to withdraw, he cannot, but must wait and see whether the condition is satisfied.

In the absence of express provision there is no set time limit for the satisfaction of the condition of delivery. However, there will inevitably come a time when the vendor will be entitled to withdraw if the condition has not been satisfied.

Upon the satisfaction of the condition the deed is treated as having been delivered on the date of the conditional delivery (see *Alan Estates* v *W.G. Stores* [1982] Ch 511).

Prior to s. 1(5) coming into force, an agent, such as a solicitor, could only be appointed to deliver a deed on behalf of another if that appointment was itself made by deed. Section 1(5) now allows authority to be given without a deed so that the task of delivery may be delegated by the client to his solicitor. The date of the deed in those circumstances would be the date upon which the vendor's solicitor hands the deeds over on completion. Thus, s. 1(5) will no doubt greatly reduce the circumstances in which deeds in escrow are used.

SECTION 4: CONVEYANCE TO SELF

Law of Property Act 1925

72. Conveyances by a person to himself, &c.

(1) In conveyances made after the twelfth day of August, eighteen hundred and fifty-nine, personal property, including chattels real, may be conveyed by a person to

himself jointly with another person by the like means by which it might be conveyed by him to another person.

(2) In conveyances made after the thirty-first day of December, eighteen hundred and eighty-one, freehold land, or a thing in action, may be conveyed by a person to himself jointly with another person, by the like means by which it might be conveyed by him to another person; and may, in like manner, be conveyed by a husband to his wife, and by a wife to her husband, alone or jointly with another person.

(3) After the commencement of this Act a person may convey land to or vest land in himself.

(4) Two or more persons (whether or not being trustees or personal representatives) may convey, and shall be deemed always to have been capable of conveying, any property vested in them to any one or more of themselves in like manner as they could have conveyed such property to a third party; provided that if the persons in whose favour the conveyance is made are, by reason of any fiduciary relationship or otherwise, precluded from validly carrying out the transaction, the conveyance shall be liable to be set aside.

Note
In *Rye* v *Rye* [1962] AC 496 it was held by Viscount Simonds, Lord MacDermott and Lord Denning that the Law of Property Act 1925, s. 72(3) does not enable a person to grant a lease to himself of land of which he is the owner.

SECTION 5: TRANSFER OF EQUITABLE INTERESTS

Law of Property Act 1925

53. Instruments required to be in writing

(1) Subject to the provision hereinafter contained with respect to the creation of interests in land by parol—

(a) no interest in land can be created or disposed of except by writing signed by the person creating or conveying the same, or by his agent thereunto lawfully authorised in writing, or by will, or by operation of law;

(b) a declaration of trust respecting any land or any interest therein must be manifested and proved by some writing signed by some person who is able to declare such trust or by his will;

(c) a disposition of an equitable interest or trust subsisting at the time of the disposition, must be in writing signed by the person disposing of the same, or by his agent thereunto lawfully authorised in writing or by will.

(2) This section does not affect the creation or operation of resulting, implied or constructive trusts.

SECTION 6: INCOMPLETE TRANSFERS OR CREATIONS

We have already seen that any conveyance of a legal estate or interest in land must comply with the Law of Property Act 1925, s. 52, as amended by the Law of Property (Miscellaneous Provisions) Act 1989, s. 1. This provision applies not only to freehold estates in land but to leaseholds as well. What is the effect of an incomplete transfer or creation of a leasehold interest in land?

Walsh v Lonsdale
(1882) 21 ChD 9 (CA)

The defendant entered into a written agreement to grant a seven year lease of a mill to the plaintiff but no formal lease. The contract stated that rent was to be payable on demand by the defendant, one year in advance. The plaintiff had been in possession of the mill for six months. The defendant distrained (i.e. he removed some of the plaintiff's chattels) for the rent he had claimed. The plaintiff then commenced an action for damages for illegal distress and for specific performance of the agreement. Held: the defendant had a right to distrain.

JESSEL MR: . . . There is an agreement for a lease under which possession has been given. Now since the Judicature Act . . . [t]here is only one Court, and the equity rules prevail in it. The tenant holds under an agreement for a lease. He holds, therefore, under the same terms in equity as if a lease had been granted, it being a case in which both parties admit that relief is capable of being given by specific performance. That being so, he cannot complain of the exercise by the landlord of the same rights as the landlord would have had if a lease had been granted. On the other hand, he is protected in the same way as if a lease had been granted; he cannot be turned out by six months' notice as a tenant from year to year. He has a right to say, 'I have a lease in equity, and you can only re-enter if I have committed such a breach of covenant as would if a lease had been granted have entitled you to re-enter according to the terms of a proper proviso for re-entry.' That being so, it appears to me that being a lessee in equity he cannot complain of the exercise of the right of distress merely because the actual parchment has not been signed and sealed.

Notes
1. *Walsh* v *Lonsdale* (following the earlier case of *Parker* v *Taswell* (1858) 2 DeG & J 559 and *Doe dem. Thomson* v *Amey* (1840) 12 Ad & El 476) treats an incomplete transfer or creation of a lease as an agreement for a lease, enabling either party to call for specific performance if there is either written evidence of the lease or part performance.
2. After the execution of the informal lease the purchaser has an 'estate contract' which, in unregistered land, should be registered as a class C(iv) land charge under the Land Charges Act 1972, s. 2(4).
3. An analogous doctrine to that in *Walsh* v *Lonsdale* applies to the informal creation of easements — see *McManus* v *Cooke* (1887) 35 ChD 681.
4. The rule in *Walsh* v *Lonsdale* has been applied where a company is in possession as tenant of premises under an agreement embodied in a consent order of the court, so as to treat the parties as if a formal instrument had been executed to give effect to the terms of the order (*Tottenham Hotspur Football & Athletic Co.* v *Princegrove Publishers* [1974] 1 WLR 113) and where the lessor had no legal estate but was entitled, under an agreement of which specific performance would be granted, to call for the legal fee simple (*Industrial Properties (Barton Hill) Ltd* v *Associated Electrical Ltd* [1977] QB 580). See Albrey (1974) 90 LQR 149.
5. The doctrine in *Walsh* v *Lonsdale* applies only to agreements for leases *where specific performance of the agreement would be granted* (see Farwell J in

Manchester Brewery v *Coombs* [1901] 2 Ch 608, at page 211). If specific performance is not available the parties will be governed by the common law relating to unsealed documents. (See also *Coatsworth* v *Johnson* (1886) 55 LJ QB 220.)

6. It may be the case (although it is difficult to find authority to support the proposition) that equity would apply the doctrine in *Walsh* v *Lonsdale* to the improper creation of other legal interests.

Question
What effect does the Law of Property (Miscellaneous Provisions) Act 1989 have on the doctrine in *Walsh* v *Lonsdale*?

SECTION 7: OPTIONS TO PURCHASE LAND

The vendor of property may wish to give the purchaser a right to purchase further land within a specified period of time. This he can achieve by granting the purchaser an option to purchase such land. The option to purchase the land may form part of the main transaction for the sale of land or 'stand on its own'. However, an option to purchase land must comply with the rule against perpetuities, must contain terms which are sufficiently certain and, where an option 'stands on its own', there must be consideration, even if only of a nominal amount (*Mountford* v *Scott* [1975] Ch 258).

The traditional analysis of an option is that it is an irrevocable standing offer, to be accepted by whatever means specified by the vendor. Thus in *Helby* v *Matthews* [1895] AC 471 there are references to it being 'a binding offer'. A different analysis was made however in *Griffith* v *Pelton* [1958] Ch 205, where it was treated as 'a conditional contract . . . which the grantee is entitled to convert into a concluded contract of purchase'. That analysis was questioned by Buckley J in *Beesly* v *Hallwood Estates* [1960] 1 WLR 549. Later decisions have reiterated the traditional view, for example Russell LJ in *Mountford* v *Scott* [1975] Ch 258, where an option was described as 'an irrevocable offer to sell'.

The need for a correct analysis is imperative since the Law of Property (Miscellaneous Provisions) Act 1989, s. 2 came into force, replacing s. 40 of the Law of Property Act 1925. If a 'contract for the sale . . . of an interest in land' is, for the purpose of s. 2(1), the agreement by which the option was granted, then there is no difficulty, provided that agreement incorporates all the terms and is signed by or on behalf of the vendor and purchaser respectively. However, if the letter or other document exercising the option is deemed to make the contract, this document must comply with s. 2 and must not only be signed by the purchaser, but must also be counter-signed by the vendor. Such a counter-signature would appear to undermine the basis of an option to purchase, which is a flexible conveyancing tool, as the flexibility depends upon the exercise of the option being a unilateral act; it would destroy its very nature and purpose if the grantee had to obtain the grantor's counter-signature to the notice by which it was exercised.

Spiro v *Glencrown Properties*
[1991] 1 All ER 600 (ChD)

This first instance decision is the first in which the nature of an option to purchase has been discussed since the Act came into effect. The plaintiff granted the defendant an option to purchase certain land. This option was in writing, complying with the provisions of s. 2. The defendant gave notice in writing exercising the option but failed to complete. The plaintiff sued for breach of contract, but the defendant argued that as the letter exercising the option had been signed only by one party (i.e. the purchaser himself), it was void for non-compliance with s. 2. Held: that the grant of the option is a contract for the purposes of s. 2, and the notice exercising the option by the purchaser is not a contract that needs to comply with s. 2.

HOFFMANN J: The language of s. 2 places no obstacle in the way of construing the grant of the option as the relevant contract. An option to buy land can properly be described as a contract for the sale of that land conditional upon the exercise of the option. A number of eminent judges have so described it. In *Helby* v *Matthews* [1895] AC 471 at 482, [1895–9] All ER Rep 821 at 827, which concerned the sale of a piano on hire purchase, Lord Macnaghten said:

> The contract, as it seems to me, on the part of the dealer was a contract of hiring coupled with a conditional contract or undertaking to sell. On the part of the customer it was a contract of hiring only until the time came for making the last payment.

In *Griffith* v *Pelton* [1957] 3 All ER 75 at 83, [1958] Ch 205 at 25, which raised the question of whether the benefit of an option was assignable, Jenkins LJ said:

> An option in gross for the purchase of land is a conditional contract for which purchase by the grantee of the option from the grantor which the grantee is entitled to convert into a concluded contract of purchase, and to have carried to completion by the grantor, on giving the prescribed notice and otherwise complying with the conditions on which the option is made exercisable in any particular case.

In the context of s. 2, it makes obvious sense to characterise it in this way. So far, therefore, the case seems to me to be clear.

The purchaser however submits that I am constrained by authority to characterise an option as an irrevocable offer which does not become a contract for the sale of land until it has been accepted by the notice which exercises the option. It follows that the 'contract for the sale . . . of an interest in land' within the meaning of s. 2 can only have been made by the letter.

The first case upon which the purchaser relies is *Helby* v *Matthews*; the very case in which, as I have said, Lord Macnaghten characterised an option to purchase as a conditional contract to sell. Lord Herschell LC and Lord Watson, however, expressed themselves rather differently. Lord Herschell LC said ([1895] AC 471 at 477, [1895–9] All ER Rep 821 at 824):

> . . . when a person has, for valuable consideration, bound himself to sell to another on certain terms, if the other chooses to avail himself of the binding offer, he may, in popular language, be said to have agreed to sell, though an agreement to sell in this sense, which is in truth merely an offer which cannot be withdrawn, certainly does not connote an agreement to buy, and it is only in this sense that there can be said to have been an agreement to sell in the present case.

Lord Watson said ([1895] AC 471 at 479–480, [1895–9] All ER Rep 821 at 826):

> In order to constitute an agreement for sale and purchase, there must be two parties who are mutually bound by it. From a legal point of view the appellant was in exactly the same position as if he had made an offer to sell on certain terms, and had undertaken to keep it open for a definite period.

It is however important to read these statements in the context in which they were made. The question in *Helby* v *Matthews* was whether, during the currency of the hire, the hirer had 'agreed to buy' the goods within the meaning of the Factors Act 1889. The purpose of the 1889 Act was to give a buyer, who was in possession but had not yet acquired title, the power to confer title upon a third party who took in good faith. It is not surprising that the House of Lords decided that a person who had at the relevant time no obligation to acquire or pay for the goods had not 'agreed to buy' them within the meaning of the 1889 Act. The language and purpose of the statute requires one to look at the arrangement from the buyer's point of view. And the essence of an option is that while the seller may be said to be conditionally bound, the buyer is free. In the *Helby* v *Matthews* context it was therefore true to say that pending exercise of the option, the position of the buyer was *as if* he had been made an offer which the seller could not withdraw.

But the concept of an offer is of course normally used as part of the technique for ascertaining whether the parties have reached that mutual consent which is a necessary element in the formation of a contract. In this primary sense, it is of the essence of an offer that by itself it gives rise to no legal obligations. It was for this reason that Diplock LJ said in *Varty (Inspector of Taxes)* v *British South Africa Co.* [1964] 2 All ER 975 at 982, [1965] Ch 508 at 523:

> To speak of an enforceable option as an 'irrevocable offer' is juristically a contradiction in terms, for the adjective 'irrevocable' connotes the existence of an obligation on the part of the offeror, while the noun 'offer' connotes the absence of any obligation until the offer has been accepted.

This does not mean that in Diplock LJ's opinion, Lord Herschell LC and Lord Watson were speaking nonsense. They were not using 'offer' in its primary sense but, as often happens in legal reasoning, by way of metaphor or analogy. Such metaphors can be vivid and illuminating but prove a trap for the unwary if pressed beyond their original context. As I said recently in another connection, '. . . there are dangers in reasoning from the metaphor as if it expressed a literal truth rather than from the underlying principle which the metaphor encapsulates' (se *Re K, re F* [1988] 1 All ER 358 at 361, [1988] Ch 310 at 314).

Here the underlying principles are clear enough. The granting of the option imposes no obligation upon the purchaser and an obligation upon the vendor which is contingent upon the exercise of the option. When the option is exercised, vendor and purchaser come under obligations to perform as if they had concluded an ordinary contract of sale. And the analogy of an irrevocable offer is, as I have said, a useful way of describing the position of the purchaser between the grant and exercise of the option. Thus in the recent case of *J. Sainsbury plc* v *O'Connor (Inspector of Taxes)* [1990] STC 516 at 532 Millett J used it to explain why the grantee of an option to buy shares did not become the beneficial owner until he had exercised the option.

But the irrevocable offer metaphor has much less explanatory power in relation to the position of the vendor. The effect of the 'offer' which the vendor has made is, from his point of view, so different from that of an offer in its primary sense that the metaphor is of little assistance. Thus in the famous passage in *London and South Western Rly Co.*

v *Gomm* (1882) 20 ChD 562 at 581, [1881–5] All ER Rep 1190 at 1193 Jessel MR had no use for it in explaining why the grant of an option to buy land confers an interest in the land upon the grantee.

> The right to call for a conveyance of the land is an equitable interest or equitable estate. In the ordinary case of a contract for purchase there is no doubt about this, and an option for repurchase is not different in its nature. A person exercising the option has to do two things, he has to give notice of his intention to purchase, and to pay the purchase-money; but as far as the man who is liable to convey is concerned, his estate or interest is taken away from him without his consent, and the right to take it away being vested in another, the covenant giving the option must give that other an interest in the land.

The fact that the option binds the vendor contingently to convey was the reason why an option agreement was held to fall within s. 40 of the Law of Property Act 1925: see *Richards* v *Creighton Griffiths (Investments) Ltd* (1972) 225 EG 2104, where Plowman J rejected a submission that it was merely a contract not to withdraw an offer. Similarly in *Weeding* v *Weeding* (1861) I John & H 424 at 430–431, 70 ER 812 at 815 Page Wood V-C held that the grant of an option to buy land was sufficient to deem that land converted into personalty for the purposes of the grantor's will, even though the option had not yet been exercised when he died. Page Wood V-C said:

> I cannot agree with the argument that there is no contract. It is as much a conditional contract as if it depended on any other contingency than the exercise of an option by a third person such as, for example, the failure of issue of a particular person.

Thus in explaining the vendor's position, the analogy to which the courts usually appeal is that of a conditional contract. This analogy might also be said to be imperfect, because one generally thinks of a conditional contract as one in which the contingency does not lie within the sole power of one of the parties to the contract. But this difference from the standard case of a conditional contract does not destroy the value of the analogy in explaining the *vendor's* position. So far as he is concerned, it makes no difference whether or not the contingency is within the sole power of the purchaser. The important point is that his estate or interest is taken away from him without his consent.

Griffith v *Pelton* [1957] 3 All ER 75, [1958] Ch 205, to which I have already referred, was another case in which the irrevocable offer analogy was unhelpful. The rule is that an offer in the primary sense can be accepted only by the person to whom it is made. The offeree cannot assign to someone else the right to accept so that someone other than the grantee could accept it, Jenkins LJ (in the passage which I have already cited) characterised the option as a conditional contract and said ([1957] 3 All ER 75 at 83, [1958] Ch 205 at 225):

> The conditional contract constituted by the grant of the option is a chose in action the benefit of which can (if the terms of the contract are such as to show that it is not merely personal to the grantor) be assigned by the grantee to anyone he chooses, subject to any restriction imposed by the contract as to the persons in whose favour assignment is permissible.

> . . . The purchaser's argument requires me to say that 'irrevocable offer' and 'conditional contract' are mutually inconsistent concepts and that I must range myself under one or other banner and declare the other to be heretical. I hope that I have demonstrated this to be a misconception about the nature of legal reasoning. An option is not strictly speaking either an offer or a conditional contract. It does not have all the

incidents of the standard form of either of these concepts. To that extent it is a relationship sui generis. But there are ways in which it resembles each of them. Each analogy is in the proper context a valid way of characterising the situation created by an option. The question in this case is not whether one analogy is true and the other false, but which is appropriate to be used in the construction of s. 2 of the Law of Property (Miscellaneous Provisions) Act 1989.

There is only one case in which, as it seems to me, the adoption of the irrevocable offer metaphor was allowed to dictate the result without regard to the context. This was *Beesly* v *Hallwood Estates Ltd* [1960] 2 All ER 314, [1960] 1 WLR 549 in which Buckley J decided that an option was not a 'contract ... to convey or create a legal estate' within the meaning of that part of the definition of an estate contract in s. 10(1) of the Land Charges Act 1925. He arrived at this conclusion on the ground that the option was not a contract to convey but only an irrevocable offer. It seems to me, with respect to Buckley J, that this was a misuse of the irrevocable offer metaphor. The purpose of including estate contracts in the Land Charges Act 1925 was to enable a purchaser to obtain notice of contracts which created interests binding upon the land. For this purpose, as Jessel MR pointed out in *Gomm's* case, there is no difference between an option and an ordinary contract of sale. In both cases the land is bound by an agreement which entitles a third party, either conditionally or unconditionally, to demand a conveyance. A purposive construction of s. 10(1) therefore requires that one characterise the option from the point of view of its effect on the land in the hands of the grantor. For this purpose, it is more appropriate to regard it as a conditional contract than an irrevocable offer. In fact Buckley J was able to give effect to the manifest intention of Parliament because the definition of an estate contract went on to say 'including a contract conferring ... a valid option of purchase'. He was therefore able to hold that an option was an estate contract, but only by treating the word 'including' as extending the meaning of the previous words. In my judgment this was unnecessary. The option would have been an estate contract even without the additional words.

Mr Douglas, for the purchaser, relied strongly upon the decision of the House of Lords in *United Scientific Holdings Ltd* v *Burnley BC, Cheapside Land Development Co. Ltd* v *Messels Service Co.* [1977] 2 All ER 62, [1978] AC 904 as authority for the universal application of the irrevocable offer characterisation. That case concerned the rule that the conditions for the exercise of an option, including any time stipulations, must be strictly complied with. The rule had been developed by analogy with the rule that an ordinary offer can be accepted only by strict compliance with the conditions which it lays down. The Court of Appeal had extended the analogy to a notice under a rent review clause in a lease. The House of Lords held that this further extension was unjustifiable. Their Lordships distinguished the ordinary option to purchase or to extend the lease from the activation of a rent review clause. In the former case, said Lord Simon of Glaisdale ([1977] 2 All ER 62 at 85, [1978] AC 904 at 945–946):

> ... the parties, on the exercise of the option, are brought into a new legal relationship. It was argued ... that the rent review clauses were also such unilateral terms. I cannot agree. The operation of the rent review clauses does not at all change the relationship of the parties, which remains that of landlord and tenant throughout the currency of the lease whether or not the machinery of the rent review clauses is operated.

The reasoning of the other Law Lords was similar. It was rightly submitted on behalf of the purchaser in this case that the House of Lords thereby endorsed the irrevocable offer analogy for ordinary options. But the endorsement was in the context of the rule that there must be strict compliance with the conditions of acceptance. The case is no authority for extending its application in a different context.

Perhaps the most helpful case for present purposes is *Re Mulholland's Will Trusts, Bryan* v *Westminster Bank Ltd* [1949] 1 All ER 460. A testator had let premises to the Westminster Bank on a lease which included an option to purchase. He appointed the bank his executor and trustee and after his death the bank exercised the option. It was argued for his widow and children that the bank was precluded from exercising the option by the rule that a trustee cannot contract with himself. Wynn-Parry J was pressed with the irrevocable offer metaphor, which, it was said, led inexorably to the conclusion that when the bank exercised the option, it was indeed entering into a contract with itself. But the judge held that if one considered the purpose of the self-dealing rule, which was to prevent a trustee from being subjected to a conflict of interest and duty, the only relevant contract was the grant of the option. The rule could only sensibly be applied to a consensual transaction. While for some purposes it might be true to say that the exercise of the option brought the contract into existence, there could be no rational ground for applying the self-dealing rule to the unilateral exercise of a right granted before the trusteeship came into existence. The judge quoted the passage I have cited from Jessel MR in *Gomm's* case and said ([1949] 1 All ER 460 at 464):

> As I understand that passage, it amounts to this, that, as regards this option, there was between the parties only one contract, namely the contract constituted by the provisions in the lease which I have read creating the option. The notice exercising the option did not lead, in my opinion, to the creation of any fresh contractual relationship between the parties, making them for the first time vendors and purchasers, nor did it bring into existence any right in addition to the right conferred by the option.

The contrast between this passage and my citation from Lord Simon of Glaisdale in *United Scientific Holdings* is a striking illustration of how in different contexts the law can accommodate analogies which appear to lead to diametrically opposing conclusions.

In my judgment there is nothing in the authorities which prevents me from giving s. 2 the meaning which I consider to have been the clear intention of the legislature. On the contrary, the purposive approach taken in cases like *Mulholland* encourages me to adopt a similar approach to s. 2. And the plain purpose of s. 2 was, as I have said, to prescribe the formalities for recording the consent of the parties. It follows that in my view the grant of the option was the only 'contract for the sale or other disposition of an interest in land' within the meaning of the section and the contract duly complied with the statutory requirements. There must be judgment for the plaintiff against both defendants with costs.

Notes

1. See P. F. Smith, 'Options to purchase — a nasty twist' [1991] Conv 140; M. Thomas, 'The legal basis of an option to purchase land' [1991] NILQ 359.
2. An option to purchase must be distinguished from a right of pre-emption (i.e. a right of first refusal).

Kling v *Keston Properties*
(1983) 49 P & C R 212 (ChD)

The grantor gave the grantee a right of pre-emption over a garage in Flood Street, Chelsea. Was this right of pre-emption enforceable by the grantee against a purchaser of the garage from the grantor?

Acquisition of Land: Contract and Conveyance

VINELOTT J: The question whether a right of pre-emption or first refusal over land creates an equitable interest in the land capable of binding a purchaser was for many years a controversial one. It was settled so far as this court is concerned by the decision of the Court of Appeal in *Pritchard* v *Briggs* [1980] Ch 338... Under [the Land Charges Act 1925] and under the Land Charges Act 1972 (which is a consolidating Act) the contracts registrable as estate contracts expressly include a contract conferring 'a valid option or right of pre-emption or any other like right.' The survivor of the owners, a Major Lockwood, in fact sold the land to the defendants, purportedly in pursuance of the right of pre-emption. After the death of Major Lockwood, the plaintiff gave notice exercising the option. Goff LJ was of the opinion that the right of pre-emption created a merely personal right and did not create an interest in land even after the conditions for its exercise had been satisfied. Accordingly the defendants could not claim priority over the plaintiff's option. In his opinion the Land Charges Act 1972, in so far as it provided for registration of a right of pre-emption as an estate contract, proceeded on a wrong view of the law. However, Templeman and Stephenson LJJ took a different view of the nature and effect of a right of pre-emption. [Vinelott J quotes the passage from *Prichard* v *Briggs*, see page 29.]

Note
See Charles Harpum, 'Rights of pre-emption: monsters not ugly ducklings' [1980] CLJ 35.

5 ACQUISITION OF LAND: ADVERSE POSSESSION

SECTION 1: INTRODUCTION

Most legal systems have realised the necessity of fixing some definite period of time within which persons must bring an action. In land law persons who have been unlawfully dispossessed of their land must pursue their claim within a definite period of time otherwise their estate or interest in that land may be extinguished under the doctrine of adverse possession. The present law is governed by the Limitation Act 1980 (based upon the recommendations of the Law Reform Committee's 21st Report 1977 (Final Report on Limitation of Actions) (Cmnd 6923)).

Limitation Act 1980

15. Time limit for actions to recover land
(1) No action shall be brought by any person to recover any land after the expiration of twelve years from the date on which the right of action accrued to him or, if it first accrued to some person through whom he claims, to that person.

Note
The Act also applies to a foreclosure action, to settled land and land held on a trust for sale, to actions for the recovery of rent and forfeiture for breach of a condition (see *post*). It should be noted that a beneficiary's interest under a trust for sale is deemed to be money under the doctrine of conversion, yet the interest is regarded as an interest in land for the purposes of adverse possession.
There are certain cases where the 12-year period is increased.

Limitation Act 1980

Schedule 1

10. Subject to paragraph 11 below, section 15(1) of this Act shall apply to the bringing of an action to recover any land by the Crown or by any spiritual or eleemosynary corporation sole with the substitution for the reference to twelve years of a reference to thirty years.

Notes
1. The usual 12-year period applies to a corporation aggregate.
2. An action to recover land brought *against* the Crown etc. is subject to the usual 12-year period.

The underlying philosophy of the doctrine of adverse possession was summed up by Lord St Leonards in *Dundee Harbour Trustees* v *Dougall* (1852) 1 Macq 317, at p. 321:

> All statutes of limitation have for their object the prevention of the rearing up of claims at great distances of time when evidences are lost; and in all well-regulated countries the quieting of possession is held an important point of policy.

See also M. Dockray, 'Why do we need adverse possession?' [1985] Conv 272.

SECTION 2: THE RUNNING OF TIME

A: PRESENT INTERESTS

Time begins to run when:

(a) the owner is dispossessed or discontinues his possession of the land; and
(b) adverse possession of the land is taken by some other person.

Dispossession occurs where a person comes in and drives out the owner and discontinuance occurs where the owner leaves the land and is followed in possession by other persons — see Fry J in *Rains* v *Buxton* (1880) 14 Ch D 537.

Limitation Act 1980

Schedule 1

Accrual of right of action in case of present interests in land

1. Where the person bringing an action to recover land, or some person through whom he claims, has been in possession of the land, and has while entitled to the land been dispossessed or discontinued his possession, the right of action shall be treated as having accrued on the date of the dispossession or discontinuance.

2. Where any person brings an action to recover any land of a deceased person (whether under a will or on intestacy) and the deceased person—

(a) was on the date of his death in possession of the land or, in the case of a rentcharge created by will or taking effect upon his death, in possession of the land charged; and

(b) was the last person entitled to the land to be in possession of it;

the right of action shall be treated as having accrued on the date of his death.

3. Where any person brings an action to recover land, being an estate or interest in possession assured otherwise than by will to him, or to some person through whom he claims, and—

(a) the person making the assurance was on the date when the assurance took effect in possession of the land or, in the case of a rentcharge created by the assurance, in possession of the land charged; and

(b) no person has been in possession of the land by virtue of the assurance;

the right of action shall be treated as having accrued on the date when the assurance took effect.

Right of action not to accrue or continue unless there is adverse possession

8.–(1) No right of action to recover land shall be treated as accruing unless the land is in the possession of some person in whose favour the period of limitation can run (referred to below in this paragraph as 'adverse possession'); and where . . . any such right of action is treated as accruing on a certain date and no person is in adverse possession on that date, the right of action shall not be treated as accruing unless and until adverse possession is taken of the land.

Notes

1. Whether the possession of the squatter is adverse or not is a matter of fact depending on the circumstances of the case, but adverse possession has always been regarded as possession inconsistent with the title of the true owner. See Bramwell LJ in *Leigh* v *Jack* (1879) 5 Ex D 264. This approach was first criticised in the case of *Powell* v *McFarlane* (1977) 38 P & CR 452, where Slade LJ said (at pp. 470–71):

> Factual possession signifies an appropriate degree of physical control. It must be a single and [exclusive] possession . . . thus an owner of land and a person intruding on that land without his consent cannot both be in possession of the land at the same time. The question what acts constitute a sufficient degree of exclusive physical control must depend on the circumstances, in particular the nature of the land and the manner in which land of that nature is commonly used or enjoyed.

See Paul Jackson, 'The animus of squatting' (1980) 96 LQR 333.

2. The most recent analysis of this issue can be found in the following case.

Buckinghamshire County Council v Moran
[1989] 3 WLR 152; [1989] 2 All ER 225 (CA)

The plaintiffs bought a plot of land adjacent to the defendant's house and garden on 20 October 1955. It was not developed and was to be used at some time in the future for road development. The defendant's predecessors in title had maintained the disputed land since 1967. They mowed the grass, trimmed the hedges and started using the property for their own purposes. On 28 July 1971, the house was conveyed to the defendant. The land was described in the conveyance as 'together with . . . all such rights estate title and interests as the vendors may have in or over' the plot. The defendant when he moved in locked the gates so as to prevent any access onto the land other than through the defendant's garden. On 20 January 1976, the defendant wrote to the plaintiffs pointing out the use made of the land since 1967 and adding it 'has always been my firm understanding that the land should be kept by the owner of [the house] if and until the proposed' road diversion. On 25 March 1967, the defendant's solicitors wrote to the council claiming that the defendant had acquired title to the plot by adverse possession. Held: the defendant had established a good claim to title by adverse possession.

SLADE LJ: I turn then to consider the first of the two requisite elements of possession. First, as at 28 October 1973 did the defendant have factual possession of the plot? I venture to repeat what I said in *Powell* v *McFarlane*, 38 P & CR 452 [pp. 470–71, at page 128] . . .

On the evidence it would appear clear that by 28 October 1973 the defendant had acquired complete and exclusive physical control of the plot. He had secured a complete enclosure of the plot and its annexation to Dolphin Place. Any intruder could have gained access to the plot only by way of Dolphin Place, unless he was prepared to climb the locked gate fronting the highway or to scramble through one or other of the hedges bordering the plot. The defendant had put a new lock and chain on the gate and had fastened it. He and his mother had been dealing with the plot as any occupying owners might have been expected to deal with it. They had incorporated it into the garden of Dolphin Place. They had planted bulbs and daffodils in the grass. They had maintained it as part of that garden and had trimmed the hedges. I cannot accept Mr Douglas's submission that the defendant's acts of possession were trivial. It is hard to see what more he could have done to acquire complete physical control of the plot by October 1983. In my judgment, he had plainly acquired factual possession of the plot by that time.

However, as the judge said, the more difficult question is whether the defendant had the necessary animus possidendi. As to this, Mr Douglas accepted the correctness of the following statement (so far as it went) which I made in *Powell* v *McFarlane*, 38 P & CR 452, 471, 472:

> the animus possidendi involves the intention, in one's own name and on one's own behalf, to exclude the world at large, including the owner with the paper title if he be not himself the possessor, so far as is reasonably practicable and so far as the process of the law will allow.

At least at first sight the following observations of Lord Halsbury LC in *Marshall* v *Taylor* [1895] 1 Ch 641, 645, which were referred to by Hoffmann J in his judgment, are very pertinent to the present case:

> The true nature of this particular strip of land is that it is enclosed. It cannot be denied that the person who now says he owns it could not get to it in any ordinary way. I do not deny that he could have crept through the hedge, or, if it had been a brick wall, that he could have climbed over the wall; but that was not the ordinary

and usual mode of access. That is the exclusion — the dispossession — which seems to me to be so important in this case.

As a number of authorities indicate, enclosure by itself prima facie indicates the requisite animus possidendi. As Cockburn CJ said in *Seddon* v *Smith* (1877) 36 LT 168, 169: 'Enclosure is the strongest possible evidence of adverse possession.' Russell LJ in *George Wimpey & Co. Ltd* v *Sohn* [1967] Ch 487, 511A, similarly observed: 'Ordinarily, of course, enclosure is the most cogent evidence of adverse possession and of dispossession of the true owner.' While Mr Douglas pointed out that the plot was always accessible from the north where no boundary demarcation existed, it was only accessible from the defendant's own property, Dolphin Place. In my judgment, therefore, he must be treated as having enclosed it.

Mr Douglas, however, submitted that even if enclosure had occurred, the defendant's intention must be assessed in the light of the particular circumstances of this case. The defendant knew that the council had acquired and retained the plot with the specific intention of building a road across it at some future time. The council had no use for the land in the interim. It was for all practical purposes waste land. None of the defendant's acts, he submitted, were inconsistent with the council's known future intentions. He invoked, inter alia, the words of Cockburn CJ in *Leigh* v *Jack*, 5 ExD 264, 271, which, he submitted, applied in the present case:

> I do not think that any of the defendant's acts were done with the view of defeating the purpose of the parties to the conveyances; his acts were those of a man who did not intend to be a trespasser, or to infringe upon another's right. The defendant simply used the land until the time should come for carrying out the object originally contemplated.

If the defendant had stopped short of placing a new lock and chain on the gate, I might perhaps have felt able to accept these submissions. . . . I agree with the judge in his saying (1988) LGR 472, 479:

> . . . I do not think that if the council, on making an inspection, had found the gate newly padlocked, they could have come to any conclusion other than that [the defendant] was intending to exclude everyone, including themselves, from the land.

The other main point which Mr Douglas has argued in support of this appeal has caused me slightly more difficulty. In his submission there can be no sufficient animus possidendi to constitute adverse possession for the purpose of the Act of 1980 unless there exists the intention to exclude the owner with the paper title in *all* future circumstances. The defendant's oral statements to Mr Harris in the conversation of 10 November 1975, as recorded in the attendance note, do appear to have constituted an implicit acknowledgment by the defendant that he would be obliged to leave the plot if in the future the council required it for the purpose of constructing the proposed new road. The letter of 18 December 1975, which I have concluded should be admitted in evidence, contains an express acknowledgment of this nature. If the intention to exclude the owner with the paper title in all future circumstances is a necessary constituent of the animus possidendi, the attendance note and the letter of 18 December 1975 show that this constituent was absent in the present case.

There are some dicta in the authorities which might be read as suggesting that an intention to *own* the land is required. Sir Nathaniel Lindly MR, for example, in *Littledale* v *Liverpool College* [1900] 1 Ch 19, 23, referred to the 'acts of ownership' relied upon by the plaintiffs. Russell LJ in *George Wimpey & Co. Ltd* v *Sohn* [1967] Ch 487, 510, said:

... I am not satisfied that the actions of the predecessors in bricking up the doorway and maintaining a lock on the gate to the roadway were necessarily referable to an intention to occupy the [land] as their own absolute property.

At one point in my judgment in *Powell* v *McFarlane*, 38 P & CR 452, 478, I suggested:

> any objective informed observer might probably have inferred that the plaintiff was using the land simply for the benefit of his family's cow or cows, during such periods as the absent owner took no steps to stop him, without any intention to appropriate the land as his own.

Nevertheless, I agree with the judge that 'what is required for this purpose is not an intention to own or even at intention to acquire ownership but an intention to possess' — that is to say, an intention for the time being to possess the land to the exclusion of all other persons, including the owner with the paper title. No authorities cited to us establish the contrary proposition. The conversation with Mr Harris, as recorded in the attendance note and the letter of 18 December 1975, to my mind demonstrate the intention of the defendant for the time being to continue in possession of the plot to the exclusion of the council unless and until the proposed by-pass is built. The form of the conveyance to the defendant and of the contemporaneous statutory declaration which he obtained from Mr and Mrs Wall, are, of course entirely consistent with the existence of an intention on his part to take and keep adverse possession of the plot, at least unless and until that event occurred.

In the light of the line of authorities to which we have been referred, beginning with *Leigh* v *Jack*, 5 ExD 264, I have already accepted that the court should be slow to make a finding of adverse possession in a case such as the present. However, as the judge pointed out, in none of those earlier cases, where the owner with the paper title successfully defended his title, was there present the significant feature of complete enclosure of the land in question by the trespasser. On the evidence in the present case he was, in my judgment, right in concluding that the defendant had acquired adverse possession of the plot by 28 October 1973 and had remained in adverse possession of it ever since. There is no evidence that any representative of the council has even set foot on the plot since that date.

This appeal, which has been well argued on both sides, should in my judgment be dismissed.

Notes

1. See *Marsden* v *Miller*, LEXIS, 16 January 1992, where Scott LJ said:

> It is well-established that in order to obtain or to retain possession of land both a mental element and a factual element are requisite. The factual element must involve an appropriate degree of exclusive physical control. The mental elements, the so-called *animus possidendi*, must consist of an intention to take possession to the exclusion of all others . . .

Scott LJ therefore approved Slade LJ in *Powell* v *McFarlane* 38 P & CR 452 (see page 128).

2. Ferris J in *Colchester Borough Council* v *Smith* [1991] 2 All ER 29 at first instance approved Slade LJ in *Buckinghamshire CC* v *Moran* [1989] 3 WLR 152 (see page 128 *et seq.*).

3. See *Colchester Borough Council* v *Smith* [1992] 2 All ER 561 (CA). At some time between 1958 and 1960 D was granted a tenancy of a 3 acre plot of land by P. D used the land for agricultural purposes and, without P's permission, extended his agricultural activities to adjoining land that P owned. In March 1967 D wrote to P asking if he would re-let the land to him. P refused to do this, but said D could stay on the land without charge until December 1967 so long as he would leave the land on short notice. P said that a tenancy might also be available from the end of the year. In 1973 P notified D that contractors were to enter the land. In 1974 P acquired more land and D started to use it.

In 1982 P challenged D's right to use the land and D claimed to have rights over the land not forming part of the original tenancy, by means of adverse possession. In 1983 P and D entered into an agreement whereby D, by means of Clause 4 said that he was in possession of the land not forming part of the original tenancy by means of a bare licence or tenancy at will and that he had not obtained the land by means of adverse possession. Held: the agreement was a compromise agreement made between P and D which was entered into to resolve the dispute between them. The agreement had not been entered into under undue influence and had been made in good faith and was therefore binding on D.

4. See J. Martin, [1988] Conv 357, for a commentary on the recent cases in the area of adverse possession.

Questions
1. What effect does the decision in *Buckinghamshire CC* v *Moran* have on a squatter's claim to a disputed piece of land? (See Gerard McCormack, 'Adverse possession — the future enjoyment fallacy' [1989] Conv 211.)
2. Is the decision in *Colchester Borough Council* v *Smith* reconcilable with s. 17 of the Limitation Act 1980?

B: FUTURE INTERESTS

Limitation Act 1980

15. Time limit for actions to recover land
 (2) Subject to the following provisions of this section, where—
  (a) the estate or interest claimed was an estate or interest in reversion or remainder or any other future estate or interest and the right of action to recover the land accrued on the date on which the estate or interest fell into possession by the determination of the preceding estate or interest; and
  (b) the person entitled to the preceding estate or interest (not being a term of years absolute) was not in possession of the land on that date;
no action shall be brought by the person entitled to the succeeding estate or interest after the expiration of twelve years from the date on which the right of action accrued to the person entitled to the preceding estate or interest or six years from the date on which the right of action accrued to the person entitled to the succeeding estate or interest, whichever period last expires.

 (3) Subsection (2) above shall not apply to any estate or interest which falls into possession on the determination of an entailed interest and which might have been barred by the person entitled to the entailed interest.

(4) No person shall bring an action to recover any estate or interest in land under an assurance taking effect after the right of action to recover the land had accrued to the person by whom the assurance was made or some person through whom he claimed or some person entitled to a preceding estate or interest, unless the action is brought within the period during which the person by whom the assurance was made could have brought such an action.

(5) Where any person is entitled to any estate or interest in land in possession and, while so entitled, is also entitled to any future estate or interest in that land, and his right to recover the estate or interest in possession is barred under this Act, no action shall be brought by that person, or by any person claiming through him, in respect of the future estate or interest, unless in the meantime possession of the land has been recovered by a person entitled to an intermediate estate or interest.

(6) Part I of Schedule 1 to this Act contains provisions for determining the date of accrual of rights of action to recover land in the cases there mentioned.

Schedule 1

Accrual of right of action in case of future interests

4. The right of action to recover any land shall, in a case where—
    (a) the estate or interest claimed was an estate or interest in reversion or remainder or any other future estate or interest; and
    (b) no person has taken possession of the land by virtue of the estate or interest claimed;
be treated as having accrued on the date on which the estate or interest fell into possession by the determination of the preceding estate or interest.

C: FORFEITURE OR BREACH OF CONDITION

Limitation Act 1980

Schedule 1

Accrual of right of action in case of forfeiture or breach of condition

7.—(1) Subject to sub-paragraph (2) below, a right of action to recover land by virtue of a forfeiture or breach of condition shall be treated as having accrued on the date on which the forfeiture was incurred or the condition broken.

(2) If any such right has accrued to a person entitled to an estate or interest in reversion or remainder and the land was not recovered by virtue of that right, the right of action to recover the land shall not be treated as having accrued to that person until his estate or interest fell into possession, as if no such forfeiture or breach of condition had occurred.

D: SETTLED LAND AND LAND HELD ON TRUST

Limitation Act 1980

18. Settled land and land held on trust

(1) Subject to section 21(1) and (2) of this Act, the provisions of this Act shall apply to equitable interests in land, including interests in the proceeds of the sale of land held upon trust for sale, as they apply to legal estates.

Accordingly a right of action to recover the land shall, for the purposes of this Act but not otherwise, be treated as accruing to a person entitled in possession to such an equitable interest in the like manner and circumstances, and on the same date, as it would accrue if his interest were a legal estate in the land (and any relevant provision of Part I of Schedule 1 to this Act shall apply in any such case accordingly).

(2) Where the period prescribed by this Act has expired for the bringing of an action to recover land by a tenant for life or a statutory owner of settled land—

    (a) his legal estate shall not be extinguished if and so long as the right of action to recover the land of any person entitled to a beneficial interest in the land either has not accrued or has not been barred by this Act; and

    (b) the legal estate shall accordingly remain vested in the tenant for life or statutory owner and shall devolve in accordance wih the Settled Land Act 1925;

but if and when every such right of action has been barred by this Act, his legal estate shall be extinguished.

(3) Where any land is held upon trust (including a trust for sale) and the period prescribed by this Act has expired for the bringing of an action to recover the land by the trustees, the estate of the trustees shall not be extinguished if and so long as the right of action to recover the land of any person entitled to a beneficial interest in the land or in the proceeds of sale either has not accrued or has not been barred by this Act; but if and when every such right of action has been so barred the estate of the trustees shall be extinguished.

(4) Where—

    (a) any settled land is vested in a statutory owner; or

    (b) any land is held upon trust (including a trust for sale);

an action to recover the land may be brought by the statutory owner or trustees on behalf of any person entitled to a beneficial interest in possession in the land or in the proceeds of sale whose right of action has not been barred by this Act, notwithstanding that the right of action of the statutory owner or trustees would apart from this provision have been barred by this Act.

Actions in respect of trust property or the personal estate of deceased persons

21. Time limit for actions in respect of trust property

(1) No period of limitation prescribed by this Act shall apply to an action by a beneficiary under a trust, being an action—

    (a) in respect of any fraud or fraudulent breach of trust to which the trustee was a party or privy; or

    (b) to recover from the trustee trust property or the proceeds of trust property in the possession of the trustee, or previously received by the trustee and converted to his use.

(2) Where a trustee who is also a beneficiary under the trust receives or retains trust property or its proceeds as his share on a distribution of trust property under the trust, his liability in any action brought by virtue of subsection (1)(b) above to recover that property or its proceeds after the expiration of the period of limitation prescribed by this Act for bringing an action to recover trust property shall be limited to the excess over his proper share.

This subsection only applies if the trustee acted honestly and reasonably in making the distribution.

(3) Subject to the preceding provisions of this section, an action by a beneficiary to recover trust property or in respect of any breach of trust, not being an action for which a period of limitation is prescribed by any other provision of this Act, shall not be brought after the expiration of six years from the date on which the right of action accrued.

For the purposes of this subsection, the right of action shall not be treated as having accrued to any beneficiary entitled to a future interest in the trust property until the interest fell into possession.

Schedule 1

Possession of beneficiary not adverse to others interested in settled land or land held on trust for sale

9. Where any settled land or any land held on trust for sale is in the possession of a person entitled to a beneficial interest in the land or in the proceeds of sale (not being a person solely or absolutely entitled to the land or the proceeds), no right of action to recover the land shall be treated for the purposes of this Act as accruing during that possession to any person in whom the land is vested as tenant for life, statutory owner or trustee, or to any other person entitled to a beneficial interest in the land or the proceeds of sale.

E: TENANCIES AND LEASEHOLDS

(a) Reversioner on a lease

Time never runs against the reversioner until the lease expires. For example, X grants Y a 50-year lease of Blackacre and Y is dispossessed by Z. The 12-year period begins to run against Y from date he is dispossessed, but against X from the date the lease determines. Z can therefore retain the land against Y for the rest of the term, but X can recover it from Z at the end of the term or within 12 years of that date.

(b) Tenant

A tenant cannot claim the freehold title of the land he occupies against his landlord during the term of the lease, because he occupies the land with permission and in accordance with the terms of the lease.

Smirk v Lyndale Developments Ltd
[1975] 1 Ch 317 (CA)

P occupied a house under a weekly service tenancy commencing in 1955, the house belonging to P's employers. The terms of the tenancy were set out in a rentbook. The plaintiff began to cultivate adjoining land which also belonged to the employers. This was done without their permission. In 1967, the house and land were bought by the defendants who issued the plaintiff with a new rentbook. The defendants began to develop the land in 1973 and the plaintiff sought a declaration that he had a good possessory title to the land, or alternatively that he held the land as an extension of the locus of his tenancy. Held:

(1) (agreeing with Pennycuick V-C) the plaintiff had occupied the land by way of an addition to the tenancy of his house;

(2) (reversing Pennycuick V-C) the purchase of the land and the handing over of a new rentbook were wholly ineffective to operate as a surrender and regrant of the lease.

PENNYCUICK V-C [on the first point only in the Chancery Division of the High Court]: . . . I turn now to the law applicable where a tenant takes possession of adjoining land — a tenant, during the currency of his tenancy, who takes possession of adjoining land belonging to his landlord. The law on this point, if I may respectfully say so, has got into something of a tangle.

I will refer first to *Kingsmill* v *Millard* (1855) 11 Exch 313 [Pennycuick V-C quotes from Parke B's judgment] . . .

It will be observed that in his judgment Parke B in terms states that the presumption that the tenant has inclosed for the benefit of the landlord applies, irrespective of whether the inclosed land is part of the waste or belongs to the landlord; and indeed he uses the word 'encroachment' as appropriate in either case. He then goes on to state in terms, following and agreeing what Alderson B said in the course of the argument, that in order to displace the presumption there must be communication to the landlord. That decision of high authority seems to me to be in accordance with justice and common sense, and unless I were compelled to do otherwise by subsequent authority, I would certainly adopt it. I should add, as is perhaps obvious, as appears in some of the later cases, that the presumption may be rebutted by any form of express or implied agreement or, in some cases, as Parke B says, by estoppel.

The next case is *Whitmore* v *Humphries* (1871) LR 7 CP 1, where Willes J says, at pp. 4–5:

> This case raises a question upon a branch of the law which involves considerations of some nicety. By the rule of law applicable to this subject the landlord is entitled at the determination of the tenancy to recover from the tenant, not only the land originally demised, but also any land which the tenant may have added to it by encroachment from the waste, such encroachment being deemed to be made by him as tenant as an addition to his holding, and consequently for the benefit of his landlord, unless it is made under circumstances which show an intention to hold it for his own benefit alone, and not as part of his holding under the landlord. This rule undoubtedly applies when the encroachment is made over land belonging to the landlord, and no inquiry appears ever to have been made in such cases, whether it was made with the consent of the landlord or not. . . . The rule, however, goes further than this. It is not confined to cases where the encroachment is upon land to which the landlord is entitled, it applies to cases where the land encroached upon does not belong to the landlord . . .

and he then goes on to deal with the position where the encroachment is upon land to which the landlord is not entitled. Willes J continues, at p. 5:

> The rule is based upon the obligation of the tenant to protect his landlord's rights, and to deliver up the subject of his tenancy in the same condition, fair wear and tear excepted, as that in which he enjoyed it. There is often great temptation and opportunity afforded to the tenant to take in adjoining land which may or may not be his landlord's and it is considered more convenient and more in accordance with the rights of property that the tenant who has availed himself of the opportunity afforded him by his tenancy to make encroachments, should be presumed to have intended to make them for the benefit of the reversioner, except under circumstances pointing to an intention to take the land for his own benefit exclusively. . . . The reason of the rule . . . appears to be quite independent of the question, whether the encroachment was made with the assent of the landlord.

. . .

Then comes *Tabor* v *Godfrey* (1895) 64 LJQB 245. The headnote runs as follows:

> The tenant under a lease for years encroached upon and occupied a piece of land belonging to his landlord and adjoining the demised premises for a period of more

Acquisition of Land: Adverse Possession

than twelve years. The landlord during the term brought an action for an injunction and damages for trespass:— *Held*, that the action would not lie. The tenant must be deemed to have occupied the piece of ground as part of the holding, and he was entitled so to occupy it during the remainder of his lease.

. . .

So far there is no difficulty on the authorities. [Pennycuick V-C then discusses the cases which are inconsistent with *Kingsmill*, namely *Lord Hastings* v *Saddler* (1898) 79 LT 355 and *J F Perrott & Co. Ltd* v *Cohen* [1951] KB 705.]

. . .

Having been through the authorities I propose, as I have said earlier, to adopt and apply the principle laid down in *Kingsmill* v *Millard*, 11 Exch 313.

To return to the present case, there is nothing on the facts which could in any way rebut the presumption, which it seems to me is applicable here, namely, that the tenant, the plaintiff, was occupying the plots by way of an addition to land comprised with his tenancy, and not otherwise adversely to the landlord. I need only add on this point that if, contrary to my view, the unilateral intention of the plaintiff was relevant, the plaintiff's very candid evidence of intention would be fatal to his own case.

(c) Non-payment of rent

Limitation Act 1980

19. Time limit for actions to recover rent
No action shall be brought, or distress made, to recover arrears of rent, or damages in respect of arrears of rent, after the expiration of six years from the date on which the arrears become due.

Note
There is no effect on the landlord's title to the land.

(d) Rights of re-entry
See Limitation Act 1980, sch. 1 para. 7(2), at page 133.

Limitation Act 1980

38. Interpretation
(7) References in this Act to a right of action to recover land shall include references to a right to enter into possession of the land or, in the case of rentcharges and tithes, to distrain for arrears of rent or tithe, and references to the bringing of such an action shall include references to the making of such an entry or distress.

(e) Periodic tenancies
See Limitation Act 1980, sch. 1, para. 5.

Hayward v *Chaloner*
[1968] 1 QB 107 (CA)

In 1939, the rector of a parish entered into an oral tenancy to rent some land for 10s a year. The land was used as an addition to a garden. From 1942 onwards the landlords did not insist on the payment of rent. In 1955, the plaintiffs purchased the disputed land and some other land. In 1966, the defendant, who was the incumbent rector, claimed title to the land under the Limitation Act 1939. Held: (Lord Denning MR dissenting), the rector had established an unassailable possessory title to the disputed land.

RUSSELL LJ: Section 4(3) of the Limitation Act, 1939, enacts that no action shall be brought by any person to recover any land after the expiration of twelve years from the date on which the right of action accrued to him or to a person through whom he claims. Section 9(2) provides that if there is a periodic tenancy not in writing, the tenancy shall be deemed (for the purposes of the Limitation Act) to be determined at the expiration of the first such period, and accordingly the right of action of the person entitled shall be deemed to have accrued at the date of such deemed determination: but if rent is received after such deemed determination, the right of action is deemed to have accrued on the date of the last receipt of rent.

In the present case there was a periodic tenancy, not in writing: the last payment of rent was in May, 1942, by the then rector, Mr McCormick, so that the right of action must by section 9(2) for the purposes of the Limitation Act be deemed to have then accrued, and the plaintiffs' action in 1966 to recover possession was clearly forbidden by section 4(3). . . .

I have no doubt that for this purpose the possession of a tenant is to be considered adverse once the period covered by the last payment of rent has expired so that section 10(1) does not bear further upon section 9(2). Nor do I doubt the applicability of section 9(2) to the present case just because the freeholders were content that the rector should not pay his rent and did not bother to ask for it for all those years. In *Moses* v *Lovegrove* [1952] 2 QB 533, in this court it was assumed on all hands that when section 9 apparently operates, adverse possession starts: see especially Lord Evershed, and Romer LJ ibid. 538–540, 543. The principle clearly accepted was that once the period covered by the last payment of rent expired, the tenant ceased to be regarded by the Limitation Acts as the tenant. This case was not cited to the county court judge. A similar assumption was made in *Nicholson* v *England* [1926] 2 KB 93, under the then existing principles which section 10(1) was designed to embody. Textbooks to the same effect include Cheshire's Modern Law of Real Property, 9th edn. (1962), pp. 797, 798; Megarry & Wade's Textbook of the Law of Real Property, 3rd edn. (1966), p. 1010: and Preston & Newsom on Limitation of Actions, 3rd edn. (1953), p. 89. I am not aware that the contrary view has been anywhere expressed, and in my judgment the cases relied upon by the county court judge of *Leigh* v *Jack* (1879) 5 ExD 264, and *Williams Bros. Direct Supply Ltd* v *Raftery* [1958] 1 QB 159 have no bearing on a question arising under section 9(2) of the Act. In my judgment, therefore, a possessory title has been acquired to this property.

F: MORTGAGES

Limitation Act 1980

16. Time limit for redemption actions
When a mortgagee of land has been in possession of any of the mortgaged land for a period of twelve years, no action to redeem the land of which the mortgagee has been so in possession shall be brought after the end of that period by the mortgagor or any person claiming through him.

29. Fresh accrual of action on acknowledgment or part payment

(1) Subsections (2) and (3) below apply where any right of action (including a foreclosure action) to recover land ... or any right of a mortgagee of personal property to bring a foreclosure action in respect of the property has accrued.

(2) If the person in possession of the land, benefice or personal property in question acknowledges the title of the person to whom the right of action has accrued—

(a) the right shall be treated as having accrued on and not before the date of the acknowledgment; and

(b) in the case of a right of action to recover land which has accrued to a person entitled to an estate or interest taking effect on the determination of an entailed interest against whom time is running under section 27 of this Act, section 27 shall thereupon cease to apply to the land.

(3) In the case of a foreclosure or other action by a mortgagee, if the person in possession of the land, benefice or personal property in question or the person liable for the mortgage debt makes any payment in respect of the debt (whether of principal or interest) the right shall be treated as having accrued on and not before the date of the payment.

(4) Where a mortgagee is by virtue of the mortgage in possession of any mortgaged land and either—

(a) receives any sum in respect of the principal or interest of the mortgage debt; or

(b) acknowledges the title of the mortgagor, or his equity of redemption;

an action to redeem the land in his possession may be brought at any time before the expiration of twelve years from the date of the payment or acknowledgment.

(5) Subject to subsection (6) below, where any right of action has accrued to recover —

(a) any debt or other liquidated pecuniary claim; or

(b) any claim to the personal estate of a deceased person or to any share or interest in any such estate;

and the person liable or accountable for the claim acknowledges the claim or makes any payment in respect of it the right shall be treated as having accrued on and not before the date of the acknowledgment or payment.

(6) A payment of a part of the rent or interest due at any time shall not extend the period for claiming the remainder then due, but any payment of interest shall be treated as a payment in respect of the principal debt.

(7) Subject to subsection (6) above, a current period of limitation may be repeatedly extended under this section by further acknowledgments or payments, but a right of action, once barred by this Act, shall not be revived by any subsequent acknowledgment or payment.

G: POSTPONEMENT OF PERIOD

(a) Disability

Limitation Act 1980

28. Extension of limitation period in case of disability

(1) Subject to the following provisions of this section, if on the date when any right of action accrued for which a period of limitation is prescribed by this Act, the person to whom it accrued was under a disability, the action may be brought at any time before the expiration of six years from the date when he ceased to be under a disability or died (whichever first occurred) notwithstanding that the period of limitation has expired.

(2) This section shall not affect any case where the right of action first accrued to some person (not under a disability) through whom the person under a disability claims.

(3) When a right of action which has accrued to a person under a disability accrues, on the death of that person while still under a disability, to another person under a disability, no further extension of time shall be allowed by reason of the disability of the second person.

(4) No action to recover land or money charged on land shall be brought by virtue of this section by any person after the expiration of thirty years from the date on which the right of action accrued to that person or some person through whom he claims.

38. Interpretation

(2) For the purposes of this Act a person shall be treated as under a disability while he is an infant, or of unsound mind.

(3) For the purposes of subsection (2) above a person is of unsound mind if he is a person who, by reason of mental disorder within the meaning of the Mental Health Act 1983 is incapable of managing and administering his property and affairs.

(b) Fraud, concealment and mistake

Limitation Act 1980

32. Postponement of limitation period in case of fraud, concealment or mistake

(1) Subject to subsection (3) below, where in the case of any action for which a period of limitation is prescribed by this Act, either—
   (a) the action is based upon the fraud of the defendant; or
   (b) any fact relevant to the plaintiff's right of action has been deliberately concealed from him by the defendant; or
   (c) the action is for relief from the consequences of a mistake;
the period of limitation shall not begin to run until the plaintiff has discovered the fraud, concealment or mistake (as the case may be) or could with reasonable diligence have discovered it.

References in this subsection to the defendant include references to the defendant's agent and to any person through whom the defendant claims and his agent.

(2) For the purposes of subsection (1) above, deliberate commission of a breach of duty in circumstances in which it is unlikely to be discovered for some time amounts to deliberate concealment of the facts involved in that breach of duty.

(3) Nothing in this section shall enable any action—
   (a) to recover, or recover the value of, any property; or
   (b) to enforce any charge against, or set aside any transaction affecting, any property;
to be brought against the purchaser of the property or any person claiming through him in any case where the property has been purchased for valuable consideration by an innocent third party since the fraud or concealment or (as the case may be) the transaction in which the mistake was made took place.

(4) A purchaser is an innocent third party for the purposes of this section—
   (a) in the case of fraud or concealment of any fact relevant to the plaintiff's right of action, if he was not a party to the fraud or (as the case may be) to the concealment of that fact and did not at the time of the purchase know or have reason to believe that the fraud or concealment had taken place; and

(b) in the case of mistake, if he did not at the time of the purchase know or have reason to believe that the mistake had been made.

Notes
1. It is thought that the term 'fraud' in the Limitation Act 1980 bears its usual meaning and necessarily implies dishonesty, whereas the term 'deliberate concealment' is something less than fraud and may be said to apply whenever the conduct of the defendant or his agent has been such as to hide from the plaintiff the existence of his right of action, in such circumstances that it would be inequitable to allow the defendant to rely on the lapse of time as a bar to the claim' (per Denning MR in *Applegate* v *Moss* [1971] 1 QB 406, at p. 413, when discussing the meaning of 'fraudulent concealment', the corresponding provision in the Limitation Act 1939).
2. The provisions of s. 32(1)(c) apply only 'where the mistake is an essential ingredient of the cause of action' (per Pearson J in *Phillips-Higgins* v *Harper* [1954] 1 QB 411, at p. 419.

H: STARTING TIME RUNNING AFRESH

This can occur where there is:
(a) effective assertion by the owner of his rights;
(b) acknowledgement of the owner's rights;
(c) part payment of principal or interest by a person in possession or his agent.

Limitation Act 1980

30. Formal provisions as to acknowledgments and part payments
(1) To be effective for the purposes of section 29 of this Act, an acknowledgment must be in writing and signed by the person making it.

31. Effect of acknowledgment or part payment on persons other than the maker or recipient
(1) An acknowledgment of the title to any land, benefice, or mortgaged personalty by any person in possession of it shall bind all other persons in possession during the ensuing period of limitation.
(2) A payment in respect of a mortgage debt by the mortgagor or any other person liable for the debt, or by any person in possession of the mortgaged property, shall, so far as any right of the mortgagee to foreclose or otherwise to recover the property is concerned bind all other persons in possession of the mortgaged property during the ensuing period of limitation.
(3) Where two or more mortgagees are by virtue of the mortgage in possession of the mortgaged land, an acknowledgment of the mortgagor's title or of his equity of redemption by one of the mortgagees shall only bind him and his successors and shall not bind any other mortgagee or his successors.
(4) Where in a case within subsection (3) above the mortgagee by whom the acknowledgment is given is entitled to a part of the mortgaged land and not to any ascertained part of the mortgage debt the mortgagor shall be entitled to redeem that part of the land on payment, with interest, of the part of the mortgage debt which bears

the same proportion to the whole of the debt as the value of the part of the land bears to the whole of the mortgaged land.

(5) Where there are two or more mortgagors, and the title or equity of redemption of one of the mortgagors is acknowledged as mentioned above in this section, the acknowledgment shall be treated as having been made to all the mortgagors.

(6) An acknowledgment of any debt or other liquidated pecuniary claim shall bind the acknowledgor and his successors but not any other person.

(7) A payment made in respect of any debt or other liquidated pecuniary claim shall bind all persons liable in respect of the debt or claim.

(8) An acknowledgment by one of several personal representatives of any claim to the personal estate of the deceased person or to any share or interest in any such estate, or a payment by one of several personal representatives in respect of any such claim, shall bind the estate of the deceased person.

(9) In this section 'successor', in relation to any mortgagee or person liable in respect of any debt or claim, means his personal representatives and any other person on whom the rights under the mortgage or, as the case may be, the liability in respect of the debt or claim devolve (whether on death or bankruptcy or the disposition of property or the determination of a limited estate or interest in settled property or otherwise).

Note
See s. 29 at page 139.

SECTION 3: THE NATURE OF THE INTEREST ACQUIRED

See J. A. Omotola, 'The nature of interest acquired by adverse possession of land under the Limitation Act 1939' (1973) 37 Conv 85; H. W. R. Wade, 'Real property — title in ejectment — possession' [1956] CLJ 177. Students may also find it useful to read the judgment of the High Court of Australia in *Allen v Roughley* [1956] 29 ALJ 603.

(a) Title of former owner

Limitation Act 1980

17. Extinction of title to land after expiration of time limit
Subject to—
    (a) section 18 of this Act; and
    (b) section 75 of the Land Registration Act 1925;
at the expiration of the period prescribed by this Act for any person to bring an action to recover land (including a redemption action) the title of that person to the land shall be extinguished.

Note
There are two exceptions to s. 17:

    (a) in the case of settled land or land held on a trust for sale, the trustees' title to the legal estate is not extinguished until the beneficiaries have been barred;

(b) in the case of registered land, see section 5 at page 149 *et seq.*

(b) Title of 'squatter'

The nature of the squatter's title was described by Lord Radcliffe in *Fairweather* v *St Marylebone Property Co. Ltd* [1963] AC 510, at p. 513:

He is not at any stage of his possession a successor to the title of the man he has dispossessed. He comes in and remains in always by right of possession, which in due course becomes incapable of disturbance as time exhausts the one or more periods allowed by statute for successful intervention. His title, therefore, is never derived through but arises always in spite of the dispossessed owner. At one time during the 19th century it was thought that section 34 of the Act of 1833 had done more than this and effected a statutory transfer of title from dispossessed to dispossessor at the expiration of the limitation period. There were eminent authorities who spoke of the law in just these terms. But the decision of the Court of Appeal in 1892 in *Tichborne* v *Weir* (1892) 67 LT 735 put an end to this line of reasoning by holding that a squatter who dispossessed a lessee and 'extinguished' his title by the requisite period of occupation did not become liable in covenant to the lessee's landlord by virtue of any privity of estate. The point was fully considered by the members of the court and they unanimously rejected the idea that the effect of the limitation statute was to make a 'Parliamentary conveyance' of the dispossessed lessee's title or estate to the dispossessing squatter.

In my opinion this principle has been settled law since the date of that decision. It formed the basis of the later decision of the Divisional Court in *Taylor* v *Twinberrow* [1930] 2 KB 16, 23. I think that this statement needs only one qualification: a squatter does in the end get a title by his possession and the indirect operation of the Act and he can convey a fee simple.

(c) Third party rights

In re Nisbet and Potts' Contract
[1906] 1 Ch 386 (CA)

The facts of this case appear at page 404.

ROMER LJ: . . . I think that with regard to a subsequent squatter, dealing in the first place with the time before that squatter has acquired any statutory right by lapse of time, inasmuch as he could not say he was a purchaser of a legal estate without notice, he would be bound by the covenant during his squatting, and accordingly the covenant, if he sought to break it, could be enforced against him at the instance and on behalf of the covenantee.

Now that being, in my opinion, the position of the squatter before he has acquired a statutory right under the Statute of Limitations, let me consider what would be the position of a squatter after a twelve years' occupation under the statute. By that occupation he has no doubt acquired a statutory title as against the covenantor or the heirs or assigns of the land of the covenantor who during those twelve years has, or have been, so remiss as not to eject him; but he does not thereby of necessity become entitled to hold the land free from the obligation of the negative covenant. That obligation is one existing against the title of the true owner of the land. The right of the true owner to the land has, no doubt, gone as against the successful squatter, who has acquired a title against him under the statute, but the original equitable right of the covenantee still exists. It was not a right that could be barred by the operation of the Statute of Limitations in favour of the statutory squatting owner.... the covenantee would, in my opinion, be no more barred by the operation of the Statute of Limitations by not taking proceedings against the squatter during the twelve years than he would have been barred by not taking proceedings against the true owner, had that true owner remained in possession during that period.

(d) **Dispossession of lease**

Fairweather v *St Marylebone Property Co. Ltd*
[1963] AC 510 (HL)

The freehold owner of two adjoining properties, Nos 311 and 315, built a shed in the back gardens. Three-quarters of the shed was in the garden of No. 315 and the entrance and rest of the shed was in No. 311. In 1894 both properties were let by separate 99-year leases. M, who was the sub-lessee of No. 311, used the shed as his own and it was conceded that the occupation was adverse to the occupier of No. 315. M acquired title to the shed by adverse possession against the tenants of No. 315 by 1932. In 1951, M sub-let No. 311 to P for a term of 21 years. In 1958, M bought the freehold to No. 315 subject to the 99-year lease. That lease was subsequently surrendered to them. In 1960, P assigned the remainder of his 21-year lease of No. 311 to the appellant. F, the respondents, claimed possession of the part of the shed in their garden. The appellant claimed the respondents were not entitled to possession until the 99-year lease expired. Held: (Lord Morris of Borth-y-Gest dissenting) the respondents were entitled to possession.

LORD DENNING: It is quite clear from the Statutes of Limitation that in the year 1932 the 'title' of the leaseholder to the land was 'extinguished.' What does this mean? There are four suggestions to consider.

The first suggestion is that the title of the leaseholder to the shed is extinguished completely, not only against the squatter, but also against the freeholder. So that the leasehold interest disappears altogether, and the freeholder becomes entitled to the land. I reject this suggestion completely.... The correct view is that the freehold is an estate in reversion within section 6(1) of the Act of 1939, and time does not run against the freeholder until the determination of the lease: see *Doe d. Davy* v *Oxenham* 7 M & W 131.

The second suggestion is that the title of the leaseholder to the shed is extinguished so far as the leaseholder is concerned — so that he is no longer entitled to the shed – but that the leasehold interest itself persists and is vested in the squatter. In other words, the squatter acquired a title which is 'commensurate' with the leasehold interest which has been extinguished. This suggestion was made in 1867 in the first edition of Darby and Bosanquet's book [Statutes of Limitation] at p. 390, and it was accepted in 1889 as correct by the court in Ireland in *Rankin* v *M'Murtry* (1889) 24 LR Ir 290. But it has since been disapproved. If it were correct, it would mean that the squatter, would be in the position of a statutory assignee of the shed, and he would by reason of privity of estate, be liable on the covenants and subject to the conditions of the lease. I reject this suggestion also: for the simple reason that the operation of the Statutes of Limitation is merely negative. It destroys the leaseholder's title to the land but does not vest it in the squatter. The squatter is not liable on the repairing covenants: see *Tichborne* v *Weir* 67 LT 735. Nor, when the leasehold is a tenancy from year to year, does he step into the shoes of the tenant so as to be himself entitled to six months' notice to quit: see *Taylor* v *Twinberrow* [1930] 2 KB 16.

The third suggestion is that the *title* of the leaseholder is extinguished but that his *estate* in the land is not. This is too fine a distinction for me. And so it was for Parliament. For Parliament itself uses the two words as if they meant the same: see section 16 of the Limitation Act, 1939, and section 75 of the Land Registration Act, 1925.

The fourth suggestion is that the title of the leaseholder to the shed is extinguished *as against the squatter*, but remains good as *against the freeholder*. This seems to me the only acceptable suggestion. If it is adopted, it means that time does not run against the freeholder until the lease is determined — which is only just. It also means that until that time the freeholder has his remedy against the leaseholder on the covenants, as he should have; and can also re-enter for forfeiture, as he should be able to do: see *Humphry* v *Damion* (1612) 3 CroJac 300, and can give notice to determine on a 'break' clause or notice to quit, as the case may be. Further, it means that if the leaseholder should be able to induce the squatter to leave the shed — or if the squatter quits and the leaseholder resumes possession — the leaseholder is at once in the same position as he was originally, being entitled to the benefits and subject to the burdens of the lease in regard to the shed. All this seems to me eminently reasonable but it can only be achieved if, despite the presence of the squatter, the title of the leaseholder remains good as against the freeholder.

On this footing it is quite apparent that at the date of the surrender, the leaseholder had something to surrender. He still had his title to the shed as against the freeholder and was in a position to surrender it to him. The maxim nemo dat quod non habet has no application to the case at all.

But there still remains the question: What was the effect of the surrender? There ar here two alternatives open:

(1) On the one hand, it may be said that the surrender operated to *determine* the term, just as a forfeiture does. If this is correct, it would mean that the freeholder would be entitled to possession at once as soon as the leaseholder surrendered the house. He could evict the squatter by virtue of his freehold estate against which the squatter could say nothing. And time would begin to run against the freeholder as soon as the surrender took place. This view is based on *Ecclesiastical Commissioners of England and Wales* v *Rowe* (1880) 5 App Cas 736, HL, and section 6(1) of the Limitation Act, 1939.

(2) On the other hand, it may be said that the surrender operated as an *assignment* by the leaseholder to the freeholder of the rest of the 99 years. If this is correct, it would mean that the freeholder could not evict the squatter because the freeholder would be 'claiming through' the leaseholder and would be barred for the rest of the 99 years, just as the leaseholder would be: see section 4(3) of the Limitation Act. Time would not begin to run against the freeholder until the 99 years expired. This view is based on *Walter* v *Yalden* [1902] 2 KB 304.

My Lords, I have come to the clear conclusion that a surrender operates as a determination of the term. It is not an assignment of it. I am aware that no less an authority than Lindley LJ once said that 'the surrender of the term only operated as an assignment of the surrenderor's interest in it': see *David* v *Sabin* [1893] 1 Ch 523, 533; 9 TLR 240, CA. But if that be true, it is not by any rule of the common law, only by force of statute: and then only in the case of underleases, not in the case of trespasser or squatter.

At common law, if a leaseholder made an underlease and afterwards surrendered his term to the freeholder, then the freeholder could not evict the underlessee during the term of the underlease: see *Pleasant (Lessee of Hayton)* v *Benson* (1811) 14 East 234. But this was not because there was any assignment from surrenderor to surrenderee. It is clear that, upon the surrender, the head term was determined altogether. It was extinguished completely, so much so that the freeholder could not sue the underlessee on the covenants or enforce the proviso for re-entry: see *Webb* v *Russell* (1789) 3 Term Rep 393. The underlessee could enjoy the property without payment of rent and without performance of the covenants and conditions until the end of the term of the underlease: see *Ecclesiastical Commissioners for England* v *Treemer* [1893] 1 Ch 166, 174; 9 TLR 78. This was remedied by the statutes of 1740 and 1845, which have been re-enacted in sections 139 and 150 of the Law of Property Act, 1925. Under those statutes, on a surrender of the head lease, an underlessee becomes a direct tenant of the freeholder on the terms of his underlease. So that the surrender does operate as if it were an assignment of the surrenderor's interest. But those statutes have no application to trespassers or squatters.

The question may be asked: why did the common law on a surrender protect the underlessee from eviction? The answer is to be found in Coke upon Littleton II, p. 338b, where it is said that 'having regard to the parties to the surrender, the estate is absolutely drowned... But having regard to strangers, who were not parties or privies thereunto, lest by a voluntary surrender they may receive prejudice touching any right or interest they had before the surrender, the estate surrendered hath in consideration of law a continuance.' This passage applies in favour of an underlessee so as to protect him from eviction during the term of his underlease: but it does not apply in favour of a trespasser. The reason for the difference is because the underlessee comes in under a grant from the lessee; and the lessee cannot, by a surrender, derogate from his own grant: see *Davenport's* case (1608) 8 Co Rep 144b and *Mellor* v *Watkins* (1874) LR 9 QB 400, 405, by Blackburn J. But a trespasser comes in by wrong and not by grant of the lessee. If the lessee surrenders his term, the freeholder is at once entitled to evict the trespasser for the simple reason that, on the surrender, the lease is determined, and there is no bar whatever to the freeholder recovering possession: see *Ecclesiastical Commissioners of England and Wales* v *Rowe* 5 App Cas 736. And I see no reason why the same reasoning should not apply even though, at the date of the surrender, the trespasser is a squatter who has been there more than 12 years. For, as against the freeholder, he is still a trespasser. The freeholder's right to possession does not arise until the lease is determined by the surrender. It then comes into being and time begins to run against him under section 6(1) of the Limitation Act, 1939.

The only reason, it seems to me, which can be urged against this conclusion is that it means that a squatter's title can be destroyed by the leaseholder and freeholder putting their heads together. It is said that they can by a surrender — or by a surrender and regrant — destroy the squatter's title completely and get rid of him. So be it. There is no way of preventing it. But I would point out that, if we were to deny the two of them this right, they could achieve the same result in another way. They could easily do it by the leaseholder submitting to a forfeiture. If the leaseholder chooses not to pay the rent, the freeholder can determine the lease under the proviso for re-entry. The squatter cannot stop him. He cannot pay the rent without the authority of the leaseholder. He cannot apply for relief against forfeiture. The squatter's title can thus be defeated by a forfeiture — or by a forfeiture and regrant — just as it can by a surrender — or by a surrender and regrant. So there is nothing in the point.

My Lords, so far as these questions under the Limitation Acts are concerned, I must say that I see no difference between a surrender or merger or a forfeiture. On each of those events the lease is determined and the freeholder is entitled to evict the squatter, even though the squatter has been on the land during the lease for more than 12 years: and on the determination of the lease, time then begins to run against the freeholder. It follows that, in my opinion, *Walter* v *Yalden* [1902] 2 KB 304 was wrongly decided and *Taylor* v *Twinberrow* [1930] 2 KB 16 was rightly decided.

One word about section 75(1) of the Land Registration Act, 1925. That point was not raised in the county court and its availability depends on facts which were not proved. I do not think it is open to the appellant here. But in any case I doubt if that puts registered land on a very different footing from unregistered land. It is machinery so as to apply the Limitation Acts to registered land but it does not alter the substantive position very materially. The registered leaseholder clearly remains liable on the covenants and subject to the conditions of the lease, including the proviso for re-entry: and I do not see why, on a surrender, the freeholder should not recover possession from a squatter, just as he can on a forfeiture. The freeholder has no notice of the trust in favour of the squatter and his interests are not to be prejudiced by the fact that the leasehold is registered. I say no more because the point is not available here. Suffice it to say that for the reasons I have given, I would dismiss this appeal.

Notes
1. Lord Morris, in his minority judgment, said that the tenant could not surrender what he did not have, namely, a right to immediate possession.
2. The decision in *Fairweather* v *St Marylebone Property Co. Ltd* has been criticised on the ground that a landlord relying on surrender must be claiming through the lessee and could not therefore prejudice the squatter's right to possession until the term had expired. See, in particular, H. W. R. Wade, 'Landlord, tenant, and squatter' (1962) 78 LQR 541.
3. The majority reasoning in this case has been expressly approved of in the case of *Tickner* v *Buzzacott* [1965] Ch 426.

SECTION 4: SUCCESSIVE SQUATTERS

(a) Where the squatter dies or transfers his interest to another before the lapse of the 12-year period

Asher v Whitlock
(1865) LR 1 QB 1 (Ct Exch Ch)

W inclosed some waste land in 1842 and some more adjoining land in 1850. He then built a cottage on the land and lived there until he died in 1860, occupying the inclosed land. The period of limitation at that time was 20 years. W devised the land to his wife as long as she should remain unmarried, with the remainder to his daughter in fee. W's widow and daughter resided at the property and D married the widow in 1861. All lived in the property but the daughter died in 1863 and the widow died shortly afterwards, leaving D in occupation alone. In 1865, the daughter's heir-at-law brought an action of ejectment against the defendant. Held: the plaintiff was entitled to recover the property.

COCKBURN LJ: . . . [A]s soon as the testator died, the estate became vested in the widow; and immediately on the widow's marriage the daughter had a right to possession; the defendant however anticipates her, and with the widow takes possession. But just as he had no right to interfere with the testator, so he had no right against the daughter, and had she lived she could have brought ejectment; although she died without asserting her right, the same right belongs to her heir. . . . On the simple ground that possession is good title against all but the true owner, I think the plaintiffs entitled to succeed, and that the rule should be discharged.

(b) Where the squatter abandons his possession and such possession is not taken by another

Limitation Act 1980

Schedule 1

8.—(2) Where a right of action to recover land has accrued and after its accrual, before the right is barred, the land ceases to be in adverse possession, the right of action shall no longer be treated as having accrued and no fresh right of action shall be treated as accruing unless and until the land is again taken into adverse possession.

(c) Where the squatter abandons his possession and after an interval of time possession is taken by a different squatter

In such a case it follows from the Limitation Act 1980, sch. 1, para. 8(2), that the time which has accrued to the original possessor would not be available for the subsequent possessor.

(d) Where there is a succession of squatters

Where a squatter dispossesses another squatter and the first squatter abandons his claim, then the second squatter can add the time enjoyed on the land by the first squatter to his own in order to achieve the 12 years necessary for adverse possession. See *Mount Carmel Investments Ltd* v *Peter Thurlow Ltd* [1988] 3 All ER 129, where Nicholls LJ said:

If squatter A is dispossessed by squatter B, squatter A can recover possession from squatter B and he has 12 years to do so, time running from his dispossesion. But squatter A may permit squatter B to take over the land in circumstances which, on ordinary principles of law, would preclude A from subsequently ousting B. For example, if A sells or gives his interest in the property, insecure as it may be, to B.

SECTION 5: ADVERSE POSSESSION AND REGISTERED LAND

Rights that are in the course of being acquired under the Limitation Act 1980 are overriding interests (see Land Registration Act 1925, s. 70(1)(f), at page 65). Thus anyone who purchases the registered estate from the proprietor will take the estate subject to the squatter's rights which will continue to run against the purchaser.

Once the squatter has been in possession for the necessary period, then the Land Registration Act 1925, s. 75 operates.

Land Registration Act 1925

75. Acquisition of title by possession

(1) The Limitation Acts shall apply to registered land in the same manner and to the same extent as those Acts apply to land not registered, except that where, if the land were not registered, the estate of the person registered as proprietor would be extinguished, such estate shall not be extinguished but shall be deemed to be held by the proprietor for the time being in trust for the person who, by virtue of the said Acts, has acquired title aganst any proprietor, but without prejudice to the estates and interests of any other person interested in the land whose estate or interest is not extinguished by those Acts.

(2) Any person claiming to have acquired a title under the Limitation Acts to a registered estate in the land may apply to be registered as proprietor thereof.

(3) The registrar shall, on being satisfied as to the applicant's title, enter the applicant as proprietor either with absolute, good leasehold, qualified, or possessory title, as the case may require, but without prejudice to any estate or interest protected by any entry on the register which may not have been extinguished under the Limitation Acts, and such registration shall, subject as aforesaid, have the same effect as the registration of a first proprietor; but the proprietor or the applicant or any other person interested may apply to the court for the determination of any question arising under this section.

(4) ...

(5) Rules may be made for applying (subject to any necessary modifications) the provisions of this section to cases where an easement, right or privilege has been acquired by prescription.

Spectrum Investment v Holmes
[1981] 1 WLR 221 (ChD)

A 99-year lease was made in 1902. D was a registered assignee of the lessee but by 1968 H had acquired a title by adverse possession against D under the Limitation Act 1939. He applied for and obtained registration as proprietor of the leasehold interest with possessory title. The title under which D was registered was then closed. In 1975, D purported to surrender the lease to S, the freeholder's successor in title, who was then the registered proprietor with absolute title to the freehold. S claimed possession against H. Held:

(1) D's title was closed, she was no longer the registered proprietor of the lease and was unable to surrender it. The term of the lease had vested in the defendant (H) and only she could dispose of it.

(2) D was not entitled to rectification of the register so as to reinstate herself as registered proprietor of the lease since the registrar had registered H's possessory title under the mandatory duty imposed on him by the Land Registration Act 1925, s. 75.

BROWNE-WILKINSON J: ... The plaintiff submits that the Land Registration Act 1925 introduces mere machinery for proving title to and transferring land and does not affect the substantive rights which parties enjoy under the general law. Accordingly, it is said that the rights of the plaintiff (as established by *St Marylebone Property Co.* v

Fairweather [1963] AC 510) must be reflected in the provisions of the Act of 1925 and are preserved by the words in section 11 which expressly provide that registration with possessory title 'shall not affect or prejudice the enforcement of any estate, right, or interest (whether in respect of the lessor's title or otherwise) adverse to or in derogation of' the proprietor with possessory title. So, it is said, having obtained a surrender of the lease from Mrs David, the plaintiff's right to possession as against the defendant is preserved.

There is in my judgment a short answer to the claim by the plaintiff. Accepting for the moment the broad proposition that the Act of 1925 was not intended to alter substantive rights, it undoubtedly was intended to alter the manner in which such rights were to be established and transferred. The surrender by Mrs David to the plaintiff is the linchpin of the plaintiff's claim. But in my judgment that surrender has not been effected by the only means authorised by the Land Registration Act 1925 for the disposal of a registered leasehold interest by act of the parties. At the date of the alleged surrender the lease was registered under title no. NGL 65073 in the name of the defendant. Mrs David was not registered as proprietor, her title no. LN 66166 having been taken off the register. By virtue of section 69(1) the effect of the registration of the defendant as proprietor of the lease was, as against Mrs David, to vest the term or deem it to be vested in the defendant.

Section 69(4) provides: 'The estate for the time being vested in the proprietor shall only be capable of being disposed of or dealt with by him in manner authorised by this Act.'

In my judgment the effect of these provisions is that, so long as the defendant is registered as proprietor of the lease, only she can dispose of it. Moreover by virtue of sections 21 and 22, even the defendant can only do so by a registered disposition. Accordingly, in my judgment there has, as yet, been no valid surrender of the lease and the plaintiff's claim fails in limine. . . .

For these reasons, in my judgment there has, as yet, been no surrender of the term by Mrs David to the plaintiff. Therefore, the plaintiff's claim fails since, so long as the term exists, it has no immediate right to possession. However, in order to determine the real issue between the parties I gave leave for Mrs David to be joined as co-plaintiff. If she is entitled to rectification of the register, she may therafter be able to execute the necessary registered surrender and, if she can, the plaintiff's claim to possession would be unanswerable.

Mr Charles's submissions for the defendant were very far-reaching. He submitted that the whole scheme of the Land Registration Act 1925 shows that the position of the squatter on registered land is totally different from that of a squatter on unregistered land as laid down by the House of Lords in *St Marylebone Property Co. Ltd* v *Fairweather* [1963] AC 510. He submits that section 75(2) makes it clear that the squatter who has obtained title against the documentary lessee is entitled to apply to be registered as proprietor of the documentary lessee's registered estate in the land, i.e. as proprietor of the lease itself. Section 75(3) then requires the registrar, if satisfied of the facts, to effect such registration. Accordingly it is said that what was done in the present case was quite correct: the defendant is rightly registered as proprietor of the lease itself. As a result, it is said, the legal term of years is vested in the defendant by a parliamentary conveyance contained in section 69 of the Act. By virtue of sections 9 and 11 of the Act the defendant as registered proprietor is deemed to have vested in her the possession of the leasehold interest, subject to the express and implied obligations in the lease and subject to any rights of the freeholder adverse to her interest. Therefore, Mr Charles submits, the scheme of the Land Registration Act 1925 is to produce exactly the result which the House of Lords held was not the result in relation to unregistered land, namely, to make the squatter the successor in title to the documentary lessee by parliamentary conveyance, the squatter taking subject to and with the benefit of the covenants in the lease.

This is a formidable and far reaching submission. But, on the other side I was strongly pressed with authority suggesting that squatter's rights were the same over both registered and unregistered land. In *St Marylebone Property Co. Ltd* v *Fairweather* [1963] AC 510 it emerged at a late stage in the proceedings that the land there in question was registered land. The squatter was not registered as proprietor of the lease, but contended that the provisions of section 75(1) of the Act (which makes the documentary lessee as registered proprietor a trustee for the squatter) prevented the documentary lessee from surrendering the term to the freeholder. It was not proved at what date the documentary lessee was registered, and on that ground it was held that section 75 had no application. But Lord Radcliffe said, at pp. 542–543:

> I do not think, therefore, that the appellant can succeed on this point. I only wish to add that at present I am not at all satisfied that section 75(1) does create a trust interest in the squatter of the kind that one would expect from the words used. So to hold would raise difficulties which I do not now explore; and the trust of the dispossessed owner's title under subsection (1) must somehow be reconciled with the provision under subsection (2) for the squatter to apply to register his own title, which would presumably be his independent possessory title acquired by the adverse possession.

To similar effect are the remarks of Sir John Pennycuick in *Jessamine Investment Co.* v *Schwartz* [1978] QB 264, 275:

> I should be very reluctant to introduce a substantive distinction in the application of a provision of the Limitation Act to registered land and unregistered land respectively, based upon what is plainly a conveyancing device designed to adapt that provision to the former class of land.

Although these are obiter dicta, they are obviously of some weight in supporting the contention that the position of a squatter does not vary according to whether the land is registered or unregistered.

Finally, the words of section 75(1) itself state that the Limitation Acts shall apply to registered land 'in the same manner and to the same extent' as it applies to unregistered land, and then goes on to state exceptions.

On the other hand, I take into account the recent decision of the House of Lords in *Williams & Glyn's Bank Ltd* v *Boland* (decided since the conclusion of the argument in this case) [1980] 3 WLR 138 which shows that, if the words of the Land Registration Act 1925 are clear, they are to be given their natural meaning and not distorted so as to seek to produce uniformity in the substantive law as between registered and unregistered land. I therefore approach this question on the basis that one would expect that substantive legal rights would be the same whether the land is registered or unregistered but that clear words in the Act of 1925 must be given their natural meaning even if this leads to a divergence.

I do not find it necessary to reach any conclusion on the far-reaching propositions which Mr Charles put forward, since I think that I can decide this case on quite a narrow ground, leaving it to others to resolve the more fundamental questions. In my judgment, if Mrs David is to succeed in any claim to have the defendant deleted from the register as proprietor of the lease, she (Mrs David) must show at least that the registration of the defendant was not a mandatory requirement of the provisions of the Land Registration Act 1925. It is clear from the references in section 75(3) that section

75 applies to a leasehold interest. Under section 75(3) the registrar is under a mandatory duty to register the squatter on the application made by the squatter under section 75(2) if the registrar is satisfied as to the squatter's title. For what does the squatter make application? I will read section 75(2) again: 'Any person claiming to have acquired a title under the Limitation Acts to a registered estate in the land may apply to be registered as proprietor thereof.'

To my mind the words are clear and unequivocal: the squatter claims to have acquired a title to 'a registered estate in the land' (i.e. the leasehold interest) and applies to be registered as a proprietor '*thereof*' (my emphasis). Therefore under section 75(2), references to the squatter having acquired title to a registered estate must include the rights which under the Limitation Act 1939 the squatter acquires in relation to leasehold interests. Section 75(2) then refers to the squatter applying to be registered as proprietor 'thereof.' This word can, in my judgment, only refer back to the registered estate in the land against which the squatter has acquired title under the Act of 1939, i.e. the leasehold interest. The clear words of the Act therefore seem to require that, once the 12 years have run, the squatter is entitled to be registered as proprietor of the lease itself, and is bound to be so registered if he applies for registration. It follows that in my judgment the defendant (as the squatter) is correctly registered as proprietor of the lease itself in accordance with the clear requirements of section 75. If that is right, Mrs David cannot be entitled to rectification of the register as against the defendant, and she can therefore never get into a position in which she is competent to surrender the lease to the plaintiff.

I am conscious that in so deciding I am reaching a conclusion which produces at least a limited divergence between squatter's rights over registered and unregistered land. Once the squatter is rightly registered as proprietor under section 75(3) the documentary lessee and the freeholder can no longer defeat the squatter's rights by a surrender. But I am not deciding anything as to the position during the period between the date when the squatter obtains his title by adverse possession and the date on which he obtains registration of it. This is the period covered by section 75(1) which is the subsection on which Lord Radcliffe in *St Marylebone Property Co. Ltd* v *Fairweather* [1963] AC 510, 542, and Sir John Pennycuick in *Jessamine Investment Co.* v *Schwartz* [1978] QB 264, 275, were commenting. It may well be, as their dicta suggest, that during the period preceding any registration of the squatter's rights, the documentary lessee (as registered proprietor of the lease) and the freeholder can deal with the legal estate without reference to a person whose rights are not recorded on the register. But once the Act provides for registration of the squatter's title, it must in my judgment follow that the squatter's rights (once registered) cannot be overriden. The difference between registered and unregistered land in this respect is an inevitable consequence of the fact that the Land Registration Act 1925 provides for registration of the squatter as proprietor and that registered proprietors have rights.

Note

In unregistered land the effect of adverse possession by the squatter against the tenant is to leave the relationship of landlord and tenant otherwise intact. If the tenant surrenders his lease to the landlord, the landlord is entitled to possession and can thus recover the land from the squatter. See the remarks of Sir John Pennycuick in *Jessamine Investments Co.* v *Schwartz* [1978] QB 264, at p. 275, quoted above.

Acquisition of Land: Adverse Possession

Questions
1. 'I only wish to add that at present I am not at all satisfied that s. 75(1) [of the Land Registration Act 1925] does create a trust interest in the squatter of the kind that one would expect from the words used.' Do you agree with Lord Radcliffe in *Fairweather* v *St Marylebone Property Co. Ltd*?
2. Have the courts followed Sir John Pennycuick's dicta in subsequent decisions?

See P. H. Kenny, 'Limitation and registered leases' [1982] Conv 201; Colin Sydenham, '*Spectrum Investment Co.* v *Holmes*' [1981] Conv 157; P. F. Smith, 'Limitation and the Land Registration Act 1925' (1981) 131 NLJ 718; E. G. Nugee, 'Limitation and the Land Registration Act' (1981) 131 NLJ 774.

Students may also find the following articles useful: M. Dockray, 'Adverse possession and intention' [1982] Conv 256, at p. 345; A. Everton, 'Built in a night . . .' (1971) 35 Conv 249; S. A. Wiren, 'The plea of the ius tertii in ejectment' (1925) 41 LQR 139; A. D. Hargreaves, 'Terminology and title in ejectment' (1940) 56 LQR 376; Mary Welstead, 'Proprietary estoppel and the acquisition of possessory title' [1991] Conv 280.

3. A recent Home Office Consultation Paper, 'Squatting', has suggested that in certain situations where there is unlawful occupation of property the criminal law should provide remedies in order to give adequate redress to dispossessed owners. Do you think that the criminal law should be employed in such a manner?

4. Compare and contrast the ways in which the law upholds the acquisition of property rights and title to land by long usage. (See chapter 12 and Michael Goodman, 'Active Possession or Prescription? Problems of Conflicts' (1968) 32 Conv 270.)

6 LEASEHOLD INTERESTS AND COVENANTS

SECTION 1: ESSENTIALS FOR A VALID LEASE

A lease is one of the two legal estates capable of subsisting in relation to land after 1925 (Law of Property Act 1925, s. 1(1) and (5)). In order to subsist as a legal estate, however, it must satisfy the definition of 'term of years absolute' in s. 205(1)(xxvii) of the Law of Property Act 1925 (see chapter 2). The effect of the grant of a leasehold estate is that the fee simple owner grants to the lessee, for a fixed period of time, the right to deal with the property as though he owns it absolutely, subject to certain conditions. Until the period of the lease ends the fee simple owner is not entitled to physical possession of the land, only the reversion on the lease. While the period of the lease endures both the landlord and the tenant can assign their interests in the land to third parties. When this is done the original landlord or tenant who assigned his interest no longer has any rights in the land or under the lease. The tenant of the land can also grant a sub-tenancy or sub-lease. Clearly the grant by the tenant must be for a term less than the tenant's existing interest under the lease.

In order for there to be a valid grant of a lease the following conditions must be fulfilled:

(a) The term and commencement date must be certain.
(b) Rent or some other monetary payment will usually be paid by the lessee or tenant.
(c) The lessee or tenant must enjoy exclusive possession of the premises.

A: THE TERM AND COMMENCEMENT DATE MUST BE CERTAIN

There are two aspects to this requirement before the lease can take effect:

(a) the date for the commencement of the lease must be either fixed or ascertainable; and
(b) the maximum duration must be either fixed or ascertainable.

Lace v *Chantler* [1944] 1 KB 368 (CA)

A tenancy was granted 'for the duration of the war'. Held: the lease was not valid, since although the date of the commencement was certain, the maximum duration of the lease was neither fixed nor ascertainable.

Note
A lease may be for a discontinuous period of time and still be valid — see *Cottage Holiday Associates* v *Customs and Excise Commissioners* [1983] 1 QB 735, where the lease was for one week a year, for 80 years on a time-share basis. It was held that this was a lease of a cottage for a discontinuous period of 80 years.

Prudential Assurance Co. Ltd v *London Residuary Body & Others* [1992] 3 WLR 279 (HL)

The owner (O) of a strip of land sold it to the council, who intended to use it to widen a road at a future date. The council in the meantime leased the land back to O. The terms in the memorandum of agreement said 'the tenancy shall continue until the . . . land is required by the council for the purposes of the widening of the road'.

The council at a later date decided not to widen the road and the reversion passed to D_1. O assigned the tenancy to P. D_1 served P with a notice to quit and then sold the land to D_2, D_3 and D_4.

Held: all lease and tenancy agreements must be created for a term which is of certain duration. The lease which was created in this case was for an uncertain period and therefore void.

The land was however held on a yearly tenancy, which came about because of the tenant's possession and payment of rent (see page 185 *et seq.*).

LORD TEMPLEMAN: A demise for years is a contract for the exclusive possession and profit of land for some determinate period. Such an estate is called a 'term'. Thus *Coke upon Littleton*, 19th ed. (1832), vol. I, para. 45b said that:

['Terminus'] in the understanding of the law does not only signify the limits and limitation of time, but also the estate and interest that passes for that time.

Blackstone's Commentaries, 1st ed. (1766), Book II, said, at p. 143:

Every estate which must expire at a period certain and prefixed, by whatever words created, is an estate for years. And therefore this estate is frequently called a term, *terminus*, because its duration or continuance is bounded, limited and determined: for every such estate must have a certain beginning, and certain end.

In *Say* v *Smith* (1563) 1 Plowd. 269 a lease for a certain term purported to add a term which was uncertain; the lease was held valid only as to the certain term. Anthony Brown J is reported to have said, at p. 272:

> every contract sufficient to make a lease for years ought to have certainty in three limitations, viz. in the commencement of the term, in the continuance of it, and in the end of it; so that all these ought to be known at the commencement of the lease, and words in a lease, which don't make this appear, are but babble . . . And these three are in effect but one matter, showing the certainty of the time for which the lessee shall have the land, and if any of these fail, it is not a good lease, for then there wants certainty.

The Law of Property Act 1925, taking up the same theme provided, by section 1(1), that:

> The only estates in land which are capable of subsisting or of being conveyed or created at law are — (a) An estate in fee simple absolute in possession; (b) A term of years absolute.

Section 205(1)(xxvii) was in these terms:

> 'Term of years absolute' means a term of years . . . either certain or liable to determination by notice, re-entry, operation of law, or by a provision for cesser on redemption, or in any other event (other than the dropping of a life, or the determination of a determinable life interest); . . . and in this definition the expression 'term of years' includes a term for less than a year, or for a year or years and a fraction of a year or from year to year; . . .

The term expressed to be granted by the agreement in the present case does not fall within this definition.

Ancient authority, recognised by the Act of 1925, was applied in *Lace* v *Chantler* [1944] KB 368.

. . .

My Lords, I consider that the principle in *Lace* v *Chantler* [1944] KB 368 reaffirming 500 years of judicial acceptance of the requirement that a term must be certain applies to all leases and tenancy agreements. A tenancy from year to year is saved from being uncertain because each party has power by notice to determine at the end of any year. The term continues until determined as if both parties made a new agreement at the end of each year for a new term for the ensuing year. A power for nobody to determine or for one party only to be able to determine is inconsistent with the concept of a term from year to year: see *Warner* v *Browne*, 8 East 165 and *Cheshire Lines Committee* v *Lewis & Co.*, 50 LJQB 121. In *In re Midland Railway Co.'s Agreement* [1971] Ch 725 there was no 'clearly expressed bargain' that the term should continue until the crack of doom if the demised land was not required for the landlord's undertaking or if the undertaking ceased to exist. In the present case there was no 'clearly expressed bargain' that the tenant shall be entitled to enjoy his 'temporary structures' in perpetuity if Walworth Road is never widened. In any event principle and precedent dictate that it is beyond the power of the landlord and the tenant to create a term which is uncertain.

A lease can be made for five years subject to the tenant's right to determine if the war ends before the expiry of five years. A lease can be made from year to year subject to a fetter on the right of the landlord to determine the lease before the expiry of five years unless the war ends. Both leases are valid because they create a determinable certain term of five years. A lease might purport to be made for the duration of the war subject to the tenant's right to determine before the end of the war. A lease might be made from year to year subject to a fetter on the right of the landlord to determine the lease before the war ends. Both leases would be invalid because each purported to create an uncertain term. A term must either be certain or uncertain. It cannot be partly certain because the tenant can determine it at any time and partly uncertain because the landlord cannot determine it for an uncertain period. If the landlord does not grant and the tenant does not take a certain term the grant does not create a lease.

The decision of the Court of Appeal *In re Midland Railway Co.'s Agreement* [1971] Ch 725 was taken a little further in *Ashburn Anstalt* v *Arnold* [1989] Ch 1. That case, if it was correct, would make it unnecessary for a lease to be of a certain duration. In an agreement for the sale of land the vendor reserved the right to remain at the property after completion as licensee and to trade therefrom without payment of rent

> save that it can be required by Matlodge [the purchaser] to give possession on not less than one quarter's notice in writing upon Matlodge certifying that it is ready at the expiration of such notice forthwith to proceed with the development of the property and the neighboruing property involving, inter alia, the demolition of the property.

The Court of Appeal held that this reservation created a tenancy. The tenancy was not from year to year but for a term which would continue until Matlodge certified that it was ready to proceed with the development of the property. The Court of Appeal held that the term was not uncertain because the vendor could either give a quarter's notice or vacate the property without giving notice. But of course the same could be said of the situation in *Lace* v *Chantler* [1944] KB 368. The cumulative result of the two Court of Appeal authorities *In re Midland Railway Co.'s Agreement* [1971] Ch 725 and *Ashburn's* case [1989] Ch 1 would therefore destroy the need for any term to be certain.

In the present case the Court of Appeal were bound by the decisions *In re Midland Railway Co.'s Agreement* and *Ashburn's* case. In my opinion both these cases were wrongly decided. A grant for an uncertain term does not create a lease. A grant for an uncertain term which takes the form of a yearly tenancy which cannot be determined by the landlord does not create a lease. I would allow the appeal. The trial judge, Millett J, reached the conclusion that the six months' notice served by the London Residuary Body was a good notice. He was of course bound by the Court of Appeal decisions but managed to construe the memorandum of agreement so as to render clause 6 ineffective in fettering the right of the landlord to serve a notice to quit after the landlord had ceased to be a road widening authority. In the circumstances this question of construction need not be considered. For the reasons which I have given the order made by Millett J must be restored. The plaintiffs must pay the costs of the second to fourth defendants before the House and in the courts below.

Note

Prior to the House of Lords' decision in *Prudential Assurance Co. Ltd* v *London Residuary Body* it was thought that a lease for a term which was not limited to expire by the effluxion of term but which was determinable by the landlord or the tenant giving specified notice to the other party was nevertheless of certain duration — see *Ashburn Anstalt* v *Arnold* [1989] Ch 1 and also *Canadian Imperial Bank of Commerce* v *Bello* (1991) *The Times*, 18 November 1991.

(a) Future leases

Law of Property Act 1925

149. Abolition of *interesse termini*, and as to reversionary leases and leases for lives

(3) A term, at a rent or granted in consideration of a fine, limited after the commencement of this Act to take effect more than twenty-one years from the date of the instrument purporting to create it, shall be void, and any contract made after such commencement to create such a term shall likewise be void; but this subsection does not apply to any term taking effect in equity under a settlement, or created out of an equitable interest under a settlement, or under an equitable power for mortgage, indemnity or other like purposes.

Weg Motors Ltd v *Hales* [1962] 1 Ch 49 (CA)

In 1937, G charged certain premises by way of a legal mortgage to S. In July 1938, G granted a lease of the premises to W for a term of 21 years from 25 December 1938. By a separate agreement made by the same parties, W was given an option to take a further lease for 21 years at the same rent, exercisable at any time before 25 December 1959. The further lease was to commence from the date of the exercise of the option at which time G would accept surrender of any unexpired residue of the old lease. Held: the option agreement was not void as a type of contract coming within s. 149(3) of the Law of Property Act 1925. No term would be created unless and until the option was exercised.

Note
To come within the provision of s. 149(3) the term must *inevitably* commence outside the 21-year period. See *In re Strand & Savoy Properties Ltd* v *Cumbrae Properties Ltd* [1960] 1 Ch 582.

(b) Leases for life

The period of a person's life is uncertain, and therefore a lease for life will offend against the rule that a lease must be of an ascertainable duration. The definition of a term of years in s. 205(1)(xxvii) of the Law of Property Act 1925 cannot include a lease for life or a lease until a person dies. However, see the Law of Property Act 1925, s. 149(6) below.

Law of Property Act 1925

149. Abolition of *interesse termini*, and as to reversionary leases and leases for lives

(6) Any lease or underlease, at a rent, or in consideration of a fine, for life or lives or for any term of years determinable with life or lives, or on the marriage of the lessee, or any contract therefor, made before or after the commencement of this Act, or created by virtue of Part V of the Law of Property Act, 1922, shall take effect as a lease, underlease or contract therefor, for a term of ninety years determinable after the death or marriage (as the case may be) of the original lessee, or of the survivor of the original

lessees, by at least one month's notice in writing given to determine the same on one of the quarter days applicable to the tenancy, either by the lessor or the persons deriving title under him, to the person entitled to the leasehold interest, or if no such person is in existence by affixing the same to the premises, or by the lessee or other persons in whom the leasehold interest is vested to the lessor or the persons deriving title under him:

Provided that—

(a) this subsection shall not apply to any term taking effect in equity under a settlement or created out of an equitable interest under a settlement for mortgage indemnity, or other like purposes;

(b) the person in whom the leasehold interest is vested by virtue of Part V of the Law of Property Act, 1922, shall, for the purposes of this subsection, be deemed as original lessee;

(c) if the lease, underlease, or contract therefor is made determinable on the dropping of the lives of persons other than or besides the lessees, then the notice shall be capable of being served after the death of any person or of the survivor of any persons (whether or not including the lessees) on the cesser of whose life or lives the lease, underlease, or contract is made determinable, instead of after the death of the original lessee or of the survivor of the original lessees;

(d) if there are no quarter days specially applicable to the tenancy, notice may be given to determine the tenancy on one of the usual quarter days.

(c) Leases until marriage
See the Law of Property Act 1925, s. 149(6) above.

(d) Perpetually renewable leases
A perpetually renewable lease again has no definite boundary and could in theory last forever. But:

Law of Property Act 1922

Fifteenth Schedule

Provisions Relating to Perpetually Renewable Leases and Underleases

1. Conversion of perpetually renewable leases into long terms
(1) Land comprised in a perpetually renewable lease which was subsisting at the commencement of this Act shall, by virtue of this Act, vest in the person who at such commencement was entitled to such lease, for a term of two thousand years, to be calculated from the date at which the existing term or interest commenced, at the rent and subject to the lessees' covenants and conditions (if any) which under the lease would have been payable or enforceable during the subsistence of such term or interest.

(2) The rent, covenants and conditions (if any) shall (subject to the express provisions of this Act to the contrary) be payable and enforceable during the subsistence of the term created by this Act; and that term shall take effect in substitution for the term or interest created by the lease, and be subject to the like power of re-entry (if any) and other provisions which affected the term or interest created by the lease, but without any right of renewal.

2. Conversion of perpetually renewable underleases into long terms
(1) Land comprised in any underlease, which at the commencement of this Act was perpetually renewable and was derived out of a head term affected by this Act, shall, by

virtue of this Act, vest in the person who at such commencement was entitled to the subterm or interest for a term of two thousand years less one day, to be calculated from the date at which the head term created by this Act commenced, at the rent and subject to the underlessee's covenants and conditions (if any) which under the underlease would have been payable or enforceable during the subsistence of such subterm or interest.

(2) The rent, covenants and conditions (if any) shall (subject to the express provisions of this Act to the contrary) be payable and enforceable during the subsistence of the subterm created by this Act; and that subterm shall take effect in substitution for the subterm or interest created by the underlease, and be subject to the like power of re-entry (if any) and other provisions which affected the subterm or interest created by the underlease, but without any right of renewal.

(3) The foregoing provisions of this section shall also apply to any perpetually renewable subterm or interest which, at the commencement of this Act, was derived out of any other subterm or interest, but so that in every case the subterm created by this Act shall be one day less in duration than the derivative term created by this Act, out of which it takes effect.

5. Dispositions purporting to create perpetually renewable leaseholds
A grant, after the commencement of this Act, of a term, subterm, or other leasehold interest with a covenant or obligation for perpetual renewal, which would have been valid if this Part of this Act had not been passed, shall (subject to the express provisions of this Act) take effect as a demise for a term of two thousand years or in the case of a subdemise for a term less in duration by one day than the term out of which it is derived, to commence from the date fixed for the commencement of the term, subterm, or other interest, and in every case free from any obligation for renewal or for payment of any fines, fees, costs, or other money in respect of renewal.

Marjorie Burnett Ltd v *Barclay*
(1981) 258 EG 642 (ChD)

A lease was made between P and X in August 1971, and at some time between 1971 and 1975 the lease was assigned to D. The lease was expressed for a term of seven years from 24 June 1971. Clause 6 of the agreement provided 'If the tenant shall be desirous of taking a new lease of the demised premises after the expiration of the term hereby granted . . . then the landlord will at or before the expiration of the term hereby granted, if there shall then be no subsisting breach of any of the tenant's obligations under this present lease grant to the tenant a new lease of the premises hereby demised for a further term of seven years, to commence from and after the expiration of the term hereby granted at a rent to be agreed between the parties . . . And such lease shall also contain a like covenant for renewal for a further term of seven years on the expiration of the term granted.'

NOURSE J: . . . I must bear in mind that the leaning of the courts has been against perpetual renewals. I have to find expressly in the lease a covenant or obligation for perpetual renewal. And I have to look ahead to see what the second lease will contain when the requirements of the covenant for renewal in the first have been duly observed.

I now return to clause 6 of the lease. What the landlord has to do, if the tenant gives it notice of his desire to take a new lease, is to grant to the tenant a new lease of the demised premises for a further term of seven years at a rent to be agreed, and if not agreed to be fixed in the manner specified. Then it is provided that such lease shall also contain a like covenant for renewal for a further term of seven years on the expiration of the term thereby granted.

Mr Henty [for the plaintiff] really puts his case on this primary question in two ways. First, he takes the simple course of asking me to see what provisions the second lease would contain if it were to be granted pursuant to clause 6. He says that it would inevitably be at a different rent from the £650 reserved by the first lease. Then he says that the second lease would contain a like covenant for renewal for a further term of seven years as that contained in clause 6 of the first lease. But that covenant ends with the part of clause 6 which deals with the provisions for fixing the rent in default of agreement. It does not seem to me that the second lease could possibly contain the words 'and such lease shall also contain a like covenant for renewal for a further term of seven years on the expiration of the term thereby granted', because those words are not part of the covenant for renewal and to include them would be to go further than clause 6 requires. And so I agree with Mr Henty that the second lease would be at a new rent and that it would contain the whole of clause 6 except for the last three lines or so which I have just quoted. On that footing it is clear that there is no express covenant or obligation for perpetual renewal. Indeed the contrary is the case. There is an express provision in the lease to the effect that it can be renewed twice only.

That would in itself be enough to dispose of the primary question in these proceedings. But Mr Henty goes on to take a second point, which appears to me to be one of equal force, and that is this. He says that even supposing his first argument were wrong I must bear in mind that what will happen if this is a perpetually renewable lease is that it will be converted by the 1922 Act into a lease for a term of 2,000 years. He says, and I can see no answer to this, that the notion of a 2,000-year term is completely inimical to a lease which contains provisions for rent review every seven years. And so again he says that as a matter of construction clause 6 could not possibly have the effect for which the defendant has contended. I agree with that contention also.

In the circumstances it seems clear to me that the plaintiff company is entitled to the primary delcaration which it seeks. On that footing it is not necessary for me to consider the second possible alternative raised by the originating summons.

Note
See H. W. Wilkinson, 'Renewable leases' 25 June 1981 NLJ 683.

(e) Periodic tenancy
As Gray says in his book, *Elements of Land Law*, at p. 437:

> In view of its open-ended nature the periodic tenancy is not viewed in English law as an aggregated series of distinct terms. Instead the units of time which constitute the periodic tenancy are seen as comprising one unbroken term which, unless and until duly determined, perpetually elongates itself by the superaddition of a fresh unit or period.

See Lord Templeman's judgment in *Prudential Assurance Co. Ltd* v *London Residuary Body & Others* [1992] 3 WLR 279, page 155 *et seq*.

B: RENT

A lease or tenancy is usually a commercial undertaking, and therefore rent or some other monetary payment will be paid by the lessee or tenant. Nevertheless, the reservation of rent is not an essential requirement of a valid lease (see *Knight's Case* (1588) 5 Co Rep 54b, 55a), although lack of it may prevent a tenant from receiving certain forms of statutory protection, for example under the Rent Act 1977, s. 5(1) as amended by s. 32 of the Housing Act 1988. If rent is reserved, however, it must be certain.

Greater London Council v Connolly
[1970] 2 QB 100 (CA)

The plaintiff increased the rents of some tenants by an average of 7s 6d a week by giving them notices informing them of the increase. The tenants' books contained a condition which said that the rent was 'liable to be increased or decreased on notice being given'. Held: the rent payable was not uncertain, even though it was open to variation, as the amount due could be ascertained with certainty at any particular time.

LORD DENNING MR: It is next said that the rent is uncertain, and that the condition is, therefore, invalid by the law of landlord and tenant. It is clear law that a rent must be certain. But that does not mean that it must be certain at the date of the lease. Rent is sufficiently certain if it can be calculated with certainty at the time when payment comes to be made. Here the notice of increase enabled the rent to be calculated with certainty as at the time when the increase was to operate, i.e., September 30, 1968 ...

Notes
1. An option to renew a lease at 'such rent as might be agreed between the parties' was held to be void for uncertainty in the absence of an arbitration clause or some other supplementary agreement fixing the rent. See *King's Motors (Oxford) Ltd v Lax* [1970] 1 WLR 426.
2. Where an option to renew a lease is expressed to be exercisable at a price to be determined according to some stated formula, but without any effective machinery being provided for determining that formula, then the court has jurisdiction to determine it. Similarly, if rent is to be fixed 'having regard to the market value of the premises' or is quantified as the current 'market rental' then the lease is not invalid (see *Sudbrook Trading Estates Ltd v Eggleton* [1983] 1 AC 444, *Brown v Gould* [1972] 1 Ch 53). See Paul Robertshaw, 'Options, Pre-emptions and Certainty of Consideration' (1972) 36 Conv 317; John Murdoch 'Enforcement of provision for valuation' (1982) 98 LQR 539.
3. Rent need not be expressly reserved in money terms. 'The rendering of services can constitute rent at common law' as can the rendering of chattels, see Sachs LJ in *Barnes v Barratt* [1970] 2 QB 657, 666.

C: EXCLUSIVE POSSESSION

For there to be a valid lease the lessee or tenant must be given exclusive possession of the premises.

Street v *Mountford*
[1985] AC 809 (HL)

By a purported 'licence agreement' S granted M the right to occupy two rooms for a licence fee, determinable on 14 days' notice. The agreement specifically declared that M understood there would be no tenancy capable of protection under the Rent Acts. M and her husband had exclusive possession of the rooms. Held: the agreement gave M a tenancy over the land not a licence.

LORD TEMPLEMAN: My Lords, there is no doubt that the traditional distinction between a tenancy and a licence of land lay in the grant of land for a term at a rent with exclusive possession. In some cases it was not clear at first sight whether exclusive possession was in fact granted. . . .

In the case of residential accommodation there is no difficulty in deciding whether the grant confers exclusive possession. An occupier of residential accommodation at a rent for a term is either a lodger or a tenant. The occupier is a lodger if the landlord provides attendance or services which require the landlord or his servants to exercise unrestricted access to and use of the premises. A lodger is entitled to live in the premises but cannot call the place his own. In *Allan* v *Liverpool Overseers* (1874) LR 9 QB 180, 191–192 Blackburn J said:

> A lodger in a house, although he has the exclusive use of rooms in the house, in the sense that nobody else is to be there, and though his goods are stowed there, yet he is not in exclusive occupation in that sense, because the landlord is there for the purpose of being able, as landlords commonly do in the case of lodgings, to have his own servants to look after the house and the furniture, and has retained to himself the occupation, though he has agreed to give the exclusive enjoyment of the occupation to the lodger.

If on the other hand residential accommodation is granted for a term at a rent with exclusive possession, the landlord providing neither attendance nor services, the grant is a tenancy; any express reservation to the landlord of limited rights to enter and view the state of the premises and to repair and maintain the premises only serves to emphasise the fact that the grantee is entitled to exclusive possession and is a tenant. In the present case it is conceded that Mrs Mountford is entitled to exclusive possession and is not a lodger. Mr Street provided neither attendance nor services and only reserved the limited rights of inspection and maintenance and the like set forth in clause 3 of the agreement. On the traditional view of the matter, Mrs Mountford not being a lodger must be a tenant.

There can be no tenancy unless the occupier enjoys exclusive possession; but an occupier who enjoys exclusive possession is not necessarily a tenant. He may be owner in fee simple, a trespasser, a mortgagee in possession, an object of charity or a service occupier. To constitute a tenancy the occupier must be granted exclusive possession for a fixed or periodic term certain in consideration of a premium or periodical payments. The grant may be express, or may be inferred where the owner accepts weekly or other periodical payments from the occupier.

Occupation by service occupier may be eliminated. A service occupier is a servant who occupies his master's premises in order to perform his duties as a servant. In those circumstances the possession and occupation of the servant is treated as the possession and occupation of the master and the relationship of landlord and tenant is not created;

see *Mayhew* v *Suttle* (1854) 4 El & Bl 347. The test is whether the servant requires the premises he occupies in order the better to perform his duties as a servant:

> Where the occupation is necessary for the performance of services, and the occupier is required to reside in the house in order to perform those services, the occupation being strictly ancillary to the performance of the duties which the occupier has to perform, the occupation is that of a servant; *per* Mellor J, in *Smith* v *Seghill Overseers* (1875) LR 10 QB 422, 428.

The cases on which Mr Goodhart relies begin with *Booker* v *Palmer* [1942] 2 All ER 674. The owner of a cottage agreed to allow a friend to install an evacuee in the cottage rent free for the duration of the war. The Court of Appeal held that there was no intention on the part of the owner to enter into legal relationships with the evacuee. Lord Greene MR, said, at p. 677:

> To suggest there is an intention there to create a relationship of landlord and tenant appears to me to be quite impossible. There is one golden rule which is of very general application, namely, that the law does not impute intention to enter into legal relationships where the circumstances and the conduct of the parties negative any intention of the kind. It seems to me that this is a clear example of the application of that rule.

> ... If the agreement satisfied all the requirements of a tenancy, then the agreement produced a tenancy and the parties cannot alter the effect of the agreement by insisting that they only created a licence....

It was also submitted that in deciding whether the agreement created a tenancy or a licence, the court should ignore the Rent Acts. If Mr Street has succeeded, where owners have failed these past 70 years, in driving a coach and horses through the Rent Acts, he must be left to enjoy the benefit of his ingenuity unless and until Parliament intervenes. I accept that the Rent Acts are irrelevant to the problem of determining the legal effect of the rights granted by the agreement. Like the professed intention of the parties, the Rent Acts cannot alter the effect of the agreement.

[Lord Templeman discusses the case of *Marcroft Wagons Ltd* v *Smith* [1951] 2 KB 496 – see page 172.]

Errington v *Errington and Woods* [1952] 1 KB 290 concerned a contract by a father to allow his son to buy the father's house on payment of the instalments of the father's building society loan. Denning LJ referred, at p. 297, to the judgment of Lord Greene MR in *Booker* v *Palmer* [1942] 2 All ER 674, 677 where, however, the circumstances and the conduct of the parties negatived any intention to enter into legal relationships. Denning LJ continued, at pp. 297–298:

> We have had many instances lately of occupiers in exclusive possession who have been held to be not tenants, but only licensees. When a requisitioning authority allowed people into possession at a weekly rent: ... when a landlord told a tenant on his retirement that he could live in a cottage rent free for the rest of his days: ... when a landlord, on the death of the widow of a statutory tenant, allowed her daughter to remain in possession, paying rent for six months: *Marcroft Wagons Ltd* v *Smith* [1951] 2 KB 496; when the owner of a shop allowed the manager to live in a flat above the shop, but did not require him to do so, and the value of the flat was taken into account at £1 a week in fixing his wages: ... in each of those cases the occupier was held to be a licensee and not a tenant.... The result of all these cases is that, although a person who is let into exclusive possession is prima facie to be considered a tenant,

nevertheless he will not be held to be so if the circumstances negative any intention to create a tenancy. Words alone may not suffice. Parties cannot turn a tenancy into a licence merely by calling it one. But if the circumstances and the conduct of the parties show that all that was intended was that the occupier should be granted a personal privilege, with no interest in the land, he will be held to be a licensee only.

In *Errington* v *Errington and Woods* [1952] 1 KB 290 and in the cases cited by Denning LJ at p. 297 there were exceptional circumstances which negatived the prima facie intention to create a tenancy, notwithstanding that the occupier enjoyed exclusive occupation. The intention to create a tenancy was negatived if the parties did not intend to enter into legal relationships at all, or where the relationship between the parties was that of vendor and purchaser, master and service occupier, or where the owner, a requisitioning authority, had no power to grant a tenancy. These exceptional circumstances are not to be found in the present case where there has been the lawful, independent and voluntary grant of exclusive possession for a term at a rent.

If the observations of Denning LJ are applied to the facts of the present case it may fairly be said that the circumstances negative any intention to create a mere licence. Words alone do not suffice. Parties cannot turn a tenancy into a licence merely by calling it one. The circumstances and the conduct of the parties show that what was intended was that the occupier should be granted exclusive possession at a rent for a term with a corresponding interest in the land which created a tenancy.

In *Cobb* v *Lane* [1952] 1 TLR 1037, an owner allowed her brother to occupy a house rent free. The county court judge, who was upheld by the Court of Appeal, held that there was no intention to create any legal relationship and that a tenancy at will was not to be implied. This is another example of conduct which negatives any intention of entering into a contract, and does not assist in distinguishing a contractual tenancy from a contractual licence.

In *Facchini* v *Bryson* [1952] 1 TLR 1386, an employer and his assistant entered into an agreement which, inter alia, allowed the assistant to occupy a house for a weekly payment on terms which conferred exclusive possession. The assistant did not occupy the house for the better performance of his duty and was not therefore a service occupier. The agreement stipulated that 'nothing in this agreement shall be construed to create a tenancy between the employer and the assistant.' Somervell LJ said, at p. 1389:

> If, looking at the operative clauses in the agreement, one comes to the conclusion that the rights of the occupier, to use a neutral word, are those of a lessee, the parties cannot turn it into a licence by saying at the end 'this is deemed to be a licence;' nor can they, if the operative paragraphs show that it is merely a licence, say that it should be deemed to be a lease.

Denning LJ referred to several cases including *Errington* v *Errington and Woods* and *Cobb* v *Lane* and said, at pp. 1389–1390:

> In all the cases where an occupier has been held to be a licensee there has been something in the circumstances, such as a family arrangement, an act of friendship or generosity, or such like, to negative any intention to create a tenancy . . . . In the present case, however, there are no special circumstances. It is a simple case where the employer let a man into occupation of a house in consequence of his employment at a weekly sum payable by him. The occupation has all the features of a service tenancy, and the parties cannot by the mere words of their contract turn it into

something else. Their relationship is determined by the law and not by the label which they choose to put on it: . . .

The decision, which was thereafter binding on the Court of Appeal and on all lower courts, referred to the special circumstances which are capable of negativing an intention to create a tenancy and reaffirmed the principle that the professed intentions of the parties are irrelevant. The decision also indicated that in a simple case a grant of exclusive possession of residential accommodation for a weekly sum creates a tenancy.

In *Murray Bull & Co. Ltd* v *Murray* [1953] 1 QB 211 a contractual tenant held over, paying rent quarterly. McNair J found, at p. 217:

> both parties intended that the relationship should be that of licensee and no more . . . The primary consideration on both sides was that the defendant, as occupant of the flat, should not be a controlled tenant.

In my opinion this case was wrongly decided. McNair J citing the observations of Denning LJ in *Errington* v *Errington and Woods* [1952] 1 KB 290, 297 and *Marcroft Wagons Ltd* v *Smith* [1951] 2 KB 496 failed to distinguish between first, conduct which negatives an intention to create legal relationships, secondly, special circumstances which prevent exclusive occupation from creating a tenancy and thirdly, the professed intention of the parties. In *Murray Bull & Co. Ltd* v *Murray* the conduct of the parties showed an intention to contract and there were no relevant special circumstances. The tenant holding over continued by agreement to enjoy exclusive possession and to pay a rent for a term certain. In those circumstances he continued to be a tenant notwithstanding the professed intention of the parties to create a licence and their desire to avoid a controlled tenancy.

In *Addiscombe Garden Estates Ltd* v *Crabbe* [1958] 1 QB 513 the Court of Appeal considered an agreement relating to a tennis club carried on in the grounds of a hotel. The agreement was: 'described by the parties as a licence . . . the draftsman has studiously and successfully avoided the use either of the word "landlord" or the word "tenant" throughout the document' *per* Jenkins LJ at p. 522. On analysis of the whole of the agreement the Court of Appeal came to the conclusion that the agreement conferred exclusive possession and thus created a tenancy. Jenkins LJ said, at p. 522:

> The whole of the document must be looked at; and if, after it has been examined, the right conclusion appears to be that, whatever label may have been attached to it, it in fact conferred and imposed on the grantee in substance the rights and obligations of a tenant, and on the grantor in substance the rights and obligations of a landlord, then it must be given the appropriate effect, that is to say, it must be treated as a tenancy agreement as distinct from a mere licence.

In the agreement in the *Addiscombe* case it was by no means clear until the whole of the document had been narrowly examined that exclusive possession was granted by the agreement. In the present case it is clear that exclusive possession was granted and so much is conceded. In these circumstances it is unnecessary to analyse minutely the detailed rights and obligations contained in the agreement.

In the *Addiscombe* case Jenkins LJ referred, at p. 528, to the observations of Denning LJ in *Errington and Errington and Woods* to the effect that 'The test of exclusive possession is by no means decisive.' Jenkins LJ continued:

> I think that wide statement must be treated as qualified by his observations in *Facchini* v *Bryson* [1952] 1 TLR 1386, 1389; and it seems to me that, save in exceptional cases of the kind mentioned by Denning LJ in that case, the law remains

that the fact of exclusive possession, if not decisive against the view that there is a mere licence, as distinct from a tenancy, is at all events a consideration of the first importance.

Exclusive possession is of first importance in considering whether an occupier is a tenant; exclusive possession is not decisive because an occupier who enjoys exclusive possession is not necessarily a tenant. The occupier may be a lodger or service occupier or fall within the other exceptional categories mentioned by Denning LJ in *Errington v Errington and Woods* [1952] 1 KB 290. . . .

In *Abbeyfield (Harpenden) Society Ltd* v *Woods* [1968] 1 WLR 374 the occupier of a room in an old people's home was held to be a licensee and not a tenant. Lord Denning MR said, at p. 376:

> The modern cases show that a man may be a licensee even though he has exclusive possession, even though the word 'rent' is used, and even though the word 'tenancy' is used. The court must look at the agreement as a whole and see whether a tenancy really was intended. In this case there is, besides the one room, the provision of services, meals, a resident housekeeper, and such like. The whole arrangement was so personal in nature that the proper inference is that he was a licensee.

As I understand the decision in the *Abbeyfield* case the court came to the conclusion that the occupier was a lodger and was therefore a licensee, not a tenant.

In *Shell-Mex and B.P. Ltd* v *Manchester Garages Ltd* [1971] 1 WLR 612 the Court of Appeal after carefully examining an agreement whereby the defendant was allowed to use a petrol company's filling station for the purposes of selling petrol, came to the conclusion that the agreement did not grant exclusive posession to the defendant who was therefore a licensee. At p. 615 Lord Denning MR in considering whether the transaction was a licence or a tenancy said:

> Broadly speaking, we have to see whether it is a personal privilege given to a person (in which case it is a licence), or whether it grants an interest in land (in which case it is a tenancy). At one time it used to be thought that exclusive possession was a decisive factor. But that is not so. It depends on broader considerations altogether. Primarily on whether it is personal in its nature or not: see *Errington* v *Errington and Woods* [1952] 1 KB 290.

In my opinion the agreement was only 'personal in its nature' and created 'a personal privilege' if the agreement did not confer the right to exclusive possession of the filling station. No other test for distinguishing between a contractual tenancy and a contractual licence appears to be understandable or workable.

[Lord Templeman discusses the facts of *Heslop* v *Burns* [1974] 1 WLR 1241 (see page 171 *et seq.*).]

In *Marchant* v *Charters* [1977] 1 WLR 1181 a bedsitting room was occupied on terms that the landlord cleaned the rooms daily and provided clean linen each week. It was held by the Court of Appeal that the occupier was a licensee and not a tenant. The decision in the case is sustainable on the grounds that the occupier was a lodger and did not enjoy exclusive possession. But Lord Denning MR said, at p. 1185:

> What is the test to see whether the occupier of one room in a house is a tenant or a licensee? It does not depend on whether he or she has exclusive possession or not. It does not depend on whether the room is furnished or not. It does not depend on whether the occupation is permanent or temporary. It does not depend on the label which the parties put upon it. All these are factors which may influence the decision

but none of them is conclusive. All the circumstances have to be worked out. Eventually the answer depends on the nature and quality of the occupancy. Was it intended that the occupier should have a stake in the room or did he have only permission for himself personally to occupy the room, whether under a contract or not? In which case he is a licensee.

But in my opinion in order to ascertain the nature and quality of the occupancy and to see whether the occupier has or has not a stake in the room or only permission for himself personally to occupy, the court must decide whether upon its true construction the agreement confers on the occupier exclusive possession. If exclusive possession at a rent for a term does not constitute a tenancy then the distinction between a contractual tenancy and a contractual licence of land becomes wholly unidentifiable.

In *Somma* v *Hazelhurst* [1978] 1 WLR 1014, a young unmarried couple H and S occupied a double bedsitting room for which they paid a weekly rent. The landlord did not provide services or attendance and the couple were not lodgers but tenants enjoying exclusive possession. But the Court of Appeal did not ask themselves whether H and S were lodgers or tenants and did not draw the correct conclusion from the fact that H and S enjoyed exclusive possession. The Court of Appeal were diverted from the correct inquiries by the fact that the landlord obliged H and S to enter into separate agreements and reserved power to determine each agreement separately. The landlord also insisted that the room should not in form be let to either H or S or to both H and S but that each should sign an agreement to share the room in common with such other persons as the landlord might from time to time nominate. The sham nature of this obligation would have been only slightly more obvious if H and S had been married or if the room had been furnished with a double bed instead of two single beds. If the landlord had served notice on H to leave and had required S to share the room with a stange man, the notice would only have been a disguised notice to quit on both H and S. The room was let and taken as residential accommodation with exclusive possession in order that H and S might live together in undisturbed quasi-connubial bliss making weekly payments. The agreements signed by H and S constituted the grant to H and S jointly of exclusive possession at a rent for a term for the purposes for which the room was taken and the agreement therefore created a tenancy. Although the Rent Acts must not be allowed to alter or influence the construction of an agreement, the court should, in my opinion, be astute to detect and frustrate sham devices and artificial transactions whose only object is to disguise the grant of a tenancy and to evade the Rent Acts. I would disapprove of the decision in this case that H and S were only licensees and for the same reason would disapprove of the decision in *Aldrington Garages Ltd* v *Fielder* (1978) 37 P & CR 461 and *Sturolson & Co.* v *Weniz* (1984) 272 EG 326.

In the present case the Court of Appeal, 49 P & CR 324 held that the agreement dated 7 March 1983 only created a licence. Slade LJ, at p. 329 accepted that the agreement and in particular clause 3 of the agreement 'shows that the right to occupy the premises conferred on the defendant was intended as an exclusive right of occupation, in that it was thought necessary to give a special and express power to the plaintiff to enter . . . .' Before your Lordships it was conceded that the agreement conferred the right of exclusive possession on Mrs Mountford. Even without clause 3 the result would have been the same. By the agreement Mrs Mountford was granted the right to occupy residential accommodation. The landlord did not provide any services or attendance. It was plain that Mrs Mountford was not a lodger. Slade LJ proceeded to analyse all the provisions of the agreement, not for the purpose of deciding whether his finding of exclusive possession was correct, but for the purpose of assigning some of the provisions of the agreement to the category of terms which he thought are usually to be found in a tenancy agreement and of assigning other provisions to the category of terms which he thought are usually to be found in a licence. Slade LJ may or may not have been right that in a letting of a furnished room it was 'most unusual to find a provision in a tenancy agreement obliging the tenant to keep his rooms in a "tidy condition"' (p. 329). If Slade LJ was right about this and other provisions there is still no logical method of evaluating the results of his survey. Slade LJ reached the conclusion that 'the agreement bears all the hallmarks of a licence rather than a tenancy save for the one important feature of exclusive occupation': p. 329. But in addition to the hallmark of exclusive occupation of residential accommodation there were the hallmarks of weekly payments for a periodical term. Unless these three hallmarks are decisive, it really becomes impossible to distinguish a contractual tenancy from a contractual licence save by reference to the professed intention of the parties or by the judge awarding marks for drafting. Slade LJ was finally impressed by the statement at the foot of the agreement by Mrs Mountford. 'I understand and accept that a licence in the above form does not and is not intended to give me a tenancy protected under the Rent Acts.' Slade LJ said, at p. 330:

> it seems to me that, if the defendant is to displace the express statement of intention embodied in the declaration, she must show that the declaration was either a deliberate sham or at least an inaccurate statement of what was the true substance of the real transaction agreed between the parties; . . .

My Lords, the only intention which is relevant is the intention demonstrated by the agreement to grant exclusive possession for a term at a rent. Sometimes it may be difficult to discover whether, on the true construction of an agreement, exclusive possession is conferred. Sometimes it may appear from the surrounding circumstances that there was no intention to create legal relationships. Sometimes it may appear from the surrounding circumstances that the right to exclusive possession is referable to a legal relationship other than a tenancy. Legal relationships to which the grant of exclusive possession might be referable and which would or might negative the grant of an estate or interest in the land include occupancy under a contract for the sale of the land, occupancy pursuant to a contract of employment or occupancy referable to the holding of an office. But where as in the present case the only circumstances are that residential accommodation is offered and accepted with exclusive possession for a term at a rent, the result is a tenancy.

The position was well summarised by Windeyer J sitting in the High Court of Australia in *Radaich* v *Smith* (1959) 101 CLR 209, 222, where he said:

> What then is the fundamental right which a tenant has that distinguishes his position from that of a licensee? It is an interest in land as distinct from a personal permission to enter the land and use it for some stipulated purpose or purposes. And how is it to be ascertained whether such an interest in land has been given? By seeing whether the grantee was given a legal right of exclusive possession of the land for a term or from year to year or for a life or lives. If he was, he is a tenant. And he cannot be other than a tenant, because a legal right of exclusive possession is a tenancy and the creation of such a right is a demise. To say that a man who has, by agreement with a landlord, a right of exclusive possession of land for a term is not a tenant is simply to contradict the first proposition by the second. A right of exclusive possession is secured by the right of a lessee to maintain ejectment and, after his entry, trespass. A reservation to the landlord, either by contract or statute, of a limited right of entry, as for example to view or repair, is, of course, not inconsistent with the grant of exclusive possession. Subject to such reservations, a tenant for a term or from year to year or for a life or lives can exclude his landlord as well as strangers from the demised premises. All this is long established law: see *Cole on Ejectment* (1857) pp. 72, 73, 287, 458.

My Lords, I gratefully adopt the logic and the language of Windeyer J. Henceforth the courts which deal with these problems will, save in exceptional circumstances, only be concerned to inquire whether as a result of an agreement relating to residential accommodation the occupier is a lodger or a tenant. In the present case I am satisfied that Mrs Mountford is a tenant, that the appeal should be allowed, that the order of the Court of Appeal should be set aside and that the respondent should be ordered to pay the costs of the appellant here and below.

Note
See Stuart Bridge, '*Street* v *Mountford* — *no hiding place*' [1986] Conv 344; D. N. Clarke, '*Street* v *Mountford*' The question of intent — a view from down under' [1986] Conv 39; Stuart Anderson, 'Licences: traditional law revived?' (1985) 48 MLR 712; Stephen Tromans, 'Leases and licences in the lords' [1985] CLJ 351; A. J. Waite, 'Leases and licences: the true distinguishing test' (1987) 50 MLR 226.

SECTION 2: DISTINCTION BETWEEN A LEASE AND A LICENCE

It is important that a lease be distinguished from a licence, since the former confers a proprietary interest on the grantee which is enforceable against third parties. The latter (in most situations) confers a mere personal right on the grantee which does not bind third parties, (see page 37 *et seq.*). Furthermore, the Rent Acts and Housing Act 1988 do not apply to licences, but do apply to tenancies. The distinction between the two concepts, however, has been problematic, since both can involve the payment of a sum of money (rent) in return for exclusive possession of the property for a fixed period of time.

A: FACTORS TO DETERMINE THE CATEGORY

(a) Exclusive possession
The concept of exclusive possession was formerly one of the primary factors in determining whether there was a tenancy or not: if exclusive possession was granted there was a tenancy rather than a licence (see *Lynes* v *Snaith* [1899] 1 QB 486). Although the test of exclusive possession remains important, it is not always decisive. If exclusive possession is not granted, then the arrangement can only be a licence. However, the grant of exclusive possession no longer excludes the possibility of a licence, so that either a licence or a tenancy may have been created.

The mere reservation by the landlord of a right to enter the premises and view, repair and maintain them does not negate the grant of exclusive possession. In fact, in *Street* v *Mountford* [1985] AC 809 (see page 163 *et seq.*) it was said that this emphasises that the grantee is entitled to exclusive possession and is a tenant. The importance of the decision in *Street* v *Mountford* is that it reinstates the pre-eminence of the test of exclusive possession in the lease-licence distinction. Prior to this the test that had come to the forefront was the expressed intention test, which the Court of Appeal in

Street v *Mountford* 49 P & CR 324 had endorsed. Here Slade LJ said (at p. 330) '[the parties'] true intentions are the decisive consideration in determining whether an agreement creates a tenancy . . . or a licence'. Exclusive possession was merely an 'important pointer'.

Questions
1. What problems, if any, did the 'expressed intention' test give rise to?
2. What do you understand by the terms 'exclusive possession' and 'exclusive occupation'? Is such a distinction important?

(b) The '*Facchini* v *Bryson*' test

The House of Lords in *Street* v *Mountford* endorsed the *Facchini* v *Bryson* [1952] TLR 1386 list of situations where, although exclusive possession at a rent for a term was given, the situation was such that would not necessarily constitute a tenancy. The *Facchini* v *Bryson* category was formulated by Denning LJ, where he said:

> In all the cases where an occupier has been held to be a licensee there has been something in the circumstances, such as a family arrangement, an act of friendship or generosity, or such like, to negative any intention to create a tenancy. In such circumstances it would be obviously unjust to saddle the owner with a tenancy, with all the momentous consequences that that entails nowadays, when there was no intention to create a tenancy at all. . . .

(i) *Acts of friendship or generosity*

Heslop v Burns
[1974] 1 WLR 1241 (CA)

T employed W for a few weeks as an office cleaner. Because W and her husband were living in poor circumstances, T provided them with a cottage rent free. They moved into several other cottages and houses owned by T. There was no formal arrangement as to the terms upon which W and her husband occupied the cottage. No rent was demanded and T paid the rates and the cost of maintaining the property. From 1954 to 1968, T visited the cottage every day and had meals there. Held: as there was no arrangement regarding the terms on which the property was held, and having regard to the circumstances of the case, it was impossible to infer an intention to create legal relations between the parties. W and her husband therefore held the property as licensees not tenants at will.

SCARMAN LJ: In the present case I think that one can find something very akin to a family arrangement. After all, we are considering the occupation of a house which is described by the lady most concerned as the 'second home' of Mr Timms. We are certainly considering a whole course of dealing within the realm of friendship, and we are certainly faced with very great generosity shown over a long number of years by Mr Timms to the defendants' family. When one considers the peculiar circumstances of this case and considers them sympathetically, as one is bound to do, it becomes very difficult to see how in principle this case can be distinguished from *Cobb* v *Lane* and very difficult to see how, even upon the two assumptions that I have made in favour of Mr Wall, there is here any evidence upon which it is possible to infer a tenancy at will.

(ii) *Intention*

Marcroft Wagons v *Smith*
[1951] 2 KB 496 (CA)

T was a tenant of a house and he died. His tenancy devolved to his wife who lived in the property with her daughter until she also died. The daughter sought to have the tenancy transferred to her own name but the landlord refused as the house was soon to be used to accommodate an employee of the landlord. Nevertheless, the landlord accepted a sum of money from the daughter which was equivalent to two weeks' rent, and she then continued to pay the same sum to the landlord as the wife had. Held: the daughter was a mere licensee.

ROXBURGH J: Generally speaking, when a person, having a sufficient estate in land, lets another into exclusive possession, a tenancy results, and there is no question of a licence. But the inference of a tenancy is not necessarily to be drawn where a person succeeds on a death to occupation of rent-controlled premises and a landlord accepts some rent while he or the occupant, or both of them, is or are considering his or their position. If this is all that happened in this case, then no tenancy would result.

(c) Provision of services

Markou v *Da Silvaesa*
(1986) 52 P & CR 204 (CA)

By an agreement the 'grantor' agreed to provide the grantee with a housekeeper, lighting of common parts of the property, cleaning of common parts of the property, window cleaning, service to the front door, a telephone, cleaning of the flat, the collection of rubbish, the provision and laundering of bed linen and hot water.

RALPH GIBSON LJ: . . . the obligation to provide attendance and services is not conclusive that the occupier is a licensee: provision of the attendance or services must, as set out in Lord Templeman's speech, require the landlord or his servants to exercise unrestricted access to and use of the premises. . . . I take the meaning of the word 'unrestricted' in this context to be primarily concerned with the landlord's need to go into and out of the lodger's rooms at the convenience of the landlord and without the lodger being there to let the landlord in. The amount and frequency of the attendance and services agreed to be provided are relevant but the question to be answered is whether, in all the circumstances, having regard to the landlord's obligations, it is clear that the landlord requires unrestricted access and has reserved the right to exercise such access in order to look after the house and the furniture. Where an agreement describes attendance and services, as in this case, without specifying the extent or frequency of them, the court may and, as I think, should treat the agreement as imposing upon the landlord an obligation to provide the attendance and services to an extent and frequency and standard which are in all the circumstances reasonable. Such a standard upon the material before the learned judge in this appeal could not be regarded as either extensive or elaborate; it would be of the order of removing rubbish daily or at least every other day, cleaning once a week and laundering sheets fortnightly. The evidence later put in by Mr Silvaesa did not show anything different except for the fact that he asserts that these appellants cleaned the flat themselves.

The learned judge, in my opinion, was right in reaching the conclusion that, if the written agreement represented the agreement between the parties, then, upon its true construction, these appellants were lodgers and not tenants. The agreement does require the landlord to provide attendance and services which require the landlord and his servants to exercise unrestricted access to and use of the room. Possession and control of the room are reserved by clause 2 of the agreement to the landlord for the purposes of discharging the obligation to provide attendance and services and that shows, in my judgment, that exclusive possession was not given. The right to require the lodger to move from one room to another could not, as I think, by itself be conclusive to show that there was no grant of exclusive occupation of the room for residential accommodation if the terms otherwise showed that there was such a grant; but the reservation of the right . . . seems to me wholly consistent with the status of lodger and of an intention on the part of the landlord to look after the house and furniture by himself or his servants and to retain to himself the occupation.

Note
The provision of services is not a decisive factor in itself. If, however, the landlord provides services which require him or his servants to exercise unrestricted access and care of the premises, the occupier is a licensee.

(d) Descriptive labels and sham agreements
The House of Lords decision in *Street* v *Mountford* confirms the doctrine that the descriptive label which the parties attach to the agreement is evidence of the parties' intention, but is not conclusive.

University of Reading v *Johnson-Houghton*
(1985) 276 EG 1353 (QB)

Over a period of years P, the owner of the land, had granted to D (and his predecessors) a right to use 'gallops'. All the grants had been expressed to be 'licences'. On the expiry of the term of the current grant, P wanted the new grant to contain a declaration that it did not create a tenancy. D refused, as he believed that he already had a tenancy. He continued to use the gallops. Held: D had a tenancy.

LEONARD J: [Leonard J discusses the authority in *Street* v *Mountford* relating to this point.]

From these authorities I derive the following propositions. First of all, it does not matter what the grant is expressed to be; in other words, whether it is expressed to be a lease or a licence. It is the true nature of the deed which the court will determine and uphold by its judgment. Second, the determining factor is whether the defendant in this case had the right to exclusive possession of the gallops and the hatched land; in other words, whether he had the right in general to exclude the owner during the currency of the agreement.

Note
The decision in *University of Reading* v *Johnson* confirms *Addiscombe Garden Estates Ltd* v *Crabbe* [1958] 1 QB 513. The agreement here was described as a licence but it was held that the agreement taken as a whole, although described as such, was on its true construction one of landlord and tenant not that of licensor and licensee (see pages 166–7).

See *Somma* v *Hazlehurst* [1978] 1 WLR 1014, page 168.

(e) Joint occupation

Hadjiloucas v *Crean* [1987] 3 All ER 1008 (CA)

A and B together agreed with the owner of premises to take a furnished two-roomed flat with separate kitchen and bathroom for a term of six months. They were each given an identical copy of documents purporting to be licences which stated 'The Licensor shall grant and the Licensee accept a licence to share with ONE others each be separately licensed by the Licensor and to the intent that the Licensee shall not have exclusive possession' of the premises. Both A and B were individually responsible for the whole rent of the flat. After a time, B left. B had arranged with the owner for R to take her place, although A had not been consulted. Held:

(1) Where two or more persons occupied a flat at the same time there was no presumption that between them they had a right to exclusive possession.

(2) The right of the landlord to nominate new occupants may merely be evidence of parallel tenancies in relation to identifiable separate parts of the premises but was a factor to be strongly considered.

(3) All the facts must be taken into account in deciding whether the agreement created a joint tenancy or two separate licences.

Note
This case was followed in the House of Lords in the next two cases.

A G Securities v *Vaughan; Antoniades* v *Villiers*
[1988] 3 All ER 1058; [1988] 3 WLR 1205 (HL)

In the first case, A granted a right to occupy a furnished four-bedroomed flat to four individual flat sharers under separate agreements. Each agreement was termed a 'licence'. Each was made at a different time and on different terms. Each agreement provided that each occupant had various rights but 'without the right to exclusive possession of any part of the . . . flat'. When an occupant left a new one was chosen by the mutual agreement of A and the other occupants.

In the second case, an unmarried couple took a flat from R, under separate but identical agreements described as 'licences'. The agreements stated that the occupants were not to have exclusive possession and clause 16 said 'The

licensor shall be entitled at any time to use the rooms together with the licensee and to permit other person to use all of the rooms together with the licensee'.
Held:

(1) In the first case the effect of the agreements was not to create a collective joint tenancy of the flat. The agreements were independent of one another, commenced on different dates, covered different periods and provided for different payments to be made. Each agreement therefore created a licence.
(2) In the second case the agreements were interdependent. In the circumstances they should be taken together as a single transaction. R knew that the couple were living as husband and wife. The true nature of the arrangement was to create a joint tenancy. The purported retention by the owner of the right to share the occupation with the tenants was a sham.

LORD OLIVER: There is an air of total unreality about [the] documents [in *Antoniades* v *Villiers*] read as separate and individual licences in the light of the circumstance that the appellants were together seeking a flat as a quasi-matrimonial home. A separate licensee does not realistically assume responsibility for all repairs and all outgoings. . . . It cannot realistically have been contemplated that the respondent would either himself use or occupy any part of the flat or put some other person in to share accommodation specifically adapted for the occupation by a couple living together. . . . The unreality is enhanced by the reservation of the right of eviction without court order, which cannot seriously have been thought to be effective, and by the accompanying agreement not to get married, which can only have been designed to prevent a situation arising in which it would be quite impossible to argue that the 'licensees' were enjoying separate rights of occupation.

The conclusion seems to me irresistible that these two so-called licences, executed contemporaneously and entered into in the circumstances already outlined, have to be read together as constituting in reality one single transaction under which the appellants became joint occupiers. That of course does not conclude the case because the question still remains: what is the effect?

The document is clearly based on the form of document which was upheld by the Court of Appeal as an effective licence in *Somma* v *Hazlehurst* [1978] 2 All ER 1011, [1978] 1 WLR 1014. That case, which rested on what was said to be the impossibility of the two licensees having between them exclusive possession, was overruled in *Street* v *Mountford* [1985] 2 All ER 289, [1985] AC 809. It was, however, a case which related to a single room and it is suggested that a similar agreement relating to premises containing space which could, albeit uncomfortably, accommodate another person is not neccesarily governed by the same principle. On the other hand, in this case the trial judge found that apart from the few visits by the respondent (who, on all but one occasion, sought admission by knocking on the door) no one shared with the appellants and that they had exclusive possession. He held that the licences were 'artificial transactions designed to evade the Rent Acts', that a tenancy was created and that the appellants occupied as joint tenants.

His decision was reversed by the Court of Appeal on, broadly, the grounds that he had erred in treating the subsequent conduct of the parties as admissible as an aid to construction of the agreements and that, in so far as the holding above referred to constituted a finding that the licences were a sham, that was unsupported by the evidence inasmuch as the appellants' intention that they should enjoy exclusive possession was not shared by the respondent (see [1988] 2 All ER 309, [1988] 3 WLR 139). The licences could not, therefore, be said to mask the real intention of the parties and fell to be construed by reference to what they said in terms.

If the documents fall to be taken seriously at their face value and to be construed according to their terms, I see, for my part, no escape from the conclusion at which the Court of Appeal arrived. If it is once accepted that the respondent enjoyed the right, whether he exercised it or not, to share the accommodation with the appellants, either himself or by introducing one or more other persons to use the flat with them, it is, as it seems to me, incontestable that the appellants cannot claim to have had exclusive possession. The appellants' case therefore rests, as counsel for the appellants frankly admits, on upholding the judge's approach that the true transaction contemplated was that the appellants should jointly enjoy exclusive possession and that the licences were mere sham or window-dressing to indicate legal incidents which were never seriously intended in fact, but which would be inconsistent with the application to that transaction of the Rent Acts. Now to begin with, I do not, for my part, read the notes of the judge's judgment as showing that he construed the agreement in the light of what the parties subsequently did. I agree entirely with the Court of Appeal that if he did that he was in error. But, though subsequent conduct is irrelevant as an aid to construction, it is certainly admissible as evidence on the question of whether the documents were or were not genuine documents giving effect to the parties' true intentions. Broadly what is said by counsel for the appellants is that nobody acquainted with the circumstances in which the parties had come together and with the physical layout and size of the premises could seriously have imagined that the clauses in the licence which, on the face of them, contemplate the respondent and an apparently limitless number of other persons moving in to share the whole of the available accommodation, including the bedroom, with what, to all intents and purposes, was a married couple committed to paying £174 a month in advance, were anything other than a smoke-screen; and the fact the respondent, who might be assumed to want to make the maximum profit out of the premises, never sought to introduce anyone else is at least some indication that that is exactly what it was. Adopting the definition of a sham formulated by Purchas LJ in *Hadjiloucas* v *Crean* [1987] 3 All ER 1008 at 1014, [1988] 1 WLR 1006 at 1013, counsel for the appellants submits that the licences clearly incorporate clauses by which neither party intended to be bound and which were obviously a smoke-screen to cover the real intentions of both contracting parties. In the Court of Appeal Bingham LJ tested the matter by asking two questions, viz ([1987] 3 All ER 1008 at 317, [1988] 3 WLR 139 at 149): (1) on what grounds, if one party had left the premises, could the remaining party have been made liable for anything more than the £87 which he or she had agreed to pay? and (2) on what ground could they have resisted a demand by the respondent to introduce a further person into the premises? For my part, however, I do not see how this helps. The assumed negative answers prove nothing, for they rest on the assumption that the licences are not sham documents, which is the very question in issue.

If the real transaction was, as the judge found, one under which the appellants became joint tenants with exclusive possession, on the footing that the two agreements are to be construed together, then it would follow that they were together jointly and severally responsible for the whole rent. It would equally follow that they could effectively exclude the respondent and his nominees.

Although the facts are not precisely on all fours with *Somma* v *Hazlehurst* [1978] 2 All ER 1011, [1978] 1 WLR 1014, they are strikingly similar and the judge was, in my judgment, entitled to conclude that the appellants had exclusive possession of the

premises. I read his finding that 'the licences are artificial transactions designed to evade the Rent Acts' as a finding that they were sham documents designed to conceal the true nature of the transaction. There was, in my judgment, material on which he could properly reach this conclusion and I, too, would allow the appeal.
...

Taking first, by way of example, the position in [*AG Securities* v *Vaughan*] of the first occupier to be let into the permises on the terms of one of these agreements, it is, in my judgment, quite unarguable, once any question of sham is out of the way, that he has an estate in the premises which entitles him to exclusive possession. His right, which is, by definition, a right to share use and occupation with such other persons not exceeding three in number as the licensor shall introduce from time to time, is clearly inconsistent with any exclusive possession in him alone even though he may be the only person in physical occupation at a particular time. He has no legal title which will permit him to exclude other persons to whom the licensor may choose to grant the privilege of entry. That must equally apply to the additional licensees who join him. None of them has individually nor have they collectively the right or power lawfully to exclude a further nominee of the licensor within the prescribed maximum.

I pause to note that it has never been contended that any individual occupier has a tenancy of a particular room in the flat with a right to use the remainder of the flat in common with the tenants of other rooms. I can envisage that as a possibility in cases of arrangements of this kind if the facts support the marking out with the landlord's concurrence of a particular room as the exclusive domain of a particular individual. But to support that there would, I think, have to be proved the grant of an identifiable part of the flat and that simply does not fit with the system described in the evidence of the instant case.

The real question, and it is this on which the respondents rely, is what is the position when the flat is occupied concurrently by all four licensees? What is said then is that, since the licensor has now exhausted, for the time being, his right of nomination, the four occupants collectively have exclusive possession of the premises because they can collectively exclude the licensor himself. Because, it is argued, (1) they have thus exclusive possession and (2) there is an ascertainable term during which all have the right to use and occupy and (3) they are occupying in consideration of the payment of periodic sums of money, *Street* v *Mountford* [1985] 2 All ER 289, [1985] AC 809 shows that they are collectively tenants of the premises. They are not lodgers. Therefore they must be tenants. And, because each is not individually a tenant, they must together be joint tenants.

My Lords, there appear to me to be a number of fallacies here. In the first place, the assertion of an exclusive possession rests, as it seems to me, on assuming what it is sought to prove. If, of course, each licence agreement creates a tenancy, each tenant will be sharing with other persons whose rights to be there rest on their own estates which, once they have been granted, they enjoy in their own right independently of the landlord. Collectively they have the right to exclude everyone other than those who have concurrent estates. But if the licence agreement is what it purports to be, that is to say merely an agreement for permissive enjoyment as the invitee of the landlord, then each shares the use of the premises with other invitees of the same landlord. The landlord is not excluded for he continues to enjoy the premises through his invitees, even though he may for the time being have precluded himself by contract with each from withdrawing the invitation. Second, the fact that under each agreement an individual has the privilege of user and occupation for a term which overlaps the term of user and occupation of other persons in the premises does not create a single indivisible term of occupation for all four consisting of an amalgam of the individual overlapping periods. Third, there is no single sum of money payable in respect of use and occupation. Each person is individually liable for the amount which he has agreed, which may differ in practice from the amounts paid by all or some of the others.

The respondents are compelled to support their claims by a stange and unnatural theory that, as each occupant terminates his agreement, there is an implied surrender by the other three and an implied grant of a new joint tenancy to them together with the new incumbent when he enters under his individual agreement. With great respect to the majority in the Court of Appeal, this appears to me to be entirely unreal. For my part, I agree with the dissenting judgment of Sir George Waller in finding no unity of interest, no unity of title, certainly no unity of time and, as I think, no unity of possession. I find it impossible to say that the agreements entered into with the respondents created either individually or collectively a single tenancy either of the entire flat or of any part of it. I agree that the appeal should be allowed.

Notes
1. See also *Stribling* v *Wickham* (1989) 27 EG 81 (CA), where the court had to decide whether a number of agreements, each purporting to be a licence, created a joint tenancy. Parker LJ said:

> ... [I]n determining whether a number of agreements, each purporting to grant a mere individual licence, collectively create a joint tenancy:
> (a) The court must construe the agreements in the light of the surrounding circumstances which will include any relationship between the prospective occupiers, the course of negotiations, the nature and extent of the accommodation and the intended and actual mode of occupation of the accommodation.
> (b) The actual mode of accommodation may not be used as a guide to construction of the documents but may be used as an aid to determining whether any parts of the agreements should be ignored when determining upon their construction, as being parts which were never intended to be acted upon but which were put in solely for the purpose of disguising the grant of tenancy.
> (c) The task of the court is to determine the true nature ... or substance and reality ... of the transaction.
> (d) There will be many factors which will assist in the determination of the nature of the transaction and of the question whether any and which provisions of the agreement were never intended to be acted upon, some of which are specified in the passages which I have quoted and others of which may be found in other parts of their lordships' speeches which I do not quote because to do so would unnecessarily lengthen this judgment. What appears to me to be clear is that their lordships were not purporting to set out an exhaustive list of such factors but were merely stating the particular factors which in the particular cases had led them to reach their conclusion.
> (e) The fact that the agreements under consideration by the court were all entered into at one time by way of replacement of earlier agreements will not be significant if the earlier agreements were entered into separately.

2. See J. L. Barton, 'Concurrent licensees' (1990) 106 LQR 215; P. V. Baker 'Exclusive possession determined' (1989) 105 LQR 165; Jonathan Hill,

'Shared accommodation and exclusive possession' (1989) 52 MLR 408; Charles Harpum, Leases, licenses, sharing and shams' [1989] CLJ 19.

(f) Payment of rent

Lord Templeman, in *Street* v *Mountford*, said that the grant must be 'at a rent for a term' in order for there to be a tenancy. Rent has, however, never been a necessary criterion to give rise to a tenancy or a lease (see page 162).

The case of *Ashburn Anstalt* v *Arnold* [1989] Ch 1 seems to uphold the established view and cast doubt on Lord Templeman's statement, for in that case it was held that although no rent was payable, the agreement nevertheless gave the grantee exclusive possession of the premises for a certain period of time and thus created a tenancy, even though the agreement was expressed in terms of a licence.

See A. J. Oakley, 'Licences and leases — a return to orthodoxy' [1988] CLJ 353. See also the first instance decision of Ferris J in *Colchester Borough Council* v *Smith* [1991] 2 All ER 29.

(g) Occupation through employment

Norris v *Checksfield* [1991] 1 WLR 1241 (CA)

An employer owned a bungalow and allowed his employee to occupy it. Before taking possession the employee signed an agreement referring to his licence to occupy the bungalow which said that such a licence would terminate if and when his employment did. The employer deducted £5 per week from the employee's wages to allow for his occupation of the bungalow. The employer dismissed the employee. Held: even if an employee is given exclusive possession of premises owned by his employer and pays rent, that does not necessarily imply that there is a tenancy, provided the employee is genuinely required to occupy it for the better performance of his duties.

B: PUBLIC AUTHORITIES AND THE LEASE LICENCE DISTINCTION

Westminster City Council v *Clark*
[1992] 1 All ER 695 (HL)

P placed D into temporary accommodation in a hostel for single men to fulfil its duty under the Housing Act 1985. D was granted a 'licence to occupy' a room which was allocated to him and he paid a weekly charge for the room. The agreement between P and D stated that D did not have exclusive possession of the room, that P could change D's room without giving him notice of such a change, that D could only occupy the room in common with P and that the agreement did not create the relationship of landlord and tenant. P sought to terminate the agreement after there had been breaches of the agreement. D claimed that he was a tenant. Held: D was not a tenant but a mere licensee.

[Lord Templeman discusses *Street* v *Mountford*, *AG Securities* v *Vaughan* and *Antoniades* v *Villiers*.]

The question is whether upon the true construction of the licence to occupy and in the circumstances in which Mr Clarke was allowed to occupy room E, there was a grant by the council to Mr Clarke of exclusive possession of room E.

From the point of view of the council the grant of exclusive possession would be inconsistent with the purposes for which the council provided the accommodation at Cambridge Street. It was in the interests of Mr Clarke and each of the occupiers of the hostel that the council should retain possession of each room. If one room became uninhabitable another room could be shared between two occupiers. If one room became unsuitable for an occupier he could be moved elsewhere. If the occupier of one room became a nuisance he could be compelled to move to another room where his actions might be less troublesome to his neighbours. If the occupier of a room had exclusive possession he could prevent the council from entering the room save for the purpose of protecting the council's interests and not for the purpose of supervising and controlling the conduct of the occupier in his interests. If the occupier of a room had exclusive possession he could not be obliged to comply with the terms of the conditions of occupation. Mr Clarke could not, for example, be obliged to comply with the directions of the warden or to exclude visitors or to comply with any of the other conditions of occupation which are designed to help Mr Clarke and the other occupiers of the hostel and to enable the hostel to be conducted in an efficient and harmonious manner. The only remedy of the council for breaches of the conditions of occupation would be the lengthy and uncertain procedure required by the 1985 Act to be operated for the purpose of obtaining possession from a secure tenant. In the circumstances of the present case I consider that the council legitimately and effectively retained for themselves possession of room E and that Mr Clarke was only a licensee with rights corresponding to the rights of a lodger. In reaching this conclusion I take into account the object of the council, namely the provision of temporary accommodation for vulnerable homeless persons, the necessity for the council to retain possession of all the rooms in order to make and administer arrangements for the suitable accommodation of all the occupiers and the need for the council to retain possession of every room not only in the interests of the council as the owners of the hostel but also for the purpose of providing for the occupier supervision and assistance. For many obvious reasons it was highly undesirable for the council to grant to any occupier of a room exclusive possession which obstructed the use by the council of all the rooms of the hostel in the interests of every occupier. By the terms of the licence to occupy Mr Clarke was not entitled to any particular room, he could be required to share with any other person as required by the council and he was only entitled to 'occupy accommodation in common with the Council whose representative may enter the accommodation at any time'. It is accepted that these provisions of the licence to occupy were inserted to enable the council to discharge its responsibilities to the vulnerable persons accommodated at the Cambridge Street hostel and were not inserted for the purpose of enabling the council to avoid the creation of a secure tenancy. The conditions of occupancy support the view that Mr Clarke was not in exclusive occupation of room E. He was expressly limited in his enjoyment of any accommodation provided for him. He was forbidden to entertain visitors without the approval of the council staff and was bound to comply with the council's warden or other staff in charge of the hostel. These limitations confirmed that the council retained possession of all the rooms of the hostel in order to supervise and control the activities of the occupiers, including Mr Clarke. Although Mr Clarke physcially occupied room E he did not enjoy possession exclusively of the council.

This is a very special case which depends on the peculiar nature of the hostel maintained by the council, the use of the hostel by the council, the totality, immediacy and objectives of the powers exercisable by the council and the restrictions imposed on Mr Clarke. The decision in this case will not allow a landlord private or public to free himself from the Rent Acts or from the restrictions of a secure tenancy merely be adopting or adapting the language of the licence to occupy. The provisions of the licence to occupy and the circumstances in which that licence was granted and continued lead to the conclusion that Mr Clarke has never enjoyed that exclusive possession which he claims. I would therefore allow the appeal and restore the order for possession made by the trial judge.

See also *Tower Hamlets LBC* v *Miah* (1991) *The Times*, 17 December.

C: HAS *STREET* v *MOUNTFORD* ANY APPLICATION TO NON-RESIDENTIAL TENANCIES?

Dresden Estates v *Collinson*
[1987] 1 EGLR 45 (CA)

C entered into a written agreement with D, described throughout as a licence, for the occupation of a unit in industrial premises. Provisions were included for payment of a 'licence fee' of £200 per month. Several terms, described as 'agreements' were similar to standard terms in business tenancies, for example, C agreed to pay general and water rates and to allow D and the necessary workmen and contractors to enter the premises to carry out any work deemed necessary by D. The agreement expressly said that C was not entitled to exclusive possession of the premises. Held: the court must look at the intention of the parties. The agreement indicated that there was a licence between the parties not a lease.

GLIDEWELL LJ: . . . *Street* v *Mountford*, as I have said, was concerned with residential premises. Mr Coveney conceded that there was no material difference, at least for present purposes, between the law applicable to residential premises and the law applicable to business premises. As a broad, general proposition that may be right, but I am not sure that his concession may not have gone too far in this respect, that the attributes of residential premises and business premises are often quite different.

The passage that I have already quoted from the speech of Lord Templeman [[1985] AC 809, at p. 817H], where he says in effect that all you have to decide in relation to residential premises is whether the occupier is a tenant or a lodger, is, of course, of itself not applicable to business premises because there is no such person as a lodger in relation to business premises. For myself, I think that the indicia, which may make it more apparent in the case of a residential tenant or a residential occupier that he is indeed a tenant, may be less applicable or be less likely to have that effect in the case of some business tenancies.

LLOYD LJ: Clause 2 of the agreement looks like an agreement for a tenancy, despite the numerous references to 'Licence', 'Licensor' and 'Licensee'. In particular, the grant of a limited right to the licensor to enter for the purpose of carrying out work is consistent only with a tenancy. The grant of an *unlimited* right of entry would be consistent with a licence, even superfluous. But the grant of a *limited* right would seem to have no place at all in a licence.

But when one comes to clause 4 the agreement wears a different complexion. Clause 4(b) confers on the licensor the right to require the licensee to transfer to other premises. Mr Coveney argues that that is a right which the licensor can exercise during the continuance of the licence. It is a right which is wholly inconsistent with a right to exclusive possession during the continuance of the agreement and is therefore wholly inconsistent with a tenancy.

Mr Rank meets that argument in this way. He submits that a notice under clause 4(b) must, in reality and of necessity, bring the old agreement to an end. There is no way in which the existing agreement can be made to apply to the new premises. The parties must, therefore, have contemplated that, on the exercise of the right under 4(b), they would enter into a new agreement. In support of that argument, Mr Rank says it is significant that the period of notice required under clause 4(b), namely three months, is the same as the period of notice to terminate the agreement under clause 4(e).

If that argument of Mr Rank's be correct, then it would undermine the basis of Mr Coveney's argument that the licensor can require the licensee to move to other premises during the continuance of the agreement.

Mr Coveney replies by drawing attention to the words of clause 4(b), 'this occupation'. He suggests that that means that the agreement was indeed to be capable of continuing after the transfer to new premises. No doubt the parties could have reached the same result by giving notice to terminate and then entering into a new agreement. But that is not what clause 4(b) contemplates.

I was nearly persuaded by Mr Rank's submission, and, like Glidewell LJ, I would pay tribute to his excellent argument, as indeed to the arguments on both sides. But Mr Rank's construction of the agreement does not, in my judgment, do full justice to clause 4(b). That means that clause 2 points in one direction and clause 4 points in another. Looking at the agreement as a whole, I agree with Glidewell LJ that clause 4 must prevail. If that be right, then the appeal must be allowed.

I would only add, like Glidewell LJ, that our decision today should not be regarded as providing a way round the decision of the House of Lords in *Street* v *Mountford* [1985] AC 809. It will be in only a limited class of case that a provision such as is found in clause 4(b) would be appropriate. If it is included in an agreement where it is not appropriate, then it will not carry the day.

Note

It was suggested by Ferris J in *Colchester BC* v *Smith*, at first instance, that although *Street* v *Mountford* relates to residential accommodation, there seemed to be no reason why the principle was not applicable to agricultural land.

Questions

1. Do you think that the decision in *Street* v *Mountford* at first instance, has created more problems than it has solved?

2. Arabella has recently moved to Cardiff to study law. She has found great difficulty obtaining accommodation and has ultimately found a one-bedroomed self-contained flat in a house near to the University. The owner, who also lives in the house, has presented her with a document headed 'Licence Agreement'. The main terms of the agreement are as follows:

   1. This agreement is intended to create a licence and not a tenancy.
   4. The monthly rent of £150 will be paid by the licensee in advance of the first day of each month.

Leasehold Interests and Covenants

    5. The licensor retains possession of the flat, but undertakes not to enter the flat without prior notice to the licensee, apart from in cases of emergency.
    7. The licence will commence on 1 October 1992 and will terminate on 30 September 1993.

Advise Arabella of the effect of this agreement.

SECTION 3: FORM OF A LEASE

The creation or transfer of a legal lease must be made by means of a deed, unless the lease is to take effect in possession and is for a term of less than three years (see chapter 4, section 3).

A legal periodic tenancy (see section 4, *post*) may be created without any kind of formality, even though there is a possibility that it will endure for a period of more than three years. See *Kushner* v *Law Society* [1952] 1 KB 264.

If a lease for less than three years contains an option to renew it, such an option does not convert the lease into a term exceeding three years, even if the tenant will ultimately enjoy possession of the land for a period exceeding three years. The option merely has the effect of creating a new term, which if in itself is for less than three years is valid. Leases for life, if granted at a rent or in consideration of a fine, are automatically converted into a 90-year term (Law of Property Act 1925, s. 149(6)). In such a case, since the term of 90 years comes about through operation of law it is immune from the provisions of s. 52(1) of the Law of Property Act 1925 (s. 52(2)(g)).

Failure to execute the assignment or create the lease in the correct form means that the lease may take effect in equity as a contract to create a lease (estate contract) in certain situations (see chapter 4, section 5; *Walsh* v *Lonsdale*). The effect of the decision in *Walsh* v *Lonsdale* is to convert a defective legal lease into a valid equitable one. It has thus been said, by Cotton LJ in *Lowther* v *Heaver* (1889) 41 ChD 248, at p. 264, that an agreement for a lease is as good as the lease itself. There are situations, however, when the equitable lease falls short of a legal one:

    (a) The equitable lease is dependent upon the grant of the discretionary remedy of specific performance. If the contract is one where equity cannot or will not grant specific performance, then the tenant is merely left with an action for breach of contract, and his rights will be those given to a periodic tenant where the tenancy is implied by law. (For a criticism of this, see S. Gardner, 'Equity, Estate Contracts and the Judicature Acts: *Walsh* v *Lonsdale* Revisited' (1987) 7 OJLS 60.)
    (b) The tenant of an equitable lease under this doctrine will not get the benefit of the Law of Property Act 1925, s. 62, since this section specifically refers to a 'conveyance ' of a legal estate. Easements and other rights can be implied in the tenant's favour by means of s. 62 but they cannot be so implied if the lease is an equitable one under *Walsh* v *Lonsdale* (see chapter 4).

(c) There is no privity of estate between the landlord and tenant in the case of an equitable lease. Certain covenants 'run with the land' only if there is privity of estate (see page 198 *et seq.*).

(d) As a contract to create a lease is an equitable interest, then in the system of unregistered conveyancing the interest does not have the superior status that a legal lease would have, and therefore has to be registered as a class C(iv) land charge against the name of the landlord. If it is not registered it is void against a purchaser of a legal estate for money or money's worth (Land Charges Act 1972, s. 4(6)). See *Hollington Bros Ltd v Rhodes* (chapter 2).

In registered conveyancing, the holder of such an equitable interest should protect the interest as a minor interest. If this is not done, then the interest will be ineffective against the transferee of the landlord's registered title. If the holder of the equitable lease is in occupation of the property, then he may have an overriding interest that does not need protection by registration (see *Grace Rymer Investments v Waite* [1958] Ch 831, at p. 849).

Coatsworth v *Johnson*
(1886) 55 LJ QB 220 (CA)

P and D entered into an agreement for a 21-year lease of a farm and P entered into possession. P served notice to quit for breach of a covenant contained in the agreement and intended to be incorporated into the lease. At that time no rent had become due or been paid. Held: the plaintiff could not recover possession.

LINDLEY LJ: It must be taken as a fact that there was no lease in force between this plaintiff and his landlord, that there was an agreement for a lease, and that the plaintiff had entered into possession under that agreement. To assert that such a state of facts makes the agreement equivalent to a lease, and to assume that a court of equity would necessarily in such a case make a decree for specific performance of the agreement, on the ground that a court of equity considers that to be done which ought to be done — a doctrine which requires to be taken with some reservation — is, I think, an error. Here the plaintiff had entered into certain covenants, and had made default with regard to some of those covenants, so that he could not have obtained a decree for specific performance of that agreement....

Note
At law, if the formalities are not complied with the lease is void. However, a legal lease may come into operation in the following circumstances: A tenancy at will (see *ante*) arises by implication where a tenant enters into possession of the property with the landlord's consent, even though the formally executed lease is invalid. Once a periodic rent is offered by the tenant at will and that rent is accepted by the landlord, the tenancy at will is converted by implication of law into a periodic tenancy, the duration of which is governed, prima facie, by the period for which the rent is payable (see *Martin v Smith* (1874) LR 9 Exch 50).

SECTION 4: TYPES OF LEASES AND TENANCIES

(a) Fixed term leases
These are leases of a fixed duration. The duration can vary from a few weeks to many years, although the shorter the duration the more likely the arrangement is to be called a tenancy; and the longer it is the more likely it is to be called a lease. This lease will terminate, without any notice to quit being issued, on the natural effusion of time. It can be terminated before this, however, if a tenant is in breach of one of his obligations under the lease, or if notice to quit is served, provided that there is provision for such in the lease.

(b) Periodic tenancies
This is a tenancy which runs from week to week, or month to month, or quarter to quarter, or year to year. These tenancies can be created expressly or by operation of law. They continue until they are determined by the appropriate notice being given. Where a periodic tenancy is held by two or more persons as joint tenants, it can be determined by a valid notice to quit given by one joint tenant without the knowledge or consent of the others (*Hammersmith and Fulham London Borough Council* v *Monk* (1991) *The Times*, 6 December 1991).

Periodic tenancies arise by operation of law whenever a person is in occupation of the land with the owner's permission, not as a licensee nor for an agreed period, and the rent is assessed by reference to the period paid and accepted.

(i) *Where a tenant at will pays a yearly rent*

Adler v Blackman [1953] 1 QB 146 (CA)

D held a weekly tenancy but then entered into an agreement with L for a 12-month tenancy. D remained in occupation after the expiration of the 12-month term, continuing to pay the weekly rent of £3. Held: this was a weekly tenancy.

(ii) *Where a tenant at sufferance pays a yearly rent*

Dougal v McCarthy [1893] 1 QB 736 (CA)

T held premises under a tenancy agreement expressed to be for one year at a rent of £140 per annum, payable quarterly in advance. T remained in possession after the expiry of the term and L demanded a further quarter's rent. T did not pay further rent but wrote to the landlord indicating that they would discontinue the tenancy and that the landlord could take possession prior to the commencement of the next quarter. Held: there was a tenancy from year to year on the terms of the former lease so far as they were not inconsistent with the tenancy.

(c) Tenancy at will

This arises when a tenant occupies land with the consent of the owner and either party is able to terminate the arrangement at will.

A tenancy at will must be capable of continuing indefinitely. Unless the parties agree that the tenancy is to be rent free, the tenant must pay an agreed sum. If there is no agreed rent and the tenant offers and landlord accepts some payment of rent which is referable to a year or a part of a year, then the tenancy at will is converted into a periodic tenancy, the period being determined by reference to the frequency of rent payments.

Javad v *Aqil* [1991] 1 All ER 243 (CA)

P was negotiating a lease of premises to D and allowed D into possession on payment of a quarter's rent in advance, even though the terms of the lease had not been finalised. While negotiations continued, D made two further quarterly payments. When an agreement could not be reached P gave D notice to quit. Held: the inferred intention in such circumstances was to create a tenancy at will, not a periodic tenancy, until terms were agreed for the lease.

(d) Tenancy at sufferance

This arises when a tenant who has enjoyed a valid tenancy holds over after the expiry of the valid tenancy, and it is the absence of the landlord's consent that distinguishes this from the previous category. The tenancy may be determined at any time. See *Wheeler* v *Mercer* [1957] AC 416.

(e) Tenancy by estoppel

See A. M. Prichard, 'Tenancy by estoppel' (1964) 80 LQR 370.

Where a person with no estate in land purports to grant a lease of the land, then such a grant cannot pass an actual estate. Nevertheless, even though the lessor's want of title was apparent to both parties, the lessor is estopped from repudiating the tenancy and the tenant is estopped from denying its existence. As between the two estoppel parties the tenancy possesses all the characteristics of a true tenancy. The covenants contained in the lease are enforceable between the parties and their successors in title, but the estoppel does not bind strangers.

(i) *'Feeding the estoppel'*

Church of England Building Society v *Piskor*
[1954] Ch 553 (CA)

D agreed to purchase the residue of a 99-year lease and went into occupation prior to completion. D then entered into purported weekly tenancies with other parties in respect of parts of the premises, to which the Rent Restriction Acts applied. The purchase was then completed and a legal mortgage dated on the day of completion charged the premises to P. The charge contained a term that the power of leasing conferred by s. 99(1) of the Law of Property Act 1925 was excluded. Held: the assignment and creation of the legal charge could not be regarded as a single transaction. For a scintilla of time a legal interest in the premises had vested in the purchasers before they could execute a charge in favour of the plaintiffs. The tenancy by estoppel which had been created in favour of the tenants was therefore fed by the legal estate which had vested in the borrowers, and the tenants' rights took priority over the rights of the plaintiffs.

ROMER LJ: ... The theory that a purchase, which is completed by payment of money which has been provided in part by a third party, and a mortgage by the purchaser of the property sold to secure the repayment of that money to the lender, constitutes only one transaction, if the instruments are executed at more or less the same time, is a conception which has a prima facie appeal, but it does not, on analysis, in my opinion, truly reflect the legal effect of what takes place. The mortgage of the purchased property cannot have any operation in law (whatever rights it may give rise to in equity or by estoppel) unless and until the purchaser is in a position to vest a legal term in the property, as security, in the mortgagee, and he is not and cannot be in a position to do this until he himself has acquired from the vendor the legal estate out of which the mortgage term is capable of being created. From this it follows that the execution and delivery of the conveyance (if the property is freehold) or of the assignment (in the case of a leasehold) by the vendor to the purchaser must of necessity constitute an essential preliminary to the vesting in the mortgagee of a subsidiary interest in the property. Mr Lightman pressed upon us the necessity of looking at the substance rather than the form of the transaction which took place in the present case and referred us to such cases as *Meux* v *Smith* [11 Sim 410] in support of that proposition. I am very willing to do so, but the substance of the transaction was that the purchasers were to purchase property with money lent in part by the building society and give the society a mortgage on the property for the loan. All this has in fact been done and the society has got its security but, look at it how one will, the fact remains that the purchasers could not have given the society the legal charge which the society required unless, at the time when the charge was executed, the purchaser were the owners of the legal interest in the property charged. That this was recognized by the society itself is sufficiently shown by the fact that there appears in the schedule to the charge the statement that the premises were then (that is to say, at the moment of the delivery of the charge) vested in the mortgagors — a circumstance of evidence upon which Danckwerts J relied in *Woolwich Equitable Building Society* v *Marshall* [[1952] Ch 1]. I agree with Danckwerts J that the plaintiffs, having inserted that statement in the charge, cannot very well complain if the statement is regarded as true. Even without this element, however, I should still regard the legal interest in the purchased premises as having become vested in the purchasers prior to the execution of the charge for, as I say, unless this sequence of interests is observed, the charge would have been wholly ineffective in law to achieve its immediate purpose. I agree with Mr Alcock's submission that a composite transaction cannot be regarded as being one transaction, unless it is not only one but one and indivisible; and that two transactions, each possessing a legal individuality of its own, do not coalesce into one merely because they are dependent on each other.

The whole object of the plaintiffs in trying to displace the view which is both logical and in conformity with conveyancing practice, namely, that the completion of the purchase preceded by however short a time the execution and delivery of the mortgage, is to defeat the claim of the sitting tenants. But for the Rent Restriction Acts the point would have had no importance and would, I suppose, never have been taken at all, for the society could have determined the tenancies by the service of notices to quit; and I find myself unable to treat as one what were, in law, two palpably distinct transactions merely for the purpose of enabling the society to evict persons, who were already in occupation, but whose existence or rights the society had never troubled to inquire about at all.

Note
The estoppel takes effect from the time the tenant goes into possession and continues after he has given up possession, unless he has been evicted by a holder of the paramount title.

(ii) *Covenants in leases*

Industrial Properties (Barton Hill) Ltd v *Associated Electrical Industries Ltd*
[1977] 2 WLR 726 (CA)

In 1959 the owners of an industrial estate, who in fact were trustees, agreed to sell part of it to P, subject to a lease to the predecessors of D. The purchase price was paid and the agreement for sale registered but no conveyance was ever executed. In 1966 D took a new lease of the premises. During the negotiations P's solicitors innocently but mistakenly told D's solicitors that the lessor was the freeholder. The lease was for 21 years from Christmas 1966, and contained a covenant by the lessee to keep the premises in good and tenantable repair and condition. The lease was executed and D occupied the premises and paid rent. After seven years, and in accordance with the terms of the lease, it was determined by P. When D gave up possession the premises were in a worse condition than when they had entered. P claimed damages against D for breach of the repair covenant. Held: a lessee is estopped from disputing his lessor's title not only during the currency of the lease but also after the expiry of the lease unless after termination of the lessee's possession a claim is made against him by title paramount in respect of some period of the lease. D here had undisturbed possession for the whole term of the lease. The innocent misrepresentation that the lessor was the freeholder had done no harm to D. They were estopped from disputing their landlord's title and liable on the repairing covenants in the lease.

LORD DENNING MR: ... In the course of the discussion we were referred to many authorities, old and new. I have considered them all — and others, too — but the result can be stated thus: If a landlord lets a tenant into possession under a lease, then, so long as the tenant remains in possession *undisturbed by any adverse claim* — then the tenant cannot dispute the landlord's title. Suppose the tenant (not having been disturbed) goes out of possession and the landlord sues the tenant on the covenant for rent or for breach of covenant to repair or to yield up in repair. The tenant cannot say to the landlord: 'You are not the true owner of the property.' Likewise, if the landlord, on the tenant's holding over, sues him for possession or for use and occupation or mesne profits, the tenant cannot defend himself by saying: 'The property does not belong to you, but to another.'

But if the tenant is disturbed *by being evicted by title paramount or the equivalent* of it, then he can dispute the landlord's title. Suppose the tenant is actually turned out by the third person — or if the tenant, without going out, acknowledges the title of the third person by attorning to him — or the tenant contests the landlord's claim on an indemnity from the third person — or there is anything else done which is equivalent to an eviction by title paramount — then the tenant is no longer estopped from denying the landlord's title: see *Wilson* v *Anderton* (1830) 1 B & Ad 450, 457, *per* Littledale J. The tenant, being thus disturbed in his possession, can say to the landlord: 'You were not truly the owner at the time when you demanded and received the rent from me. I am liable to pay mesne profits to this other man. So you must repay me the rent which I overpaid you. Nor am I liable to you on the covenants during the time you were not the owner.' See *Newsome* v *Graham* (1829) 10 B & C 234, *Mountnoy* v *Collier* (1853) 1 E & B 630 and *Watson* v *Lane* (1856) 11 Exch 769. The tenant can also claim damages for the eviction if there is, as here, an express covenant for quiet enjoyment covering interruption by title paramount.

Short of eviction by title paramount, or its equivalent, however, the tenant is estopped from denying the title of the landlord. It is no good his saying: 'The property does not belong to you but to a third person' unless that third person actually comes forward and successfully makes an adverse claim — by process in the courts or by the tenant's attornment; or acknowledgment of it as by the tenant defending on an indemnity. If the third person, for some reason or other, makes no adverse claim or is debarred from making it, the tenant remains estopped from denying the landlord's title. This is manifestly correct: for, without an adverse claim, it would mean that the tenant would be enabled to keep the property without paying any rent to anybody or performing any covenants. That cannot be right. That was the reasoning adopted by the Court of Queen's Bench in *Biddle* v *Bond* (1865) 6 B & S 225, a case of a bailor and bailee, but the court treated it as the same as landlord *v* tenant.

Note
See Paul Jackson, 'Tenancies by estoppel and decisions *per incuriam*' (1977) 40 MLR 718; Jeffrey W. Price, '*National Westminster Bank* v *Hart*' [1984] Conv 64; Jill Martin, 'Tenancies by estoppel, equitable leases and priorities' [1978] Conv 137.

(iii) *Determination of landlord's title*

National Westminster Bank v Hart [1983] 1 QB 773 (CA)

D were sub-tenants of some property and discovered in 1978 that they had been paying rent to leaseholders whose title had expired in 1967. D withheld their rent until P, an executor of the leaseholders, showed proof of title. Held: D was under no obligation to continue to pay rent after the landlord's title to the property had determined and D was not estopped from relying on the determination and withholding rent simply because they had been paying rent without knowledge of that determination. There is no requirement that a third party should claim the title before a tenant can withhold rent.

SECTION 5: TERMINATION OF LEASES AND TENANCIES

(a) Expiry
A lease or tenancy may determine automatically at the end of its fixed term, and in such a case the tenant need not be given any notice to quit. There are

certain situations, however, where the expiry of the term does not automatically determine the tenant's rights, for example certain types of residential tenancies that have protection under statute.

(b) Forfeiture
A lease may be determined by forfeiture if a covenant in the lease is breached. (See further page 193 *et seq.*).

(c) Notice to quit
In the case of periodic tenancies, notice may be given by the landlord to the tenant or vice versa. In the absence of any express provision the period of the notice is governed by the common law as amended by statute. At common law a yearly tenancy may be determined by at least half a year's notice expiring at the end of a year of the tenancy. In other cases the notice must be at least one full period and must (unless agreed otherwise) expire on the last day of a completed period of the tenancy.

Protection from Eviction Act 1977

5. Validity of notices to quit

(1) No notice by a landlord or a tenant to quit any premises let (whether before or after the commencement of this Act) as a dwelling shall be valid unless—
   (a) it is in writing and contains such information as may be prescribed, and
   (b) it is given no less than 4 weeks before the date on which it is to take effect.

(2) In this section 'prescribed' means prescribed by regulations made by the Secretary of State by statutory instrument, and a statutory instrument containing any such regulations shall be subject to annulment in pursuance of a resolution of either House of Parliament.

(3) Regulations under this section may make different provision in relation to different descriptions of lettings and different circumstances.

(d) Surrender
A lease can be terminated when a tenant surrenders his interest to his immediate landlord and the landlord accepts the surrender. A surrender may be either express or implied by operation of the law.

(i) *Express surrender* An express surrender of a lease of a term not exceeding three years must be made by means of a deed, since the surrender of the term is in effect a disposition of an estate in land (see Law of Property Act 1925, s. 52). It was possible, however, before the Law of Property (Miscellaneous Provisions) Act 1989, that an oral surrender evidenced in writing or acts of part performance could have been sufficient in equity (see *Hoggett* v *Hoggett* (1980) 39 P & CR 121, at p. 126).

(ii) *Surrender by operation of law* This occurs when the tenant consciously does an act which is inconsistent with the continuance of the tenancy and the landlord concurs. The doctrine is based on estoppel.

Foster v *Robinson* [1951] 1 KB 149 (CA)

Foster, who managed a farm, let a cottage to X, at a rent of £3.5s a half year. X worked on the farm when the cottage was first let and continued to do so after Foster let the farm itself. By 1946 X grew too old and infirm to work but Foster agreed to let X live rent free at the cottage for the rest of his life on the basis that the original tenancy would immediately cease. This X agreed to. The defendant was X's daughter and had been living at the cottage for nine years prior to his death. She claimed to be entitled to remain in the cottage paying the old rent. Held: Foster was entitled to possession on the grounds that the original tenancy had been surrendered in 1946 by operation of the law.

(e) Merger

This occurs when the tenant acquires the landlord's reversion or where a third party acquires both.

Law of Property Act 1925

185. Merger

There is no merger by operation of law only of any estate the beneficial interest in which would not be deemed to be merged or extinguished in equity.

(f) Disclaimer

A lease may be terminated by a disclaimer, for example where a tenant denies his landlord's title. The tenant's lease is then automatically liable to forfeiture, because repudiation of the landlord's title is incompatible with the tenant's obligation not to prejudice the landlord's interests.

Disclaimer may also occur under the Insolvency Act 1986, whereby a trustee in bankruptcy has the power to disclaim property which is vested in him and which is of an onerous nature. Thus if the lease is close to expiring and imposes some sort of liability on the tenant, for example to repair, the trustee in bankruptcy may disclaim the lease, with the leave of the court.

(g) Enlargement

Law of Property Act 1925

153. Enlargement of residue of long terms into fee simple estates

(1) Where a residue unexpired of not less than two hundred years of a term, which, as originally created, was for not less than three hundred years, is subsisting in land, whether being the whole land originally comprised in the term, or part only thereof,—

(a) without any trust or right of redemption affecting the term in favour of the freeholder, or other person entitled in reversion expectant on the term; and

(b) without any rent, or with merely a peppercorn rent or other rent having no money value, incident to the reversion, or having had a rent, not being merely a peppercorn rent or other rent having no money value, originally so incident, which subsequently has been released or has become barred by lapse of time, or has in any other way ceased to be payable;

the term may be enlarged into a fee simple in the manner, and subject to the restrictions in this section provided.

(2) This section applies to and includes every such term as aforesaid whenever created, whether or not having the freehold as the immediate reversion thereon; but does not apply to—

    (i) Any term liable to be determined by re-entry for condition broken; or

    (ii) Any term created by subdemise out of a superior term, itself incapable of being enlarged into fee simple.

(3) This section extends to mortgage terms, where the right of redemption is barred.

(4) A rent not exceeding the yearly sum of one pound which has not been collected or paid for a continuous period of twenty years or upwards shall, for the purposes of this section, be deemed to have ceased to be payable:

Provided that, of the said period, at least five years must have elapsed after the commencement of this Act.

(5) Where a rent incident to a reversion expectant on a term to which this section applies is deemed to have ceased to be payable for the purposes aforesaid, no claim for such rent or for any arrears thereof shall be capable of being enforced.

(6) Each of the following persons, namely—

    (i) Any person beneficially entitled in right of the term, whether subject to any incumbrance or not, to possession of any land comprised in the term, and, in the case of a married woman without the concurrence of her husband, whether or not she is entitled for her separate use or as her separate property, . . .;

    (ii) Any person being in receipt of income as trustee, in right of the term, or having the term vested in him in trust for sale, whether subject to any incumbrance or not;

    (iii) Any person in whom, as personal representative of any deceased person, the term is vested, whether subject to any incumbrance or not;

shall, so far as regards the land to which he is entitled, or in which he is interested in right of the term, in any such character as aforesaid, have power by deed to declare to the effect that, from and after the execution of the deed, the term shall be enlarged into a fee simple.

(7) Thereupon, by virtue of the deed and of this Act, the term shall become and be enlarged accordingly, and the person in whom the term was previously vested shall acquire and have in the land a fee simple instead of the term.

(8) The estate in fee simple so acquired by enlargement shall be subject to all the same trusts, powers, executory limitations over, rights, and equities, and to all the same covenants and provisions relating to user and enjoyment, and to all the same obligations of every kind, as the term would have been subject to if it had not been so enlarged.

(9) But where—

    (a) any land so held for the residue of a term has been settled in trust by reference to other land, being freehold land, so as to go along with that other land, or, in the case of settlements coming into operation before the commencement of this Act, so as to go along with that other land as far as the law permits; and

    (b) at the time of enlargement, the ultimate beneficial interest in the term, whether subject to any subsisting particular estate or not, has not become absolutely and indefeasibly vested in any person, free from charges or powers of charging created by a settlement; the estate in fee simple acquired as aforesaid shall, without prejudice to any conveyance for value previously made by a person having a contingent or defeasible interest in the term, be liable to be, and shall be, conveyed by means of a subsidiary vesting instrument and settled in like manner as the other land, being freehold land, aforesaid, and until so conveyed and settled shall devolve beneficially as if it had been so conveyed and settled.

(10) The estate in fee simple so acquired shall, whether the term was originally created without impeachment of waste or not, include the fee simple in all mines and minerals which at the time of enlargement have not been severed in right or in fact, or have not been severed or reserved by an inclosure Act or award.

(h) Frustration

National Carriers Ltd v Panalpina [1981] AC 675 (HL)

D occupied a warehouse under a ten-year lease which contained a covenant not to use the property other than as a warehouse unless the landlord gave consent. Due to another building becoming dangerous, the street which provided the only access to the warehouse was closed for 20 months and D was effectively unable to use the premises. D claimed the lease was frustrated by the events. Held: (Lord Hailsham, Lord Wilberforce, Lord Simon and Lord Roskill) although the doctrine of frustration theoretically could apply to leases, D had failed to show that the doctrine could be applied in these circumstances, particularly because of the likely length of continuance of the lease after the interruption of user in relation to the term originally granted.

SECTION 6: REMEDIES FOR BREACH OF COVENANTS

A: LANDLORD'S REMEDIES FOR BREACH OF COVENANT BY THE TENANT

(a) Forfeiture of the lease

See Law Commission Report on 'Forfeiture of Tenancies' 1985 (Law Com. No. 142); P. F. Smith, 'Reform of the law of forfeiture' [1986] Conv 165.

A landlord can forfeit the tenancy at any time if a tenant is in breach of a covenant *provided* that a right of entry or re-entry is reserved in the lease. A landlord's right of re-entry amounts to a proprietary interest in the land. If the right of re-entry is annexed to an equitable term of years it is equitable, whereas if it is exercisable in respect of a legal term of years absolute it is legal and therefore enforceable against everyone.

A landlord can enforce his right of re-entry:

(i) By physically entering the land. If, however, he uses force in re-entering, he may commit an offence under ss. 6 and 7 of the Criminal Law Act 1977. If the property is let as a dwelling house, it is an offence to enter the premises to enforce a forfeiture other than by court proceedings, if there is any person lawfully residing on the premises (Rent Act 1977, s. 98(1)).

(ii) By issuing a writ for possession of the property, and if the court makes an order for possession that determines the lease.

The law leans against forfeiture, however, and the tenant may be able to obtain relief from forfeiture.

(i) *Relief from forfeiture for non-payment of rent* If the landlord had reserved a right of re-entry, then at common law he had to make a formal demand for rent. The position is now governed by the Common Law Procedure Act 1852.

Common Law Procedure Act 1852

210. Proceedings in ejectment by landlord for nonpayment of rent
In all cases between landlord and tenant, as often as it shall happen that one half year's rent shall be in arrear, and the landlord or lessor, to whom the same is due, hath right by law to re-enter for the nonpayment thereof, such landlord or lessor shall and may, without any formal demand or re-entry, serve a writ in ejectment for the recovery of the demised premises, . . . which service . . . shall stand in the place and stead of a demand and re-entry; and in case of judgment against the defendant for nonappearance, if it shall be made appear to the court where the said action is depending, by affidavit, or be proved upon the trial in case the defendant appears, that half a year's rent was due before the said writ was served, and that no sufficient distress was to be found on the demised premises, countervailing the arrears then due, and that the lessor had power to re-enter, then and in every such case the lessor shall recover judgment and execution, in the same manner as if the rent in arrear had been legally demanded, and a re-entry made; and in case the lessee or his assignee, or other person claiming or deriving under the said lease, shall permit and suffer judgment to be had and recovered on such trial in ejectment, and execution to be executed thereon, without paying the rent and arrears, together with full costs, and without proceedings for relief in equity within six months after such execution executed, then in such case the said lessee, his assignee, and all other persons claiming and deriving under the said lease, shall be barred and foreclosed from all relief or remedy in law or equity, other than by bringing error for reversal of such judgment, in case the same shall be erroneous; and the said landlord or lessor shall from thenceforth hold the said demised premises discharged from such lease; . . .

Note
The loss to the tenant may be greater than his fault, however, and therefore equity has intervened. Equity does not deny the landlord's right of forfeiture, but if the tenant pays the due rent and expenses the landlord has incurred equity may restore the tenant's rights. This is now embodied in statute.

Supreme Court Act 1981

38. Relief against forfeiture for non-payment of rent
   (1) In any action in the High Court for the forfeiture of a lease for non-payment of rent, the court shall have power to grant relief against forfeiture in a summary manner, and may do so subject to the same terms, and conditions as to the payment of rent, costs or otherwise as could have been imposed by it in such an action immediately before the commencement of this Act.
   (2) Where the lessee or a person deriving title under him is granted relief under this section, he shall hold the demised premises in accordance with the terms of the lease without the necessity for a new lease.

Notes
1. Since this is an equitable remedy, the relief afforded to the tenant is discretionary.

2. A claim must be brought within six months of actual re-entry by the landlord, and the tenant can apply for relief either at the time the action is brought or at the time of re-entry.
3. The effect of the granting of relief is that the tenancy continues on its former terms.

(ii) *Relief for other breaches* See David Hayton, 'Section 146 notices and negative covenants' [1974] CLJ 54.

Law of Property Act 1925

146. Restrictions on and relief against forfeiture of leases and underleases
(1) A right of re-entry or forfeiture under any proviso or stipulation in a lease for a breach of any covenant or condition in the lease shall not be enforceable, by action or otherwise, unless and until the lessor serves on the lessee a notice—
    (a) specifying the particular breach complained of; and
    (b) if the breach is capable of remedy, requiring the lessee to remedy the breach; and
    (c) in any case, requiring the lessee to make compensation in money for the breach;
and the lessee fails, within a reasonable time thereafter, to remedy the breach, if it is capable of remedy, and to make reasonable compensation in money, to the satisfaction of the lessor, for the breach.

(2) Where a lessor is proceeding, by action or otherwise, to enforce such a right of re-entry or forfeiture, the lessee may, in the lessor's action, if any, or in any action brought by himself, apply to the court for relief; and the court may grant or refused relief, as the court, having regard to the proceedings and conduct of the parties under the foregoing provisions of this section, and to all the other circumstances, thinks fit; and in case of relief may grant it on such terms, if any, as to costs, expenses, damages, compensation, penalty, or otherwise, including the granting of an injunction to restrain any like breach in the future, as the court, in the circumstances of each case, thinks fit.

(4) Where a lessor is proceeding by action or otherwise to enforce a right of re-entry or forfeiture under any covenant, proviso, or stipulation in a lease, or for non-payment of rent, the court may, on application by any person claiming as under-lessee any estate or interest in the property comprised in the lease or any part thereof, either in the lessor's action (if any) or in any action brought by such person for that purpose, make an order vesting, for the whole term of the lease or any less term, the property comprised in the lease or any part thereof in any person entitled as under-lessee to any estate or interest in such property upon such conditions as to execution of any deed or other document, payment of rent, costs, expenses, damages, compensation, giving security, or otherwise, as the court in the circumstances of each case may think fit, but in no case shall any such under-lessee be entitled to require a lease to be granted to him for any longer than he had under his original sub-lease.

(5) For the purposes of this section—
    (a) 'Lease' includes an original or derivative under-lease; also an agreement for a lease where the lessee has become entitled to have his lease granted; also a grant at a fee farm rent, or securing a rent by condition;
    (b) 'Lessee' includes an original or derivative under-lessee, and the persons deriving title under a lessee; also a grantee under any such grant as aforesaid and the persons deriving title under him;

(c) 'Lessor' includes an original or derivative under-lessor, and the persons deriving title under a lessor; also a person making such grant as aforesaid and the persons deriving title under him;

(d) 'Under-lease' includes an agreement for an under-lease where the under-lessee has become entitled to have his under-lease granted;

(e) 'Under-lessee' includes any person deriving title under an under-lessee.

(8) This section does not extend—

(i) To a covenant or condition against assigning, underletting, parting with the possession, or disposing of the land leased where the breach occurred before the commencement of this Act; or

(ii) In the case of a mining lease, to a covenant or condition for allowing the lessor to have access to or inspect books, accounts, records, weighing machines or other things, or to enter or inspect the mine or the workings thereof.

(9) This section does not apply to a condition for forfeiture on the bankruptcy of the lessee or on taking in execution of the lessee's interest if contained in a lease of—

(a) Agricultural or pastoral land;
(b) Mines or minerals;
(c) A house used or intended to be used as a public-house or beershop;
(d) A house let as a dwelling-house, with the use of any furniture, books, works of art, or other chattels not being in the nature of fixtures;
(e) Any property with respect to which the personal qualifications of the tenant are of importance for the preservation of the value or character of the property, or on the ground of neighbourhood to the lessor, or to any person holding under him.

(10) Where a condition of forfeiture on the bankruptcy of the lessee or on taking in execution of the lessee's interest is contained in any lease, other than a lease of any of the classes mentioned in the last sub-section, then—

(a) if the lessee's interest is sold within one year from the bankruptcy or taking in execution, this section applies to the forfeiture condition aforesaid;

(b) if the lessee's interest is not sold before the expiration of that year, this section only applies to the forfeiture condition aforesaid during the first year from the date of the bankruptcy or taking in execution.

(11) This section does not, save as otherwise mentioned, affect the law relating to re-entry or forfeiture or relief in case of non-payment of rent.

(12) This section has effect notwithstanding any stipulation to the contrary.

Notes

1. The landlord must give the tenant a reasonable time to comply with the notice, and what is reasonable depends on the breach. Breaches can be divided into two categories, namely, irremediable breaches and remediable breaches. Parting with possession to a subtenant and using property for immoral purposes come within the former class. Where the breach is irremediable a short period of time only need be given to the tenant before proceedings are brought.

2. The court has a discretion in granting relief. It can have regard to the conduct of the parties and the circumstances of the case (see *Central Estates (Belgravia) Ltd* v *Woolgar (No. 2)* [1972] 3 All ER 610).

3. Section 146 does not apply to all kinds of leases. A s. 146 notice need not be served:

(a) in a breach of a covenant to pay rent;

(b) in a breach of a covenant to allow inspection in a mining lease;
(c) in the case of the bankruptcy of a tenant of a lease of agricultural land, a mining lease, a lease of a public house, a lease of a furnished house and a lease of any property where the personal qualifications of the tenant are important.

In any such case the landlord can forfeit immediately. In all other cases s. 146(10) of the Law of Property Act 1925 applies.

If a landlord forfeits a tenant's lease, then any subtenancy automatically comes to an end (see *Official Custodian for Charities* v *Mackey* [1985] Ch 168). The subtenant may apply for relief from forfeiture even if the tenant is not entitled to do so. See S. Tromans, 'Forfeiture of Leases' [1986] Conv 187.

4. Where, instead of obtaining a court order for possession, a landlord has forfeited the lease by re-entry as a result of a breach of covenant by the tenant, the court can allow the tenant relief from forfeiture under s. 146(2), whether or not the tenant has applied for relief prior to the landlord's re-entry — *Billson* v *Residential Apartments Ltd* [1992] 2 WLR 15 (HL).

(iii) *Waiver of breach* A landlord may lose his right to forfeit the lease by either expressly or impliedly waiving the breach of covenant. An implied waiver occurs where the landlord, with knowledge of the tenant's breach, does some act that shows he regards the tenancy as continuing. The effect of the waiver depends on the nature of the breach. If the breach is a once and for all breach, which would include a breach of a covenant not to assign, then the waiver by the landlord results in him losing his right to forfeit altogether. If the breach is of a continuing nature, then the waiver merely operates for the period in which the breach was accepted.

(b) Distress

This is a remedy whereby the landlord is allowed to seize goods on the tenant's premises and sell them in order to recoup arrears of rent. The conditions for distress to apply are as follows:

(i) Distress can only be levied if there are arrears of rent, and arises as soon as rent is in arrears.
(ii) The remedy of distress cannot be used if forfeiture is to be employed.
(iii) Distress cannot be levied between sunset and sunrise, nor on a Sunday.
(iv) Entry to the premises cannot be made by breaking an outer door, but inner doors can be broken.
(v) Entry can be made through an open window, but not through a closed window which may be unlocked.
(vi) Certain goods cannot be distrained, for example, clothes and bedding (to a value of £100); tools of a trade (to a value of £100); perishable foods and tenants' fixtures.

(c) Damages for breach of covenant

(d) Action for arrears of rent

(e) **Injunction**

(f) **Damage for waste**

B: TENANT'S REMEDIES FOR BREACH OF COVENANT BY THE LANDLORD

The landlord's liability frequently arises as a result of breach of his repairing covenants. The tenant's remedies include:

(a) Damages for breach of covenants.
(b) Specific performance.
(c) Self-help. In *Lee-Parker* v *Izzet* [1971] 1 WLR 1688, it was said that a tenant has a right to carry out the covenanted repairs himself and deduct the cost of those repairs from future payments of rent. There are three conditions necessary for this remedy to apply:

  (i) there must be a breach of a repair covenant;
  (ii) the tenant must give notice to the landlord of the repairs needed;
  (iii) expenditure on the repairs must be fair and reasonable.

(d) Injunction.
(e) Appointment of a receiver.

SECTION 7: ENFORCEABILITY OF LEASEHOLD COVENANTS

See Law Commission Working Paper No. 95 'Landlord and Tenant Privity of Contract of Estate: Duration of Liability of Parties to Leases'. See also David Gordon, 'The burden and benefit of the rules of assignment' [1987] Conv 103.

A: GENERAL

Prima facie a covenant in a lease is binding only between the contracting parties to the covenant since there is privity of contract between the parties. The obligation between the two original contracting parties will continue even if one or both of the parties has disposed of their interest in the property (see *Thursby* v *Plant* (1670) 1 Wms Saund 230). This is because covenants are usually worded in such a way that they relate not only to the covenantor's acts and omissions but also to those of his successors in title and persons deriving title under him. The limited scope of the privity of contract doctrine was thought to be highly undesirable, since both the landlord and the tenant have interests that can be assigned to third parties and which should impose obligations directly onto those assignees. So in what circumstances can a person other than the original lessor and lessee sue and be sued on the covenants contained in the lease? Enforceability in other situations depends upon:

(a) whether the covenants 'touch and concern' the land;
(b) the existence of privity of estate;
(c) the lease being in the correct form.

B: COVENANTS TOUCHING AND CONCERNING THE LAND

Covenants which are of a personal nature, or which are collateral to the lease are enforceable only between the original contracting parties. They cannot 'run with the land', i.e. bind assignees of the original parties to the lease, since they do not affect the subject matter of the lease itself. A covenant touches and concerns the land if it has direct reference to the land, i.e. affects the nature, quality or value of the land, or the mode of using or enjoying the land. Not only must the covenant have direct reference to the land, it must also affect the landlord *qua* landlord or the tenant *qua* tenant — it must have some reference to the relationship of landlord and tenant. A surety covenant was held to touch and concern the land in *Kumar* v *Dunning* [1987] 2 All ER 801. Browne-Wilkinson V-C said '... the acid test whether or not a benefit is collateral is that laid down by Best J [in *Vyvyan* v *Arthur* (1823) 1B & C 410, 417] namely "is the covenant beneficial to the owner for the time being of the covenantee's land, and to no one else?" ... a covenant simply to pay a sum of money, whether by way of insurance premium, compensation or damages, is a covenant capable of touching and concerning the land provided that the existence of the covenant, and the right to payment thereunder, affects the value of the land in whomsoever it is vested for the time being.'

Thomas v *Hayward*
(1869) LR 4 Exch 311 (Court of Exchequer)

Here the lessee covenanted to use the premises as a public house and the lessor covenanted not to build or keep any house for the sale of spirits or beers within half a mile of the public house.

BRAMWELL B: The covenant does not touch or concern the thing demised. It touches the beneficial occupation of the thing, but not the thing itself; and this becomes manifest when it is considered that, supposing the lessee's covenant to carry on the sale of spirits on the premises to be discharged by agreement between the lessor and lessee, or that without such discharge, the lessee, in fact, discontinued the business, the defendant's covenant would obviously in no way concern the land. This shows that the covenant relates only to the mode of occupying the land, not to the land itself. It does not, therefore, run with the land so as to enable the plaintiff to sue upon it.

Notes
1. Compare, however, *Fleetwood* v *Hull* (1889) 23 QBD 35, where a covenant to keep a public house so that there would be no ground to suspend the licence, was held to touch and concern the land as it affected the *use of the premises* by the tenant.
2. A covenant allowing the tenant to purchase the fee simple during the term of the lease does not touch and concern the land since it affects the parties as

vendor and purchaser not as landlord and tenant (see *Woodall* v *Clifton* [1905] 2 Ch 257). See, however, the following case.

In re Button's Lease [1964] Ch 263 (ChD)

Land was leased to T by a lease dated 10 August 1955. By clause 4(d) of the lease, T could purchase the freehold reversion by giving L three months' notice in writing of such a desire to purchase. T, on 28 February 1957, with L's consent, assigned the property to P for the unexpired term. The assignment made no mention of the option. By a second assignment dated 17 March 1960, the benefit of the option was specifically assigned to P. Held: an option creates a chose in action or an equitable interest in the land which in principle can be assigned, unless the terms of the lease provide otherwise. There was nothing in the present lease to that effect, and therefore the option could be assigned to P.

Notes
1. If a covenant 'touches and concerns' the land, then, in theory it is capable of passing either with the reversion or with the land. In *Horsey Estate Ltd* v *Steiger* [1899] 2 QB 79, Lord Russell of Killowen said (at p. 89):

> Is, then, the condition in question one the burden of which runs with the land so that its obligation binds the assignee of the lease? The answer to this question depends, in this case, upon whether it is a condition touching the thing demised or is merely collateral. I say 'in this case' because there are undoubtedly collateral covenants or conditions, which on equitable principles, but only in a restrictive sense, bind the assignee. But this principle is confined to covenants and conditions of a negative character, and depends upon notice. But apart from cases of this class the true principle is that no covenant or condition which affects merely the person, and which does not affect the nature, quality, or value of the thing demised or the mode of using or enjoying the thing demised, runs with the land: see *Mayor of Congleton* v *Pattison* [(1808) 10 East 130].

2. The Law of Property Act 1925, ss. 141 and 142 (see pages 204 and 207) have replaced the phrase 'touching and concerning the land' with the phrase 'having reference to the subject-matter of the lease'.

C: PRIVITY OF ESTATE

Privity of estate describes the relationships that exist between the parties who hold the same estates as those which were originally created in the lease. It is something which is temporary in nature.

D: ASSIGNMENT BY THE ORIGINAL LESSEE

If the original lessee assigns his lease, then the assignee will want to know:

(a) whether covenants in the lease in favour of the lessee are enforceable by the assignee against the landlord (i.e. does the benefit of the covenant run with the land)?

(b) whether covenants in the lease in favour of the lessor bind the assignee (i.e., does the burden run with the land)?

Spencer's Case
(1583) 5 Co Rep 16a (Court of King's Bench)

S and his wife leased land to X who covenanted for himself, his executors and administrators that he, his executors, administrators or assigns would build a brick wall on the land. He assigned to J, who assigned to C. Held: there was no liability on C.

1. When the covenant extends to a thing *in esse*, parcel of the demise, the thing to be done by force of the covenant is *quodammodo* annexed and appurtenant to the thing demised, and shall go with the land, and shall bind the assignee although he be not bound by express words: but when the covenant extends to a thing which is not in being at the time of the demise made, it cannot be appurtenant or annexed to the thing which hath no being: as if the lessee covenants to repair the houses demised to him during the term, that is parcel of the contract, and extends to the support of the thing demised, and therefore is *quodammodo* annexed appurtenant to houses, and shall bind the assignee although he be not bound expressly by the covenant: but in the case at Bar, the covenant concerns a thing which was not *in esse* at the time of the demise made, but to be newly built after, and therefore shall bind the covenantor, his executors, or administrators, and not the assignee, for the law will not annex the covenant to a thing which hath no being.

2. It was resolved that in this case, if the lessee had covenanted for him and his assigns, that they would make a new wall upon some part of the thing demised, that for as much as it is to be done upon the land demised, that it should bind the assignee; for although the covenant doth extend to a thing to be newly made, yet it therefore shall bind the assignee by express words. So on the other side, if a warranty be made to one, his heirs and assigns, by express words, the assignee shall take benefit of it, and shall have a *warrantia chartae* . . . But although the covenant be for him and his assigns, yet if the thing to be done be merely collateral to the land, and doth not touch or concern the thing demised in any sort, there the assignee shall not be charged. As if the lessee covenants for him and his assigns to build a house upon the land of the lessor which is no parcel of the demise, or to pay any collateral sum to the lessor, or to a stranger, it shall not bind the assignee, because it is merely collateral, and in no manner touches or concerns the thing that was demised, or that is assigned over; and therefore in such case the assignee of the thing demised cannot be charged with it, no more than any other stranger.

. . .

4. It was resolved, that if a man makes a feoffment by this word *dedi*, which implies a warranty, the assignee of the feoffee shall not vouch; but if a man makes a lease for years by this word *concessi* or *demisi*, which implies a covenant, if the assignee of the lessee be evicted, he shall have a writ of covenant; for the lessee and his assignee hath the yearly profits of the land which shall grow by his labour and industry for an annual rent, and therefore it is reasonable when he hath applied his labour, and employed his

cost upon the land, and be evicted (whereby he loses all), that he shall take such benefit of the demise and grant, as the first lessee might, and the lessor hath no other prejudice than what his special contract with the first lessee hath bound him to.

Notes
1. The case draws a distinction between covenants relating to things in existence (*in esse*) and covenants relating to things not yet in existence (*in posse*). Before 1925, the former would bind all assignees, whereas the latter does not, unless the covenant was made for the lessee and on behalf of all his assigns.
2. In order for covenants to run where there has been an assignment by the lessee and to enable the assignee to be affected by the covenant, two conditions must be met:

(a) privity of estate must exist between the assignee and the landlord or the person against whom or by whom enforcement is sought; and
(b) the covenant must touch and concern the land.

Law of Property Act 1925

79. Burden of covenants relating to land
(1) A covenant relating to any land of a covenantor or capable of being bound by him, shall, unless a contrary intention is expressed, be deemed to be made by the covenantor on behalf of himself his successors in title and the persons deriving title under him or them, and, subject as aforesaid, shall have effect as if such successors and other persons were expressed.

This subsection extends to a covenant to do some act relating to the land, notwithstanding that the subject-matter may not be in existence when the covenant is made.

(2) For the purposes of this section in connexion with covenants restrictive of the user of land 'successors in title' shall be deemed to include the owners and occupiers for the time being of such land.

(3) This section applies only to covenants made after the commencement of this Act.

Note
Where the original lessee has assigned his interest and a covenant has subsequently been breached, the landlord has a choice of suing either the original lessee (by means of privity of contract) or the present lessee. If the landlord has proceeded against the original lessee, that person will wish to recoup his losses and can do so in one of two ways:

(a) The original lessee can recover directly from the present lessee, relying on the rule in *Moule* v *Garrett* (1872) LR 7 Ex 101.

(b) The original lessee can sue the person to whom he directly assigned the lease, if the present lessee is not such a person, by means of the Law of Property Act 1925, s. 77.

Law of Property Act 1925

77. Implied covenants in conveyances subject to rents

(1) In addition to the covenants implied under the last preceding section, there shall in the several cases in this section mentioned, be deemed to be included and implied, a covenant to the effect in this section stated, by and with such persons as are hereinafter mentioned, that is to say:—

(C) In a conveyance for valuable consideration, other than a mortgage, of the entirety of the land comprised in a lease, for the residue of the term or interest created by the lease, a covenant by the assignee or joint and several covenants by the assignees (if more than one) with the conveying parties and with each of them (if more than one) in the terms set out in Part IX of the Second Schedule to this Act. Where a rent has been apportioned in respect of any land, with the consent of the lessor, the covenants in this paragraph shall be implied in the conveyance of that land in like manner as if the apportioned rent were the original rent reserved, and the lease related solely to that land:

Second Schedule
PART IX
COVENANT IN A CONVEYANCE FOR VALUABLE CONSIDERATION, OTHER THAN A MORTGAGE, OF THE ENTIRETY OF THE LAND COMPRISED IN A LEASE FOR THE RESIDUE OF THE TERM OR INTEREST CREATED BY THE LEASE

That the assignees, or the persons deriving title under them, will at all times, from the date of the conveyance or other date therein stated, duly pay all rent becoming due under the lease creating the term or interest for which the land is conveyed, and observe and perform all the covenants, agreements and conditions therein contained and thenceforth on the part of the lessees to be observed and performed:

And also will at all times, from the date aforesaid, save harmless and keep indemnified the conveying parties and their estates and effects, from and against all proceedings, costs, claims and expenses on account of any omission to pay the said rent or any breach of any of the said covenants, agreement and conditions.

Note
It is common practice for an assignor to expressly indemnify himself against future breaches, but s. 77(1)(C) implies such a covenant into assignment.

Question
Do you think that the original tenant should remain liable throughout the whole term of the lease for any breaches of covenant by his assignees?

E: ASSIGNMENT BY THE ORIGINAL LESSOR

The reversioner will want to know:
(a) Whether covenants in the lease in favour of the lessor run with the land (i.e. does the benefit of the covenant run with the reversion)?
(b) Whether covenants in the lease in favour of the lessee bind the reversioner (i.e. does the burden run with the land)?

At common law the grantee of a reversion could only sue upon implied covenants in the lease not express ones. This rule has now been abrogated by statute.

Law of Property Act 1925

141. Rent and benefit of lessee's covenants to run with the reversion

(1) Rent reserved by a lease, and the benfit of every covenant or provision therein contained, having reference to the subject-matter thereof, and on the lessee's part to be observed or performed, and every condition of re-entry and other condition therein contained, shall be annexed and incident to and shall go with the reversionary estate in the land, or in any part thereof, immediatley expectant on the term granted by the lease, notwithstanding severance of that reversionary estate, and without prejudice to any liability affecting a covenantor or his estate.

(2) Any such rent, covenant or provision shall be capable of being recovered, received, enforced, and taken advantage of, by the person from time to time entitled, subject to the term, to the income of the whole or any part, as the case may require, of the land leased.

(3) Where that person becomes entitled by conveyance or otherwise, such rent, covenant or provision may be recovered, received, enforced or taken advantage of by him notwithstanding that he becomes so entitled after the condition of re-entry of forfeiture has become enforceable, but this subsection does not render enforceable any condition of re-entry or other condition waived or released before such person becomes entitled as aforesaid.

(4) This section applies to leases made before or after the commencement of this Act, but does not affect the operation of—

(a) any severance of the reversionary estate; or

(b) any acquisition by conveyance or otherwise of the right to receive or enforce any rent covenant or provision;

effected before the commencement of this Act.

Notes

1. In order for a covenant to run on assignment of the reversion the covenant must 'have reference to the subject matter of the lease'.

2. There is no requirement for privity of estate when relying on ss. 141 and 142.

London and County (A & D) Ltd v Wilfred Sportsman Ltd
[1971] Ch 764 (CA)

Two properties (No. 5 and No. 6) were leased to H for a term of 21 years from August 1961. The leases allowed re-entry if rent was unpaid for 21 days after becoming payable, and a prohibition against assigning without consent. H assigned both properties to G, who subleased No. 6 to D. In June 1963, G obtained a licence to assign the leases to M, and G covenanted to pay the rent if M defaulted. On the assignment from G to M of August 1963, M charged his interest in No. 5 to P.

M paid no rent from March 1964. G made payments under the guarantee and took the rent due from D under the sublease. In March 1965, P, as mortgagee obtained an order for possession of No. 5 against M and M left the premises. D went into possession of No. 5 in anticipation of the grant of a new sub-tenancy of both premises to D. In August 1965, the head landlord granted a new reversionary lease to G seven days longer than the original leases and expressed to be 'subject to and with the benefit of' M's lease. P claimed possession of No. 5 from D. G claimed the original lease of No. 5 had been forfeited and no rent had been paid with respect to that lease since the new lease had been granted. P claimed the payments made by G under the guarantee were rent, therefore forfeiture never arose.

Held: by virtue of the Law of Property Act 1925, s. 141, an assignee of the reversion could sue and re-enter for arrears of rent at the date of the assignment even when the right to re-enter had arisen before the assignment. Therefore G could re-enter and forfeit M's lease.

Note
The next case extended the doctrine in *London and County (A & D) Ltd* v *Wilfred Sportsman Ltd*, to cover breaches before assignment.

Arlesford Trading Co. Ltd v *Servansingh*
[1971] 3 All ER 113 (CA)

The defendant took a 99-year lease of premises from D Ltd and D Ltd granted the defendant a 99-year lease. The defendant covenanted to pay a ground rent and service charges to the lessor and his successor in title. The lease stipulated that all obligations of the lessee and rights of the lessor should be incidental to the reversion expectant on the lease and should pass and devolve therewith. The rent and service charges were not paid. The defendant assigned the lease to J. The assignment was facilitated by D Ltd giving a receipt in respect of rent and service charges, though it was in fact unpaid. D Ltd then conveyed the freehold reversion to the plaintiffs. Held: by virtue of s. 141 of the Law of Property Act 1925, an assignee of the reversion can sue an original lessee for breaches that occurred before the assignment.

RUSSELL LJ: Now it has been established in this court that an assignee of the reversion can claim, against the lessee, arrears of rent accrued prior to the assignment, and to re-enter on the ground of the failure to have paid such arrears; this is by force of s. 141 of the Law of Property Act 1925: see *London and County (A & D) Ltd* v *Wilfred Sportsman Ltd (Greenwoods (Hosiers and Outfitters) Ltd, third party)*. In that case, however, the claim to re-enter and forfeit the lease was against the original lessee (and his chargee). It is pointed out that in the present case the defendant assigned his lease before the reversion was assigned to the plaintiffs and that there has never been privity of estate between the plaintiffs and the defendant, contrary to what appears from the note of the judgment to have been the judge's view. But it is argued for the plaintiffs that an original lessee remains at all times liable under the lessee's covenants throughout the lease, and that assignment of the reversion does not automatically release him from that liability. This argument is in our judgment correct; so that if there is no special feature in this case the plaintiffs undoubtedly have a right as assignee of the reversion, and with it of the benefit of the lessee's covenants for rent etc to sue for arrears of rent.

Was there a special feature which denies the plaintiffs the right to sue the defendant? It is plain that Drayville Properties Ltd could not have asserted against the assignee of the lease (or his mortgagee) that there was any subsisting breach of the covenant for rent. This is because of the production of the receipt for the June 1969 instalment. It was manifestly the intention that the lease should be assigned 'clean', so to speak, of any liability for those three unpaid instalments. Equally, the plaintiffs could not have asserted against the assignee of the term (or his mortgagee) the failure in the payment of those three instalments. But does it follow from that that the postponed obligation of the defendant to pay those three instalments no longer had sufficiently the quality of an obligation to pay rent etc under the lease to enable the assignee of the reversion to assert against the defendant that the benefit of that obligation was assigned together with the reversion? In our judgment the answer is in the negative. The obligation on the defendant remained on him in his capacity as lessee under the lease, and the ability to enforce against him passed with the reversion to the plaintiffs.

Re King
[1963] Ch 459 (CA)

T granted a lease of property to E who covenanted to keep the premises in repair during the term; to keep the premises insured; and to lay out all moneys received under any such policy of insurance in rebuilding or repairing the premises. In 1907, the lease was assigned to K. In 1944, the premises were destroyed by fire but they could not be rebuilt because of wartime and post-war restrictions. In 1945, the insurance moneys were paid and invested in the joint names of the lessor and the lessee their respective solicitors having come to a written agreement that the moneys were 'charged with the [lessee's] liability'. In 1946, T assigned this reversion to G. In 1949, K died. In 1960, G assigned his reversion to London County Council under a compulsory purchase order. G claimed to be a creditor for damages for breach of covenants in the lease. Held: K's executors were not liable to G. A landlord who had assigned his reversion could not then sue the lessee for breaches that had occurred before the assignment.

UPJOHN LJ: I turn, then, to a consideration of the meaning of section 141 and construe the language used in its ordinary and natural meaning, which seems to me quite plain and clear. To illustrate this, consider the case of a lease containing a covenant to build a house according to certain detailed specifications before a certain day. Let me suppose that after that certain day the then lessor assigns the benefit of the reversion to an assignee, and at the time of the assignment the lessee has failed to perform the covenant to build. Who can sue the lessee for breach of covenant? It seems to me clear that the assignee alone can sue. Upon the assignment the benefit of every covenant on the lessee's part to be observed and performed is annexed and incident to and goes with the reversionary estate. The benefit of that covenant to build, therefore, passed; as it had been broken, the right to sue also passed as part of the benefit of the covenant and, incidentally, also the right to re-enter, if that has not been waived. I protest against the argument that because a right to sue is itself a chose in action it, therefore, has become severed from, and independent of, the parent covenant; on the contrary it remains part of it. The right to sue on breach is merely one of the bundle of rights that are contained in the concept 'benefit of every covenant'.... To return to my example. Suppose the right to sue for breach of that covenant did not pass, and that right remained in the assignor, then the assignee would take the lease without the benefit of that covenant and he could never enforce it. So he has not got the benefit of every covenant contained in the lease and the words of the section are not satisfied. That cannot be right....

Then suppose the lease contains a covenant to keep in repair which is broken at the date of the assignment, and that at all material times the premises were out of repair; that is, a continuing breach. It is an a fortiori case to the example I have just dealt with. Indeed, with all respect to the argument to the contrary, you cannot give any sensible meaning to the words of the section unless the entire benefit of a repairing covenant has passed, leaving the assignor without remedy against the lessee. Look at the absurd results if that were not so. The assignor of the reversion remains at liberty to sue the lessee for breaches down to the moment of the assignment. After assignment he sues and obtains judgment for certain damages. But then the premises are still out of repair and the breach continues. The assignee claims to re-enter or to sue because the premises are out of repair. What is the situation of the lessee? Either he has to pay damages twice or pay damages to the assignor and then reinstate the premises because otherwise the assignee will re-enter. This is impossible. Alternatively, the assignee's right to re-enter or to sue in respect of post-assignment breaches is in some way adversely affected by reason of the fact that the assignor has recovered a judgment for damages for pre-assignment breaches; therefore, the benefit of the covenant to keep in repair did not pass wholly to him even in respect of post-assignment breaches. That directly contradicts the words of the section....

In my judgment Tagg's claims fail and I would allow this part of the appeal.

Question
If the original landlord sells the reversion on the lease, can he still sue the original tenant on any covenants made between himself and the tenant?

Burden of Covenant

Law of Property Act 1925

142. Obligation of lessor's covenants to run with reversion

(1) The obligation under a condition or of a covenant entered into by a lessor with reference to the subject-matter of the lease shall, if and as far as the lessor has power to bind the reversionary estate immediately expectant on the term granted by the lease, be annexed and incident to and shall go with that reversionary estate, or the several parts thereof, notwithstanding severance of that reversionary estate, and may be taken advantage of and enforced by the person in whom the term is from time to time vested by conveyance, devolution in law, or otherwise; and, if and as far as the lessor has power to bind the person from time to time entitled to that reversionary estate, the obligation aforesaid may be taken advantage of and enforced against any person so entitled.

(2) This section applies to leases made before or after the commencement of this Act, whether the severance of the reversionary estate was effected before or after such commencement:

Provided that, where the lease was made before the first day of January eighteen hundred and eighty-two, nothing in this section shall affect the operation of any severance of the reversionary estate effected before such commencement.

This section takes effect without prejudice to any liability affecting a covenantor or his estate.

Notes
1. The reversioner cannot be made liable for breaches committed by the landlord prior to the assignment of the reversion (see *Pettiward Estates* v *Shepherd* [1986] 6 CL 1186).
2. The term 'covenant' in this section has an extended meaning and is not restricted to those made by deed (*Weg Motors Ltd* v *Hales* [1962] Ch 49).

F: ENFORCEMENT BY AND AGAINST SUB-TENANTS

The rules relating to the running of covenants apply only when there has been an assignment of the whole of the lease or the whole of the term. If the lessee has created a sub-tenancy, how can the enforcement of covenants be achieved?

(a) Forfeiture
See Law of Property Act 1925, s. 79.

If a sub-tenant breaches a covenant contained in the head lease, then any right of re-entry expressly reserved by the landlord in the head lease becomes exercisable against the final assignee of the original tenant. The effect of re-entry is to forfeit not only the final assignee's lease, but also that of the sub-tenants so that both are trespassers, subject, of course, to any relief against forfeiture which either may have.

(b) *Tulk* v *Moxhay* (1848) 2 Ph 774
(See chapter 11.)

A landlord may be able to obtain a remedy in equity (i.e. an injunction or damages) against a sub-tenant if the rule in *Tulk* v *Moxhay* is complied with. For this the following conditions need to be met:

(i) the covenant must be negative in substance;
(ii) the covenant must touch and concern the land;
(iii) there must be no intention that the sub-tenant should not be liable for the covenants expressed in the sublease;
(iv) the sub-tenant must have actual, constructive or imputed notice of the existence of the covenant.

In unregistered land, restrictive covenants between lessor and lessee are not registrable as land charges and therefore must be protected under the doctrine of notice. In registered land, such covenants are not capable of protection by the entry of a notice on the register, but are automatically binding on the transferee by means of the Land Registration Act 1925, s. 23(1)(a), and s. 2.

A sub-tenant cannot sue the head landlord by means of the rules relating to leasehold covenants for any breach of covenants in the head lease. However, he can sue the original landlord by means of the Law of Property Act 1925, s. 78.

Law of Property Act 1925

78. Benefit of covenants relating to land

(1) A covenant relating to any land of the covenantee shall be deemed to be made with the covenantee and his successors in title and the persons deriving title under him or them, and shall have effect as if such successors and other persons were expressed.

For the purposes of this subsection in connexion with covenants restrictive of the user of land 'successors in title' shall be deemed to include the owners and occupiers for the time being of the land of the covenantee intended to be benefited.

(2) This section applies to covenants made after the commencement of this Act, but the repeal of section fifty-eight of the Conveyancing Act, 1881, does not affect the operation of covenants to which that section applied.

Note
See *Smith and Snipes Hall Farm* v *River Douglas Catchment Board* [1949] 2 KB 500 (chapter 11).

A sub-tenant can sue an assignee of the reversion under the rule in *Tulk* v *Moxhay*.

Question
How can leasehold covenants be enforced by and against a lessor and his assignees against and by a person who derives his title by means of adverse possession? See *Tichborne* v *Weir* (1892) 67 LT 735 and *Nisbet and Potts' Contract* [1905] 1 Ch 391.

SECTION 8: ENFORCEMENT OF LEASEHOLD COVENANTS IN AN AGREEMENT FOR A LEASE

The rules for the enforceability of covenants in an equitable lease differ somewhat from those relating to a legal lease.

(a) Liability of the original tenant to an assignee of the landlord's reversion
In *Rickett* v *Green* [1910] 1 KB 253, Darling J said:

Before dealing with that point I ought to say that I think that the learned judge rightly construed s. 10 of the Act as giving the assignee of the reversion, who has a right of re-entry, the power to avail himself of the procedure to recover possession authorized by s. 139 of the County Courts Act, 1888, although the half-year's rent in arrear is composed of rent partly due before and partly due after the date of the assignment. Having thus construed s. 10, the question occurred to him whether this tenancy agreement was a 'lease' within the meaning of s. 10 of the Act of 1881, inasmuch as the agreement was dated December 19, 1907, and the three years were to run from December 25, 1907, so that the lease was one exceeding three years from the making thereof and, not being under seal, was void at law under s. 3 of the Real Property Act, 1845. Though at law it may be void as a lease, still in equity it is looked upon as a lease, and in my judgment it must be treated, as between the parties, as if it were a lease under seal. A Court of Equity would look upon the matter as if a lease under seal had been granted. Upon the case to which we have been referred the county court judge came to a right conclusion upon this point, and the agreement must be treated as a 'lease' for the purposes of s. 10 of the Act of 1881, and for other purposes also.

Note
The relevant provision is now contained in s. 141(1) of the Law of Property Act 1925.

(b) Liability of the assignee of the reversion to the original tenant
This is governed by the Law of Property Act 1925, s. 142(1), and applies, according to Lord Evershed in *Weg Motors Ltd* v *Hales* [1962] 1 Ch 49, at p. 73, to both legal and equitable leases.

(c) Liability of assignees
Traditional legal theory has held that the doctrine in *Spencer's Case* (1583) 5 Co Rep 16a (see page 201) has no application to equitable leases. The reason for this seems to stem from the fact that there is no 'privity of estate' in such a lease, since there can be no 'estate' in the legal sense of the word as the relationship is based in equity.

Purchase v *Lichfield Brewery Company*
[1915] 1 KB 184 (KB)

A purported deed of assignment from a tenant to assignees was never executed by the assignees and they did not take possession of the premises. Held: the assignees were not liable for the rent.

LUSH J: . . . The only point which the county court judge decided was that the present case was governed by *Williams* v *Bosanquet* [1 Brod & B 238]. In my view that case does not apply. The lease in question there was under seal. It was assigned by deed to mortgagees. That was a valid assignment. The only question was whether the mortgagees, not having taken possession, were bound by the covenants in the lease. It was held that they were bound. in this case there was no lease under seal. No term was created as between lessor and lessee. Therefore the question decided in *Williams* v *Bosanquet* [1 Brod & B 238] does not arise in this case. Consequently the judgment of the county court judge cannot stand on the grounds on which he has based it.
Then can the judgment be supported on other grounds? I do not think it is necessary to say how the case might have stood if the defendants had ever taken possession. They are liable, if at all, on the principle of *Walsh* v *Lonsdale* [21 ChD 9]. In that case the tenant was in possession under the agreement. In the present case the defendants never did take possession. The agreement contained a provision against assigning. The defendants were only mortgagees. It does not follow from *Walsh* v *Lonsdale* [21 ChD 9] that a Court of Equity would decree specific performance against mere mortgagees who only took an assignment by way of security. In my opinion it would leave the parties to their position at law. Accordingly the matter stands thus: A tenant under an agreement, whose only title to call himself a lessee depends on his right to assignees. The assignees never had a term vested in them because no term was ever created; therefore there was never privity of estate. They never went into possession or were recognized by the landlord; therefore there was never privity of contract. It is impossible that specific performance of a contract can be decreed against a person with whom there is neither

privity of contract nor privity of estate. Therefore these assignees hare not liable to perform the terms of the agreeement and this appeal must be allowed.

Note
If this decision is correct, it is limited in that it applies only to the recovery of damages. The landlord or the assignee of the reversion may apply for equitable remedies since there is an equitable lease in existence, i.e. an injunction or forfeiture.

Boyer v Warbey
[1953] 1 QB 234 (CA)

A flat was leased for three years and the lease was not made under seal. The lease contained a covenant by the tenant (T) to pay £40 towards redecorating the premises on the expiration of the lease. Before the lease expired T assigned the lease to D. D claimed that since the lease was not under seal the covenant could not run with the land. Held: D was bound.

DENNING LJ: Seeing that the agreement touched and concerned the thing demised, it ran with the land so as to bind the assignee, the tenant, as soon as he entered into possession. I know that before the Judicature Act, 1873, it was said that the doctrine of covenants running with the land only applied to covenants under seal and not to agreements under hand: see *Elliott* v *Johnson* [(1866) LR 2 QB 120]. But since the fusion of law and equity, the position is different. The distinction between agreements under hand and covenants under seal has been largely obliterated. There is no valid reason nowadays why the doctrine of covenants running with the land — or with the reversion — should not apply equally to agreements under hand as to covenants under seal; and I think we should so hold, not only in the case of agreements for more than three years which need the intervention of equity to perfect them, but also in the case of agreements for three years or less which do not.

Benefit of a Covenant

The right to the *benefit* of a covenant may be enforced. A covenant is a promise under seal and gives the parties rights which are capable of being enforced by the law and therefore capable of being assigned under the normal rules governing the assignment of choses in action.

Manchester Brewery v Coombs
[1901] 2 Ch 608 (ChD)

By a yearly tenancy agreement made under seal, A took hotel premises from B and covenanted with B 'and their successors in title' to purchase beer only from B. The agreement was only executed by A who took possession under its terms. Later, B sold their business, including the property, to C and A soon stopped buying his beer from C. Held: the covenant ran with the land.

FARWELL J: [Farwell J decided the covenant was not a personal one.] The last point taken by Mr Younger rests on the fact that the agreement of December 10, 1892, was not executed by the landlords. Having regard to the construction that I have put on the covenant, it could not be contended that it is not of such a nature as to run with the land. But it is said that, in order to arrive at the conclusion that it does run with the land, the Court must first find that an estate has been duly created at law in the land with which the covenant can run, or in other words, that there must be privity of estate between lessor and lessee, and that such estate can only be created by deed duly executed by the lessor, and that this is borne out by 32 Hen. 8, c. 34, which applies only to leases by deed. This is undoubtedly sound — e.g., it has been held that a lease by mortgagor and mortgagee, in which the covenants to repair were with the mortgagor and his assigns, did not enable an assign of the mortgagee to maintain an action on the covenant: *Webb v Russell* [(1789) 3 TR 393, 402; 1 RR 725]. Lord Kenyon there says: 'It is not sufficient that a covenant is concerning the land, but, in order to make it run with the land, there must be a privity of estate between the covenanting parties. But here 'the mortgagor' had no interest in the land of which a Court of Law could take notice; though he had an equity of redemption, an interest which a Court of Equity would take notice of.' And in *Standen* v *Chrismas* [10 QB 135] it was held that 32 Hen. 8, c. 34, applied to leases by deed only, and that when the lease was not under seal the assignee of the reversion could not maintain assumpsit on the contract against the lessee for failure to repair. The reason is obvious; if the contract was regarded as personal, the right to sue on it was not assignable at law; and, if it was not by deed, there was no estate in which the right to sue could be inherent. The law is stated with great lucidity by Wilde CJ in *Bickford* v *Parson* [(1848) 5 CB 920, 929]: 'It was well said by Shepherd, arguendo, in *Webb* v *Russell* [(1789) 3 TR 393, 402; 1 RR 725], that "there are three relations at common law, which may exist between the lessor and the lessee and their respective assignees; first, *privity of contract*, which is created by the contract itself, and subsists for ever between the lessor and lessee; secondly, *privity of estate*, which subsists between the lessee, or his assignee in possession of the estate, and the assignee of the reversioner; and, thirdly, *privity of contract and estate*, which both exist where the term and reversion remain in the original covenantors. The statute 32 Hen. 8, c. 34, seems to have created a fourth relation, *a privity of contract in respect of the estate*, as between the assignees of the reversion and the lessees or their assignees. The statute annexes, or rather creates, a privity of contract between those who have privity of estate; and, when the one fails, the other fails with it. At common law, the covenant did not pass by an assignment of the reversion, for, it was a mere personal contract."' If, therefore, the plaintiffs had been suing in covenant or in assumpsit on contract before the Judicature Acts, I think they would have failed. But it by no means follows that the plaintiffs would have failed in every form of action, even before the Judicature Acts; still less that they must fail now. Before the Judicature Acts the plaintiffs might have succeeded if they had sued on the new contract implied from the conduct of the tenant and the assignee of the landlord, instead of suing on the original contract between the tenant and the landlord . . .

There is, moreover, another point which is fatal to the defendant. The defendant holds under an agreement for a lease from Broadbents, Limited, under which he has been in possession and paid rent for several years. The whole contract has been performed up to the present time, except that the legal estate has not been actually demised. The defendant would have no defence to an action for specific performance, the sole object of which would be to compel him to accept the legal estate. If Broadbents, Limited, had not parted with the legal estate, I see no reason why they should not now execute the deed in order to complete the transaction. The present plaintiffs are the assigns of the benefit of the agreement both by implication from the conveyance of the land subject to the lease, and by the express words of clause 26 of the agreement of March 29, 1899. The plaintiffs could, therefore, obtain specific performance in this Court of the contract so far as it is incomplete. In saying this I do not forget that this is a yearly tenancy only, and that Wood V-C in *Clayton* v *Illingworth* [(1853) 10 Hare 451] refused to grant specific performance of a tenancy from year to year; but the reasons given by the Vice-Chancellor are inapplicable to the present case. He said there was nothing to shew in that case that there was to be any lease under seal at all; here the tenant executes under seal. He said that equity interposes to grant specific performance in cases where the legal remedy is inadequate, and that there was nothing in the case before him to shew why the remedy at law would not be adequate. Here the defendant's whole contention rests on the ground that the plaintiffs have no legal remedy, and the grant of specific performance is necessary to give them their full rights. It is well settled that the assign of one of the parties to a contract can obtain specific performance of that contract against the other contracting party; and, although it is usually necessary in such an action to make the assignor a party, I do not think that it is essential in a case like the present, where the sub-contract is no longer in fieri, and there are no equities between the parties to the original contract, and no suggestion of any reason for making the original contractor a party. The managing director of Broadbents was called as a witness, and no question was put to him suggesting any reason for Broadbents, Limited, being made parties. Holding, therefore, as I do, that the plaintiffs could obtain specific performance against the defendant, I find it laid down by the Court of Appeal that since the Judicature Acts there are not in such a case as this two estates as there were formerly, one at common law by reason of the payment of the rent, and another in equity under the agreement, but the tenant holds under the same terms, and has the same rights and liabilities as if a lease had been granted: *Walsh* v *Lonsdale* [21 ChD 9], approved by Cotton LJ in *Lowther* v *Heaver* [(1889) 41 ChD 248, 264)], and explained by Lord Esher in *Swain* v *Ayres* [21 QBD 289, 292] and *Foster* v *Reeves* [[1892] 2 QB 255]. Although it has been suggested that the decision in *Walsh* v *Lonsdale* [21 ChD 9] takes away all differences between the legal and equitable estate, it, of course, does nothing of the sort, and the limits of its applicability are really somewhat narrow. It applies only to cases where there is a contract to transfer a legal title, and an act has to be justified or an action maintained by force of the legal title to which such contract relates. It involves two questions: (1) Is there a contract of which specific performance can be obtained? (2) If Yes, will the title acquired by such specific performance justify at law the act complained of, or support at law the action in question? It is to be treated as though before the Judicature Acts there had been, first, a suit in equity for specific performance, and then an action at law between the same parties; and the doctrine is applicable only in those cases where specific performance can be obtained between the same parties in the same court, and at the same time as the subsequent legal question falls to be determined. Thus, in *Walsh* v *Lonsdale* [21 ChD 9], the landlord under an agreement for a lease for a term of seven years distrained. Distress is a legal remedy and depends on the existence at law of the relation of landlord and tenant; but the agreement between the same parties, if specifically enforced, created that relation. It was clear that such an agreement would be enforced in the same court and between the same parties: the act of distress was therefore held to be lawful. So in the present case I have already stated that specific performance can be granted between the parties to this action. I must treat it therefore as granted, and I then find that the result justifies this action. It is not necessary to call in aid this doctrine in matters that are purely equitable; its existence is due entirely to the divergence of legal and equitable rights between the same parties, nor does it affect the rights of third parties. Thus, a contract by a landowner to sell the fee simple of land in possession to A. would not enable A. to maintain an action of ejectment or trespass against a third person, because such actions are purely legal actions requiring the legal estate and possession respectively to support them, and the contract relied on is not made with the defendant. The case of *Friary, Holroyd, and Healey's Breweries* v *Singleton* [[1899] 1 Ch 86; 2 Ch 261] turned on the construction of the word 'assigns'. In that case the plaintiffs had a contract to buy from the lessor a public house subject to a lease which contained a covenant to sell the freehold at a certain price on six months' notice being given by the lessor, his executors, administrators, or assigns. The only notice given was given by the plaintiffs, and it was held that they were not assigns within the meaning of the clause. *Walsh* v *Lonsdale* 21 ChD 9 was cited, but Romer LJ held that it had no application. The real point was that the notice was given by the wrong person, that such notice was a condition precedent, and the objection would have been just as fatal if the action had been brought in the name of the original landlord. The reversal in the Court of Appeal turned on a question of fact only. I hold, therefore, on this point, that the plaintiffs, being clearly entitled in this Court against the defendant to specific performance of the agreement under which the defendant has been for years and still is in possession of the land, can sue him on the covenants in the same manner as they could have done if Broadbents had actually executed the original agreement. . . .

The result is that I grant the injunction as asked, and order the defendant to pay the costs of the action.

Note
The following case concerns the application of estoppel to assignees.

Rodenhurst Estates Ltd v *W H Barnes Ltd*
[1936] 2 All ER 3 (CA)

T leased a property and the lease contained a covenant against assigning without the landlord's consent. T agreed with C that C would buy his business from him and take over T's lease. The landlords granted a licence to assign and C took over possession and payment of the rent, although no formal deed of assignment was executed. C defaulted on payment of the rent. They claimed they were merely equitable assignees of the lease and that they were not liable for the payment of rent as there was no privity of contract between the landlords and C. *Held*: C was estopped from so claiming.

SCOTT LJ: . . . To my mind none of the cases prevents the application here of the ordinary principles of the law of estoppel. It is quite clear that an equitable assignee does not become privy to the estate as between himself and the lessor of the lease, and, consequently, a lessor cannot sue an equitable assignee as such for either the rent or breach of covenant. Where, however, the equitable assignee leads the lessor to understand quite definitely that he, the equitable assignee, is more than an equitable assignee and has the term as a legal assignee, then, if the landlord acts upon that representation in such a way as to alter his position, you have every constituent of a common law estoppel. In this case the particular form of estoppel that is applicable is described in the third paragraph of the propositions of Brett, J, in *Carr* v *London & North Western Railway Co.* at p. 317:

> If a man, whatever his real meaning may be, so conducts himself that a reasonable man would take his conduct to mean a certain representation of facts, and that it was a true representation, and that the latter was intended to act upon it in a particular way, and he with such belief does act in that way to his damage, the first is estopped from denying that the facts were as represented.

Questions
1. In what way does the enforceability of obligations by and against successors in title of the original contracting parties differ with regard to leaseholds to freeholds?
2. Examine the doctrine of privity of estate and the way in which it operates in land law.

SECTION 9: COMMONHOLDS

See the Law Commission Report, 'Commonhold freehold flats and freehold ownership of other interdependent buildings' (Cm 179, July 1987, HMSO).

'Commonhold' can be described as a method whereby the owner of a flat can have the fee simple of his own flat, and with the other flat owners have collective rights and obligations over the common parts of the property.

Lord Chancellor's Department, 'Commonhold — A Consultation Paper' (Cm 1345, November 1990, HMSO).

Question
Why has it been thought necessary to introduce a third kind of tenure, i.e. the commonhold, in addition to the fee simple absolute and the term of years absolute? What will it achieve that the others do not?

See H. W. Wilkinson, 'Commonhold within our grasp' [1991] Conv 170; H. W. Wilkinson, 'Commonhold not plain sailing' [1991] Conv 70.

What is a 'commonhold'?
3.1 A 'commonhold' is a freehold development of two or more 'units' which share services and facilities and so require a system for communal management, and for the ownership of any common parts. A commonhold must consist of at least two units because the concept of shared services and facilities is of the essence of the commonhold system. The 'promoter' of a commonhold (ie, the person who establishes it) might be the developer of a new development, or the persons interested in an existing one, such as the freeholder and leaseholders of a block of long-leasehold flats.

3.2 The most obvious example of a commonhold is that of a block of flats where, at present, the flats would be owned on a long-leasehold basis. But there would be nothing in the commonhold legislation to prevent commonholds from being established for non-residential purposes (though the rules of a particular commonhold could include restrictions as to use of the kind which might now be found in leases). The system might equally be adopted for commercial or mixed-use developments, and the units do not have to be horizontally divided (ie, like flats). Thus, it could also be used for housing or industrial estates, or even shopping precincts with flats or offices above. Equally, it could be applied to agricultural buildings and surrounding farmland.

7 LICENCES

SECTION 1: THE NATURE OF A LICENCE

Vaughan LJ in *Thomas* v *Sorrell* (1673) Vaugh 330, said (at p. 351):
'A dispensation or licence properly passeth no interest, nor alters or transfers property in anything, but only makes an action lawful, which without it had been unlawful.'

A licence is a permission given by the occupier of land allowing a person to do some act which would otherwise be a trespass.

Since a licence is a mere permission it did not originally confer upon the holder an interest in the land and it could be revoked at any time. The law relating to licences has developed so that it is not now possible to revoke all types of licences so easily.

SECTION 2: CATEGORIES OF LICENCES

At common law there are three kinds of licences:

(a) The bare licence.
(b) The licence coupled with a grant or an interest.
(c) The contractual licence.

A: BARE LICENCES

A bare licence is a mere permission given to the licensee to enter the licensor's land; for example, a licence given to a postman to deliver mail to a house. Such a licence is gratuitous, confers no interest on the licensee, and the licensor can withdraw the permission at any time, whereupon the licensee becomes a trespasser.

B: LICENCES COUPLED WITH A GRANT OR AN INTEREST

A licence may be coupled with another right or interest, and it may in such a case be irrevocable. This occurs when the licensee is granted a proprietary interest in the land or in a chattel on the land *and* is given permission to enter the land in order to enjoy the interest; for example, X is given a right to cut timber on Y's land. Such a grant must be effected in the correct manner, namely by deed, if the grant is of a *profit à prendre*, although the doctrine of *Walsh* v *Lonsdale* (1882) 21 ChD 9 would apply.

In *Wood* v *Leadbitter* (1845) 13 M & W 838, Alderson B said:

It may further be observed, that a license under seal (provided it be a mere license) is as revocable as a license by parol; and, on the other hand, a license by parol, coupled with a grant, is as irrevocable as a license by deed, provided only that the grant is of a nature capable of being made by parol. But where there is a license by parol, coupled with a parol grant, or pretended grant, of something which is incapable of being granted otherwise than by deed, there the license is a mere license; it is not an incident to a valid grant, and it is therefore revocable. Thus, a license by A to hunt in his park, whether given by deed or by parol, is revocable; it merely renders the act of hunting lawful, which, without the license, would have been unlawful. If the license be, as put by Chief Justice Vaughan, a license not only to hunt, but also to take away the deer when killed to his own use, this is in truth a grant of the deer, with a license annexed to come on the land: and supposing the grant of the deer to be good, then the license would be irrevocable by the party who had given it; he would be estopped from defeating his own grant, or act in the nature of a grant. But suppose the case of a parol license to come on my lands, and there to make a watercourse, to flow on the land of the licensee. In such a case there is no valid grant of the watercourse, and the license remains a mere license, and therefore capable of being revoked. On the other hand, if such a license were granted by deed, then the question would be on the construction of the deed, whether it amounted to a grant of the watercourse; and if it did, then the license would be irrevocable.

C: CONTRACTUAL LICENCES

Contractual licences are licences supported by consideration; for example, where a person buys a ticket to the theatre to watch a play.

At common law this type of licence was said to be revocable.

Wood v *Leadbitter* (1845) 13 M & W 838

P bought a ticket to a race meeting and was forcefully ejected from the racecourse even though he had paid one guinea to enter the premises and view the races. He sued for assault and false imprisonment. Held: his action failed. The licensor could revoke the licence at any time, and once he did so the licensee became a trespasser who had refused to leave when asked to. Reasonable force could therefore be used to eject him. The only remedy available to him was to sue for breach of contract, but for this he would receive merely nominal damages.

(a) Situation post-Judicature Acts 1873-75

Hurst v Picture Theatres Ltd
[1915] 1 KB 1 (CA)

P bought a ticket for the cinema and was forcefully ejected before the film had finished. Held: (Phillimore LJ dissenting) P could recover damages for assault and false imprisonment.

BUCKLEY LJ: Let me at the outset say what *Wood* v *Leadbitter* seems to me to have decided. It affirmed that a mere license, whether or not it be under seal, by which I mean a licence not coupled with an interest or a grant whether it be under seal or not, is revocable. It affirmed also that if there be a license coupled with an interest or coupled with a grant, it is not, or at any rate in general is not, revocable. . . .

The position of matters now is that the Court is bound under the Judicature Act to give effect to equitable doctrines. The question we have to consider is whether, having regard to equitable considerations, *Wood* v *Leadbitter* is now law, meaning that *Wood* v *Leadbitter* is a decision which can be applied in its integrity in a Court which is bound to give effect to equitable considerations. In my opinion, it is not. Cozens-Hardy J, as he then was, the present Master of the Rolls, in the case of *Lowe* v *Adams* said this [1901] 2 Ch 598, at p. 600: 'Whether *Wood* v *Leadbitter* is still good law having regard to *Walsh* v *Lonsdale*' — which is a decision of the Court of Appeal — 'is very doubtful.' The present Lord Parker, then Parker J, in the case of *Jones* v *Earl of Tankerville* says this [1909] 2 Ch 440, at p. 443: 'An injunction restraining the revocation of the licence, when it is revocable at law, may in a sense be called relief by way of specific performance, but it is not specific performance in the sense of compelling the vendor to do anything. It merely prevents him from breaking his contract, and protects a right in equity which but for the absence of a seal would be a right at law, and since the Judicature Act it may well be doubted whether the absence of a seal in such a case can be relied on in any Court.' What was relied on in *Wood* v *Leadbitter*, and rightly relied on at that date, was that there was not an instrument under seal, and therefore there was not a grant, and therefore the licensee could not say that he was not a mere licensee, but a licensee with a grant. That is now swept away. It cannot be said as against the plaintiff that he is a licensee with no grant merely because there is not an instrument under seal which gives him a right at law.

There is another way in which the matter may be put. If there be a licence with an agreement not to revoke the licence, that, if given for value, is an enforceable right. If the facts here are, as I think they are, that the licence was a licence to enter the building and see the spectacle from its commencement until its termination, then there was included in that contract a contract not to revoke the licence until the play had run to its termination. It was then a breach of contract to revoke the obligation not to revoke the licence, and for that the decision in *Kerrison* v *Smith* [1897] 2 QB 445 is an authority.

Note
The House of Lords settled the matter in the next case.

Winter Garden Theatre (London) Ltd v Millennium Productions Ltd
[1948] AC 173 (HL)

A granted a licence to M to use a theatre for various productions over the period of six months with an option to continue use after the original period.

The agreement made no express provision for the revocation of the licence. Held: whether a contractual licence is revocable or not depends upon the terms of the agreement.

LORD UTHWATT: My view as to the construction of the agreement renders it unnecessary to consider whether *Hurst* v *Picture Theatres, Ltd* [1915] 1 KB 1 was rightly decided, or to express any concluded opinion on the question of the remedies now open in every court to a bare licensee who claims that the licensor has in breach of his bargain affected to revoke it. I merely confess my present inability to see any answer to the propositions of law stated by the Master of the Rolls in his judgment in the case under appeal. The settled practice of the courts of equity is to do what they can by an injunction to preserve the sanctity of a bargain. To my mind, as at present advised, a licensee who has refused to accept the wrongful repudiation of the bargain which is involved in an unauthorized revocation of the licence is as much entitled to the protection of an injunction as a licensee who has not received any notice of revocation; and, if the remedy of injunction is properly available in the latter case against unauthorized interference by the licensor, it is also available in the former case. In a court of equity, wrongful acts are no passport to favour.

Note

In the House of Lords the licence was construed as being revocable and so all views were *obiter*. In the Court of Appeal the licence was construed as being irrevocable and the licensee was protected by the grant of an injunction.

Hurst v *Picture Theatres Ltd* and the *Winter Garden* case were considered by Megarry J in the following case.

Hounslow London Borough Council v Twickenham Garden Developments Ltd
[1971] 1 Ch 233 (Ch D)

MEGARRY J: There is, however, an alternative route to irrevocability, namely, by means of a contract. Let it be assumed that there is no 'interest' which can be coupled with a licence, but merely a contract. This, per se, may preclude revocation. In *Hurst* v *Picture Theatres Ltd* [1915] 1 KB 1, 10, Buckley LJ put the point shortly. (See page 218)....

This point was developed further in the *Winter Garden* case in the Court of Appeal [1946] 1 All ER 678. [Megarry J outlined the facts of the case] The House of Lords reversed the decision of the Court of Appeal in favour of the licensees, the difference between the two decisions being essentially one of construction. The Court of Appeal held that the licensors had no power to revoke the licence, whereas the House of Lords held that they had that power. Nothing that I can see in the speeches in the House of Lords suggests that the Court of Appeal was wrong in the law which that court applied to an irrevocable licence. Indeed, Lord Uthwatt confessed that he found Lord Greene MR's propositions of law unanswerable: see [1948] AC 173, 202.

Lord Greene MR, at p. 680, first disposed of any concept that a contractual licence was an entity distinct from the contract:

> Counsel for the respondents put in the forefront of his argument a proposition of this nature. There is a thing called a licence, which is something which, so to speak, has a separate existence, distinct from the contract which creates it; and there is a rule of law governing that particular thing which says that a licence is determinable at will.

> That seems to me to be putting the matter on the wrong footing. A licence created by a contract is not an interest. It creates a contractual right to do certain things which otherwise would be a trespass. It seems to me that, in considering the nature of such a licence and the mutual rights and obligations which arise under it, the first thing to do is to construe the contract according to ordinary principles. There is the question whether or not the particular licence is revocable at all and, if so, whether by both parties or by only one. There is the question whether it is revocable immediately or only after the giving of some notice. Those are questions of construction of the contract. It seems to me quite inadmissible to say that the question whether a licence is revocable at all can be, so to speak, segregated and treated by itself, leaving only the other questions to be decided by reference to the true construction of the contract. As I understand the law, rightly or wrongly, the answers to all these questions must depend on the terms of the contract when properly construed in the light of any relevant and admissible circumstances.

Whereas in equity, at all events, a contract for a grant or conveyance may be regarded as bringing into being some estate or interest in the land, separate from the contract that creates it, a licence is no separate entity but merely one of the manifestations of the contract. I think that the speech of Lord Simon in the House of Lords is at least consistent with this view: see [1948] AC 173, 189, 191.

Secondly, Lord Greene MR said, at p. 684:

> The respondents have purported to determine the licence. If I have correctly construed the contract their doing so was a breach of contract. It may well be that, in the old days, that would only have given rise to a right to sue for damages. The licence would have stood revoked, but after the expiration of what was the appropriate period of grace the licensees would have been trespassers and could have been expelled, and their right would have been to sue for damages for breach of contract, as was said in *Kerrison* v *Smith* [1897] 2 QB 445. But the matter requires to be considered further, because the power of equity to grant an injunction to restrain a breach of contract is, of course, a power exercisable in any court. The general rule is that, before equity will grant such an injunction, there must be, on the construction of the contract, a negative clause express or implied. In the present case it seems to me that the grant of an option which, if I am right, is an irrevocable option, must imply a negative undertaking by the licensor not to revoke it. That being so, in my opinion, such a contract could be enforced in equity by an injunction. Then the question would arise, at what time can equity interfere? If the licensor were threatening to revoke, equity, I apprehend, would grant an injunction to restrain him from carrying out that threat. But supposing he has in fact purported to evoke, is equity then to say: 'We are now powerless. We cannot stop you from doing anything to carry into effect your wrongful revocation'? I apprehend not. I apprehend equity would say: 'You have revoked and the licensee had no opportunity of stopping you doing so by an injunction; but what the court of equity can do is to prevent you from carrying that revocation into effect and restrain you from doing anything under it.' In the present case, nothing has been done. The appellants are still there. I can see no reason at all why, on general principles, equity should not interfere to restrain the licensors from acting upon the purported revocation, that revocation being, as I consider, a breach of contract. Looking at it in that rather simple way, one is not concerned with the difficulties which are suggested to arise from the decision of this court in *Hurst* v *Picture Theatres Ltd* [1915] 1 KB 1.

James Jones & Sons Ltd v *Earl of Tankerville* [1909] 2 Ch 440 does not appear to have been cited, but the views of Parker J at p. 443 seem to have been similar.

Quite apart, then, from the question whether the contractor has a licence coupled with an interest, there is the question whether the contractor has a contractual licence which either expressly or by implication is subject to a negative obligation by the borough not to revoke it. If this is so, then, on the law laid down by the Court of Appeal, equity would interfere to prevent the borough from revoking the licence or, if it had been revoked, from acting on the revocation. A fortiori, equity would refuse to grant the borough an injunction to enforce the revocation.

(b) Inferred contractual licences

Tanner v *Tanner* [1975] 3 All ER 776 (CA)

M and W formed a relationship. W was a tenant of a flat, where M visited her. In 1970, the parties decided to purchase a house to provide accommodation for W and the children of the relationship. The house was purchased in M's name and financed by a mortgage. W made no contribution to the purchase price, but gave up her flat that had Rent Act protection and purchased furniture and furnishings for the house. W occupied the ground floor in the house and the rest was let. M stopped paying W maintenance for the children. M moved in with W but later formed a relationship with another woman whom he married. M tried to persuade W to leave the property. He first offered her a lump sum but, when this was refused he claimed W had only a licence to occupy and he sought to terminate it. An order for possession was granted and W vacated the property but appealed. Held: on the facts a contract should be inferred in terms that M granted W a licence to occupy the house for herself and the children so long as they were of school age and the accommodation was reasonably required by them. W had given good consideration in that she had surrendered the tenancy of her flat and looked after M's children. The licence was not revocable at will, and W was entitled to damages for the loss of a contractual licence.

Chandler v *Kerley* [1978] 2 All ER 942 (CA)

H and W bought a house as a family home, partly financed by a mortgage. H paid the mortgage instalments. Some two years later the marriage broke down and H left W to live with their children in the house. H continued to pay the mortgage. W met P and became his mistress. H was unable to afford future mortgage instalments and agreed with W to sell the property. The mortgagees were threatening possession proceedings when P offered to purchase the property at a substantially reduced price of £10,000. The house was sold to P at that price on the understanding that W would continue to live there and he would join her there. A few weeks after completing the purchase P served a notice on W purporting to terminate her licence to occupy the house. W refused to leave. Held: W had a contractual licence which was determinable on reasonable notice, and in this case that was thought to be 12 months. She did not have a licence to remain for life, which would have tied up P's capital indefinitely.

Hardwick v Johnson [1978] 2 All ER 935 (CA)

M purchased a home in her own name for her son (S) and daughter-in-law (D) to live in. It was arranged that the couple would pay £7 per week to M although it was not clear whether the sum was payment for rent or money towards payment of the purchase price. After making some payments to M, the rent fell into arrears but M waived payment. The marriage broke down. M asked D to vacate the premises as no rent was being paid and M wished to sell the house. D then offered to pay £7 a week to M. M served a notice on S purporting to determine D's right of occupation whether it was a tenancy or a licence. D remained in the property with a new-born child. M brought proceedings against S and D claiming possession of the house and arrears of the monthly instalments. Held: the arrangements amounted to the grant of a licence which was equitable (Lord Denning MR) or contractual (Roskill and Browne LJJ). S and D could live in the house provided that they paid M £28 a month. The courts would impute to the parties their common intention to determine the legal relationship. The licence was not conditional on the marriage succeeding.

Horrocks v Forray
[1976] 1 All ER 737 (CA)

H and W married. D was H's mistress. D gave birth to a daughter of the relationship, and H then wholly supported D to the extent of £4,000–£5,000 a year and the provision of accommodation. D then married another man and had a child by him, but the marriage was short-lived and she divorced. Her relationship with H continued and H bought a house in Kensington for D and the children to live in. The house was transferred into his sole name and, for tax reasons, was never transferred to D. H was killed. H's executors wrote to D telling her to leave the property. She refused to do so. She said that from the circumstances of the relationship with H a contract was to be inferred whereby she had subordinated her 'mode of life and choice of residence' to H in return for an undertaking that he maintain her and her family, and that she thus had an irrevocable licence to remain in the property. Held: there could be no express or implied contract in the absence of an intention shared by both parties to affect their legal relationship.

SCARMAN J: Counsel for the defendant has sought to persuade the court that a contract is to be inferred from a course of conduct, from the development of the relationship between the parties and its course over a period of years. This submission is, as a matter of law, open to him. That has been clearly decided, as I understand it, in two cases in the Court of Appeal to which he has referred us: *Ward* v *Byham* [1956] 2 All ER 318 and *Tanner* v *Tanner* [1975] 3 All ER 776. In each of those cases, however, the relationship of man and mistress was either broken or on the point of collapse. The parties to the relationship, the man and the woman, had to consider what best should be done for the innocent product of their relationship, the illegitimate children. In a very real sense, both in *Ward* v *Byham* [1956] 2 All ER 318 and in *Tanner* v *Tanner* [1975] 3 All ER 776, the man and the woman were making arrangements for the future at arm's length. The woman was concerned for herself and her children: the man was concerned to limit and define his financial responsibilities towards the woman and the children. Here is a fertile area for the growth of an inference of a legally binding contract; and for myself I do not find it surprising, when I look at the facts in *Ward* v *Byham* [1956] 2 All ER 318 or *Tanner* v *Tanner* [1975] 3 All ER 776, that the court came to the conclusion that a contract was to be inferred from the conduct of the parties. But how different is this case. Right up to the death of the man there was a continuing, warm relationship of man and mistress. He was maintaining his mistress in luxurious, even, so the judge thought, extravagant, style, and, we now know, in a style beyond his means; his estate is now at risk of being insolvent.

Questions
1. Have the courts shown a willingness to imply or infer the existence of a contractual licence in family situations?
2. How can the decision of *Tanner* v *Tanner* be reconciled with that of *Greasley* v *Cooke* [1980] 1 WLR 1306?

(c) Specific performance of a contractual licence

Verrall v Great Yarmouth Borough Council
[1981] 1 QB 202 (CA)

D granted a licence of a hall to the National Front. Following a change in the council's political control, it then purported to revoke the licence. Held: an injunction or specific performance could be used to protect any interest, including a licence of a transient nature.

LORD DENNING MR: Since the *Winter Garden* case, it is clear that once a man has entered under his contract of licence, he cannot be turned out. An injunction can be obtained against the licensor to prevent his being turned out. On principle it is the same if it happens before he enters. If he has a contractual right to enter, and the licensor refuses to let him come in, then he can come to the court and in a proper case get an order for specific performance to allow him to come in.

(d) Contractual licences and third parties

The problem with enforceability of a contractual licence against third parties arises because a contract made between A and B is not capable of imposing a burden on C due to the doctrine of privity of contract. The protection given to a licensee is of limited use if the licence is binding and irrevocable against the licensor but not enforceable against a transferee. The only remedy available for the licensee in such a situation would be to claim damages against the licensor.

(i) *Traditional view*

King v David Allen and Sons, Billposting Ltd
[1916] 2 AC 54 (HL)

An agreement, which was made in writing between P and D, allowed P to fix posters and advertisements to the walls of a cinema which was to be built on

D's property. The permission was to last for a period of four years at a rent of £12 per annum, and P was to have the exclusive right of using the wall for advertisements during the licence period. Subsequently D leased the cinema to T and assigned to T his interest in the agreement between himself and P. The lease contained no reference to the agreement. T refused P the permission granted by the agreement. Held: the agreement gave rise to a mere personal obligation and not an interest in land. D was liable to P for damages only.

LORD BUCKMASTER: The matter then is left in this way. There is a contract between the appellant and the respondents which creates nothing but a personal obligation. It is a licence given for good and valuable consideration and to endure for a certain time. But I fail to see — although I have done my best to follow the many authorities which the learned Solicitor-General has thought it right to place before our consideration — that there is any authority for saying that any such document creates rights other than those I have described. A case of *Wilson* v *Tavener* [1901] 1 Ch 578 was indeed referred to, but it really affords no assistance, for there the right conferred was to erect a hoarding upon the defendant's ground, while in the present case the sole right is to fix bills against a flank wall, and it is unreasonable to attempt to construct the relationship of landlord and tenant or grantor and grantee of an easement out of such a transaction, and I find it difficult to see how it can be reasonably urged that anything beyond personal rights was ever contemplated by the parties. Those rights have undoubtedly been taken away by the action on the part of the company, who have been enabled to prevent the respondents from exercising their rights owing to the lease granted by Mr King, and he is accordingly liable in damages, although it was certainly not with his will, and indeed against his own express desire, that the company has declined to honour his agreement.

Clore v *Theatrical Properties Ltd and Westby & Co. Ltd*
[1936] 3 All ER 483 (CA)

An indenture contained a provision that 'the lessor doth hereby demise and grant unto the lessee the free and exclusive use of all the refreshment rooms . . . of the theatre . . . for the purpose only of the supply and the accommodation of the visitors to the theatre and for no other purpose whatsoever'. The lessor's consent was required before assignment or sub-letting. The terms 'lessor' and 'lessee' were defined to include their executors, administrators and assigns. An assignee of the lessor sought to prevent assignees of the lessee from exercising the rights granted by the indenture. Held: the indenture was a licence not a lease, enforceable as a personal contract and could only be enforced by persons between whom there was privity of contract.

LORD WRIGHT MR: . . . I think that this court is bound by the decisions in previous cases to hold that this document does not convey any interest in land but is merely a personal contract embodying a licence. On that ground the learned judge decided this matter and I agree with him and in particular with his final conclusion in that the rights mentioned in the document are purely contractual. It follows from this that there is no circumstance which enables the present appellants to assert any rights against the present respondent because there is no contractual nexus between them.

(ii) *Contractual licences binding on third parties*

Errington v Errington & Woods
[1952] 1 KB 290 (CA)

F purchased a home in his own name using his own capital and a mortgage advance. The house was to be a home for his newly married son S. F paid the rates but told S and S's wife that he would transfer the property to them if they lived in the house, paying the mortgage instalments until the last one was paid. S's wife looked after the building society's book. F died. S and S's wife had occupied the property up until F's death, paying the instalments. S then left his wife and moved in with his mother. S's wife remained in the property and continued paying the mortgage. S's mother sought possession. Held: S's wife and S were contractual licensees. They could not be evicted as long as they paid the instalments.

DENNING LJ: The father's promise was a unilateral contract — a promise of the house in return for their act of paying the instalments. It could not be revoked by him once the couple entered on performance of the act, but it would cease to bind him if they left it incomplete and unperformed, which they have not done. If that was the position during the father's lifetime, so it must be after his death. If the daughter-in-law continues to pay all the building society instalments, the couple will be entitled to have the property transferred to them as soon as the mortgage is paid off; but if she does not do so, then the building society will claim the instalments from the father's estate and the estate will have to pay them. I cannot think that in those circumstances the estate would be bound to transfer the house to them, any more than the father himself would have been.

. . . [A]lthough a person who is let into exclusive possession is prima facie to be considered to be a tenant, nevertheless he will not be held to be so if the circumstances negative any intention to create a tenancy. Words alone may not suffice. Parties cannot turn a tenancy into a licence merely by calling it one. But if the circumstances and the conduct of the parties show that all that was intended was that the occupier should be granted a personal privilege, with no interest in the land, he will be held to be a licensee only. In view of these recent cases I doubt whether *Lynes* v *Snaith* [1899] 1 QB 486, and the case of the gamekeeper referred to therein, would be decided the same way today.

Applying the foregoing principles to the present case, it seems to me that, although the couple had exclusive possession of the house, there was clearly no relationship of landlord and tenant. They were not tenants at will but licensees. They had a mere personal privilege to remain there, with no right to assign or sub-let. They were, however, not bare licensees. They were licensees with a contractual right to remain. As such they have no right at law to remain, but only in equity, and equitable rights now prevail. I confess, however, that it has taken the courts some time to reach this position. At common law a licence was always revocable at will, notwithstanding a contract to the contrary: *Wood* v *Leadbitter* (1845) 13 M & W 838. The remedy for a breach of the contract was only in damages. That was the view generally held until a few years ago: see, for instance, what was said in *Booker* v *Palmer* [1942] 2 All ER 674, 677 and *Thompson* v *Park* [1944] KB 408, 410. The rule has, however, been altered owing to the interposition of equity.

Law and equity have been fused for nearly 80 years, and since 1948 it has been clear that, as a result of the fusion, a licensor will not be permitted to eject a licensee in breach of a contract to allow him to remain: see *Winter Garden Theatre, London* v *Millennium Productions Ld* [1946] 1 All ER 678, 680; [1948] AC 173, 191 *per* Lord Greene, and in the House of Lords *per* Lord Simon; nor in breach of a promise on which the licensee has acted, even though he gave no value for it: see *Foster* v *Robinson* [1951] 1 KB 149, 156, where Sir Raymond Evershed MR said that as a result of the oral arrangement to let the man stay, he was entitled as licensee to occupy the premises without any payment of rent for the rest of his days. This infusion of equity means that contractual licences now have a force and validity of their own and cannot be revoked in breach of the contract. Neither the licensor nor anyone who claims through him can disregard the contract except a purchaser for value without notice. . . .

In the present case it is clear that the father expressly promised the couple that the property should belong to them as soon as the mortgage was paid, and impliedly promised that so long as they paid the instalments to the building society they should be allowed to remain in possession. They were not purchasers because they never bound themselves to pay the instalments, but nevertheless they were in a position analogous to purchasers. They have acted on the promise, and neither the father nor his widow, his successor in title, can eject them in disregard of it. The result is that in my opinion the appeal should be dismissed and no order for possession should be made.

Notes
1. If *Errington* v *Errington and Woods* is correctly decided, then it reverses the rule in *Wood* v *Leadbitter* that contractual licences are to all intents and purposes revocable.
2. Denning LJ said that the original contractual arrangement gave the daughter-in-law an 'equitable right' to remain in the property for as long as the instalments were paid. This equitable right it is thought could be enforced against a third party according to the doctrine of notice.
3. It would seem that the enforceability of contractual licences against third parties developed from the concept of a licence coupled with an equity (compare a licence coupled with a grant). Lord Denning MR in *National Provincial Bank Ltd* v *Hastings Car Mart Ltd* [1964] Ch 665, at p. 684, said that a licence coupled with an equity arises if:

> the owner of the land grants a licence to another to go upon the land and occupy it for a specific period or a prescribed purpose, and on the faith of that authority the licensee enters into occupation and does work, or in some other way alters his position to his detriment, then the owner cannot revoke the licence at his will. He cannot revoke the licence so as to defeat the period or purpose for which it was granted. A court of equity will restrain him from so doing. Not only will it restrain him, but it will restrain any successor in title who takes the land with knowledge of the arrangement that has been made.

Questions
1. Do you agree with the way in which Denning LJ developed the concept of a licence coupled with equity?
2. What is the difference between a licence by estoppel (see page 236 *et seq.*) and a licence coupled with an equity? Are there similarities between the two concepts?

See A. Briggs, 'Licences: back to basics' [1981] Conv 212; M. P. Thompson, 'Licences, questioning the basics' [1983] Conv 50.

Note
See *National Provincial Bank Ltd* v *Ainsworth* [1965] AC 1175, per Lord Wilberforce:

> ... the legal position of contractual licensees, as regards 'purchasers,' is very far from clear. The Court of Appeal has attempted to reach a generalisation by which licences, or at least licences coupled with occupation, are binding upon 'purchasers' but I note that the members of that court are not wholly agreed as to this doctrine. No doubt the time will come when this whole subject will have to be reviewed; this is not the occasion for it and I think that it would be undesirable now to say anything which might impede the development of this branch of the law. Neither contractual licences nor those licences where money has been expended by the licensee in my view afford any useful analogy or basis upon which to determine the character of the wife's rights.
>
> I would only add, with reference to the authorities (1) that I must not be taken as accepting the arguments placed before the Court of Appeal whereby such cases as *King* v *David Allen & Sons, Billposting Ltd* and *Clore* v *Theatrical Properties Ltd* and *Westby & Co. Ltd* are put on one side as not, or no longer, relevant authorities; (2) that, while accepting the actual decision I do not find that the case of *Errington* v *Errington and Woods*, even if reconcilable with the two cases I have mentioned, is of assistance as to the transmissibility of contractual licences. The Court of Appeal in that case seem to have treated it simply as one of contract and not to have focused their argument on the precise legal position of the plaintiff, i.e., whether she was the legal personal representative or the successor in title of the licensor.

Questions
1. What additional legal issues would have been involved if the land in *Errington* v *Errington and Woods* had been registered land? See A. D. Hargreaves, 'Licenced possessors' (1953) 69 LQR 466; H. W. R. Woods, 'Licences and third parties' (1952) 68 LQR 337.
2. The subsequent constraints that have been imposed on the *Tulk* v *Moxhay* doctrine represent a 'decisive repudiation of the notion that the mere fact that an equitable remedy was available was enough to turn a contract into an interest in land binding purchasers with notice' (H. W. R. Wade (1952) 68 LQR 337, at p. 348). What is the relevance of this statement to the law of licences?

Binions v Evans
[1972] 1 Ch 359 (CA)

D was the widow of an estate employee who had lived in a cottage rent free during his employment. The trustees of the estate allowed D to continue living rent free in the cottage, which they owned, following her husband's death and entered into an agreement with D 'to provide a temporary home' for her to 'reside in and occupy' the property as tenant at will 'free of rent for the rest of her life or until as hereafter provided'. D did have some obligations as a tenant. The tenancy could 'be determined at any time' by D giving notice to the trustees of not less than four weeks. The tenancy was to determine on death, if not before.

The trustees agreed to sell the cottage to P subject to the tenancy and inserted a special clause in the contract for sale to protect D. Because of D's tenancy the price of the cottage was reduced. P then gave D notice to quit. Held: all the Court of Appeal held that D was protected, but gave different reasons. Lord Denning said the agreement amounted to a contractual licence, resulting in an equitable interest. Megaw and Stephenson LJJ said D was a tenant for life under the Settled Land Act 1925.

LORD DENNING MR: Seeing that the defendant has no legal estate or interest in the land, the question is what right has she? At any rate, she has a contractual right to reside in the house for the remainder of her life or as long as she pleases to stay. I know that in the agreement it is described as a tenancy: but that does not matter. The question is: What is it in reality? To my mind it is a licence, and no tenancy. It is a privilege which is personal to her. On all the modern cases, which are legion, it ranks as a contractual licence, and not a tenancy: see *Shell-Mex and B.P. Ltd* v *Manchester Garages Ltd* [1971] 1 WLR 612.

What is the status of such a licence as this? There are a number of cases in the books in which a similar right has been given. They show that a right to occupy for life, arising by contract, gives to the occupier an equitable interest in the land: just as it does when it arises under a settlement: see *In re Carne's Settled Estates* [1899] 1 Ch 324 and *In re Boyer's Settled Estates* [1916] 2 Ch 404. The courts of equity will not allow the landlord to turn the occupier out in breach of the contract: see *Foster* v *Robinson* [1951] 1 KB 149, 156; nor will they allow a purchaser to turn her out if he bought with knowledge of her right — *Errington* v *Errington and Woods* [1952] 1 KB 290, 299.

It is instructive to go back to the cases before the Supreme Court Judicature Act 1873. They show that, if a landlord, by a memorandum in writing, let a house to someone, let us say to a widow, at a rent, for her life or as long as she pleased to stay, the courts of equity would not allow the landlord to turn her out in breach of his contract. If the landlord were to go to the courts of law and obtain an order in ejectment against her, as in *Doe d. Warner* v *Browne*, 8 East 165, the courts of equity would grant an injunction to restrain the landlord from enforcing his rights at law, as in *Browne* v *Warner* (1808) 14 Ves 409. The courts of equity would give the agreement a construction, which Lord Edon LC called an "equitable construction," and construe it as if it were an agreement to execute a deed granting her a lease of the house for her life — *Browne* v *Warner*, 14 Ves 156, 158. They would order the landlord specifically to perform the contract, so construed, by executing such a deed. This court did so in *Zimbler* v *Abraham* [1903] 1 KB 577. This means that she had an equitable interest in the land. So much so that if a purchaser wished to buy her interest from her, he had to pay her its full value as such. Malins V-C so held in *In re King's Leasehold Estates* (1873) LR 16 Eq 521, 527, where he described it as an "equitable interest." It follows that, if the owner sold his reversion to another, who took with notice of the widow's interest, his sucessor could not turn her out any more than he could. She would have, I should have thought, at least as strong a case as the occupier in *Webb* v *Paternoster* (1619) Poph

Licences

151, which received the blessing of Lord Upjohn in *National Provincial Bank Ltd* v *Hastings Car Mart Ltd* [1965] AC 1175, 1239.

Suppose, however, that the defendant did not have an equitable interest at the outset, nevertheless it is quite plain that she obtained one afterwards when the Tredegar Estate sold the cottage. They stipulated with the plaintiffs that they were to take the house "subject to" the defendant's rights under the agreement. They supplied the plaintiffs with a copy of the contract: and the plaintiffs paid less because of her right to stay there. In these circumstances, this court will impose on the plaintiffs a constructive trust for her benefit: for the simple reason that it would be utterly inequitable for the plaintiffs to turn the defendant out contrary to the stipulation subject to which they took the premises. That seems to me clear from the important decision of *Bannister* v *Bannister* [1948] 2 All ER 133, which was applied by the judge, and which I gladly follow.

This imposing of a constructive trust is entirely in accord with the precepts of equity. As Cardozo J once put it: "A constructive trust is the formula through which the conscience of equity finds expression," see *Beatty* v *Guggenheim Exploration Co.* (1919) 225 NY 380, 386: or, as Lord Diplock put it quite recently in *Gissing* v *Gissing* [1971] AC 886, 905, a constructive trust is created "whenever the trustee has so conducted himself that it would be inequitable to allow him to deny to the cestui que trust a beneficial interest in the land acquired."

I know that there are some who have doubted whether a contractual licensee has any protection against a purchaser, even one who takes with full notice. We were referred in this connection to Professor Wade's article Licences and Third Parties in (1952) 68 LQR 337, and to the judgment of Goff J in *In re Solomon, A Bankrupt, Ex parte Trustee of the Property of the Bankrupt* v *Solomon* [1967] Ch 573. None of these doubts can prevail, however, when the situation gives rise to a constructive trust. Whenever the owner sells the land to a purchaser, and at the same time stipulates that he shall take it "subject to" a contractual licence, I think it plain that a court of equity wll impose on the purchaser a constructive trust in favour of the beneficiary. It is true that the stipulation (that the purchaser shall take it subject to the rights of the licensee) is a stipulation for the benefit of one who is not a party to the contract of sale; but, as Lord Upjohn said in *Beswick* v *Beswick* [1968] AC 58, 98, that is just the very case in which equity will "come to the aid of the common law." It does so by imposing a constructive trust on the purchaser. It would be utterly inequitable that the purchaser should be able to turn out the beneficiary. It is to be noticed that in the two cases which are said to give rise to difficulty *King* v *David Allen and Sons, Billposting Ltd* [1916] 2 AC 54 and *Clore* v *Theatrical Properties Ltd and Westby & Co. Ltd* [1936] 3 All ER 483, there was no trace of a stipulation, express or implied, that the purchaser should take the property subject to the right of the contractual licensee. In the first case, if Mr King had protected himself by stipulating that the company should take the lease "subject to the rights of David Allen," I cannot think that he would have been held liable in damages. In the second case the documents were exceedingly complicated, but if Mr Clore had acquired the theatre "subject to the rights of the licensees," I cannot suppose that this court would have allowed him to disregard those rights.

In many of these cases the purchaser takes *expressly* "subject to" the rights of the licensee. Obviously the purchaser then holds the land on an imputed trust for the licensee. But, even if he does not take expressly "subject to" the rights of the licensee, he may do so *impliedly*. At any rate when the licensee is in actual occupation of the land, so that the purchaser must know he is there, and of the rights which he has: see *Hodgson* v *Marks* [1971] Ch 892. Whenever the purchaser takes the land impliedly subject to the rights of the contractual licensee, a court of equity will impose a constructive trust for the beneficiary. So I still adhere to the proposition I stated in *Errington* v *Errington and*

Woods [1952] 1 KB 290, 299; and elaborated in *National Provincial Bank Ltd* v *Hastings Car Mart Ltd* [1964] Ch 665, 686–689, namely, that, when the licensee is in actual occupation, neither the licensor nor anyone who claims through him can disregard the contract except a purchaser for value without notice.

5. *Conclusion*

In my opinion the defendant, by virtue of the agreement, had an equitable interest in the cottage which the court would protect by granting an injunction against the landlords restraining them from turning her out. When the landlords sold the cottage to a purchaser "subject to" her rights under the agreement, the purchaser took the cottage on a constructive trust to permit the defendant to reside there during her life, or as long as she might desire. The courts will not allow the purchaser to go back on that trust. I entirely agree with the judgment of Judge Bulger. I would dismiss this appeal.

STEPHENSON LJ: Apart from authority, I would not have thought that such an interest could be understood to amount to a tenancy for life within the meaning of the Settled Land Act 1925, and I would have thought that the other terms of her tenancy (as I think it ought properly to be called) are inconsistent with a power to ask for the legal estate to be settled on her or to sell the cottage. But *Bannister* v *Bannister* [1948] 2 All ER 133 is a clear decision of this court that such words as have been used in this agreement (excepting, I must concede, the words "as tenant at will of them") create a life interest determinable (apart from the special considerations introduced by the Settled Land Act 1925) on the beneficiary ceasing to occupy the premises and the landlords hold the cottage on trust to permit her to occupy it "during her life or as long as she lives" as Judge Bulger held, and subject thereto in trust for them.

I therefore find it unnecessary to consider or decide the vexed questions (1) whether this agreement is or creates an irrevocable contractual licence to occupy, and (2) whether such a licence has been elevated to a status equivalent to an estate or interest in land by decisions of this court such as *Errington* v *Errington and Woods* [1952] 1 KB 290 or *Foster* v *Robinson* [1951] 1 KB 149 or still awaits legislation before it can so achieve transmissibility to subsequent purchasers with notice: see the rival views set out by Goff J in *In re Solomon, A Bankrupt, Ex parte Trustee of the Property of the Bankrupt* v *Solomon* [1967] Ch 573, 582–586.

Questions

1. In *Binions* v *Evans* Lord Denning had to contend with the earlier cases of *Clore* v *Theatrical Properties Ltd* [1936] 3 All ER 483 and *King* v *David Allan and Sons, Billposting Ltd* [1916] 2 AC 54. How did he distinguish those cases from *Binions* v *Evans*?

2. How did Megaw and Stephenson LJJ give Mrs Evan's an interest under the Settled Land Act 1925? (See estoppel and constructive trusts re *Binions* v *Evans*.)

3. Do you think that there is any substance to the argument that Mrs Evans could have had a tenancy of some kind in *Binions* v *Evans*?

Ashburn Anstalt v *Arnold*
[1989] Ch 1 (CA)

FOX LJ (obiter): It is not in doubt that the actual decision [in *Errington* v *Errington and Woods*] was correct. It could be justified on one of three grounds. (i) There was a contract to convey the house on completion of the payments giving rise to an equitable interest in the form of an estate contract which would be binding on the widow: see *Megarry & Wade, The Law of Real Property*, 5th ed. (1984), p. 806. The widow was not a purchaser for value. (ii) The daughter-in-law had changed her position in reliance upon a representation binding on the widow as a privy of the representor: see *Spencer Bower and Turner, Estoppel by Representation*, 3rd ed. (1977), p. 123. (iii) The payment of the instalments by the son or the daughter-in-law gave rise to direct proprietary interests by way of constructive trust, though it is true that, until *Gissing* v *Gissing* [1971] AC 886, the law relating to constructive trusts in this field was not much considered.

Accordingly, it does not appear to have been necessary, in order to produce a just result, to have accepted the broad principle stated, at p. 299, in the passage which we have quoted, that "Neither the licensor nor anyone who claims through him can disregard the contract except a purchaser for value without notice." That statement itself is not supported by any citation of authority, and indeed we do not think it could have been supported on the authorities. None of the cases prior to *Errington* v *Errington and Woods* to which we have referred, except *Thomas* v *Sorrell*, Vaugh. 330, is mentioned in the judgments and it does not appear that any was cited. . . .

It must, we think, be very doubtful whether this court's decision in *Errington* v *Errington and Woods* [1952] 1 KB 290 is consistent with its earlier decisions in *Daly* v *Edwardes*, 83 LT 548; *Frank Warr & Co.* v *London County Council* [1904] 1 KB 713 and *Clore* v *Theatrical Properties Ltd* [1936] 3 All ER 483. That decision cannot be said to be in conflict with any later decision of the House of Lords, because the House expressly left the effect of a contractual licence open in the *Hastings Car Mart* case. But there must be very real doubts whether *Errington* can be reconciled with the earlier decisions of the House of Lords in *Edwardes* v *Barrington*, 85 LT 650, and *King* v *David Allen and Sons (Billposting) Ltd* [1916] 2 AC 54. It would seem that we must follow those cases or choose between the two lines of authority. It is not, however, necessary to consider those alternative courses in detail, since in our judgment the House of Lords cases, whether or not as a matter of strict precedent they conclude this question, state the correct principle which we should follow.

Our reasons for reaching this conclusion are based upon essentially the same reasons as those given by Russell LJ in the *Hastings Car Mart* case [1964] Ch 665, 697 and by Professor Wade in the article, "Licences and Third Parties" (1952) 68 LQR 337, to which Russell LJ refers. Before *Errington* the law appears to have been clear and well understood. It rested on an important and intelligible distinction between contractual obligations which gave rise to no estate or interest in the land and proprietary rights which, by definition, did. The far-reaching statement of principle in *Errington* was not supported by authority, not necessary for the decision of the case and per incuriam in the sense that it was made without reference to authorities which, if they would not have compelled, would surely have persuaded the court to adopt a different ratio. Of course, the law must be free to develop. But as a response to problems which had arisen, the *Errington* rule (without more) was neither practically necessary nor theoretically convincing. By contrast, the finding on appropriate facts of a constructive trust may well be regarded as a beneficial adaptation of old rules to new situations.

Note
See J. Hill, 'Leases, licences and third parties' (1988) 51 MLR 226; Adrian Briggs, 'Contractual licences: a reply' [1983] Conv 285: M. P. Thompson, [1983] Conv 471; M. P. Thompson, 'Leases, licences & the demise of *Errington*: *Ashburn Anstalt* v *WJ Arnold & Co.*' [1988] Conv 201; Jill Martin,

'Contractual licence or tenant for life?' (1972) 36 Conv 266; G. C. Cheshire, 'A new equitable interest in land' (1953) 16 MLR 1; R. J. Smith, 'Licences and constructive trusts "The law is what it ought to be"' [1973] CLJ 123; J. A. Hornby, 'Tenancy for life or licence' (1977) 93 LQR 561.

(e) Constructive trusts

Even if a person has a contractual licence in relation to the property which does not constitute an interest in land, the courts have, in a few cases, decided the person's occupation on the basis of a constructive trust. The existence of a contractual licence does not preclude the court from imposing a constructive trust if it is in the interests of justice to do so, or to prevent unjust enrichment. Such an imposition will create a property interest for the occupier which will bind third parties.

Bannister v Bannister
[1948] 2 All ER 133 (CA)

P orally undertook that D could live in a cottage rent free for as long as she desired and in reliance on that undertaking D sold P that cottage and an adjacent one. D retained the use of one room. P's undertaking was not referred to in the conveyance to him. P wanted to recover possession of the room D was occupying. Held: D had a life interest in the cottage under a constructive trust which was created by the oral agreements.

SCOTT LJ: It is, we think, clearly a mistake to suppose that the equitable principle on which a constructive trust is raised against a person who insists on the absolute character of a conveyance to himself for the purpose of defeating a beneficial interest, which, according to the true bargain, was to belong to another, is confined to cases in which the conveyance itself was fraudulently obtained. The fraud which brings the principle into play arises as soon as the absolute character of the conveyance is set up for the purpose of defeating the beneficial interest, and that is the fraud to cover which the Statute of Frauds or the corresponding provisions of the Law of Property Act, 1925, cannot be called in aid in cases in which no written evidence of the real bargain is available. Nor is it, in our opinion, necessary that the bargain on which the absolute conveyance is made should include any express stipulation that the grantee is in so many words to hold as trustee. It is enough that the bargain should have included a stipulation under which some sufficiently defined beneficial interest in the property was to be taken by another. The above propositions are, we think, clearly borne out by the cases to which we were referred of *Booth* v *Turle* (1873) LR 16 Eq 182, *Chattock* v *Muller* (1878) 8 ChD 177, *Re Duke of Marlborough* [1894] 2 Ch 133, and *Rochefoucauld* v *Boustead* [1897] 1 Ch 196. We see no distinction in principle between a case in which property is conveyed to a purchaser on terms that the entire beneficial interest in some part of it is to be retained by the vendor (as in *Booth* v *Turle*) and a case, like the present, in which property is conveyed to a purchaser on terms that a limited beneficial interest in some part of it is to be retained by the vendor. We are, accordingly, of opinion that the third ground of objection to the learned county court judge's conclusion also fails. His finding that there was no fraud in the case cannot be taken as meaning that it was not fraudulent in the plaintiff to insist on the absolute character of the conveyance for the purpose of defeating the beneficial interest which he had agreed the defendant

Licences

should retain. The conclusion that the plaintiff was fraudulent, i
necessarily follows from the facts found, and, as indicated above, the fa
have been innocent of any fraudulent intent in taking the conveyance in
is for this purpose immaterial. The failure of the third ground of objecti
also destroys the second objection based on want of writing and the provisions of ss. 53
and 54 of the Law of Property Act, 1925.

Note
P had obtained the property more cheaply by falsely representing to D that she
could remain in the cottage. Thus the property had been obtained by fraud.

Questions
1. Could the contractual licence argument have been used by the defendant
in *Bannister* v *Bannister*? Could there be a licence by estoppel? See also *Binions*
v *Evans* (above), where the majority held that the widow was to have an
equitable life interest in the property under a Settled Land Act settlement.
2. The defendant in *Bannister* v *Bannister* became a tenant for life under the
Settled Land Act 1925 and she therefore had the power to sell the property.
What do you think of such a result? Is it in line with the intention of the
parties?

Note
Binions v *Evans* may also be legally justified on the ground that the defendant
had a contract which was enforceable against the estate. The purchaser knew
of the existence of this contract and was therefore liable in tort for interference
with a contract.

Ungurian v *Lesnoff* [1989] 3 WLR 840 (Ch D)

D gave up her flat in Poland, her Polish nationality and an academic career
in order to live with P. P bought a house in London, registered in his sole
name, in which he and D lived with D's two sons of a previous marriage and
one of P's sons. D made considerable improvements to the house. The
relationship ended after some four years and P left D in the house. Held: it
could be inferred from the particular circumstances that the common
intention was that D should reside in the property for life, P holding it on
constructive trust for her so to do. Therefore the house became settled land
within the Settled Land Act 1925.

Note
Vinelott J here followed the majority view in *Binions* v *Evans*.

Re Sharpe (a Bankrupt) [1980] 1 WLR 219 (ChD)

D borrowed £12,000 from his aunt to enable him to buy a property for
£17,000. It was lent partly in reliance on an agreement that the aunt would
live with D and his wife in the property and that they would look after her.

A receiving order was made against D, and his trustee-in-bankruptcy sought possession so that the property could be sold with vacant possession. The aunt claimed to have either a beneficial interest or irrevocable licence to occupy. Held: where there was a common assumption that one party to a transaction was to have a right to occupy the property, and that person expended money or otherwise acted to his detriment in reliance on that assumption, the other party would be bound by the arrangement. The court, in such circumstances, would imply an irrevocable licence or a constructive trust. Here the aunt had an irrevocable licence to live in the house until the loan was repaid. The licence arose under a constructive trust and gave rise to an interest in the property binding on third parties.

Note
This case could have been dealt with under estoppel principles rather than those of constructive trusts.

See Jill Martin, 'Constructive trusts and licences: *Re Sharpe*' [1980] Conv 207; Gordon Woodman, 'Social interests in the development of constructive trusts' (1980) 96 LQR 336.

Question
Can it be argued that the aunt had an interest under a resulting trust in *Re Sharpe*?

Note
See also *Hussey* v *Palmer* [1972] 3 All ER 744 (CA), where an elderly widow was invited to live with a daughter and son-in-law and she paid the cost of building an extra bedroom onto the house for her to live in. It was held (Cairns LJ dissenting) that she acquired an equitable interest in the property because justice and good conscience required it by means of a resulting (or constructive) trust.

See *Lyus* v *Prowsa Developments* (chapter 3), a case on the imposition of a constructive trust to protect minor interests.

Ashburn Anstalt v Arnold
[1989] Ch 1 (CA)

FOX LJ: The constructive trust principle, to which we now turn, has been long established and has proved to be highly flexible in practice. It covers a wide variety of cases from that of a trustee who makes a profit out of his trust or a stranger who knowingly deals with trust properties, to the many cases where the courts have held that a person who directly or indirectly contributes to the acquisition of a dwelling house purchased in the name of and conveyed to another has some beneficial interest in the property. The test, for the present purposes, is whether the owner of the property has so conducted himself that it would be inequitable to allow him to deny the claimant an interest in the property: see *Gissing* v *Gissing* [1971] AC 886, 905, *per* Lord Diplock.

[Fox LJ discusses the facts of *Bannister* v *Bannister*] . . .

In *In re Schebsman, decd* [1944] Ch 83, 89, Lord Greene MR said: "It is not legitimate to import into the contract the idea of a trust when the parties have given no indication that such was their intention." Du Parcq LJ said, at p. 104, that "the court ought not to be astute to discover indications of such an intention." We do not, however, regard either of these observations as differing from what Scott LJ said in *Bannister* v *Bannister*. It is, we think, in every case a question of what is the reasonable inference from the known facts.

We come then to four cases in which the application of the principle to particular facts has been considered.

[Fox LJ then discusses the facts of *Binions* v *Evans*.] . . . In the Court of Appeal Megaw and Stephenson LJJ decided the case on the ground that the defendant was a tenant for life under the Settled Land Act 1925. Lord Denning MR did not agree with that. He held that the plaintiffs took the property subject to a constructive trust for the defendant's benefit. In our view that is a legitimate application of the doctrine of constructive trusts. The estate would certainly have allowed the defendant to live in the house during her life in accordance with their agreement with her. They provided the plaintiffs with a copy of the agreement they made. The agreement for sale was subject to the agreement, and they accepted a lower purchase price in consequence. In the circumstances it was a proper inference that on the sale to the plaintiffs, the intention of the estate and the plaintiffs was that the plaintiffs should give effect to the tenancy agreement. If they had failed to do so, the estate would have been liable in damages to the defendant.

In *D.H.N. Food Distributors Ltd* v *Tower Hamlets Borough Council* [1976] 1 WLR 852, premises were owned by Bronze Investments Ltd but occupied by an associated company (D.H.N.) under an informal agreement between them — they were part of a group. The premises were subsequently purchased by the council and the issue was compensation for disturbance. It was said that Bronze was not disturbed and that D.H.N. had no interest in the property. The Court of Appeal held that D.H.N. had an irrevocable licence to occupy the land. Lord Denning MR said, at p. 859:

> It was equivalent to a contract between the two companies whereby Bronze granted an irrevocable licence to D.H.N. to carry on their business on the premises. In this situation Mr Dobry cited to us *Binions* v *Evans* [1972] Ch 359 to which I would add *Bannister* v *Bannister* [1948] 2 All ER 133 and *Siew Soon Wah* v *Yong Ton Hong* [1973] AC 836. Those cases show that a contractual licence (under which a person has a right to occupy premises indefinitely) gives rise to a contructive trust, under which the legal owner is not allowed to turn out the licensee. So, here. This irrevocable licence gave to D.H.N. a sufficient interest in the land to qualify them for compensation for disturbance.

Goff LJ made this a ground for his decision also.

On that authority, Browne-Wilkinson J in *In re Sharpe (A Bankrupt), Ex parte Trustee of the Bankrupt's Property* v *The Bankrupt* [1980] 1 WLR 219 felt bound to conclude that, without more, an irrevocable licence to occupy gave rise to a property interest. He evidently did so with hesitation. For the reasons whch we have already indicated, we prefer the line of authorities which determine that a contractual licence does not create a property interest. We do not think that the argument is assisted by the bare assertion that the interest arises under a constructive trust.

[Fox LJ then discusses the facts of *Lyus* v *Prowsa Developments Ltd*.] . . . The [plaintiff's] action succeeded. This again seems to us to be a case where a constructive trust could justifiably be imposed. The bank were selling as mortgagees under a charge prior in date to the contract. They were therefore not bound by the contract and on any view could give a title which was free from it. There was, therefore, no point in making the conveyance subject to the contract unless the parties intended the purchaser to give effect to the contract. Further, on the sale by the bank a letter had been written to the bank's agents, Messrs Strutt & Parker, by the first defendant's solicitors, giving an assurance that their client would take reasonable steps to make sure the interests of contractual purchasers were dealt with quickly and to their satisfaction. How far any constructive trust so arising was on the facts of that case enforceable by the plaintiffs against owners for the time being of the land we do not need to consider.

In re Sharpe [1980] 1 WLR 219 seems to us a much more difficult case in which to imply a constructive trust against the trustee in bankruptcy and his successors, and we do not think it could be done. Browne-Wilkinson J did not, in fact, do so. He felt (understandably, we think) bound by authority to hold that an irrevocable licence to occupy was a property interest. [The facts of Re Sharpe] do not suggest a need in equity to impose constructive trust obligations on the trustee or his successors.

We come to the present case. It is said that when a person sells land and stipulates that the sale should be "subject to" a contractual licence, the court will impose a constructive trust upon the purchaser to give effect to the licence: see *Binions v Evans* [1972] Ch 359, 368, *per* Lord Denning MR. We do not feel able to accept that as a general proposition. We agree with the observations of Dillon J in *Lyus v Prowsa Developments Ltd* [see page 93 *et seq.*] . . . The court will not impose a constructive trust unless it is satisfied that the conscience of the estate owner is affected. The mere fact that that land is expressed to be conveyed "subject to" a contract does not necessarily imply that the grantee is to be under an obligation, not otherwise existing, to give effect to the provisions of the contract. The fact that the conveyance is expressed to be subject to the contract may often, for the reasons indicated by Dillon J, be at least as consistent with an intention merely to protect the grantor against claims by the grantee as an intention to impose an obligation on the grantee. The words "subject to" will, of course, impose notice. But notice is not enough to impose on somebody an obligation to give effect to a contract into which he did not enter. Thus, mere notice of a restrictive covenant is not enough to impose upon the estate owner an obligation or equity to give effect to it: *London County Council v Allen* [1914] 3 KB 642.

Question

Do you think the constructive trust is being used appropriately in this area of land law?

D: LICENCES BY ESTOPPEL

Proprietary estoppel forms an exception to the rule that a person who spends money on improving the property of another cannot claim that by so doing he either has a proprietary interest in the property or is entitled to the money back.

Fry J described the nature of proprietary estoppel in the case of *Willmott v Barber* (1880) 15 ChD 96, at pp. 105–6:

It has been said that the acquiescence which will deprive a man of his legal rights must amount to fraud, and in my view that is an abbreviated statement of a very true proposition. A man is not to be deprived of his legal rights unless he has acted in such a way as would make it fraudulent for him to set up those rights. What, then, are the elements or requisites necessary to constitute fraud of that description? In the first place the plaintiff must have made a mistake as to his legal rights. Secondly, the plaintiff must have expended some money or must have done some act (not necessarily upon the defendant's land) on the faith of his mistaken belief. Thirdly, the defendant, the possessor of the legal right, must know of the existence of his own right which is inconsistent with the right claimed by the plaintiff. If he does not know of it he is in the same position as the plaintiff, and the doctrine of acquiescence is founded upon conduct with a knowledge of your legal rights. Fourthly, the defendant, the possessor of the legal right, must know of the plaintiff's mistaken belief of his rights. If he does not, there is nothing which calls upon him to assert his own rights. Lastly, the defendant, the possessor of the legal right, must have encouraged the plaintiff in his expenditure of money or in the other acts which he has done, either directly or by abstaining from asserting his legal right. Where all these elements exist, there is fraud of such a nature as will entitle the Court to restrain the possessor of the legal right from exercising it, but, in my judgment, nothing short of this will do.

The courts have recently widened the test for proprietary estoppel. *Taylors Fashions Ltd* v *Liverpool Victoria Trustee Co. Ltd* [1981] 1 All ER 897, Oliver J said (at p. 915):

Furthermore, the more recent cases indicate, in my judgment, that the application of the *Ramsden* v *Dyson* principle (whether you call it proprietary estoppel, estoppel by acquiescence or estoppel by encouragement is really immaterial) requires a very much broader approach which is directed to ascertaining whether, in particular individual circumstances, it would be unconscionable for a party to be permitted to deny that which, knowingly or unknowingly, he has allowed or encouraged another to assume to his detriment rather than to inquiring whether the circumstances can be fitted within the confines of some preconceived formula serving as a universal yardstick for every form of unconscionable behaviour.

(a) Detriment

(i) *Expenditure*

Inwards v *Baker* [1965] 2 QB 29 (CA)

S wished to buy a piece of land on which to build a bungalow for himself, but the land was too expensive. S's father, F, suggested that S built a larger bungalow on F's land. S subsequently built a bungalow on F's land. The cost of the bungalow was £300, and F and S paid approximately half each, although the bungalow was mostly built by S himself. S lived in the bungalow believing he would be allowed to live there for his lifetime or for so long as he wished. The position was never formalized. F died and, under the provisions of his will, made many years before the bungalow was built, the land vested in trustees for the benefit of a person other than S. Held:

(1) An equity arose in these circumstances through the expenditure of money on the land of another where the owner of the land induced or encouraged the other to believe that he would be allowed to remain in occupation. The court has power to determine in what way such an equity can be satisfied. In this case S should be allowed to remain in occupation of the bungalow for as long as he desired.

(2) (Per Lord Denning MR) S had a licence coupled with an equity so that a purchaser of the land with notice of S's interest would be bound by the equity, and F's successors would be similarly bound.

Dillwyn v *Llewelyn* (1862) 4 De G F & J 517

F gave possession of some of his land to one of his sons (S) and signed a memorandum to the effect that the land was a gift to the son to provide him with a house. The son, with F's consent and encouragement, built a house on the land for himself at his own expense. Held: S was entitled to call for a conveyance of the fee simple to complete the gift.

Note
But see the next case.

Western Fish Products Ltd v *Penwith District Council*
[1981] 2 All ER 204 (CA)

P bought an industrial site including a disused fertiliser factory. P intended to manufacture animal feed and pack fresh fish on the site but to do so some of the buildings had to be demolished and rebuilt and others needed alteration and repair. P claimed they had an *existing* established use of the land and the planning officer asked them to satisfy him of this claim. P supplied the information requested and received confirmation from the planning officer that the existing use was established. P proceeded to renovate and rebuild the property. The planning officer did nothing for two months and then asked that planning applications be submitted saying that the application should be 'a formality'. Four such applications were submitted. All the applications were subsequently refused and the Council authorised the service of enforcement and stop notices. P alleged that this was a case where proprietary estoppel operated. Held:

(1) Proprietary estoppel arises where P acts to his detriment in relation to his own land as a result of the encouragement of D and in the expectation of acquiring rights over D's land. It could not apply here as P was never to acquire any other person's land.
(2) The Council had a discretion which they were entitled to exercise and estoppel could not be employed to prevent it doing so or performing its statutory duty.

See also *Brinnard* v *Ewens* [1987] 2 EGLR 67.

(ii) *Detriment other than expenditure*

Jones (AE) v *Jones (FW)* [1977] 2 All ER 231 (CA)

Here S, at his father's request, gave up his job and went with his family to live in Blunderston in a home his father (F) had bought him. Held: P (who was F's widow) was estopped from dispossessing S because F would have been estopped from dispossessing him. F's conduct led S reasonably to believe that the house would be his for life and in reliance on F's conduct S had given up his house and job in Kingston and paid £1,000 towards the purchase price. He had also carried out various work on the house.

Pascoe v *Turner* [1979] 1 WLR 431 (CA)

Here M assured his former mistress (D) that a house in which they lived was hers, but it was never conveyed to her. After M left D she stayed in the house, and M allowed and encouraged her to spend a quarter of her savings on repairs, improvements and redecorating the house. Held: D had an equity in her favour and the gift should be perfected by the transfer of the fee simple to her.

Greasley v *Cooke* [1980] 3 All ER 710 (CA)

D was employed as a maid in W's house. W's son (S) formed a relationship with D and they started to live as husband and wife. On W's death the relationship between S and D continued and D lived on in the house performing the duties of housekeeper for S's brothers and sister but she was unpaid for these duties. W left the house equally to S and one other brother. S and his brother had assured D that she could live in the property rent free as long as she wished. Held: D had relied on the conduct of S and his brother and the assurances they had given her and that gave rise to an equity in her favour.

Crabb v *Arun District Council*
[1976] Ch 179 (CA)

P owned some land together with a right of way along a road (owned by D) to an access point A. P intended to divide the land into two parts in order to sell them. D agreed to allow P a further point of access at a point B and a corresponding easement. D then erected a fence on the boundary between D's and P's land and gates at points A and B. P sold the part of his land with access at point A but did not reserve any rights of way in favour of the second plot which P retained. D then removed the gates at point B and blocked it with a fence so that P's remaining land was landlocked. Held: D could not go back on his agreement as P had acted to his detriment in reliance on it.

LORD DENNING MR: The basis of this proprietary estoppel — as indeed of promissory estoppel — is the interposition of equity. Equity comes in, true to form, to mitigate the rigours of strict law. The early cases did not speak of it as "estoppel." They spoke of it as "raising an equity." If I may expand what Lord Cairns LC said in *Hughes* v *Metropolitan Railway Co* (1877) 2 App Cas 439, 448: "it is the first principle upon which all courts of equity proceed," that it will prevent a person from insisting on his strict legal rights — whether arising under a contract, or on his title deeds, or by statute — when it would be inequitable for him to do so having regard to the dealings which have taken place between the parties.

What then are the dealings which will preclude him from insisting on his strict legal rights? If he makes a binding contract that he will not insist on the strict legal position, a court of equity will hold him to his contract. Short of a binding contract, if he makes a promise that he will not insist upon his strict legal rights — then, even though that promise may be unenforceable in point of law for want of consideration or want of writing — then, if he makes the promise knowing or intending that the other will act upon it, and he does act upon it, then again a court of equity will not allow him to go back on that promise: see *Central London Property Trust Ltd* v *High Trees House Ltd* [1947] KB 130 and *Charles Rickards Ltd* v *Oppenhaim* [1950] 1 KB 616, 623. Short of an actual promise, if he, by his words or conduct, so behaves as to lead another to believe that he will not insist on his strict legal rights — knowing or intending that the other will act on that belief — and he does so act, that again will raise an equity in favour of the other; and it is for a court of equity to say in what way the equity may be satisfied. The cases show that this equity does not depend on agreement but on words or conduct. In *Ramsden* v *Dyson* (1866) LR 1 HL 129, 170 Lord Kingsdown spoke of a verbal agreement "or what amounts to the same thing, an expectation, created or encouraged." In *Birmingham and District Land Co.* v *London and North Western Railway Co.* (1888) 40 ChD 268, 277, Cotton LJ said that ". . . what passed did not make a new agreement, but . . . what took place . . . raised an equity against him." And it was the Privy Council in *Plimmer* v *Wellington Corporation* (1884) 9 App Cas 699, 713–714 who said that ". . . the court must look at the circumstances in each case to decide in what way the equity can be satisfied" giving instances.

Recent cases afford illustrations of the principle. [Lord Denning uses the cases of *Inwards* v *Baker* and *Ives* v *High* as illustrations.] In *Siew Soon Wah* v *Yong Tong Hong* [1973] AC 836 the Privy Council held that there was an "equity or equitable estoppel protecting the defendant in his occupation for 30 years." In *Bank Negara Indonesia* v *Hoalim* [1973] 2 MLJ 3 the Privy Council held that, despite the fact that the defendant had no protection under the Rent Acts, he had an equity to remain "so long as he continued to practise his profession."

The question then is: were the circumstances here such as to raise an equity in favour of the plaintiff? True the defendants on the deeds had the title to their land, free of any access at point B. But they led the plaintiff to believe that he had or would be granted a right of access at point B. At the meeting of July 26, 1967, Mr Alford and the plaintiff told the defendants' representative that the plaintiff intended to split the two acres into two portions and wanted to have an access at point B for the back portion; and the defendants' representative agreed that he should have this access. I do not think the defendants can avoid responsibility by saying that their representative had no authority to agree this. They entrusted him with the task of setting out the line of the fence and the gates, and they must be answerable for his conduct in the course of it: see *Attorney-General to the Prince of Wales* v *Collom* [1916] 2 KB 193, 207; and *Moorgate Mercantile Co. Ltd* v *Twitchings* [1976] QB 225, 243.

The judge found that there was "no definite assurance" by the defendants' representative, and "no firm commitment," but only an "agreement in principle," meaning I suppose that, as Mr Alford said, there were "some further processes" to be gone through before it would become binding. But if there were any such processes in the mind of the parties, the subsequent conduct of the defendants was such as to dispense with them. The defendants actually put up the gates at point B at considerable expense. That certainly led the plaintiff to believe that they agreed that he should have the right of access through point B without more ado.

The judge also said that, to establish this equity or estoppel, the defendants must have known that the plaintiff was selling the front portion without reserving a right of access for the back portion. I do not think this was necessary. The defendants knew that the plaintiff *intended* to sell the two portions separately and that he would need an access at point B as well as point A. Seeing that they knew of his intention — and they did nothing to disabuse him but rather confirmed it by erecting gates at point B — it was their conduct which led him to act as he did: and this raises an equity in his favour against them.

In the circumstances it seems to me inequitable that the council should insist on their strict title as they did; and to take the high-handed action of pulling down the gates without a word of warning: and to demand of the plaintiff £3,000 as the price for the easement. If he had moved at once for an injuncton in aid of his equity — to prevent them removing the gates — I think he should have been granted it. But he did not do so. He tried to negotiate terms, but these failing, the action has come for trial. And we have the question: in what way now should the equity be satisfied?

Here equity is displayed at its most flexible, see *Snell's Principles of Equity*, 27th ed. (1973), p. 568, and the illustrations there given. If the matter had been finally settled in 1967, I should have thought that, although nothing was said at the meeting in July 1967, nevertheless it would be quite reasonable for the defendants to ask the plaintiff to pay something for the access at point B, perhaps — and I am guessing — some hundreds of pounds. But, as Mr Millett pointed out in the course of the argument, because of the defendants' conduct, the back land has been landlocked. It has been sterile and rendered useless for five or six years: and the plaintiff has been unable to deal with it during that time. This loss to him can be taken into account. And at the present time, it seems to me that, in order to satisfy the equity, the plaintiff should have the right of access at point B without paying anything for it.

I would, therefore, hold that the plaintiff, as the owner of the back portion, has a right of access at point B over the verge on to Mill Park Road and a right of way along that road to Hook Lane without paying compensation. I would allow the appeal and declare that he has an easement, accordingly.

(b) Expectation or belief

Ramsden v *Dyson*
(1866) LR 1 HL 129 (HL)

T, a yearly tenant, carried out building works at the demised premises in the hope and belief that the landlord would grant him a new lease for 60 years. The landlord refused to do so and T claimed to be entitled in equity to such a lease. Held: (Lord Kingsdown dissenting) there was merely a tenancy from year to year.

LORD CRANWORTH: If a stranger build on my land, supposing it to be his own, and I, knowing it to be mine do not interfere, but leave him to go on, equity considers it to be dishonest in me to remain passive and afterwards to interfere and take the profit. But if a stranger build knowingly upon my land, there is no principle of equity which prevents me from insisting on having back my land, with all the additional value which the occupier has imprudently added to it. If a tenant of mine does the same thing, he cannot insist on refusing to give up the estate at the end of his term. It was his own folly to build.

Inwards v *Baker*
[1965] 2 QB 29 (CA)

The facts of this case appear at page 237.

LORD DENNING MR: The son appeals to this court. We have had the advantage of cases which were not cited to the county court judge — cases in the last century, notably *Dillwyn* v *Llewelyn* (1862) 4 De GF & J 517 and *Plimmer* v *Wellington Corporation* (1884) 9 App Cas 699, PC. This latter was a decision of the Privy Council which expressly affirmed and approved the statement of the law made by Lord Kingsdown in *Ramsden* v *Dyson* (1866) LR 1 HL 129, 170. It is quite plain from those authorities that if the owner of land requests another, or indeed allows another, to expend money on the land under an expectation created or encouraged by the landlord that he will be able to remain there, that raises an equity in the licensee such as to entitle him to stay. He has a licence coupled with an equity. Mr Goodhart urged before us that the licensee could not stay indefinitely. The principle only applied, he said, when there was an expectation of some precise legal term. But it seems to me, from *Plimmer's* case in particular, that the equity arising from the expenditure on land need not fail "merely on the ground that the interest to be secured has not been expressly indicated . . . the court must look at the circumstances in each case to decide in what way the equity can be satisfied." 9 App Cas 699, 713–4, PC.

(c) Encouragement

The person to whom the equity is given must have been encouraged by the encouragor or his agent (*Moorgate Mercantile Co. Ltd* v *Twitchings* [1976] 1 QB 225), or by a predecessor in title (*Jones (AE)* v *Jones (FW)* [1977] 2 All ER 231).

(i) *Active encouragement* See *Inwards* v *Baker* (above), *Pascoe* v *Turner* (above). In *Griffiths* v *Williams* (1977) 248 EG 947 (CA), D was the daughter of T and lived in a house owned by T for most of her life. T allowed and encouraged D to spend money on the property, assuring D that the house was hers. T's will left the property to her granddaughter. Held: the daughter had a right to an interest in the property.

(ii) *Passive encouragement* In *Steed* v *Whitaker* (1740) Barn Ch 220, a purchaser of land (P) expended money building on it unaware of a mortgage over the land. The mortgagee stood by and allowed P to do so. In such a case an equity will arise in P's favour.

See, however, *Taylors Fashions Ltd* v *Liverpool Victoria Trustees Co. Ltd* [1981] 1 All ER 897 (above) and *Greasley* v *Cooke*.

(d) No bar to equity

See *Western Fish Products Ltd* v *Penwith District Council*, at page 238.

In *Somerset Coal Canal Co.* v *Harcourt* (1858) 2 De G & J 596, although an encouragor stood by whilst improvements were made, the equity that arose could not be enforced because the encouragor was a minor at the relevant time.

(e) Satisfaction of the equity

If a claim for proprietary estoppel is upheld, then there are a number of different ways in which it can be fulfilled.

Licences

(i) *The action brought by the encouragor could be dismissed*   In such a case the equity would be given effect to by way of a defence.

(ii) *Injunction*   An injunction, which would stop the encouragor from interfering with possession of the land, could be granted.

(iii) *Equitable lien*   The person who has acted to his detriment may be given an equitable lien on the property for the amount of his expenditure, and in such a case the person would be treated as a mortgagee in possession. See *Hussey* v *Palmer* [1972] 1 WLR 1286, where a trust was imposed in proportion to the expenditure incurred.

Dodsworth v Dodswoth (1973) 228 EG 115 (CA)

Here A expended money on a bungalow relying on the owner's promise that A could reside there. There was an equity in A's favour but the facts did not warrant the creation of rights of occupation in A's favour. Instead an order for possession against A was made, conditional upon the owner repaying the cost of improvements effected by A.

Note
If it appears A has already had sufficient satisfaction for his expenditure no relief will be granted (*AG* v *Balliol College, Oxford* (1744) 9 Mod Rep 407).

(iv) *Title*   See *Dillwyn* v *Llewelyn* and *Pascoe* v *Turner* (above), where the court effected the encouragee's equity by a transfer of the land. These cases seem to indicate that the courts will fulfil the equity by this means where there has been an imperfect gift of the land or where there has been an oral abandonment of the land.

Lim Teng Huan v Ang Swee Chuan [1992] 1 WLR 113 (PC)

P and D purchased some land jointly but it was transferred into their fathers' names. At his own expense D started to erect a house on the land. Some years later P and D signed an agreement in which P confirmed that the building works were being done with his consent. The agreement provided that P was to exchange his share in the land for some unspecified land which D expected to receive. On the death of both fathers, P, as his father's administrator, claimed that he was the owner of an undivided one-half share in the land. Held: the agreement was evidence of the parties' intentions and D completed the construction in reliance on the agreement although it was unenforceable. It would thus be unconscionable to allow P to prevent D acquiring a sole interest in the house and land on paying compensation to P. Therefore, provided D paid P compensation, P would be estopped from denying D's title.

(v) *Lease*

Taylor Fashions Ltd v Liverpool Victoria Trustees Co. Ltd [1981] 1 All ER 897

X owned the freehold of two shops — 21 and 22 Westover Road. In 1948, they leased No. 22 to T for a term of 28 years, with an option to renew for a further 14 years if T installed a lift. T did not register the option under the Land Charges Act 1925. X then sold the freehold of both shops to D who were adjoining owners (No. 20). No. 21 was then leased back to X for a term of 42 years, but D was given the right to determine the lease of No. 21 if T failed to exercise his option in respect of No. 22. D was made fully aware of the terms of the lease including the option to renew. P purchased T's lease of No. 22 and proceeded to instal a lift, believing that they would be entitled to exercise the option. D knew of and acquiesced in the installation of the lift. In 1963, X took a lease from D in respect of No. 20 and carried out alterations to combine Nos 20 and 21 into a single shop. The lease of No. 20 was for a term of 14 years with an option to renew for a further 14 years and this was done so that the leases of No. 20 and 21 would run parallel. D was given the right to determine the lease of No. 22 if T failed to exercise his option. P sought to exercise his option over No. 22 in 1976, and served a notice accordingly. D claimed that the notice was void for want of registration. Similarly, D claimed the leases of Nos 20 and 21 were invalid. D served notices to quit on P and X. P said that even if the option was void for want of registration, D were estopped from denying P's rights in view of P's expenditure on the installation of the lift.

Held:

(1) There was no evidence that D had in any way created or encouraged P's mistaken belief.

(2) D were estopped from asserting the invalidity of the option against X. When D offered the leases to X in 1948 and in 1963 they impliedly represented that the option granted to P was valid because X's renewal was made to depend upon its validity and exercise. Also, in 1963 D encouraged X to incur expenditure and alter their position irrevocably by taking additional premises relying on the belief that the option was valid. It was therefore inequitable and unconscionable for D to frustrate X's expectation which D themselves created and X were entitled to specific performance.

See also *J. T. Developments Ltd* v *Quinn* [1991] 2 EGLR 257 where the Court of Appeal (Glidewell LJ dissenting) held that D were entitled to a lease by means of proprietary estoppel where an agent of the Plaintiffs told D that they would be granted a new tenancy of premises on the same terms as those granted to a neighbouring shop and D carried out improvements to the kitchen as a result.

(vi) *Easement*

ER Ives Investment Ltd v High
[1967] 2 QB 379

The facts of this case appear at page 40.

LORD DENNING MR: One thing is quite clear. Apart from this point about the Land Charges Act, 1925, Mr High would have in equity a good right of way across the yard. This right arises in two ways:
1. *Mutual benefit and burden*
The right arises out of the agreement of November 2, 1949, and the subsequent action taken on it: on the principle that "he who takes the benefit must accept the burden." When adjoining owners of land make an agreement to secure continuing rights and benefits for each of them in or over the land of the other, neither of them can take the benefit of the agreement and throw over the burden of it. This applies not only to the original parties, but also to their successors. The successor who takes the continuing benefit must take it subject to the continuing burden. This principle has been applied to neighbours who send their water into a common drainage system: see *Hopgood* v *Brown* [1955] 1 WLR 213; [1955] 1 All ER 550, CA; and to purchasers of houses on a building estate who had the benefit of using the roads and were subject to the burden of contributing to the upkeep: see *Halsall* v *Brizell* [1957] Ch 169; [1957] 2 WLR 123; [1957] 1 All ER 371. The principle clearly applies in the present case. The owners of the block of flats have the benefit of having their foundations in Mr High's land. So long as they take that benefit, they must shoulder the burden. They must observe the condition on which the benefit was granted, namely, they must allow Mr High and his successors to have access over their yard: cf. *May* v *Belleville* [1905] 2 Ch 605. Conversely, so long as Mr High takes the benefit of the access, he must permit the block of flats to keep their foundations in his land.
2. *Equity arising out of acquiescence*
The right arises out of the expense incurred by Mr High in building his garage as it is now, with access only over the yard: and the Wrights standing by and acquiescing in it, knowing that he believed he had a right of way over the yard. By so doing the Wrights created in Mr High's mind a reasonable expectation that his access over the yard would not be disturbed. That gives rise to an "equity arising out of acquiescence." It is available not only against the Wrights but also their successors in title. The court will not allow that expectation to be defeated when it would be inequitable so to do. It is for the court in each case to decide in what way the equity can be satisfied: see *Inwards* v *Baker* [1965] 2 QB 29; *Ward* v *Kirkland* [1966] 1 WLR 601 and the cases cited therein. In this case it could only be satisfied by allowing Mr High and his successors to have access over the yard so long as the block of flats has its foundations in his land.

(vii) *A perpetual licence*

Plimmer v Mayor Councillors and Citizens of the City of Wellington
(1884) 9 App Cas 699 (PC)

Land became vested in the respondents (R) by means of the Wellington Harbour Board and Corporation Land Act 1880. A claimed to have an estate or interest in the land and sought compensation under the Public Works Act

1882. A's lessor had erected a wharf on the land in question and, later, a jetty. A year after the jetty was built the Government asked A's lessor to extend the jetty and build a warehouse. This he did for them at some expense. Thereafter the Government used, paid for and improved the land with the lessor's knowledge and approval. Held: When the wharf was erected the lessor must be deemed to have occupied the ground under a revocable license. The request to extend the jetty and the subsequent expenditure showed that both parties contemplated that the lessor would be allowed to continue using the existing jetty, as the extension of it would otherwise be useless to them. Following the extension of the jetty the licence ceased to be revocable at the will of the Government, and the lessor acquired an indefinite right to the jetty in connection with his operations as a wharfinger. Such an equitable right is an 'estate or interest in, to or out of land' within the wide meaning of the relevant Act which directs the court should do what is reasonable and just when considering compensation.

SIR ARTHUR HOBHOUSE: In fact, the Court must look at the circumstances in each case to decide in what way the equity can be satisfied.

In this case their Lordships feel no great difficulty. In their view, the licence given by the Government to John Plimmer, which was indefinite in point of duration but was revocable at will, became irrevocable by the transactions of 1856, because those transactions were sufficient to create in his mind a reasonable expectation that his occupation would not be disturbed; and because they and the subsequent dealings of the parties cannot be reasonably explained on any other supposition. Nothing was done to limit the use of the jetty in point of duration. The consequence is that Plimmer acquired an indefinite, that is practically a perpetual, right to the jetty for the purposes of the original licence, and if the ground was afterwards wanted for public purposes, it could only be taken from him by the legislature.

(viii) *A licence for as long as the encouragor wishes to use the premises as his home* See *Inwards* v *Baker* [1965] 2 QB 29.

(ix) *A licence to remain until a loan is repaid* See *Re Sharpe* [1980] 1 WLR 219.

Note
It is unclear whether the benefit of a licence based on estoppel can be transferred to a third party. In *Inwards* v *Baker,* the son's right to remain in the bungalow for as long as he wished was not transferable and created a more personal right. However, in *ER Ives Investment* v *High* the benefit of High's interest would run with the land. See the New South Wales case of *Hamilton* v *Geraghty* (1901) 1 SR NSW Eq 81.

Questions
1. If the court decides to give effect to an encouragee's equity, and does so by giving that person a life interest, does the licensee become a tenant for life under the Settled Land Act 1925, and if so what is the legal effect?
2. What could the following licences be registered as in registered land:

(a) a licence coupled with a grant or interests;
(b) a contractual licence;
(c) a licence by estoppel.

3. Do you think that the doctrine of estoppel should be employed in a *Paddington Building Society* v *Mendelsohn* situation?

Note
See Paul Todd, 'Estoppel licences and third party rights' [1981] Conv 347; Graham Battersby, 'Contractual and estoppel licences as proprietary interests in land' [1991] Conv 36; Stephen Moriarty, 'Licences and land law: legal principles and public policies' (1984) 100 LQR 376; M. P. Thompson, 'From representation to expectation: estoppel as a cause of action' [1973] CLJ 257.

8 STRICT SETTLEMENTS AND TRUSTS FOR SALE

SECTION 1: INTRODUCTION

A settlement is a disposition of property which creates a succession of interests in the property, for example Blackacre to A for life, remainder to B absolutely. We have already seen in chapter 2 that since 1925 a life interest can no longer exist as a legal estate in land, because of the effect of the Law of Property Act 1925, s. 1. Therefore, such an interest is equitable of necessity and must exist under a trust.

There are two methods by which successive interests in land can be created, both of which involve trusts:

(a) The strict settlement (governed by the Settled Land Act 1925).
(b) The trust for sale (governed by the Law of Property Act 1925).

A strict settlement describes the arrangement which exists whenever successive beneficial interests in land are created in favour of a number of persons, provided such land is not land held under a trust for sale. For example, Blackacre to A for life, remainder to B in fee simple. In such a situation A is known as the tenant for life and B the remainderman. In a strict settlement, unlike a conventional trust, the tenant for life will hold the legal estate, will be beneficially entitled to it during his lifetime and will have extensive powers of management and disposition. Usually the legal estate will remain with the first tenant for life until his death, whereupon it will devolve to the trustees who will convey it to the person next entitled. The trustees will often be appointed in the instrument creating the settlement.

A trust for sale arises when the terms of the trust impose upon the trustees a *duty* to sell the property and hold the proceeds of such a sale upon the trusts as declared by the settlor. For example, a settlor leaves Blackacre to A and B (the trustees) on trust to sell the land and hold the proceeds of sale for C for life, then to D absolutely. In such a situation the duty to sell imposes an obligation on the trustees to do so. Under a trust for sale the trustees will, as in a conventional trust, have the legal estate in the land and will have the powers of management and control over the property.

When successive interests are created, a trust for sale must be expressly employed (except where imposed by statute), or the Settled Land Act will apply and the arrangement will be a strict settlement. Strict settlements and trusts for sale are mutually exclusive concepts.

SECTION 2: STRICT SETTLEMENTS

A: DEFINITION OF A STRICT SETTLEMENT

See Law Commission Report on Trusts of Land 1989, Law Com No. 181.

Settled Land Act 1925

1. What constitutes a settlement
  (1) Any deed, will, agreement for a settlement or other agreement, Act of Parliament, or other instrument, or any number of instruments, whether made or passed before or after, or partly before and partly after, the commencement of this Act, under or by virtue of which instrument or instruments any land, after the commencement of this Act, stands for the time being—
   (i) limited in trust for any persons by way of succession; or
   (ii) limited in trust for any person in possession—
     (a) for an entailed interest whether or not capable of being barred or defeated;
     (b) for an estate in fee simple or for a term of years absolute subject to an executory limitation, gift, or disposition over on failure of his issue or in any other event;
     (c) for a base or determinable fee or any corresponding interest in leasehold land;
     (d) being an infant, for an estate in fee simple or for a term of years absolute; or
   (iii) limited in trust for any person for an estate in fee simple or for a term of years absolute contingently on the happening of any event; or
   (v) charged, whether voluntarily or in consideration of marriage or by way of family arrangement, and whether immediately or after an interval, with the payment of any rentcharge for the life of any person, or any less period, or of any capital, annual, or periodical sums for the portions, advancement, maintenance, or otherwise for the benefit of any persons, with or without any terms of years for securing or raising the same;
creates or is for the purposes of this Act a settlement and is in this Act referred to as a settlement, or as the settlement, as the case requires:
  Provided that, where land is the subject of a compound settlement, references in this Act to the settlement shall be construed as meaning such compound settlement, unless the context otherwise requires.
  (2) Where an infant is beneficially entitled to land for an estate in fee simple or for a term of years absolute and by reason of an intestacy or otherwise there is no

instrument under which the interest of the infant arises or is acquired, a settlement shall be deemed to have been made by the intestate, or by the person whose interest the infant has acquired.

(4) An estate or interest not disposed of by a settlement and remaining in or reverting to the settlor, or any person deriving title under him, is for the purposes of this Act an estate or interest comprised in the subject of the settlement and coming to the settlor or such person under or by virtue of the settlement.

(5) Where—
   (a) a settlement creates an entailed interest which is incapable of being barred or defeated, or a base or determinable fee, whether or not the reversion or right of reverter is in the Crown, or any corresponding interest in leasehold land; or
   (b) the subject of a settlement is an entailed interest, or a base or determinable fee, whether or not the reversion or right of reverter is in the Crown, or any corresponding interest in leasehold land;
the reversion or right of reverter upon the cesser of the interest so created or settled shall be deemed to be an interest comprised in the subject of the settlement, and limited by the settlement.

(6) Subsections (4) and (5) of this section bind the Crown.

(7) This section does not apply to land held upon trust for sale.

Notes
1. Under s. 1(1)(i), the land need not be expressly limited in trust for persons by way of succession in order to give rise to a Settled Land Act settlement. The trust may arise by operation of law where, for example, a court gives protection to a licensee for the period of his or her life (see *Bannister* v *Bannister* [1948] 2 All ER 133 and *Binions* v *Evans* [1972] Ch 359 (Lord Denning dissenting) at pages 232 and 227 *et seq.*).
2. For an example of a limitation subject to a gift over, see *Re Richardson* [1904] 2 Ch 777, where a testatrix (T) gave her residuary estate to C (her niece) on condition that C lived at a particular house and looked after T's sister, M, providing a home for her throughout M's life or as long as M wished. There was a gift over to a second niece upon a similar condition should C fail to fulfil the condition. If neither niece fulfilled the condition, then the estate was to be held upon trust for M for life with trusts over on her death. M was insane and in an asylum. It was held that C was the person with the powers of the tenant for life under the Settled Land Act 1882. The condition to provide a home for M was void in so far as it prevented C from exercising the power of sale. C was entitled to sell the house and was entitled to the proceeds of sale.
3. A conveyance of a legal estate of land to an infant is not possible because of the Law of Property Act 1925, s. 1(6), which says that a legal estate in land is not capable of being held by an infant. Thus any such conveyance or disposition takes effect as an agreement by the settlor to execute a settlement by means of a vesting deed in the trustees' favour, and a trust instrument in the infant's favour (Settled Land Act 1925 s. 27(1)).
4. For an example of a 'springing interest' within s. 1(1)(iii), see *Re Bird* [1927] 1 Ch 210, where the testator devised all his residuary estate to trustees

upon trust to pay the net annual income thereof to A for his life, and after A's death, to hold the capital and income of the residuary estate on trust for all of A's children who were male and attained the age of 21. A left three sons, but only the eldest attained the age of 21. Clauson J said:

> In my opinion [the words of s. 1(1)(iii) of the Settled Land Act 1925] apply to this case for this reason: the son who has attained 21 appears to me to be a person of whom it is true to say that under the will land is limited in trust for him, for an estate in fee simple contingent on the happening of the various events, which would result in his being the only son left to claim the land, and that . . . justifies me in holding that, as regards that land, the will operates as a settlement under the Settled Land Act 1925.

5. Section 1(1)(v) covers arrangements of a family nature, for example where the settlor gives the legal estate to X but charges it with an annuity for his wife and children. Such sums of money should come from the income of the property, which would usually go to the tenant for life. The section covers only payments for 'portions, advancement, maintenance or otherwise for the benefit of any persons' and therefore if the property charged with the rent-charge does not fall within the provisions of the section the imposition of the rent-charge does not make the land settled land.

Law of Property (Amendment) Act 1926

1. Conveyances of legal estates subject to certain interests

(1) Nothing in the Settled Land Act, 1925, shall prevent a person on whom the powers of a tenant for life are conferred by paragraph (ix) of subsection (1) of section twenty of that Act from conveying or creating a legal estate subject to a prior interest as if the land had not been settled land.

(2) In any of the following cases, namely—

(a) where a legal estate has been conveyed or created under subsection one of this section, or under section sixteen of the Settled Land Act, 1925, subject to any prior interest, or

(b) where before the first day of January, nineteen hundred and twenty-six, land has been conveyed to a purchaser for money or money's worth subject to any prior interest whether or not on the purchase the land was expressed to be exonerated from, or the grantor agreed to indemnify the purchaser against, such prior interest,

the estate owner for the time being of the land subject to such prior interest may, notwithstanding any provision contained in the Settled Land Act, 1925, but without prejudice to any power whereby such prior interest is capable of being overreached, convey or create a legal estate subject to such prior interest as if the instrument creating the prior interest was not an instrument or one of the instruments constituting a settlement of the land.

(3) In this section "interest" means an estate, interest, charge or power of charging subsisting, or capable of arising or of being exercised, under a settlement, and, where a prior interest arises under the exercise of a power, "instrument" includes both the instrument conferring the power and the instrument exercising it.

B: MACHINERY NECESSARY TO CREATE A SETTLEMENT

(a) Inter vivos

Settled Land Act 1925

4. Authorised method of settling land inter vivos

(1) Every settlement of a legal estate in land inter vivos shall, save as in this Act otherwise provided, be effected by two deeds, namely, a vesting deed and a trust instrument and if effected in any other way, shall not operate to transfer or create a legal estate.

(2) By the vesting deed the land shall be conveyed to the tenant for life or statutory owner (and if more than one as joint tenants) for the legal estate the subject of the intended settlement;

Provided that, where such legal estate is already vested in the tenant for life or statutory owner, it shall be sufficient, without any other conveyance, if the vesting deed declares that the land is vested in him for that estate.

(3) The trust instrument shall—
   (a) declare the trusts affecting the settled land;
   (b) appoint or constitute trustees of the settlement;
   (c) contain the power, if any, to appoint new trustees of the settlement;
   (d) set out, either expressly or by reference, any powers intended to be conferred by the settlement in extension of those conferred by this Act;
   (e) bear any ad valorem stamp duty which may be payable (whether by virtue of the vesting deed or otherwise) in respect of the settlement.

5. Contents of vesting deeds

(1) Every vesting deed for giving effect to a settlement or for conveying settled land to a tenant for life or statutory owner during the subsistence of the settlement (in this Act referred to as a "principle vesting deed") shall contain the following statements and particulars, namely:—
   (a) A description, either specific or general, of the settled land;
   (b) A statement that the settled land is vested in the person or persons to whom it is conveyed or in whom it is declared to be vested upon the trusts from time to time affecting the settled land;
   (c) The names of the persons who are the trustees of the settlement;
   (d) Any additional or larger powers conferred by the trust instrument relating to the settled land which by virtue of this Act operate and are exercisable as if conferred by this Act on a tenant for life;
   (e) The name of any person for the time being entitled under the trust instrument to appoint new trustees of the settlement.

(2) The statements or particulars required by this section may be incorporated by reference to an existing vesting instrument, and, where there is a settlement subsisting at the commencement of this Act, by reference to that settlement and to any instrument whereby land has been conveyed to the uses or upon the trusts of that settlement, but not (save as last aforesaid) by reference to a trust instrument nor by reference to a disentailing deed.

(3) A principal vesting deed shall not be invalidated by reason only of any error in any of the statements or particulars by this Act required to be contained therein.

(b) By will

Settled Land Act 1925

6. Procedure in the case of settlements by will
Where a settlement is created by the will of an estate owner who dies after the commencement of this Act—
    (a)   the will is for the purposes of this Act a trust instrument; and
    (b)   the personal representatives of the testator shall hold the settled land on trust, if and when required so to do, to convey it to the person who, under the will, or by virtue of this Act, is the tenant for life or statutory owner, and, if more than one, as joint tenants.

9. Procedure in the case of settlements and of instruments deemed to be trust instruments
(1) Each of the following settlements or instruments shall for the purposes of this Act be deemed to be a trust instrument, and any reference to a trust instrument contained in this Act shall apply thereto, namely:—
    (i)   An instrument executed, or, in case of a will, coming into operation, after the commencement of this Act which by virtue of this Act is deemed to be a settlement;
    (ii)   A settlement which by virtue of this Act is deemed to have been made by any person after the commencement of this Act;
    (iii)   An instrument inter vivos intended to create a settlement of a legal estate in land which is executed after the commencement of this Act, and does not comply with the requirements of this Act with respect to the method of effecting such a settlement; and
    (iv)   A settlement made after the commencement of this Act (including a settlement by the will of a person who dies after such commencement) of any of the following interests—
        (a)   an equitable interest in land which is capable, when in possession, of subsisting at law; or
        (b)   an entailed interest; or
        (c)   a base or determinable fee or any corresponding interest in leasehold land,
but only if and when the interest settled takes effect free from all equitable interests and powers under every prior settlement (if any).

(2) As soon as practicable after a settlement, or an instrument which for the purposes of this Act is deemed to be a trust instrument, takes effect as such, the trustees of the settlement may, and on the request of the tenant for life or statutory owner shall, execute a principal vesting deed, containing the proper statements and particulars, declaring that the legal estate in the settled land shall vest or is vested in the person or persons therein named, being the tenant for life or statutory owner, and including themselves if they are the statutory owners, and such deed shall, unless the legal estate is already so vested, operate to convey or vest the legal estate in the settled land to or in the person or persons aforesaid and, if more than one, as joint tenants.

(3) If there are no trustees of the settlement, then (in default of a person able and willing to appoint such trustees) an application under this Act shall be made to the court for the appointment of such trustees.

C: INCOMPLETELY CONSTITUTED SETTLEMENTS

Settled Land Act 1925

13. Dispositions not to take effect until vesting instrument is made
Where a tenant for life or statutory owner has become entitled to have a principal

vesting deed or a vesting assent executed in his favour, then until a vesting instrument is executed or made pursuant to this Act in respect of the settled land, any purported disposition thereof inter vivos by any person, other than a personal representative (not being a disposition which he has power to make in right of his equitable interests or powers under a trust instrument), shall not take effect except in favour of a purchaser of a legal estate without notice of such tenant for life or statutory owner having become so entitled as aforesaid but, save as aforesaid, shall operate only as a contract for valuable consideration to carry out the transaction after the requisite vesting instrument has been executed or made, and a purchaser of a legal estate shall not be concerned with such disposition unless the contract is registered as a land charge.

Nothing in this section affects the creation or transfer of a legal estate by virtue of an order of the court or the Minister or other competent authority.

Note
The paralysing effect of s. 13 does not apply in the following situations:

(a) where the disposition is made by personal representatives, since they are allowed to sell settled land in the course of administering the estate;

(b) where the settlement comes to an end and the land ceases to be settled land (see *Re Alefounder's Will Trusts* [1927] 1 Ch 360);

(c) where the beneficiaries are of full age and wish to terminate the settlement;

(d) where land has become settled because it has been voluntarily subjected to family charges. In such a case the tenant for life may sell the land subject to the charges without executing a vesting deed (Law of Property (Amendment) Act 1926, s. 1).

D: THE TENANT FOR LIFE

(a) Who is the tenant for life?

Settled Land Act 1925

19. Who is tenant for life

(1) The person of full age who is for the time being beneficially entitled under a settlement to possession of settled land for his life is for the purposes of this Act the tenant for life of that land and the tenant for life under that settlement.

(2) If in any case there are two or more persons of full age so entitled as joint tenants, they together constitute the tenant for life for the purposes of this Act.

(3) If in any case there are two or more persons so entitled as joint tenants and they are not of full age, such one or more of them as is or are for the time being of full age is or (if more than one) together constitute the tenant for life for the purposes of this Act, but this subsection does not affect the beneficial interests of such of them as are not for the time being of full age.

(4) A person being tenant for life within the foregoing definitions shall be deemed to be such notwithstanding that, under the settlement or otherwise, the settled land, or his estate or interest therein, is incumbered or charged in any manner or to any extent, and notwithstanding any assignment by operation of law or otherwise of his estate or interest under the settlement, whether before or after it came into possession, other than an assurance which extinguishes that estate or interest.

Strict Settlements and Trusts for Sale

20. Other limited owners having powers of tenant for life

(1) Each of the following persons being of full age shall, when his estate or interest is in possession, have the powers of a tenant for life under this Act, (namely):—

(i) A tenant in tail, including a tenant in tail after possibility of issue extinct, and a tenant in tail who is by Act of Parliament restrained from barring or defeating his estate tail, and although the reversion is in the Crown, but not including such a tenant in tail where the land in respect whereof he is so restrained was purchased with money provided by Parliament in consideration of public services;

(ii) A person entitled to land for an estate in fee simple or for a term of years absolute with or subject to, in any of such cases, an executory limitation, gift, or disposition over on failure of his issue or in any other event;

(iii) A person entitled to a base or determinable fee, although the reversion or right of reverter is in the Crown, or to any corresponding interest in leasehold land;

(iv) A tenant for years determinable on life, not holding merely under a lease at a rent;

(v) A tenant for the life of another, not holding merely under a lease at a rent;

(vi) A tenant for his own or any other life, or for years determinable on life, whose estate is liable to cease in any event during that life, whether by expiration of the estate, or by conditional limitation, or otherwise, or to be defeated by an executory limitation, gift, or disposition over, or is subject to a trust for accumulation of income for any purpose;

(vii) A tenant by the curtesy;

(viii) A person entitled to the income of land under a trust or direction for payment thereof to him during his own or any other life, whether or not subject to expenses of management or to a trust for accumulation of income for any purpose, or until sale of the land, or until forfeiture, cesser or determination by any means of his interest therein, unless the land is subject to an immediate binding trust for sale;

(ix) A person beneficially entitled to land for an estate in fee simple or for a term of years absolute subject to any estates, interests, charges, or powers of charging, subsisting or capable of being exercised under a settlement;

117. Definitions

(xxviii) "Tenant for life" includes a person (not being a statutory owner) who has the powers of a tenant for life under this Act, and also (where the context requires) one of two or more persons who together constitute the tenant for life, or have the powers of a tenant for life; . . .

Notes

1. An annuitant has been held not to be a tenant for life (*Re Jefferys* [1939] Ch 205).
2. If the interest granted amounts in effect to a life interest, then the grantee becomes the tenant for life. In *Re Carne's Settled Estates* [1899] 1 Ch 324, for example, a house was held on trust for a woman to occupy for as long as she wished. The woman became the tenant for life.
3. Leases at a rent for a term of years determinable on the death of the tenant do not come within the ambit of s. 20(1)(iv), since such leases are converted into a term for 90 years by s. 149(6) of the Law of Property Act 1925 (see pages 158–9). Thus such a tenant cannot be a tenant for life — see *Re Catling* [1931] 2 Ch 359, where the testator gave his widow the right to take a yearly tenancy of a house at a nominal rent of £1 per annum. Section 149(6) of the Law of

Property Act 1925 does not apply, however, where the term takes effect under a settlement.

(b) No tenant for life
In certain situations there will be no tenant for life, despite the land being settled land. This can occur:

(i) where the person entitled to the land is an infant;
(ii) where there is no one who is entitled to the whole of the income (for example, *Re Frewen* [1926] Ch 580, where the person entitled in possession was entitled to only part of the income from the trust, the remainder to be accumulated, and *Re Jefferys* [1939] Ch 205, where a fixed annuity of £150 was to be paid);
(iii) where no person is entitled to any income from the trust, i.e. where there is a discretionary trust (see *Re Gallenga Will Trusts* [1938] 1 All ER 106).

Settled Land Act 1925

23. Powers of trustees, etc when there is no tenant for life
(1) Where under a settlement there is no tenant for life nor, independently of this section, a person having by virtue of this Act the powers of a tenant for life then—
    (a) any person of full age on whom such powers are by the settlement expressed to be conferred; and
    (b) in any other case the trustees of the settlement;
shall have the powers of a tenant for life under this Act.

26. Infants, how to be affected
(1) Where an infant is beneficially entitled in possession to land for an estate in fee simple or for a term of years absolute or would if of full age be a tenant for life of or have the powers of a tenant for life over settled land, then, during the minority of the infant—
    (a) if the settled land is vested in a personal representative, the personal representative, until a principal vesting instrument has been executed pursuant to the provisions of this Act; and
    (b) in every other case, the trustees of the settlement;
shall have, in reference to the settled land and capital money, all the powers conferred by this Act and the settlement on a tenant for life, and on the trustees of the settlement.

E: THE TRUSTEES OF THE SETTLEMENT

Settled Land Act 1925

30. Who are trustees for purposes of Act
(1) Subject to the provisions of this Act, the following persons are trustees of a settlement for the purposes of this Act, and are in this Act referred to as the "trustees of the settlement" or "trustees of a settlement," namely—
    (i) the persons, if any, who are for the time being under the settlement, trustees with power of sale of the settled land (subject or not to the consent of any person), or with power of consent to or approval of the exercise of such a power of sale, or if there are no such persons; then

(ii) the persons, if any, for the time being, who are by the settlement declared to be trustees thereof for the purposes of the Settled Land Acts, 1882 to 1890, or any of them, or this Act, or if there are no such persons; then

(iii) the persons, if any, who are for the time being under the settlement trustees with power of or upon trust for sale of any other land comprised in the settlement and subject to the same limitations as the land to be sold or otherwise dealt with, or with power of consent to or approval of the exercise of such power of sale, or, if there are no such persons; then

(iv) the persons, if any, who are for the time being under the settlement trustees with future power of sale, or under a future trust for sale of the settled land, or with power of consent to or approval of the exercise of such a future power of sale, and whether the power or trust takes effect in all events or not, or, if there are no such persons; then

(v) the persons, if any, appointed by deed to be trustees of the settlement by all the persons who at the date of the deed were together able, by virtue of their beneficial interests or by the exercise of an equitable power, to dispose of the settled land in equity for the whole estate the subject of the settlement.

(2) Paragraphs (i), (iii) and (iv) of the last preceding subsection take effect in like manner as if the powers therein referred to had not by this Act been made exercisable by the tenant for life or statutory owner.

(3) Where a settlement is created by will, or a settlement has arisen by the effect of an intestacy, and apart from this subsection there would be no trustees for the purposes of this Act of such settlement, then the personal representatives of the deceased shall, until other trustees are appointed, be by virtue of this Act the trustees of the settlement, but where there is a sole personal representative, not being a trust corporation, it shall be obligatory on him to appoint an additional trustee to act with him for the purposes of this Act, and the provisions of the Trustee Act, 1925, relating to the appointment of new trustees and the vesting of trust property shall apply accordingly.

31. As to trustees of compound settlements

(1) Persons who are for the time being trustees for the purposes of this Act of an instrument which is a settlement, or is deemed to be a subsisting settlement for the purposes of this Act, shall be the trustees for the purposes of this Act of any settlement constituted by that instrument and any instruments subsequent in date or operation.

Where there are trustees for the purposes of this Act of the instrument under which there is a tenant for life or statutory owner but there are no trustees for those purposes of a prior instrument, being one of the instruments by which a compound settlement is constituted, those trustees shall, unless and until trustees are appointed of the prior instrument or of the compound settlement, be the trustees for the purposes of this Act of the compound settlement.

34. Appointment of trustees by court

(1) If at any time there are no trustees of a settlement, or where in any other case it is expedient, for the purposes of this Act, that new trustees of a settlement be appointed, the court may, if it thinks fit, on the application of the tenant for life, statutory owner, or of any other person having, under the settlement, an estate or interest in the settled land, in possession, remainder or otherwise, or, in the case of an infant, of his testamentary or other guardian or next friend, appoint fit persons to be trustees of the settlement.

(2) The persons so appointed, and the survivors and survivor of them, while continuing to be trustees or trustee, and, until the appointment of new trustees, the personal representatives or representative for the time being of the last surviving or continuing trustee, shall become and be the trustees or trustee of the settlement.

Note
The trustees have the following functions in relation to the settlement:

(a) They must receive and hold capital money.

(b) Where there is no tenant for life the trustees must act as statutory owner (Settled Land Act 1925, s. 102).

(c) They receive notices from the tenant for life when he wishes to exercise certain powers conferred on him the by the Settled Land Act 1925.

(d) They must give their consent to certain powers being exercised by the tenant for life.

(e) They must execute a deed of discharge when a settlement comes to an end.

(f) They must execute a vesting deed when a settlement is improperly created.

(g) They must act as special personal representatives when a tenant for life dies and the settlement continues.

(h) They must exercise the powers of a tenant for life if the tenant for life wishes to acquire an interest in the legal estate for himself.

(i) Where a tenant for life has parted with his equitable interest and then unreasonably refuses to exercise his powers or consent to the trustees exercising them, then the court may order the trustees to exercise the powers of the tenant for life.

(j) They have a general supervisory role over the settlement.

F: THE POWERS OF THE TENANT FOR LIFE

The tenant for life, since the reforms of the Settled Land Act 1882, has been given extensive powers of management, and even sale, which allow him to deal with the land in a similar manner to a fee simple owner, which can be contrary to the wishes expressed by the settlor. Any gain made from the exercise of such a power must, however, be held on trust for the beneficiaries of the settlement.

The powers available to the tenant for life can be divided into five different categories:

(a) Powers exercisable by the tenant for life giving notice to the trustees of his intention to exercise them.

(b) Powers exercisable with the consent of the trustees.

(c) Powers exercisable with the consent of the trustees or the court.

(d) Powers exercisable with the consent of the court.

(e) Powers exercisable without the tenant for life either giving notice to or obtaining the consent of the trustees or the court.

Such powers cannot be excluded.

Any provision tending to induce a tenant for life not to exercise his powers is likewise void, but a settlor can, however, extend the statutory powers — Settled Land Act 1925, ss. 106 and 109.

Where there is a conflict between the Act and the settlement the Act prevails.

(a) Powers exercisable on giving notice to trustees
Such notice must be made in writing and be given to at least two trustees or a trust corporation at least one month before the transaction. In most situations notice of general intention is sufficient, without details of the specific transaction, but this is not so in the case of a mortgage. See Settled Land Act 1925, s. 101.

(i) *Power of sale or exchange*   See SLA 1925, ss. 38, 39 and 40.

(ii) *Power to grant leases*   See SLA 1925, ss. 41, 42.

(iii) *Power to grant options*   See SLA 1925, s. 51

(iv) *Power to mortgage*   See SLA 1925, s. 71.

(b) Powers exercisable with the consent of the trustees
Such powers include the power:

(i) to compromise or settle disputes (Settled Land Act 1925, s. 58(1));
(ii) to release rights imposed on other land for the benefit of settled land (Settled Land Act 1925, s. 58(2)).

(c) Powers exercisable with the consent of the trustees or the court

(i) *To cut and sell timber*   See SLA 1925, s. 66.

(ii) *To dispose of the principal mansion house*   See SLA 1925, s. 65.

(d) Powers exercisable with the consent of the court

(i) *To sell heirlooms*   See SLA 1925, s. 67.

(ii) *To effect any transaction not otherwise authorised by the Act or settlement if it will benefit the land or the beneficiaries*   See SLA 1925, s. 64.

(iii) *To grant building or mining leases for terms longer than allowed in the Act*   See SLA 1925, s. 46.

(e) Powers exercisable without the tenant for life either giving notice to or obtaining consent of the trustees or the court

(i) *To make improvements*   See SLA 1925, ss. 75, 83 and 84.

(ii) *Power to accept surrender of leases*

(iii) *To take leases of other lands*

(iv) *To make leases of less than 21 years*

G: NATURE OF POWERS OF THE TENANT FOR LIFE

(a) Non-assignability of powers

The powers of the tenant for life are non-assignable and incapable of being released while the land remains settled land (Settled Land Act 1925, s. 104(1)). Therefore, in a settlement to X for life, remainder to Y absolutely, where X sells his life interest to Z, the power to grant leases, for example, is exercisable by X not by Z as X retains the legal estate. Nevertheless, notice of any intended transaction must be given to Z and Z's interest is protected in that he:

>   (a) shall be entitled to the same or the like estate or interest in or charge on the land, money, or securities for the time being representing the land, money or securities compromised in the assignment, as he had by virtue of the assignment in the last-mentioned land, money or securities; and
>   (b) if the assignment so provides, or if it takes effect by operation of the law or bankruptcy, and after notice thereof to the trustees of the settlement, no investment or application of capital money for the time being affected by the assignment shall be made without the consent of the assignee, except an investment in securities authorised by statute for the investment of trust money — Settled Land Act 1925, s. 104(4)(a) and (b).

However—

Settled Land Act 1925

24. As to a tenant for life who has parted with his interest

(1) If it is shown to the satisfaction of the court that a tenant for life, who has by reason of bankruptcy, assignment, incumbrance, or otherwise ceased in the opinion of the court to have a substantial interest in his estate or interest in the settled land or any part thereof, has unreasonably refused to exercise any of the powers conferred on him by this Act, or consents to an order under this section, the court may, on the application of any person interested in the settled land or the part thereof affected, make an order authorising the trustees of the settlement, to exercise in the name and on behalf of the tenant for life, any of the powers of a tenant for life under this Act, in relation to the settled land or the part thereof affected, either generally and in such manner and for such period as the court may think fit, or in a particular instance, and the court may by the order direct that any documents of title in the possession of the tenant for life relating to the settled land be delivered to the trustees of the settlement.

(2) While any such order is in force, the tenant for life shall not, in relation to the settled land or the part thereof affected, exercise any of the powers thereby authorised to be exercised in his name and on his behalf, but no person dealing with the tenant for life shall be affected by any such order, unless the order is for the time being registered as an order affecting land.

(3) An order may be made under this section at any time after the estate or interest of the tenant for life under the settlement has taken effect in possession, and

notwithstanding that he disposed thereof when it was an estate or interest in remainder or reversion.

In Re Thornhill's Settlement [1941] 1 Ch 24

When a tenant for life became bankrupt he ceased to take any part in the management of the agricultural estate of which he was in possession. He refused to perform the functions of a tenant for life and the farms became derelict as he refused to let them when they were vacant. Held: Because his actions amounted to an unreasonable refusal by the tenant for life to exercise his powers of leasing and sale, rather than mere neglect, the court could make an order under Settled Land Act 1925, s. 24(1) vesting all such powers in the Public Trustee as trustee of the settlement.

Settled Land Act 1925

105. Effect of surrender of life estate to the next remainderman
(1) Where the estate or interest of a tenant for life under the settlement has been or is absolutely assured with intent to extinguish the same, either before or after the commencement of this Act, to the person next entitled in remainder or reversion under the settlement, then, ... the statutory powers of the tenant for life under this Act shall, in reference to the property affected by the assurance, and notwithstanding the provisions of the last preceding section, cease to be exercisable by him, and the statutory powers shall thenceforth become exercisable as if he were dead, but without prejudice to any incumbrance affecting the estate or interest assured, and to the rights to which any incumbrancer would have been entitled if those powers had remained exercisable by the tenant for life.

This subsection applies whether or not any term of years or charge intervenes, or the estate of the remainderman or reversioner is liable to be defeated, and whether or not the estate or interest of the tenant for life under the settlement was in possession at the date of the assurance.

(b) Fiduciary nature of powers

Settled Land Act 1925

107. Tenant for life trustee for all parties interested
(1) A tenant for life or statutory owner shall, in exercising any power under this Act, have regard to the interests of all parties entitled under the settlement, and shall, in relation to the exercise thereof by him, be deemed to be in the position and to have the duties and liabilities of a trustee for those parties.

Notes
1. In ***Re Earl of Radnor's Will Trusts*** (1890) 45 ChD 402, Lord Esher said (at p. 417):

[The tenant for life] must take all the circumstances of the family, and of each member of the family who may be affected by what he is about to do; he must consider them carefully, and must consider them in the way that an honest outside trustee would consider them; then he must come to what, is his judgment, is the right thing to do under the circumstances — not the best thing, but the right thing to do.

2. In ***Middlemas v Stevens*** [1901] 1 Ch 574 (ChD), a husband had provided by his will that his widow should have a right to the use and enjoyment of a house, rent free, so long as she personally resided there during her widowhood. As she intended to re-marry she proposed to grant a 21-year lease of the house to her intended husband using powers of leasing given to a tenant for life under the Settled Land Act. The plaintiffs, who were the remaindermen, objected. Held: the defendant's exercise of her powers was not bona fide and could be prevented. Joyce J said: 'A tenant for life in exercising any of the powers conferred by the Settled Land Acts must have regard to the interests of all parties entitled under the settlement'.

Compare the following case.

Wheelwright v Walker (No. 1) (1883) 23 ChD 752 (ChD)

Land was settled on the defendant (T) for life and after his death on trust for sale for the defendant's daughter (D). T was about 70 years of age. In July 1880, D and her husband contracted to sell her reversion to the plaintiff. A month after the Settled Land Act 1882 came into effect, in January 1883, T advertised the estate for sale under the powers of that Act. P sought an injunction to prevent T from selling, as P wanted to occupy the estate when T died. Also, no Settled Land Act trustees had been appointed. Held: the tenant for life had power to sell under the Act provided he complied with the provisions of it. However, as there were no trustees to whom notice could be given an injunction would be granted restraining the tenant for life from selling until such trustees had been appointed.

H: CHANGE OF OWNERSHIP

Settled Land Act 1925

7. Procedure on change of ownership

(1) If, on the death of a tenant for life or statutory owner, or of the survivor of two or more tenants for life or statutory owners, in whom the settled land was vested, the land remains settled land, his personal representatives shall hold the settled land on trust, if and when required so to do, to convey it to the person who under the trust instrument or by virtue of this Act becomes the tenant for life or statutory owner and, if more than one, as joint tenants.

(2) If a person by reason of attaining full age becomes a tenant for life for the purposes of this Act of settled land, he shall be entitled to require the trustees of the settlement, personal representatives, or other persons in whom the settled land is vested, to convey the land to him.

(3) If a person who, when of full age, will together with another person or other persons constitute the tenant for life for the purposes of this Act of settled land attains that age, he shall be entitled to require the tenant for life, trustees of the settlement,

personal representatives or other persons in whom the settled land is vested to convey the land to him and the other person or persons who together with him constitute the tenant for life as joint tenants.

(4) If by reason of forfeiture, surrender, or otherwise the estate owner of any settled land ceases to have the statutory powers of a tenant for life and the land remains settled land, he shall be bound forthwith to convey the settled land to the person who under the trust instrument, or by virtue of this Act, becomes the tenant for life or statutory owner and, if more than one, as joint tenants.

(5) If any person of full age becomes absolutely entitled to the settled land (whether beneficially, or as a personal representative, or as trustee for sale, or otherwise) free from all limitations, powers, and charges taking effect under the settlement, he shall be entitled to require the trustees of the settlement, personal representatives, or other persons in whom the settled land is vested, to convey the land to him, and if more persons than one being of full age become so entitled to the settled land they shall be entitled to require such persons as aforesaid to convey the land to them as joint tenants.

8. Mode and costs of conveyance, and saving of rights of personal representatives and equitable chargees

(1) A conveyance by personal representatives under either of the last two preceding sections may be made by an assent in writing signed by them which shall operate as a conveyance.

(4) Where the land is or remains settled land a conveyance under either of the last two preceding sections shall—
    (a) if by deed, be a principal vesting deed; and
    (b) if by an assent, be a vesting assent, which shall contain the like statements and particulars as are required by this Act in the case of a principle vesting deed.

Administration of Estates Act 1925

22. Special executors as respects settled land

(1) A testator may appoint, and in default of such express appointment shall be deemed to have appointed, as his special executors in regard to settled land, the persons, if any, who are at his death the trustees of the settlement thereof, and probate may be granted to such trustees specially limited to the settled land.

In this subsection "settled land" means land vested in the testator which was settled previously to his death and not by his will.

(2) A testator may appoint other persons either with or without such trustees as aforesaid or any of them to be his general executors in regard to his other property and assets.

Re Bridgett & Hayes' Contract
[1928] Ch 163 (ChD)

T was the tenant for life of settled land and in her will appointed B to be her sole executor. J was the sole surviving trustee of the settlement of which T was the tenant for life. The settlement ended upon the death of T. B contracted to sell the land to H. H objected and claimed that title should have been made by J, the sole surviving trustee of the settlement, as he was T's special personal representative under the Administration of Estates Act 1925, s. 22(1). Held: the section did not apply and B was able to give good title.

ROMER J: It is common ground that up to the date of her death Mrs Emily Margaret Thornley, who was the tenant for life of the property now in question, had vested in her the legal estate in the property. It is common ground that, that being so, on her death this legal estate passed to her personal representative by virtue of sub-ss. 1 and 3 of s. 1 of the Administration of Estates Act, 1925. But then it is said that by virtue of s. 22, sub-s. 1, of that Act, in such a case as this the lady must be deemed to have appointed as her special executor in regard to this land the person who up to the date of her death was sole surviving trustee for the purposes of the Settled Land Act. Let me assume that that was so. On January 17, 1926, she died, and on April 7, 1926, a general grant of probate of her will was made to Thomas William Bridgett, a person whom she had thereby appointed as executor. As from that date, at any rate, wherever the legal estate in this property may have been as between the date of her death and this act of probate, the legal estate in this land vested in Thomas William Bridgett, and, while that act of probate remains unrevoked, he can in my opinion properly convey the legal estate to the purchaser. Sect. 204 of the Law of Property Act, 1925, sub-s. 1, says this: "An order of the Court under any statutory or other jurisdiction shall not, as against a purchaser, be invalidated on the ground of want of jurisdiction, or of want of any concurrence, consent, notice, or service, whether the purchaser has notice of any such want or not." Sect. 22, sub-s. 1 (if the purchaser is right as to its application at all to this case), provided that probate might have been granted to this sole surviving trustee. In point of fact the Court of Probate did not grant probate to him, but granted probate to Thomas William Bridgett. That being so, it appears to me that s. 204 of the Law of Property Act applies to the case with regard to the taking of a conveyance from the legal personal representative. Further, the purchaser would be protected in the event of any subsequent revocation of that grant of probate by s. 37, sub-s. 1, of the Administration of Estates Act, 1925. It can hardly be doubted that in this case, if the purchaser does take a conveyance from the person to whom the grant of probate was granted, he would be acting in good faith, within the meaning of s. 55, sub-s. 1 (xviii), of the Act.

The only difficulty I think as regards that point is caused by sub-s. 1 (xi) of the last mentioned section, which says: "'Personal representative' means the executor, original or by representation, or administrator for the time being of a deceased person." At present the only executor of this deceased person is Thomas William Bridgett. But then it adds: "and 'executor' includes a person deemed to be appointed executor as respects settled land." I think however that these later words only refer to the case where in the circumstances it is proper that the word "executor" should be so read as to include a person deemed to be appointed executor as respects settled land, and that the definition when read in connection with s. 1 cannot have the effect of vesting in the person who is deemed to be appointed special executor the legal estate in settled land where the Court of Probate has granted general administration to somebody else.

The point still remains as to whether s. 22, sub-s. 1, applies to the present case, it being conceded on both sides that on the death of this lady the settlement came to an end. Let me read the words of s. 22, sub-s. 1: . . . Sect. 22 is the first of three sections which are introduced under the general heading "Special Provisions as to Settled Land." In ss. 23 and 24 it is I think reasonably clear that "settled land" means land which after the death of the testator continues to be settled land, and the words in s. 22, sub-s. 1, "'settled land' means land vested in the testator which was settled previously to his death and not by his will" refer in terms only to that particular sub-section. I cannot help thinking that these words were merely designed for the purpose of making it clear that s. 22, sub-s. 1, did not apply to a case where the land was settled by the will of a testator. However, I have to deal with the words as I find them, and that being so I must read the earlier part of the sub-section as follows: "A testator may appoint and in default of such express appointment shall be deemed to have appointed as his special executors in regard to land vested in the testator which was settled previously to his death the persons if any who are at his death the trustees of the settlement thereof." So far down to the words "previously to his death" the section applies to the present case, because here land was vested in the testatrix and it had been settled previously to her death. Then the sub-section says she shall be deemed to have appointed as her special executors the persons, if any, who are at her death the trustees of the settlement. Now before any one can go to the Court of Probate and get probate specially limited to the settled land granted to him, he must be in a position to say to the Court that he is to be deemed to have been appointed special executor of this land, because at the death of the testator he was trustee of the settlement thereof. But in my opinion he is not in a position to make that statement if the settlement comes to an end the moment the testator dies. It is to be observed that the sub-section does not refer to the persons who immediately before the death of the testator were the trustees of the settlement, but to the persons who at his death are the trustees of the settlement.

The words "persons who are at his death the trustees of the settlement" cannot to my mind mean persons who are trustees notwithstanding his death, especially when it is realized that the section is dealing with the testator's will, which comes into operation only when he is dead.

For these reasons I think this sub-section does not apply in a case like the present, where, upon the death of the testatrix in question, the settlement existing up to that date comes to an end.

I: PROTECTION OF PURCHASERS

If the correct procedure is followed, then on a sale by the tenant for life, the beneficial interests under the settlement can be 'overreached' and the purchaser obtains title to the land free from those interests, irrespective of whether he has notice of them or not. The beneficiaries' interests will then be in the purchase money not in the land (see Section 4 for a more detailed discussion of the concept of overreaching). The purchaser can obtain the benefit of the overreaching machinery only if the purchase money is paid to at least two trustees or a trust corporation and he purchases a *legal* estate for money or money's worth.

See also the Settled Land Act 1925, s. 13 at pages 253–4.

Settled Land Act 1925

18. Restrictions on dispositions of settled land where trustees have not been discharged

(1) Where land is the subject of a vesting instrument and the trustees of the settlement have not been discharged under this Act, then—

(a) any disposition by the tenant for life or statutory owner of the land, other than a disposition authorised by this Act or any other statute, or made in pursuance of any additional or larger powers mentioned in the vesting instrument, shall be void, except for the purpose of conveying or creating such equitable interests as he has power, in right of his equitable interests and powers under the trust instrument, to convey or create; and

(b) if any capital money is payable in respect of a transaction, a conveyance to a purchaser of the land shall only take effect under this Act if the capital money is paid to or by the direction of the trustees of the settlement or into court; and

(c) notwithstanding anything to the contrary in the vesting instrument, or the trust instrument, capital money shall not, except where the trustee is a trust corporation, be paid to or by the direction of fewer persons than two as trustees of the settlement.

(2) The restrictions imposed by this section do not affect—

(a) the right of a personal representative in whom the settled land may be vested to convey or deal with the land for the purposes of administration;

(b) the right of a person of full age who has become absolutely entitled (whether beneficially or as trustee for sale or personal representative or otherwise) to the settled land, free from all limitations, powers, and charges taking effect under the trust instrument, to require the land to be conveyed to him;

(c) the power of the tenant for life, statutory owner, or personal representative in whom the settled land is vested to transfer or create such legal estates, to take effect in priority to the settlement, as may be required for giving effect to any obligations imposed on him by statute, but where any capital money is raised or received in respect of the transaction the money shall be paid to or by the direction of the trustees of the settlement or in accordance with an order of the court.

95. Trustees' receipts

The receipt or direction in writing of or by the trustees of the settlement, or where a sole trustee is a trust corporation, of or by that trustee, or of or by the personal representatives of the last surviving or continuing trustee, for or relating to any money or securities, paid or transferred to or by the direction of the trustees, trustee, or representatives, as the case may be, effectually discharges the payer or transferor therefrom, and from being bound to see to the application or being answerable for any loss or misapplication thereof, and, in case of a mortgagee or other person advancing money, from being concerned to see that any money advanced by him is wanted for any purpose of this Act, or that no more than is wanted is raised.

Note
See the Settled Land Act 1925, s. 101.

Settled Land Act 1925

110. Protection of purchasers, etc

(1) On a sale, exchange, lease, mortgage, charge, or other disposition, a purchaser dealing in good faith with a tenant for life or statutory owner shall, as against all parties entitled under the settlement, be conclusively taken to have given the best price, consideration, or rent as the case may require, that could reasonably be obtained by the tenant for life or statutory owner, and to have complied with all the requisitions of this Act.

(2) A purchaser of a legal estate in settled land shall not, except as hereby expressly provided, be bound or entitled to call for the production of the trust instrument or any information concerning that instrument or any ad valorem stamp duty thereon, and whether or not he has notice of its contents he shall, save as hereinafter provided, be bound and entitled if the last or only principal vesting instrument contains the statements and particulars required by this Act to assume that—

(a) the person in whom the land is by the said instrument vested or declared to be vested is the tenant for life or statutory owner and has all the powers of a tenant for life under this Act, including such additional or larger powers, if any, as are therein mentioned;

   (b) the persons by the said instrument stated to be the trustees of the settlement, or their successors appearing to be duly appointed, are the properly constituted trustees of the settlement;

   (c) the statements and particulars required by this Act and contained (expressly or by reference) in the said instrument were correct at the date thereof;

   (d) the statements contained in any deed executed in accordance with this Act declaring who are the trustees of the settlement for the purposes of this Act are correct;

   (e) the statements contained in any deed of discharge, executed in accordance with this Act, are correct:

Provided that, as regards the first vesting instrument executed for the purpose of giving effect to—

   (a) a settlement subsisting at the commencement of this Act; or
   (b) an instrument which by virtue of this Act is deemed to be a settlement; or
   (c) a settlement which by virtue of this Act is deemed to have been made by any person after the commencement of this Act; or
   (d) an instrument inter vivos intended to create a settlement of a legal estate in land which is executed after the commencement of this Act and does not comply with the requirements of this Act with respect to the method of effecting such a settlement;
a purchaser shall be concerned to see—

      (i)   that the land disposed of to him is comprised in such settlement or instrument;
      (ii) that the person in whom the settled land is by such vesting instrument vested, or declared to be vested, is the person in whom it ought to be vested as tenant for life or statutory owner;
      (iii) that the persons thereby stated to be the trustees of the settlement are the properly constituted trustees of the settlement.

   (3) A purchaser of a legal estate in settled land from a personal representative shall be entitled to act on the following assumptions:—

      (i)   If the capital money, if any, payable in respect of the transaction is paid to the personal representative, that such representative is acting under his statutory or other powers and requires the money for purposes of administration;

      (ii) If such capital money is, by the direction of the personal representative paid to persons who are stated to be the trustees of a settlement, that such persons are the duly constituted trustees of the settlement for the purposes of this Act, and that the personal representative is acting under his statutory powers during a minority;

      (iii) In any other case, that the personal representative is acting under his statutory or other powers.

   (4) Where no capital money arises under a transaction, a disposition by a tenant for life or statutory owner shall; in favour of a purchaser of a legal estate, have effect under this Act notwithstanding that at the date of the transaction there are no trustees of the settlement.

   (5) If a conveyance of or an assent relating to land formerly subject to a vesting instrument does not state who are the trustees of the settlement for the purposes of this Act, a purchaser of a legal estate shall be bound and entitled to act on the assumption that the person in whom the land was thereby vested was entitled to the land free from all limitations, powers, and charges taking effect under that settlement, absolutely and beneficially, or, if so expressed in the conveyance or assent, as personal representative, or trustee for sale or otherwise, and that every statement of fact in such conveyance or assent is correct.

Note
There has been a great deal of uncertainty about the position where a purchaser has dealt in good faith with a person he thought was the absolute owner, but who was in fact the tenant for life making an unauthorised transaction.

Weston v Henshaw [1950] Ch 510 (ChD)

In 1921, some property was conveyed in fee simple by a father (F) to his son (S), but in 1927 S sold the fee simple back to F. In 1931, F settled the property on his wife for life, then on S for life with remainder to F's grandson on attaining the age of 25. F died in 1931 and, when his wife died in 1940 the property was vested in S by means of a vesting assent. S was given all the deeds save for the grant of probate. In 1944, S used the conveyance of 1921 to obtain money on security of a charge over the property in favour of the defendants. The deeds executed after 1921 had been concealed from the mortgagees so that S appeared to be the absolute owner of the property, although he was merely the tenant for life. When S died the grandson sought a declaration that the charge (and further charges) were void as against him under Settled Land Act, s. 18. The mortgagee claimed to be protected by s. 110(1). Held: the charges were void as against the grandson.

Note
The decision in *Weston v Henshaw* was doubted in the following later case.

Re Morgan's Lease
[1972] Ch 1 (ChD)

In 1950, a tenant for life (M) demised some business premises to the plaintiffs (P) for a term of 10 years. On the expiry of the lease M purported as absolute owner to grant a lease to P for a further term of seven years with an option to renew, on similar terms. P believed M to be an absolute owner. M died in 1962. D was the administratrix, and in 1965 she executed a vesting assent of the legal estate in reversion to herself and the other defendants on trust for sale. The defendants refused to renew the lease when P sought to exercise their option. Held:

(1) A tenant who acted in good faith when dealing with the tenant for life could rely on section 110 of the Settled Land Act 1925 whether the transaction was completed or not.

(2) For section 110 to apply a purchaser need only act in good faith and need not know he was dealing with a tenant for life.

UNGOED-THOMAS J: I come now to the third issue on the first question, whether section 110 of the Settled Land Act 1925 only applies if the purchaser knows that the other party to the transaction is a tenant for life. The landlords' submission was

Strict Settlements and Trusts for Sale

founded on *Weston* v *Henshaw* [1950] Ch 510. [Ungoed-Thomas J outlines the facts of the case.] Danckwerts J observed, at p. 519:

> I am satisfied, however, that that subsection [i.e., section 110 (1)] applies only to a person who is dealing with the tenant for life or statutory owner as such, whom he knows to be a limited owner, and with regard to whom he might be under a duty.

The passage, unfortunately, does not set out the reasoning which led to the conclusion, and I confess to some difficulty in appreciating what was the relevant duty which the person dealing with the life tenant might be under to the life tenant, as contrasted with the limitation which was imposed upon the purchaser by the section. Unfortunately, too, *Mogridge* v *Clapp* [1892] 3 Ch 382 was not brought to the judge's notice.

The headnote of *Mogridge* v *Clapp* [1892] 3 Ch 382, so far as I need read it, states:

> In October 1884, one H, purporting to demise as absolute owner (which he believed himself to be), granted a building lease of certain land to the plaintiff for the term of 99 years. The plaintiff made no inquiry as to H's title, but assumed that he was the absolute owner of the land demised. The defendant afterwards agreed to purchase the lease of the demised land from the plaintiff; but, on investigating the title, he discovered that the land had, under a will, belonged to H's deceased wife, and that H was only tenant by the curtesy. A tenant by the curtesy has, under section 58 (1) (viii) of the Settled Land Act 1882, all the powers of a tenant for life; but the lease, though complying with the enabling sections of the Settled Land Acts, contained no reference thereto; and at its date there were no trustees of the will, to whom the notices required by section 45 of the Settled Land Act 1882, in the case of a lease by a tenant for life, could be given.

Kay LJ refers to section 54 of the Settled Land Act 1882, the predecessor of section 110 of the Settled Land Act 1925, at p. 400:

> Section 54 provides that on a sale, lease, etc., a purchaser or lessee, dealing in good faith with a tenant for life, shall, as against the parties entitled under the settlement, be conclusively taken to have given the best price or rent "and to have complied with all the requisitions of this Act." This section confirms the view that in the case of a lessee dealing in good faith the remedy, if any, of the persons entitled under the settlement for any neglect of the provisions of the Act is to be against the tenant for life in his fiduciary character, not against the lessee, and is not to affect the validity of the lease.

A little later Kay LJ says, at p. 401:

> If the lessee knew that there were no trustees, or that the tenant for life had not given the trustees notice, he might, by accepting the lease under such circumstances, be implicated in the breach of fiduciary duty by the tenant for life. It might be said that he was not dealing then in good faith with the tenant for life. Good faith in that connection must mean or involve a belief that all is being regularly and properly done; and if the lessee has not that belief, it may be said that section 54 of the Act of 1882 does not protect him against an action by other persons entitled under the settlement.

Then he expresses his "present opinion" "that if the lease were otherwise unobjectionable it could not be set aside because the lessee knew there were no trustees"; and he later adds that it was not necessary to give a decided opinion on that point "because I do not think that the lessee in this case had either knowledge or notice such as to make his acceptance of the lease a dealing not in good faith with the lessor."

Here Kay, LJ, sitting in the Court of Appeal with Lindley LJ and Bowen LJ, seems to me to treat it as self-evident that a person dealing with a life tenant without knowing that he was a life tenant would be entitled to rely on section 110 of the Settled Land Act 1925; and, with the greatest respect for the decision in *Weston* v *Henshaw* [1950] Ch 510, that is the conclusion to which I would come independently of authority. There is, in the section, no express provision limiting its benefit to a purchaser who knows that the person with whom he is dealing is a tenant for life. On its face it reads as free of limitation and as applicable to a person without such knowledge as to a person who has it. There is a limitation, namely, that the purchaser must act in good faith; but that limitation reads as applicable to a purchaser with such knowledge as without. So, despite the insertion of the limitation of good faith on the part of the purchaser, there is no insertion of the limitation for which the landlords contend. Thus my conclusion is that section 110 applies whether or not the purchaser knows that the other party to the transaction is tenant for life.

That disposes of the first question.

The second question is whether the landlords have shown absence of good faith, within the meaning of section 110 (1) of the Settled Land Act 1925 on the part of the tenants. The landlords have rightly disavowed any suggestion of dishonesty on the part of the tenants. Quite clearly there was none whatsoever. It is submitted that the tenants knew, in 1960, that the £475 rent provided for in the option was less than was or would be obtainable under a lease in the terms of the option lease. I am, however, satisfied that this is not so for reasons which, I trust, will sufficiently appear from my consideration of question 3 (b) when I deal with the quantum of rent. However, assuming that the landlords' submission so far is correct, they then, on that footing, suggest that it follows that the tenants were not dealing in good faith. But the tenants did not know that the life tenant was a life tenant, and thought that he was absolute owner. Therefore even if they thought that the option rent was or would be less than would be obtainable under a lease on the terms of the option lease, that would clearly not establish any lack of good faith on their part; and if, contrary to my view, knowledge that they were dealing with a person who was tenant for life was required to bring the tenants within section 110 (1) of the Settled Land Act 1925, then they were not within it and this question does not arise at all.

Questions
1. Which do you think is the better decision, *Weston* v *Henshaw* or *Re Morgan's Lease*?
2. Is the decision in *Weston* v *Henshaw* in line with the policy of the 1925 legislation?

J: TERMINATION OF A SETTLEMENT

Settled Land Act 1925

3. Duration of settlements
Land not held upon trust for sale which has been subject to a settlement shall be deemed for the purposes of this Act to remain and be settled land, and the settlement shall be deemed to be a subsisting settlement for the purposes of this Act so long as—
 (a) any limitation, charge, or power of charging under the settlement subsists, or is capable of being exercised; or
 (b) the person who, if of full age, would be entitled as beneficial owner to have that land vested in him for a legal estate is an infant.

Note
See also s. 110(2), at page 266.

K: SETTLEMENTS AND REGISTERED LAND

Where a settlement is made of registered land, the settled land is registered in the name of the estate owner and the beneficial interests are minor interests.

Land Registration Act 1925

49. Rules to provide for notices of other rights, interests and claims
(2) A notice shall not be registered in respect of any estate, right, or interest which (independently of this Act) is capable of being overridden by the proprietor under a trust for sale or the powers of the Settled Land Act 1925, or any other statute, or of a settlement, and of being protected by a restriction in the prescribed manner:

Provided that notice of such an estate right or interest may be lodged pending the appointment of trustees of a disposition on trust for sale or a settlement, and if so lodged, shall be cancelled if and when the appointment is made and the proper restriction (if any) is entered.

74. Notice of trust not to affect registered dealing
Subject to the provisions of this Act as to settled land, neither the registrar nor any person dealing with a registered estate or charge shall be affected with notice of a trust express implied or constructive, and references to trusts shall, so far as possible, be excluded from the register.

86. Registration of settled land
(1) Settled land shall be registered in the name of the tenant for life or statutory owner.
(2) [See chapter 3, page 68.]
(3) There shall also be entered on the register such restrictions as may be prescribed, or may be expedient, for the protection of the rights of the persons beneficially interested in the land, and such restrictions shall (subject to the provisions of this Act relating to releases by the trustees of a settlement and to transfers by a tenant for life whose estate has ceased in his lifetime) be binding on the proprietor during his life, but shall not restrain or otherwise affect a disposition by his personal representative.
(5) References in this Act to the "tenant for life" shall, where the context admits, be read as referring to the tenant for life, statutory owner, or personal representative who is entitled to be registered.

SECTION 3: TRUSTS FOR SALE

A: DEFINITION

Law of Property Act 1925

205. General definitions
(xxix) "Trust for sale," in relation to land, means an immediate binding trust for sale, whether or not exercisable at the request or with the consent of any person, and

with or without a power at discretion to postpone the sale; "trustees for sale" mean the persons (including a personal representative) holding land on trust for sale; and "power to postpone a sale" means power to postpone in the exercise of a discretion;

Note
The terms 'trust for sale', 'immediate' and 'binding' need to be examined.

(a) Trust for sale
There is no trust for sale unless there is a duty imposed on the trustees *to sell* the property and not merely a power to sell it. An examination of the terms of the document purporting to create the trust for sale will determine this question, with one exception — the Law of Property Act 1925, s. 25(4).

Law of Property Act 1925

25. Power to postpone sale
(4) Where a disposition or settlement coming into operation after the commencement of this Act contains a trust either to retain or sell land the same shall be construed as a trust to sell the land with power to postpone the sale.

Note
If the settlor does not impose a duty on the trustee to sell but merely imposes a power of sale, the trustees become trustees under the Settled Land Act 1925 and the land becomes settled land (Settled Land Act 1925, ss. 30(1)(i) and 109, at pages 256–7).

Settled Land Act 1925

108. Saving for and exercise of other powers
(1) Nothing in this Act shall take away, abridge, or prejudicially affect any power for the time being subsisting under a settlement, or by statute or otherwise, exercisable by a tenant for life, or (save as hereinafter provided) by trustees with his consent, or on his request, or by his direction, or otherwise, and the powers given by this Act are cumulative.

(2) In case of conflict between the provisions of a settlement and the provisions of this Act, relative to any matter in respect whereof the tenant for life or statutory owner exercises or contracts or intends to exercise any power under this Act, the provisions of this Act shall prevail; and, notwithstanding anything in the settlement, any power (not being merely a power of revocation or appointment) relating to the settled land thereby conferred on the trustees of the settlement or other persons exercisable for any purpose, whether or not provided for in this Act, shall, after the commencement of this Act, be exercisable by the tenant for life or statutory owner as if it were an additional power conferred on the tenant for life within the next following section of this Act and not otherwise.

(3) If a question arises or a doubt is entertained respecting any matter within this section, the tenant for life or statutory owner, or the trustees of the settlement, or any other person interested, under the settlement may apply to the court for its decision thereon, and the court may make such order respecting the matter as the court thinks fit.

(b) Immediate

This means that the trust for sale must take effect immediately not at a future date. For example, a gift of Blackacre to Harry when he attains the age of 25 creates a strict settlement, not a trust for sale.

In Re Herklots' Will Trusts
[1964] 1 WLR 583 (ChD)

The testatrix provided that the residue of her estate should be held on trust for sale, with a subsequent direction that the income of the residue be given to G for life and that G be permitted to reside in the house during her life for as long as she wished. The plaintiff was given a share in the residue after G's death. The testatrix later executed a codicil directing her trustees to 'transfer to the [plaintiff] absolutely if he desires it my house aforesaid in part settlement of the one third share to which he may in due course become entitled under' the will. G and a co-trustee proposed to sell the house as tenant for life. The plaintiff sought an injunction to prevent the sale, claiming that it was subject to a trust for sale. Held: the house was held on trust for sale with a prohibition against sale in G's lifetime without the plaintiff's consent.

(c) Binding

There has been some uncertainty as to the meaning of the term 'binding'. In its primary sense it clearly emphasises the mandatory nature of the trustees' obligation to sell the land in a trust for sale (although the date of the sale is ultimately their decision) rather than a mere discretion or power being placed on them to sell the land. The courts, however, have held that the term 'binding' has other meanings.

Re Leigh's Settled Estates (No. 1)
[1926] Ch 852 (ChD)

T was a tenant in tail of settled land which was subject to a jointure rent charge created by a deceased tenant for life in favour of his widow. In 1923, T disentailed. The fee simple was conveyed, subject to the jointure, to trustees upon trust for sale but with power to postpone sale which was not to take place without T's consent. The trustees were to stand possessed of the net proceeds of sale and the rents and profits until sale upon the trusts of a settlement. Under this settlement certain annuities were to be paid to certain beneficiaries out of the income and the balance was to be paid to T. Was the settlement created in 1923 a strict settlement, or was the land held on trust for sale? Held: the land was settled land.

TOMLIN J: The question is what is meant by "an immediate binding trust for sale." Of course an immediate trust for sale is an intelligible conception where immediate is used as distinct from future; a binding trust for sale in its simplest form would be something the opposite of one that was not binding, but it is difficult to suppose that this is the contrast which was intended to be indicated by the use of this phrase. There must be, it seems to me, some significance in the word "binding" here. It is incredible that the word should have no meaning. It has presumably been inserted for some definite purpose, and it is the duty of the Court to attribute to it some intelligible meaning. The expression "unless the land is subject to an immediate binding trust for sale" must I think mean unless the land that is the total subject matter of the settlement is subject to a trust for sale which operates in relation to the whole subject matter of the settlement and is immediately exercisable, although possibly with the limitation, that it is treated as immediately exercisable "whether or not exercisable at the request or with the consent of any person and with or without a power at discretion to postpone the sale." If that be the meaning of the phrase it may well be that, where the subject matter of the settlement is the whole unencumbered fee simple, there is no immediate binding trust for sale so long as there is not a trust for sale which is capable of overriding all charges having under the settlement priority to the trust for sale. In the present case there is no trust for sale capable of overriding all prior charges. The trust for sale under the conveyance of December, 1923, is not capable of overriding the annuity which arose under the will of 1860. It is true that the annuitant entered into a special contract with the trustees of that conveyance that in connection with any sale under the trust for sale she would, if desired, concur to release her annuity, but the trust for sale itself is not a trust for sale which overrides that annuity.

Re Parker's Settled Estates
[1928] Ch 247 (ChD)

A was tenant for life of settled land. In 1901, A married and appointed by deed a jointure rent charge to his wife, if she survived him. A also created a portions charge over the land in favour of the younger children of his marriage. There was only one such child, who was an infant on 1 January 1926. In 1924, A's elder son B disentailed and the land was conveyed to trustees for sale. During A's life the income was payable in various amounts to A, B, A's wife and A's younger children under the terms of a trust deed. Held: the land was settled land under the Settled Land Act 1925.

ROMER J: Now "trust for sale" is defined as meaning, in relation to land, an immediate binding trust for sale whether or not exercisable at the request or with the consent of any person, and it was contended before me that the land is not held upon an immediate binding trust for sale within the meaning which it was said had been given to those words by Tomlin J in *In re Leigh's Settled Estates* [1926] Ch 852. In that case the learned judge came to the conclusion that where the subject-matter of a settlement is the whole unincumbered fee simple, "the land" is not "subject to an immediate binding trust for sale," so long as there is not a trust for sale which is capable of overriding all charges having, under the settlement, priority to the trust for sale. At the time that this decision was given the Law of Property (Amendment) Act, 1926, had not been passed, so that the learned judge was not dealing with sub-s. 7 of s. 1 of the Settled Land Act. He was merely dealing with s. 20, sub-s. 1 (viii.), of the Act. But I feel some little doubt as to whether the learned judge held that "the land" in the case before him was not subject to any trust for sale, inasmuch as the subject-matter of the trust was merely the fee simple subject to the incumbrance, or whether he held that no land can ever be subject to a binding trust for sale, unless the trustees have power to overreach prior equitable interests. If the latter be the real reason of his decision, I find myself, with the greatest respect, unable to follow it. For it means that there cannot be, within the meaning of the Settled Land Act, any trust for sale of land that is subject to equitable interests; unless the trustees have a legal estate and are either two or more individuals approved or appointed by the Court, or the successors in office of such individuals or a trust corporation.

... The conclusion, however, that I come to as a result of a consideration of all the Acts is that the words "trust for sale," when used in reference to land that is subject to a prior equitable interest, are not confined to cases where that equitable interest can be overreached by the trustees. It may be said that in that case no effect is given to the word "binding." But the word may quite conceivably have been inserted to meet a case of a revocable trust for sale such as existed in *In re Goodall's Settlement* [1909] 1 Ch 440, and even if this be not so I should prefer to treat the word as mere surplusage, inserted ex majore cautela, rather than give to it a meaning that would exclude from being trusts for sale innumerable trusts which are indubitably trusts for sale, as that phrase has always been understood by lawyers hitherto, and which would either exclude them without any apparent reason from a very large number of the general provisions of the Acts relating to "trusts for sale," or would necessitate the Court holding that the context required some other meaning to be attributed to that expression.

There is therefore, in my opinion, a trust for sale in the present case affecting the legal estate in fee simple vested in the trustees of the 1924 deed. But is there a trust for sale that brings the present case within the exception to s. 1 of the Settled Land Act introduced by the new sub-s. 7? In my opinion there is not. It is, I think, reasonably clear that that sub-section only applies where "the land" that would otherwise be the subject of a settlement under sub-s. 1 is held upon trust for sale.

Now in *In re Leigh's Settled Estates* [the trust for sale did], however, affect the whole legal estate in the land that was the subject-matter of the alleged settlement; and if "trust for sale" means what I think it does, it may well be that, in view of the subsequent enactment of sub-s. 7 of s. 1, the land was excluded from the definition of settled land, even though the trustees, for the moment, had not power to override the family charge: see as to this the observations of Sargant LJ in *In re Ryder and Steadman's Contract* [1927] 2 Ch 62, 83. For although by virtue of s. 117, sub-s. 1 (ix.), of the Settled Land Act, land includes an interest in land not being an undivided share, it is impossible to read what are commonly called "the curtain" provisions of the Settled Land Act and the Law of Property Act without seeing the importance attached to the possession of the legal estate; and it would, I think, be proper and in accordance with the general spirit of the Acts to regard all cases in which the whole legal estate, that would otherwise be comprised in a settlement, is vested in trustees for sale, as coming within sub-s. 7 of s. 1. But in the present case there is a legal estate in the term of 1000 years which cannot be disposed of under the trust for sale, and which, upon the coming into force of the Law of Property Act, 1925, would seem to have vested in the trustees of the portions term by virtue of para. 3 of Part II of Schedule 1 of that Act. The whole legal estate which is the subject-matter of the settlement is not therefore subjected to a trust for sale, and in my opinion sub-s. 7 has no application to the case.

Re Norton
[1929] 1 Ch 84 (ChD)

ROMER J: The first question that arises upon this summons is whether the compound settlement came to an end on the death of the second Lord Norton. The solution of that question depends upon the answer to be given to the further question whether, on the death of Lord Norton, the land, which previously had been the subject-matter of the settlement, was held upon trust for sale within the meaning of s. 3 of the Settled Land Act, 1925. That section, as amended, says: "Land not held upon trust for sale which has been subject to a settlement shall be deemed for the purposes of this Act to remain and be settled land, and the settlement shall be deemed to be a subsisting settlement for the purposes of this Act so long as: (a) any limitation, charge, or power of charging under the settlement subsists, or is capable of being exercised." It is quite clear from that, that this land remains settled land after the death of the second Lord Norton, unless upon the happening of that event the land became held upon trust for sale. I had occasion recently in the case of *In re Parker's Settled Estates* [1928] Ch 247 to consider the meaning of the phrase "trust for sale" as used in sub-s. 7 of s. 1 of the Settled Land Act, and for reasons that I then gave I came to the conclusion that land was not settled land where the whole legal estate, which would be otherwise subject to a settlement, was held upon trust for sale. But I also came to the conclusion that the land in question there was settled land, because there was outstanding in certain trustees a legal estate in a term of years for securing portions. The whole legal estate subject to the settlement was not therefore held upon trust for sale.

That being so, what I have to consider here is whether, on the death of Lord Norton, the legal estate in the whole subject-matter of the settlement, which undoubtedly had existed up to that date, was thereafter held upon trust for sale. Up to his death he had had the legal estate in fee simple, and that was the legal estate which was the subject of the settlement. On his death it vested in his personal representatives, his special representatives to whom probate had been granted, and was not vested in the trustees for sale. I must accordingly turn to s. 7 of the Act which is the section that provides what is to be done with the legal estate which becomes vested in his personal representatives on the death of a tenant for life, and for the purposes of the present case I need only refer to sub-s. 5, which is in these terms: "If any person of full age becomes absolutely entitled to the settled land (whether beneficially, or as personal representative, or as trustee for sale, or otherwise) free from all limitations, powers, and charges taking effect under the settlement, he shall be entitled to require the trustees of the settlement, personal representatives, or other persons in whom the settled land is vested, to convey the land to him." But the trustees for sale in this case have not become absolutely entitled to the settled land free from all charges taking effect under the settlement. There are certain equitable rent-charges which take effect in priority to the trust for sale. That being so, it appears to me that not only was the whole legal estate the subject-matter of the settlement not held upon trust for sale upon the death of the second Lord Norton, but that the trustees for sale as such had not, and have not now, a right to call for the legal estate. So far, I must, as it seems to me, come to the conclusion that on the death of the second Lord Norton the land did not cease to be settled land, but continued to be settled land and is still settled land.

B: CREATION OF A TRUST FOR SALE

A trust for sale may arise expressly from an act of the parties' on the express wording of the documents, or by means of statute in the following situations:

(a)   Where a person dies intestate.

Administration of Estates Act 1925

33. Trust for sale

(1)   On the death of a person intestate as to any real or personal estate, such estate shall be held by his personal representatives—

(a) as to the real estate upon trust to sell the same; and
(b) as to the personal estate upon trust to call in sell and convert into money such part thereof as may not consist of money,
with power to postpone such sale and conversion for such a period as the personal representatives, without being liable to account, may think proper, and so that any reversionary interest be not sold until it falls into possession, unless the personal representatives see special reason for sale, and so also that, unless required for purposes of administration owing to want of other assets, personal chattels be not sold except for special reason.

(b) Where two or more persons are jointly entitled to the land. See chapter 9.

(c) Where land that is vested in trustees by way of mortgage becomes discharged from the debtor's right of redemption.

Law of Property Act 1925

31. Trust for sale of mortgaged property where right of redemption is barred
(1) Where any property, vested in trustees by way of security, becomes, by virtue of the statutes of limitation, or of an order for foreclosure or otherwise, discharged from the right of redemption, it shall be held by them on trust for sale.

C: THE POWERS OF THE TRUSTEES FOR SALE

(a) Power to postpone sale

Law of Property Act 1925

25. Power to postpone sale
(1) A power to postpone sale shall, in the case of every trust for sale of land, be implied unless a contrary intention appears.
(2) Where there is a power to postpone the sale, then (subject to any express direction to the contrary in the instrument, if any, creating the trust for sale) the trustees for sale shall not be liable in any way for postponing the sale, in the exercise of their discretion, for any indefinite period; nor shall a purchaser of a legal estate be concerned in any case with any directions respecting the postponement of a sale.

Notes
1. In *Re Rooke* [1953] Ch 716, a direction by a testator to his trustees to sell his farm 'as soon as possible after my death' was held to amount to a contrary intention.
2. Since there is a trust and therefore an obligation to sell the land, any trustee or person beneficially entitled can in theory insist on an immediate sale. If the co-trustees refuse to join in the sale, or if any requisite consents cannot be obtained, then an application can be made under s. 30 of the Law of Property Act 1925.
3. It would seem that anyone who has a proprietary right under a trust for sale can apply under s. 30 (see *Stevens* v *Hutchinson* [1953] Ch 299, at p. 305).

Law of Property Act 1925

30. Powers of court where trustees for sale refuse to exercise powers

(1) If the trustees for sale refuse to sell or to exercise any of the powers conferred by either of the last two sections, or any requisite consent cannot be obtained, any person interested may apply to the court for a vesting or other order for giving effect to the proposed transaction or for an order directing the trustees for sale to give effect thereto, and the court may make such order as it thinks fit.

Re Mayo
[1943] Ch 302 (ChD)

One of three trustees holding land on trust for sale asked the court to exercise its discretion under s. 30 when two trustees were not willing to agree a sale.

SIMONDS J: The result of the residuary devise, having regard to the provisions of s. 36 of the Settled Land Act, 1925, was that the property was held on trust for sale, but, superadded to that trust, there is a statutory power of postponement. It appears to me that the judicial discretion conferred by s. 30 of the Law of Property Act, 1925, must be exercised in the same way as the discretion which is exercisable by the court in the case of an instrument containing an express trust for sale. The trust for sale will prevail, unless all three trustees agree in exercising the power to postpone. The principle is established by *In re Roth* (1896) 74 LT 50, and *In re Hilton* [1909] 2 Ch 548. Here there is no suggestion of mala fides on the part of the testator's son, who claims that the sale should not be postponed. If that were established, the position would be different, but in the present case I think that the son is reasonable in asking for the property to be sold.

Note
The court will not order a sale if such an order would defeat the object of the trust.

Re Buchanan-Wollaston's Conveyance [1939] Ch 738 (ChD)

Four neighbours purchased a piece of land which was conveyed to them as joint tenants, and entered into a deed of covenant by which they agreed to preserve the land as an open space. One of the parties, having sold his house, wanted the land to be sold contrary to the wishes of the other. Held:

(1) The conveyance created a trust for sale.
(2) The court would not compel immediate execution of the trust as the object of the trust was expressed in the deed of covenant and that object was still alive.

Note
See chapter 9 for a further discussion of s. 30.

(b) Consent and consultation

Law of Property Act 1925

26. Consents to the execution of a trust for sale
(1) If the consent of more than two persons is by the disposition made requisite to the execution of a trust for sale of land, then, in favour of a purchaser, the consent of any two of such persons to the execution of the trust or to the exercise of any statutory or other powers vested in the trustees for sale shall be deemed sufficient.
(2) Where the person whose consent to the execution of any such trust or power is expressed to be required in a disposition is not sui juris or becomes subject to disability, his consent shall not, in favour of a purchaser, be deemed to be requisite to the execution of the trust or the exercise of the power; but the trustees shall, in any such case, obtain the separate consent of the parent or testamentary or other guardian of an infant or of the ... receiver (if any) of a person suffering from mental disorder.
(3) Trustees for sale shall so far as practicable consult the persons of full age for the time being beneficially interested in possession in the rents and profits of the land until sale, and shall, so far as consistent with the general interest of the trust, give effect to the wishes of such persons, or, in the case of dispute, of the majority (according to the value of their combined interests) of such persons, but a purchaser shall not be concerned to see that the provisions of this subsection have been complied with.
In the case of a trust for sale, not being a trust for sale created by or in pursuance of the powers conferred by this or any other Act, this subsection shall not apply unless the contrary intention appears in the disposition creating the trust.
(4) This section applies whether the trust for sale is created before or after the commencement or by virtue of this Act.

Notes
1. See *Re Herklots' Will Trusts* at page 273.
2. If the trustees fail to obtain the requisite consents they will be in breach of trust.
3. The effect of s. 26(3) is to curtail the principle established in *Re Mayo*, so that the wishes of the majority of the beneficiaries should guide the trustees unless this is contrary to the general nature of the trust.
4. A problem occurs where the same persons are acting as trustees and beneficiaries and the property is their only home. See *Bull* v *Bull* [1955] 1 QB 234.

(c) Settled Land Act powers

Law of Property Act 1925

28. Powers of management, etc conferred on trustees for sale
(1) Trustees for sale shall, in relation to land or to manorial incidents and to the proceeds of sale, have all the powers of a tenant for life and the trustees of a settlement under the Settled Land Act, 1925, including in relation to the land the powers of management conferred by that Act during a minority: and where by statute settled land is or becomes vested in the trustees of the settlement upon the statutory trusts, such trustees and their successors in office shall also have all the additional or larger powers

(if any) conferred by the settlement on the tenant for life, statutory owner, or trustees of the settlement and (subject to any express trust to the contrary) all capital money arising under the said powers shall, unless paid or applied for any purpose authorised by the Settled Land Act, 1925, be applicable in the same manner as if the money represented proceeds of sale arising under the trust for sale.

All land acquired under this subsection shall be conveyed to the trustees on trust for sale.

The powers conferred by this subsection shall be exercised with such consents (if any) as would have been required on a sale under the trust for sale, and when exercised shall operate to overreach any equitable interests or powers which are by virtue of this Act or otherwise made to attach to the net proceeds of sale as if created by a trust affecting those proceeds.

(2) Subject to any direction to the contrary in the disposition on trust for sale or in the settlement of the proceeds of sale, the net rents and profits of the land until sale, after keeping down costs of repairs and insurance and other outgoings shall be paid or applied, except so far as any part thereof may be liable to be set aside as capital money under the Settled Land Act, 1925, in like manner as the income of investments representing the purchase money would be payable or applicable if a sale had been made and the proceeds had been duly invested.

Note

The powers of the tenant for life under the Settled Land Act 1925 cannot be curtailed by any provision inserted in the settlement (see page xxx). It should be noted there is no such corresponding provision in trusts for sale limiting the powers of the trustees for sale.

(d) Delegation

Law of Property Act 1925

29. Delegation of powers of management by trustees for sale

(1) The powers of and incidental to leasing, accepting surrenders of leases and management, conferred on trustees for sale whether by this Act or otherwise, may, until sale of the land, be revocably delegated from time to time, by writing, signed by them, to any person of full age (not being merely an annuitant) for the time being beneficially entitled in possession to the net rents and profits of the land during his life or for any less period: and in favour of a lessee such writing shall, unless the contrary appears, be sufficient evidence that the person named therein is a person to whom the powers may be delegated, and the production of such writing shall, unless the contrary appears, be sufficient evidence that the delegation has not been revoked.

(2) Any power so delegated shall be exercised only in the names and on behalf of the trustees delegating the power.

(3) The persons delegating any power under this section shall not, in relation to the exercise or purported exercise of the power, be liable for the acts or defaults of the person to whom the power is delegated, but that person shall, in relation to the exercise of the power by him, be deemed to be in the position and to have the duties and liabilities of a trustee.

(4) Where, at the commencement of this Act, an order made under section seven of the Settled Land Act, 1884, is in force, the person on whom any power is thereby conferred shall, while the order remains in force, exercise such power in the names and

on behalf of the trustees for sale in like manner as if the power had been delegated to him under this section.

D: RE-INVESTMENT IN LAND

Re Wakeman [1945] Ch 177

The trustees for sale wanted to invest the proceds of the sale of some land in the purchase of other land. The will gave the trustees power to invest it in any investments authorised by the law. The land sold was the only land in the residuary estate. Held: there was no land capable of being the subject matter of the testator's will and therefore there was no trust for sale. Section 205(1)(xxix) of the Law of Property Act 1925 defines trustees for sale as being persons who are holding *land* on trust for sale.

Re Wellsted's Will Trusts [1949] Ch 296

The trustees for sale wanted to invest the proceeds of sale of land and other investments in the purchase of land. The Court of Appeal held that where the trustees for sale retain some land then they may invest the proceeds of sale of land provided such proceeds can be traced, in the purchase of further land. Cohen LJ reserved judgment on whether *Re Wakeman* had been correctly decided.

E: REGISTERED LAND AND TRUSTS FOR SALE

Land Registration Act 1925

94. Land held on trust for sale
(1) Where registered land is subject to a trust for sale, express or implied, whether or not there is power to postpone the sale, the land shall be registered in the names of the trustees for sale.
(2) Where an order, obtained under section seven of the Settled Land Act 1884, is in force at the commencement of this Act, the person authorised by the order to exercise any of the powers conferred by the Settled Land Act 1925, may, in the names and on behalf of the proprietors, do all such acts and things under this Act as may be requisite for giving effect on the register to the powers authorised to be exercised in like manners as if such person were registered as proprietor of the land, and a copy of the order shall be filed at the registry.
(3) Where, by virtue of any statute, registered land is made subject to a trust for sale, the trustees for sale (unless already registered) shall be registered as proprietors thereof, and shall in the prescribed manner apply for registration accordingly, and no fee shall be charged in respect of such registration or consequential alteration of the register, but this subsection has effect subject to the provisions of this Act relating to the registration of the Public Trustee and the removal of an undivided share from the register before the title to the entirety of the land is registered.

95. Restriction on number of trustees
The statutory restrictions affecting the number of persons entitled to hold land on trust for sale and the number of trustees of a settlement apply to registered land.

Note
The interests of the beneficiaries are minor interests whether or not a restriction has been entered on the title, and a purchaser who complies with the restriction can take the land free of the beneficial interests.

SECTION 4: OVERREACHING — STRICT SETTLEMENTS AND TRUSTS FOR SALE

Provided that certain conditions are met, a purchaser of land will take it free from certain interests that subsist in relation to it, irrespective of whether or not he has notice of them. The owner of such an interest will cease to have an interest in the land itself but will instead have a corresponding right to the purchase money (compare rights that are void for want of registration or unenforceable against a purchaser without notice where the owner's interest becomes valueless).

A conveyance to a purchaser of a legal estate for money or money's worth will overreach *certain* legal interests in the land and any equitable interest or power affecting the land, irrespective of whether or not the purchaser has notice of it, in the following situations:

(a) where the conveyance is made under the Settled Land Act 1925; or
(b) where the conveyance is made by trustees for sale; or
(c) where the conveyance is made by a mortgagee or a personal representative in the exercise of his powers; or
(d) where the conveyance is made under an order of the court; and

in all four cases above, provided that the capital money arising from the transaction is paid, in the case of a strict settlement or a trust for sale, to at least two trustees or a trust corporation, in the case of a conveyance made by a mortgagee or a personal representative, or in the case of a conveyance made under a court order then in accordance with the court order.

Settled Land Act 1925

72. Completion of transactions by conveyance
(1) On a sale, exchange, lease, mortgage, charge, or other disposition, the tenant for life may, as regards land sold, given in exchange, leased, mortgaged, charged, or otherwise disposed of, or intended so to be, or as regards easements or other rights or privileges sold, given in exchange, leased, mortgaged, or otherwise disposed of, or intended so to be, effect the transaction by deed to the extent of the estate or interest vested or declared to be vested in him by the last or only vesting instrument affecting the settled land or any less estate or interest, in the manner requisite for giving effect to the sale, exchange, lease, mortgage charge, or other disposition, but so that a mortgage shall be effected by the creation of a term of years absolute in the settled land or by charge by way of legal mortgage, and not otherwise.

(2) Such a deed, to the extent and in the manner to and in which it is expressed or intended to operate and can operate under this Act, is effectual to pass the land conveyed, or the easements, rights, privileges or other interests created, discharged from all the limitations, powers, and provisions of the settlement, and from all estates,

interests, and charges subsisting or to arise thereunder, but subject to and with the exception of—
    (i) all legal estates and charges by way of legal mortgage having priority to the settlement; and
    (ii) all legal estates and charges by way of legal mortgage which have been conveyed or created for securing money actually raised at the date of the deed; and
    (iii) all leases and grants at fee-farm rents or otherwise, and all grants of easements, rights of common, or other rights or privileges which—
        (a) were before the date of the deed granted or made for value in money or money's worth, or agreed so to be, by the tenant for life or statutory owner, or by any of his predecessors in title, or any trustees for them, under the settlement, or under any statutory power, or are at that date otherwise binding on the successors in title of the tenant for life or statutory owner; and
        (b) are at the date of the deed protected by registration under the Land Charges Act, 1925 [now Land Charges Act 1972], if capable of registration thereunder.
    (3) Notwithstanding registration under the Land Charges Act, 1925 [now Land Charges Act 1972], of—
    (a) an annuity within the meaning of Part II of that Act;
    (b) a limited owner's charge or a general equitable charge within the meaning of that Act;
a disposition under this Act operates to overreach such annuity or charge which shall, according to its priority, take effect as if limited by the settlement.

Notes

1. There is not a general power to overreach the rights of persons who are not the beneficiaries under the settlement, and s. 72(2) lists the interests that are not capable of being overreached.
2. Section 72(3) outlines those rights that arise prior to the settlement that are capable of being overreached.

A: OVERREACHING IN A TRUST FOR SALE

Law of Property Act 1925

2. Conveyances overreaching certain equitable interests and powers
    (1) A conveyance to a purchaser of a legal estate in land shall overreach any equitable interest or power affecting that estate, whether or not he has notice thereof, if—
    (i) the conveyance is made under the powers conferred by the Settled Land Act, 1925, or any additional powers conferred by a settlement, and the equitable interest or power is capable of being overreached thereby, and the statutory requirements respecting the payment of capital money arising under the settlement are complied with;
    (iii) the conveyance is made by a mortgagee or personal representative in the exercise of his paramount powers, and the equitable interest or power is capable of being overreached by such conveyance, and any capital money arising from the transaction is paid to the mortgagee or personal representative;
    (iv) the conveyance is made under an order of the court and the equitable interest or power is bound by such order, and any capital money arising from the transaction is paid into, or in accordance with the order of, the court.

(2) Where the legal estate affected is subject to a trust for sale, then if at the date of a conveyance made after the commencement of this Act under the trust for sale or the powers conferred on the trustees for sale, the trustees (whether original or substituted) are either—

    (a) two or more individuals approved or appointed by the court or the successors in office of the individuals so approved or appointed; or

    (b) a trust corporation,

any equitable interest or power having priority to the trust for sale shall, notwithstanding any stipulation to the contrary, be overreached by the conveyance, and shall, according to its priority, take effect as if created or arising by means of a primary trust affecting the proceeds of sale and the income of the land until sale.

(3) The following equitable interests and powers are excepted from the operation of subsection (2) of this section, namely—

    (i) Any equitable interest protected by a deposit of documents relating to the legal estate affected;

    (ii) The benefit of any covenant or agreement restrictive of the user of land;

    (iii) Any easement, liberty, or privilege over or affecting land and being merely an equitable interest (in this Act referred to as an "equitable easement");

    (iv) The benefit of any contract (in this Act referred to as an "estate contract") to convey or create a legal estate, including a contract conferring either expressly or by statutory implication a valid option to purchase, a right of pre-emption, or any other like right;

    (v) Any equitable interest protected by registration under the Land Charges Act, 1925 [now the Land Charges Act 1972], other than—

        (a) an annuity within the meaning of Part II of that Act;

        (b) a limited owner's charge or a general equitable charge within the meaning of that Act.

(4) Subject to the protection afforded by this section to the purchaser of a legal estate, nothing contained in this section shall deprive a person entitled to an equitable charge of any of his rights or remedies for enforcing the same.

(5) So far as regards the following interests, created before the commencement of this Act (which accordingly are not within the provisions of the Land Charges Act, 1925 [now the Land Charges Act 1972]), namely—

    (a) the benefit of any covenant or agreement restrictive of the user of the land;

    (b) any equitable easement;

    (c) the interest under a puisne mortgage within the meaning of the Land Charges Act, 1925 [now the Land Charges Act 1972], unless and until acquired under a transfer made after the commencement of this Act;

    (d) the benefit of an estate contract, unless and until the same is acquired under a conveyance made after the commencement of this Act;

a purchaser of a legal estate shall only take subject thereto if he has notice thereof, and the same are not overreached under the provisions contained or in the manner referred to in this section.

27. Purchaser not to be concerned with the trusts of the proceeds of sale which are to be paid to two or more trustees or to a trust corporation

(1) A purchaser of a legal estate from trustees for sale shall not be concerned with the trusts affecting the proceeds of sale of land subject to a trust for sale (whether made to attach to such proceeds by virtue of this Act or otherwise), or affecting the rents and profits of the land until sale, whether or not those trusts are declared by the same instrument by which the trust for sale is created.

(2) Notwithstanding anything to the contrary in the instrument (if any) creating a

trust for sale of land or in the settlement of the net proceeds, the proceeds of sale or other capital money shall not be paid to or applied by the direction of fewer than two persons as trustees for sale, except where the trustee is a trust corporation, but this subsection does not affect the right of a sole personal representative as such to give valid receipts for, or direct the application of, proceeds of sale or other capital money, nor, except where capital money arises on the transaction, render it necessary to have more than one trustee.

Notes
1. It is somewhat anomalous to say that the doctrine of overreaching applies in the case of a trust for sale, for a trust for sale is subject to the equitable doctrine of conversion. Generally the doctrine of conversion arises where there is a binding obligation to exchange one type of property (for example, realty in the case of a trust for sale) for another (personalty in a trust for sale). Under the doctrine of conversion the property to be exchanged is treated as if it were the property for which it is to be exchanged, as from the time the obligation becomes binding. Conversion operates in the course of a trust for sale because in a trust for sale, there is a *binding obligation* placed on the trustees to sell the property, i.e. a *duty* to sell. There is a maxim in equity which says that equity regards done that which ought to be done, and therefore equity regards the trustees as if they have sold the property and are holding the proceeds of sale for the beneficiaries. In a trust for sale there is conversion from the moment that the instrument creating the trust comes into effect, so that land held on trust for sale is deemed to be *personalty even though it is unsold*. (See Section 5, *post*.)
2. What is the effect of non-compliance with s. 27? Where an interest is not overreachable in unregistered land the old doctrine of notice applies. This can be illustrated by the case of *Caunce* v *Caunce* [1969] 1 WLR 286 (see chapter 2). In registered land, if the beneficiary's interest is a minor interest then the purchaser would have notice of it because it would have been entered as a restriction on the register, and therefore the purchaser should insist on the appointment of a second trustee. However, if the beneficiary's interest is an overriding interest and s. 27 is not complied with, then the purchaser will be bound by the beneficiary's interest. (See *Williams & Glyn's Bank* v *Boland* in chapter 3.) If money is paid to two trustees, however, then the overreaching machinery will take effect (see *City of London Building Society* v *Flegg* in chapter 3).

B: OVERREACHING IN AD HOC SETTLEMENTS AND TRUSTS FOR SALE

An ad hoc settlement or trust for sale is one where there are 'guaranteed trustees'. By this we mean that either the trustees are appointed by the court, or there is a trust corporation acting as the trustee of the settlement or trust for sale. In such a case equitable rights having priority to the settlement or trust for sale are overreached with the exception of:

(a) equitable interests protected by the deposit of documents relating to the legal estate affected;
(b) restrictive covenants;
(c) equitable easements;
(d) estate contracts;
(e) equitable interests protected by registration under the Land Charges Act 1972 other than:
   (i) annuities,
   (ii) a limited owner's charge,
   (iii) general equitable charges.

Questions
1. In what circumstances can there be a 'single trustee for sale'?
2. Can such a trustee ever pass to the purchaser a title that is free from the beneficial interests:

(a) if the title is unregistered;
(b) if the title is registered?

SECTION 5: NATURE OF A BENEFICIARY'S INTEREST UNDER A TRUST FOR SALE

See A. E. Boyle, 'Trusts for sale and the doctrine of conversion' [1981] Conv 108; M. P. Thompson, 'Dispositions by trustees for sale' [1988] Conv 108; M. J. Pritchard, 'Trusts for sale — the nature of the beneficiary's interest' [1971] CLJ 44; Humphrey Forrest, 'Trusts for sale and co-ownership: a case for reform' [1978] Conv 194; Stephen Cretney, 'A technical and tricky matter' (1971) 34 MLR 441.

The trustees' duty to sell the land in a trust for sale causes the doctrine of conversion to operate so that the beneficiaries' interests are, from the date of conversion of the trust for sale, in capital money and not land.

In *Irani Finance Ltd* v *Singh* [1971] Ch 59, Cross LJ said (at p. 80):

The whole purpose of the trust for sale is to make sure, by shifting the equitable interests away from the land and into the proceeds of sale, that a purchaser of the land takes free from the equitable interests. To hold these to be equitable interests in the land itself would be to frustrate this purpose. Even to hold that they have equitable interests in the land for a limited period, namely, until the land is sold, would, we think, be inconsistent with the trust for sale being an "immediate" trust for sale working an immediate conversion, which is what the Law of Property Act, 1925, envisages (see section 205 (1) (xxix)), though, of course, it is not in fact only such a limited interest that the plaintiffs are seeking to charge.

The problem in this area occurs because many statutes refer to 'land' and not the proceeds of sale of land. Therefore, the question is whether 'land' includes a beneficiary's interest under a trust for sale for the purposes of various statutes. Professor Cretney, however, points out ((1971) 34 MLR 441):

A beneficiary under a trust for sale of land can be said to have an interest in the land itself at least in the following ways. (1) He may, with the concurrence of the other beneficiaries, compel the transfer of the land to himself [*Saunders* v *Vautier* (1841) 4 Beav 115; *cf.* the trustees' power to partition land held on trust for tenants in common: s. 28 (3) of the Law of Property Act 1925]. (2) If the trust is imposed by law, he has a right to be consulted by the trustees as to the exercise of their powers over the land; they are obliged to give effect to the beneficiaries' wishes [Law of Property Act 1925, s. 26 (3), which applies only to trusts imposed by statute: Law of Property Amendment Act 1926, Sched. It could be argued that this shows legislative recognition of the need to distinguish between cases where the trust for sale should be regarded as machinery, on the one hand, and those where it has been expressly chosen, when its logical consequences may be implemented]. (3) Even if some of the trustees wish to execute the trust (rather than use their power to postpone sale) the court may refuse to permit this (contrary to the general principle that even a minority may compel the execution of an imperative obligation) [*Re Mayo* [1943] Ch 302: *cf. Re 90 Thornhill Rd, Tolworth, Surrey* [1970] Ch 261] if some particular purpose for which the land was acquired still subsists, or it would be inequitable to do so [*Re Buchanan-Wollaston's Conveyance* [1989] Ch 738; *Re Hyde's Conveyance* [1952] noted in LJ 58; *Bedson* v *Bedson* [1965] 2 QB 666; *Rawlings* v *Rawlings* [1964] P 398]. (4) For purposes of construction, although a devise of "all my freehold and copyhold land" is inapt to carry an interest under a trust for sale [*Re Kempthorne* [1930] 1 Ch 268] yet a gift of a "share and interest" in land has been held to suffice [*Re Newman* [1930] 2 Ch 409, see particularly *per* Farwell J at p. 414; and see also *Re Warren* [1932] 1 Ch 32].

It is thus chimerical to suppose that a single "correct" answer can be given to the problem whether the benficiary's interest is or is not an "interest in land": in some ways it is, in others it is not. It is submitted that the right approach is therefore to ask for what purposes the land has been subjected to the trust, and what is the policy of the legislation under which the question arises.

In the following case a beneficial interest under a trust for sale for the purposes of the Law of Property Act 1925, s. 40 was examined.

Cooper v *Critchley*
[1955] Ch 431 (CA)

P and D held the fee simple of some premises on trust for sale as joint tenants on trust for themselves in equal shares. The premises were leased to a company which operated from there. P and D were the only directors and shareholders of the company. P negotiated with D for the sale of P's interest in the premises and the company to D. P alleged that there was an agreement for sale and sought specific performance. A draft contract had been drawn up but never signed. D denied that the various written and oral negotiations had given rise to a binding contract. Held: there was no enforceable agreement for sale as the parties had never reached the stage of a concluded contract.

JENKINS LJ: . . . [F]or certain purposes of disposition and devolution, the proceeds of sale to arise under a trust for sale of land are by virtue of the equitable doctrine of conversion to be considered as personalty, but the question in this case is whether, for the purposes of section 40 of the Law of Property Act, 1925, an interest in the proceeds which arise under a trust for sale of land is an interest in land within the meaning of that section. [Jenkins LJ then discusses the cases of *In re Fox* [1913] 2 Ch 75 and *In re Witham* [1922] 2 Ch 413 and continues:]

There is thus authority — not, it is true, relating to this particular Act — for the proposition that in Acts of Parliament the expression "interest in land" may include an interest in the proceeds of sale of land; and I would be disposed, with little hesitation, to give the words a similar meaning in section 40 of the Law of Property Act, 1925, were it not for the definition of land contained in section 205 (1) (ix) of the Law of Property Act, 1925, which states: "'Land' includes land of any tenure" — there follows a long enumeration of particulars ending with "an easement, right, privilege, or benefit in, over, or derived from land; but not an undivided share in land." One may also refer to paragraph (x), which provides: "'Legal estates' mean the estates, interests and charges, in or over land (subsisting or created at law) which are by this Act authorized to subsist or to be created as legal estates; 'equitable interests' mean all the other interests and charges in or over land or in the proceeds of sale thereof; an equitable interest 'capable of subsisting as a legal estate' means such as could validly subsist or be created as a legal estate under this Act."

The definition of land in section 205 (1) (ix) of this Act does, in so many words, exclude an undivided share in land; but that does not, to my mind, conclude the matter. The interest here in question is not an undivided share in land: it is a right to a share of the proceeds to arise from a sale of land, and paragraph (ix) does not say that such a right is not an interest in land, while paragraph (x) classes together as "equitable interests" interests in land or the proceeds of sale thereof. Moreover, the definitions in section 205 of the Act of 1925 are assigned subject to the qualification "unless the context otherwise requires." Section 40 of the Act of 1925, as is well known, replaced section 4 of the Statute of Frauds, and there is to my mind little doubt that, before the Law of Property Act, 1925, an interest in the proceeds to arise from a sale of land would, notwithstanding the equitable doctrine of conversion, have ranked as an interest in land for the purposes of section 4 of the old statute. I am reluctant to construe section 40 of the Act of 1925 as altering the law in this respect.

Accordingly, I would be disposed to hold that a share in the proceeds to arise from a sale of land is an interest in land within the meaning of section 40. But if I am wrong in my inclination to accept the proposition in these general terms, I think that in a case such as this, where the transaction to which the contract relates is a sale by one to the other of two legal joint tenants of land, each of whom is beneficially entitled to one-half of the proceeds to arise from its sale, and who, moreover, are joint lessors under a lease to which the property is subject, and by virtue of the transaction the purchaser will acquire, subject to and with the benefit of the lease, the whole estate, legal and beneficial, in the entirety of the land, the contract cannot well be regarded as anything else than a contract for the sale of an interest in land and, were it necessary for us to do so, I would so hold.

Note

In *Elias* v *Mitchell* the beneficial interest for the purpose of s. 54(1) of the Land Registration Act 1925 was examined.

Elias v *Mitchell*
[1972] Ch 652 (ChD)

The plaintiff and first defendant were partners. The partnership deed contained a provision that the parties would hold the property of the business on trust for the partners in equal shares. The freehold property owned by the business was registered in the name of the first defendant as sole proprietor. The partnership ended in August 1970. In October 1970, the first defendant transferred the property to the second defendant who had no notice of the partnership. Before the second defendant applied for registration of the transfer, the plaintiff lodged a caution against dealings with the property under s. 54 of the Land Registration Act 1925. Held: for the purposes of the Land Registration Act 1925 the plaintiff, as a tenant in common under a trust for sale, had an interest in the proceeds of sale of land which constituted a 'minor interest' within the definition in s. 3(xv).

PENNYCUICK V-C: I will first consider this matter apart from authority. When one reads the definition of "minor interests" in section 3 (xv) it seems to me perfectly clear that although what is defined is simply "minor interests," that is intended as a definition of minor interests in land. The opening words "interests not capable of being disposed of or created by registered dispositions and capable of being overridden . . . by the proprietors unless protected as provided by this Act . . ." relate straight back to section 2 (1): ". . . all other interests in registered land . . . shall take effect in equity as minor interests. . ." Reading those two subsections together it seems to me clear that the entire subject matter of the definition of "minor interests" consists of interests in land. Then one finds in section 3 (xv) (a) that interests under a trust for sale are expressly included among minor interests; and it follows that those particular interests under a trust for sale are treated, for the purpose of this Act, as being minor interests in land.

Then one comes to section 54 (1): "Any person interested . . . howsoever, in any land . . . may lodge a caution. . ." If it is right to say that an interest in the proceeds of sale being by definition a minor interest is, within the intendment of this Act, an interest in land, then there is no doubt that a person interested in the proceeds of sale is a person interested in land for the purpose of section 54 (1) and can accordingly lodge a caution. If there were any doubt on this point, it would, I think, be set at rest by section 101 (3) which provides that minor interests may be protected by entry on the register of cautions. So that subsection in terms provides that minor interests, which by definition include interests under a trust for sale, may be protected by entry on the register, and that means that such interests are interests in land within the scope of section 54. . . .

It seems to me that the general principle to be applied in this connection is, if I may say so, correctly set out in the obiter statement made by Jenkins LJ in *Cooper* v *Critchley* [1955] Ch 431, 439. One must look at the particular Act and see whether in the context of that particular Act an expression such as "interest in land" is or is not apt to cover an interest in the proceeds of sale of land. I do not find anything in the other authorities which I have cited which leads me to a different conclusion from that which I have expressed on the construction of the relevant sections of the Land Registration Act viewed in the context of that Act.

Note
In the case of *Williams & Glyn's Bank* v *Boland* [1981] AC 487, the nature of a beneficial interest under a trust for sale for the purpose of the Land Registration Act 1925, s. 70(1)(g) was examined. See chapter 3, pages 72–3.

Irani Finance Ltd v *Singh*
[1971] Ch 59 (CA)

The first and second defendants held registered land as legal and equitable joint tenants under a trust for sale. There was a mortgage over the property which was subsequently assigned to the third defendant. The plaintiff was owed money by the first and second defendants and obtained a charging order under s. 35(1) of the Administration of Justice Act 1956 in respect of each of them, charging the land or 'interest in land' of each defendant with payment of the judgment debt. This section provides:

> (1) The High Court and any county court may, for the purpose of enforcing a judgment or order of those courts respectively for the payment of money to a person, by order impose on any such land or interest in land of the debtor as may be specified in the order a charge for securing the payment of any moneys due or to become due under the judgment or order. . . . (3) The Land Charges Act, 1925, and the Land Registration Act, 1925, shall apply in relation to orders under subsection (1) of this section as they apply in relation to other writs or orders affecting land issued or made for the purpose of enforcing judgments, but, save as aforesaid, a charge imposed under the said subsection (1) shall have the like effect and shall be enforceable in the same courts and in the same manner as an equitable charge created by the debtor by writing under his hand: . . .

Held: (approving Buckley J's decision at first instance) a charge against an 'interest in land' could not be made under s. 35 of the Administration of Justice Act 1956 unless that interest was registrable under the Land Charges Act 1925 or the Land Registration Act 1925. The plaintiff's interest could not be charged under s. 35 as the defendants each had only an interest in the proceeds of sale of land, under a trust for sale, not an interest in land.

BUCKLEY J: The case turns upon the proper interpretation to be placed upon the expression "such land or interest in land" in section 35 (1), and it has been strenuously argued on behalf of the plaintiffs in the present case that anyone who has an interest in the proceeds of sale of land which is held upon a trust for sale has, while the land remains unsold, an interest in the land capable of answering those words in section 35 (1). It is no doubt true that, in a sense, a person who has a beneficial interest in property held on trust for sale has an interest in that specific property while it remains unsold. He is at least concerned to see that the trustees do not allow the property to go to waste, that they do not misapply it in any way, and that they perform their fiduciary duties in respect of the subject-matter in a proper way, and those interests are, in one sense at any rate, certainly capable of being described as an interest in the subject-matter of the trust for sale. This sort of question received some consideration by the Court of Appeal in *Cooper* v *Critchley* [1955] Ch 431, CA. . . .

[Buckley J then discusses Jenkins LJ's judgment in *Cooper* v *Critchley*.] The language in which those observations are framed in the judgment of Jenkins LJ, who delivered the leading judgment, makes it clear, I think, that they were obiter dicta not necessary for the decision, which went, as I have said, upon the question of whether or not the parties had reached a concluded bargain. But they are dicta which indicate that in the view of the Court of Appeal references to an "interest in land" may in appropriate circumstances include an interest in the proceeds of sale of land. In the course of his remarks Jenkins LJ referred to a number of authorities indicating such a use of the expression "interest in land."

What I have to consider, in my judgment, is whether in interpreting section 35 of the Act of 1956 it would be right for me to construe the reference in that section to an interest in land in that wide sense, or whether I ought to consider it in some more restricted sense, having regard to the fact that what is referred to is an interest in land — and I emphasise the word "land." The Legislature has for some reason apparently thought it right, over a long period, that this special assistance which is afforded to judgment creditors by way of a charge upon property of the judgment debtor should be restricted to land and should not extend to other types of property, such as stocks and shares, money in the bank, debts due to the judgment creditor, or perhaps a fund in court. Upjohn J, when he was considering section 195 of the 1925 Act, took the view that, although the language of that section differed from the language of the section in the Act of 1838, the intention of the Legislature was in substance to reproduce the earlier law, subject only to such express modifications as were to be found in the section, and I think that I must approach the construction of section 35 of the Act of 1956 with the inclination to suppose that the Legislature did not intend to alter the law further than is made clear by the language of the section.

It is clear from a number of authorities that a charge on the proceeds of sale of land subject to a trust for sale is not registrable under the Land Charges Act, 1925, or under the Land Regisration Act, 1925, and the reference in section 35 (3) of the Act of 1956 to those two Acts supports the view I have just expressed — namely, that it would not be right that I should construe subsection (1) in such a way as to effect a change in the law with regard to the subject-matter of the charging orders, so as to admit of charging orders on proceeds of sale of land held on trust for sale, unless there is some strong and clear indication that that was the intention of the Legislature. To a lawyer the beneficial interest of a person whose interest arises under a trust for sale and is a beneficial interest in the proceeds of sale is not one which is appropriately described as being "an interest in the land," although, as I have indicated, in a non-technical use of language, the beneficiary may be said to have a real interest in the land, or at any rate in the way in which the trustees deal with the land. But he has no estate or interest in the land itself, although he may be entitled to receive the rents and profits so long as the land remains unsold.

In this view I am supported by an unreported decision of Diplock J in *J. Bibby & Sons Ltd* v *Wawrszkowicz* (October 28, 1957). In that case the defendant and his wife held property, which was vested in them, on trust for sale, and in trust for themselves beneficially as tenants in common. A judgment was obtained against the defendant and the master made an order, charging his interest in the land in question under section 35 of the Administration of Justice Act, 1956. The question was whether his interest was an interest in land within the meaning of subsection (1) of that section, and so was a proper subject-matter for a charging order. Diplock J reached the conclusion, following the decisions in *Thomas* v *Cross* (1865) 2 Dr & Sm 423 and *Stevens* v *Hutchinson* [1953] Ch 299, to which I have already referred, that the interest was not such as to form a proper subject-matter of the charging order, and he took the view that he was fortified in that opinion by the references in section 35 (3) to the Land Charges Act, 1925, and the Land Registration Act, 1925. He had been referred to *Cooper* v *Critchley* [1955] Ch 431 which he pointed out related to section 40 of the Law of Property Act, 1925, and which must, he said, be looked at in that context and the history of that legislative provision. Accordingly, he discharged the master's order. That decision, it seems to me, is precisely in point in the present case, and unless I could think that it was clearly mistaken I think I ought to proceed in the present case upon the same reasoning. It is, in fact, the reasoning that commends itself to my own mind. Accordingly, I feel no difficulty in following the decision of Diplock J in *J. Bibby*

& Sons Ltd v Wawrszkowicz which leads me to the conclusion that neither of the first and second defendants had at the relevant times any such interest in 11 Cambridge Road as could be the subject of an effective charging order under section 35 of the Act of 1956.

It is said that the third defendants, not being parties to those proceedings, would have no locus standi to get those charging orders set aside and that the third defendants cannot challenge the charging orders. The third defendants do not seek to dispute that the charging orders have been made. What they contend is that having regard to the facts of the case the charging orders were ineffective to create any equitable charge on the defendants' interests in the property, which is the subject-matter with which I am concerned, that is to say, 11 Cambridge Road, or its proceeds of sale, and consequently that the orders do not create any such interest in the plaintiffs as to entitle the plaintiffs to redeem the third defendants' mortgage.

In my judgment those contentions are sound and in the circumstances I reach the conclusion that the plaintiffs fail on this application.

Cedar Holdings Ltd v *Green*
[1981] Ch 129 (CA)

The defendants were married and the matrimonial home was registered in their joint names. The defendants divorced and the former husband, and another woman who pretended to be his wife together executed a legal charge of the property in the plaintiff's favour. The plaintiffs later found out about the fraud and brought proceedings seeking, *inter alia* a declaration that the former husband had charged to the plaintiffs all his beneficial interest in the house under the trust for sale. The former wife counter-claimed and sought a declaration that the house was not subject to any charge. Held: the property expressed to be charged was land, and the beneficial interests in the proceeds of sale of the land held on the statutory trusts for sale was not an interest in that land within the meaning of s. 63(1) of the Law of Property Act 1925.

BUCKLEY LJ: In section 63 we are concerned with the expression "interest in the property conveyed or expressed or intended so to be." This, as it seems to me, focuses attention upon the particular subject matter conveyed or expressed or intended to be conveyed. If, as in the present case, that subject matter is land it would seem to me a strong thing to construe the word "interest" in such a way as to make a conveyance effectual to pass property which is not land in any sense.

The device of the statutory trust for sale in respect of property vested in co-owners must have been very prominent in the minds of those who framed the 1925 property legislation. Had they intended the Law of Property Act 1925 section 63, to have a different kind of operation from that which the Conveyancing Act 1881, section 63, had been designed to achieve, I would certainly have expected some indication of this fact in section 63. Instead, section 63 of the Act of 1881 was left intact by the amending Act (Law of Property Act 1922) and was consolidated without any change in its language into the Act of 1925. In my judgment, upon the true construction of section 63 a beneficial interest in the proceeds of sale of land held upon the statutory trusts is not an interest in that land within the meaning of the section and a conveyance of that land is not effectual to pass a beneficial interest in the proceeds of sale. It follows that, in my judgment, in the present case the legal charge executed by the first defendant was not effectual to charge his beneficial interest in the proceeds of sale of 12 Preston Road.

Questions
1. Can it be said with certainty whether a beneficiary under a trust for sale has an interest in land or an interest in the proceeds of sale of land?
2. What are the reasons for the court's decisions in *Cooper* v *Critchley*, *Elias* v *Mitchell* and *Irani Finance* v *Singh* and *Cedar Holdings* v *Green*?

9 CO-OWNERSHIP OF LAND

SECTION 1: INTRODUCTION

Co-ownership of land arises whenever two or more persons hold an interest in land at the same time, i.e., whenever there is concurrent ownership of land. There are two different kinds of co-ownership in English law, the joint tenancy and the tenancy in common.

Law of Property Act 1925

34. Effect of future dispositions to tenants in common

(1) An undivided share in land shall not be capable of being created except as provided by the Settled Land Act, 1925, or as hereinafter mentioned.

(2) Where, after the commencement of this Act, land is expressed to be conveyed to any persons in undivided shares and those persons are of full age, the conveyance shall (notwithstanding anything to the contrary in this Act) operate as if the land had been expressed to be conveyed to the grantees, or, if there are more than four grantees, to the four first named in the conveyance, as joint tenants upon the statutory trusts hereinafter mentioned and so as to give effect to the rights of the persons who would have been entitled to the shares had the conveyance operated to create those shares:

Provided that, where the conveyance is made by way of mortgage the land shall vest in the grantees or such four of them as aforesaid for a term of years absolute (as provided by this Act) as joint tenants subject to cesser on redemption in like manner as if the mortgage money had belonged to them on a joint account, but without prejudice to the beneficial interests in the mortgage money and interest.

(3) A devise bequest or testamentary appointment, coming into operation after the commencement of this Act, of land to two or more persons in undivided shares shall operate as a devise bequest or appointment of the land to the trustees (if any) of the will for the purposes of the Settled Land Act, 1925, or, if there are no such trustees, then to the personal representatives of the testator, and in each case (but without prejudice to the rights and powers of the personal representatives for purposes of administration) upon the statutory trusts hereinafter mentioned.

Co-ownership of Land

(4) Any disposition purporting to make a settlement of an undivided share in land shall only operate as a settlement of a corresponding share of the net proceeds of sale and of the rents and profits until sale of the entirety of the land.

35. Meaning of the statutory trusts

For the purposes of this Act land held upon the "statutory trusts" shall be held upon the trusts and subject to the provisions following, namely, upon trust to sell the same and to stand possessed of the net proceeds of sale, after payment of costs, and of the net rents and profits until sale after payment of rates, taxes, costs of insurance, repairs, and other outgoings, upon such trusts, and subject to such powers and provisions, as may be requisite for giving effect to the rights of the persons (including an incumbrancer of a former undivided share or whose incumbrance is not secured by a legal mortgage) interested in the land and the right of a person who, if the land had not been made subject to a trust for sale by virtue of this Act, would have been entitled to an entailed interest in an undivided share in the land, shall be deemed to be a right to a corresponding entailed interest in the net proceeds of sale attributable to that share.

Where—
   (a) an undivided share was subject to a settlement, and
   (b) the settlement remains subsisting in respect of other property, and
   (c) the trustees thereof are not the same persons as the trustees for sale,

then the statutory trusts include a trust for the trustees for sale to pay the proper proportion of the net proceeds of sale or other capital money attributable to the share to the trustees of the settlement to be held by them as capital money arising under the Settled Land Act, 1925.

36. Joint tenancies

(1) Where a legal estate (not being settled land) is beneficially limited to or held in trust for any persons as joint tenants, the same shall be held on trust for sale, in like manner as if the persons beneficially entitled were tenants in common, but not so as to sever their joint tenancy in equity.

(2) No severance of a joint tenancy of a legal estate, so as to create a tenancy in common in land, shall be permissible, whether by operation of law or otherwise, but this subsection does not affect the right of a joint tenant to release his interest to the other joint tenants, or the right to sever a joint tenancy in an equitable interest whether or not the legal estate is vested in the joint tenants:

Provided that where a legal estate (not being settled land) is vested in joint tenants beneficially, and any tenant desires to sever the joint tenancy in equity, he shall give to the other joint tenants a notice in writing of such desire or do such other acts or things as would, in the case of personal estate, have been effectual to sever the tenancy in equity, and thereupon under the trust for sale affecting the land the net proceeds of sale, and the net rents and profits until sale, shall be held upon the trusts which would have been requisite for giving effect to the beneficial interests if there had been an actual severance.

Nothing in this Act affects the right of a survivor of joint tenants, who is solely and beneficially interested, to deal with his legal estate as if it were not held on trust for sale.

(3) Without prejudice to the right of a joint tenant to release his interest to the other joint tenants no severance of a mortgage term or trust estate, so as to create a tenancy in common, shall be permissible.

Settled Land Act 1925

36. Undivided shares to take effect behind a trust for sale of the land

(1) If and when, after the commencement of this Act, settled land is held in trust for persons entitled in possession under a trust instrument in undivided shares, the

trustees of the settlement (if the settled land is not already vested in them) may require the estate owner in whom the settled land is vested (but in the case of a personal representative subject to his rights and powers for purposes of administration), at the cost of the trust estate, to convey the land to them, or assent to the land vesting in them as joint tenants, and in the meantime the land shall be held on the same trusts as would have been applicable thereto if it had been so conveyed to or vested in the trustees.

(2) If and when the settled land so held in trust in undivided shares is or becomes vested in the trustees of the settlement, the land shall be held by them (subject to any incumbrances affecting the settled land which are secured by a legal mortgage, but freed from any incumbrances affecting the undivided shares or not secured as aforesaid, and from any interests, powers and charges subsisting under the trust instrument which have priority to the trust for the persons entitled to the undivided shares) upon the statutory trusts.

(3) If the state owner refuses or neglects for one month after demand in writing to convey the settled land so held in trust in undivided shares in manner aforesaid, or if by reason of his being outside the United Kingdom or being unable to be found, or by reason of the dissolution of a corporation, or for any other reason, the court is satisfied that the conveyance cannot otherwise be made, or cannot be made without undue delay or expense, the court may, on the application of the trustees of the settlement, make an order vesting the settled land in them on the statutory trusts.

(4) An undivided share in land shall not be capable of being created except under a trust instrument or under the Law of Property Act, 1925, and shall then only take effect behind a trust for sale.

(5) Nothing in this section affects the priority inter se of any incumbrances whether affecting the entirety of the land or an undivided share.

(6) For the purposes of this section land held upon the statutory trusts shall be held upon the trusts and subject to the provisions following, namely, upon trust to sell the same, with power to postpone the sale of the whole or any part thereof, and to stand possessed of the net proceeds of sale, after payment of costs, and of the net rents and profits until sale, after payment of rates, taxes, costs of insurance, repairs, and other outgoings, upon such trusts and subject to such powers and provisions as may be requisite for giving effect to the rights of the persons interested in the settled land, and the right of a person who, if the land had not been made subject to a trust for sale by virtue of this Act, would have been entitled to an entailed interest in an undivided share in the land, shall be deemed to be a right to a corresponding entailed interest in the net proceeds of sale attributable to that share.

(a) Joint tenancy

Here the joint tenants are considered to be a single owner of the whole estate or interest which is subject to the joint tenancy. No single joint tenant holds any specific share in the land but each has a *potential* share equal to that of the other joint tenants. There is unity of possession (which there must be for all forms of co-ownership), title, time and interest. One co-owner cannot, generally, bring an action for trespass against another, unless one co-owner is ousting another by the act complained of.

Generally a co-owner cannot be made to pay rent to another. However, in *Dennis* v *McDonald* [1981] 2 All ER 632 (aff'd [1982] 1 All ER 590 (CA)), F and M were unmarried and lived together with their children. The house had been purchased in their joint names and was held on trust for sale for themselves as tenants in common. F was violent to M and she left the property taking the children with her. F stayed in the house and was later joined by three of the five children of M. M applied under s. 30 of the Law of Property Act 1925 for either an order for the sale of the house, or alternatively, for rent from F to compensate M for being out of occupation. Held: F and M were regarded as trustees for each other and also beneficiaries of the property. M was entitled to compensation from F as she had been ousted and F had exclusive enjoyment of the property: such compensation was consistent with the discharge of the trust and was assessed at half the fair rent for an unfurnished letting.

See Jill Martin, 'A co-owner's liability to pay rent' [1982] Conv 305; Frank Webb, 'Cohabitational homes' [1982] 98 LQR 519.

One of the characteristics of a joint tenancy is the right of survivorship or *jus accrescendi*, which means that on the death of one or more joint tenants their interests will not pass via their estate, but will accrue to the surviving joint tenant or tenants. This continues until only one surviving joint tenant remains and that joint tenant will be solely entitled to the property. Therefore a joint tenant cannot devise the share of his joint tenancy in his will. A joint tenant can, however, 'sever' the joint tenancy and convert it into a tenancy in common during his lifetime, thus avoiding the *jus accrescendi* rule.

There are situations, however, where the right of survivorship does not benefit both joint tenants equally. For example, Blackacre to X and Y during Y's life. If Y dies before X, then Blackacre cannot accrue to X.

(b) Tenancy in common

Here each co-owner owns an individual distinct share in the land. Such shares need not be equal, although the share does not in any way represent any particular piece of land. Each co-owner has a share in all the land and the shares are known as individual shares. The right of survivorship does not apply to a tenancy in common, and therefore each co-owner can effectively dispose of his interest both during his lifetime and on his death.

SECTION 2: POSITION IN LAW AND EQUITY

Since 1925, only one form of co-ownership can exist *at law*, the joint tenancy. The tenancy in common cannot exist at law, only in equity — see Law of Property Act 1925, ss. 1(6) and 34(1). Therefore, there can be no tenancy in common of a legal estate, only of the equitable interest, and in such a case the legal estate is held on a joint tenancy. For example, in a conveyance of Blackacre to A, B and C as tenants in common, the legal estate in Blackacre will be held by A, B and C as *joint tenants* and the equitable interest will be held by A, B and C as tenants in common. In a conveyance of Blackacre to A, B and C as joint tenants however, the legal estate in Blackacre will be held by A, B and C as joint tenants, and the equitable interest will be also held by A, B and C as joint tenants.

The effect of subjecting concurrent ownership to a trust for sale is that the co-owners hold the property as trustees for themselves on trust for sale as beneficiaries. Therefore the co-owners will hold the legal estate as trustees for themselves as beneficiaries whether or not the equitable estate is subject to a joint tenancy or a tenancy in common. The fact that all forms of co-ownership must exist behind the trust for sale means that the doctrine of conversion applies (see pages 282 *et seq.*).

The object of the 1925 legislation was to subject all forms of concurrent ownership to a trust for sale, except for joint owners taking as tenants for life where the land remains settled land (Settled Land Act 1925, s. 19(2)).

Do tenancies in common that arise by means of an implied, resulting or constructive trust come within the 1925 legislation, and are they subjected to a trust for sale?

Bull v *Bull*
[1955] 1 QB 234 (CA)

P purchased a house with his mother which was conveyed into P's sole name. Contributions to the purchase money were unequal, with P paying the greater share. P later married and arranged that his mother would occupy two rooms, P and his wife occupying the other rooms. The parties then fell into dispute and P gave his mother notice to quit. Held:

(1) The mother was an equitable tenant in common and entitled, concurrently with P, to possession of the premises until the house was sold.

(2) The property was subject to a *statutory trust for sale* (per curiam) and P could not sell it without his mother's consent or an order of the court.

DENNING LJ: The son is, of course, the legal owner of the house; but the mother and son are, I think, equitable tenants in common. Each is entitled in equity to an undivided share in the house, the share of each being in proportion to his or her respective contribution. The rights of equitable tenants in common as between themselves have never, so far as I know, been defined; but there is plenty of authority about the rights of legal owners in common. Each of them is entitled to the possession of the land and to the use and enjoyment of it in a proper manner. Neither can turn out the other; but if one of them should take more than his proper share the injured party can bring an action for an account. If one of them should go so far as to oust the other he is guilty of a trespass: see *Jacobs* v *Seward* (1872) LR 5 HL 464. Such being the rights of legal tenants in common, I think that the rights of equitable tenants in common are the same, save only for such differences as are necessarily consequent on the interest being equitable and not legal. It is well known that equity follows the law; and it does so in these cases about tenants in common as in others.

In support of this view I would refer to the words used by Sir Joseph Jekyll MR over 200 years ago in *Cowper* v *Cowper* (1734) 2 P Wms 753: "The law is clear, and courts of equity ought to follow it in their judgments concerning titles to equitable estates; otherwise great uncertainty and confusion would ensue." I realize that since 1925 there has been no such thing as a legal tenancy in common: see section 1(6) of the Law of Property Act, 1925. All tenancies in common now are equitable only and they take effect behind a trust for sale: see section 36(4) of the Settled Land Act, 1925. Nevertheless, until a sale takes place these equitable tenants in common have the same right to enjoy the land as legal tenants used to have. Their position was well stated by Maugham J in *In re Warren* [1932] 1 Ch 32, 47. "There is no doubt that, since the coming into force of the Law of Property Act, 1925, the position of undivided owners is different from what it was before. That Act, for the purpose of simplifying the law, has introduced provisions for undivided shares, and has made petition actions unnecessary and obsolete. But in substance the beneficial interests of the undivided owners in regard to enjoyment so long as the land remains unsold have not been altered, and it is true to say that the ordinary layman possessed of an undivided share in land would be quite unaware of any alteration in his rights as the result of the Act."

My conclusion, therefore, is that, when there are two equitable tenants in common, then, until the place is sold, each of them is entitled concurrently with the other to the possession of the land and to the use and enjoyment of it in a proper manner; and that neither of them is entitled to turn out the other.

The question may be asked: What is to happen when the two fall out, as they have done here? The answer is that the house must then be sold and the proceeds divided between mother and son in the proper proportions. The son is the legal owner and he holds it on the statutory trusts for sale. He cannot at the present moment sell the house because he cannot give a valid receipt for the proceeds. It needs two trustees to give a receipt: see section 14 of the Trustee Act, 1925. The son could get over this difficulty by appointing another trustee (under section 36(6) of the Trustee Act, 1925) who would agree with him to sell the house. The two trustees would no doubt have to consider the mother's wishes, but as the son appears to have made the greater contribution he could in theory override her wishes about a sale: see section 26(3) of the Law of Property Act, 1925. The difficulty of the two trustees would be a practical difficulty because, so long as the mother is there, they could not sell with vacant possession.

The mother is entitled to rely on her equitable interest as tenant in common, which is preserved by two sections of the Law of Property Act, 1925. The first is section 14 which provides that the Act "shall not prejudicially affect the interest of any person in possession or in actual occupation of land to which he may be entitled in right of such possession or occupation." The second is section 35 which says that the trust for sale is subject to such provisions as may be requisite for giving effect to the rights of the persons interested in the land. The mother here is in possession and in actual occupation as equitable co-owner and by virtue of that interest she could not be turned out by the trustees except with her consent. In this situation if the trustees wished to sell with vacant possession the only thing they could do would be to apply to the court under section 30 of the Law of Property Act, 1925, on the ground that the mother's consent could not be obtained. The court could then make such order as it thought fit and this would include, I think, an order to turn the mother out if it was right and proper for such an order to be made: compare *In re Buchanan-Wollaston's Conveyance* [1939] Ch 738 and *In re Hyde's Conveyance* (1952) LJN 58.

Questions
1. Would the position be different if there was a joint tenancy arising by means of an implied, resulting or constructive trust?
2. What is the problem of conveying land to co-owners, one of whom is a minor? Does it make a difference if the co-ownership is a joint tenancy or a tenancy in common?

Note
See F. R. Crane, '*Bull* v *Bull*' (1955) 19 Conv 146.

Trustee Act 1925

34. Limitation of the number of trustees

(2) In the case of settlements and dispositions on trust for sale of land made or coming into operation after the commencement of this Act—

  (a) the number of trustees thereof shall not in any case exceed four, and where more than four persons are named as such trustees, the four first named (who are able and willing to act) shall alone be the trustees, and the other persons named shall not be trustees unless appointed on the occurrence of a vacancy;

  (b) the number of the trustees shall not be increased beyond four.

Note
See also Law of Property Act 1925, s. 34(2), at page 294.

If the correct method of a conveyance upon a trust for sale is not employed, then there are several provisions in the Law of Property Act 1925 designed to ensure that the effect of the transaction is the same as if a tenancy in common had been effectively limited under a trust for sale:

  (a) the Law of Property Act 1925, s. 34(2);
  (b) the Law of Property Act 1925, s. 34(3);
  (c) the Law of Property Act 1925, s. 42.

Law of Property Act 1925

42. Provisions as to contracts

(6) Any contract to convey an undivided share in land made before or after the commencement of this Act, shall be deemed to be sufficiently complied with by the conveyance of a corresponding share in the proceeds of sale of the land in like manner as if the contract had been to convey that corresponding share.

SECTION 3: CREATION OF A JOINT TENANCY

In order for there to be a joint tenancy, the so-called 'four unities' must be present — time, title, possession and interest.

  (a) *Unity of time* Each of the interests of the co-owner must vest at the same time.

  (b) *Unity of title* Each co-owner must claim title under the same document or act.

  (c) *Unity of possession* Each co-owner is equally entitled to possession of the whole land and can sue if excluded from a particular part.

  (d) *Unity of interest* The interest of each co-owner must be identified. Each interest must be the same in its duration, extent and nature.

If there is no unity of possession, then there is no co-ownership; if one of the other unities is missing there may be a tenancy in common, but not a joint tenancy. However, even if the four unities are present there may still not be a joint tenancy if words of severance are used. Words of severance are words which indicate that the parties are to be regarded as having separate shares in the property. Words which have been held to be words of severance are:

'equally' (*Lewen* v *Dodd* (1595) Cro Eliz 443);
'in equal shares' (*Payne* v *Webb* (1874) LR 19 Eq 26);
'between' (*Lashbrook* v *Cock* (1816) 2 Mer 70);
'to be divided between' (*Peat* v *Chapman* (1750) 1 Ves Sen 542);
'share and share alike' (*Heathe* v *Heathe* (1740) 2 Atk 121).

Question
A conveyance contained the following addendum: 'To hold in fee simple as beneficial joint tenants in common equal shares.' What is the effect of such words?

See Vinelott J in *Joyce* v *Barker Bros (Builders) Ltd* (1980) 40 P & CR 512 and Millett J in *Martin* v *Martin* (1987) 54 P & CR 238.

Note
In certain circumstances a rebuttable equitable presumption arises that a tenancy in common has been created. (This presumption overrides the common-law presumption which favours a joint tenancy.) The equitable presumption arises in the following situations:

(a) When the purchase money provided for the property by the co-owners was provided by those persons in unequal shares. In such a situation the legal estate will be held by the owners as joint tenants on trust for themselves as tenant in common in such proportions as they contributed. See *Bull* v *Bull*, at page 298. Such a presumption can, of course, be rebutted by evidence to the contrary.

(b) Where two or more persons advance money on a mortgage, whether in equal or unequal shares.

(c) Where land is partnership property. See *Barton* v *Morris* [1985] 2 All ER 1032, at page 310.

(d) Where joint purchasers of the land used it for their individual business purposes.

Malayan Credit Ltd v *Jack Chia – MPH Ltd* [1986] AC 549 (PC)

A and R took a five year lease of some office space which they agreed to use and pay for in the proportions of 62 per cent 38 per cent respectively. They were invoiced separately and paid rent, survey fees etc. pro rata. The parties fell into dispute and R applied for an order for the sale of the lease and equal division of the net proceeds or, alternatively an order for an equal partition of the premises. The lease did not contain any words of severance and therefore A and R were joint tenants at law, but the question before the court was how it was held in equity. Held: it was possible to have unequal beneficial interests where the legal estate was held by joint tenants and the case did not fall into any of the usual three categories, viz unequal contributors to the purchase price, co-mortgagees or partners. Where circumstances are sufficient to show that the beneficial interest was intended to be held by the parties as tenants in common such as in this case then equity will give effect to that intention.

SECTION 4: SEVERANCE OF A JOINT TENANCY

A joint tenant who wishes his property to pass to another person (other than the joint tenant or tenants) can achieve such a result by converting the joint tenancy into a tenancy in common during his lifetime, but not by his will on death. Thus severance of a joint tenancy, if there are two joint tenants, only takes effect in equity, converting the equitable joint tenancy into a tenancy in common, while at law the joint tenancy remains. The joint tenant who is severing will take an equal portion of the interest as a tenant in common.

The position is somewhat different if there are more than two joint tenants. If one of the joint tenants severs a joint tenancy where there are, say, three joint tenants, then the effect is that the three remain joint tenants at law holding the equitable interest on trust for the unsevering co-owners as joint tenants and the severing co-owners as tenant in common.

There are various ways in which severance can be effected.

(a) Notice in writing
See the Law of Property Act 1925, s. 36(2).

Law of Property Act 1925

196. Regulations respecting notices
(4) Any notice required or authorised by this Act to be served shall also be sufficiently served, if it is sent by post in a registered letter addressed to the lessee, lessor, mortgagee, mortgagor, or other person to be served, by name, at the aforesaid place of abode or business, office, or counting-house, and if that letter is not returned through the post office undelivered; and that service shall be deemed to be made at the time at which the registered letter would in the ordinary course be delivered.

Re 88 Berkeley Road, London, NW9 [1971] Ch 648

P and D were joint tenants of their home, both at law and in equity. D decided to sever the joint tenancy and her solicitors sent a notice of severance to P by recorded delivery. The letter arrived whilst P was away from the house and was accepted by D himself. P never acknowledged receipt of the letter and claimed she never received it. Held: even though P had never received the letter, the provisions of s. 196(4) set out the conditions under which notices under the 1925 Act were deemed to have been served, including notices of severance under s. 36(2). The notice of severance, sent by recorded delivery to P's address, was sufficient notice under s. 36(2) to sever the joint tenancy not withstanding the fact that it had not been received by P herself. P was therefore not entitled to D's half-share of the property by survivorship.

In Re Draper's Conveyance
[1969] 1 Ch 486 (ChD)

A husband (H) and wife (W) were joint tenants at law and in equity of a house. W commenced divorce proceedings and, between obtaining a decree nisi and the pronouncement of a decree absolute, W issued a summons under s. 17 of the Married Women's Property Act 1882 seeking the sale of the house and the division of the proceeds of sale in accordance with the parties' interests in the property. W obtained an order accordingly but the house was still unsold and H was still in occupation when he died intestate. Held: the summons under s. 17 of the Married Women's Property Act 1882, coupled with the affidavit in support of it, severed the beneficial joint tenancy during the husband's lifetime.

PLOWMAN J: Mr Cooke, as I say, puts it in two ways: first, he submits that the wife's conduct was such as to effect a severance of the joint tenancy, and in relation to that matter he relies on the summons of February 11, 1966, in the Probate, Divorce and Admiralty Division, coupled with the orders which were made by that court, coupled with the plaintiff's solicitor's letter of June 7, 1966. And he says, either as a result of those three matters or as a result of any of them, the joint tenancy became severed by conduct, and he referred me to the decision of Havers J in *Hawkesley* v *May* [1956] 1 QB 304. The part of that case which is relevant for present purposes depends upon these facts, which I read from the headnote [1936] 1 QB 304, 305: "A settled fund was held by trustees upon trusts under which on attaining the age of 21 the plaintiff and his younger sister became absolutely entitled as joint tenants." The question was whether that joint tenancy had become severed, and Havers J said [1956] 1 QB 304, 313:

> The joint tenancy was capable of being severed by the plaintiff on attaining the age of 21. There are a number of ways by which a joint tenancy may be severed. In *Williams* v *Hensman* (1861) 1 J & H 546, Page Wood V-C, in the course of his judgment, said, Ibid. 557: 'A joint-tenancy may be severed in three ways: in the first place, an act of any one of the persons interested operating upon his own share may create a severance as to that share. The right of each joint-tenant is a right by survivorship only in the event of no severance having taken place of the share which is claimed under the jus accrescendi. Each one is at liberty to dispose of his own interest in such manner as to sever it from the joint fund — losing, of course, at the same time, his own right of survivorship. Secondly, a joint-tenancy may be severed by mutual agreement. And, in the third place, there may be a severance by any course of dealing sufficient to intimate that the interests of all were mutually treated as constituting a tenancy in common. When the severance depends on an inference of this kind without any express act of severance, it will not suffice to rely on an intention, with respect to the particular share, declared only behind the backs of the other persons interested.'

Havers J continued [1956] 1 QB 304, 313:

> The first method indicated, namely, an act of any one of the persons interested operating upon his own share, obviously includes a declaration of intention to sever by one party.

Then, after referring to *Walmsley* v *Foxhall* (1870) 40 LJ Ch 28 he said [1956] 1 QB 304, 314:

This being the state of the authorities, I hold that on the plaintiff attaining the age of 21 he was entitled to the income of his share of the fund. As regards the severance, I hold that when the sister wrote the letter dated March 18, 1942, in which she said: 'Thank you for your letter of 17th instant with the particulars of the investments. I should like the dividends to be paid into my account at Martins Bank, 208 Kensington High Street' (which was a letter in reply to the first defendant) that was a sufficient act on her part to constitute a severance of the joint tenancy. If I am wrong about that, there clearly was a severance when her share of the trust funds were transferred to her in September, 1942.

So from that case I derive this; a declaration by one of a number of joint tenants of his intention to sever operates as a severance. Mr Cooke also, as I have said, relied upon the notice in writing which under section 36 (2) of the Law of Property Act, 1925, is allowed in the case of a joint tenancy in land, although not in personalty, and he submits that the summons to which I have alrady referred, although not signed, amounted to a notice in writing on the part of the wife that she desired to sever the joint tenancy in equity. I say "although not signed by the wife or by anybody on her behalf" because there is no requirement in the subsection of a signature.

Dealing with the matter there, and ignoring for a moment certain matters which were submitted by Mr McCulloch, it seems to me that Mr Cooke's submissions are right whether they are based on the new provision in section 36 (2) of the Law of Property Act, 1925, or whether they are based on the old law which applied to severing a joint tenancy in the case of a personal estate. It seems to me that that summons, coupled with the affidavit in support of it, clearly evinced an intention on the part of the wife that she wished the property to be sold and the proceeds distributed, a half to her and a half to the husband. And if that is right then it seems to me that that is wholly inconsistent with the notion that a beneficial joint tenancy in that property is to continue, and therefore, apart from these objections to which I will refer in a moment, I feel little doubt that in one way or the other this joint tenancy was severed in equity before the end of February, 1966, as a result of the summons which was served on the husband and as a result of what the wife stated in her affidavit in support of the summons.

But then certain matters were submitted to me by Mr McCulloch on behalf of the wife, which I think fall under two heads. In the first place I was referred to certain observations which were made by Lord Denning MR in *Bedson* v *Bedson* [1965] 2 QB 666. That was a case in which a wife, in September, 1964, applied to the County court under section 17 of the Married Women's Property Act, 1882, for an order that the property together with the fixtures, fittings, car, stock and goodwill be sold, and the proceeds divided between herself and her husband in equal shares. And then the headnote goes on to state that no matrimonial proceedings had at any relevant date been begun.

But Lord Denning in the course of his judgment had certain things to say about the severance of the joint tenancy in the matrimonial home. He said [1965] 2 QB 666, 678: "(3) So long as the house is in the possession of the husband and wife as joint tenants or one of them, there can be no severance of their equitable interests: see section 36 (1) (3)." That is a reference to the Law of Property Act, 1925. "Neither of them can sell his or her equitable interest separately. If he or she could do so, it would mean that the purchaser could insist on going into possession himself — with the other spouse there — which is absurd. It would mean also that one of them could, of his own head, destroy the right of survivorship which was the essence of the joint tenancy. That cannot be correct."

If I may say so, it is not easy to understand what it is in section 36 (1) and (3) of the Law of Property Act, 1925, on which Lord Denning was relying as authority for the proposition that so long as the house is in the possession of the husband and wife as joint tenants or one of them there can be no severance of their equitable interests.

Then Lord Denning MR added [1965] 2 QB 666, 683:

"One further point: I am of opinion that, while the husband is in possession of the house, there can be no severance of the joint tenancy. The wife cannot sell her interest separately. In case I am wrong about this, I think we should make an order restraining the wife from doing so. It would be quite intolerable that she should, for instance, be able to sell her interest to her mother and get her to run him out. The jurisdiction in this behalf is amply covered by *Lee* v *Lee* [1952] 2 QB 489n, which has been approved by the House of Lords."

Mr McCulloch points out that in the present case the husband continued in possession until January of 1967 which was some time after the orders of the Divorce court had been made. However, Russell LJ in the same case took a different view about the severance of beneficial joint tenancies. He said [1965] 2 QB 666, 690:

"I am unable to accept the legal proposition of Lord Denning MR that when husband and wife are joint tenants of the legal estate in the matrimonial home and also beneficial joint tenants in respect of it, neither can, so long as one is in possession, sell his or her beneficial interest therein or otherwise sever the beneficial joint tenancy. The proposition is, I think, without the slightest foundation in law or in equity. If anything, it appears to be an attempt to revive to some extent the long defunct tenancy by entireties which, as I have already remarked, was doomed by the Married Women's Property Act, 1882, itself. It may indeed be that either the wife's claim in this case, or the notation in the business accounts of the husband of her interest has long since operated as a severance.

If I have to choose between those two statements I respectfully express my preference for that of Russell LJ. It is interesting to note that he referred to the possibility that the wife's claim in that case might have operated by itself as a severance, and, as I have already stated, I take the view that in this case the summons issued by the wife in the Divorce Division coupled with the affidavit which she swore in support of that summons did operate to sever her beneficial joint tenancy.

Note
Compare the following case.

Harris v *Goddard*
[1983] 3 All ER 242 (CA)

H and W were married joint tenants in equity of premises that comprised of both residential accommodation and a shop. In 1979, W petitioned for divorce and asked, *inter alia*, 'that such order may be made by way of transfer of property and/or settlement of property and/or variation of settlement in respect of the former matrimonial home . . . and otherwise as maybe just'. H died before the hearing of the petition. The issue was whether the words of the petition severed the joint tenancy under s. 36(2) of the Law of Property Act 1925. Held: the petition did not show an intention to sever the joint tenancy immediately, but was a mere invitation to the court at a future date to consider whether to exercise its jurisdiction or not. Thus there was no severance.

LAWTON LJ: I start with s. 36. It dealt with beneficial joint tenancies, which must mean all joint tenancies, including those held by husbands and wives. The section makes no special provisions by way of giving extra rights or raising presumptions in favour of spouses. When severance is said to arise under s. 36(2), not from the giving of a notice in writing, but from '[doing] . . . other acts or things' which would, in the case of personal estate, have been effectual to sever a joint tenancy in equity, the fact that the parties were married may make the drawing of inferences easier. It is, in my judgment, only in this limited evidential context that the existence of the married state has any relevance. In reaching ths conclusion I have followed what Russell LJ said in *Bedson* v *Bedson* [1965] 3 All ER 307 at 318–319, [1965] 2 QB 666 at 689–690 rather than the obiter statement of Lord Denning MR in the same case (see [1965] 3 All ER 307 at 311, [1965] 2 QB 666 at 677). Lord Denning MR said that spouses holding as beneficial joint tenants cannot sever their interests so as to convert them into tenancies in common. The trial judge seems to have been influenced to some extent by what Lord Denning MR said. Since in this case severance is said to have come about by a notice in writing the sole question is whether that which is said to be the notice did show that Mrs Harris desired to sever the joint tenancy.

In *Williams* v *Hensman* (1861) John & H 546, 70 ER 862 Page Wood V-C said that a joint tenancy could be severed in three ways, that is by disposal of one of the interests, by mutual agreement and 'by any course of dealing sufficient to intimate that the interests of all were mutually treated as constituting a tenancy in common'. The words in s. 36(2) 'do such other acts or things as would . . . have been effectual to sever the tenancy, put into statutory language the other ways of effecting severance to which Page Wood V-C referred in *Williams* v *Hensman*. The words 'and any tenant desires to sever the joint tenancy in equity, he shall give to the other joint tenants a notice in writing of such desire' operate to extend the mutual agreement concept of severance referred to in *Williams* v *Hensman*. Unilateral action to sever a joint tenancy is now possible. Before 1925 severance by unilateral action was only possible when one joint tenant disposed of his interest to a third party. When a notice in writing of a desire to sever is served pursuant to s. 36(2) it takes effect forthwith. It follows that a desire to sever must evince an intention to bring about the wanted result immediately. A notice in writing which expresses a desire to bring about the wanted result at some time in the future is not, in my judgment, a notice in writing within s. 36(2). Further the notice must be one which shows an intent to bring about the consequences set out in s. 36(2), namely that the net proceeds of the statutory trust for sale 'shall be held upon the trust which would have been requisite for giving effect to the beneficial interests if there had been an actual severance'. I am unable to accept the submission of counsel for the plaintiffs that a notice in writing which shows no more than a desire to bring the existing interest to an end is a good notice. It must be a desire to sever which is intended to have the statutory consequences. Paragraph 3 of the prayer of the petition does no more than invite the court to consider at some future time whether to exercise its jurisdiction under s. 24 of the 1973 Act and, if it does, to do so in one or more of three different ways. Orders under s. 24(1)(a) and (b) could bring co-ownership to an end by ways other than by severance. It follows, in my judgment, that para 3 of the prayer of the petition did not operate as a notice in writing to sever the joint tenancy in equity. This tenancy had not been severed when Mr Harris died, with the consequence that Mrs Harris is entitled to the whole of the fund held by the first and second defendants as trustees. I wish to stress that all I am saying is that para 3 in the petition under consideration in this case did not operate as a notice of severance.

Perhaps this case should be a cautionary tale for those who draft divorce petitions when the spouses hold property as joint tenants in equity. The decision of Plowman J in *Re Draper's Conveyance, Nihan* v *Porter* [1967] 3 All ER 853, [1969] 1 Ch 486 is an example of how starting legal proceedings can sever a joint tenancy . . . Plowman J adjudged that the summons and the affidavit together effected a severance during the lifetime of the husband. I agree that it did; but it is not clear from the judgment whether the judge regarded the summons or the affidavit or both as notices in writing or whether the service of the summons and the filing of the affidavit were acts which were effectual to sever the joint tenancy. I do not share the doubts about the correctness of this judgment on this point which Walton J expressed in *Nielson-Jones* v *Fedden* [1974] 3 All ER 38 at 50, [1975] Ch 222 at 236 relying on *Re Wilks, Child* v *Bulmer* [1891] 3 Ch 59. The fact that the wife in *Re Draper's Conveyance* could have withdrawn the summons is a factor which could have been taken into account in deciding whether what was done was effectual to sever the joint tenancy in equity. The weight of that factor would have depended on all the other circumstances and was in that case clearly negligible.

Note
See (1984) 100 LQR 161 (J. M. T.); Stephen Coneys, 'How not to sever a joint tenancy: *Harris* v *Goddard*' [1984] Conv 148.

(b) Alienation of interest
If a joint tenant alienates his interest *inter vivos*, then this will have the effect of the assignee becoming a tenant in common, but the other co-owners, as between themselves, remain joint tenants. See *Re Gorman (a bankrupt)* [1990] 1 WLR 616 where the court held that a joint tenancy could be severed by the bankruptcy of one of two joint tenants. It is at the moment of adjudication of bankruptcy that the property vests in the trustee causing an involuntary alienation which results in the severance of the joint tenancy, *not* at any earlier time such as the presentation of the bankruptcy petition — see *In re Dennis (a Bankrupt)* [1992] 3 WLR 204.

An act of partial alienation is a sufficient act of severance — for example, a mortgage.

Where one joint tenant enters into a contract to settle or sell his share, then this may be a sufficient act of alienation to sever the joint tenancy. See *Burgess* v *Rawnsley*, below.

(c) Forfeiture
If one tenant kills another, then the right of survivorship will not operate since a person is not allowed to benefit from a criminal act.

(d) Acquisition of larger interest by a joint tenant
If a joint tenant acquires an interest which is greater than that of his co-owners, then that destroys the joint tenancy.

(e) Mutual agreement

Burgess v *Rawnsley*
[1975] Ch 429 (CA)

H and D bought a house in their joint names 'as joint tenants' in 1967, and each paid half of the purchase price. D did not move into the property but

H lived there. D agreed orally with H, in 1968, to sell her share to H at a certain price. She then, apparently, changed her mind and refused to sell. H died in 1971. The plaintiff was H's daughter and administratrix and brought an action claiming that there was a resulting trust, or alternatively that the joint tenancy had been severed. Held: the oral agreement for sale was sufficient to sever the beneficial joint tenancy, even though such an agreement could not have been specifically enforced.

LORD DENNING MR: [W]as there a severance of the beneficial joint tenancy? The judge said:

I hold that there has been a severance of the joint tenancy brought about by the conduct of the defendant in asking £750 for her share which was agreed to.

In making that statement the judge made a little slip. She did not ask £750. But it was a slip of no importance. The important finding is that there was an agreement that she would sell her share to him for £750. Almost immediately afterwards she went back upon it. Is that conduct sufficient to effect a severance?

Mr Levy submitted that it was not. He relied on the recent decision of Walton J in *Nielson-Jones* v *Fedden* [1975] Ch 222, given subsequently to the judgment of the judge here. Walton J held that no conduct is sufficient to sever a joint tenancy unless it is irrevocable. Mr Levy said that in the present case the agreement was not in writing. It could not be enforced by specific performance. It was revocable and was in fact revoked by Mrs Rawnsley when she went back on it. So there was, he submitted, no severance.

Walton J founded himself on the decision of Stirling J in *In re Wilks, Child* v *Bulmer* [1891] 3 Ch 59. He criticised *Hawkesley* v *May* [1956] 1 QB 304 and In *re Draper's Conveyance* [1969] 1 Ch 486, and said that they were clearly contrary to the existing well-established law. He went back to *Coke upon Littleton*, 189a, 299b and to *Blackstone's Commentaries*. Those old writers were dealing with legal joint tenancies. *Blackstone* said, 8th ed. (1778), vol. II, pp. 180, 185:

> The properties of a joint estate are derived from its unity, which is fourfold; the unity of interest, the unity of title, the unity of time, and the unity of possession: . . . an estate in joint tenancy may be severed and destroyed . . . by destroying any of its constituent unities.

and he gives instances of how this may be done. Now that is all very well when you are considering how a legal joint tenancy can be severed. But it is of no application today when there can be no severance of a legal joint tenancy; and you are only considering how a beneficial joint tenancy can be severed. The thing to remember today is that equity leans against joint tenants and favours tenancies in common.

Nowadays everyone starts with the judgment of Sir William Page Wood V-C in *Williams* v *Hensman* (1861) 1 John & Hem 546, 557 . . . In that passage Page Wood V-C distinguished between severance "by mutual agreement" and severance by a "course of dealing." That shows that a "course of dealing" need not amount to an agreement, expressed or implied, for severance. It is sufficient if there is a course of dealing in which one party makes clear to the other that he desires that their shares should no longer be held jointly but be held in common. I emphasise that it must be made clear to the other party. That is implicit in the sentence in which Page Wood V-C says:

> "it will not suffice to rely on an intention, with respect to the particular share, declared only behind the backs of the other persons interested."

Similarly it is sufficient if both parties enter on a course of dealing which evinces an intention by both of them that their shares shall henceforth be held in common and not jointly. As appears from the two cases to which Page Wood V-C referred of *Wilson* v *Bell*, 5 Ir Eq R 501 and *Jackson* v *Jackson*, 9 Ves Jun 591.

I come now to the question of notice. Suppose that one party gives a notice in writing to the other saying that he desires to sever the joint tenancy. Is that sufficient to effect a severance? I think it is. It was certainly the view of Sir Benjamin Cherry when he drafted section 36 (2) of the Law of Property Act 1925. . . . The word "other" is most illuminating. It shows quite plainly that, in the case of personal estate one of the things which is effective in equity to sever a joint tenancy is "a notice in writing" of a desire to sever. So also in regard to real estate.

Taking this view, I find myself in agreement with Havers J in *Hawkesley* v *May* [1956] 1 QB 304, 313–314, and of Plowman J in *In re Draper's Conveyance* [1969] 1 Ch 486. I cannot agree with Walton J [1975] Ch 222, 234–235, that those cases were wrongly decided. It would be absurd that there should be a difference between real estate and personal estate in this respect. Suppose real estate is held on a joint tenancy on a trust for sale and is sold and converted into personal property. Before sale, it is severable by notice in writing. It would be ridiculous if it could not be severed afterwards in like manner. I look upon section 36 (2) as declaratory of the law as to severance by notice and not as a new provision confined to real estate. A joint tenancy in personal estate can be severed by notice just as a joint tenancy in real estate.

It remains to consider *Nielson-Jones* v *Fedden* [1975] Ch 222. In my view it was not correctly decided. The husband and wife entered upon a course of dealing sufficient to sever the joint tenancy. They entered into negotiations that the property should be sold. Each received £200 out of the deposit paid by the purchaser. That was sufficient. Furthermore there was disclosed in correspondence a declaration by the husband that he wished to sever the joint tenancy: and this was made clear by the wife. That too was sufficient.

I doubt whether *In re Wilks, Child* v *Bulmer* [1891] 3 Ch 59 can be supported. A young man who had just become 21 applied to the court to have one third of a joint fund paid out to him. He died just before the application was heard. Stirling J held that, if he had died just after, there would have been a severance: but, as he died just before, there was not. Ironically enough too, the delay was not on his side. It was the delay of the court. Nowadays I think it should have been decided differently. The application was a clear declaration of his intention to sever. It was made clear to all concerned. There was enough to effect a severance.

It remains to apply these principles to the present case. I think there was evidence that Mr Honick and Mrs Rawnsley did come to an agreement that he would buy her share for £750. That agreement was not in writing and it was not specifically enforceable. Yet it was sufficient to effect a severance. Even if there was not any firm agreement but only a course of dealing, it clearly evinced an intention by both parties that the property should henceforth be held in common and not jointly.

On these grounds I would dismiss the appeal.

Note

The agreement can be express or implied from the conduct of the parties.

See David Hayton, 'Joint tenancies — severance' [1976] CLJ 20; J. F. Garner, 'Severance of a joint tenancy' (1975) 40 Conv 77.

(f) Course of dealing

In *Burgess* v *Rawnsley* [1975] 1 Ch 429, Sir John Pennycuick said (at p. 447):

[Course of dealing] covers only acts of the parties, including, it seems to me, negotiations which, although not otherwise resulting in any agreement, indicate a common intention that the joint tenancy should be regarded as severed.

... An uncommunicated declaration by one party to the other or indeed a mere verbal notice by one party to another clearly cannot operate as a severance.

Note
There can be severance of a joint tenancy where one joint tenant negotiates with another for some re-arrangement of interest, even if the negotiations break down.

Barton v Morris [1985] 2 All ER 1032 (ChD)

H and W were cohabitees. In August 1979 they bought a property together in their joint names to run as a guest house. The house cost £40,000 and £39,100 was paid for by W by contributing initially to the purchase price and subsequently paying off the mortgage. H contributed the remaining £900. The business was run as an equal partnership, the accounts treated the property as a partnership asset and profits and losses were divided equally. In March 1982, W died intestate. Held: the treatment of the property as a partnership asset in the accounts did not indicate an intention of either H or W to sever the joint tenancy by a course of dealing. The intention at the time of purchase to create a joint tenancy was apparent and there was not evidence to suggest that the parties had changed their intention nor that the interests of each of them were in fact being treated as being a tenancy in common.

Questions
1. Do you think that the commencement of an action concerning the joint tenancy is sufficient to sever it?
2. What did Page Wood V-C mean in *Williams* v *Hensman* (1861) 1 John & H 546 by the term 'mutual conduct'?

SECTION 5: TERMINATION OF CO-OWNERSHIP

Severance converts a joint tenancy into a tenancy in common. Co-ownership can be terminated completely, however, in the following ways:

(a) Partition
Partition has the effect of destroying the unity of possession necessary for co-ownership by allowing the land to be physically divided. See the Law of Property Act 1925, s. 28(3).

(b) Sale of legal estate
If the legal estate is conveyed to a third party, then the co-ownership is destroyed. The purchaser will take the property free of all beneficial interests which are overreached, provided he pays the purchase money to two trustees.

(c) Union in sole ownership

Co-ownership clearly terminates if the estate becomes owned by one joint tenant. This may occur:

(i) On the release by one joint tenant of his interests to another. See Law of Property Act 1925, ss. 36(2) and 72.

(ii) On the survival of the last joint tenant where no severance has been effected in equity.

Section 36(2) of the Law of Property Act 1925 says that nothing affects 'the right of a survivor of joint tenants, who is solely and beneficially interested, to deal with his legal estate as if it were not held on trust for sale.' The problem is that if the survivor tries to sell the property, the purchaser will require proof that none of the deceased joint tenants severed the joint tenancy during their lifetime. The survivor can always appoint a second trustee in order to bring into operation the overreaching machinery.

The Law of Property (Joint Tenants) Act 1964 was passed to remedy this.

Law of Property (Joint Tenants) Act 1964

1. Assumptions on sale of land by survivor of joint tenants

(1) For the purposes of section 36(2) of the Law of Property Act 1925, as amended by section 7 of and the Schedule to the Law of Property (Amendment) Act 1926, the survivor of two or more joint tenants shall, in favour of a purchaser of the legal estate, be deemed to be solely and beneficially interested if he conveys as beneficial owner or the conveyance includes a statement that he is so interested.

Provided that the foregoing provisions of this subsection shall not apply if, at any time before the date of the conveyance by the survivor—

(a) a memorandum of severance (that is to say a note or memorandum signed by the joint tenants or one of them and recording that the joint tenancy was severed in equity on a date therein specified) had been endorsed on or annexed to the conveyance by virtue of which the legal estate was vested in the joint tenants; or

(b) a bankruptcy order made against any of the joint tenants, or a petition for such an order, had been registered under the Land Charges Act 1925 [now the Land Charges Act 1972], being an order or petition of which the purchaser has notice, by virtue of the registration, on the date of the conveyance by the survivor.

(2) The foregoing provisions of this section shall apply with the necessary modifications in relation to a conveyance by the personal representatives of the survivor of joint tenants as they apply in relation to a conveyance by such a survivor.

Note

The Act does not apply to registered land.

For the relationship between co-owners, see pages 296–7.

SECTION 6: LAW OF PROPERTY ACT 1925, s. 30

See R. Schuz, 'Section 30, Law of Property Act 1925 and unmarried cohabitees' (1982) 12 Fam Law 108; M. P. Thompson, 'Cohabitation, co-ownership and section 30' [1984] Conv 103.

...perty is held on a trust for sale, there is a duty on the trustees to ...perty and a mere power to postpone such sale. If the power is to ...ity over the duty, then the trustees must be unanimous in their ... to postpone sale. If one trustee wishes to sell the property, ...onally it has been thought that the land should be sold.

Whenever there is a dispute between the co-owners as to whether the property should be sold, an application can be made to the court under s. 30 of the Law of Property Act 1925. The courts have regarded the legal nature of a trust for sale as imposing a binding obligation on the trustees to sell the property, and thus the recalcitrant trustee would normally be ordered to co-operate and convey the land along with the others (see *Re Mayo* [1983] Ch 302, chapter 8). In *Buchanan-Wollaston's Conveyance* [1939] Ch 738, however, the court decided to look at the underlying purpose of the trust in deciding whether to order a sale or not.

A: THE UNDERLYING PURPOSE TEST

Re Evers's Trust
[1980] 3 All ER 399 (CA)

P and D lived together as man and wife in P's home. They had a child and D's two children from a previous marriage came to live with them also. In 1978, P and D purchased a house as joint tenants. The purchase price was largely funded by a joint mortgage and both P and D contributed substantially though unequally to make up the balance. In 1979, the relationship ended. P left D and the three children in the house. D would not agree to sell the property so P applied to the court for an order under s. 30 of the Law of Property Act 1925. Held: the court said that in 'family' cases, where an application had been made under s. 30 the court had to take into account both the primary purpose of the trust (i.e. sale) and its underlying purpose (i.e. provision of a home) when exercising its discretion. In the circumstances then existing the Court decided to dismiss P's application and leave him to re-apply when the circumstances had changed.

ORMROD LJ: The powers of the court under s. 30 of the Law of Property Act 1925 are different from the powers which it has under s. 24 of the Matrimonial Causes Act 1973; the ambit of the discretion is consequently different. Under s. 24 the court is empowered to make orders between former husbands and wives, 'adjusting' their respective property rights; under s. 30 the court is concerned with the effect to be given to existing property rights, a much more restricted function. Cases arising under s. 24, therefore, are not relevant to cases arising under s. 30, although some of the considerations to be taken into account are common to both classes.

Section 30 of the Law of Property Act 1925 . . . gives the court a discretion to intervene to deal, inter alia, with the situation which arises when the trustees under a trust for sale are unable or unwilling to agree that the property should be sold. In such circumstances, the court can order a sale of the property, and if appropriate impose terms, or it can decline to make an order, leaving the property unsold unless and until the trustees reach agreement or the court makes an order at some future date.

The usual practice in these cases has been to order a sale and a division of the proceeds of sale, thus giving effect to the express purpose of the trust. But the trust for sale has become a very convenient and much used conveyancing technique. Combined with the statutory power in the trustees to postpone the sale, it can be used to meet a variety of situations, in some of which an actual sale is far from the intentions of the parties at the time when the trust for sale comes into existence. So, when asked to exercise its discretionary powers under s. 30 to execute the trust, the court must have regard to its underlying purpose. [Ormrod LJ discusses the facts of *Re Buchanan-Wollaston's Conveyance*:] At first instance Farwell J refused the order, saying ([1939] Ch 217 at 223):

> The question is this: Will the court assist the plaintiff to do an act which would be directly contrary to his contract with the other parties, since it was plainly the intention of the parties to the said contract that the land should not be sold save with the consent of them all?

His decision was upheld in this court, but on a broader basis. Greene MR said ([1939] 2 All ER 302 at 308, [1939] Ch 738 at 747):

> ... it seems to me that the court of equity, when asked to enforce the trust for sale, whether one created by a settlement or a will or one created by the statute, must look into all the circumstances of the case and consider whether or not, at the particular moment and in the particular circumstances when the application is made to it, it is right and proper that such an order shall be made. In considering a question of that kind, in circumstances such as these, the court is bound to look at the contract into which the parties have entered and to ask itself the question whether or not the person applying for execution of the trust for sale is a person whose voice should be allowed to prevail.

Some twenty years later, in *Jones* v *Challenger* [1960] 1 All ER 785 at 787, [1961] 1 QB at 181, Devlin LJ reviewed the authorities and affirmed this principle:

> This simple principle [i.e. that in a trust for sale there is a duty to sell] cannot prevail where the trust itself or the circumstances in which it was made show that there was a secondary or collateral object besides that of sale. Simonds, J in his judgment in *Re Mayo* ([1943] 2 All ER 440, [1943] Ch 302) said that if there were mala fides, the position would be different. If it be not mala fides, it is at any rate wrong and inequitable for one of the parties to the trust to invoke the letter of the trust in order to defeat one of its purposes, whether that purpose be written or unwritten, and the court will not permit it.

In *Jones* v *Challenger* a house had been purchased by a husband and wife jointly as a home. Subsequently the marriage broke down, the wife left and committed adultery and applied to the court for an order for sale of the property, a leasehold with only a few years to run. The husband continued to live in the house on his own; there were no children. In these circumstances the court decided that the house should be sold. Devlin LJ said ([1960] 1 All ER 785 at 789, [1961] 1 QB 176 at 183):

> In the case which we have to consider, the house was acquired as the matrimonial home. That was the purpose of the joint tenancy and, for so long as that purpose was still alive, I think that the right test to be applied would be that in *Re Buchanan-Wollaston*. But with the end of the marriage, that purpose was dissolved and the primacy of the duty to sell was restored.

Had there been children whose home was still in the property, the conclusion in that case might have been different. Later Devlin LJ said ([1960] 1 All ER 785 at 789, [1961] 1 QB 176 at 184): 'The true question is whether it is inequitable for the wife, once the matrimonial home has gone, to want to realise her investment?'

In *Burke* v *Burke* [1974] 2 All ER 944, [1974] 1 WLR 1063, however, children were involved. On the husband's application under s. 17 the registrar ordered a sale, but postponed it for a year or so to give the wife, who had custody of the children, an opportunity to find an alternative home for them. This court upheld the registrar's order. The application was actually made under s. 17 of the Married Women's Property Act 1882. That section is purely procedural and the principles are the same as under s. 30. In giving the leading judgment Buckley LJ took the view that the trust for sale was an immediate binding trust subject to the discretionary power in the court to postpone the execution of the trust for sale, and that the court must have regard to all the relevant circumstances of the case and to the situation of both the beneficial owners. The interests of the children in that case, he thought were ([1974] 2 All ER 944 at 947–948, [1974] 1 WLR 1063 at 1067)—

> interests which are only incidentally to be taken into consideration in that sort of way. They are, as I say, proper to be taken into consideration so far as they affect the equities in the matter as between the two persons entitled to the beneficial interests in the property. But it is not, I think, right to treat this case as though the husband was obliged to make provision for his children by agreeing to retain the property unsold. To do so is, as I think, and as was urged on us by counsel for the husband, to confuse with a problem relating to property, considerations which are relevant to maintenance.

He expressed disagreement with an obiter dictum of Salmon LJ in the earlier case of *Rawlings* v *Rawlings* [1964] 2 All ER 804 at 814, [1964] P 398 at 419 where he said:

> If there were young children the position would be different. One of the purposes of the trust would no doubt have been to provide a home for them, and whilst that purpose still existed, a sale would not generally be ordered.

Buckley LJ was plainly anxious to make it clear that the children themselves in such circumstances were not objects of the trust and, therefore, had no beneficial interests in the property, and so were in that sense only 'incidental' to the problem, but we do not think that Salmon LJ thought otherwise. The court in *Burke* v *Burke* was not referred to the *Buchanan-Wollaston* case, so Buckley LJ does not seem to have considered, in so many words, whether or not the primary purpose of the trust, i.e. for sale, 'the letter of the trust' in the words of Devlin LJ in *Jones* v *Challenger* [1960] 1 All ER 785 at 787, [1961] 1 QB 178 at 181, had been affected by the underlying purpose, quoting Devlin LJ again, 'written or unwritten' of providing a home, not only for the parents but also for the children. The dictum of Salmon LJ appears, therefore, to be more in line with the judgments of this court in the *Buchanan-Wollaston* case and in *Jones* v *Challenger*. Moreover, it is now supported by a dictum of Lord Denning MR in *Williams* v *Williams* [1977] 1 All ER 28 at 30, [1976] Ch 278 at 285: 'The court, in executing the trust, should regard the primary object as being to provide a home and not a sale.'

This approach to the exercise of the discretion given by s. 30 has considerable advantages in these 'family' cases. It enables the court to deal with substance (that is, reality) rather than form (that is, convenience of conveyancing); it brings the exercise of the discretion under this section, so far as possible, into line with the exercise of the discretion given by s. 24 of the Matrimonial Causes Act 1973; and it goes some way to eliminating differences between legitimate and illegitimate children in accordance with present legislative policy (see for example the Family Law Reform Act 1969, Part II).

[Ormrod LJ then discusses the facts of the present case.]

The irresistible inference from these facts is that, as the judge found, they purchased this property as a family home for themselves and the three children. It is difficult to imagine that the mother, then wholly responsible for two children and partly for the third, would have invested nearly all her capital in the purchase of this property if it was not to be available to her as a home for the children for the indefinite future. It is inconceivable that the father, when he agreed to this joint adventure, could have thought otherwise or contemplated the possibility of an early sale without the consent of the mother. The underlying purpose of the trust was, therefore, to provide a home for all five of them for the indefinite future. Unfortunately, the relationship between the father and the mother broke down very soon, and the parties separated at the beginning of August 1979 in circumstances of great bitterness. This is clearly shown by two dates. On 20th July 1979 the mother issued her originating summons in the wardship proceedings, and on 2nd August 1979 the father issued his application under s. 30 for an order for sale of the property.

... Under s. 30 the primary question is whether the court should come to the aid of the applicant at the 'particular moment, and in the particular circumstances when the application is made to it' (*Re Buchanan-Wollaston's Conveyance* [1939] 2 All ER 302 at 308, [1939] Ch 738 at 747). In the present case, at the present moment and in the existing circumstances, it would be wrong to order a sale. But circumstances may change unpredictably. It may not be appropriate to order a sale when the child reaches 16 years, a purely arbitrary date, or it may become appropriate to do so much sooner, for example on the mother's remarriage or on it becoming financially possible for her to buy the father out. In such circumstances it will probably be wiser simply to dismiss the application while indicating the sort of circumstances which would, prima facie, justify a further application. The ensuing uncertainty is unfortunate, but, under this section, the court has no power to adjust property rights or to redraft the terms of the trust. Ideally, the parties should now negotiate a settlement on the basis that neither of them is in a position to dictate terms. We would, therefore, dismiss the father's appeal, but would vary the order to dismiss the application on the mother's undertaking to discharge the liability under the mortgage, to pay the outgoings and maintain the property, and to indemnify the father so long as she is occupying the property.

Note

1. See *Smith* v *Smith and Smith* (1976) 120 SJ 100, where the court ordered a sale of the property where the underlying purpose of the trust had ended.
2. Clearly, much litigation in this area surrounds matrimonial and quasi-matrimonial property where the relationship between the parties has broken down. If the parties are married and the marriage has broken down, then an application can be made under the Matrimonial Causes Act 1973 (as amended by the Matrimonial and Family Proceedings Act 1984) to determine the property rights between the parties. The Act gives the court a wide jurisdiction to order a distribution of the spouses' property. In such a case the court need not have regard to the parties' actual legal or equitable rights. If the parties are unmarried and the relationship breaks down, then they can only rely on s. 30. The test to be applied by the courts in such a situation is the underlying purpose test, but the underlying purpose may itself be unclear.

In *Re Evers' Trusts* the court thought that the underlying purpose was to provide a *family home,* and therefore no sale would be ordered while that purpose was still in existence. However, in the case of *Re Holliday* [1981] Ch

405 (CA), the court thought the purpose of the trust was to provide a *matrimonial home*, and the interests of the children are taken into account only in as far as they affect the equities of the persons entitled to the beneficial interests in the property.

3. The court has no power to adjust the parties' property rights under s. 30, only to give effect to existing property rights.

4. The court may refuse to order a sale if such a sale would be inequitable.

Bedson v *Bedson* [1965] 2 QB 666 (CA)

A husband carried on a draper's business from a property consisting of a shop on the ground floor and living accommodation above. The property was vested in the husband and his wife as joint tenants on trust for sale. The parties separated and the wife sought an order for sale under the Married Women's Property Act 1882 and equal division of the sale proceeds. Held: the wife was not able to insist on the sale of the property as that would defeat the contemplated purposes of providing a matrimonial home and a business through which the husband could provide for himself and his children.

B: INSOLVENCY AND SECTION 30

Charging Orders Act 1979

1. Charging orders

(1) Where, under a judgment or order of the High Court or a county court, a person (the "debtor") is required to pay a sum of money to another person (the "creditor") then, for the purpose of enforcing that judgment or order, the appropriate court may make an order in accordance with the provisions of this Act imposing on any such property of the debtor as may be specified in the order a charge for securing the payment of any money due or to become due under the judgment or order.

(5) In deciding whether to make a charging order the court shall consider all the circumstances of the case and, in particular, any evidence before it as to—

    (a) the personal circumstances of the debtor, and

    (b) whether any other creditor of the debtor would be likely to be unduly prejudiced by the making of the order.

2. Property which may be charged

(1) Subject to subsection (3) below, a charge may be imposed by a charging order only on—

    (a) any interest held by the debtor beneficially—

        (i) in any asset of a kind mentioned in subsection (2) below, or

        (ii) under any trust, or

    (b) any interest held by a person as trustee of a trust ("the trust"), if the interest is in such an asset or is an interest under another trust and—

        (i) the judgment or order in respect of which a charge is to be imposed was made against that person as trustee of the trust, or

        (ii) the whole beneficial interest under the trust is held by the debtor unencumbered and for his own benefit, or

(iii) in a case where there are two or more debtors all of whom are liable to the creditor for the same debt, they together hold the whole beneficial interest under the trust unencumbered and for their own benefit.

(2) The assets referred to in subsection (1) above are—
   (a) land,
   (b) securities of any of the following kinds—
      (i) government stock,
      (ii) stock of any body (other than a building society) incorporated within England and Wales,
      (iii) stock of any body incorporated outside England and Wales or of any state or territory outside the United Kingdom, being stock registered in a register kept at any place within England and Wales,
      (iv) units of any unit trust in respect of which a register of the unit holders is kept at any place within England and Wales, or
   (c) funds in court.

(3) In any case where a charge is imposed by a charging order on any interest in an asset of a kind mentioned in paragraph (b) or (c) of subsection (2) above, the court making the order may provide for the charge to extend to any interest or dividend payable in respect of the asset.

Notes
1. By s. 2 of the Act, the property which may be charged includes a beneficial interest which a debtor may have in land.
2. Such a charge, however, would be equitable only and therefore could be overreached on the sale of the legal estate. Such an interest can be protected by means of the Law of Property Act 1925, s. 137.
3. The effect of a charging order is that the court can appropriate the home to provide security for a debt. The charge has the ancillary effect of conferring an interest in the property on the chargee, and this charge gives the chargee *locus standi* to apply for the sale of the home under s. 30.
   See also the Law of Property Act 1925, s. 137 (chapter 12, pages 476 *et seq.*).
4. With regard to matrimonial property and insolvency, see Catherine Hand, 'Bankruptcy and the family home' [1983] Conv 219; Catherine Hand, 'Bankruptcy: refusal to order a sale of the matrimonial home' (1981) 97 LQR 200; Angela Sydenham, '*Re Holliday* and *Re Evers's Trust*' [1981] Conv 79; Claire Palley, 'Wives, creditors and the matrimonial home' (1969) 20 NILQ 132; Nigel P. Gravells, 'Creditors and the family home: the exercise of discretion' (1985) OLJS 132.

First National Securities v *Hegerty* [1985] QB 850 (CA)

H and W purchased property with the aid of a mortgage. The property was vested in them as joint tenants. Although bought to be a home for H and W and their child when H retired H never lived there. In December 1979, H executed a legal charge on the house in favour of P and emigrated with the money he borrowed on that security. W's signature had been forged in order to obtain this loan, of which she had no knowledge. When the loan repayments fell into arrears P obtained judgment and later a charging order.

W appealed as her application for ancillary relief in divorce proceedings was pending and she sought to have P's application transferred to the Family Division. Held: a charging order could properly be made in favour of P. The court have a discretion and in all the circumstances it was properly exercised.

STEPHENSON LJ: I have, however, come to the conclusion (1) that the court should not use its powers under Part II of the Matrimonial Causes Act 1973 to override the claims of a creditor seeking security for a debt by a charging order; (2) that it should not discharge or vary a charging order so as to prefer a wife's claim to such a creditor's; (3) that it can, and often should, postpone the enforcement of a charging order until the hearing of any application under section 30 of the Law of Property Act 1925, when the court can decide between the competing claims of wife and creditor.

Note
Compare the following case.

Harman v *Glencross* [1986] Fam 81 (CA)

H and W purchased a house in 1970 and it was vested in joint names. The purchase was financed by a mortgage and, when H left the house in 1980, it was also subject to two futher bank charges. W continued to live in the house with the children of the marriage. W started divorce proceedings in January 1981 and sought an order for the transfer of the property into her own name. In May 1981 D, a former business partner of H, obtained judgment against him for moneys owed. In September 1981 D obtained a charging order absolute, but W had had no notice of those proceedings. W applied for the charging order to be varied. The matter was transfered to the family division and the charging order was varied to be subject to any order made in relation to W's ancillary relief claim. Held: W was interested in the property and could properly apply for a variation of the charging order. In exercising its discretion to vary the order the court should look at all the circumstances of the case.

Note
See Jean Warburton, 'Victory for the sprinter: *Harman* v *Glenross*' [1986] Conv 218.

Austin-Fell v *Austin-Fell*
[1990] 2 All ER 455 (Fam Div)

Here there were competing claims by a divorced wife and a judgment creditor of the husband to the equity in a former matrimonial home. The equity was insufficient to enable a charging order to be made in favour of the husband's creditor immediately and to allow sufficient funds to be used to provide protection for the accomodation of the wife. The court decided here that in the circumstances a postponed enforcement order represented the fairest balance between the interests of the parties.

WAITE J: When the judgments of the Court of Appeal in *Harman* v *Glencross* are read as a whole in the context of the facts with which they were dealing, they plainly refute the idea that there can ever be automatic predominance for any claim, whether it be the wife's claim for permanent adequate protection of her right of accommodation or the creditor's claim for permanent protection of his debt. Every case depends, as Fox LJ said, on striking a fair balance between the normal expectations of the creditor and the hardship to the wife and children if a charging order is made (see [1986] 1 All ER 545 at 562, [1986] Fam 81 at 104). The use of the expression 'hardship' in that formula necessarily implies that there will be instances in which the wife and/or children will be compelled, in the interests of justice to the judgment creditor, to accept a provision for their security of accommodation which falls below the level of adequacy....

C: BANKRUPTCY AND SECTION 30

(a) Setting aside transactions

On the bankruptcy of a person the whole of his property vests in the trustee in bankruptcy. It is the trustee's duty to get in, realise and distribute the bankrupt's estate according to the provisions of the Insolvency Act 1986. The law for 'setting aside' transactions is contained in the Bankruptcy Act 1914, s. 42 and the Law of Property Act 1925, s. 172 for bankruptcies occurring before 29 December 1986 and the Insolvency Act 1986, for bankruptcies after that date.

Law of Property Act 1925

172. Voluntary conveyances to defraud creditors voidable

(1) Save as provided in this section, every conveyance of property, made whether before or after the commencement of this Act, with intent to defraud creditors, shall be voidable, at the instance of any person thereby prejudiced.

(2) This section does not affect the operation of a disentailing assurance, or the law of bankruptcy for the time being in force.

(3) This section does not extend to any estate or interest in property conveyed for valuable consideration and in good faith or upon good consideration and in good faith to any person not having, at the time of the conveyance, notice of the intent to defraud creditors.

Insolvency Act 1986

423. Transactions defrauding creditors

(1) This section relates to transactions entered into at an under-value; and a person enters into such a transaction with another person if—

    (a) he makes a gift to the other person or he otherwise enters into a transaction with the other on terms that provide for him to receive no consideration;

    (b) he enters into a transaction with the other in consideration of marriage; or

    (c) he enters into a transaction with the other for a consideration the value of which, in money or money's worth, is significantly less than the value, in money or money's worth, of the consideration provided by himself.

(2) Where a person has entered into such a transaction, the court may, if satisfied under the next subsection, make such order as it thinks fit for—
   (a) restoring the position to what it would have been if the transaction had not been entered into, and
   (b) protecting the interests of persons who are victims of the transaction.

(3) In the case of a person entering into such a transaction, an order shall only be made if the court is satisfied that it was entered into by him for the purpose—
   (a) of putting assets beyond the reach of a person who is making, or may at some time make, a claim against him, or
   (b) of otherwise prejudicing the interests of such a person in relation to the claim which he is making or may make.

(4) In this section "the court" means the High Court or—
   (a) if the person entering into the transaction is an individual, any other court which would have jurisdiction in relation to a bankruptcy petition relating to him;
   (b) if that person is a body capable of being wound up under Part IV or V of his Act, any other court having jurisdiction to wind it up.

(5) In relation to a transaction at an undervalue, references here and below to a victim of the transaction are to a person who is, or is capable of being, prejudiced by it; and in the following two sections the person entering into the transaction is referred to as "the debtor".

Re Densham (a bankrupt)
[1975] 1 WLR 1519 (ChD)

Shortly after their marriage, M and W purchased a house for themselves. The bulk of the purchase price was provided by a mortgage advance, and the balance came from their joint savings. Although the purchase was joint the house was transferred into the sole name of M. M had been stealing money, some £13,000, from his employers. In March 1973, M and W jointly borrowed £900 on a second mortgage to pay for some home improvements. M's employers discovered his thefts and made M bankrupt. W applied for a declaration that M held the house on trust for herself and the trustee in bankruptcy. Held:

(1) There was a common intention of the parties at the time of purchase of the property that the house should belong to them jointly. An agreement could be inferred from the parties' conduct that the property was to be held jointly (see Section 7) and M held as constructive trustee.

(2) The agreement was void against the trustee in bankruptcy under s. 42 of the Bankruptcy Act 1914, which provides that:

Any settlement of property, not being a settlement made before and in consideration of marriage, or made in favour of a purchaser or incumbrancer in good faith and for valuable consideration [then there is another exception, which is not relevant for present purposes, and the section proceeds:] shall, if the settlor becomes bankrupt within two years after the date of the settlement, be void against the trustee in the bankruptcy, and shall, if the settlor becomes bankrupt at any subsequent time within ten years after the date of the settlement, be void against the trustee in the bankruptcy, unless the parties claiming under the settlement can prove that the settlor was, at the time of making the settlement, able to pay all his debts without the aid of the property comprised in the settlement, and that the interest of the settlor in such property passed to the trustee of such settlement on the execution thereof.

GOFF LJ: There remains only the question of sale and possession. It is clear now on the authority of my own case, *Re Turner (a bankrupt)* [1974] 1 WLR 1556, that I have a discretion; that where, as here, there are no other assets and the co-owner is not in a position to make any proposition to the trustee, his voice should normally prevail in equity, because of his statutory duty. Counsel for the bankrupt and the wife asks me to refuse a sale at this stage, but it is clear that he is seeking, and he fairly admitted this, indefinite postponement. He stresses the nervous illness which all her troubles have brought on the wife. I have seen her distressed condition in the box and I have every sympathy for her. He also stressed the possible harmful effects on the children, particularly the boy I have mentioned. That, I must and do consider also, but, as appears in *Burke* v *Burke* [1974] 2 All ER 944, that has only an indirect bearing. On the other hand, I have the telling factors of the trustee's statutory duty and the inability to offer anything. In addition, I am not being asked to postpone the sale to achieve some particular remedial purpose, such as to enable a course of treatment to be completed, or anything of that sort, but indefinitely, merely in the hope that the blow of losing their home when it falls, as it must sooner or later, will be less severe. Further, the wife, though entirely bona fide, has been party to reckless expenditure, despite what should have been a warning to her. If they were so well off, as appeared, why should she need to go out to work to save for a house? Again, the bankruptcy has resulted from stealing, and the principal creditor is the employer from whom the money was stolen. Also the thief will himself be enjoying the house if it be not sold while his creditors wait for their money, and, of course, the wife's beneficial share in this case is less than a half. A further factor of no small importance is that the local authority is trying to find alternative accommodation and, in fact, has made one offer. That seems to have been in many ways unsatisfactory — the garden or yard was full of junk — but there is no reason to suppose that they will not find something else. And, of course, this family must be prepared to make sacrifices and accept a much reduced home.

Therefore, in my judgment, I must make an order in the terms of paras 4 and 5 of the trustee's notice of motion, but, in all the circumstances, I shall allow a generous time for possession. I propose, therefore, to say that completion should be not earlier than six months from the date of the order and I make an order for delivery up of possession within six months or subsequently 14 days after service of the order on the bankrupt and the wife. I say only 14 days there because that part arises only if the bankrupt and the wife are in default in giving up possession within the six months I have allowed.

(b) Petitions for sale by the trustee in bankruptcy

When a person is declared bankrupt his property automatically vests in the trustee in bankruptcy. Where land is held jointly by the bankrupt and another person, the legal title does not vest in the trustee since a legal joint tenancy cannot be severed. The equitable joint tenancy, however, is severed and the bankrupt's share vests in the trustee in bankruptcy together with the co-owner. It is then that the trustee in bankruptcy has *locus standi* to apply to the court for an order under s. 30.

The court is then faced not solely with balancing the interests of the various members within the family, but with balancing the interests of the family against those of the creditors. The court, in deciding whether to order a sale of the family home, is not guided by whether the wife/husband or trustee are being reasonable in their requests for preservation or sale of the matrimonial home, but by 'whose voice in equity ought, in all the circumstances to prevail' *Re Turner* [1974] 1 WLR 1556, per Goff at p. 1558.

Insolvency Act 1986

336. Rights of occupation etc. of bankrupt's spouse

(1) Nothing occurring in the initial period of the bankruptcy (that is to say, the period beginning with the day of the presentation of the petition for the bankruptcy order and ending with the vesting of the bankrupt's estate in a trustee) is to be taken as having given rise to any rights of occupation under the Matrimonial Homes Act 1983 in relation to a dwelling house comprised in the bankrupt's estate.

(2) Where a spouse's rights of occupation under the Act of 1983 are a charge on the estate or interest of the other spouse, or of trustees for the other spouse, and the other spouse is adjudged bankrupt—

　　(a) the charge continues to subsist notwithstanding the bankruptcy and, subject to the provisions of that Act, binds the trustee of the bankrupt's estate and persons deriving title under that trustee, and

　　(b) any application for an order under section 1 of that Act shall be made to the court having jurisdiction in relation to the bankruptcy.

(3) Where a person and his spouse or former spouse are trustees for sale of a dwelling house and that person is adjudged bankrupt, any application by the trustee of the bankrupt's estate for any order under section 30 of the Law of Property Act 1925 (powers of court where trustees for sale refuse to act) shall be made to the court having jurisdiction in relation to the bankruptcy.

(4) On such an application as is mentioned in subsection (2) or (3) the court shall make such order under section 1 of the Act of 1983 or section 30 of the Act of 1925 as it thinks just and reasonable having regard to—

　　(a) the interests of the bankrupt's creditors,

　　(b) the conduct of the spouse or former spouse, so far as contributing to the bankruptcy,

　　(c) the needs and financial resources of the spouse or former spouse,

　　(d) the needs of any children, and

　　(e) all the circumstances of the case other than the needs of the bankrupt.

(5) Where such an application is made after the end of the period of one year beginning with the first vesting under Chapter IV of this Part of the bankrupt's estate in a trustee, the court shall assume, unless the circumstances of the case are exceptional, that the interests of the bankrupt's creditors outweigh all other considerations.

Notes

1. Apart from exceptional circumstances, a creditor's interests prevail over those of a bankrupt's spouse where an application for sale is made a year after the bankruptcy. A question remains as to what is the position where applications are made within the one-year period.

2. Section 336 of the Insolvency Act 1986 covers the situation of spouses but does not expressly mention cohabitees, nor any other relationship.

Insolvency Act 1986

337. Rights of occupation of bankrupt

(1) This section applies where—

(a) a person who is entitled to occupy a dwelling house by virtue of a beneficial estate or interest is adjudged bankrupt, and

(b) any persons under the age of 18 with whom that person had at some time occupied that dwelling house had their home with that person at the time when the bankruptcy petition was presented and at the commencement of the bankruptcy.

(2) Whether or not the bankrupt's spouse (if any) has rights of occupation under the Matrimonial Homes Act 1983—

(a) the bankrupt has the following rights as against the trustee of his estate—

(i) if in occupation, a right not to be evicted or excluded from the dwelling house or any part of it, except with the leave of the court,

(ii) if not in occupation, a right with the leave of the court to enter into and occupy the dwelling house, and

(b) the bankrupt's rights are a charge, having the like priority as an equitable interest created immediately before the commencement of the bankruptcy, on so much of his estate or interest in the dwelling house as vests in the trustee.

(3) The Act of 1983 has effect, with the necessary modifications, as if—

(a) the rights conferred by paragraph (a) of subsection (2) were rights of occupation under that Act,

(b) any application for leave such as is mentioned in that paragraph were an application for an order under section 1 of that Act, and

(c) any charge under paragraph (b) of that subsection on the estate or interest of the trustee were a charge under that Act on the estate or interest of a spouse.

(4) Any application for leave such as is mentioned in subsection (2)(a) or otherwise by virtue of this section for an order under section 1 of the Act of 1983 shall be made to the court having jurisdiction in relation to the bankruptcy.

(5) On such an application the court shall make such order under section 1 of the Act of 1983 as it thinks just and reasonable having regard to the interests of the creditors, to the bankrupt's financial resources, to the needs of the children and to all the circumstances of the case other than the needs of the bankrupt.

(6) Where such an application is made after the end of the period of one year beginning with the first vesting (under Chapter IV of this Part) of the bankrupt's estate in a trustee, the court shall assume, unless the circumstances of the case are exceptional, that the interests of the bankrupt's creditors outweigh all other considerations.

Note

Again, s. 337 does not expressly deal with cohabitees.

Question

What factors would the courts consider to be relevant to cases concerning cohabitees?

Re Citro
[1990] 3 All ER 952 (CA)

A partnership involving two brothers went bankrupt and receiving orders were made against them, both jointly and individually. Each was named as having a half share in a matrimonial home and no other capital. One of the brothers lived apart from his wife, and she was in occupation of the matrimonial home with their three children. The second brother lived with his wife and three children. The trustee in bankruptcy applied to the court under s. 30 of the Law of Property Act 1925 for a sale of both the matrimonial homes. Held: generally, where one spouse becomes bankrupt, his creditors' rights will prevail over the right of the other spouse. The position is the same whether or not the spouses are living together. Hardship to the occupying spouse or young children caused by their eviction was not an exceptional circumstance (Sir George Waller dissenting). If it would cause great hardship to the creditors to postpone the payment of their debts then that could amount to an exceptional circumstance. Thus, in this case, the original charging orders which were postponed until the youngest child reached 16 years were varied so that their enforcement was postponed for no longer than six months.

NOURSE LJ: One of the consequences of the 1925 property legislation is that the legal estate in any property which is beneficially owned jointly or in common is necessarily held on trust for sale and is thus subject to the jurisdiction of the court under s. 30. From its inception the section was one of wide application. But it seems that before *Jones* v *Challenger* it had not been the means of making an order for the sale of a former matrimonial home (see [1960] 1 All ER 785 at 787, [1961] 1 QB 176 at 180).

In that case Devlin LJ considered the earlier authorities on the section and distinguished between those where the purpose behind the joint acquisition had been investment and no more and those where there had been a secondary or collateral purpose, either expressed or to be inferred from the circumstances. In the first category was *Re Mayo, Mayo* v *Mayo* [1943] 2 All ER 440 at 441, [1943] Ch 302 at 304, where Simonds J said: 'The trust for sale will prevail, unless all three trustees agree in exercising the power to postpone.' Chief amongst the authorities in the second category was *Re Buchanan-Wollaston's Conveyance, Curtis* v *Buchanan-Wollaston* [1939] 2 All ER 302 at 308, [1939] Ch 738 at 747, where Lord Greene MR said that the court must ask itself 'whether or not the person applying for execution of the trust for sale is a person whose voice should be allowed to prevail'.

Devlin LJ said ([1960] 1 All ER 785 at 789, [1961] 1 QB 176 at 183–184):

In the case we have to consider, the house was acquired as the matrimonial home. That was the purpose of the joint tenancy and, for so long as that purpose was still alive, I think that the right test to be applied would be that in *Re Buchanan-Wollaston*. But with the end of the marriage, that purpose was dissolved and the primacy of the duty to sell was restored. No doubt there is still a discretion. If the husband wanted time to obtain alternative accommodation, the sale could be postponed for that purpose . . . If he was prepared to buy out the applicant's interest, it might be proper to allow it . . . Let it be granted that the court must look into all the circumstances; if when the examination is complete, it finds that there is no inequity in selling the property, then it must be sold. The test is not what is reasonable. It is reasonable for the husband to want to go on living in the house, and reasonable for the wife to want her share of the trust property in cash. The true question is whether it is inequitable for the wife, once the matrimonial home has gone, to want to realise her investment? Nothing said in the cases which I have cited can be used to suggest that it is, and in my judgment it clearly is not. The conversion of the property into a form in which both parties can enjoy their rights equally is the prime object of the trust; the preservation of the house as a home for one of them singly is not an object at all. If the true object of the trust is made paramount, as it should be, there is only one order that can be made.

Before turning to the subsequent bankruptcy decisions, I should state that, with regard to the distinction made in *Jones* v *Challenger*, I look on the secondary purpose behind the joint acquisition of Domenico and Mary Citro's home as having come to an end, whereas the secondary purpose behind the joint acquisition of Carmine and Josephine Citro's home still exists.

In *Re a debtor, ex p the trustee* v *Solomon* [1966] 3 All ER 255, [1967] Ch 573 the husband's trustee in bankruptcy applied for an order for the sale of the matrimonial home under s. 30. Although the marriage was still subsisting, the husband had deserted the wife more than ten years earlier. Goff J gave four reasons for his conclusion that a sale of the property ought to be ordered (see [1966] 3 All ER 255 at 264, [1967] Ch 573 at 588–589). His first reason, in line with *Jones* v *Challenger* and *Rawlings* v *Rawlings* [1964] 2 All ER 804, [1964] P 398, was that the marriage, thought not legally at an end, was in fact virtually so. His fourth reason was ([1966] 3 All ER 255 at 264, [1967] Ch 573 at 589): '... because this is not a question between the husband and the wife, but between the wife and the trustee in bankruptcy on behalf of the husband's creditors.'

In *Boydell* v *Gillespie* (1970) 216 EG 1505 the husband had executed a deed of arrangement whereby he assigned to a trustee for his creditors a number of interests, including his half share of the beneficial interest in the matrimonial home where he and his wife were living. On the application of the trustee, Plowman J ordered a sale of all the properties, including the matrimonial home. He distinguished an earlier decision, *Re Hardy's Trust, Sutherst* v *Sutherst* (1970) 114 SJ 864, where it had been the simple case of a dispute between husband and wife, and continued (at 1507):

Here it was not the husband who was trying to get the wife out of the matrimonial home; it was a husband and wife who were united in trying to prevent the trustee under the deed of arrangement from selling the house with vacant possession for the benefit of [the husband's] creditors. There was no dispute in the matter as between the defendants themselves. He [his Lordship] did not think that [the wife] was entitled to pray this doctrine in aid for the purpose of depriving [the husband's] creditors of their rights under the deed of arrangement.

Re Turner (a bankrupt), ex p the trustee of the bankrupt v *Turner* [1975] 1 All ER 5, [1974] 1 WLR 1556, another decision of Goff J, was also a case where a bankrupt husband was living with his wife in the matrimonial home. The husband's trustee in bankruptcy sought an order for sale. The trustee was represented by counsel, but the husband and wife appeared in person. In applying the guiding principle, Goff J thought that the trustee's claim based on his statutory duty gave him the stronger claim and required his voice to be treated as the one which ought to prevail in equity. The judge found support in *Boydell* v *Gillespie* (1970) 216 EG 1505, although he observed that it did not appear whether *Jones* v *Challenger* [1960] 1 All ER 785, [1961] 1 QB 176 and *Solomon* case's had been brought to Plowman J's attention. Having quoted from the report of Plowman J's judgment, Goff J continued ([1975] 1 All ER 5 at 8, [1974] 1 WLR 1556 at 1559):

Plowman J there rejected the claim of the wife to pray in aid the doctrine of *Re Hardy's Trust* and I think that I ought to follow the conclusion of Plowman J and say that, in the circumstances of this case, the wife is not entitled to pray in aid the *Jones* v *Challenger* line of cases, and is not entitled to deprive the husband's creditors in the bankruptcy of their share in the matrimonial home.

Re Densham (a bankrupt), ex p the trustee of the bankrupt v *Densham* [1975] 3 All ER 726, [1975] 1 WLR 1519, a third decision of Goff J, was yet another case where a bankrupt husband was living with his wife in the matrimonial home, although there the wife's beneficial interest in it was less than a half. Goff J made an order for sale, but his reasoning did not add anything of general value to the earlier authorities. However, for the first time in the bankruptcy cases, consideration was given to the effect of there being young children of the marriage. Counsel for the husband and the wife stressed the possible harmful effects on the children, but Goff J, following *Burke* v *Burke* [1974] 2 All ER 944, [1974] 1 WLR 1063, thought that that had only an indirect bearing on the matter (see [1975] 3 All ER 726 at 738, [1975] 1 WLR 1519 at 1531).

In *Re Bailey (a bankrupt), ex p the trustee of the bankrupt* v *Bailey* [1977] 2 All ER 26, [1977] 1 WLR 278 the parties had been divorced in 1974 and the husband became bankrupt in 1975. On an application by the husband's trustee in bankruptcy, the wife contended that the order for sale should be postponed until the son of the marriage had completed his full-time education in the summer of 1978. The Divisional Court in bankruptcy, on appeal from the county court, rejected that contention and ordered a sale within a short period. Much of the judgments were taken up with a discussion as to how far the interests of children could be taken into account and both Megarry V-C and Walton J, also following *Burke* v *Burke* [1974] 2 All ER 944, [1974] 1 WLR 1063, thought that their interests were only incidentally to be taken into consideration. Megarry V-C said that the matrimonial property cases were not cases in which matters of commercial obligation arose, as in the case of bankruptcy, where the claims of the creditors as asserted through the trustee in bankruptcy must be considered (see [1977] 2 All ER 26 at 30, [1977] 1 WLR 278 at 282). Walton J, having accepted that the children's welfare was a very big factor to be taken into account in the matrimonial cases, said ([1977] 2 All ER 26 at 31, [1977] 1 WLR 278 at 283):

> But when one has cases which are between the trustee in bankruptcy and a former spouse, or indeed, an existing spouse (because it sometimes works out that way) of the bankrupt then the situation is vastly different ...

I now come to *Re Holliday* [1980] 3 All ER 385, [1981] Ch 405, which, as I have said, is the only reported bankruptcy decision in which a sale within a short period has not been ordered. It is also the only previous case in which the bankruptcy decisions have been considered by this court. It must therefore be examined with some care.

So far as material, the facts in *Re Holliday* were these. The parties were married in 1962 and had three children, born in 1965, 1968 and 1973. The matrimonial home was jointly acquired in 1970. In 1974 the husband left the wife and ceased to live in the matrimonial home. The wife petitioned for divorce and a decree nisi was pronounced in 1975. On or shortly before 3 March 1976 the wife gave notice of her intention to bring on her application for ancillary relief, whereupon, on that same day, the husband filed his own bankruptcy petition, asking for immediate adjudication. A receiving order was then and there made against him and he was at once adjudicated bankrupt. In due course his trustee in bankruptcy applied to the court for an order for the sale of the matrimonial home. The wife responded by launching a motion to annul the adjudication. Foster J dismissed the wife's application and later made an order for the sale of the matrimonial home within a short period.

The wife's appeal to this court came first before Buckley, Goff LJJ and Sir David Cairns. It was held that Foster J had been correct in deciding that the husband could not pay his debts and that the bankruptcy petition had not been an abuse of the process of the court. That appeal was dismissed accordingly. The leading judgment was given by Goff LJ, who, in turning to the wife's appeal against the order for sale, dealt with

Co-ownership of Land

the position where there has been no bankruptcy ([1980] 3 All ER 385 at 391, [1981] Ch 405 at 415):

> Where the property in question is a matrimonial home, then the provision of a home for both parties is a secondary or collateral object of the trust for sale (see per Devlin LJ in *Jones* v *Challenger* [1960] 1 All ER 785 at 787, [1961] 1 QB 177 at 181) and the court will not ordinarily order a sale if the marriage be still subsisting and no question of bankruptcy has supervened. Where, however, the marriage has come to an end by divorce or death of one of the parties, or is dead in fact, though still subsisting at law, then apart from any question how far the secondary or collateral object can be said to be still subsisting if there are young or dependent children, though there remains a discretion it is one in which, as I see it, some very special circumstances need to be shown to induce the court not to order a sale (see *Jones* v *Challenger* and *Rawlings* v *Rawlings* [1964] 2 All ER 804, [1964] P 398).

Goff LJ then considered how far the interests of children were to be taken into consideration where no bankruptcy had supervened. Again he preferred the view expressed by Buckley LJ in *Burke* v *Burke* [1974] 2 All ER 944, [1974] 1 WLR 1063, that is to say that the existence of young or dependent children did not prolong the secondary purpose, but was a factor incidentally to be taken into account so far as it affected the equities in the matter (see [1980] 3 All ER 385 at 392, [1981] Ch 405 at 417). Next, he held that, where the beneficial interest of one of the parties to a marriage was vested in a trustee in bankruptcy, the matter could be dealt with in the Chancery Division under s. 30, even though proceedings for ancillary relief were pending in the Family Division. Having then referred to the previous bankruptcy decisions, he concluded that the court had to exercise its discretion in accordance with the guiding principle (see above), for which purpose there ought to be an adjournment so that the parties could consider the position and file further evidence, if advised.

Sir David Cairns agreed with the judgment of Goff LJ. Buckley LJ also agreed and added some short observations of his own. He said ([1980] 3 All ER 385 at 395, [1981] Ch 405 at 421):

> When considering whether in the existing circumstances a sale should be ordered or not, the conflicting legal and moral claims to be taken into account and weighed against each other are, as I am at present inclined to think, those of the creditors asserted through the trustee in bankruptcy on the one hand (rather than any claim of the trustee in bankruptcy) and those of the wife on the other, taking all relevant facts, including the existence of the children, into account.

The matter came back for further consideration on fresh evidence in May 1980. Goff LJ having died in the meantime, the parties agreed that the matter should be disposed of by the other two members of the court. In the course of stating the facts, Buckley LJ said that the value of the equity of redemption in the matrimonial home might be taken to be of the order of £26,500. The only creditors who called for consideration in the husband's bankruptcy were his former solicitors, to whom he owed about £1,260 for costs, his bank, to whom he owed about £5,000, and the wife's mother, to whom he owed about £250 in respect of a loan. Those debts added up to about £6,500 and about £7,500 was needed in order fully to discharge the obligations and expenses under the bankruptcy. On the other side, the wife would have needed something between £20,000 and £25,000 to buy another house of comparable capacity in the neighbourhood, she was without capital and her present income was of the order of £87 per week.

Buckley LJ, having said that the wife's situation was attributable to the husband's former conduct, which seemed to afford the wife strong and justifiable grounds for saying that it would be unfair to her to enforce the trust for sale at that juncture, continued ([1980] 3 All ER 385 at 397, [1981] Ch 405 at 424):

> Of course, the creditors are entitled to payment as soon as the debtor is in a position to pay them. They are entitled to payment forthwith; they have an unassailable right to be paid out of the assets of the bankrupt. But in my view, when one of those assets is an undivided share in land in respect of which the debtor's right to an immediate sale is not an absolute right, that is an asset in the bankruptcy which is liable to be affected by the interest of any other party interested in that land, and if there are reasons which seem to the court to be good reasons for saying that the trust for sale of the land should not be immediately enforced, then that is an asset of the bankruptcy which is not immediately available because it cannot be immediately realised for the benefit of the creditors.

He concluded that the house should not be sold, without the consent of the wife or pursuant to an order of the court, before 1 July 1985, some five years in the future.

Sir David Cairns agreed that in all the circumstances of the case the voice of the wife, on behalf of herself and the children, should prevail to the extent that the sale of the house should be deferred for a substantial period. He continued ([1980] 3 All ER 385 at 398, [1981] Ch 405 at 425):

> I reach that view because I am satisfied that it would at present be very difficult, if not impossible, for the wife to secure another suitable home for the family in or near Thorpe Bay; because it would be upsetting for the children's education if they had to move far away from their present schools, even if it were practicable, having regard to the wife's means, to find an alternative home at some more distant place; because it is highly unlikely that postponement of the payment of the debts would cause any great hardship to any of the creditors; and because none of the creditors thought fit themselves to present a bankruptcy petition and it is quite impossible to know whether any one of them would have done so if the debtor had not himself presented such a petition.

In referring to the earlier cases, he said that the trustee had succeeded there because no sufficiently substantial case of hardship of dependants had been established.

Finally, there is *Re Lowrie (a bankrupt)* [1981] 3 All ER 353, another case where the husband and wife were living in the matrimonial home. The husband having been adjudicated bankrupt in 1979, his trustee applied to the county court for an order for sale, which order was made but suspended for 30 months. The trustee appealed successfully to the Divisional Court in bankruptcy, which ordered a sale within a short period. In giving the first judgment, Walton J said (at 355–356):

> ... one must always look at the whole of the circumstances of the case, and in exceptional circumstances there is no doubt that the trustee's voice will not be allowed to prevail in equity and the sale will not be ordered. A brilliant example of just such a situation is to be found in *Re Holliday (a bankrupt)* [1980] 3 All ER 385, [1981] Ch 405, where the petition in bankruptcy had been presented by the husband himself as a tactical move, and quite clearly as a tactical move, to avoid a transfer of property order in favour of his wife, or ex-wife, at a time when no creditors whatsoever were pressing and he was in a position in the course of a year or so out of a very good income to discharge whatever debts he had. He had gone off leaving the wife in the matrimonial home, which was the subject matter of the application, with responsibility for all the children on her own. One can scarcely, I think, imagine a more exceptional set of facts, and the court gave effect to those exceptional facts.

Co-ownership of Land

He then reviewed the facts in detail and concluded that there were no exceptional circumstances which justified a postponement of the order for sale. Although Goulding J had more difficulty in coming to that conclusion, he agreed with Walton J that the appeal must be allowed. He continued (at 358-359):

> In all cases where a home is the subject of co-ownership between a trustee in bankruptcy for the benefit of the bankrupt's creditors on the one hand and the wife of the bankrupt on the other, the court, in exercising its discretionary jurisdiction to order or not to order a sale pursuant to s. 30 of the Law of Property Act 1925, has to effect a comparison of merits and hardship which in its nature is very difficult, because the position of creditors on the one hand and a family on the other are in themselves hard to compare.

In my view Walton J, in describing the circumstances in which the trustee's voice will not prevail as 'exceptional', stated a correct test. Alternatively, he might have described them as 'special', which to my mind means exactly the same thing.

The broad effect of these authorities can be summarised as follows. Where a spouse who has a beneficial interest in the matrimonial home has become bankrupt under debts which cannot be paid without the realisation of that interest, the voice of the creditors will usually prevail over the voice of the other spouse and a sale of the property ordered within a short period. The voice of the other spouse will only prevail in exceptional circumstances. No distinction is to be made between a case where the property is still being enjoyed as the matrimonial home and one where it is not.

What then are exceptional circumstances? As the cases show, it is not uncommon for a wife with young children to be faced with eviction in circumstances where the realisation of her beneficial interest will not produce enough to buy a comparable home in the same neighbourhood, or indeed elsewhere; and, if she has to move elsewhere, there may be problems over schooling and so forth. Such circumstances, while engendering a natural sympathy in all who hear of them, cannot be described as exceptional. They are the melancholy consequences of debt and improvidence with which every civilised society has been familiar. It was only in *Re Holliday* that they helped the wife's voice to prevail; and then only, as I believe, because of one special feature of that case.

One of the reasons for the decision given by Sir David Cairns was that it was highly unlikely that postponement of payment of the debts would cause any great hardship to any of the creditors, a matter of which Buckley LJ no doubt took account as well. Although the arithmetic was not fully spelt out in the judgments, the net value of the husband's half share of the beneficial interest in the matrimonial home was about £13,250, against which had to be set debts of about £6,500 or £7,500 as the sum required to obtain a full discharge. Statutory interest at 4% on £6,500 for five years would have amounted to no more than £1,300, which, when added to the £7,500, would make a total of less than £9,000, well covered by the £13,250. Admittedly, it was detrimental to the creditors to be kept out of a commercial rate of interest and the use of the money during a further period of five years. But, if the principal was safe, one can understand that that detriment was not treated as being decisive, even in inflationary times. It must indeed be exceptional for creditors in a bankruptcy to receive 100p in the pound plus statutory interest in full and the passage of years before they do so does not make it less exceptional. On the other hand, without that special feature, I cannot myself see how the circumstances in *Re Holliday* could fairly have been treated as exceptional. I am confirmed in that view by the belief that it would be shared by Balcombe LJ, who in *Harman v Glencross* [1986] 1 All ER 545 at 556, [1986] Fam 81 at 95 said that the decision in *Re Holliday* was very much against the run of the recent authorities. I would not myself have regarded it as an exceptional circumstance that the husband had presented his own petition, even 'as a tactical move'. That was not something of the creditors' choosing and could not fairly have been held against them. I do not say that in other cases there might not be other exceptional circumstances. They must be identified if and when they arise.

If *Re Holliday* is put on one side, are the bankruptcy cases, all of which were decided at first instance or in the Divisional Court in bankruptcy, consistent with the principles stated in *Jones* v *Challenger*? I will take first the case where the property is no longer being enjoyed as the matrimonial home, either because the marriage has been dissolved or because the bankrupt spouse has gone to live elsewhere and the marriage is dead in fact if not in law. The decisions in this category are *Solomon's* case [1966] 3 All ER 255, [1967] Ch 573 and *Re Bailey* [1977] 2 All ER 26, [1977] 1 WLR 278. Here it is clear that there is no inconsistency, because, even if he was not bankrupt, the husband would usually be entitled to demand a sale. His trustee in bankruptcy cannot be in any worse position than he himself.

The more interesting question is whether there is an inconsistency in the case where the property is still being enjoyed as the matrimonial home, as it was in *Boydell* v *Gillespie* (1970) 216 EG 1505, *Re Turner* [1975] 1 All ER 5, [1974] 1 WLR 1556, *Re Densham* [1975] 3 All ER 726, [1975] 1 WLR 1519 and *Re Lowrie* [1981] 3 All ER 353. It would have been open to the wife in each of those cases to argue that the secondary purpose was still existing, that the husband's beneficial interest to which the trustee had succeeded was, in the words of Buckley LJ in *Re Holliday* [1980] 3 All ER 385 at 397, [1981] Ch 405 at 424, 'an asset in the bankruptcy which is liable to be affected by the interest of any other party interested in that land' and that the trustee had no greater right to demand a sale than the husband himself. That argument may have been advanced in *Boydell* v *Gillespie* and I think it likely that Goff J had it in mind in *Re Turner*. Perhaps it was unfortunate that there the husband and wife represented themselves, because after that the point appears to have got lost. In none of the decisions is there to be found any overt consideration of the argument or any reasoned explanation of its rejection. They simply assume that there is no distinction between the two cases.

Here I should state that counsel who appears for the bankrupts and their wives has not argued for any distinction between these two cases, notwithstanding that the secondary purpose behind the joint acquisition of Carmine and Josephine Citro's home still exists. Having been puzzled by the point myself and having thought it right to consider it, I have come to a clear conclusion that the assumption made in the earlier decisions is correct. Shortly stated, my reasoning is this. In the husband and wife cases exemplified by *Jones* v *Challenger* it is held that neither spouse has a right to demand a sale of the property while the purpose of its enjoyment as a matrimonial home still exists. In order to be so enjoyed it must be occupied by the spouses jointly. As a matter of property law, the basis of their joint occupation is their joint ownership of the beneficial interest in the home. Although the vesting of one of their interests in a trustee for creditors does not in itself destroy the secondary purpose of the trust, the basis for their joint occupation has gone. It must, I think, be implicit in the principle of *Jones* v *Challenger* that the secondary purpose can only exist while the spouses are not only joint occupiers of the home but joint owners of it as well.

I am therefore of the opinion that the earlier authorities, as I have summarised them, correctly state the law applicable to the present case. Did Hoffmann J correctly apply it to the facts which were before him? I respectfully think that he did not. First, for the reasons already stated, the personal circumstances of the two wives and their children, although distressing, are not by themselves exceptional. Second, I think that the judge erred in fashioning his orders by reference to those which might have been made in the Family Division in a case where bankruptcy had not supervened. That approach, which tends towards treating the home as a source of provision for the children, was effectively disapproved by the earlier and uncontroversial part of the decision of this court in *Re Holliday* [1980] 3 All ER 385, [1981] Ch 405. Third, and perhaps most significantly, he did not ask himself the critical question whether a further postponement of payment of their debts would cause hardship to the creditors. It is only necessary to look at the substantial deficiencies referred to earlier in this judgment in order to see that it would. Since then a further 18 months' interest has accrued and the trustee has incurred the costs of these proceedings as well.

In all the circumstances, I think that these cases are clearly distinguishable from *Re Holliday* and ought to have been decided accordingly. Part at least of the reason why they were not was that the points with which we have been concerned were not as fully argued below as they have been here. In particular, a close examination of the figures in order to see whether a postponement would cause increasing hardship to the creditors was not undertaken. That is not to imply any criticism of counsel. It is a characteristic of our system that the higher court often seems partial toward thinking that the important point is the one which was not taken in the lower court.

Finally, I refer to s. 336 of the Insolvency Act 1986, which, although it does not apply to either of these cases, will apply to such cases in the future. In sub-s (5) of that section the court is required, in the circumstances there mentioned, to 'assume, unless the circumstances of the case are exceptional, that the interests of the bankrupt's creditors outweigh all other considerations'. I have no doubt that that section was intended to apply the same test as that which has been evolved in the previous bankruptcy decisions, and it is satisfactory to find that it has. I say that not least because s. 336 only applies to the rights of occupation of those who are or have been married. The case law will continue to apply to unmarried couples, who nowadays set up house together in steadily increasing numbers. A difference in the basic tests applicable to the two classes of case would have been most undesirable.

I would allow both appeals by deleting the provisos for postponement from the orders of Hoffmann J and substituting short periods of suspension, the length of which can be discussed with counsel.

Note
See A. M. M. Lawson, 'Bankruptcy and the family home: *Re Citro*' [1991] Conv 302; Gareth Miller, 'Occupation of the family home and the Insolvency Act 1986' [1986] Conv 393.

Questions
1. Do you think that the court exercises its discretion under s. 30 differently in cases where there is a dispute between the partners *inter se,* as opposed to cases where there is a dispute between the partners and a chargee or trustee in bankruptcy?
2. Do you agree with Nourse LJ when he says that 'Where a spouse who has a beneficial interest in the matrimonial home has become bankrupt under debts which cannot be paid without the realisation of that interest, the voice of the creditors will usually prevail over the voice of the other spouse and a sale of the property ordered within a short period. The voice of the other spouse will only prevail in exceptional circumstances?'

SECTION 7: MATRIMONIAL AND QUASI MATRIMONIAL PROPERTY

See Law Commission Report No. 175 Family Law — Matrimonial Property; Law Commission Report No. 52 Family Law — First Report on Family Property: A New Approach; Law Commission Report No. 86 Third Report on Family Property: The Matrimonial Home (Co-ownership and Occupational Rights) and Household Goods.

When examining the area of ownership of family property it may be useful to look at the following situations:

A: LEGAL ESTATE VESTED IN BOTH PARTIES

In this situation, if the conveyance contains an express declaration of the beneficial interests of the parties, then that is proof of their interests and the express declaration is given effect to, in the absence of fraud, mistake, undue influence or evidence to the contrary. It is thought that such evidence will include evidence that at the date of the conveyance the parties had a common interest that the property be held in some other way and this intention was not carried out.

Goodman v *Gallant* [1986] Fam 106 (CA)

H and W were beneficial joint owners of a matrimonial home vested in H's sole name. The parties separated and W remained in the home. M came to live with W and together they purchased H's interest. The conveyance to M and W stated that this property was held 'upon trust to sell . . . until sale upon trust for themselves as joint tenants'. M and W separated and W gave written notice of severance claiming she owned three-quarters of the interest in the property. She applied to court for a declaration as to the beneficial interest of each party. Held: the provision in the conveyance expressly declaring the parties' beneficial interests is conclusive. On severance of the joint tenancy each party was entitled to half the proceeds of sale.

No express declaration of trust

Bernard v *Josephs* [1982] 3 All ER 162 (CA)

P and D were engaged when they bought a house for themselves. The house was transferred into their joint names, without any express declaration of trust and was subject to a mortgage for the full purchase price, again in their joint names. Other contributions, for example to improvement costs, were unequal. Held: when there is no express declaration of trust there is no presumption that the parties should always take equal shares. Their respective interests must be ascertained according to the circumstances, including the nature of the relationship, the contributions made by each to the purchase and the joint finances of the home. The shares could be determined either (per Lord Denning MR and Kerr LJ) by calculating the contributions made by each party in cash, kind or services up to, and sometimes after the time of separation or (per Griffiths LJ) by ascertaining the intention of the parties at the time of the purchase having regard to their respective contributions, both at the time of purchase and afterwards.

See also *Springette* v *Defoe* (1992) *The Independent*, 24 March.

B: LEGAL ESTATE VESTED IN ONE PARTY ALONE

Where the legal estate is vested in one of the parties' names alone and contributions are made by another party, then in the absence of any express agreement outlining how the property is to be held, the courts have determined the parties' interests in the land by means of the resulting or constructive trust, the contractual licence and estoppel. If the parties are married the provisions of the Matrimonial Causes Act 1973 can also be employed to determine or vary the parties' beneficial interests. See also the Matrimonial Proceedings and Property Act 1970.

Matrimonial Proceedings and Property Act 1970

37. Contributions by spouse in money or money's worth to the improvement of property

It is hereby declared that where a husband or wife contributes in money or money's worth to the improvement of real or personal property in which or in the proceeds of sale of which either or both of them has or have a beneficial interest, the husband or wife so contributing shall, if the contribution is of a substantial nature and subject to any agreement between them to the contrary express or implied, be treated as having then acquired by virtue of his or her contribution a share or an enlarged share, as the case may be, in that beneficial interest of such an extent as may have been then agreed or, in default of such agreement, as may seem in all the circumstances just to any court before which the question of the existence or extent of the beneficial interest of the husband or wife arises (whether in proceedings between them or in any other proceedings).

Note
The contributions to the property can be of two kinds:

(a) *Initial contributions to the purchase price of the property.* Where both parties contribute to the purchase price of the property and the property is vested in the sole name of one of the parties, then the property is deemed to be held by the party with the legal estate as trustee for himself and other contributor as beneficiaries in proportion to the contributions made by means of a resulting trust.

However, when a husband transfers or purchases a house in the name of the wife, there is a presumption, known as the presumption of advancement, which says that such a transfer is intended to act as a gift to the wife absolutely (see *Tinker* v *Tinker* (1970) P 136). Such a presumption can be rebutted by evidence showing that no outright gift to the wife was intended. The presumption is now considered to be weak in cases involving husband and wife and is easily rebuttable (see *Pettitt* v *Pettitt* [1970] AC 777).

If, however, a wife transfers or purchases a house in the name of the husband, there is no presumption of advancement, merely a presumed resulting trust in her favour (see *Mercier* v *Mercier* [1903] 2 Ch 98).

(b) *Subsequent contributions.* These can be divided into subsequent financial contributions (e.g., making mortgage repayments), and subsequent non-financial contributions (e.g., looking after the house and family at the expense of going out to work). Are such types of contributions sufficient to give a person a beneficial interest in the property by means of a constructive or a resulting trust? The test to determine whether the contributor should have an interest in the property is whether there was a common intention at the time of aquisition of the property that the contributor should have an interest in the property *and* as a result of that common intention the contributor has acted to his/her detriment and made contributions to the property. The courts have taken two approaches when answering this question.

(i) *Narrow view.* The House of Lords in the cases of *Pettit* v *Pettit* [1970] AC 777 and *Gissing* v *Gissing* [1970] 2 All ER 780 was discouraging to the claimant in this type of situation. In the former case the wife was the sole owner and the husband had effected improvements to the house. He was nevertheless held not to have any beneficial interest in the house. In the latter case the husband was the sole owner and the wife had bought furniture and contributed to the household expenses. The court said that on the facts of the case there was no evidence to show that there was a *common intention* that she should have any beneficial interest in the property.

(ii) *Wide view taken by Denning.* The court has been willing to find a beneficial share for a cohabitant who has contributed either:

(a) to the improvements of the house; or
(b) in money's worth to the household by being a housekeeper, mother, etc.

Grant v Edwards
[1986] Ch 638 (CA)

M and W set up home together, and property was purchased and put into the name of M and his brother partly to increase the chances of obtaining a mortgage. M told W that her name would be kept off the title deeds because it would prejudice her in the matrimonial proceedings pending with her husband. W made a very substantial contribution to general household expenses. Held:

(1) If both parties shared a common intention that they would each have a beneficial interest in the property and if the contributor acted to his/her detriment due to that intention then equity would infer a trust.
(2) The excuse given by M for W's name not being included on the title deeds raised the inference of a common intention that W should have a beneficial an interest in the property. In reliance upon that intention W had

contributed more to the household expenses than would otherwise be regarded as a normal contribution, and that substantial contribution enabled M to make the mortgage repayments. W had acted to her detriment.

BROWNE-WILKINSON V-C: In my judgment, there has been a tendency over the years to distort the principles as laid down in the speech of Lord Diplock in *Gissing* v *Gissing* [1971] AC 886 by concentrating on only part of his reasoning. For present purposes, his speech can be treated as falling into three sections: the first deals with the nature of the substantive right; the second with the proof of the existence of that right; the third with the quantification of that right.

1. *The nature of the substantive right*: [1971] AC 886, 905B–G
If the legal estate in the joint home is vested in only one of the parties ("the legal owner") the other party ("the claimant"), in order to establish a beneficial interest, has to establish a constructive trust by showing that it would be inequitable for the legal owner to claim sole beneficial ownership. This requires two matters to be demonstrated: (a) that there was a common intention that both should have a beneficial interest; (b) that the claimant has acted to his or her detriment on the basis of that common intention.

2. *The proof of the common intention*
   (a) Direct evidence (p. 905H). It is clear that mere agreement between the parties that both are to have beneficial interests is sufficient to prove the necessary common intention. Other passages in the speech point to the admissibility and relevance of other possible forms of direct evidence of such intention: see pp. 907C and 908C.
   (b) Inferred common intention (pp. 906A–908D). Lord Diplock points out that, even where parties have not used express words to communicate their intention (and therefore there is no direct evidence), the court can infer from their actions an intention that they shall both have an interest in the house. This part of his speech concentrates on the types of evidence from which the courts are most often asked to infer such intention viz. contributions (direct and indirect) to the deposit, the mortgage instalments or general housekeeping expenses. In this section of the speech, he analyses what types of expenditure are capable of constituting evidence of such common intention: he does not say that if the intention is proved in some other way such contributions are essential to establish the trust.

3. *The quantification of the right* (pp. 908D–909)
Once it has been established that the parties had a common intention that both should have a beneficial interest *and* that the claimant has acted to his detriment, the question may still remain "what is the extent of the claimant's beneficial interest?" This last section of Lord Diplock's speech shows that here again the direct and indirect contributions made by the parties to the cost of acquisition may be crucially important.

If this analysis is correct, contributions made by the claimant may be relevant for four different purposes, viz.: (1) in the absence of direct evidence of intention, as evidence from which the parties' intentions can be inferred; (2) as corroboration of direct evidence of intention; (3) to show that the claimant has acted to his or her detriment in reliance on the common intention: Lord Diplock's speech does not deal directly with the nature of the detriment to be shown; (4) to quantify the extent of the beneficial interest.

I have sought to analyse Lord Diplock's speech for two reasons. First, it is clear that the necessary common intention can be proved otherwise than by reference to contributions by the claimant to the cost of acquisition. Secondly, the remarks of Lord Diplock as to the contributions made by the claimant must be read in their context.

In cases of this kind the first question must always be whether there is sufficient direct evidence of a common intention that both parties are to have a beneficial interest. Such direct evidence need have nothing to do with the contributions made to the cost of acquisition. Thus in *Eves* v *Eves* [1975] 1 WLR 1338 the common intention was proved by the fact that the claimant was told that her name would have been on the title deeds but for her being under age. Again, in *Midland Bank Plc* v *Dobson* (unreported), 12 July 1985; Court of Appeal (Civil Division) Transcript No. 381 of 1985 this court held that the trial judge was entitled to find the necessary common intention from evidence which he accepted that the parties treated the house as "our house" and had a "principle of sharing everything." Although, as was said in the latter case, the trial judge has to approach such direct evidence with caution, if he does accept such evidence the necessary common intention is proved. One would expect that in a number of cases the court would be able to decide on the direct evidence before it whether there was such a common intention. It is only necessary to have recourse to inferences from other circumstances (such as the way in which the parties contributed, directly or indirectly, to the cost of acquisition) in cases such as *Gissing* v *Gissing* [1971] AC 886 and *Burns* v *Burns* [1984] Ch 317 where there is no direct evidence of intention.

Applying those principles to the present case, the representation made by the defendant to the plaintiff that the house would have been in the joint names but for the plaintiff's matrimonial disputes is clear direct evidence of a common intention that she was to have an interest in the house: *Eves* v *Eves* [1975] 1 WLR 1338. Such evidence was in my judgment sufficient by itself to establish the common intention: but in any event it is wholly consistent with the contributions made by the plaintiff to the joint household expenses and the fact that the surplus fire insurance moneys were put into a joint account. . . .

But as Lord Diplock's speech in *Gissing* v *Gissing* [1971] AC 886, 905D and the decision in *Midland Bank Plc.* v *Dobson* (unreported) make clear, mere common intention by itself is not enough: the claimant has also to prove that she has acted to her detriment in the reasonable belief by so acting she was acquiring a beneficial interest.

There is little guidance in the authorities on constructive trusts as to what is necessary to prove that the claimant so acted to her detriment. What "link" has to be shown between the common intention and the actions relied on? Does there have to be positive evidence that the claimant did the acts in conscious reliance on the common intention? Does the court have to be satisfied that she would not have done the acts relied on but for the common intention, e.g. would not the claimant have contributed to household expenses out of affection for the legal owner and as part of their joint life together even if she had no intere... in the house? Do the acts relied on as a detriment have to be inherently referable to the house, e.g. contribution to the purchase or physical labour on the house?

I do not think it is necessary to express any concluded view on these questions in order to decide this case. *Eves* v *Eves* [1975] 1 WLR 1338 indicates that there has to be some "link" between the common intention and the acts relied on as a detriment. In that case the acts relied on did inherently relate to the house (viz. the work the claimant did to the house) and from this the Court of Appeal felt able to infer that the acts were done in reliance on the common intention. So, in this case, as the analysis of Nourse LJ makes clear, the plaintiff's contributions to the household expenses were essentially linked to the payment of the mortgage instalments by the defendant: without the plaintiff's contributions, the defendant's means were insufficient to keep up the mortgage payments. In my judgment where the claimant has made payments which, whether directly or indirectly, have been used to discharge the mortgage instalments, this is a sufficient link between the detriment suffered by the claimant and the common

Co-ownership of Land

intention. The court can infer that she would not have made such payments were it not for her belief that she had an interest in the house. On this ground therefore I find that the plaintiff has acted to her detriment in reliance on the common intention that she had a beneficial interest in the house and accordingly that she has established such beneficial interest.

I suggest that in other cases of this kind, useful guidance may in the future be obtained from the principles underlying the law of proprietary estoppel which in my judgment are closely akin to those laid down in *Gissing* v *Gissing* [1971] AC 886. In both, the claimant must to the knowledge of the legal owner have acted in the belief that the claimant has or will obtain an interest in the property. In both, the claimant must have acted to his or her detriment in reliance on such belief. In both, equity acts on the conscience of the legal owner to prevent him from acting in an unconscionable manner by defeating the common intention. The two principles have been developed separately without cross-fertilisation between them: but they rest on the same foundation and have on all other matters reached the same conclusions.

. . .

What then is the extent of the plaintiff's interest? It is clear from *Gissing* v *Gissing* [1971] AC 886 that, once the common intention and the actions to the claimant's detriment have been proved from direct or other evidence, in fixing the quantum of the claimant's beneficial interest the court can take into account indirect contributions by the plaintiff such as the plaintiff's contributions to joint household expenses: see *Gissing* v *Gissing* [1971] AC 886, 909A and D–E. In my judgment, the passage in Lord Diplock's speech at pp. 909G–910A is dealing with a case where there is no evidence of the common intention other than contributions to joint expenditure: in such a case there is insufficient evidence to prove any beneficial interest and the question of the extent of that interest cannot arise.

Where, as in this case, the existence of some beneficial interest in the claimant has been shown, prima facie the interest of the claimant will be that which the parties intended: *Gissing* v *Gissing* [1971] AC 886, 908G. In *Eves* v *Eves* [1975] 1 WLR 1338, 1345G Brightman LJ plainly felt that a common intention that there should be a joint interest pointed to the beneficial interests being equal. However, he felt able to find a lesser beneficial interest in that case without explaining the legal basis on which he did so. With diffidence, I suggest that the law of proprietary estoppel may again provide useful guidance. If proprietary estoppel is established, the court gives effect to it by giving effect to the common intention so far as may fairly be done between the parties. For that purpose, equity is displayed at its most flexible: see *Crabb* v *Arun District Council* [1976] Ch 179. Identifiable contributions to the purchase of the house will of course be an important factor in many cases. But in other cases, contributions by way of the labour or other unquantifiable actions of the claimant will also be relevant.

Taking into account the fact that the house was intended to be the joint property, the contributions to the common expenditure and the payment of the fire insurance moneys into the joint account, I agree that the plaintiff is entitled to a half interest in the house.

C: THE CURRENT VIEW

Burns v *Burns* [1984] 1 All ER 244 (CA)

A house was acquired and transferred into M's sole name. W made no direct contribution to the purchase moneys nor to the mortgage repayments. M and W cohabited for 17 years, during which time W made some contributions to the housekeeping and the household furnishings and also looked after the children. Held: where parties are unmarried and property is purchased in the name of one of them (A), but the other (B) makes no direct contribution to the purchase price and there is no express agreement or declaration regarding the beneficial interests in the property then, prima facie, the person into whose name that property is conveyed is to be treated as the sole legal and beneficial owner. It is only if the courts can impute from the conduct of both A and B, before separation, a common intention that both were to have a beneficial interest in the property, that such an interest may arise. It can only arise where B has made a substantial financial contribution towards the household expenses which could be related to the *acquisition* of the property. On the facts of this case no such common intention could be imputed.

Lloyd's Bank Plc v *Rosset*
[1990] 1 All ER 1111 (HL)

The facts of this case appear at page 78.

LORD BRIDGE: Even if there had been the clearest oral agreement between Mr and Mrs Rosset that Mr Rosset was to hold the property in trust for them both as tenants in common, this would, of course, have been ineffective since a valid declaration of trust by way of gift of a beneficial interest in land is required by s. 53(1) of the Law of Property Act 1925 to be in writing. But if Mrs Rosset had, as pleaded, altered her position in reliance on the agreement this could have given rise to an enforceable interest in her favour by way either of a constructive trust or of a proprietary estoppel.
...

On any view the monetary value of Mrs Rosset's work expressed as a contribution to a property acquired at a cost exceeding £70,000 must have been so trifling as to be almost de minimis. I should myself have had considerable doubt whether Mrs Rosset's contribution to the work of renovation was sufficient to support a claim to a constructive trust in the absence of writing to satisfy the requirements of s. 51 of the Law of Property Act 1925 even if her husband's intention to make a gift to her of half or any other share in the equity of the property had been clearly established or if he had clearly represented to her that that was what he intended. But here the conversations with her husband on which Mrs Rosset relied, all of which took place before November 1982, were incapable of lending support to the conclusion of a constructive trust in the light of the judge's finding that by that date there had been no decision that she was to have any interest in the property. The finding that the discussions 'did not exclude the possibility' that she should have an interest does not seem to me to add anything of significance.

These considerations lead me to the conclusion that the judge's finding that Mr Rosset held the property as constructive trustee for himself and his wife cannot be supported and it is on this short ground that I would allow the appeal. In the course of the argument your Lordships had the benefit of elaborate submissions as to the test to be applied to determine the circumstances in which the sole legal proprietor of a dwelling house can properly be held to have become a constructive trustee of a share in the beneficial interest in the house for the benefit of the partner with whom he or she has cohabited in the house as their shared home. Having in this case reached a conclusion on the facts which, although at variance with the views of the courts below, does not seem to depend on any nice legal distinction and with which, I understand, all your Lordships agree, I cannot help doubting whether it would contribute anything to the illumination of the law if I were to attempt an elaborate and exhaustive analysis of the relevant law to add to the many already to be found in the authorities to which our attention was directed in the course of the argument. I do, however, draw attention to one critical distinction which any judge required to resolve a dispute between former partners as to the beneficial interest in the home they formerly shared should always have in the forefront of his mind.

The first and fundamental question which must always be resolved is whether, independently of any inference to be drawn from the conduct of the parties in the course of sharing the house as their home and managing their joint affairs, there has at any time prior to acquisition, or exceptionally at some later date, been any agreement, arrangement or understanding reached between them that the property is to be shared beneficially. The finding of an agreement or arrangement to share in this sense can only, I think, be based on evidence of express discussions between the partners, however imperfectly remembered and however imprecise their terms may have been. Once a finding to this effect is made it will only be necessary for the partner asserting a claim to a beneficial interest against the partner entitled to the legal estate to show that he or she has acted to his or her detriment or significantly altered his or her position in reliance on the agreement in order to give rise to a constructive trust or proprietary estoppel.

In sharp contrast with this situation is the very different one where there is no evidence to support a finding of an agreement or arrangement to share, however reasonable it might have been for the parties to reach such an arrangement if they had applied their minds to the question, and where the court must rely entirely on the conduct of the parties both as the basis from which to infer a common intention to share the property beneficially and as the conduct relied on to give rise to a constructive trust. In this situation direct contributions to the purchase price by the partner who is not the legal owner, whether initially or by payment of mortgage instalments, will readily justify the inference necessary to the creation of a constructive trust. But, as I read the authorities, it is at least extremely doubtful whether anything less will do.

The leading cases in your Lordships' House are *Pettitt* v *Pettitt* [1969] 2 All ER 385, [1970] AC 777 and *Gissing* v *Gissing* [1970] 2 All ER 780, [1971] AC 886. Both demonstrate situations in the second category to which I have referred and their Lordships discuss at great length the difficulties to which these situations give rise. The effect of these two decisions is very helpfully analysed in the judgment of Lord MacDermott LCJ in *McFarlane* v *McFarlane* [1972] NI 59.

Outstanding examples on the other hand of cases giving rise to situations in the first category are *Eves* v *Eves* [1975] 3 All ER 768, [1975] 1 WLR 1338 and *Grant* v *Edwards* [1986] 2 All ER 426, [1986] Ch 638. In both these cases, where the parties who had cohabited were unmarried, the female partner had been clearly led by the male partner to believe, when they set up home together, that the property would belong to them jointly. In *Eves* v *Eves* the male partner had told the female partner that the only reason why the property was to be acquired in his name alone was because she was under 21 and that, but for her age, he would have had the house put into their joint names. He admitted in evidence that this was simply an 'excuse'. Similarly, in *Grant* v *Edwards* the female partner was told by the male partner that the only reason for not acquiring the property in joint names was because she was involved in divorce proceedings and that, if the property were acquired jointly, this might operate to her prejudice in those proceedings. As Nourse LJ put it ([1986] 2 All ER 426 at 433, [1986] Ch 638 at 649):

Just as in *Eves* v *Eves*, these facts appear to me to raise a clear inference that there was an understanding between the plaintiff and the defendant, or a common intention, that the plaintiff was to have some sort of proprietary interest in the house; otherwise no excuse for not putting her name onto the title would have been needed.

The subsequent conduct of the female partner in each of these cases, which the court rightly held sufficient to give rise to a constructive trust or proprietary estoppel supporting her claim to an interest in the property, fell far short of such conduct as would by itself have supported the claim in the absence of an express representation by the male partner that she was to have such an interest. It is significant to note that the share to which the female partners in *Eves* v *Eves* and *Grant* v *Edwards* were held entitled were one-quarter and one-half respectively. In no sense could these shares have been regarded as proportionate to what the judge in the instant case described as a 'qualifying contribution' in terms of the indirect contributions to the acquisition or enhancement of the value of the houses made by the female partners.

I cannot help thinking that the judge in the instant case would not have fallen into error if he had kept clearly in mind the distinction between the effect of evidence on the one hand which was capable of establishing an express agreement or an express representation that Mrs Rosset was to have an interest in the property and evidence on the other hand of conduct alone as a basis for an inference of the necessary common intention.

Note
For post-*Rosset* litigation, see *Ungurian* v *Lesnoff* in chapter 7.

Hammond v *Mitchell*
[1991] 1 WLR 1127 (Fam Div)

H and M lived together in a bungalow which H bought in his own name by means of a building society mortgage. In time the mortgage was replaced by a series of bank loans which were also used to finance extensions to the property and buying additional land. To facilitate the loan M agreed that such interest as she had in the bungalow was to be postponed to the bank's interest. M also agreed to the bungalow being mortgaged by H to fund various business ventures which M supported and took part in. H had a business in Spain and bought a house there, where they lived there for a short time. The relationship broke down. H brought an action for possession of the bungalow against M. Held: the beneficial rights of the parties to both the bungalow and property in Spain had to be determined strictly in accordance with their equitable rights. The court had to consider whether there had been any agreement or understanding reached by them expressly and relied upon in later conduct by M to her detriment. If there was not, the court had to consider whether an intention to share beneficial ownership could be imputed.

There was evidence to show that there was an express understanding that M should have had a beneficial interest in the bungalow. By her actions she had significantly altered her own position and acted to her own potential detriment.

Co-ownership of Land

There was no such agreement or understanding regarding the Spanish property and no evidence to justify imputing a common intention for M to have a beneficial interest in it.

WAITE J: The template for that analysis has recently been restated by the House of Lords and the Court of Appeal in *Lloyds Bank Plc.* v *Rosset* [1991] 1 AC 107 and *Grant* v *Edwards* [1986] Ch 638. The court first has to ask itself whether there have at any time prior to acquisition of the disputed property, or exceptionally at some later date, been discussions between the parties leading to any agreement, arrangement or understanding reached between them that the property is to be shared beneficially. Any further investigation carried out by the court will vary in depth according to whether the answer to that initial inquiry is "Yes" or 'No." If there have been discussions of that kind and the answer is therefore "Yes," the court then proceeds to examine the subsequent course of dealing between the parties for evidence of conduct detrimental to the party without legal title referable to a reliance upon the arrangement in question. If there have been no such discussions and the answer to that initial inquiry is therefore "No," the investigation of subsequent events has to take the form of an inferential analysis involving a scrutiny of all events potentially capable of throwing evidential light on the qustion whether, in the absence of express discussion, a presumed intention can be spelt out of the parties' past course of dealing.

Question

How, if at all, has Lord Bridge altered the test for acertaining whether a party can acquire a beneficial interest in land where that person is not the legal owner of the property?

Does Waite J add anything to Lord Bridge's test?

10 EASEMENTS AND PROFITS À PRENDRE

SECTION 1: THE NATURE OF AN EASEMENT

An easement is an incorporeal hereditament. It is a right attached to one piece of land (the dominant land) which allows the owner of that land to use the land of another (the servient land) in a certain way, or prohibits use of the servient land in a particular way by the other person.

An easement confers no proprietary right on the owner of the land affected, but it does impose a restriction upon that owner's rights over the land.

SECTION 2: CHARACTERISTICS OF A VALID EASEMENT

In order for an easement to be valid it must come within the four criteria outlined in *Re Ellenborough Park*.

Re Ellenborough Park
[1956] Ch 131 (CA)

The vendors owned Ellenborough Park and some surrounding land. The land around the park was sold to X and Y for building purposes. The conveyances of the various building plots granted the purchasers 'the full enjoyment . . . at all times in common with the other persons to which such easements may be granted of the pleasure ground [Ellenborough Park] . . . but subject to the payment of a fair and just proportion of the costs, charges and expenses of keeping in good order and condition the said [Park]'. Each purchaser covenanted on behalf of himself, his heirs, executors, administrators and assigns to pay a fair proportion of the expenses of making the park and keeping it in good condition. P became the owner of the park and sought to prevent the purchaser of the plot from using the Park. Held: the right to use the park as a collective garden was an easement known to the law which was appurtenant to the plots bought by the original purchasers.

EVERSHED MR: The substantial question in the case ... is one of considerable interest and importance. It is clear from our brief recital of the facts that, if the house owners are now entitled to an enforceable right in respect of the use and enjoyment of Ellenborough Park, that right must have the character and quality of an easement as understood by, and known to, our law. ...

For the purposes of the argument before us Mr Cross and Mr Goff were content to adopt, as correct, the four characteristics formulated in Dr Cheshire's *Modern Real Property*, 7th ed., pp. 456 et seq. They are (1) there must be a dominant and a servient tenement: (2) an easement must "accommodate" the dominant tenement: (3) dominant and servient owners must be different persons, and (4) a right over land cannot amount to an easement, unless it is capable of forming the subject matter of a grant. ...

We pass, accordingly, to a consideration of the first of Dr Cheshire's conditions — that of the accommodation of the alleged dominant tenements by the rights as we have interpreted them. For it was one of the main submissions by Mr Cross on behalf of the appellant that the right of full enjoyment of the park, granted to the purchaser by the conveyance of December 23, 1864, was insufficiently connected with the enjoyment of the property conveyed, in that it did not subserve some use which was to be made of that property; and that such a right accordingly could not exist in law as an easement. In this part of his argument, Mr Cross was invoking a principle which is, in our judgment, of unchallengeable authority, expounded, in somewhat varying language, in many judicial utterances, of which the judgments in *Ackroyd* v *Smith* (1850) 10 CB 164 are, perhaps, most commonly cited. We think it unnecessary to review the authorities in which the principle has been applied; for the effect of the decisions is stated with accuracy in Dr Cheshire's *Modern Real Property*, 7th ed., at p. 457. After pointing out that "one of the fundamental principles concerning easements is that they must be not only appurtenant to a dominant tenement, but also connected with the normal enjoyment of the dominant tenement" and referring to certain citations in support of that proposition the author proceeded: "We may expand the statement of the principle thus: a right enjoyed by one over the land of another does not possess the status of an easement unless it accommodates and serves the dominant tenement, and is reasonably necessary for the better enjoyment of that tenement, for if it has no necessary connexion therewith, although it confers an advantage upon the owner and renders his ownership of the land more valuable, it is not an easement at all, but a mere contractual right personal to and only enforceable between the two contracting parties." [Evershed MR then discusses the judgment of Willes J in *Bailey* v *Stephens* (1862) 12 CBNS 91, where it was said "We do not think that Willes J was intending to say that the right of a man to use another person's property for the purposes of his own estate cannot amount to an easement, unless it is incapable of being in fact enjoyed by anyone other than the grantee of the right".]

Can it be said, then, of the right of full enjoyment of the park in question, which was granted by the conveyance of December 23, 1864, and which, for reasons already given, was, in our view, intended to be annexed to the property conveyed to Mr Porter, that it accommodated and served that property? It is clear that the right did, in some degree, enhance the value of the property, and this consideration cannot be dismissed as wholly irrelevant. It is, of course, a point to be noted; but we agree with Mr Cross's submission that it is in no way decisive of the problem; it is not sufficient to show that the right increased the value of the property conveyed, unless it is also shown that it was connected with the normal enjoyment of that property. It appears to us that the question whether or not this connexion exists is primarily one of fact, and depends largely on the nature of the alleged dominant tenement and the nature of the right granted. As to the former, it was in the contemplation of the parties to the conveyance of 1864 that the property conveyed should be used for residential and not commercial purposes.... As to the nature of the right granted, the conveyance of 1864 shows that the park was to be kept and maintained as a pleasure ground or ornamental garden.... On these facts Mr Cross submitted that the requisite connexion between the right to use the park and the normal enjoyment of the houses which were built around it or near it had not been established.... The park became a communal garden for the benefit and enjoyment of those whose houses adjoined it or were in its close proximity. Its flower beds, lawns and walks were calculated to afford all the amenities which it is the purpose of the garden of a house to provide; and, apart from the fact that these amenities extended to a number of house-holders, instead of being confined to one (which on this aspect of the case is immaterial), we can see no difference in principle between Ellenborough Park and a garden in the ordinary signification of that word. It is the collective garden of the neighbouring houses, to whose use it was dedicated by the owners of the estate and as such amply satisfied, in our judgment, the requirement of connexion with the dominant tenements to which it is appurtenant. The result is not affected by the circumstance — that the right to the park is in this case enjoyed by some few houses which are not immediately fronting on the park. The test for present purposes, no doubt, is that the park should constitute in a real and intelligible sense the garden (albeit the communal garden) of the houses to which its enjoyment is annexed. But we think that the test is satisfied as regards these few neighbouring, though not adjacent, houses. We think that the extension of the right of enjoyment to these few houses does not negative the presence of the necessary "nexus" between the subject-matter enjoyed and the premises to which the enjoyment is expressed to belong....

We turn next to Dr Cheshire's fourth condition for an easement — that the right must be capable of forming the subject-matter of a grant. As we have earlier stated, satisfaction of the condition in the present case depends on a consideration of the questions whether the right conferred is too wide and vague, whether it is inconsistent with the proprietorship or possession of the alleged servient owners, and whether it is a mere right of recreation without utility or benefit.

To the first of these questions the interpretation which we have given to the typical deed provides, in our judgment, the answer; for we have construed the right conferred as being both well defined and commonly understood. In these essential respects the right may be said to be distinct from the indefinite and unregulated privilege which, we think, would ordinarily be understood by the Latin term "jus spatiandi," a privilege of wandering at will over all and every part of another's field or park, and which, though easily intelligible as the subject-matter of a personal licence, is something substantially different from the subject-matter of the grant in question, namely, the provision for a limited number of houses in a uniform crescent of one single large but private garden.

Our interpretation of the deed also provides, we think, the answer to the second question; for the right conferred no more amounts to a joint occupation of the park with its owners, no more excludes the proprietorship or possession of the latter, than a right of way granted through a passage, or than the use by the public of the gardens of Lincoln's Inn Fields (to take one of our former examples) amount to joint occupation of that garden with the London County Council, or involve an inconsistency with the possession or proprietorship of the council as lessees....

Mr Cross relied, upon this part of this case, on the recent decision of *Copeland* v *Greenhalf* [1952] Ch 488 ...

The third of the questions embraced in Dr Cheshire's fourth condition rests primarily on a proposition stated in Theobald's *The Law of Land*, 2nd ed. (1929), at p.

263, where it is said that an easement "must be a right of utility and benefit and not one of mere recreation and amusement." The passage in Theobald is justified by reference to two cases: *Mounsey* v *Ismay* (1865) 3 H & C 486, 492, and *Solomon* v *Vintners Co* (1859) 4 H&N 585, 593. The second of these cases was concerned with a right of support, and appears only to be relevant for present purposes on account of an intervention in the course of the argument on the part of Pollock C B and Baron Bramwell, in which it was suggested that one who had for a long period played rackets against the wall of a neighbour would have a right not to have the wall pulled down. ...

As appears from what has been stated earlier, the right to the full enjoyment of Ellenborough Park, which was granted by the 1864 and other relevant conveyances, was, in substance, no more that a right to use the park as a garden in the way in which gardens are commonly used. In a sense, no doubt, such a right includes something of a jus spatiandi, inasmuch as it involves the principle of wandering at will round each part of the garden, except of course, such parts as comprise flower beds, or are laid out for some other purpose, which renders walking impossible or unsuitable. We doubt, nevertheless, whether the right to use and enjoy a garden in this manner can with accuracy be said to constitute a mere jus spatiandi. Wandering at large is of the essence of such a right and constitutes the main purpose for which it exists. A private garden, ... is an attribute of the ordinary enjoyment of the residence to which it is attached, and the right of wandering in it is but one method of enjoying it. On the assumption, however, that the right now in question does constitute a jus spatiandi, or that it is analogous thereto, it becomes necessary to consider whether the right, which is in question in these proceedings, is, for that reason, incapable of ranking in law as an easement. ... [Evershed refers to Farwell J's judgments in *International Tea Stores Co.* v *Hobbs* [1903] 2 Ch 165 and *Attorney General* v *Antrobus* [1905] 2 Ch 188 where it was said that a jus spatiandi is 'not known to our law'].

Duncan v *Louch* 6 QB 904, on the other hand, decided more than 100 years ago but not, as we have observed, quoted to Farwell J in either of the two cases which we have cited, is authoritative in favour of the recognition by our law as an easement of a right closely comparable to that now in question which, if it involves in some sense a just spatiandi, is nevertheless properly annexed and appurtenant to a defined hereditament. ...

For the reasons which we have stated, Danckwerts J came, in our judgment, to a right conclusion in this case and, accordingly, the appeal must be dismissed.

(a) Dominant and servient land

An easement cannot exist *in gross*, i.e. it cannot exist independently of the ownership of land. There must be a dominant tenement which benefits from the easement and a servient tenement over which the easement is exercisable.

Cresswell J said in *Ackroyd* v *Smith* (1850) 10 CB 164:

> Upon the same principle, it appears to us that such a right, unconnected with the enjoyment or occupation of the land, cannot be annexed as an incident to it: nore can a way appendant to a house or land be granted away, or made in gross; for, no one can have such a way but he who has the land to which it is appendant: Bro. Abr. Graunt, pl. 130 (a). If a way be granted in gross, it is personal only, and cannot be assigned.

Question

What is the rationale for the rule that an easement cannot exist *in gross*? Do you think such a rule should be maintained in English law? See M. R. Sturley, 'Easements in gross' (1980) 96 LQR 557.

(b) An easement must accommodate the dominant tenement
An easement must be connected with the normal use and enjoyment of the dominant tenement, as opposed to conferring a mere personal or commercial advantage on the owner of the dominant land (*Ackroyd* v *Smith*).

Hill v *Tupper* (1863) 2 H & C 121 (Ct Exchequer)

P leased premises situated on the bank of a canal from a canal company. The lease purported to give P the 'sole and exclusive right' to put or use boats on the canal and let them for hire for pleasure purposes only. D was the owner of an inn which was also next to the canal. D let out boats on the canal for fishing purposes and P sued D, alleging that his exclusive easement had been disturbed. Held: P's right was not a right that accommodated the land but was a mere licence that was personal to him.

Note
The easement must *accommodate* the dominant land and this means that the dominant and servient tenements must have a degree of proprinquity to each other even if they are not necessarily adjoining. In *Todrick* v *Western National Omnibus Co. Ltd* [1934] Ch 561, it was said that a right of way can be made appurtenant to land with which it has no physical contiguity.

See also *Bailey* v *Stephens* (1862) 12 CB(NS) 91, a case on the same issue but regarding profits à prendre.

(c) The dominant and servient owners must be different
In *Roe* v *Siddons* (1888) 22 QBD 224 (CA), Fry LJ said (at p. 236):

... Of course, strictly speaking, the owner of two tenements can have no easement over one of them in respect of the other. When the owner of Whiteacre and Blackacre passes over the former to Blackacre, he is not exercising a right of way in respect of Blackacre; he is merely making use of his own land to get from one part of it to another.

(d) The right must be capable of forming the subject matter of a grant
Every easement, except those arising under statute, must lie in grant (see page 354 *et seq.*). This means that:

(i) there must be a capable grantee;
(ii) there must be a capable grantor;
(iii) there must be certainty of description; and
(iv) the right must be of a type generally recognised by the law as capable of being an easement.

(i) *Capable grantee* The grantee must be a legal person or body of persons. If the right is given to a fluctuating body of individuals (such as the inhabitants of a village) rather than a person or class of persons, the right is not an easement but it may be a local customary right (see *Mercer* v *Denne* [1905] 2

Ch 538, where certain inhabitants were allowed to dry their nets on the foreshore).

(ii) *Capable grantor*   The grantor must be entitled to make the grant.

(iii) *Certainty of description*   The right granted must be sufficiently capable of description. Therefore there can be no easement of privacy (*Browne* v *Flower* [1911] 1 Ch 219) or of view (*Aldred's Case* (1610) 9 Co Rep 57b), although the latter can be achieved by means of a restrictive covenant (see *Wakeham* v *Wood* (1981) 43 P & CR 40).

Harris v *De Pinna* (1886) 33 ChD 238 (CA)

P and D occupied adjoining premises. P erected structures for storing and seasoning timber on his land. The structures were left open on D's side for air and light. D held his land under a lease and, by arrangement with the freehold owner, was to build two warehouses on the land. He demolished the existing buildings and started to build the warehouses up to the boundary with P's premises. P claimed that by so doing D would interfere with P's access of light and air from D's yard. Held: a right to the uninterrupted access of air and light not coming by any definite channel, but coming over a general unlimited surface, could not amount to an easement.

Cable v *Bryant*
[1908] 1 Ch 259 (ChD)

P bought land from H, who retained adjoining land. P's land had a stable on it which was ventilated by apertures. The access to air was necessarily over H's land. H conveyed the land to D, and the lessee of that land joined in to merge the lease. D erected a hoarding which prevented air reaching the apertures of P's stable. Held: D was prevented from so doing.

NEVILLE J: It has been said, first of all, that the right to air is different in its nature from the right to light, and cannot be granted as an easement at all. Now with regard, first of all, to the question of the right of air, cases have been cited shewing that a general right to air cannot be acquired by prescription, and it is suggested — and I think has been suggested in some of the cases — that even where a right to air has been enjoyed through a particular aperture in the house or other dominant tenement an easement with respect to air cannot be acquired. That seems to have been thought to be the case by Fry J in the fairly recent case of *Hall* v *Lichfield Brewery Co.* 49 LJ (Ch) 655, in which he refers to the proposition of Littledale J supporting his view. Now I think that the cases that I have referred to and the case of *Aldin* v *Latimer Clark, Muirhead & Co.* [1894] 2 Ch 437 are authorities to the contrary, and I think, also, one must not lose sight of the observations of Lord Selborne in the case of *Dalton* v *Angus* 6 App Cas 740 in the House of Lords. It appears to me that in its result there is the distinction between the acquisition of a right to light and of a right to air. The measure of interference with light and with air which entitles the plaintiff to relief of course may differ to a very considerable extent, but it appears to me that both the right to light and the right to air through a particular aperture in a house or building on the dominant tenement is capable of being acquired by prescription.

Note
But see the following case.

Bryant v Lefever
(1879) 4 CPD 172 (CA)

D was the lessee of premises adjacent to P. By stacking timber on D's roof and increasing the height of a wall, D blocked the free flow of air to P's chimneys, causing them to smoke. Held: Free access of air was not an easement capable of being granted.

COTTON LJ: The first question is whether the plaintiff has, either as a natural right of property, or as an easement, a right as against the defendants to have the access of air to his chimney without any interruption by the defendants. In my opinion he has no such right.

In my opinion, it would be a contradiction in terms to say that a man has a natural right against his neighbour in respect of a house, which is an artificial addition to, and not a user of the land; that the owner of the house has, as against his neighbour, no natural rights in respect of his house is shewn by the cases as to subjacent and lateral support. These shew, that while every owner of property has, independently of user, a natural right to support for his land, if he adds buildings to his land, and thereby requires an increased support, he, in the absence of express grant, can only acquire a right to such support by user; that is, by way of easement.

The right, if any, of the plaintiff to the uninterrupted flow of air to his chimney must therefore be by way of easement. Cases to prevent, or to claim damages for interference with ancient lights, are frequently spoken of as cases of light and air, and the right relied on as a right to the access of light and air. But these are inaccurate. The cases, as a rule, relate solely to the interference with the access of light, and in no case has any injunction been granted to restrain interference with the access of air. It is unnecessary to say whether, if the uninterrupted flow of air through a definite aperture or channel over a neighbour's property has been enjoyed as of right for a sufficient period, a right by way of easement could be acquired. No such point is raised in this case, and I am of opinion that a right by way of easement to the access of air over the general surface of a neighbour's land cannot be acquired by such enjoyment. For this *Webb* v *Bird* (1861) 10 CBNS 268 is an authority, and as the last decision in that case was in the Exchequer Chamber, it would be sufficient to rely upon the authority of that case. But I think it better to say that I entirely agree with that decision, and with the reasons given in this case by Lord Justice Bramwell. In my opinion, therefore, the plaintiff has no right in respect of the flow of air to and from his chimney.

Question
Can a right of *jus spatiandi*, i.e. the right to wander at will over all and every part of another person's field, ever amount to an easement? See *Re Ellenborough Park*, at page 342.

(iv) *Right of a type generally recognised by the law as capable of being an easement*   The category of easements is not closed, 'the category of servitudes and easements must alter and expand with the changes that take place in the circumstances of mankind' (per Lord St Leonards in *Dyce* v *Lady James Hay* (1852) 1 Macq 305, at p. 312). Nevertheless, the courts have exhibited a reluctance to recognise a right as being an easement unless it is similar in its nature to existing easements.

SECTION 3: FACTORS WHICH NEGATE AN EASEMENT

Even if a right complies with the four conditions listed above, it is unlikely to be an easement in the following situations:

(a) Where the right involves expenditure of money by the servient owner

Regis Property Co. Ltd v *Redman* [1956] 2 QB 612 (CA)

Landlords of a flat covenanted with the tenant to use their 'best endeavours . . . to maintain at all times a reasonable and adequate supply of hot water for domestic purposes . . . and to keep the radiators (if any) . . . sufficiently and adequately heated through the central heating installation . . .' Held: the right to receive hot water and central heating was not a right of nature contemplated by s. 62 of the Law of Property Act 1925 and could not, therefore, pass under that section (see page 356).

Note
There are exceptions to this:

Crow v *Wood*
[1971] 1 QB 77 (CA)

The facts of this case appear at pages 400–1. Held: the right to have a fence or wall kept in good repair by a neighbour is a right in the nature of an easement.

LORD DENNING MR: [the right to have a fence or wall kept in good repair] was described by Gale as a 'spurious easement'. But it has been treated in practice by the courts as being an easement. Professor Glanville Williams writes in his book on the *Liability for Animals*: 'If we put aside these questions of theory and turn to the practice of the courts, there seems to be little doubt that fencing is an easement.' In *Jones* v *Price* [1965] 2 QB 618, 633, Willmer LJ said: 'It is clear that a right to require the owner of adjoining land to keep the boundary fence in repair is a right which the law will recognise as a quasi-easement.' Diplock LJ pointed out ([1965] 2 All ER 634, [1965] 2 QB at 639) that it is a right of such a nature that it can be acquired by prescription, which imports that it lies in grant, for prescription on a presumed grant.

Liverpool City Council v *Irwin* [1977] AC 239 (HL)

A council, P, sought possession of a maisonette where tenants were withholding rent. The tenants claimed P was in breach of its duty to repair and maintain various common parts of the building including lifts, staircases, rubbish chutes and passages. The only written document in relation to the tenancy was a form of 'conditions of tenancy', with a further form annexed to it describing the various conditions and obligations of the tenants. None of P's obligations were mentioned and only the tenants had signed the document. Held: the existing contract of letting was incomplete as showing only matters relating to the tenant. The complete contract had to be determined. The common parts were retained by P and an easement therefore had to be implied for the tenants to use the stairs, lifts and rubbish chutes. It was implicit that P was under an obligation to maintain the common means of access to the maisonettes, as there was no express obligation placed on the tenants and circumstances required that the obligation be placed on P.

See also *King* v *South Nottinghamshire DC* (1991) *The Times*, 3 December.

(b) Where the right is negative in nature
If the right gives the owner of the dominant tenement a right to stop his neighbour from doing something on the servient land, then the right is unlikely to be an easement since the courts are reluctant to allow an easement preventing the servient owner from developing his own land.

Phipps* v *Pears
[1965] 1 QB 76 (CA)

O was the freehold owner of two houses No. 14 and No. 16, which shared a party wall. No. 16 was demolished and rebuilt, with one wall built right up against the old party wall. O sold No. 16 to P and later sold No. 14 to D. D demolished No. 14. Rain entered No. 16 through the exposed wall as it had not been rendered, and the property suffered weather damage. P sought damages. Held: there was no easement of protection from the weather known to the law.

LORD DENNING MR: There are two kinds of easements known to the law: positive easements, such as a right of way, which give the owner of land *a right himself to do something* on or to his neighbour's land: and negative easements, such as a right of light, which gives him *a right to stop his neighbour doing something* on his (the neighbour's) own land. The right of support does not fall neatly into either category. It seems in some way to partake of the nature of a positive easement rather than a negative easement. The one building, by its weight, exerts a thrust, not only downwards, but also sideways on to the adjoining building or the adjoining land, and is thus doing something to the neighbour's land, exerting a thrust on it, see *Dalton* v *Angus* (1881) 6 App Cas 740, *per* Lord Selborne LC. But a right to protection from the weather (if it exists) is entirely negative. It is a right to stop your neighbour pulling down his own house. Seeing that it is a negative easement, it must be looked at with caution. Because the law has been very chary of creating any new negative easements.

Take this simple instance: Suppose you have a fine view from your house. You have enjoyed the view for many years. It adds greatly to the value of your house. But if your neighbour chooses to despoil it, by building up and blocking it, you have no redress. There is no such right known to the law as a right to a prospect or view, see *Bland* v

Moseley cited by Lord Coke in *Aldred's* case (1610) 9 Co Rep 51b. The only way in which you can keep the view from your house is to get your neighbour to make a covenant with you that he will not build so as to block your view. Such a covenant is binding on him by virtue of the contract. It is also binding in equity on anyone who buys the land from him with notice of the covenant. But it is not binding on a purchaser who has no notice of it, see *Leech* v *Schweder* (1874) 9 Ch App 463.

Take next this instance from the last century. A man built a windmill. The winds blew freely on the sails for thirty years working the mill. Then his neighbour built a schoolhouse only 25 yards away which cut off the winds. It was held that the miller had no remedy, for the right to wind and air, coming in an undefined channel, is not a right known to the law, see *Webb* v *Bird* (1861) 10 CBNS 268; (1862) 13 CBNS 841. The only way in which the miller could protect himself was by getting his neighbour to enter into a covenant.

The reason underlying these instances is that if such an easement were to be permitted, it would unduly restrict your neighbour in his enjoyment of his own land. It would hamper legitimate development, see *Dalton* v *Angus* (1881) 6 App Cas 740 *per* Lord Blackburn. Likewise here, it we were to stop a man pulling down his house, we would put a brake on desirable improvement. Every man is entitled to pull down his house if he likes. If it exposes your house to the weather, that is your misfortune. It is no wrong on his part. Likewise every man is entitled to cut down his trees if he likes, even if it leaves you without shelter from the wind or shade from the sun; see the decision of the Master of the Rolls in Ireland in *Cochrane* v *Verner* (1895) 29 ILT 571. There is no such easement known to the law as an easement to be protected from the weather. The only way for an owner to protect himself is by getting a covenant from his neighbour that he will not pull down his house or cut down his trees. Such a covenant would be binding on him in contract: and it would be enforceable on any successor who took with notice of it. But it would not be binding on one who took without notice.

Note

In **Sedgwick Forbes Bland Payne Group Ltd** v **Regional Properties Ltd** (1981) 257 EG 64, it was suggested that a right to protection against the weather by a roof might be an easement. Oliver J said (at p. 70):

> ... Mr Colyer submits that [*Phipps* v *Pears*] is really restricted to the case of adjoining tenements in a vertical plan and that it can have no application to a case such as this where the only object of the superior premises is the protection of the inferior premises, or the subjacent premises, from the onslaught of the elements. I do not propose to decide that question on this motion. I think that it would be quite wrong that I should do so. There is this authority of the Court of Appeal which is of course binding upon me. I have the strongest suspicion that the somewhat wide expressions used by the Master of the Rolls might not have been formulated having in mind the sort of position that one has here. I am not prepared to say; at any rate so far as this ground of attack on Mr Colyer is concerned, that it is unarguable. It seems to be that there are arguments which can be advanced in favour of the submission which he makes, serious arguments, which will have to be dealt with on total review of all the authorities when it comes to the trial because a motion of this sort is not of course an appropriate proceeding for deciding what is on any analysis a very difficult question of law.

See R. E. Megarry, *'Phipps v Pears'* (1964) 80 LQR 318; H. W. Wilkinson, 'Protection against the weather' (1964) 27 MLR 614; H. W. Wilkinson (1965) 28 MLR 264; J. F. Garner (1964) 27 MLR 768. See also *Bradburn v Lindsay* [1983] 2 All ER 408.

(c) Where the claim amounts to exclusive or joint user

Copeland v Greenhalf
[1952] Ch 488 (ChD)

P owned premises, including an orchard. A piece of land about 150 feet long and about 15 feet wide provided access to the orchard from the highway. D occupied premises opposite P's land from which he operated his business as a wheelwright. With P's full knowledge, D had from time to time parked vehicles on the strip. D claimed to have a right to continue to use the strip in this way in the course of his business. Held: the right which D exercised was too extensive to constitute an easement in law.

UPJOHN J: I think that the right claimed goes wholly outside any normal idea of an easement, that is, the right of the owner or the occupier of a dominant tenement over a servient tenement. This claim (to which no closely related authority has been referred to me) really amounts to a claim to a joint user of the land by the defendant. Practically, the defendant is claiming the whole beneficial user of the strip of land on the south-east side of the track there; he can leave as many or as few lorries there as he likes for as long as he likes; he may enter on it by himself, his servants and agents to do repair work thereon. In my judgment, that is not a claim which can be established as an easement. It is virtually a claim to possession of the servient tenement, if necessary to the exclusion of the owner; or, at any rate, to a joint user, and no authority has been cited to me which would justify the conclusion that a right of this wide and undefined nature can be the proper subject matter of an easement. It seems to me that to succeed, this claim must amount to a successful claim of possession by reason of long adverse possession. I say nothing, of course, as to the creation of such rights by deeds or by covenant, I am dealing solely with the question of a right arising by prescription.

Note
See, however, the following cases:

Wright v Macadam [1949] 2 KB 744 (CA)

D let a top floor flat to P. The initial tenancy was for one week but P remained there and was later granted a new tenancy. Throughout P's seven year period of occupation P had been allowed by D to use a garden shed to store coal. D then demanded an additional rent in respect of the shed. Held: the right to use the shed was an easement.

Miller v Emcer Products Ltd
[1956] Ch 304 (CA)

A tenant took premises under a formal demise which gave the tenant a right to use two lavatories on the upper floors of the premises. Those upper floors were occupied by X, who had a title superior to that of the landlord. X prevented the tenant from using one of the lavatories. The tenant sued the landlord for breach of covenant. Held: the right the landlord had purported to grant was a legal easement.

ROMER LJ: In my judgment the right had all the requisite characteristics of an easement. There is no doubt as to what were intended to be the dominant and servient tenements respectively, and the right was appurtenant to the former and calculated to enhance its beneficial use and enjoyment. It is true that during the times when the dominant owner exercised the right, the owner of the servient tenement would be excluded, but this in greater or less degree is a common feature of many easements (for example, rights of way) and does not amount to such an ouster of the servient owner's rights as was held by Upjohn J to be incompatible with a legal easement in *Copeland* v *Greenhalf* [1952] Ch 488. No case precisely in point on this issue was brought to our attention, but the right to use a lavatory is not dissimilar, I think, to the right to use a neighbour's kitchen for washing, the validity of which was an easement was assumed without question in *Heywood* v *Mallalieu* (1883) 25 ChD 357. No objection can fairly be made based upon uncertainty, and it follows, in my judgment, that the right may properly be regarded as an easement which the lessors were professing to grant for a term of years; and such an easement would rank as an interest in or over land capable of being created at law by virtue of section 1 (2) of the Law of Property Act, 1925.

Grigsby v *Melville*
[1974] 1 WLR 80 (CA)

H owned premises which had been divided into a shop and a cottage. H conveyed the cottage to P's predecessor in title and soon after conveyed the shop to D. The conveyance to P's predecessor in title conveyed to him 'all such rights and easements or . . . quasi-easements as may now be enjoyed in connection with the property', excepting and reserving to the vendor all rights, easements and quasi-easements as may be enjoyed with the shop premises. There was a cellar running under the cottage but the only practical access to it was via the shop. In 1962, D and her husband started using the cellar for storage. P later discovered that D was using the cellar and objected. D claimed to have an easement. Held: D and her husband's claim failed as it amounted to a virtual exclusive right of user which was so extensive as to be incapable of constituting an easement at law. In any event, the original business use of the cellar which existed whilst the properties were in common ownership had ceased.

BRIGHTMAN J (at first instance): Mr Ainger countered by observing that *Copeland* v *Greenhalf* was inconsistent with *Wright* v *Macadam* [1949] 2 KB 744, an earlier decision of the Court of Appeal in which it was held that the right of a tenant to store domestic coal in a shed on the landlord's land could exist as an easement for the benefit of the demised premises. I am not convinced that there is any real inconsistency between the two cases. The point of the decision in *Copeland* v *Greenhalf* [1952] Ch 488, was that the right asserted amounted in effect to a claim to the whole beneficial user of the servient tenement and for that reason could not exist as a mere easement. The precise facts in *Wright* v *Macadam* [1949] 2 KB 744, in this respect are not wholly clear fromt he report and it is a little difficult to know whether the tenant had exclusive use of the coal shed or of any defined portion of it. To some extent a problem of this sort may be one of degree.

In the case before me, it is, I think, clear that the defendant's claim to an easement would give, to all practical intents and purposes, an exclusive right of user over the whole of the confined space representing the servient tenement. I think I would be at liberty, if necessary, to follow *Copeland v Greenhalf* [1952] Ch 488. I doubt, however, whether I need express any concluded view on this aspect of the case. The cellar was, on the evidence enjoyed in connection with Church Hill for the exclusive purpose of accommodating a brine bin for the better conduct of the butcher's business then carried on at Church Hill. When the properties were divided, that business ceased and it was never contemplated that it would be resumed because the two properties were divided for the purpose of making them into two private dwelling houses. Consequently the function performed by the cellar for the benefit of Church Hill came to an end because there was no business, and it was never contemplated that there would thereafter be a business, which could be served by the cellar. In other words, the mode in which the occupant of Church Hill had used the cellar had terminated for good and all prior to the Natinvil conveyance. For that reason I decide that the claim to an easement of storage fails.

SECTION 4: VALID LEGAL EASEMENTS

In order for a valid legal easement to be created two conditions must be fulfilled:

(a) The easement must be held 'for an interest equivalent to an estate in fee simple absolute in possession or for a term of years absolute' (Law of Property Act 1925, s. 1(2)(a)).

(b) The easement must be created in the correct way, i.e. by means of deed, statute or prescription.

If the easement is not created in the correct manner and is granted for a period of more than three years, it can be equitable only and if an easement is equitable it must, in addition, be registered in the correct manner (see pages 24 and 25).

SECTION 5: ACQUISITION OF EASEMENTS

All easements must lie in grant, except those acquired by statute.

A: ACQUISITION BY EXPRESS GRANT OR RESERVATION

If a legal easement is expressly granted or reserved, the grant must be made either by means of a deed (complying with the statutory requirements of a deed outlined in s. 52(1) of the Law of Property Act 1925 as amended by s. 1 of the Law of Property (Miscellaneous Provisions) Act 1989) or by means of a validly executed will (complying with the requirements of s. 9 of the Wills Act 1837). If these requirements are not complied with, then at common law the grant is deemed to be a mere licence (see *Wood v Leadbitter* (1845) 13 M & W 838).

Nevertheless the easement could be valid as an equitable easement, if made before the Law of Property (Miscellaneous Provisions) Act 1989 came into force, provided it was made in writing, or orally with sufficient acts of part peformance, and the agreement was one that was specifically enforceable (see *Walsh* v *Lonsdale*, at page 117 *et seq.*). Since s. 2 of the 1989 Act came into force, all contracts for the sale or disposition of land must be made in writing. Therefore it is thought that oral easements will no longer be valid in equity, but easements in writing will be, provided that the writing complies with the requirements of s. 2.

May v *Belleville*
[1905] 2 Ch 605 (ChD)

Two farms, White Lodge and Coxhill, were in common ownership from 1867 to 1902, but let to different tenants. The tenants of Coxhill had used a right of way over White Lodge throughout that period. The freehold owner entered an agreement to sell White Lodge, the terms of which provided that there were reserved to the vendor, his heirs and assigns the owners and occupiers for the time being of Coxhill, all rights of way exercised by them in respect of Coxhill over any portion of White Lodge. Although a reservation of benefit was included in the conveyance in the same terms, that conveyance was never executed by the purchaser. The purchaser went into possession of White Lodge. Held: the purchaser took with notice of the reservation and was therefore bound by it, as would be his successors in title.

BUCKLEY J: The conveyance as executed by the vendor was not executed by Jay. The agreement of May 16, 1902, had been signed by Probyn Dighton on Jay's behalf, and had incorporated the words in the conditions reserving the rights to which I have referred. Under that conveyance Jay took possession. Was Jay, then, entitled to say that inasmuch as the right of way could only be created by grant, and he did not execute the deed, there existed no right of way, and that the reservation effected nothing? In other words, if there were rights of way previously exercised in respect of such farms, can he say, by reason of his non-execution of the deed, "I am not bound by that"? In my judgment he cannot. Suppose that Jay were the defendant in this action. He is a person who has taken possession of the property under a conveyance which shews that he is to make a certain grant. What right has he to say that he is not bound in equity to give effect to the terms upon which he so obtained possession? The Statute of Frauds does not apply; there is part possession; the bargain is shewn by the terms of the conveyance. Jay can be called upon by the plaintiffs to give effect to the terms upon which he obtained possession, namely, the creation of those rights of way.

McManus v *Cooke*
(1887) 35 ChD 681 (ChD)

P and D owned adjoining houses. They verbally agreed that P would demolish and rebuild a party-wall after which each party would be allowed to make a lean-to skylight, part of which would rest on the party wall. P rebuilt the wall and erected a lean-to skylight in accordance with the agreement. D then erected a skylight but it was not built as a lean-to and it obstructed the access of light to P's premises. Held: the agreement gave each party an easement of light over the other party's land. P had performed his part of the agreement and could enforce it against D.

KAY J: These authorities seem to me to establish the following propositions: (1) The doctrine of part-performance of a parol agreement, which enables proof of it to be given notwithstanding the *Statute of Frauds*, though principally applied in the case of contracts for the sale or purchase of land, or for the acquisition of an interest in land, has not been confined to those cases. (2) Probably it would be more accurate to say it applies to all cases in which a Court of Equity would entertain a suit for specific performance if the alleged contract had been in writing. (3) The most obvious case of part-performance is where the defendant is in possession of land of the plaintiff under the parol agreement. (4) The reason for the rule is that where the defendant has stood by and allowed the plaintiff to fulfil his part of the contract, it would be fraudulent to set up the statute. (5) But this reason applies wherever the defendant has obtained and is in possession of some substantial advantage under a parol agreement which, if in writing, would be such as the Court would direct to be specifically performed. (6) The doctrine applies to a parol agreement for an easement, though no interest in land is intended to be acquired.

I have no doubt that the present case comes within the principle of these decisions.

I find the Defendant in possession of an easement of light over the Plaintiff's land by reason of the Plaintiff having taken down and re-erected at a less height a boundary wall partly on the Defendant's and partly on the Plaintiff's land. By the same act the Defendant has been put in possession of a larger space on his side of the wall; the new wall erected being much thinner than the old one.

These acts could not have been done by the Plaintiff and these advantages could not have been obtained by the Defendant without some agreement between them. According to *Morphett* v *Jones* 1 Swans 172 the Court is bound to inquire what that agreement was. I find it to be one by which the Plaintiff was to have, as his part of the arrangement, a better light to his skylight over the Defendant's land, and this was to be secured to him by the construction, in an agreed position, of a lean-to skylight on the Defendant's side.

The Defendant having obtained all the advantages which this agreement was intended to give him, it would be a fraud on his part to refuse to carry out his part of the agreement, and to resist an attempt to compel him to do so by insisting on the Statute of Frauds.

Therefore, if the statute applies — as in my opinion it should — the equitable rule in cases of part-performance applies also.

Question
Do you think that *May* v *Belleville* and *McManus* v *Cooke* would be decided in the same way if they were heard before the courts today?

(a) Express reservation
An easement is reserved when the owner of a piece of land wishes, on the sale of part of the land, to retain for himself an easement over the land being sold. When a vendor wishes to reserve an easement in such a situation, he should do so expressly in the conveyance.

Law of Property Act 1925

65. Reservation of legal estates

(1) A reservation of a legal estate shall operate at law without any execution of the conveyance by the grantee of the legal estate out of which the reservation is made, or any regrant by him, so as to create the legal estate reserved, and so as to vest the same in possession in the person (whether being the grantor or not) for whose benefit the reservation is made.

(2) A conveyance of a legal estate expressed to be made subject to another legal estate not in existence immediately before the date of the conveyance, shall operate as a reservation, unless a contrary intention appears.

(3) This section applies only to reservations made after the commencement of this Act.

Note
Prior to Law of Property Act 1925, a reservation had to be executed by the grantee and the easement would operate by means of a regrant from him since easements could not be reserved at common law. Section 65 reverses this.

(b) Law of Property Act 1962, s. 62

Law of Property Act 1962

62. General words implied in conveyances

(1) A conveyance of land shall be deemed to include and shall by virtue of this Act operate to convey, with the land, all buildings, erections, fixtures, commons, hedges, ditches, fences, ways, waters, water-courses, liberties, privileges, easements, rights, and advantages whatsoever, appertaining or reputed to appertain to the land, or any part thereof, or, at the time of conveyance, demised, occupied, or enjoyed with, or reputed or known as part or parcel of or appurtenant to the land or any part thereof.

Notes
1. The effect of s. 62 is that easements, profits, other rights appurtenant to the land, privileges and quasi-easements which are enjoyed in respect of the land are acquired by the grantee without the need for general words being expressly mentioned in the conveyance.
2. Section 62 can be excluded by an express term to the contrary.
3. The effect of s. 62 may be more far reaching than at first appears, since the section says that all privileges pass with the land at the date of the conveyance. For example, if X leases a flat to Y and allows Y, as a gesture of goodwill and friendship, to use a lavatory on the third floor instead of on the second floor, then, on the renewal of the lease, if made by conveyance, such a privilege will pass by means of s. 62.

Wright v *Macadam*
[1949] 2 KB 744

The facts of this case appear at page 352. Held: the right to use the coalshed passed with the agreement by means of s. 62 of the Law of Property Act

1925, even though the agreement contained no reference to the coalshed, since it was a right that the plaintiff had enjoyed prior to the agreement.

JENKINS LJ: The predecessor of s. 62 of the Act of 1925, in the shape of s. 6 of the Act of 1881 has been the subject of a good deal of judicial discussion, and I think the effect of the cases can be thus summarized. First, the section is not confined to rights which, as a matter of law, were so annexed or appurtenant to the property conveyed at the time of the conveyance as to make them actual legally enforceable rights. Thus, on the severance of a piece of land in common ownership, the quasi easements de facto enjoyed in respect of it by one part of the land over another will pass although, of course, as a matter of law, no man can have a right appendant or appurtenant to one part of his property exerciseable by him over the other part of his property. Secondly, the right, in order to pass, need not be one to which the owner or occupier for the time being of the land has had what may be described as a permanent title. A right enjoyed merely by permission is enough. The leading authority for that proposition is the case of *International Tea Stores Co.* v *Hobbs* [1903] 2 Ch 165. That was a decision of Sir George Farwell as a judge of first instance. It was a case in which the defendant, who owned two houses, let one of them for business purposes and there had been a practice of giving permission to the successive managers of the property let to pass and re-pass with their servants and so forth across a yard which was part of the property and remained in the defendant's occupation. The part of the property which had been let was later sold to the tenants, nothing being said in the conveyance about the right of way. The purchasers claimed to exercise the right of way by virtue of s. 6 of the Act of 1881. That claim was disputed, and the point was taken that it could not be a right which would pass under the implied general words inasmuch as it was only precariously enjoyed. The learned judge held that the fact that the way was permissive only was irrelevant for this purpose, and that by virtue of s. 6 of the Act of 1881 the grant included a corresponding right of way in fee simple. Dealing with the question of licence or permission, the learned judge said this: 'Unless I am prepared to say that in no case can a tenant obtain under the Conveyancing Act, 1881, a right of way unless he has enjoyed it as of right, I must hold in this case that the fact of licence makes no difference....'

The next proposition deducible from the cases is the one laid down in *Burrows* v *Lang* [1901] 2 Ch 502, which has been referred to in some of the passages I have already read. It is that the right in question must be a right known to the law. In *Burrows* v *Lang* [1901] 2 Ch 502 it was held that a so-called right to take, for the purposes of watering cattle, so much water, if any, as might happen to be left in an artificial watercourse after the owner of the watercourse had taken what he required for his own purposes, was not such a right. A certain amount of confusion has been introduced into the discussion on this aspect of the case by the circumstances that some of the learned judges have used the word 'precarious' in describing rights of a kind unknown to the law, and in particular the expression was so used by Farwell J in the case of *Burrows* v *Lang* [1901] 2 Ch 502; but in this context the precariousness enters into the character of the right as distinct from the title to the right. The right is precarious in the sense that, to take the example of the surplus water, there may be no water at all, and that the right is in itself liable to be defeated in that way. It is necessary to keep clearly in mind the distinction between 'precariousness' in the sense in which it is used in relation to quasi rights of that description, and precariousness of title as used in relation to a permissively exercised right. For the purposes of s. 62, it is only necessary that the right should be one capable of being granted at law, or, in other words, a right known to the law. If it is a right of that description it matters not, as the *International Tea Stores* case shows, that it has been in fact enjoyed by permission only. The reason for that is clear, for, on the assumption that the right is included or imported into the parcels of the conveyance by virtue of s. 62, the grant under the conveyance supplies what one may call the defect in title, and substitutes a new title based on the grant. . . .

Next, the right was, as I understand it, a right to use the coal shed in question for the purpose of storing such coal as might be required for the domestic purposes of the flat. In my judgment that is a right or easement which the law will clearly recognize, and it is a right or easement of a kind which could readily be included in a lease or conveyance by the insertion of appropriate words in the parcels. This, therefore, is not a case in which a title to a right unknown to the law is claimed by virtue of s. 62. Nor is it a case in which it can be said to have been in the contemplation of the parties that the enjoyment of the right should be purely temporary. No limit was set as to the time during which the coal shed could continue to be used. Mr Macadam simply gave his permission; that permission was acted on; and the use of the coalshed in fact went on down to August 28, 1943, and thereafter down to 1947. Therefore, applying to the facts of the present case the principles which seem to be deducible from the authorities, the conclusion to which I have come is that the right to use the coal shed was at the date of the letting of August 28, 1943, a right enjoyed with the top floor flat within the meaning of s. 62 of the Law of Property Act, 1925, with the result that (as no contrary intention was expressed in the document) the right in question must be regarded as having passed by virtue of that letting, just as it would have passed if it had been mentioned in express terms in cl. 1, which sets out the subject-matter of the lease.

. . . In my judgment the right must be regarded as carrying with it the necessary means of access, and it must be assumed that at all times down to August 28, 1943, Mrs Wright enjoyed the use of the coal shed together with the necessary access to it and from it.

Goldberg v *Edwards*
[1950] Ch 247 (CA)

D let out an annexe at the rear of his house. There were two possible means of access, one being via an outside passageway at the side of the house and the other being through the house itself. Tenants of the annexe, prior to P, had used only the outside passageway as a means of access. D then orally agreed to lease the annexe to P together with a personal right of access via the house. P went into possession and they, their servants and customers used the house as a means of access to the annexe. Six months later D demised the annexe to P with appurtenances for a period of two years with an option to renew for another two years. D subsequently granted a lease of the house to D2, who blocked P's access via the house by locking the front door. Held: at the time of the conveyance the right was a right appertaining to the demised premises within s. 62 and was therefore enforceable by P.

EVERSHED MR: What is the 'time of conveyance' within the meaning of s. 62, sub-ss. 1 and 2? The arrangement about this use of the passage appears to have been made at various dates, the last of which was January 13, 1947. The plaintiffs went into occupation of the annexe on January 18, 1947. The fitting of the bell and signboard took place after that. Several months passed (why, I know not, and it is quite immaterial) before the lease was executed on July 10, 1947, though the term was expressed to run from January 18. It is plain that before July 10 there was no written instrument whatever. Possession may no doubt have been attributable to an oral agreement of which, having regard to the position, specific performance might have been granted; but I fail to find any instrument in writing within the meaning of s. 62 before the lease of July 10. It seems to me, therefore, that the phrase 'at the time of conveyance' must mean in this case July 10. I am unable to accept the view that one should construe that as meaning at the time when the term granted by the lease is stated to have begun. On July 10, 1947, under the privilege granted, this right of ingress and egress was being enjoyed in fact. As I have held, though it is limited to the lessees themselves and does not extend to other persons, it would be capable of formulation and incorporation as a term of the lease, and it is, in my judgment, covered by s. 62. To that extent, therefore, but to that limited extent only, the plaintiffs are entitled to succeed.

(c) Limits to s. 62

Section 62 applies only where there has been a *conveyance* of the legal estate in land.

Law of Property Act 1925

205. General definitions

(ii) 'Conveyance' includes a mortgage, charge, lease, assent, vesting declaration, vesting instrument, disclaimer, release and every other assurance of property or of an interest therein by any instrument, except a will; 'convey' has a corresponding meaning; and 'disposition' includes a conveyance and also a devise, bequest, or an appointment of property contained in a will; and 'disposed of' has a corresponding meaning; . . .

Notes

1. Section 62 cannot be used in the case of equitable easements arising under the doctrine in *Walsh* v *Lonsdale*. See *Borman* v *Griffith* [1930] 1 Ch 493, where Maugham J said:

> In my opinion, a contract for a lease exceeding a term of three years does not come within the meaning of the phrase 'assurance of property or of an interest therein' as that phrase is used in s. 205, sub-s. 1 (ii.), of the Law of Property Act, 1925; and accordingly I am unable to construe the agreement of October 10, 1923, as if the general words of s. 62 of that Act were included in it.

2. Section 62 does not apply to easements in an oral lease that could be created prior to 1989 (see *Rye* v *Rye* [1962] AC 496).

3. The right must be of a kind known to the law. See *Wright* v *Macadam*, at pages 352 and 357.

4. There must be diversity of occupation or ownership before the sale or lease.

Long v *Gowlett* [1923] 2 Ch 177 (ChD)

N sold two adjacent plots of land, one to G and one to L's predecessor in title. A river ran through both plots of land. N had periodically gone to the upper part of the land, from the lower part, to carry out repair and maintenance of the river banks, including the cutting of weeds to maintain a free flow of water downstream to the mill on the lower part, now G's land. G claimed an easement to enter L's land to carry out similar works and maintain the free flow of water. G claimed that the easement had been created in his favour by means of s. 6 of the Conveyancing Act 1881 (now s. 62 of the Law of Property Act 1925). Held: G's claim was rejected. There must be diversity of ownership or occupation of the dominant and servient land for s. 62 to operate.

Note
This decision was followed in the next case.

Sovmots Investments Ltd v Secretary of State for the Environment
[1979] AC 144 (HL)

The Greater London Council were the freeholders of a site in London and granted S a 150-year lease of it. S built an office complex on the site and 36 residential maisonettes. The maisonettes were left unoccupied once built. The London Borough Council made a compulsory purchase order authorising the purchase of the maisonettes, the corridors giving access to them and some of the staircases and lifts. The council claimed that certain ancilliary rights, such as the right of support from the building below and rights of passage for water, soil, electricity etc., would pass on the conveyance of the land. Held: (Lord Russell dissenting), the ancilliary rights sought to be acquired did not pass under s. 62 of the Law of Property Act 1925 (nor under *Wheeldon* v *Burrows*, see page 367).

LORD WILBERFORCE: Under section 62 a conveyance of land operates to convey with the land all ways, watercourses, liberties, privileges, easements, rights, and advantages whatsoever, appertaining or reputed to appertain to the land, or any part thereof, or, at the time of conveyance, demised, occupied or enjoyed with, or reputed or known as part or parcel or appurtenant to the land or any part thereof.

My Lords, there are very comprehensive expressions here, but it does not take much analysis to see that they have no relevance to the situation under consideration.

The rule is a rule of intention, based on the proposition that a man may not derogate from his grant. He cannot grant or agree to grant land and at the same time deny to his grantee what is at the time of the grant obviously necessary for its reasonable enjoyment. To apply this to a case where a public authority is taking from an owner his land without his will is to stand the rule on its head: it means substituting for the intention of a reasonable voluntary grantor the unilateral, opposed, intention of the acquirer.

Moreover, and this point is relevant to a later argument, the words I have underlined show that for the rule to apply there must be actual, and apparent, use and enjoyment at the time of the grant. But no such use or enjoyment had, at Centre Point, taken place at all.

Equally, section 62 does not fit this case. The reason is that when land is under one ownership one cannot speak in any intelligible sense of rights, or privileges, or easements being exercised over one part for the benefit of another. Whatever the owner does, he does as owner and, until a separation occurs, of ownership or at least of occupation, the condition for the existence of rights, etc., does not exist: see *Bolton* v *Bolton* (1879) 11 ChD 968, 970 *per* Fry J and *Long* v *Gowlett* [1923] 2 Ch 177, 189, 198, in my opinion a correct decision.

A separation of ownership, in a case like the present, will arise on conveyance of one of the parts (e.g. the maisonettes), but this separation cannot be projected back to the stage of the compulsory purchase order so as, by anticipation to bring into existence rights not existing in fact.

Questions
1. Do you agree with the generally accepted proposition that there must be diversity of occupation or ownership of the land in order for s. 62 to operate?
2. Harvey owns the fee simple of two adjoining semi-detached houses, Greenacre and Pinkacre. He has leased Greenacre to Gertrude for a term of five years, and he has leased Pinkacre to Samphire for a term of five years. After a period of five years he sells the fee simple of Greenacre together with the second floor of Pinkacre to Gertrude as one property, and he also sells the ground floor of Pinkacre to Samphire for an estate in fee simple. Gertrude is now claiming that she has an easement of support from Samphire. Advise Gertrude.

See Stephen Tromans, 'Easements and section 62' [1985] CLJ 15.

B: ACQUISITION BY IMPLIED GRANT OR RESERVATION

Even if there is no express grant or reservation, an easement may arise by means of the intention of the parties, i.e. by means of implication.

(a) Implied reservation
When the owner of two separate tenements has enjoyed certain quasi-easements over one of them, if he sells the quasi-servient tenement certain easements may be implied in his favour over the part sold. The law, however, is reluctant to imply such easements and will do so only in the following situations:

(i)   *Easements of necessity*

Union Lighterage Co. v London Graving Dock Co.
[1902] 2 Ch 557 (CA)

A dock and wharf were adjacent and in common ownership. The owner secured the side of the dock by laying a number of tie-rods which encroached about $15\frac{1}{2}$ feet onto the wharf side of the fence, but underground. They were fastened by nuts to piles that were driven into the soil of the wharf. Only the nuts on the piles were visible The owner conveyed the wharf to P, but made no express reservation in relation to the right of support. The dock was later conveyed to D's predecessor in title and then to D. P only later discovered the tie-rods when making subsequent excavations. Held: (Vaughan Williams LJ dissenting) when the wharf was conveyed to P, there was no implied reservation of a right of support to the dock.

STIRLING LJ: In my opinion an easement of necessity, such as is referred to, means an easement without which the property retained cannot be used at all, and not one merely necessary to the reasonable enjoyment of that property. In *Wheeldon* v *Burrows* 12 ChD 31 the lights which were the subject of decision were certainly reasonably necessary to the enjoyment of the property retained, which was a workshop, yet there was held to be no reservation of it. So here it may be that the tie-rods which pass through the plaintiff's property are reasonably necessary to the enjoyment of the defendants' dock in its present condition; but the dock is capable of use without them, and I think that there cannot be implied any reservation in respect of them. Some other exceptions to the general rule are mentioned in *Wheeldon* v *Burrows* and in particular reciprocal easements, but it was not contended, and it does not appear to me that this case falls within any of them. Nor do I think that the tie-rods here form part of the corporeal structure of the dock which can be held not to have passed by the conveyance of the adjoining property.

VAUGHAN WILLIAMS LJ: . . . One exception is the case of necessity, of which a way of necessity is the most familiar instance. Another case of exception is the case of reciprocity, in which houses or other buildings are so constructed as to be mutually subservient to and dependent on each other, neither being capable of standing or being enjoyed without the support it derives from its neighbour. This exception is recognised by Lord Westbury 4 DJ & S 198 and by Thesiger LJ in *Wheeldon* v *Burrows* 12 ChD 31, the judgment of Pollock CB in *Richards* v *Rose* 9 Ex 218 being generally the authority quoted for this exception of reciprocal or mutual easements. A third exception is where that which is claimed to be reserved is not an incorporeal easement, but part and parcel of a house or other building belonging to the conveying party, but not included in the conveyance.

Note

The creation of landlocked land is one of the few situations in which the courts will imply an easement of necessity. In order for the action to succeed the vendor must show that without the easement being impliedly reserved his land could not be used at all. It is not sufficient merely to prove that the easement would be convenient for the use of the land.

Barry v *Hasseldine* [1952] Ch 835 (ChD)

D conveyed land to P's predecessor in title with no express right of access. The land was surrounded by land retained by D and by land belonging to others over which neither P nor D had rights. Held: there was an easement of necessity over D's land in favour of the grantee.

Corporation of London v *Riggs* (1880) 13 ChD 798 (ChD)

A owned a close and surrounding lands. He sold all the surrounding land, retaining the close but making no retention in the conveyance of a right of way for access. Held: there was an implied right of way of necessity over the land sold.

Question
Can a person claim an easement of necessity to go onto neighbouring land to carry out essential repairs to his property, which can only be carried out if he has access to the neighbouring land?

(ii) *Common intention* Easements will be implied in favour of the grantor if it is the common intention of the grantor and grantee that the grantor have an easement, for example mutual easements of support. It should be noted that these easements will often equate to those implied from necessity.

Re Webb's Lease
[1951] Ch 808 (CA)

L leased the upper floors of a building to T. L carried on business from the ground floor. He then granted T a 21-year lease of those floors, including the outer walls of the building. The landlord had an advertisement displayed on the outside wall of an upper floor, which had been present before the lease was granted, but for which L failed to reserve an easement. Held: the landlord had no right to claim an easement to advertise on the wall.

JENKINS LJ: As to the law applicable to the case, it is not disputed that as a general rule a grantor, whether by way of conveyance or lease, of part of a hereditament in his ownership, cannot claim any easement over the part granted for the benefit of the part retained, unless it is expressly reserved out of the grant. See (for instance) *Suffield* v *Brown* 4 De GJ & S 185; *Crossley & Sons Ltd* v *Lightowler* LR 2 Ch 478; *Wheeldon* v *Burrows* 12 ChD 31.

There are, however, certain exceptions to the general rule. Two well-established exceptions relate to easements of necessity and mutual easements such as rights of support between adjacent buildings. But it is recognized in the authorities that these two specific exceptions do not exhaust the list, which is indeed incapable of exhaustive statement, as the circumstances of any particular case may be such as to raise a necessary inference that the common intention of the parties must have been to reserve some easement to the grantor, or such as to preclude the grantee from denying the right consistently with good faith, and there appears to be no doubt that where circumstances such as these are clearly established the court will imply the appropriate reservation....

The most comprehensive statement of the area of potential exceptions is probably that contained in the speech of Lord Parker in *Pwllbach Colliery Co. Ltd* v *Woodman* [1915] AC 634, where his Lordship, after referring to the exception with respect to easements of necessity, said this:

The second class of cases in which easements may impliedly be created depends not upon the terms of the grant itself, but upon the circumstances under which the grant was made. The law will readily imply the grant or reservation of such easements as may be necessary to give effect to the common intention of the parties to a grant of real property, with reference to the manner or purposes in and for which the land granted or some land retained by the grantor is to be used. See *Jones* v *Pritchard* [1908] 1 Ch 630, and *Lyttleton Times Co. Ld* v *Warners Ld* [1907] AC 476. But it is essential for this purpose that the parties should intend that the subject of the grant or the land retained by the grantor should be used in some definite and particular manner. It is not enough that the subject of the grant or the land retained should be intended to be used in a manner which may or may not involve this definite and particular use.

...

The case which in point of actual decision goes furthest in the direction of implying reservations of easements in favour of a grantor is undoubtedly that of *Simpson* v *Weber* 133 LT 46. The question there was whether the grantor of one of two adjoining houses owned by him had by implication reserved the right to have a creeper growing in the garden of the house retained supported by a wall of the house granted over which its foliage had spread, and the right to continue the attachment of a gate forming part of the premises retained to a wall forming part of the premises granted; and the Divisional Court, reversing a county court judge, decided in favour of the grantor's successor in title on both points. Of this case I need only say that, while the physical circumstances at the date of the severance may perhaps have sufficed to support an implication of an intention common to grantor and grantee that the easements in question should be reserved, I cannot agree that the decision is good law, so far as it proceeds on the ground, given in both the two not very satisfactory reports, 'that there was no evidence that it was not the intention of the parties that the creeper and the gatepost should stay'.

In his judgment in the present case, Danckwerts, J, after citing at length from *Simpson* v *Weber* 133 LT 46, and also referring to *Liddiard* v *Waldron* [1934] 1 KB 435, *Wheeldon* v *Burrows* 12 ChD 31 and *Thomas* v *Owen* 20 QBD 225, expressed his conclusion thus:

> It does seem to me that there may be exceptional circumstances in which it is only common sense to imply some reservation, for example, the circumstances of the present case. When I see that, when the parties entered into their transaction, there was an enormous advertisement painted on the wall advertising 'Webb's for Meat, Grocery and Provisions', and a very large advertisement advertising 'Brymay', safety matches, which had been there since 1939 and before, and nothing was said between the parties about the removal of those advertisements, it seems to me common sense to imply an intention on the part of the two parties to the document that those advertisements should be allowed to remain. Therefore, I am prepared to hold that there was implied in favour of the landlord in this lease an easement until the termination of the lease to keep those two advertisements in the position in which they are, and, of course, by necessary implication, a right to repair them, paint them, or do whatever may be necessary from time to time to preserve them as effective advertisements.

I find myself unable to agree with the judge's conclusion. The question is whether the circumstances of the case as proved in evidence are such as to raise a necessary inference that the common intention of the parties was to reserve to the landlord during the twenty-one years' term some, and if so what, rights in regard to the display of advertisements over the outer walls of the demised premises, or such as to preclude the tenant from denying the implied reservation to the landlord of some such rights consistently with good faith.

That question must be approached with the following principles in mind: (i) If the landlord intended to reserve any such rights over the demised premises it was his duty to reserve them expressly in the lease of August 11, 1949 (*Wheeldon* v *Burrows* 12 ChD 31); (ii) The landlord having failed in this duty, the onus was upon him to establish the facts to prove, and prove clearly, that his case was an exception to the rule (*Aldridge* v *Wright* [1929] 2 KB 117); (iii) The mere fact that the tenant knew at the date of the lease of August 11, 1949, that the landlord was using the outer walls of the demised premises for the display of the advertisements in question did not suffice to absolve the landlord from his duty of expressly reserving any rights in respect of them he intended to claim, or to take the case out of the general rule; see *Suffield* v *Brown* 4 De GJ & S 185; *Crossley & Sons Ltd* v *Lightowler* LR 2 Ch 478. . . .

The mere fact that the tenant knew of the presence of the advertisements at the date when the lease of August 11, 1949, was granted being, as stated above, beside the point, nothing is left beyond the bare circumstance that the advertisements were not only present at the date of the grant but had been continuously present without objection by the tenant since the commencement of his original tenancy in 1939. Does this circumstance suffice to raise a necessary inference of an intention common to both parties at the date of the lease that the landlord should have reserved to him the right to maintain these advertisements throughout the twenty-one years' term thereby granted? I cannot see that it does: The most that can be said is that the facts are consistent with such a common intention. But that will not do. The landlord must surely show at least that the facts are not reasonably consistent with any other explanation. Here he manifestly fails. . . .

(b) Implied grant

It is more likely that a grant will be implied in favour of a grantee as opposed to a reservation in favour of a grantor. Such a grant will be implied in the following situations:

(a) Easements of necessity.
(b) Easements of common intention.

Wong v Beaumont Property Trust Ltd
[1965] 1 QB 173 (CA)

T took a 21 year lease of three cellars and covenanted to use the premises as a restaurant, to control and eliminate smells and odours caused by him and to comply with the health regulations. The regulations required suitable ventilation in every food room. There was no means of complying with the ventilation requirements without installing a duct affixed to the walls of the landlord's building. This was so even at the time that the lease was completed. Held: there was an easement of necessity.

LORD DENNING MR: The question is: Has the plaintiff a right to put up this duct without the landlords' consent? If he is to have any right at all, it must be by way of easement and not merely by way of implied contract. He is not the original lessee, nor are the defendants the original lessors. Each is a successor in title. As between them, a right of this kind, if it exists at all, must be by way of an easement. In particular, an easement of necessity. The law on the matter was stated by Lord Parker of Waddington in *Pwllbach Colliery Co. Ltd* v *Woodman* [1915] AC 634. . . . That is the principle which underlines all easements of necessity. If you go back to Rolle's Abridgment you will find it stated in this way (2 Rol Abr 60, pl. 17, 18): 'If I have a field inclosed by my own land on all sides, and I alien this close to another, he shall have a way to this close over my land, as incident to the grant; for otherwise he cannot have any benefit by the grant.'

I would apply those principles here. Here was the grant of a lease to the lessee for the very purpose of carrying on a restaurant business. It was to be a popular restaurant, and it was to be developed and extended. There was a covenant not to cause any nuisance; and to control and eliminate all smells; and to comply with the Food Hygiene

Regulations. That was 'a definite and particular manner' in which the business had to be conducted. It could not be carried on in that manner at all unless a ventilation system was installed by a duct of this kind. In these circumstances it seems to me that, if the business is to be carried on at all — if, in the words of Rolle's Abridgment, the lessee is to 'have any benefit by the grant' at all — he must of necessity be able to put a ventilation duct up the wall. It may be that in Blackaby's time it would not have needed such a large duct as is now needed in the plaintiff's time. But nevertheless a duct of some kind would have had to be put up the wall. The plaintiff may need a bigger one. But that does not matter. A man who has a right to an easement can use it in any proper way, so long as he does not substantially increase the burden on the servient tenement. In this case a bigger duct will not substantially increase the burden.

There is one point in which this case goes further than the earlier cases which have been cited. It is this. It was not realised by the parties, at the time of the lease, that this duct would be necessary. But it was in fact necessary from the very beginning. That seems to me sufficient to bring the principle into play. In order to use this place as a restaurant, there must be implied an easement, by the necessity of the case, to carry a duct up this wall. The county court judge so held. He granted a declaration. I agree with him.

Note
A grant may also be implied under the rule in *Wheeldon v Burrows*.

Wheeldon v Burrows
(1879) 12 ChD 31 (CA)

S owned a workshop and some adjacent land. The land was sold to P. The workshop was conveyed to X shortly afterwards. Some windows of the workshop received light from over P's land. No right to access of light had been reserved by S in the conveyance of the land to P. Held: in the absence of an express reservation of a right to access of light, no such right passed to X, and P could not be prevented from obstructing that light by building on the land.

THESIGER LJ: We have had a considerable number of cases cited to us, and out of them I think that two propositions may be stated as what I may call the general rules governing cases of this kind. The first of these rules is, that on the grant by the owner of a tenement of part of that tenement as it is then used and enjoyed, there will pass to the grantee all those continuous and apparent easements (by which, of course, I mean *quasi* easements), or, in other words, all those easements which have been necessary to the reasonable enjoyment of the property granted, and which have been and are at the time of the grant used by the owners of the entirety for the benefit of the part granted. The second proposition is that, if the grantor intends to reserve any right over the tenement granted, it is his duty to reserve it expressly in the grant. Those are the general rules governing cases of this kind, but the second of those rules is subject to certain exceptions. One of those exceptions is the well-known exception which attaches to cases of what are called ways of necessity; and I do not dispute for a moment that there may be, and probably are, certain other exceptions, to which I shall refer before I close my observations upon this case.

Both of the general rules which I have mentioned are founded upon a maxim which is as well established by authority as it is consonant to reason and common sense, viz., that a grantor shall not derogate from his grant. It has been argued before us that there is no distinction between what has been called an implied grant and what is attempted to be established under the name of an implied reservation; and that such a distinction between the implied grant and the implied reservation is a mere modern invention, and one which runs contrary, not only to the general practice upon which land has been bought and sold for a considerable time, but also to authorities which are said to be clear and distinct upon the matter. So far, however, from that distinction being one which was laid down for the first time by and which is to be attributed to Lord Westbury in *Suffield* v *Brown* 4 De GJ & S 185, it appears to me that it has existed almost as far back as we can trace the law upon the subject; and I think it right, as the case is one of considerable importance, not merely as regards the parties, but as regards vendors and purchasers of land generally, that I should go with some little particularity into what I may term the leading cases upon the subject....

These cases in no way support the proposition for which the Appellant in this case contends; but, on the contrary, support the propositions that in the case of a grant you may imply a grant of such continuous and apparent easements or such easements as are necessary to the reasonable enjoyment of the property conveyed, and have in fact been enjoyed during the unity of ownership, but that, with the exception which I have referred to of easements of necessity, you cannot imply a similar reservation in favour of the grantor of land.

Notes

1. The rule in *Wheeldon* v *Burrows* is based on the proposition that a man 'may not derogate from his grant' (see *Bayley* v *GWR Co.* (1884) 26 ChD 434).
2. Unlike s. 62, the easement in *Wheeldon* v *Burrows* must be continuous and apparent. 'Continuous and apparent' would appear to mean a user which is discoverable on 'a careful inspection by a person ordinarily conversant with the subject' (*Pyer* v *Carter* (1857) 1 H&N 916) or, as Ungoed-Thomas J said in *Ward* v *Kirkland* [1967] Ch 194, 225 '... the words "continuous and apparent" seem to be directed to there being on the servient tenement a feature which would be seen on inspection and which is neither transitory nor intermittent'.
3. The rule cannot apply to cases of compulsory purchase of land. Why is this so?
4. *Wheeldon* v *Burrows* applies only where the easement is necessary for the reasonable enjoyment of the land.

Ward v Kirkland
[1967] Ch 194

UNGOED-THOMAS J: ... [I]t would appear that the 'easements which are necessary to the reasonable enjoyment of the property conveyed' might be a separate class from 'continuous and apparent easements.' It has been recognised that there is some difficulty in these descriptions, to which I have referred, of the easements which come within the ambit of the doctrine of *Wheeldon* v *Burrows*. It has been suggested that perhaps the 'easements necessary to the reasonable enjoyment of the property conveyed' might refer to negative easements, whereas what we are concerned with here is positive easements. However that may be, I understand that there is no case in which positive easements which are not 'continuous and apparent' have been held to come within the doctrine of *Wheeldon* v *Burrows*. Here, there has certainly been continuous user, in the sense that the right has been in fact used whenever the need arose....

Here, it is conceded that it was only possible or practicable for the occupiers of the cottage to maintain the boundary wall by going onto the defendant's property as claimed in this case. That would be obvious on an inspection of the properties. But here there was no feature on the defendant's property designed or appropriate for such maintenance. The question is whether that requirement is necessary. If it is not necessary, then there are no clearly defined limits to the area of user; and if the easement extends to maintain the whole wall, as it must, then there could be no interference with that easement and therefore no building in the yard along that wall.

Professor Cheshire, in his book on *Real Property*, says [at p. 468] that

> The two words 'continuous' and 'apparent' must be read together and understood as pointing to an easement which is accompanied by some obvious and permanent mark on the land itself, or at least by some mark which will be disclosed by a careful inspection of the premises.

Then he gives instances, and says [at p. 469]:

> A right of way is not necessarily such a quasi-easement as will pass under the rule in *Wheeldon* v *Burrows*. To do so it must be apparent. There is no difficulty where there is a definite made road over the quasi-servient tenement to and for the apparent use of the quasi-dominant tenement. Such will clearly pass upon a severance of the common tenement. But the existence of a formed road is not essential, and if there are other indicia which show that the road was being used at the time of the grant for the benefit of the quasi-dominant tenement and that it is necessary for the reasonable enjoyment of that easement, it will pass to a purchaser of the latter.

It seems to me that in the absence of a continuous and apparent feature designed or appropriate for the exercise of the easement on the servient tenement, there is not a continuous and apparent easement within the requirements of *Wheeldon* v *Burrows* in the case of alleged positive easements. I, therefore, come to the conclusion that the easement claimed was not created by implication of law.

Notes
1. There must be user as of right until the date of the grant.
2. *Wheeldon* v *Burrows* is wider than s. 62, in the sense that it applies even where there has been no conveyance (see *Borman* v *Griffith* [1930] 1 Ch 493), and where there has been no diversity of ownership or occupation prior to the conveyance.

Question
Compare and contrast the rule in *Wheeldon* v *Burrows* with s. 62.

C: EASEMENTS BY PRESCRIPTION OR PRESUMED GRANT

See 14th Report of the Law Reform Committee (Cmnd 3100 1966).

There are three ways in which a claimant can obtain an easement by means of prescription or long user:

(a) at common law; or
(b) under the doctrine of lost modern grant; or
(c) by means of the Prescription Act 1832.

The doctrine of prescription is based upon the principle that although an easement should lie in grant it is unfair to deprive a person of a right that he has used for a long and continuous period simply because he cannot prove the existence of a deed.

In all three methods of prescription the following factors must be present:

(a) The user must be as of right.
(b) The user must be continuous.
(c) The user must be in fee simple.

(a) User as of right

The user must be as of right, and therefore any user which is not lawful cannot give rise to a prescriptive claim. See *Cargill* v *Gotts* [1981] 1 WLR 441, where the Court of Appeal said that there could be no easement based on prescription of a right to take water from a pond, where the plaintiff did not have a licence under the Water Resources Act 1963.

Gardner v Hodgson's Kingston Brewery Co. Ltd
[1903] AC 229 (HL)

The owner of a house used a path through the yard of an adjoining inn to the public road and had done so for over 40 years, paying the owner of the inn 15s a year. The path provided the only access to the stables. Held: the user was not of right under the Prescription Act.

LORD LINDLEY: I will take the Prescription Act first. Section 2 is the important section, and the last part of it is relied upon by the plaintiff. To bring herself within this enactment she must prove that she and her predecessors in title have enjoyed the way in question 'claiming right thereto' without interruption for forty years. The difficulty is raised by the words 'claiming right thereto,' and by the payment of the 15s. a year. I understand the words 'claiming right thereto' and the equivalent words 'as of right,' which occur in s. 5, to have the same meaning as the older expression nec vi, nec clam, nec precario. A temporary permission, although often renewed, would prevent an enjoyment from being 'as of right'; but a permanent, irrevocable permission attributable to a lost grant would not have the same effect. The common law doctrine is that all prescription presupposes a grant. But if the grant is proved and its terms are known, prescription has no place.

A title by prescription can be established by long peaceable open enjoyment only; but in order that it may be so established the enjoyment must be inconsistent with any other reasonable inference than that it has been as of right in the sense above explained. . . .

Note
In order for the user to be as of right, there must be no force, no secrecy and no permission (user *nec vi, nec clam, nec precario*).

Dalton v Angus & Co.
(1881) 6 App Cas 740 (HL)

Two dwelling houses, though built separately, were adjacent to each other and built so that each had lateral support from the soil beneath the other.

After more than 20 years, P's house was converted into a coach factory. The conversion involved the removal of internal walls which were replaced by girders inserted into a stack of brickwork. The result of this was to increase the lateral pressure upon the neighbouring property. There was no question of the conversion being concealed or done without the knowledge of the neighbour. The position remained unaltered for over 20 years until the owners of the adjoining house decided to have it demolished. The contractor they employed agreed to shore up all adjoining buildings and make good the damage. He, in turn, employed a sub-contractor to do the work on the same basis. No support was provided for P's building during the work and the factory collapsed when soil was excavated. Held: P had acquired a right of support for their factory having enjoyed that right for 20 years.

LORD SELBORNE: The inquiry on this part of the case is, as to the nature and extent of the knowledge or means of knowledge which a man ought to be shewn to possess, against whom a right of support for another man's building is claimed. He cannot resist or interrupt that of which he is wholly ignorant. But there are some things of which all men ought to be presumed to have knowledge, and among them (I think) is the fact, that, according to the laws of nature, a building cannot stand without vertical or (ordinarily) without lateral support. When a new building is openly erected on one side of the dividing line between two properties, its general nature and character, its exterior and much of its interior structure, must be visible and ascertainable by the adjoining proprietor during the course of its erection. When (as in the present case) a private dwelling-house is pulled down, and a building of an entirely different character, such as a coach or carriage factory, with a large and massive brick pillar and chimney-stack, is erected instead of it, the adjoining proprietor must have imputed to him knowledge that a new and enlarged easement of support (whatever may be its extent) is going to be acquired against him, unless he interrupts or prevents it. The case is, in my opinion, substantially the same as if a new factory had been erected, where no building stood before. Having this knowledge, it is, in my judgment, by no means necessary that he should have particular information as to those details of the internal structure of the building on which the amount or incidence of its weight may more or less depend. If he thought it material, he might inquire into those particulars, and then if information were improperly withheld from him, or if he received false or misleading information, or if anything could be shewn to have been done secretly or surreptitiously, in order to keep material facts from his knowledge, the case would be different. But here there was no evidence from which a jury could have been entitled to infer any of these things. Everything was honestly and (as far as it could be) openly done, without any deception or concealment. The interior construction of the building was, indeed, such as to require lateral support, beyond what might have been necessary if it had been otherwise constructed. But this must always be liable to happen, whenever a building has to be adapted to a particular use. The knowledge that it may or may not happen is in my opinion enough, if the adjoining proprietor makes no inquiry. I think, therefore, that in this case the kind and degree of knowledge which the adjoining proprietor must necessarily have had was sufficient; that nothing was done *clam*, and that the evidence did not raise any question on this point which ought to have been submitted to the jury.

My opinion, therefore, upon the whole case is in favour of the Respondents, the Plaintiffs in the action, and against the Appellants.

Note
If the user has been made forceably, then the claim cannot be as of right.

Eaton v *Swansea Waterworks Co.* (1851) 17 QB 267 (QBD)

P claimed to be entitled to divert water, and claimed a right to a watercourse by means of 20 years user without interruption. D had penned back the water from P's land and this prevented P from irrigating his land. These obstructions were, however, from time to time removed by P, and an employee of P's had been fined for removing such obstructions. Held: there was no enjoyment by P as of right.

Notes
1. The user must be without concealment. It must have been openly enjoyed. See *Union Lighterage Co.* v *London Graving Dock Co.*, at page 362, where rods had been sunk in the ground. Romer LJ said that an easement by prescription could only be acquired when the enjoyment has been open, that is to say, of such a character that an ordinary owner of the land, diligent in the protection of his interests, would have, or must be taken to have, a reasonable opportunity of becoming aware of that enjoyment.

See also *Liverpool Corp* v *H. Coghill & Son Ltd* [1918] 1 Ch 307.

2. Permission by the servient owner will negate any prescriptive claim — see, for example, *Gardner* v *Hodgson's Kingston Brewery Co. Ltd*, at page 370. Therefore, any right that is founded on a licence from the owner of the land cannot be the basis of an easement by prescription. The basis of a prescriptive claim is acquiescence by the servient owner but not permission. In *Dalton* v *Angus & Co.* (1881) 6 App Cas 740, Fry J said (at p. 774):

> I cannot imagine any case of acquiescence in which there is not shown to be in the servient owner:
> (1) a knowledge of the acts done;
> (2) a power in him to stop the acts or to sue in respect of them; and
> (3) an abstinence on his part from the exercise of such power.

Davies v *Du Paver* [1953] 1 QB 184 (CA)

P owned and occupied a farm (A) and claimed a prescriptive right of pasture over part of an adjoining farm (B) on the ground that the owner of farm A had exercised the right, without interruption for more than 60 years. Farm B had been occupied by sitting tenants for 55 of the 60 years. D acquired Farm B and immediately erected a fence to prevent P's user. Although P protested at the time the fence was erected and also threatened legal proceedings nothing further was done for over a year. Held: P had failed to show that D had either knowledge or the means of acquiring knowledge of the user. As D was therefore not in a position to object to the user until he took over Farm B, P could not establish a right under the Prescription Act or common law.

Diment v *NH Foot Ltd*
[1974] 2 All ER 785 (ChD)

P and D owned neighbouring farms. Between 1936 and 1967 D and his predecessor in title had used an alleged right of way between six and 10 times each year to allow vehicles to come on to D's field which was separated from the highway by a strip of P's land. P had let the farm out to tenants during this period and only came to live on the farm in 1967. She had employed a firm of surveyors to act as her agent in her absence and only visited the farm occasionally herself. The surveyor never carried out full inspections of the land and P was only told of D's use of the right of way in 1967. She sought an injunction restraining D from coming that way. Held: P had not heard before 1967 that D had been using the field over her farm, and therefore she had no actual knowledge of the user of the way across the field. There was no easement by prescription.

PENNYCUICK V-C: ... [It] is I think an enlargement of the principle stated in *Dalton v Henry Angus & Co*. The plaintiff herself did not have such knowledge and so, as far as she is concerned, she has rebutted the presumption. But what was said by counsel for the defendant company was this: that during these years the plaintiff employed a firm of chartered surveyors known as Henry Duke & Son of Dorchester to act for her in connection with Sanctions Farm including the making of agreements with the successive tenants in occupation of field 415. That is undoubtedly so. Then he said that any knowledge or imputed knowledge on the part of the plaintiff's agent must be treated for this purpose as her own knowledge as principal and went on to contend that this presumption applies as regards Henry Duke & Son, with the consequence that it could only be rebutted by showing that Henry Duke & Son did not in fact have knowledge of the user of the way, or means of such knowledge. I do not think the presumption can legitimately be carried so far where a landowner employs an agent in connection with his property. There cannot, I think, be a presumption, merely by reason of that relation and without reference to the particular circumstances, that the agent has knowledge or means of knowledge of any particular act on the land. That would be carrying this presumption altogether beyond anything that was said in *Pugh v Savage* and would, I venture to think, lead to some very odd consequences. It seems to me that where one is concerned with an agent the role of establishing knowledge or means of knowledge must rest on the other party concerned who may discharge that burden by positive evidence or inference — the inference depending on all the particular circumstances. There is no evidence here as to the precise activities carried on by Henry Duke & Son apart from the fact that they were responsible for making the tenancies and dealing with matters of rents and so forth. There is no evidence as to what members or representatives of that firm did physically on Sanctions Farm or field 415 by way of inspection and I see no ground on which I would be entitled to hold that Henry Duke & Son had knowledge or means of knowledge of the user of this by Mr Foot or the defendant company.

That is sufficient to decide this case because the defendant company has failed to establish that the plaintiff either had knowledge of the use of this way or the means of such knowledge and that is the third of Fry LJ's requirements.

Note
See also Goff J in *Healey v Hawkins* [1968] 1 WLR 1967.

(b) User must be continuous

The user must be continuous. How frequently the right must be exercised will vary according to the nature of the right.

In *Hollins v Verney* (1884) 13 QBD 304 (CA), it was said that use of a right of way on three separate occasions in 12 years was insufficient to show continual user, but in *Diment* v *NH Foot Ltd* [1974] 2 All ER 785, it was said that if a field is used on 6 to 10 occasions each year for a period of 35 years, this was sufficient user in extent and regularity to be capable of creating a right of way.

Mills v *Silver*
[1991] Ch 271 (CA)

Here D bought a derelict farm. The only access to the farm was along a track over P's adjoining land. A previous occupier of the farm had used this track, but it had not been used frequently. P knew of this use and had not sought to prevent it. Held: there was an easement in D's favour.

PARKER LJ: In *Hollins* v *Verney* (1884) 13 QBD 304 at 315 Lindley LJ, giving the judgment of the court, said:

> ... no actual user can be sufficient to satisfy the statute, unless during the whole of the statutory term (whether acts of user be proved in each year or not) the user is enough at any rate to carry to the mind of a reasonable person who is in possession of the servient tenement, the fact that a continuous right to enjoyment is being asserted, and ought to be resisted if such right is not recognised, and if resistance to it is intended.

This shows clearly that the crucial matter for consideration is whether for the necessary period the use is such as to bring home to the mind of a reasonable person that a continuous right of enjoyment is being asserted. If it is and the owner of the allegedly servient tenement knows or must be taken to know of it and does nothing about it the right is established. It is no answer for him to say, 'I "tolerated" it.' If he does nothing he will be taken to have recognised the right and not intended to resist it. He will have consented to it or acquiesced in it.

Note
User is still continuous where there is an agreement between the dominant and servient owners to vary the route of a right of way. See *Davis* v *Whitby* [1973] 1 WLR 629.

(c) User in fee simple

A prescriptive claim at common law is based on user in fee simple, and an easement can only be acquired by means of prescription for an estate in fee simple. Therefore, there can be no acquisition of an easement by means of prescription for a term of years.

Kilgour v *Gaddes*
[1904] 1 KB 457 (CA)

P and D occupied adjacent premises. Both were assignees under separate leases from a common landlord G. D and his predecessors in title had used a pump on P's premises for 40 years prior to the action. Held: no easement could be acquired.

COLLINS MR: With regard to easements such as a right of way, as was pointed out by Romer LJ during the argument, and by Palles CB in *Timmons v Hewitt* 22 LR Ir 627, the reason why a prescriptive right of way cannot be acquired by user by one tenant over land in the occupation of another tenant of the same owner is that the enjoyment of the easement in that case would not be as of right. The learned Chief Baron said in *Timmons v Hewitt* 22 LR Ir 627:

> Where the two tenements are held by termors under the same landlord, prescription does not apply; because, as pointed out by Lord Cairns in *Gayford v Moffatt* LR 4 Ch 133, 'the possession of the tenant of the demised close is the possession of his landlord; and it seems to be an utter violation of the first principles of the relation of landlord and tenant to suppose that the tenant, whose occupation of close A was the occupation of his landlord, could by that occupation acquire an easement over close B, also belonging to his landlord.' This doctrine was approved and acted upon by the Court of Common Pleas in this country in *Clancy v Byrne* (1877) IR 11 CL 355. If I am asked how it is consistent with the Prescription Act, I answer that such user and enjoyment is not as of right within the meaning of the 2nd section. It is a user by a termor, who, if he acquire the right, must acquire it as incident to the land of which he is termor, and thus for the benefit of his reversioner. Such user cannot be as of right, unless a reversioner can in law by user acquire a right against himself.

That reasoning appears to me conclusive of the present case. There was a long discussion in the course of the argument as to the possibility of a termor under one landlord acquiring for his landlord an easement by user over land in the occupation of a termor under another landlord, and as to whether an easement in such a case could be acquired, unless and until the user had continued for the period of three years after the determination of the term in the servient tenement without interference by the reversioner. That no doubt raises an interesting question, which appears to have been decided in Ireland in the case of *Beggan v McDonald* 2 LR Ir 560 contrary to the view expressed in this country in *Bright v Walker* 1 CM & R 211; 40 RR 536 and also in *Wheaton v Maple & Co.* [1893] 3 Ch 48, in neither of which cases, however, was it necessary actually to decide the point. That question, however, is not the question raised in the present case.

Pugh v Savage [1970] 2 QB 373 (CA)

P purchased a farm, which included field A, from R in 1950. A footpath ran from the highway, along a lane, which was partly on P's land, into field A. The footpath continued across field A to give access to field B and the next field, field C. Until 1966 the three fields had been in separate ownership. In 1966, the owner of field B purchased field C and let both fields to D. D was told that he had a right of way over field A. P tried to prevent D from using the right of way. D claimed to have acquired a right of way by prescription as the right had been used uninterrupted for over 30 years by his predecessors in title. It was established that R had let the farm, including field A, to his son, from 1940 to 1950 and it was argued that that tenancy defeated D's claim to a prescriptive right of way. Held: where a tenancy of a servient tenement came into existence during the course of the period of user, the grant of the tenancy is not fatal to the presumption of a grant or claim under the Prescription Act 1832, unless there is evidence that the servient owner had no knowledge of the user while the tenant was in possession.

(d) Prescription at common law

Prescription at common law is based on long user of the right claimed, stemming from time immemorial, which according to the Statute of Westminster I, 1275, c. 39, is a date fixed at 1189. Therefore, prescription at common law requires the right to be in existence at or before that date. A rule evolved whereby proof that the right existed during living memory would suffice. This has since been abrogated to 20 years. Such a claim can be rebutted, however, by proof that such a grant could not have existed since 1189, or proof of unity of possession between the dominant and servient tenements since 1189.

Bryant v Foot
(1867) LR 2 QB 161 (Ct of QB)

By a custom established for over 50 years the sum of 13s had been paid (via the rector) to a parish church as a fee in respect of every marriage. Held: (Blackburn J dissenting) in the circumstance, the fee was not legally due.

COCKBURN CJ: Taking it, therefore, that the custom to pay the fee now claimed is shewn to have existed since the year 1808, it would *prima facie* follow, according to the established rule as to presumption in such cases, that we ought to presume the previous existence of the custom for an antecedent period, extending as far back as the time of legal memory. But it is equally clear that this rule must be taken with this important qualification, that it can only be applied when the presumption of immemoriality is not rebutted, either by proof of the actual origin of the custom since the time of legal memory, or by its appearing that the custom could not possibly have existed at that date. In either of these cases the presumption is inadmissible, and the custom, whatever may have been its duration, has no binding validity in law. Furthermore, it is immaterial whether the impossibility of the origin of the custom having been beyond the time of legal memory is shewn by extrinsic evidence, or is to be gathered from the nature of the alleged custom itself, as where, in the case of an alleged customary payment, the amount is so large as to make it impossible that such a payment can have been established as far back as the reign of Richard the First. Now, when it is borne in mind that the parish of Horton is a rural parish, inhabited principally by agricultural labourers, and that a fee of 13s. on the celebration of marriage is, even in our day, for people of this class, a very high fee, it seems quite impossible to believe — looking to the relative value of money in the twelfth century and at the present day, even if the disproportion be taken at the most moderate rate — that such a payment can have been exacted and submitted to in the reign of King Richard.

(e) Lost modern grant

The difficulties in proving a prescriptive right based on common law led to the development of prescription based on lost modern grant. This doctrine is based on the legal fiction that 20 years user is sufficient evidence that a grant was made by means of a deed after 1189 but has been misplaced and lost.

Tehidy Minerals Ltd v Norman
[1971] 2 QB 528 (CA)

D owned farms and claimed rights of common grazing over land owned by P. Some of the farms had been in common ownership with the farm until 1920 when it was sold to P. D claimed that they had acquired rights in the period from January 1920 when the land ceased to be in common ownership to October 1941 when the land was requisitioned by the Ministry of Agriculture and Fisheries.

BUCKLEY LJ: The question is whether on the facts of this case enjoyment of this grazing for a period of upwards of 20 years preceding October 6, 1941, permits or requires us to presume that such enjoyment was had by virtue of grants made after January 19, 1920, but before October 6, 1921 (being 20 years before October 6, 1941), and subsequently lost, and whether we ought to act on such a presumption.

In this connection we were referred to *Angus v Dalton* (1877) 3 QBD 85; (1878) 4 QBD 162; (1881) 6 App Cas 740.... In the Queen's Bench Division (1877) 3 QBD 85, where the case was argued before Cockburn CJ, Lush and Mellor JJ, all three judges took the view that the right claimed was an easement. They all agreed in the view that the right must be based in that case upon a presumed lost grant and that such presumption was rebuttable. The majority, consisting of Cockburn CJ and Mellor J, considered that the presumption had been rebutted, but Lush J thought that this was not so. In his view, at p. 93, after 20 years' enjoyment a grant should be presumed, unless it were proved that the easement had been enjoyed by sufferance. They were all in agreement that, although the right was in the nature of an easement, it was not an easement of a kind to which the Prescription Act 1832 was applicable. In the Court of Appeal (1878) 4 QBD 162 the matter came before Thesiger, Cotton and Brett LJJ. They also all took the view that the right claimed was an easement but that such easement was not within the terms of the Prescription Act 1832, and that the claim must be based upon a presumed lost grant. They all agreed that such presumption was rebuttable, but the majority, consisting of Thesiger and Cotton LJJ, held that the presumption was not in fact rebutted, whereas Brett LJ considered that it was effectively rebutted. The case was twice argued before the House of Lords (1881) 6 App Cas 740 and on the second occasion the House was advised by seven judges, namely, Pollock B, Field, Lindley, Lopes, Manisty, Fry and Bowen JJ. Of these, four, namely, Lindley, Lopes, Fry and Bowen JJ were of opinion that the right was in the nature of an easement. Pollock B and Field and Manisty JJ were of opinion that it was a proprietary right adhering to the plaintiffs' property in his own land. The latter three judges were consequently not concerned to consider the doctrine of lost modern grant. Lindley, Lopes and Bowen JJ considered that the case was one to which the doctrine of lost modern grant was applicable. Lindley and Lopes JJ considered that in the circumstances the presumption had not been effectively rebutted, but Bowen J considered that it had been rebutted. Lindley J said at p. 765:

> But it appears to me to be contrary to the reason for the theory itself to allow such an enjoyment to be disturbed simply because it can be proved that no grant was ever in fact made.

Fry J considered that on principle the doctrine of lost modern grant ought not to apply because the owner of the servient tenement had no real opportunity of interfering with the enjoyment of the dominant owner. He considered, however, that authority precluded this view being adopted. He said, at p. 779:

I regard the right as resting, not on any principle, but solely on a series of authorities which disclose no clear ground for their existence; but as it has been established that the right in question may be acquired by the lapse of time, I think that the period of 20 years may and ought to be held a sufficient one to confer the right.

On the second occasion when the case was argued before the House of Lords the House consisted of Lord Selborne LC, Lord Blackburn, Lord Penzance, Lord Watson and Lord Coleridge. Lord Selborne considered that the right in question was an easement, and, moreover, that it was an easement to which the Prescription Act 1832 applied. With these views Lord Watson agreed. Lord Selborne went on to say, at p. 800:

> Supposing, however, that section 2 of the Prescription Act ought not to be held to apply to the easement of support, the same result would practically be reached by the doctrine, that a grant, or some lawful title equivalent to it, ought to be presumed after 20 years' user. As to this I think it unnecessary to say more than that I agree with the view of the authorities taken by Lush J, by the majority of the judges of the Court of Appeal, and by all the learned judges who attended this House (unless Bowen J, who preferred to rely on the equitable doctrine of acquiescence, is an exception) in their answer to the first two questions proposed to them by your Lordships.

These questions, stated shortly, were whether the owner of an ancient building was entitled to lateral support from the land of an adjoining owner and whether, in the circumstances of that case, 27 years' enjoyment was sufficient to confer the same right as if the plaintiffs' building were ancient. Lord Blackburn appears to have been of the opinion that the right was of a proprietary nature rather than an easement (at p. 808); but, unlike those judges who in their advice to the House of Lords took the same view of the character of the right, he thought that the plaintiff must rely on the doctrine of lost modern grant (at p. 810). He consequently proceeded to consider this doctrine and held that the presumption could not be rebutted by a finding that no grant was in fact made. Lord Coleridge, somewhat ambiguously, said that he entirely concurred in the conclusions at which the Lord Chancellor and Lord Blackburn had arrived and in the reasons which they had given for them. Lord Penzance dealt with the case on similar lines to Fry J.

Of the judges who considered the doctrine of lost modern grant in *Angus* v *Dalton* (1877) 3 QBD 85; (1878) 4 QBD 162; (1881) 6 App Cas 740, a majority in the Queen's Bench Division, consisting of Cockburn CJ, and Mellor J, thought that the presumption of a grant had been rebutted: a majority in the Court of Appeal, consisting of Thesiger and Cotton LJJ, thought that it had not been rebutted: in the House of Lords the Lord Chancellor agreed with the majority in the Court of Appeal, while Lord Blackburn was of the view that a party relying on the protection of a presumed lost modern grant ought not to be deprived of that protection by showing that no grant was originally made to him. It is hard to say just where Lord Coleridge stood, but he clearly assented to the views of the Lord Chancellor and Lord Blackburn where they coincided. Lord Penzance and Lord Watson did not find it necessary to deal with this question. Of the judges who advised the House of Lords, Lindley and Lopes JJ considered that the presumption had not been rebutted, but Bowen J thought otherwise. It is evident that the authoritative view must be sought in the judgments of the majority in the Court of Appeal, approved by the Lord Chancellor and Lord Blackburn. It appears from what was said in *Angus* v *Dalton* by Cockburn CJ and by Cotton LJ that the case proceeded upon the basis that it was admitted that in truth there had been no grant of the right of support claimed. Thesiger JL dealt with the doctrine (1878) 4 QBD 162. He said, at p. 171:

And, first, as regards easements generally, the authorities cited in the court below establish that this presumption is not 'presumptio juris et de jure' or, to use other language, is not an absolute and conclusive bar. On the other hand, these same authorities lay down that the uninterrupted enjoyment of an easement for 20 years raises, to use the words of Lord Mansfield in *Darwin* v *Upton*, 2 Will Saund 506 'such decisive presumption of a right by grant or otherwise, that unless contradicted or explained the jury ought to believe it'; and the corollary upon this proposition is stated by Bayley J in *Cross* v *Lewis* (1823) 2 B & C 686 where he says: 'I do not say that 20 years' possession confers a legal right; but uninterrupted possession for 20 years raises a presumption of right; and ever since the decision in *Darwin* v *Upton*, 2 Will Saund 506 it has been held that in the absence of any evidence to rebut the presumption, a jury should be told to act upon it.' What then is the nature of the evidence which would be held to 'contradict,' 'explain,' or 'rebut' this decisive presumption?

After referring to certain matters which he considered insufficient to displace the presumption, Thesiger LJ then went on, at p. 172:

In harmony, as it appears to me, with the last proposition, is the further proposition, that the presumption cannot be rebutted by mere proof by the owner of the servient tenement, that no grant was in fact made either at the commencement or during the continuance of the enjoyment. I am not aware that this proposition has been in terms directly decided, but it is almost impossible to suppose that among the numerous cases in which easements have been held by the courts to have been acquired by uninterrupted user for 20 years only, there must not have been many in which the owner of the servient tenement at the time when the period commenced was alive when the action was tried to contradict, if such evidence had been admissible, the fact of a grant; and if such evidence were admissible, it is almost inconceivable that in the numerous cases, in which questions of easements have been discussed, no trace of an opinion to that effect should be found in the observations of the judges. The correct view upon this point I take to be, that the presumption of acquiescence and the fiction of an agreement or grant deduced therefrom in a case, where enjoyment of an easement has been for a sufficient period uninterrupted, is in the nature of an estoppel by conduct, which, while it is not conclusive so far as to prevent denial or explanation of the conduct, presents a bar to any simple denial of the fact, which is merely the legal inference drawn from the conduct. If, instead of its being a mere legal inference, the courts had considered that it was an inference of fact to be drawn by juries like other inferences of fact, and in respect of which the servient owner might be called as a witness to negative the fact by denial of a grant ever having been made, it is difficult to understand how judges could have systematically, as the Lord Chief Justice admits they did, directed juries to find grants 'in cases in which no one had the faintest belief that any grant had ever existed, and where the presumption was known to be a mere fiction.'

He said, at p. 175:

These cases, therefore, as direct authorities go no further than to show that a legal incompetence as regards the owner of the servient tenement to grant an easement, or a physical incapacity of being obstructed as regards the easement itself, or an uncertainty and secrecy of enjoyment putting it out of the category of all ordinary known easements, will prevent the presumption of an easement by lost grant; and on the other hand indirectly, they tend to support the view, that as a general rule where no such legal incompetence, physical incapacity, or peculiarity of enjoyment, as was shown in those cases, exists, uninterrupted and unexplained user will raise the presumption of a grant, upon the principle expressed by the maxim, 'Qui non prohibet quod prohibere potest assentire videtur.'

Cotton LJ took a similar view. He said, at p. 186:

> The question of enjoyment beyond the time of living memory does not arise, but there had been upwards of 20 years' enjoyment, and this is sufficient to raise a presumption that the enjoyment has been under a modern lost grant. This is, no doubt, liable to be rebutted, and in my opinion the real question on this part of the case is, what evidence is sufficient to rebut the presumption. On this point there is very little authority, but as stated by Lord Cockburn CJ in this case 3 QBD 105, it is not necessary that the jury should come to the conclusion, that in fact there was such a grant. The easement is analogous to that of a right to light before the statute 2 & 3 Wm 4, c. 71, and in *Cross* v *Lewis* (1823) 2 B & C 686, Bayley J lays it down, and in my opinion correctly, that in such case mere dissent by the owner of the alleged servient tenement will not be sufficient to rebut the presumption. If, therefore, the parties at the trial, as stated by the Lord Chief Justice, admitted that there was not in fact any grant, this, in my opinion, was not sufficient to rebut the presumption arising from 20 years' enjoyment, or to justify a judgment for the defendants. But it may be urged this is contrary to what is said in many cases, namely, that 20 years' enjoyment raises a presumption only, and that the opinion which I have expressed will make such enjoyment confer an absolute right; but this is not so. The presumption may be rebutted by showing that the owner of the servient tenement was not capable of making a grant, as for instance, that he was tenant for life, or of unsound mind. . . .

He then referred to *Barker* v *Richardson* (1821) 4 B & A 579, where the owner at the relevant time was incapable of making a grant, and to *Webb* v *Bird* (1862) 13 CBNS 841 and *Chasemore* v *Richards* (1859) 7 HL Cas 349, where the decisions turned on the peculiar character of the rights claimed, and proceeded:

> An admission, therefore, or evidence, that in fact there was no grant, would not, in my opinion, rebut the presumption, and notwithstanding such evidence or admission, unless there was any other evidence to rebut the presumption (as for instance, evidence that the adjoining owner was incapable of making a grant), the jury ought to be directed to find that there had been a grant which has been lost.

Not only were these views explicitly approved by the Lord Chancellor but they also accord with the view of Lord Blackburn, who said (1881) 6 App Cas 826:

> Now, if the motive for introducing prescription is that given in the Digest . . . I think it irresistibly follows that the owner of a house, who has enjoyed the house with a de facto support for the period and under the conditions prescribed by law, ought to be protected in the enjoyment of that support, and should not be deprived of it by showing that it was not originally given to him.

In our judgment *Angus* v *Dalton* (1877) 3 QBD 85; (1878) 4 QBD 162; (1881) 6 App Cas 740 decides that, where there has been upwards of 20 years' uninterrupted enjoyment of an easement, such enjoyment having the necessary qualities to fulfil the requirements of prescription, then unless, for some reason such as incapacity on the part of the person or persons who might at some time before the commencement of the 20-year period have made a grant, the existence of such a grant is impossible, the law will adopt a legal fiction that such a grant was made, in spite of any direct evidence that no such grant was in fact made.

If this legal fiction is not to be displaced by direct evidence that no grant was made, it would be strange if it could be displaced by circumstantial evidence leading to the same conclusion, and in our judgment it must follow that circumstantial evidence tending to negative the existence of a grant (other than evidence establishing impossibility) should not be permitted to displace the fiction. Precisely the same reasoning must, we think, apply to a presumed lost grant of a profit à prendre as to an easement.

Note
See also *Bridle v Ruby* [1988] 3 All ER 64 (CA), where it was said that the presumption that arises from the doctrine of lost modern grant could be rebutted by alternative explanations for the use being uninterrupted, such as the granting of permission and neighbourly tolerance, but not by a mistaken belief about the legal origin of the right asserted if the mistake did not affect the conduct of the claimant or the understanding of that conduct by the owner of the servient land.

See V. T. H. Delany, 'Lessees and the doctrine of lost grant' [1958] 74 LQR 82.

(f) Prescription under the Prescription Act 1832
The object of the Act is to remove the difficulties that arise from prescription at common law:

(a) by shortening the time of legal memory;

(b) by making it impossible for a claim to be defeated by proof that at a time after 1189 the easement could not have existed.

Prescription Act 1832

1. Claims to right of common and other profits à prendre, not to be defeated after thirty years enjoyment by merely showing the commencement; after sixty years enjoyment the right to be absolute, unless had by consent or agreement

No claim which may be lawfully made at the common law, by custom, prescription, or grant, to any right of common or other profit or benefit to be taken and enjoyed from or upon any land of our sovereign lord the King, . . . or any land being parcel of the duchy of Lancaster or of the duchy of Cornwall, or of any ecclesiastical or lay person, or body corporate, except such matters and things as are herein specially provided for, and except tithes, rent, and services, shall, where such right, profit, or benefit shall have been actually taken and enjoyed by any person claiming right thereto without interruption for the full period of thirty years, be defeated or destroyed by showing only that such right, profit, or benefit was first taken or enjoyed at any time prior to such period of thirty years, but nevertheless such claim may be defeated in any other way by which the same is now liable to be defeated; and when such right, profit, or benefit shall have been so taken and enjoyed as aforesaid for the full period of sixty years, the right thereto shall be deemed absolute and indefeasible, unless it shall appear that the same was taken and enjoyed by some consent or agreement expressly made or given for that purpose by deed or writing.

2. In claims of right of way or other easement the periods to be twenty years and forty years

No claim which may be lawfully made at the common law, by custom, prescription, or grant, to any way or other easement, or to any watercourse, or the use of any water, to be enjoyed or derived upon, over, or from any land or water of our said lord the King, ... or being parcel of the duchy of Lancaster or of the duchy of Cornwall, or being the property of any ecclesiastical or lay person, or body corporate, when such way or other matter as herein last before mentioned shall have been actually enjoyed by any person claiming right thereto without interruption for the full period of twenty years, shall be defeated or destroyed by showing only that such way or other matter was first enjoyed at any time prior to such period of twenty years, but nevertheless such claim may be defeated in any other way by which the same is now liable to be defeated; and where such way or other matter as herein last before mentioned shall have been so enjoyed as aforesaid for the full period of forty years, the right thereto shall be deemed absolute and indefeasible, unless it shall appear that the same was enjoyed by some consent or agreement expressly given or made for that purpose by deed or writing.

3. Claim to the use of light enjoyed for 20 years

When the access and use of light to and for any dwelling house, workshop, or other building shall have been actually enjoyed therewith for the full period of twenty years without interruption, the right thereto shall be deemed absolute and indefeasible, any local usage or custom to the contrary notwithstanding, unless it shall appear that the same was enjoyed by some consent or agreement expressly made or given for that purpose by deed or writing.

4. Before mentioned periods to be deemed those next before suits

Each of the respective periods of years herein-before mentioned shall be deemed and taken to be the period next before some suit or action wherein the claim or matter to which such period may relate shall have been or shall be brought into question and that no act or other period shall be deemed to be an interruption, within the meaning of this statute, unless the same shall have been or shall be submitted to or acquiesced in for one year after the party interrupted shall have had or shall have notice thereof, and of the person making or authorizing the same to be made.

7. Proviso for infants, etc

Provided also, that the time during which any person otherwise capable of resisting any claim to any of the matters before mentioned shall have been or shall be an infant, idiot, non compos mentis, feme covert, or tenant for life, or during which any action or suit shall have been pending, and which shall have been diligently prosecuted, until abated by the death of any party or parties thereto, shall be excluded in the computation of the periods herein-before mentioned, except only in cases where the right or claim is hereby declared to be absolute and indefeasible.

8. What time to be excluded in computing the term of forty years appointed by this Act

Provided always, that when any land or water upon, over, or from which any such way or other convenient watercourse or use of water shall have been or shall be enjoyed or derived hath been or shall be held under or by virtue of any term or life, or any term of years exceeding three years from the granting thereof, the time of the enjoyment of any such way or other matter as herein last before mentioned, during the continuance of such terms, shall be excluded in the computation of the said period of forty years, in case the claim shall within three years next after the end or sooner determination of such term be resisted by any person entitled to any reversion expectant on the determination thereof.

Easements and Profits à Prendre

Note
The Act does not supersede other forms of common law prescriptions but creates another basis for a prescriptive claim.

(i) *Section 2* A claimant relying on the Act does not have to worry about the claim being based in legal memory. A claim cannot be defeated by evidence that user could not have been in existence since 1189; but other common law defences can be adduced to defeat a claim, whether based on the 20- or 40-year period, e.g., if the user is not as of right. The term 'as of right' has the same meaning as it does for common law prescription with the following exceptions:

(a) A written or oral consent given from time to time during the user can defeat a claim, whether the claim is based on the 20- or 40-year period.

(b) A written consent given at the beginning of the user and continuing throughout will defeat a claim irrespective of which period is used.

(c) an oral consent given at the beginning of the user and continuing throughout will defeat a claim based on the 20-year period but not one based on the 40-year period.

(ii) *Section 4* The user must be without interruption. Interruption means an overt act that interferes with the right claimed (see *Carr* v *Foster* (1842) 3 QB 581).

In **Reilly v Orange** [1955] 2 QB 112 (CA) Jenkins LJ said:

Mr Blease's argument on this part of the case is of this nature: he says that what must be shown is 20 years' uninterrupted user, and that, according to section 4, no act or matter counts as an interruption unless the same shall have been or shall be submitted to or acquiesced in for one year. It follows, says Mr Blease, that inasmuch as in this case over 19 years' user down to the commencement of the action is proved, the defendant's right is made good inasmuch as there could be no interruption acquiesced in for one year between the date of the commencement of the action and the completion of the full period of 20 years.

In support of that proposition he referred us to the well-known case of *Flight* v *Thomas* (1841) 8 Cl & Fin 231. In that case: 'A had the free access of light and air through a window of his house for nineteen years and 330 days, and B then raised a wall which obstructed the light, and the obstruction was submitted to only for 35 days, when A brought an action to remove it.' It was held: 'that the right of action was complete; that the twenty years' enjoyment was to be reckoned from the commencement of the enjoyment to the time of bringing the action; and that an interruption of the enjoyment, in whatever period of the twenty years it may happen, cannot be deemed an interruption within the meaning of the Act, unless it is acquiesced in for a whole year.'

Mr Blease seeks to apply that to the present case in this way: he says that the commencement of the action constituted an interruption, and that, inasmuch as the action was not commenced until after the alleged easement had been enjoyed for more than 19 years, the interruption so constituted could not last for the required period of one year, so that his title was complete at the time of action brought. In my view that argument cannot prevail. What the Prescription Act requires, as appears from the combined effect of section 2 and section 4, is the full period of 20 years, being 'the period next before some suit or action wherein the claim or matter to which such period may relate shall have been or shall be brought into question.' The commencement of the suit or action in my view is clearly not an interruption within the meaning of section 4, but is the event marking the date down to which the requisite period of user must be shown. What must be shown is a full 20 years reckoned down to the date of action brought. That must be an uninterrupted period, but in considering whether it is an uninterrupted period or not, interruptions not acquiesced in for at least a year are not to be counted as interruptions.

In **Ward v Kirkland** [1967] Ch 194, Ungoed-Thomas J said:

The next ground upon which the claim is based by the plaintiff is prescription. This turns, of course, on sections 2 and 4 of the Prescription Act, 1832. [His Lordship read sections 2 and 4, and continued:]

So, the enjoyment required is for 20 years before action without submitting to or acquiescing in interruption for a year. The defendant submits that in this case there was an interruption for that period. The interruption is stated to have started in October, 1958, and to have been submitted to or acquiesced in till May or June, 1960, and, of course, if that submission is correct, then the claim based on prescription is defeated. The writ was not issued until December 29, 1960, and, therefore, when the action started, there was not 20 years' enjoyment before action without interruption which had been acquiesced in or submitted to by the plaintiff for one year, if the defendant's submission is accepted.

It is clear that submission to or acquiescing in an interruption is more than mere interruption itself. In *Davies* v *Du Paver*, Birkett LJ stated that such submission or acquiescence was a state of mind. In this case, it is clear that there was no submission or acquiescence in October, 1958. At that time, the plaintiff attempted to enter the defendant's yard for the purpose of maintaining his wall. She refused him entry. His son-in-law was with him and used certain words which she chose to interpret as a request for permission and stated that as he had asked for permission, she would let him in to do the wall. The occasion was heated, and it is perfectly clear that the plaintiff did not go into the property and was not allowed into the property, because he himself was not prepared to go in by permission but was maintaining that he was entitled as of right to do the maintenance work to his wall.

Note
The user must be for a period 'next before some suit or action'. Therefore the enjoyment of the right must be for the period which immediately precedes and terminates in the action (see *Jones* v *Price* (1836) 3 Bing NC 52).

(iii) *Sections 7 and 8* Certain disabilities of the servient owner affect a claim based on the Prescription Act 1832. The disabilities are:

(a) the infancy of the servient owner;
(b) where the servient owner is a patient under the Mental Health Act 1983, or any Act which predates it;
(c) where the servient owner is a tenant for life.

All these disabilities affect a claim based on 20 years, but only (c) affects a 40-year claim. The time during which a person is under one of the disabilities is subtracted from the period of user, and time begins to run again as soon as the disability is removed. The deduction does not destroy the user. In a claim based on 40 years user a deduction is made for any period under (c) or where there has been a tenant for a term of years on the servient land.

(iv) *Easements of light and the Act*

  (a) The disabilities discussed above do not apply to easements of light.
  (b) The user need not be 'as of right', provided it is enjoyed without written agreement.
  (c) The user must have continued for 20 years next before the action in which the claim is brought (see *Hyman v Van Den Bergh* [1907] 2 Ch 516; affd [1908] 1 Ch 167).
  (d) There is only one period, 20 years.

A right of light cannot be acquired if it has been interrupted by the servient owner carrying out an adverse act lasting at least one year. The interruption can be a physical interruption of light, or can be a notional obstruction under the Rights of Light Acts 1959, as amended by the Local Land Charges Act 1975, s. 17, sch. 1.

An easement of light can be acquired by a tenant against his landlord since the prescription is not limited in respect of fee simple.

Morgan v Fear [1907] AC 425 (HL)

Two adjoining properties were let to different tenants by the same landlord. One of the tenants had enjoyed the uninterrupted right to the access of light to his property over the other property for 20 years. He therefore had an indefeasible claim against the other tenant and his successors in title. It was held that he also had such a right against the landlord and his successors in title.

Allen v Greenwood [1980] Ch 119 (CA)

Here the court considered the amount of light necessary for a greenhouse in P's garden. Held: where a right to light is acquired under s. 3 of the Prescription Act 1832 the measure of the amount of light to which the dominant land was entitled is that required for the beneficial use of the building for the ordinary purpose for which it is adapted. That could be for example, as here, where the building was a greenhouse.

Note

See A. H. Hudson, 'Light for inadequate windows' [1984] Conv 408; '*Allen v Greenwood*' [1979] Conv 298.

Questions

1. The Law Reform Committee (Cmnd 3100, 1966) said that the Prescription Act 1832 enjoyed the unenviable reputation of being 'one of worst drafted Acts on the Statute Book'. Do you agree with this view?

2. Do you consider that the law of acquisition of easements by prescription is in a satisfactory state? If not, why not, and what reforms do you consider desirable?

See H. W. Wilkinson, 'Law Reform Committee: Fourteenth Report on Acquisition of Easements and Profits by Prescription' (1967) 30 MLR 189.

Note
It should also be noted that easements can be created by means of estoppel (see pages 40–1 and 236 *et seq.*).

D: EXTENT OF RIGHTS

After an easement has been created, its content and extent can still be questioned. This would normally occur, for example, due to changes in the neighbourhood.

(a) Easements acquired by prescription
These are dependent on user, and therefore their extent will be determined by user.

British Railways Board v *Glass* [1965] Ch 538 (CA)

In 1847, a strip of land, which was part of a farm, was conveyed to a predecessor of P. The land was to be used in connection with a railway line and the vendors reserved a right of crossing, including crossing for cattle, to enable the vendors and their successors in title to cross from one part of their land to another. For many years prior to 1942, part of the farm near the crossing had been used from time to time as a caravan site for caravans and tents. The number of caravans and people on the land increased substantially after 1942 and, inevitably, the number of people using the crossing had increased. P complained of this and attempted to limit the user of the crossing. Held: (Lord Denning MR dissenting):

(1) The right of way that had been granted was for all purposes and not limited to the user contemplated when the grant was made. The reference to 'cattle' operated as an extension, rather than a limitation, to the right.

(2) A right of way to use the crossing based on prescription had been acquired by the people using the caravans. Even though there was an increase in user as a result, there was not excessive user.

Notes
1. See (1965) 81 LQR 17 (R.E.M.).
2. See *Woodhouse Co. Ltd* v *Kirkland (Derby) Ltd* [1970] 1 WLR 1185, where Plowman J considered an increase in the number of customers using a right of way which had been established by prescription. The right of way had been established for business purposes and a mere increase in customers using it did not amount to excessive user. There is an important difference between

an increase in user and user which is of a different kind or for a different purpose.

3. See also *Giles* v *County Building Constructors (Hertford) Ltd* [1971] 22 P & CR 978, where the erection of seven modern dwellings in the place of two houses was said to be an evolution not a mutation. The plaintiffs and defendant both had rights of way over a road. The plaintiffs sought to prevent increased usage of the road which would be caused by the larger number of dwellings. The plaintiffs failed.

(b) Easements acquired by express grant
Here the terms of the grant must be construed.

St Edmundsbury & Ipswich Diocesan Board of Finance v **Clark (No. 2)** [1975] 1 All ER 772 (CA)

A church authority conveyed certain land to D. The land surrounded a church. A right of way was reserved in the conveyance over a 30-yard strip of land to provide access from a public highway to the church. The strip, the only defined means of access, was wide enough for vehicles although there was no evidence that it had every been used for vehicles before the conveyance was made. D erected gates on the land which prevented vehicles passing so that the church could only be reached on foot. P claimed they were entitled to a right of way with or without vehicles over the strip of land. Held: on construction, taking into account the surrounding circumstances, the right of way was a footway only. The words must be given their natural meaning. Only where the words of reservation are wholly unambiguous could the surrounding circumstances be ignored.

Note
A right of way that has been granted for general purposes is not to be restricted to access to the land merely for such purposes as were reasonably required at the date of the grant.

Keefe v *Amor* [1965] 1 QB 334 (CA)

P's semi-detached property had the benefit of an express right of way over a strip of land which formed part of D's neighbouring property. The strip was shown on a plan and was 20 feet wide and 130 feet long. P was under a liability to contribute to the repair and upkeep of the strip of land and also a boundary wall. At the front of the property there was a wall and a gap in that wall 4 foot 6 inches wide gave access from the strip of land to the highway. Part of the strip itself was gravelled and the rest laid to flower beds. D widened the front gates to 7 foot 6 inches by widening the gap and hanging an additional gate 3 feet wide, which was kept locked. P claimed a right of way for all purposes over the strip as the entrance was now wide enough to allow vehicles to pass. D objected to the right being extended to any use which was not possible when there was the original, smaller gap. Held: the right of way was not limited by the physical characteristics of the land when the grant was made. P could use the strip for all purposes, including vehicular traffic.

Note
See also *White* v *Grand Hotel Eastbourne Ltd* [1913] 1 Ch 113, where a right of way for general purposes to a private dwelling house was not affected by the house being turned into a hotel.

Jelbert v *Davis* [1968] 1 WLR 589 (CA)

Land was conveyed to P with a right of way over the vendor's driveway 'at all times and for all purposes in common with all other persons having the like right'. The defendants were others with rights over the driveway. P obtained planning permission to use his land for a caravan site for part of the year. The defendants objected to the extra use. Held:

(1) The words of the grant were sufficiently wide to entitle P, upon construction of the words of the conveyance, to use the driveway for access to his land and the change of use of that land was immaterial.

(2) P's right was limited in extent to that contemplated at the time of the grant. P could not use the right excessively or in such a way as it would interfere unreasonably with the enjoyment of the like right by others entitled to use it.

Note
In the next case, alteration to the dominant tenement was considered.

Graham v *Philcox*
[1984] QB 747 (CA)

Combining a ground floor and first floor flat into one where a right of way was appurtenant only to the first floor flat was held not to affect the right as it would not cause excessive user.

PURCHAS LJ: The only change that has now been made is that one dwelling unit is now housed where two dwelling units were previously housed. It does not follow of necessity that the 'de facto' user of the right of way made by the members of the unit now occupying both parts of the coach house would be more than the user of that right to which the occupier personally and/or his servants, invitees and licensees would have been entitled as occupier of the dominant tenement confined to the first floor. Indeed, it is not difficult to conceive of circumstances in which it might be a good deal less. This change is entirely different from the dramatic structural changes, changes of use considered in the cases to which reference has already been made; and falls far more within the concept of the alteration to the dominant tenement which was held not to have prejudiced the right to use the coal shed in *Wright* v *Macadam* [1949] 2 KB 744, to which May LJ has already referred and upon which Mr Reid relied in support of his submission that mere alteration to the extent of the dominant tenement was not effective to destroy an easement or right. . . . The right of way having been created by direct grant and its use continuing even though under statutory protection at the time of the conveyance, the use and enjoyment of that easement fell within the terms of section 62 of the Act and the judge was in error in holding that it did not. Nor, for the reasons I have already given, can I accept the submissions made by Mr Godfrey that by enlarging the physical dimensions or indeed altering the nature of the dominant tenement from two individual flats to one dwelling house has the easement, right or advantage been destroyed. The occupier of the dominant tenement, however, will be and will remain subject to the rules requiring that the character and extent of the burden imposed upon the servient tenement must not be enlarged. For want of a better definition, this burden must be said to be commensurate with the reasonable user of the means of access by the occupier, his servants, agents, invitees or licensees occupying a single dwelling unit. If by any change in the nature of his enjoyment of the dominant tenement the occupier thereof increases the burden upon the servient tenement beyond this, then he will be liable to the consequences of excessive user which may be imposed upon any person enjoying an easement, right or benefit of this kind.

Note
In the following case, alteration to the servient tenement was considered.

Celsteel Ltd v *Alton House Holdings Ltd*
[1985] 1 WLR 204 (ChD)

Here, P had a right of access and D proposed to build a car-wash on the servient land which would have reduced the width of access from 9 metres to 4.14 metres. Held: the reduction in width would amount to a substantial interference with the right of way over the servient tenement and P was entitled to an injunction to prevent it.

SCOTT J: It has been settled law for a long time that an interference with a private right of way is not, per se, an actionable interference. In *Clifford* v *Hoare* (1874) LR 9 CP 362 a vehicular right of way had been granted over a roadway 40 feet wide. The defendant erected a building which encroached 2 feet into the roadway. It was held that this encroachment did not represent an actionable interference with the right of way. The issue was treated as depending basically on the construction of the grant. What quality of enjoyment of the right of way had been intended to be granted? Lord Coleridge CJ answered this question by saying that 'the intention was to grant the plaintiff an easement only, the reasonable use and enjoyment of an ascertained way' (at 370). Since the encroachment did not interfere with the reasonable use and enjoyment of the way, it did not represent an actionable interference. *Clifford* v *Hoare* was a case where the interference had resulted in a reduction of the width of the way by a trivial amount. In *Pettey* v *Parsons* [1914] 2 Ch 653 the issue was whether a gate across a right of way represented an actionable interference. In the view of the Court of Appeal the gate would not do so provided it were kept open during business hours. It is to be noted that the servient owner was contending for the right to maintain a closed gate across the way. Lord Cozens-Hardy MR said that an interference 'is not actionable unless it is substantial' (at 662). . . . And in *Keefe* v *Amor* [1964] 2 All ER 517 at 520, [1965] 1 QB 334 at 346 Russell LJ described as actionable 'such obstacles as impede the user of the strip for such exercise of the right granted as from time to time is reasonably required by the dominant tenant'.

There emerge from the three cases I have cited two criteria relevant to the question whether a particular interference with a right of way is actionable. The interference will be actionable if it is substantial. And it will not be substantial if it does not interfere with the reasonable use of the right of way. I must apply these criteria to the present case.

I will take first the position of the third plaintiff as lessee of garage 52. Both he and his son expressed the preference of reversing into the garage and exiting forwards. They were cross-examined at some length by counsel for Alton House, who sought to establish that it was preferable to drive in forwards and reverse out. There are advantages and disadvantages attached to each of the alternatives. Some may prefer one, others may prefer the other. In my view, a lessee whose right of way permits him to adopt either alternative as he may from time to time choose suffers actionable interference if one alternative is precluded and he is constrained always to adopt the other. To put the point another way, use of the rear driveway in order to reverse into garage 52 is a reasonable use. An obstruction which prevents that use is, accordingly, in my judgment actionable.

SECTION 6: EXTINGUISHMENT OF EASEMENTS

(a) Statute
Easements can be extinguished under various statutes, such as the Town and Country Planning Act 1971, ss. 118 and 127.

(b) Release
Release may be express or implied.

(i) *Express release* At common law a release must be made by a deed which effectively frees the servient tenement from the easement. However, even in the absence of a deed, an express agreement to release servient land from an easement may take effect in equity if the servient owner acts to his own detriment in reliance on the agreement (see *Davies* v *Marshall* (1861) 10 CB(NS) 697).

(ii) *Implied release* Release from an easement will not generally be implied merely from lack of use. However, if there is no other explanation for the non-user than the abandonment of the right by the dominant owner such an abandonment may be implied. The dominant owner can avoid this result by explaining the non-user. In *Moore* v *Rawson* (1824) 3 B & C 332, a wall with windows was replaced by a wall without any. Seventeen years had passed since the new wall was built. This was held to be an abandonment of any right to light.

An alteration in the dominant tenement rendering the right unnecessary may be regarded as evidence of an intention to abandon that right, but such a presumption is rebuttable.

(c) Unity of seisin
Easements cannot exist where the fee simple of the dominant and servient land become vested in a common owner. However, where there is common occupation without common ownership such rights are suspended but will

automatically be revived once the tenements pass again into separate occupation.

SECTION 7: PROFITS À PRENDRE

Profits confer a right on a person to take something from land which belongs to another, i.e. the servient tenement.

There are several important points to note about profits:

(a) A profit can exist 'in gross', i.e. there need not be a dominant tenement which will benefit from the profit.

(b) Profits may be acquired in the same way as an easement, i.e. by means of statute, express grant, implied grant and prescription. Where a profit is acquired under the Prescription Act 1832, the statutory periods of enjoyment are 30 years and 60 years respectively, instead of 20 and 40 years.

(c) Profits may be annexed to the land but an easement may not.

(d) Profits may be enjoyed by their owner to the exclusion of all others ('several' profits) or can be enjoyed by him in common with others (profits 'in common').

11 FREEHOLD COVENANTS

SECTION 1: GENERAL

A covenant is a promise which is contained in a deed. The deed usually takes the form of the conveyance of the freehold estate, but a covenant can be contained in a deed other than the conveyance.

A fee simple owner may wish to impose a duty upon a neighbouring fee simple owner, and this can be achieved by means of freehold covenants. For example, A owns Blackacre and sells part of his land (Whiteacre) to B. A may wish to control the way in which B uses the land. He may require B to covenant not to use Whiteacre for business purposes, or for B to construct and maintain a road between Blackacre and Whiteacre for the benefit of A and his successors in title. The former covenant is a negative or restrictive covenant and the latter is a postive covenant.

The rules for the enforcement of freehold covenants are distinct and separate from the rules for the enforcement of leasehold covenants which were discussed in chapter 6.

SECTION 2: ENFORCEABILITY BETWEEN THE ORIGINAL PARTIES

As between the original covenantee and covenantor there is privity of contract and hence the covenant can be enforced. If, however, the covenant was made for the benefit of land with which the covenantee has now parted, then the covenantee can recover only nominal damages as he has suffered no loss. At common law there was a rule that no one could sue on a deed made between the parties unless he was named as a party in the deed (*Lord Southampton* v *Brown* (1827) 6B & C 718, 719f).

Law of Property Act 1925

56. Persons taking who are not parties and as to indentures
(1) A person may take an immediate or other interest in land or other property, or the benefit of any condition, right of entry, covenant or agreement over or respecting land or other property, although he may not be named as a party to the conveyance or other instrument.
(2) A deed between parties, to effect its objects, has the effect of an indenture though not indented or expressed to be an indenture.

Note
This section abrogates the common law rule that no person can sue on a deed made *inter partes* unless he was named in the deed as a party, but it is somewhat unclear what effect s. 56 has on the doctrine of privity of contract. It would appear from *Beswick* v *Beswick* [1968] AC 58, that it does not effect a fundamental change in the law so as to allow a third party, who is not a party to a contract, to enforce it. See G. H. Treitel, 'Specific performance and third parties', (1967) 30 MLR 687.

White v *Bijou Mansions Ltd*
[1937] Ch 610 (ChD)

SIMONDS J: ... Just as under s. 5 of the Act of 1845 only that person could call it in aid who, although not a party, yet was a grantee or covenantee, so under s. 56 of this Act only that person can call it in aid who, although not named as a party to the conveyance or other instrument, is yet a person to whom that conveyance or other instrument purports to grant some thing or with which some agreement or covenant is purported to be made. To give it any other meaning appears to me to open the door to claims or assertion of rights which cannot have been contemplated by the Legislature, for if that be not the limitation which must be imposed on this section it appears to me that there is no limit and it will be open to anybody to come into Court and say: 'Here is a covenant which if enforced will redound to my advantage, therefore I claim the benefit of the section. I claim that this covenant or condition is one which should be enforced in my favour because it is for my benefit, whether intended for my benefit or not intended for my benefit would not appear to matter.' I cannot give to the section any such meaning as that. I interpret it as a section which can be called in aid only by a person in whose favour the grant purports to be made or with whom the covenant or agreement purports to be made. If that is so, whether the plaintiff's claim arises under the earlier or the later Act, he cannot sue on it in this Court because he is not a person who, under the deed of 1890, can point to any grant or any covenant purported to be made to or with him. ...

See also *In re Ecclesiastical Commissioners for England's Conveyance* [1936] Ch 430 (ChD).

Note
The effect of s. 56 would thus appear to be that if a person is expressed in the conveyance to be the one for whose benefit the covenant was made, that person is to be regarded as an original covenantee even if not a party to the deed.

SECTION 3: ENFORCEMENT OF COVENANTS AT COMMON LAW

Where a covenant is enforceable by and against the successors in title of the original covenantor and covenantee, then the covenant is said to 'run with the land'. In order for a covenant to be enforceable at common law between such assignees both the benefit and the burden of the covenant must run at common law.

A: BENEFIT OF THE COVENANT AT COMMON LAW

The rule is that the benefit of a covenant, whether positive or negative, can run with the land, provided four conditions are fulfilled:

(a) The covenant must touch and concern the land. This is the same as in leasehold covenants, see page 199 *et seq*.

(b) There must have been an intention that the benefit of the covenant should run with the land that is owned by the covenantee at the date of the covenant. See Law of Property Act 1925, s. 78(1), at page 209.

(c) The covenantee, at the time of making the covenant, must have had a legal estate in the land. Prior to 1875 the common law did not recognise the existence of equitable interests in land, and therefore covenants could only be enforced by the owner of a legal estate (see *Webb* v *Russell* (1789) 3 Term Rep 393).

(d) An assignee claiming to enforce the covenant must derive his title from or under the original covenantee. At one time the assignee seeking to enforce the covenant had to have the same legal estate in land as the original covenantee, since at common law a covenant was incidental to the estate.

Smith and Snipes Hall Farm v *River Douglas Catchment Board*
[1949] 2 All ER 179 (CA)

In order to prevent flooding, several owners of land together entered into an agreement with D by which D covenanted to widen, deepen and make good the banks of the river which ran through the owners' land and maintain the banks in order to prevent flooding. In return, the owners covenanted to contribute to the cost. Part of the land affected was conveyed to P, and the conveyance expressly stated that the land was conveyed with the benefit of the agreement between the landowners and D. P1 then leased the land to P2. The river subsequently flooded, burst its banks and flooded P1's and P2's land. P1 and P2 brought proceedings for breach of contract. D contended that there was no privity of contract and that the covenant did not run with the land. Held: the covenant was binding on the board.

TUCKER LJ: It remains to consider whether, in these circumstances, the plaintiffs, or either of them, can sue in respect of this breach. It is said for the board that the benefit of the covenant does not run with the land so as to bind a stranger who has not and never had an interest in the land to be benefited and there being no servient tenement to bear the burden. Further it is contended that such a covenant must by the terms of the deed in which it is contained relate to some specific parcel of land, the precise extent and situation of which can be identified by reference to the deed alone. It is first necessary to ascertain from the deed that the covenant is one which 'touches or concerns' the land, that is, it must either affect the land as regards mode of occupation or it must be such as *per se*, and not merely from collateral circumstances, affects the value of the land, and it must then be shown that it was the intention of the parties that the benefit thereof should run with the land. . . . With regard to the covenantor being a stranger, *The Prior's Case* (1368) YB 42 Edw 3, fo 3A pl 14 is referred to in *Spencer's Case* 5 Co Rep 16a in these words as set out in *Smith's Leading Cases* (13th ed., vol. 1, p. 55):

> [In the case of a] grandfather, father and two sons: The grandfather being seised of the manor of D, whereof a chapel was parcel: a prior, with the assent of his convent, by deed covenanted for him and his successors, with the grandfather and his heirs, that he and his convent would sing all the week in his chapel, parcel of the said manor, for the lords of the said manor and his servants, etc.; the grandfather did enfeoff one of the manor in fee, who gave it to the younger son and his wife in tail; and it was adjudged that the tenants in tail, as terre-tenants (for the elder brother was heir), should have an action of covenant against the prior, for the covenant is to do a thing which is annexed to the chapel, which is within the manor, and so annexed to the manor, as it is there said.

. . .

In *Rogers* v *Hosegood* [1900] 2 Ch 388 Farwell, J, in a passage where he refers, among others, to *The Prior's Case* (1368) YB 42 Edn 3, fo 3A pl 14 — and I quote from his judgment because, although the case went to the Court of Appeal, the Court of Appeal had to deal with a rather different point — after stating what are the requirements in order that the covenant may run with the land, says ([1900] 2 Ch 395):

> It is not contended that the covenants in question in this case have not the first characteristic, but it is said that they fail in the second. I am of opinion that they possess both. Adopting the definition of Bayley, J, in *Congleton Corpn* v *Pattison* (1808) 10 East 130 the covenant must either affect the land as regards mode of occupation, or it must be such as *per se*, and not merely from collateral circumstances, affects the value of the land. It is to my mind obvious that the value of Sir J Millais's land is directly increased by the covenants in question. If authority is needed, I would refer to *Mann* v *Stephens* (1846) 15 Sim 377, a case very similar to the present; *Vyvyan* v *Arthur* (1823) 1 B & C 410; *The Prior's Case* (1368) YB 42 Edw 3, fo 3A pl 14; *Fleetwood* v *Hull* (1889) 23 QBD 35; *White* v *Southend Hotel Co*. [1897] 1 Ch 767. I see no difficulty in holding that the benefit of a covenant runs with the land of the covenantee, while the burden of the same covenant does not run with the land of the covenantor.

In this state of the authorities it seems clear, despite some *dicta* tending to the contrary view, that such a covenant, if it runs with the land, is binding on the covenantor though a mere stranger, and that this point will not avail the board.

As to the requirement that the deed containing the covenant must expressly identify the particular land to be benefited, no authority was cited to us and in the absence of such authority I can see no valid reason why the maxim '*Id certum est quod certum reddi potest*' should not apply so as to make admissible extrinsic evidence to prove the extent and situation of the lands of the respective landowners adjoining the Eller Brook situate between the Leeds and Liverpool Canal and the River Douglas. . . . I do not find anything in the judgments in *Austerberry* v *Oldham Corpn.* (1885) 29 ChD 750 which conflicts with the law as I have endeavoured to set it out above, and I have, accordingly, arrived at the conclusion that the covenenant by the board in the agreement of April 25, 1938, is one which runs with the land referred to therein, which land is capable of identification, and that it is binding on the board; and, further, that by virtue of s. 78 (1) of the Law of Property Act, 1925, it can be enforced at the suit of the covenantee and her successors in title and the persons deriving title under her or them so that both the plaintiff Smith and the plaintiff company can sue in respect of the damage resulting to their respective interests therein by reason of the board's breach of covenant.

DENNING LJ: The law on this subject was fully expounded by Mr Smith in his note to *Spencer's* case which has always been regarded as authoritative. Such covenants [relating to land] are clearly intended, and usually expressed, to be for the benefit of whomsoever should be the owner of the land for the time being; and at common law each successive owner has a sufficient interest to sue because he holds the same estate as the original owner. The reason which Lord Coke gave for this rule is the reason which underlies the whole of the principle now under consideration. He said in his work upon Littleton that it was 'to give damages to the party grieved'. If a successor in title were not allowed to sue it would mean that the covenantor could break his contract with impunity, for it is clear that the original owner, after he has parted with the land, could recover no more than nominal damages for any breach that occurred thereafter. It was always held, however, at common law that, in order that a successor in title should be entitled to sue, he must be of the same estate as the original owner. That alone was a sufficient interest to entitle him to enforce the contract. The covenant was supposed to be made for the benefit of the owner and his successors in title, and not for the benefit of anyone else. This limitation, however, was, as is pointed out in *Smith's Leading Cases*, capable of being 'productive of very serious and disagreeable consequences', and it has been removed by section 78 of the Law of Property Act 1925, which provides that a covenant relating to any land of the covenantee shall be deemd to be made with the covenantee and his successors in title, 'and the persons deriving title under him or them' and shall have effect as if such successors 'and other persons' were expressed.

The covenant of the catchment board in this case clearly relates to the land of the covenantees. It was a covenant to do work on the land for the benefit of the land. By the statute, therefore, it is to be deemed to be made, not only with the original owner, but also with the purchasers of the land and their tenants as if they were expressed. Now if they were expressed, it would be clear that the covenant was made for their benefit; and they clearly have sufficient interest to entitle them to enforce it because they have suffered the damage. The result is that the plaintiffs come within the principle whereby a person interested can sue on a contract expressly made for his benefit.

Notes
1. The decision in this case has been criticised since s. 78 of the Law of Property Act 1925 was merely meant to be a word-saving provision abrogating the need to show an intention that the benefit of the covenant was to run. It was not intended to have substantative effect. See E. H. Scammell, 'Positive covenants in conveyances of the fee simple' (1954) 18 Conv 546, 553; H. W. R Wade, 'Covenants — a broad and reasonable view' 31 (1972) CLJ 157, 171.
2. The interpretation of the section has been followed in *Federated Homes Ltd* v *Mill Lodge Properties Ltd* [1980] 1 All ER 371 (see page 409).

3. The benefit of a covenant can also be transferred under the Law of Property Act 1925, s. 136.

Law of Property Act 1925

136. Legal assignments of things in action

(1) Any absolute assignment by writing under the hand of the assignor (not purporting to be by way of charge only) of any debt or other legal thing in action, of which express notice in writing has been given to the debtor, trustee or other person from whom the assignor would have been entitled to claim such debt or thing in action, is effectual in law (subject to equities having priortiy over the right of the assignee) to pass and transfer from the date of such notice—

(a) the legal right to such debt or thing in action;
(b) all legal and other remedies for the same; and
(c) the power to give a good discharge for the same without the concurrence of the assignor:

Provided that, if the debtor, trustee or other person liable in respect of such debt or thing in action has notice—

(a) that the assignment is disputed by the assignor or any person claiming under him; or
(b) of any other opposing or conflicting claims to such debt or thing in action;

he may, if he thinks fit, either call upon the persons making the claim thereto to interplead concerning the same, or pay the debt or other thing in action into court under the provisions of the Trustee Act, 1925.

B: BURDEN OF THE COVENANT AT COMMON LAW

Austerberry v *Corporation of Oldham*
(1885) 29 ChD 750 (CA)

A conveyed a piece of land to T, and in the conveyance T covenanted with A, his heirs and assigns, that they, their heirs and assigns would make up a road and keep it in repair and allow the public to use the road upon payment of tolls. T made the road. A then sold his lands, bounding T's land on both sides, to P. T sold their land to D. Both P and D bought with notice of the covenant to repair. Held: P could not enforce the covenant against D.

LINDLEY LJ: . . . [A]s regards the benefit running with the Plaintiff's land, the covenant is, so far as the road goes, a covenant to repair the road; what I mean by that is, there is nothing in the deed which points particularly to that portion of the road which abuts upon or fronts the Plaintiff's land — it is a covenant to repair the whole of the road, no distinction being made between the portion of that road which joins or abuts upon his land and the rest of the road; in other words, it is a covenant simply to make and maintain this road as a public highway; there is no covenant to do anything whatever on the Plaintiff's land, and there is nothing pointing to the Plaintiff's land in particular. . . . I do not overlook the fact that the Plaintiff as a frontager has certain rights of getting on to the road; and if this covenant had been so worded as to shew that there had been an intention to grant him some particular benefit in respect of that particular part of his land, possibly we might have said that the benefit of the covenant did run with this land; . . .

But it strikes me, I confess, that there is a still more formidable objection as regards the burden. Does the burden of this covenant run with the land so as to bind the Defendants? The Defendants have acquired the road under the trustees, and they are bound by such covenant as runs with the land. Now we come to face the difficulty; does a covenant to repair all this road run with the land — that is, does the burden of it descend upon those to whom the road may be assigned in future? We are not dealing here with a case of landlord and tenant. The authorities which refer to that class of cases have little, if any, bearing upon the case which we have to consider, and I am not prepared to say that any covenant which imposes a burden upon land does run with the land, unless the covenant does, upon the true construction of the deed containing the covenant, amount to either a grant of an easement, or a rent-charge, or some estate or interest in the land. A mere covenant to repair or to do something of that kind, does not seem to me, I confess, to run with the land in such a way as to bind those who may acquire it.

It is remarkable that the authorities upon this point, when they are examined, are very few, and it is also remarkable that in no case that I know of, except one which I shall refer to presently, is there anything like authority to say that a burden of this kind will run with the land. That point has often been discussed, and I rather think the conclusion at which the editors of the last edition of *Smith's* Leading Cases have come to is right, that no case has been decided which does establish that such a burden can run with the land in the sense in which I am now using that expression.

[Lindley LJ refers to the cases of *Holmes* v *Buckley* 1 Eq C Ab 27, *Morland* v *Cook* Law Rep 6 Eq 252, *Cooke* v *Chilcott* 3 ChD 694 and *Western* v *Macdermott* Law Rep 1 Eq 499]. I am not aware of any other case which either shews, or appears to shew, that a burden such as this can be annexed to land by a mere covenant, such as we have got here; and in the absence of authority it appears to me that we shall be perfectly warranted in saying that the burden of this covenant does not run with the land. After all it is a mere personal covenant. If the parties had intended to charge this land for ever, into whosesoever hands it came, with the burden of repairing the road, there are ways and means known to conveyancers by which it could be done with comparative ease; all that would have been necessary would have been to create a rentcharge and charge it on the tolls, and the thing would have been done. They have not done anything of the sort, and, therefore, it seems to me to shew that they did not intend to have a covenant which should run with the land. That disposes of the part of the case which is perhaps the most difficult.

The last point was this — that even if it did not run with the land at law, still, upon the authority of *Tulk* v *Moxhay* (1848) 2 Ph 774, the Defendants, having bought the land with notice of this covenant, take the land subject to it. . . . *Tulk* v *Moxhay* cannot be extended to covenants of this description. It appears to me, therefore, that upon all points the Plaintiff has failed, and that the appeal ought to be dismissed with costs.

Note:
See also *E & GC Ltd* v *Bate* (1935) 79 Law J News 203.

C: DEVICES TO CIRCUMVENT THE RULE IN *AUSTERBERRY*

(a) Lease instead of sale

A lease of the land could be made instead of a sale of the fee simple. Positive covenants can then be enforced under the doctrine of privity of estate. See chapter 6.

Freehold Covenants

(b) Law of Property Act 1925, s. 153
See pages 191–3.

Instead of conveying the fee simple, a long lease could be granted. Such a lease could contain the required covenants, and by s. 153 of the Law of Property Act 1925, such a lease is enlarged into a fee simple subject 'to all the same covenants . . . as the term would have been subject to if it had not been so enlarged'.

(c) Chain of indemnity covenants
The original covenantor always remains liable on the original covenants even after he has parted with the land. He can protect himself, however, by taking a covenant of indemnity from the person to whom he sells the land. Each successive purchaser can do this and a chain of indemnity covenants is thus created. The original covenantee can then secure the enforcement of positive covenants by the current owner of the land by suing the original covenantor, who in turn sues the person to whom he sold the land as that purchaser is bound by the covenant of indemnity. The same process will occur throughout the chain of indemnity so that the ultimate successor of the original covenator will effectively bear the burden of the covenant.

Question
What problems do you envisage in creating a chain of indemnity covenants?

(d) *Halsall* v *Brizell*

Halsall v *Brizell*
[1957] Ch 169 (ChD)

O and J were the owners of 40 acres of land most of which they sold as building plots. O and J retained the roads, sewers, promenade and sea wall. They entered into a deed with many of the purchasers of the plots, the object of which was to declare the trusts on which the roads and promenade were to be held and to provide payment for their maintenance. The vendors declared that they held the roads etc. on trust for the purchasers, and the purchasers covenanted to contribute towards their upkeep. The covenants by the purchasers were expressed to be for themselves, their heirs, executors and assigns. The covenants by O and J were expressed to be made with O and J, their heirs and assigns.

In 1931, F purchased a building plot and house for an estate in fee simple. The property was conveyed to him subject to the covenants in the earlier deed, so far as they related to and affected the property and were subsisting and enforceable and capable of taking effect. F let the property to five tenants.

In 1950, at an annual general meeting of the owners of the various plots it was decided to authorise the trustees to require an additional contribution by any owner who had divided his property into two or more separate flats or dwellings. F's executors refused to pay the additional sums.

UPJOHN J: . . . [I]t is conceded that it is ancient law that a man cannot take benefit under a deed without subscribing to the obligations thereunder. If authority is required for that proposition, I need but refer to one sentence during the argument in *Elliston* v *Reacher* [1908] 2 Ch 374, where Lord Cozens-Hardy MR observed: 'It is laid down in Co. Litt. 230b, that a man who takes the benefit of a deed is bound by a condition contained in it, though he does not execute it.' If the defendants did not desire to take the benefit of this deed, for the reasons I have given, they could not be under any liability to pay the obligations thereunder. But, of course, they do desire to take the benefit of this deed. They have no right to use the sewers which are vested in the plaintiffs, and I cannot see that they have any right, apart from the deed, to use the roads of the park which lead to their particular house, No. 22, Salisbury Road. The defendants cannot rely on any way of necessity or on any right by prescription, for the simple reason that when the house was originally sold in 1931 to their predecessor in title he took the house on the terms of the deed of 1851 which contractually bound him to contribute a proper proportion of the expenses of maintaining the roads and sewers, and so forth, as a condition of being entitled to make use of those roads and sewers. Therefore, it seems to me that the defendants here cannot, if they desire to use this house, as they do, take advantage of the trusts concerning the user of the roads contained in the deed and the other benefits created by it without undertaking the obligations thereunder. Upon that principle it seems to me that they are bound by this deed, if they desire to take its benefits.

Note
See F. R. Crane, (1977) 41 Conv 432; F. P. Aughterson, 'Enlargement of positive burdens — a new viability' [1985] Conv 12.

(e) Estate rentcharges
See Rentcharges Act 1977, s. 2(3)(c), (4), (5), and pages 22–3.
 A covenant to pay money or contribute to the maintenance of the property may be construed as an estate rentcharge.

(f) Right of re-entry
This may be reserved on events which amount to a breach of a positive covenant. See *Shiloh Spinners* v *Harding* [1973] AC 691, at page 31 *et seq.*; S. M. Tolson, '"Land" without earth: freehold flats in English law' (1950) 14 Conv 350.

(g) *Crow* v *Wood*

Crow v *Wood* [1971] 1 QB 77

A landowner owned a moor and several adjoining farms, each enclosed by stone walls. The farms were leased to various tenants and each was granted a right to allow sheep to go onto the moor. Each tenant was also under a duty to keep his fences and walls in good repair. From 1951 the owner started selling the farms to the tenants, including P. Each conveyance contained a right for the new owner to allow his sheep to stray onto the moor. P did not maintain the fences and walls of her farm and the defendant's sheep came onto P's land from the moor, causing damage. P sought damages and an injunction. The defendant said P was in breach of a duty to keep the walls and fences in good repair. Held: the right to have a fence or wall kept in repair was a right in the nature of an easement, and P was in breach of her duty to maintain her fences and walls.

(h) Law of Property Act 1925, s. 79
(See chapter 6.)

It would appear that s. 79 has been interpreted by the courts as being a word-saving provision. In ***Tophams Ltd v Sefton (Earl)*** [1966] 1 All ER 1039 (HL), Lord Wilberforce said: 'I should add that section 79 of the Law of Property Act 1925, itself does not have the effect of causing Tophams' covenant to run with the land: it merely extends the scope of Tophams' covenants.' Lord Upjohn added:

. . . on this aspect of the matter, I think that too much significance was placed in the courts below on the impact of s. 79(1) of the Law of Property Act, 1925. During the course of the hearing before your lordships it became common ground that, so far as relevant to any question that your lordships have to decide, it does no more than render it unnecessary in the description of the parties to the conveyance to add after Lord Sefton's name, 'his executors administrators and assigns' and after Tophams' name 'and their successors in title'. This can really have little or no weight in considering the liability of Tophams' assigns in relation to a restrictive covenant affecting land.

Question
What would be the effect on *Austerberry* v *Oldham Corporation* of construing s. 79 in the same way as s. 78 has been construed in *Federated Homes Ltd* v *Mill Lodge Properties Ltd*?

Note
See the Wilberforce Committee Report of the Committee on Positive Covenants Affecting Land 1965 (Cmnd 2719); Law Commission Report on Restrictive Covenants 1967 (Law Com No. 11); Law Commission Report on Positive and Restrictive Covenants 1984 (Law Com No. 127).

Question
How would the position of the running of the burden of covenants be altered if the proposals of Law Commission Report No. 127 were adopted?

SECTION 4: ENFORCEABILITY OF COVENANTS IN EQUITY

The restrictive nature of the common law led equity to develop rules for the enforcement of covenants by means of an injunction. Equity thought it unfair to allow a person to buy land which was subject to a covenant of which he had notice, actual or constructive, and to use the land free of that covenant. Again, for a covenant to run in equity, both the benefit and the burden must run.

Tulk v *Moxhay*
(1848) 2 Ph 774

In 1808, P, the fee simple owner of a piece of land in Leicester Square and several houses in the square, sold the land to E. In the conveyance E covenanted on behalf of himself, his heirs and assigns that he would maintain the land and keep it in an open state and that the inhabitants of Leicester Square should have access to the land. The land was conveyed eventually to D whose deed of purchase contained no such covenant with the vendor, but who took with notice of the covenant. Held: an injunction was granted preventing D breaching the covenant.

LORD COTTENHAM LC: That this Court has jurisdiction to enforce a contract between the owner of land and his neighbour purchasing a part of it, that the latter shall either use or abstain from using the land purchased in a particular way, is what I never knew disputed. Here there is no question about the contract: the owner of certain houses in the square sells the land adjoining, with a covenant from the purchaser not to use it for any other purpose than as a square garden. And it is now contended, not that the vendor could violate that contract, but that he might sell the piece of land, and that the purchaser from him may violate it without this Court having any power to interfere. If that were so, it would be impossible for an owner of land to sell part of it without incurring the risk of rendering what he retains worthless. It is said that, the covenant being one which does not run with the land, this Court cannot enforce it; but the question is, not whether the covenant runs with the land, but whether a party shall be permitted to use the land in a manner inconsistent with the contract entered into by his vendor, and with notice of which he purchased. Of course, the price would be affected by the covenant, and nothing could be more inequitable than that the original purchaser should be able to sell the property the next day for a greater price, in consideration of the assignee being allowed to escape from the liability which he had himself undertaken.

That the question does not depend upon whether the covenant runs with the land is evident from this, that if there was a mere agreement and no covenant, this Court would enforce it against a party purchasing with notice of it; for if an equity is attached to the property by the owner, no one purchasing with notice of that equity can stand in a different situation from the party from whom he purchased. . . .

I think the cases cited before the Vice-Chancellor and this decision of the Master of the Rolls perfectly right, and, therefore, that this motion must be refused, with costs.

Notes
1. The decision in *Tulk* v *Moxhay* was based on the doctrine of notice and the unconscionability of failing to restrain the defendant from committing a breach of the restrictive covenant.
2. The decision in *Tulk* v *Moxhay* is particularly significant in that it elevated a contractual right for the covenantee into a proprietary right in the land of the covenantor. This interest was then capable of running with the land. See, in particular, Simon Gardner, 'The proprietary effect of contractual obligations under *Tulk* v *Moxhay* and *De Mattos* v *Gibson*' (1982) 98 LQR 279.

Freehold Covenants

Question
Restrictive covenants are an illustration of the crossing of 'the chasm which lies between contract and property', H. W. R. Wade (1952) 68 LQR 337, 348. What is meant by this statement and can you find any other examples of this crossing of the chasm in land law?

A: BURDEN OF COVENANT

The following conditions must be satisfied in order for the burden of a covenant to run with the land under the doctrine of *Tulk* v *Moxhay*.

(a) The covenant must be negative (or restrictive) in substance. The covenant must not be one which is positive, requiring the expenditure of money. It is, however, the substance and not the form of the covenant that must be negative. See *Haywood* v *The Brunswick Permanent Benefit Building Society* [1881] 8 QBD 403.

(b) The covenant must touch and concern the land of the covenantee. In **Rogers v Hosegood** [1900] 2 Ch 388 (CA), Farwell J (at first instance, affirmed) said:

Adopting the definition of Bayley J in *Congleton Corporation* v *Pattison* (1808) 10 East 130, the covenant must either affect the land as regards mode of occupation, or it must be such as per se, and not merely from collateral circumstances, affects the value of the land.

(c) The covenant must accommodate the dominant tenement. In order for the burden of a covenant to run under *Tulk* v *Moxhay*, the covenantee must own an estate in the dominant land *and* the covenantor must own an estate in the servient land.

London County Council v *Allen*
[1914] 3 KB 642 (CA)

O obtained permission from P to develop land subject to a condition that O enter into a covenant not to build on a certain plot of land. O entered into such a covenant for himself, his heirs and assigns and other persons claiming under him. P did not possess, nor were they interested in, any neighbouring land which the covenant affected. Held: P were not entitled to enforce the covenant against O's assignees.

BUCKLEY LJ: *Tulk* v *Moxhay* established that as between the grantor of a restrictive covenant affecting certain land and the owner of adjoining land the covenantee may in equity enforce the covenant against the derivative owner taking with notice. The reasoning of Lord Cottenham's judgment in *Tulk* v *Moxhay* is that if an owner of land sells part of it reserving the rest, and takes from his purchaser a covenant that the purchaser shall use or abstain from using the land purchased in a particular way, that covenant (being one for the protection of the land reserved) is enforceable against a sub-purchaser with notice. The reason given is that, if that were not so, it would be impossible for an owner of land to sell part of it without incurring the risk of rendering what he retains worthless. If the vendor has retained no land which can be protected by the restrictive covenant, the basis of the reasoning of the judgment is swept away. . . . In the present case we are asked to extend the doctrine of *Tulk* v *Moxhay* so as to affirm that a restrictive covenant can be enforced against a derivative owner taking with notice by a person who never has had or who does not retain any land to be protected by the restrictive covenant in question. In my opinion the doctrine does not extend to that case. The doctrine is that a covenant not running with the land, but being a negative covenant entered into by an owner of land with an adjoining owner, binds the land in equity and is enforceable against a derivative owner taking with notice. The doctrine ceases to be applicable when the person seeking to enforce the covenant against the derivative owner has no land to be protected by the negative covenant. The fact of notice is in that case irrelevant.

Notes
1. See also *Formby* v *Barker* [1903] 2 Ch 539 (CA), where an assignee of the original covenantee was said to be unable to enforce the covenant as she had sold all the land to be benefited by the covenant.

In *Re Gadd's Land Transfer* [1966] Ch 56 (ChD), Buckley J held that the retention of a mere road to the land burdened by the covenant may be sufficient to enable the covenantee to enforce a restrictive covenant.

2. A lessor's interest in a reversion is a sufficient interest to allow a restrictive covenant on a head lease to be enforced against a subtenant under the rule in *Tulk* v *Moxhay*. See *Regent Oil Co. Ltd* v *J. A. Gregory (Hatch End) Ltd* [1966] Ch 402.

(d) The covenant must be intended to run with the land of the covenantor. This can be seen from the wording of the covenant itself, or failing this by means of the Law of Property Act 1925, s. 79, unless excluded.

(e) If the covenant is created after 1925 and the land is unregistered, it should be registered under the Land Charges Act 1972 (see Chapter 2). If the covenant was created before 1925, the doctrine of notice applies.

B: THE EXTENT OF *TULK* v *MOXHAY*

Once a restrictive covenant satisfies the conditions necessary for running with the land, it is enforceable against all who acquire the land, including any occupier of the land, irrespective of the character of occupation.

Adverse possession

Mander v *Falcke* [1891] 2 Ch 554 (CA)

P, the owners of a freehold reversion, were entitled to an injunction against A to prevent a use of the property in breach of a restrictive covenant, even though A had no estate or interest in the property. A had notice of the covenant and was in occupation.

Re Nisbet and Pott's Contract [1905] 1 Ch 391; [1906] 1 Ch 386 (CA)

Y purchased land from X in 1867, and covenanted not to use any building on the land for any purpose other than as a private dwelling. The land was conveyed to A, in 1872, subject to similar covenants. Z obtained title by adverse possession in the 12 years from 1878. Z's son maintained possession after Z died. B purchased the land from Z's son in 1890 and agreed to accept the possessory title instead of requiring a proved root of title of 40 years. B sold to N who agreed to sell the property to P. The question arose as to whether P would be subject to the restrictive covenants? Held: Z was not a purchaser for value and was thus bound by the covenants. N had constructive notice of the restrictive covenants entered into within 40 years of the commencement of Z's adverse possession.

Tichborne v *Weir* (1892) 67 LT 735 (CA)

D granted an 89 year lease of a house to B in 1802 containing various covenants including a covenant to repair. G took over possession of the property from B, whose whereabouts were unknown from 1836 to 1876, paying the agreed rent in the lease to D. In 1876, G assigned all his estate and interest in the lease to W who went into possession and stayed there until 1891, paying the rent due under the lease to D and then to P. W delivered up possession to P at the end of the term, in 1891. P sued W for breach of the covenant to repair contained in the lease. Held: B's right and title were not transferred by means of s. 34 of the Limitation Act 1833. Therefore, W was not liable on the covenants running with the land contained in the lease to B.

C: BENEFIT OF THE COVENANT

The benefit of a covenant may pass in any one of three ways:

(a) annexation;
(b) assignment;
(c) scheme of development.

(a) Annexation of the covenant to the dominant land
Annexation may be express, implied or statutory.

(i) *Express annexation* In order for the benefit of the covenant to run with the land the following must be fulfilled:

(a) The words of the covenant must be such as to show that the original parties intended it to run with the land. In *Rogers* v *Hosegood* [1900] 2 Ch 388, a covenant 'with the intent that the covenants . . . might so far as possible bind the premises thereby conveyed and every part thereof . . . and might enure to the benefit of the [vendors] . . . their heirs and assigns and others claiming under them to all or any of their lands adjoining or near to the said premises' was held to annex the covenants to the land. In *Renals* v *Cowlishaw* (1878) 9 ChD 125 (ChD), however, R owned a residential estate and various lands. D's predecessors in title purchased some of those lands from V and entered into covenants with V and his assigns including a covenant not to build upon part of the land. The residential estate was later bought by P's predecessors in title. The conveyance to them from V did not expressly assign the benefit of the covenants. D purchased the land with notice of the covenants. P, the then owners of the residential estate sought to enforce the original covenants against D. D claimed that they could not be enforced. The original conveyance from V did not state what land was to be benefited by the covenants. The word 'assigns' was insufficient as it could refer to assigns of the benefit of the covenant rather than assigns of the land.

The effect of express annexation is that the covenant runs automatically and is enforceable by the covenantee's successors in title, even if they do not know of its existence until after the conveyance.

(b) The dominant land must be clearly or easily identified in the conveyance creating the covenant.

(c) Even if the first two conditions are fulfilled, if the deed creating the covenant annexes it to the whole of the land of the covenantee, then such annexation will not be effective unless the covenant confers an actual benefit on all the property.

Re Ballard's Conveyance
[1937] Ch 473 (ChD)

X purchased 18 acres of a 1,700 acre estate and covenanted with the vendor, her heirs and assigns and successors that he, his heirs and assigns would be bound by certain covenants. Held: where a restrictive covenant purports to have been annexed to land but does not affect the whole of the land, the annexation is ineffective and the covenant cannot run with the land. Even if there is some part of the land which the covenant does affect, the court will not sever it and annex it to that part.

CLAUSON J: I am bound to hold that, while the covenant may concern or touch some comparatively small portion of the land to which it has been sought to annex it, it fails to concern or touch far the largest part of the land. I asked in vain for any authority which would justify me in severing the covenant and treating it as annexed to or running with such part of the land as is touched by or concerned with it, though as regards the remainder of the land, namely, such part as is not touched by or concerned with the covenant, the covenant is not and cannot be annexed to it and accordingly does not and cannot run with it. Nor have I been able through my own researches to find anything in the books which seems to justify any such course. In *Rogers* v *Hosegood* the benefit of the covenant was annexed to all or any of certain lands adjoining or near to the covenantor's land, and no such difficulty arose as faces me here; and there are many other reported cases in which, for similar reasons, no such difficulty arose. But the requirement that the covenant, in order that the benefit of it may run with certain lands, must concern or touch those lands, is categorically stated by Farwell J in the passage I have cited, in terms which are unquestionably in accord with a long line of earlier authority.

Note
See also *Earl of Leicester* v *Wells-next-the-Sea Urban District Council* [1973] Ch 110. Compare, however, the next case.

Marquess of Zetland v Driver [1939] Ch 1 (CA)

V was the tenant for life of settled land. V conveyed part of the land to P subject to a covenant which was expressed to be for the benefit and protection of 'such part or parts of the [dominant land] (a) as shall for the time being remain unsold or (b) as shall be sold by the vendor or his successors in title, with the express benefit of this covenant'. Some parts of the retained land adjoined the land sold, but other parts of the land retained were some distance away. Held: The effect of the covenant as written was to benefit the whole or any part or parts of the retained land and it was, therefore, enforceable.

Notes
1. See G. R. Y. Radcliffe, 'Some problems of the law relating to restrictive covenants' (1941) 57 LQR 203.
2. The following case deals with the situation where a successor in title acquires part of the land annexed with the benefit of the covenant.

Re Selwyn's Conveyance [1967] Ch 674 (ChD)

The Selwyn estate was conveyed to JS who sold off some parts of the estate. In 1924 JS sold one such part to P and the conveyance contained certain restrictive covenants including a covenant not to build more than one house on the land. The covenant was '[to] endure for the protection of the adjoining or neighbouring land part of or lately part of the Selwyn Estate' and was made for himself, his heirs and assigns. The land was later conveyed to the defendant. The defendant obtained planning permission to build six houses on the plot. The plaintiffs, who owned adjacent land, sought to enforce the covenants of the 1924 conveyance against the defendant. Held: the covenant was annexed to the plaintiffs' land as it benefited all parts of the Selwyn estate which was 'adjoining or neighbouring' the land of the defendants.

(ii) *Implied annexation* Implied annexation would appear to arise when the circumstances of the case are such that, although words of express annexation are not present, it is obvious that the covenant was intended to pass.

It would appear that implied annexation finds its roots in the two decisions of *Newton Abbot Co-operative Society Ltd v Williamson & Treadgold Ltd* (see page 416) and *Marten v Flight Refuelling Ltd*.

Marten v Flight Refuelling Ltd
[1962] Ch 115 (HL)

WILBERFORCE J: Before passing to the *Newton Abbot* case [1952] Ch 286, I should add that the rule as stated by the Court of Appeal in *Miles v Easter* [1933] Ch 611 seems to me to be clearly in line with other statements of principle made by the courts. In

Rogers v *Hosegood* [1900] 2 Ch 388; 16 TLR 489, CA — a leading case on annexation — Collins LJ said [1900] 2 Ch 368, 407: 'When, as in *Renals* v *Cowlishaw* (1879) 11 ChD 866, CA, there is no indication in the original conveyance, or in the circumstances attending it, that the burden of the restrictive covenant is imposed for the benefit of the land reserved, or any particular part of it, then it becomes necessary to examine the circumstances under which any part of the land reserved is sold, in order to see whether a benefit, not originally annexed to it, has become annexed to it on the sale, so that the purchaser is deemed to have bought it with the land, and this can hardly be the case when the purchaser did not know of the existence of the restrictive covenant.'

This seems to support the view that an intention to benefit may be found from surrounding or attending circumstances, as indeed is frequently done in practice in the case, mentioned by Collins LJ [1900] 2 Ch 388, 408, of building schemes.

In *Formby* v *Barker* [1903] 2 Ch 539, CA, which is one of the authorities which show that unless the covenantee retains some land intended to be benefited he cannot sue any person except the original covenantor, Vaughan Williams LJ said ibid. 550: 'I have not been able to find any case in which, after the sale of the whole of an estate in land, the benefit of a restrictive covenant has been enforced by injunction against an assignee of the purchaser at the instance of a plaintiff having no land retained by the vendor, although there are cases in which restrictive covenants seem to have been enforced at the instance of plaintiffs, other than the vendor, for the benefit of whose land it appears from the terms of the covenant, or can be inferred from surrounding circumstances, that the covenant was intended to operate.' A reference to these passages was made by Upjohn J in the *Newton Abbot* case [1952] Ch 286, but I have thought it worth while to set them out here so that they can be compared with other citations.

I would add to these a reference to the facts in *Lord Northbourne* v *Johnston & Son* [1922] 2 Ch 309, where the covenant was expressed to be with the trustees of a settlement, their heirs and assigns, the deed containing no reference to any land at all. Sargant J seems not to have doubted that it could be shown that the covenant was for the benefit of the unsold part of a particular building estate which in fact was vested in the trustees.

I pass now to the *Newton Abbot* case [1952] Ch 286. The facts were that the original covenantee was the owner of a property called Devonia, in Fore Street, Bovey Tracey, on which she carried on business as an ironmonger. The original covenantor was the purchaser from her of other properties in Fore Street opposite Devonia, and the covenant was (briefly) against carrying on the business of an ironmonger. There was no reference in the conveyance by which the covenant was imposed to any land for whose benefit it was made, the only mention of Devonia being that the vendor was described as 'of Devonia'. The action was between assigns of the covenantee's son, who inherited her estate, and assigns of the covenantors.

Upjohn J held that the benefit of the covenant was not annexed to Devonia, but held that, looking at the attendant circumstances, the land to be benefited was shown with reasonable certainty and that the land in question was Devonia.

This decision was attacked by the Attorney-General in a lively argument, and I was invited not to follow it. Of course, it relates to its own special facts, and no doubt I could leave it on one side. But I see nothing in it contrary to the principles which appear to be securely laid down. Here were two shops in common ownership facing each other in the same street, one of them, Devonia, an ironmonger's shop. The shops opposite are sold with a covenant against carrying on an ironmonger's business. What could be more obvious than that the covenant was intended for the protection or benefit of the vendor's property Devonia? To have rejected such a conclusion would, I venture to think, have involved not only an injustice but a departure from common sense. So far from declining the authority of this case, I welcome it as a useful guide. But it is only a guide, and I must ultimately reach my conclusion on the facts of the present case.

Notes
1. See E. C. Ryder, 'Restrictive covenants: the problems of implied annexation' (1972) 36 Conv (NS) 20; H. W. R. Wade, 'Covenants — "A broad and reasonable view"' [1972] CLJ 157; D. J. Hayton, 'Restrictive covenants as property interests' (1971) 87 LQR 539; P. V. Baker, 'The benefit of restrictive covenants' (1968) 84 LQR 22.
2. This decision has been criticised on the grounds that:

(a) the case did not concern the issue of annexation at all;
(b) the case increases the uncertainty in the area of annexation of covenants in that questions of implied annexation would have to be decided by the court, not by reference to documents.

(iii) *Statutory annexation*   See the Law of Property Act 1925, s. 78, at page 209.

The problem in *Re Selwyn's Conveyance* concerning the issue of implied annexation (see page 407) may be of less importance since the decision in the next case.

Federated Homes Ltd v *Mill Lodge Properties Ltd*
[1980] 1 All ER 371 (CA)

M owned some land and obtained outline planning permission to develop it for dwelling houses. Shortly afterwards part of the land was purchased by D and the conveyance to D contained a covenant against D building more than 300 dwellings on the land 'so as not to reduce the number of units which the vendor might eventually erect on the retained land under the existing planning consent'. P later became owner of two parts of the retained land. Each of the transfers in relation to the first part contained an unbroken chain of express assignments of the benefit of the restrictive covenant. However the transfer to P of the second part of the land did not contain an express assignment of the benefit of the covenant. P later obtained planning permission to build on all their retained land but discovered that D had obtained permission to build more dwellings on the land they had purchased than was permitted by the restrictive covenant. P sought to restrain D from building the extra houses. Held: where a restrictive covenant touched and concerned or related to the covenantee's land, s. 78(1) of the Law of Property Act 1925 effectively annexed the benefit of the covenant to the covenantee's land.

BRIGHTMAN LJ: An express assignment of the benefit of a covenant is not necessary if the benefit of the covenant is annexed to the land. In that event, the benefit will pass automatically on a conveyance of the land, without express mention, because it is annexed to the land and runs with it. So the issue of annexation is logically the next to be considered.

The judge said:

> The next heading with which I must deal is 'annexation', to which I will now come. It is a somewhat technical thing in the law of restrictive covenants. A good deal of argument was addressed to me on annexation by both sides. Submissions are made about express annexation, implied annexation, that is to say, annexation implied from surrounding circumstances, and annexation by assignment. In my judgment, there was in this case no 'annexation' of the benefit of the covenant to the retained land or any part of it. Section 78, in particular, of the Law of Property Act does not have the effect of annexing the benefit of the covenant to anything. It is simply a statutory shorthand for the shortening of conveyances, which it perhaps has done to some extent in this case. Annexation depends on appropriate drafting, which is not here in this case, in spite of a recent process which can perhaps be called 'a widening of the law' in these matters. The attendant circumstances moreover, positively militate against annexation because, as counsel for the defendants rightly pointed out to me (though he did so in the course of his argument on construction) the restriction in this particular case is of limited duration and plainly not applicable to ultimate purchasers of plots of the land intended to be benefited. 'Annexation', in my judgment, is for the parties to the covenant itself to achieve if they wish to, and (though those parties may no doubt provide for annexation at a later stage) I am not satisfied or prepared to hold that there is any such thing as 'delayed annexation by assignment' to which the covenantor is not party or privy.

The reference to 'delayed annexation by assignment' is to a proposition that a covenant can, on a later assignment, thereby become annexed to the land by the act of the assignor and the assignee alone.

In my judgment the benefit of this covenant was annexed to the retained land, and I think that this is a consequence of s. 78 of the Law of Property Act 1925 [he outlines s. 78] . . .

Counsel for the defendants submitted that there were three possible views about s. 78. One view, which he describes as 'the orthodox view' hitherto held, is that it is merely a statutory shorthand for reducing the length of legal documents. A second view, which was the one that counsel for the defendants was inclined to place in the forefront of his arguments, is that the section only applies, or at any rate only achieves annexation, when the land intended to be benefited is signified in the document by express words or necessary implication as the intended beneficiary of the covenant. A third view is that the section applies if the covenant in fact touches and concerns the land of the covenantee, whether that be gleaned from the document itself or from evidence outside the document.

For myself, I reject the narrowest interpretation of s. 78, the supposed orthodox view, which seems to me to fly in the face of the wording of the section. Before I express my reasons I will say that I do not find it necessary to choose between the second and third views because, in my opinion, this covenant relates to land of the covenantee on either interpretation of s. 78. Clause 5(iv) shows quite clearly that the covenant is for the protection of the retained land and that land is described in cl. 2 as 'any adjoining or adjacent property retained by the Vendor'. This formulation is sufficient for annexation purposes: see *Rogers* v *Hosegood*.

There is in my judgment no doubt that this covenant 'related to the land of the covenantee', or, to use the old-fashioned expression, that it touched and concerned the land, even if counsel for the defendants is correct in his submission that the document must show an intention to benefit identified land. The result of such application is that one must read cl. 5(iv) as if it were written: 'The purchaser hereby covenants with the vendor and its successors in title and the persons deriving title under it or them, including the owners and occupiers for the time being of the retained land, that in carrying out the development of the blue land the purchaser shall not build at a greater density than a total of 300 dwellings so as not to reduce the number of units which the vendor might eventually erect on the retained land under the existing planning consent.' I leave out of consideration s. 79 as unnecessary to be considered in this context, since Mill Lodge is the original covenantor.

The first point to notice about s. 78(1) is that the wording is significantly different from the wording of its predecessor, s. 58(1) of the Conveyancing and Law of Property Act 1881. The distinction is underlined by sub-s. (2) of s. 78, which applies sub-s. (1) only to covenants made after the commencement of the Act. Section 58(1) of the earlier Act did not include the covenantee's successors in title or persons deriving title under him or them, nor the owners or occupiers for the time being of the land of the covenantee intended to be benefited. The section was confined, in relation to realty, to the covenantee, his heirs and assigns, words which suggest a more limited scope of operation than is found in s. 78.

If, as the language of s. 78 implies, a covenant relating to land which is restrictive of the user thereof is enforceable at the suit of (1) a successor in title of the covenantee, (2) a person deriving title under the covenantee or under his successors in title, and (3) the owner or occupier of the land intended to be benefited by the covenant, it must, in my view, follow that the covenant runs with the land, because ex hypothesi every successor in title to the land, ever derivative proprietor of the land and every other owner and occupier has a right by statute to the covenant. In other words, if the condition precedent of s. 78 is satisfied, that is to say, there exists a covenant which touches and concerns the land of the covenantee, that covenant runs with the land for the benefit of his successors in title, persons deriving title under him or them and other owners and occupiers.

This approach to s. 78 has been advocated by distinguished textbook writers: see Dr Radcliffe in the *Law Quarterly Review* (1941) 57 LQR 203, Professor Wade in the *Cambridge Law Journal* [1972] CLJ 157 under the apt cross-heading 'What is wrong with section 78?', and Megarry and Wade on the *Law of Real Property* 4th edn (1975) p. 764. Counsel pointed out to us that the fourth edition of Megarry and Wade's textbook indicates a change of mind on this topic since the third edition was published in 1966.

Although the section does not seem to have been extensively used in the course of argument in this type of case, the construction of s. 78 which appeals to me appears to be consistent with at least two cases decided in this court. The first is *Smith v River Douglas Catchment Board* [1949] 2 All ER 179, [1949] 2 KB 500. In that case an agreement was made in April 1938 between certain landowners and the catchment board under which the catchment board undertook to make good the banks of a certain brook and to maintain the same, and the landowners undertook to contribute towards the cost. In 1940 the first plaintiff took a conveyance from one of the landowners of a part of the land together with an express assignment of the benefit of the agreement. In 1944 the second plaintiff took a tenancy of that land without any express assignment of the benefit of the agreement. In 1946 the brook burst its banks and the land owned by the first plaintiff and tenanted by the second plaintiff was inundated. The two important points are that the agreement was not expressed to be for the benefit of the landowner's successors in title; and there was no assignment of the benefit of the agreement in favour of the second plaintiff, the tenant. In reliance, as I understand the case, on s. 78 of the Law of Property Act 1925, it was held that the second plaintiff was entitled to sue the catchment board for damages for breach of the agreement. It seems to me that that conclusion can only have been reached on the basis that s. 78 had the effect of causing the benefit of the agreement to run with the land so as to be capable of being sued on by the tenant.

The other case, *Williams* v *Unit Construction Co. Ltd* (1951) 19 Conv NS 262, was decided by this court in 1951. There a company had acquired a building estate and had underleased four plots to Cubbin for 999 years. The underlessors arranged for the defendant company to build houses on the four plots. The defendant company covenanted with Cubbin to keep the adjacent road in repair until adopted. Cubbin granted a weekly tenancy of one house to the plaintiff without any express assignment of the benefit of the covenant. The plaintiff was injured owing to the disrepair of the road. She was held entitled to recover damages from the defendants for breach of the covenant.

We were referred to observations in the speeches of Lord Upjohn and Lord Wilberforce in *Tophams Ltd* v *Earl of Sefton* to the effect that s. 79 of the Law of Property Act 1925 (relating to the burden of covenants) achieved no more than the introduction of statutory shorthand into the drafting covenants. Section 79, in my view, involves quite different considerations and I do not think that it provides a helpful analogy.

It was suggested by counsel for the defendants that if this covenant ought to be read as enuring for the benefit of the retained land, it should be read as enuring only for the benefit of the retained land as a whole and not for the benefit of every part of it; with the apparent result that there is no annexation of the benefit to a part of the retained land when any severance takes place. He referred us to a passage in *Re Union of London and Smith's Bank Ltd's Conveyance, Miles* v *Easter* [1933] Ch 611, [1933] All ER Rep 355, which I do not think it is necessary for me to read.

The problem is alluded to in Megarry and Wade on the *Law of Real Property* 4th edn (1975) p. 763:

> In drafting restrictive covenants it is therefore desirable to annex them to the covenantee's land 'or any part or parts thereof'. An additional reason for using this form of words is that, if there is no indication to the contrary, the benefit may be held to be annexed only to the whole of the covenantee's land, so that it will not pass with portions of it disposed of separately. But even without such words the court may find that the covenant is intended to benefit any part of the retained land; and small indications may suffice, since the rule that presumes annexation to the whole only is arbitrary and inconvenient. In principle it conflicts with the rule for assignments, which allows a benefit annexed to the whole to be assigned with part, and it also conflicts with the corresponding rule for easements.

I find the idea of the annexation of a covenant to the whole of the land but not to a part of it a difficult conception fully to grasp. I can understand that a covenantee may expressly or by necessary implication retain the benefit of a covenant wholly under his own control, so that the benefit will not pass unless the covenantee chooses to assign; but I would have thought, if the benefit of a covenant is, on a proper construction of a document, annexed to the land, prima facie it is annexed to every part thereof, unless the contrary clearly appears. It is difficult to see how this court can have reached its decision in *Williams* v *Unit Construction Co Ltd* (1951) 19 Conv NS 262 unless this is right. The covenant was, by inference, annexed to every part of the land and not merely to the whole, because it will be recalled that the plaintiff was a tenant of only one of the four houses which had the benefit of the covenant. . . .

In the instant case the judge in the course of his judgment appears to have dismissed the notion that any individual plotholder would be entitled, even by assignment, to have the benefit of the covenant that I have been considering. I express no view about that. I only say this, that I am not convinced that his conclusion on that point is correct. I say no more about it.

In the end, I come to the conclusion that s. 78 of the Law of Property Act 1925 caused the benefit of the restrictive covenant in question to run with the red land and therefore to be annexed to it, with the result that the plaintiff company is able to enforce the covenant against Mill Lodge, not only in its capacity as owner of the green land, but also in its capacity as owner of the red land.

For these reasons I think that the judge reached the correct view on the right of the plaintiff company to enforce the covenant, although in part he arrived there by a different route.

Notes
1. See David Hayton, 'Revolution in restrictive covenants law?' (1980) 43 MLR 445; Paul Todd, 'Annexation after *Federated Homes*' [1985] Conv 177; G. H. Newsom, 'Annexation of restrictive covenants' [1980] JPL 371; G. H. Newsom, 'Universal annexation' (1981) 97 LQR 32; G. H. Newsom, 'Universal annexation? a postscript' (1982) 98 LQR 202; D. J. Hurst, 'The transmission of restrictive covenants' (1982) 2 Legal Studies 53.
2. The effect of this decision would appear to be that the benefit of any covenant which touches and concerns the land of the covenantee is automatically annexed to the covenantee's land when the conveyance is made.
3. If the decision is correct, the rule in *Rogers* v *Hosegood* (see page 405) seems to be abrogated.
4. The decision has been much criticised as it is said that s. 78 was designed merely as a statutory shorthand and not to impose fundamental changes to the nature of the substantive law. The decision in *Federated Homes* v *Mill Lodge Properties Ltd* can cause difficulties with regard to s. 79 (which deals with the running of the burden of a covenant) if a similar interpretation is placed on that section.
5. The decision in *Federated Homes* v *Mill Lodge Properties Ltd* was considered in the first instance decision of *Roake* v *Chadha*.

Roake v Chadha
[1984] 1 WLR 40 (ChD)

W sold land in plots. Each transfer was in the same terms and reserved certain easements to W 'and their assigns'. L bought a plot. The transfer contained a covenant with W which referred to various stipulations and was expressed to be made 'so as to bind . . . the land hereby transferred into whosesoever hands the same may come . . . but so that this covenant shall not enure for the benefit of any owner or subsequent purchaser of any part [of the estate] unless the benefit of this covenant shall be expressly assigned'. Held: despite the effect of s. 78 where a covenant relates to or touches and concerns the covenantee's land each covenant must be construed as a whole to determine whether the benefit is annexed.

HIS HONOUR JUDGE PAUL BAKER QC: As to annexation, counsel for the plaintiffs conceded that the express terms of the covenant appeared to exclude annexation, and there was no suggestion that the case fell within the category known as building schemes. Counsel for the plaintiffs, however, in an interesting argument submitted that annexation had come about through the operation of s. 78 of the 1925 Act, as interpreted in *Federated Homes Ltd* v *Mill Lodge Properties Ltd* [1980] 1 All ER 371, [1980] 1 WLR 594, a decision of the Court of Appeal. I can summarise his argument by the following four points. (1) The covenant was a covenant relating to the land of the covenantee. (2) Section 78(1) of the 1925 Act provides, as regards such covenants relating to land, that they are deemed—

to be made with the covenantee and his successors in title and the persons deriving title under him or them, and shall have effect as if such successors and other persons were expressed. For the purposes of this subsection in connexion with covenants restrictive of the user of land 'successors in title' shall be deemed to include the owners and occupiers for the time being of the land of the covenantee intended to be benefited.

(3) In the *Federated Homes* case it was held that by virtue of that section the benefit of a covenant relating to land retained by the covenantee ran with that land and was annexed to it and to every part of it. (4) The provisions of s. 78, unlike those of s. 79 relating to the burden of the covenant, cannot be excluded by the expression of a contrary intention. [Judge Baker QC outlines s. 79:] . . .

Unlike s. 78, which had a counterpart in s. 58 of the Conveyancing Act 1881, s. 79 was a new section in 1925. The important point to which attention is called is 'unless a contrary intention is expressed', and that appears in s. 79. There is no corresponding expression in s. 78. Those are the main points of the argument.

I have no difficulty in accepting that the covenant in the standard form of transfer which I have read is a covenant relating to the retained land of the covenantee, that is to say Wembley (C & W) Land Co Ltd, and that therefore s. 78 comes into play. It is the third and fourth points which have given rise to the argument in this case. I must begin, therefore, by examining the *Federated Homes* case. . . .

Counsel for the defendants in the present case has argued that accordingly the Court of Appeal's judgments in relation to the red land were obiter. I am unable to accept this view of the effect of the judgments. As it seems to me, the status of the covenant in relation to both pieces of land, the red and the green, was in issue in the case. If the defendant in subsequent proceedings had sought to challenge the validity of the covenant in relation to the red land, he could, as I would see it, be met by a plea of issue estoppel and consequently the principle underlying the court's conclusion cannot be regarded as obiter. . . .

Counsel for the defendants made a frontal attack on this use of s. 78, which he reinforced by reference to an article by G H Newsom QC 'Universal Annexation?' (1981) 97 LQR 32 which is critical of the decision. The main lines of attack are: (1) the conclusion overlooks the legislative history of s. 78 which it is said shows that it has a narrower purpose than is claimed and does not in itself bring about annexation; (2) this narrower purpose has been accepted in relation to the corresponding s. 79 (relating to burden), which I have already read, by Lord Upjohn and Lord Wilberforce in *Tophams Ltd* v *Earl of Sefton* [1966] 1 All ER 1039 at 1048, 1053, [1967] 1 AC 50 at 73, 81. Further, it is said by way of argument sub silentio that in a number of cases, notably *Marquess of Zetland* v *Driver* [1938] 2 All ER 158, [1939] Ch 1 and *Re Jeffs's Transfer, Rogers* v *Astley (No 2)* [1966] 1 All ER 937, [1966] 1 WLR 841, the argument could have been used to good effect but was not deployed.

Now, all this is very interesting, and the views of Mr Newsom are entitled to very great respect seeing that until his recent retirement he was a practitioner of long experience who had made a special study of this branch of the law. He has written a valuable monograph on it. All the same, despite counsel for the defendants' blandishments, I am not going to succumb to the temptation of joining in any such discussion. Sitting here as a judge of the Chancery Division, I do not consider it to be my place either to criticise or to defend the decisions of the Court of Appeal. I conceive it my clear duty to accept the decision of the Court of Appeal as binding on me and apply it as best I can to the facts I find here.

Counsel for the plaintiffs' method of applying it is simplicity itself. The *Federated Homes* case shows that s. 78 brings about annexation, and that the operation of the section cannot be excluded by a contrary intention. As I have indicated, he supports this last point by reference to s. 79, which is expressed to operate 'unless a contrary intention is expressed', a qualification which, as we have already noticed, is absent from s. 78. Counsel for the plaintiffs could not suggest any reason of policy why s. 78 should be mandatory, unlike, for example, s. 146 of the 1925 Act, which deals with restrictions on the right to forfeiture of leases and which, by an express provision, 'has effect notwithstanding any stipulation to the contrary'.

I am thus far from satisfied that s. 78 has the mandatory operation which counsel for the plaintiffs claimed for it. But, even if one accepts that it is not subject to a contrary intention, I do not consider that it has the effect of annexing the benefit of the covenant in each and every case irrespective of the other express terms of the covenant. I notice that Brightman LJ did not go so far as that . . .

So at least in some circumstances Brightman LJ is considering that despite s. 78 the benefit may be retained and not pass or be annexed to and run with land. In this connection, I was also referred by counsel for the defendants to Sir Lancelot Elphinstone's *Covenants Affecting Land* (1946) p. 17, where the author says, with reference to this point (and I quote from a footnote on that page): ' . . . but it is thought that, as a covenant must be construed as a whole, the court would give due effect to words excluding or modifying the operation of the section.'

The true position as I see it is that, even where a covenant is deemed to be made with successors in title as s. 78 requires, one still has to construe the covenant as a whole to see whether the benefit of the covenant is annexed. Where one finds, as in the *Federated Homes* case, the covenant is not qualified in any way, annexation may be readily inferred; but, where, as in the present case, it is expressly provided that 'this covenant shall not enure for the benefit of any owner or subsequent purchaser of any part of the Vendor's Sudbury Court Estate at Wembley unless the benefit of this covenant shall be expressly assigned', one cannot just ignore these words. One may not be able to exclude the operation of the section in extending the range of covenantees, but one has to consider the covenant as a whole to determine its true effect. When one does that, then it seems to me that the answer is plain and in my judgment the benefit was not annexed. That is giving full weight to both the statute in force and also what is already there in a covenant.

Notes
1. See Paul Todd, '*Roake* v *Chadha*' [1984] Conv 68.
2. Pre-1926 covenants were considered in the case of *J Sainsbury Plc* v *Enfield London Borough Council* [1989] 2 All ER 817.

(b) Assignment

If the benefit of a covenant is not annexed to the land, the covenantee can transfer the benefit by means of express assignment. The benefit of a covenant may be transferred at law under the Law of Property Act 1925, s. 136, as such a benefit is a chose in action. In *Re Union of London and Smith's Bank Ltd's Conveyance* [1933] Ch 611 (CA), Romer LJ outlined the conditions necessary for an assignment in equity:

It is plain, however, from these and other cases, and notably that of *Renals v Cowlishaw* 9 ChD 125, that if the restrictive covenant be taken not merely for some personal purpose or object of the vendor, but for the benefit of some other land of his in the sense that it would enable him to dispose of that land to greater advantage, the covenant, though not annexed to such land so as to run with any part of it, may be enforced against an assignee of the covenantor taking with notice, both by the covenantee and by persons to whom the benefit of such covenant has been assigned, subject however to certain conditions. In the first place, the 'other land' must be land that is capable of being benefited by the covenant — otherwise it would be impossible to infer that the object of the covenant was to enable the vendor to dispose of his land to greater advantage. In the next place, this land must be 'ascertainable' or 'certain,' to use the words of Romer and Scrutton LJJ respectively. For, although the Court will readily infer the intention to benefit the other land of the vendor where the existence and situation of such land are indicated in the conveyance or have been otherwise shown with reasonable certainty, it is impossible to do so from vague references in the conveyance or in other documents laid before the Court as to the existence of other lands of the vendor, the extent and situation of which are undefined. In the third place, the covenant cannot be enforced by the covenantee against an assign of the purchaser after the covenantee has parted with the whole of his land.

In addition, there must, apparently, be an unbroken chain of assignments, so that the benefit has been passed to the new owner (see *Re Pinewood Estate, Farnborough* [1958] Ch 280). (Cf dicta in cases such as *Rogers v Hosegood* [1900] 2 Ch 388 and *Renals v Cowlishaw* (1878) 9 ChD 125, where it was suggested that an express assignment has the effect of annexing the restrictive covenant to the dominant land, so as to automatically run with the land without any need of further express assignment.)

Newton Abbot Co-operative Society Ltd v *Williamson & Treadgold Ltd* [1952] Ch 286 (ChD)

M owned two separate premises A and B, which were opposite each other. He ran an ironmongers from A. In 1923, M sold premises B to P and the conveyance contained a covenant that the purchasers, and the person deriving title under them would not carry on the business of ironmongery in premises B. After M died in 1944 her executors vested premises A in the name of L. There was no assent in respect of the restrictive covenant. L carried on the iron-monger's business until 1948 when he sold it to BTC, assigning to them the goodwill of the business and purporting to assign the benefit of the restrictive covenant. L also granted BTC a lease of premises A for a term of 21 years. In 1949, BTC amalgamated with the plaintiff. In 1950, D, who had purchased premises B in 1947, started to sell ironmongery. The plaintiffs sought to enforce the covenant. Held:

(1) The land intended to be benefited by the covenant was not clearly identified in the 1923 conveyance. Thus, the benefit of the original covenant could not have passed with the assignment of M's premises unless expressly assigned.

(2) On M's death, the benefit of the covenant was held by M's executors on a bare trustees for L, who was therefore entitled to it in equity. Thus, although the benefit had not been expressly assigned to L he could assign it in equity on the assignment of the premises.

(3) The covenant in the 1923 conveyance benefited the land itself, not merely the business, as it increased the value of the land.

(4) The land to be benefited by a covenant need not be defined in the deed creating it provided the existence and location of the land was indicated in the deed or otherwise shown with reasonable certainty. M took the covenant for the benefit of premises A which were sufficiently identified and the assignees could therefore sue on the covenant.

Note
The question whether the benefit of a covenant can pass under the Law of Property Act 1925, s. 62, was considered in *Roake* v *Chadha*.

Roake v *Chadha*
[1984] 1 WLR 40 (ChD)

The facts of this case appear at page 413.

HIS HONOUR JUDGE PAUL BAKER QC: I must now turn to the alternative argument of the plaintiffs based on s. 62 of the 1925 Act. This argument is directed to the conveyances or transfers conveying the alleged benefited land to the predecessors of the plaintiffs, and ultimately to the respective plaintiffs themselves. In each of these transfers, so I am prepared to assume, there is to be implied the general words of s. 62:

(1) A conveyance of land shall be deemed to include and shall by virtue of this Act operate to convey, with the land, all buildings, erections, fixtures, commons, hedges, ditches, fences, ways, waters, watercourses, liberties, privileges, easements, rights, and advantages whatsoever, appertaining or reputed to appertain to the land, or any part thereof, or, at the time of conveyance, demised, occupied, or enjoyed with or reputed or known as part or parcel of or appurtenant to the land or any part thereof . . .

Then in sub-s. (2) it deals with the conveyance of land having houses and buildings and various corresponding rights in relation to buildings. I do not think I need read that subsection.

The argument is that the benefit of the covenant contained in the original transfer to the predecessors of the defendants (that is to say William Lambert) was carried by the words 'rights, and advantages whatsoever, appertaining or reputed to appertain to the land, or any part thereof'.

It seems an argument on these lines was accepted by John Mills QC, the deputy judge who gave the decision at first instance in the *Federated Homes* case, but I have not seen it, and so cannot comment on it. The proposition now contended for is not a new one. In *Rogers* v *Hosegood* [1900] 2 Ch 388, [1900–3] All ER Rep 915 it was similarly put forward as an alternative argument to an argument based on annexation. In that case however it was decided that the benefit of the covenant was annexed so that the point on the Conveyancing Act 1881, s. 6, the forerunner of s. 62 of the 1925 Act, did not have to be decided. Nevertheless, Farwell J, sitting in the Chancery Division, said ([1900] 2 Ch 388 at 398):

> It is not necessary for me to determine whether the benefit of the covenants would pass under the general words to which I have referred above, if such covenants did not run with the land. If they are not in fact annexed to the land, it may well be that the right to sue thereon cannot be said to belong, or be reputed to belong, thereto; but I express no final opinion on this point.

In the Court of Appeal the point was canvassed in argument but not referred to in the judgment of the court, which was given by Collins LJ.

In the present case, the covenant in terms precludes the benefit passing unless it is expressly assigned. That being so, as it seems to me, it is not a right appertaining or reputed to appertain to land within the meaning of s. 62 of the 1925 Act. On whether the benefit of a covenant not annexed can ever pass under s. 62, I share the doubts of Farwell J. Counsel for the defendants suggested, and there may well be something in this, that the rights referred to in s. 62 are confined to legal rights rather than equitable rights which the benefit of restrictive covenants is. But again I place it on construction. It cannot be described as a right appertaining or reputed to appertain to land when the terms of the covenant itself would seem to indicate the opposite.

(c) Scheme of development or building scheme

In *Brunner* v *Greenslade* [1971] Ch 993, Megarry J described a scheme of development (at p. 1003):

> ... A owns the entire estate and, having laid it out, himself sells individual lots to individual purchasers who enter into the covenants of the scheme. As soon as he sells a lot to the first purchaser, B, the scheme crystallises. Not only is B bound in respect of his lot to A, for the benefit of the remainder of the estate, but also A is bound, in respect of the remainder of the estate, to B, for the benefit of B's plot. It may be noted that while B is bound by the express covenants that he entered into, A may well have entered into no express covenants with B; and yet the concept of a scheme of development requires that A shall be treated as having impliedly bound himself by the provisions of the scheme. If A then sells another plot to C, C is taking part of the land that has already been subjected to the scheme in favour of B, and the covenants that he enters into are treated as being made for the benefit not only of A's remaining land but also of B's plot. If A continues to sell off one lot to each purchaser, and all the purchasers are different, in this way the whole concept of the enforceability of the covenants under a scheme of development, as between all within the area of the scheme, is readily explicable in terms of covenant, express or implied.

Where a scheme of development is proved, then each purchaser and his assignees can sue and be sued by every other purchaser and his assignee for breach of the restrictive covenants (see *Spicer* v *Martin* (1888) 14 App Cas 12).

The conditions necessary for enforceability of a scheme of development were set out in *Elliston* v *Reacher*.

Elliston v Reacher
[1908] 2 Ch 374 (ChD)

Here, the owners of a large area of land laid it out for development into separate plots and sold each plot using an identical conveyance and imposing identical restrictive covenants upon the purchasers. The covenants were said to be enforceable against a successor in title to the original covenantor.

PARKER J: I pass, therefore, to the consideration of the question whether the plaintiffs can enforce these restrictive covenants. In my judgment, in order to bring the principles of *Renals* v *Cowlishaw* (1878) 9 Ch D 125 and *Spicer* v *Martin* (1888) 14 App Cas 12 into operation it must be proved (1) that both the plaintiffs and defendants derive title under a common vendor; (2) that previously to selling the lands to which the plaintiffs and defendants are respectively entitled the vendor laid out his estate, or a defined portion thereof (including the lands purchased by the plaintiffs and defendants respectively), for sale in lots subject to restrictions intended to be imposed on all the lots, and which, though varying in details as to particular lots, are consistent and consistent only with some general scheme of development; (3) that these restrictions were intended by the common vendor to be and were for the benefit of all the lots intended to be sold, whether or not they were also intended to be and were for the benefit of other land retained by the vendor; and (4) that both the plaintiffs and the defendants, or their predecessors in title, purchased their lots from the common vendor upon the footing that the restrictions subject to which the purchases were made were to enure for the benefit of the other lots included in the general scheme whether or not they were also to enure for the benefit of other lands retained by the vendors. If these fourth points be established, I think that the plaintiffs would in equity be entitled to enforce the restrictive covenants entered into by the defendants or their predecessors with the common vendor irrespective of the dates of the respective purchases. I may observe, with reference to the third point, that the vendor's object in imposing the restrictions must in general be gathered from all the circumstances of the case, including in particular the nature of the restrictions. If a general observance of the restrictions is in fact calculated to enhance the values of the several lots offered for sale, it is an easy inference that the vendor intended the restrictions to be for the benefit of all the lots, even though he might retain other land the value of which might be similarly enhanced, for a vendor may naturally be expected to aim at obtaining the highest possible price for his land. Further, if the first three points be established, the fourth point may readily be inferred, provided the purchasers have notice of the facts involved in the three first points; but if the purchaser purchases in ignorance of any material part of those facts, it would be difficult, if not impossible, to establish the fourth point. It is also observable that the equity arising out of the establishment of the four points I have mentioned has been sometimes explained by the implication of mutual contracts between the various purchasers, and sometimes by the implication of a contract between each purchaser and the common vendor, that each purchaser is to have the benefit of all the covenants by the other purchasers, so that each purchase is in equity an assign of the benefit of these covenants. In my opinion the implication of mutual contract is not always a perfectly satisfactory explanation. It may be satisfactory where all the lots are sold by auction at the same time, but when, as in cases such as *Spicer* v *Martin*, there is no sale by auction, but all the various sales are by private treaty and at various intervals of time, the circumstances may, at the date of one or more of the sales, be such as to preclude the possibility of an actual contract. For example, a prior purchaser may be dead or incapable of contracting at the time of a subsequent purchase, and in any event it is unlikely that the prior and subsequent purchasers are ever brought into personal relationship, and yet the equity may exist between them. It is, I think, enough to say, using Lord Macnaghten's words in *Spicer* v *Martin*, that where the four points I have mentioned are established, the community of interest imports in equity the reciprocity of obligation which is in fact contemplated by each at the time of his own purchase.

Notes
1. It was further added by the case of *Reid* v *Bickerstaff* [1909] 2 Ch 305, that the area to which the scheme of development relates must be clearly defined.
2. It would appear that these conditions are merely a guide-line, and the important issue seems to be whether the parties intended the scheme of development to operate. In *Re Dolphin's Conveyance* [1970] Ch 654, a scheme was held to exist even where there was no common vendor and no lotted estate. The true construction of the various conveyances showed that the covenants were imposed for the common benefit of all the purchasers of the estate, and also the vendors. It was clearly intended that the covenants should be enforceable between the purchasers against each other, and all of them had a common interest in such enforcement. Similarly, in *Baxter* v *Four Oaks Properties Ltd* [1965] Ch 816, a scheme was said to exist even though the whole area had not been divided into lots prior to the sale. Again, the issue was whether there was direct evidence by the execution of a deed of mutual covenant that the vendor and purchasers had a common intention to create a building scheme.
3. If a scheme of development is established in an action for a breach of the restrictive covenant, it is irrelevant whether the defendant acquired title to the land before or after the date on which the plaintiff acquired his plot (see *Brunner* v *Greenslade*).
4. See *Brunner* v *Greenslade* regarding acquisition of part only of a plot.

Brunner v Greenslade [1971] Ch 993 (ChD)

In 1928, V conveyed part of an estate to P, and the latter covenanted with V by way of indemnity to observe a covenant previously entered into by V which restricted building on a certain piece of land. The covenant was expressed to be for the benefit of owners of the land capable of deriving benefit from it. P also covenanted with V not to build more than one house on each plot. The covenant was expressed to be 'for the benefit and protection of' V's estate. The land was then divided into five lots with a house on each. B purchased one lot expressly subject to the covenant contained in the 1928 conveyance. B also covenanted with P, by way of indemnity, to observe the covenant. B's neighbour then sold part of her adjoining lot to D who proposed to build a house in what was part of the garden. B applied for an injunction against D. Held: A scheme of development created an equity independent of a contract and the restrictions would be presumed to be mutually enforceable by purchasers of sub-lots, whether or not they had covenanted to that effect, in order to give effect to the original common intention.

Note
Where two plots come into common ownership and are later divided, the original covenants are automatically reserved between the subsequent owners (see *Texaco Antilles Ltd* v *Dorothy Kernochan* [1973] AC 609).

SECTION 5: DISCHARGE OF RESTRICTIVE COVENANTS

A restrictive covenant can come to an end in any of the following ways:

(a) A restrictive covenant is discharged when the dominant and servient land come into common ownership. See *Re Tiltwood, Sussex* [1978] Ch 269. However, in *Texaco Antilles Ltd* v *Kernochan* [1973] AC 609, it was said that where there is a scheme of development common ownership does not automatically discharge the covenant.

(b) Where the person entitled to the benefit of the covenant expressly releases it by acquiescing to the breach of covenant (see *Shaw* v *Applegate* [1978] 1 All ER 123).

(c) If the person entitled to the benefit of the covenant impliedly releases it by acting in such a way as to make it inequitable to enforce the covenant. See *Chatsworth Estates Co.* v *Fewell* [1931] 1 Ch 224, where Farwell J said that such a doctrine was analagous to the doctrine of estoppel.

(d) Law of Property Act 1925, s. 84.

Law of Property Act 1925

84. Power to discharge or modify restrictive covenants affecting land

(1) The Lands Tribunal shall (without prejudce to any concurrent jurisdiction of the court) have power from time to time, on the application of any person interested in any freehold land affected by any restriction arising under covenant or otherwise as to the user thereof or the building thereon, by order wholly or partially to discharge or modify any such restriction on being satisfied—

(a) that by reason of changes in the character of the property or the neighbourhood or other circumstances of the case which the Lands Tribunal may deem material, the restriction ought to be deemed obsolete, or

(aa) that in a case falling within subsection (1A) below the continued existence thereof would impede some reasonable user of the land for public or private purposes or, as the case may be, would unless modified so impede such user; or

(b) that the persons of full age and capacity for the time being or from time to time entitled to the benefit of the restriction, whether in respect of estates in fee simple or any lesser estates or interests in the property to which the benefit of the restriction is annexed, have agreed, either expressly or by implication, by their acts or omissions, to the same being discharged or modified; or

(c) that the proposed discharge or modification will not injure the persons entitled to the benefit of the restriction:

and an order discharging or modifying a restriction under this subsection may direct the applicant to pay to any person entitled to the benefit of the restriction such sum by way of consideration as the Tribunal may think it just to award under one, but not both, of the following heads, that is to say, either—

(i) a sum to make up for any loss or disadvantage suffered by that person in consequence of the discharge or modification; or

(ii) a sum to make up for any effect which the restriction had, at the time when it was imposed, in reducing the consideration then received for the land affected by it.

(1A) Subsection (1)(aa) above authorises the discharge or modification of a restriction by reference to its impeding some reasonable user of land in any case in which the Lands Tribunal is satisfied that the restriction, in impeding that user, either—
    (a) does not secure to persons entitled to the benefit of it any practical benefits of substantial value or advantage them; or
    (b) is contrary to the public interest;
and that money will be an adequate compensation for the loss or disadvantage (if any) which any such person will suffer from the discharge or modification.

(1B) In determining whether a case is one falling within subsection (1A) above, and in determining whether (in any such case or otherwise) a restriction ought to be discharged or modified, the Lands Tribunal shall take into account the development plan and any declared or ascertainable pattern for the grant or refusal of planning permissions in the relevant areas, as well as the period at which and context in which the restriction was created or imposed and any other material circumstances.

(1C) It is hereby declared that the power conferred by this section to modify a restriction includes power to add such further provisions restricting the user of or the building on the land affected as appear to the Lands Tribunal to be reasonable in view of the relaxation of the existing provisions, and as may be accepted by the applicant; and the Lands Tribunal may accordingly refuse to modify a restriction without some such addition.

(2) The court shall have power on the application of any person interested—
    (a) To declare whether or not in any particular case any freehold land is or would in any given event be affected by a restriction imposed by any instrument; or
    (b) To declare what, upon the true construction of any instrument purporting to impose a restriction, is the nature and extent of the restriction thereby imposed and whether the same is or would in any given event be enforceable and if so by whom. Neither subsections (7) and (11) of this section nor, unless the contrary is expressed, any later enactment providing for this section not to apply to any restrictions shall affect the operation of this subsection or the operation for purposes of this subsection of any other provisions of this section.

(3) The Lands Tribunal shall, before making any order under this section, direct such enquiries, if any, to be made of any government department or local authority, and such notices, if any, whether by way of advertisement or otherwise, to be given to such of the persons who appear to be entitled to the benefit of the restriction intended to be discharged, modified, or dealt with as, having regard to any enquiries notices or other proceedings previously made, given or taken, the Lands Tribunal may think fit.

(3A) On an application to the Lands Tribunal under this section the Lands Tribunal shall give any necessary directions as to the persons who are or are not to be admitted (as appearing to be entitled to the benefit of the restriction) to oppose the application, and no appeal shall lie against any such direction, but rules under the Lands Tribunal Act 1949 shall make provision whereby, in cases in which there arises on such an application (whether or not in connection with the admission of persons to oppose) any such question as is referred to in subsection (2)(a) or (b) of this section, the proceedings on the application can and, if the rules so provide, shall be suspended to enable the decision of the court to be obtained on that question by an application under that subsection, or by means of a case stated by the Lands Tribunal, or otherwise, as may be provided by those rules or by rules of court.

(5) Any order made under this section shall be binding on all persons, whether ascertained or of full age or capacity or not, then entitled or thereafter capable of

Freehold Covenants

becoming entitled to the benefit of any restriction, which is thereby discharged, modified, or dealt with, and whether such persons are parties to the proceedings or have been served with notice or not . . .

SECTION 6: REGISTERED LAND

Land Registration Act 1925

40. Creation and discharge of restrictive covenants

(1) Subject to any entry to the contrary on the register, and without prejudice to the rights of persons entitled to overriding interests (if any) and to any incumbrances entered on the register, who may not concur therein, the proprietor may in any registered disposition or other instrument by covenant, condition or otherwise, impose or make binding, so far as the law permits, any obligation or reservation with respect to the building on or other user of the registered land or any part thereof, or with respect to mines and minerals (whether registered separately or as part of the registered land), or with respect to any other thing in like manner as if the proprietor were entitled to the registered land for his own benefit.

(2) The proprietor may (subject as aforesaid) release or waive any rights arising or which may arise by reason of any covenant or condition, or release any obligation or reservation the benefit of which is annexed or belongs to the registered land, to the same extent and in the same manner as if the rights in respect of the breach or the benefit of the covenant, condition, obligation, or reservation had been vested in him absolutely for his own benefit.

This subsection shall authorise the proprietor in reference to the registered land to give any licence, consent or approval which a tenant for life is by the Settled Land Act 1925, authorised to give in reference to settled land.

(3) Entries shall be made on the register in the prescribed manner of all obligations and reservations imposed by the proprietor, of the release or waiver of any obligation or reservation, and of all obligations and reservations acquired by him for the benefit of the registered estate.

50. Notices of restrictive covenants

(1) Any person entitled to the benefit of a restrictive covenant or agreement (not being a covenant or agreement made between a lessor and lessee) with respect to the building on or other user of registered land may apply to the registrar to enter notice thereof on the register, and where practicable the notice shall be by reference to the instrument, if any, which contains the covenant or agreement, and a copy or abstract of such instrument shall be filed at the registry; and where any such covenant or agreement appears to exist at the time of first registration, notice thereof shall be entered on the register. In the case of registered land the notice aforesaid shall take the place of registration as a land charge.

(2) When such a notice is entered the proprietor of the land and the persons deriving title under him (except incumbrancers or other persons who at the time when the notice is entered may not be bound by the covenant or agreement) shall be deemed to be affected with notice of the covenant or agreement as being an incumbrance on the land.

(3) Where the covenant or agreement is discharged modified or dealt with by an order under the Law of Property Act 1925, or otherwise, or the court refuses to grant an injunction for enforcing the same, the entry shall either be cancelled or reference made to the order or other instrument and a copy of the order, judgment or instrument shall be filed at the registry.

(4) The notice shall, when practicable, refer to the land, whether registered or not for the benefit of which the restriction was made.

12 MORTGAGES

SECTION 1: INTRODUCTION

'[A] mortgage is a conveyance of land or an assignment of chattels as a security for the payment of a debt or the discharge of some other obligation for which it is given', per Lindley MR in *Santley* v *Wilde* [1899] 2 Ch 474.

SECTION 2: CREATION OF A MORTGAGE

Prior to 1926, if the land were freehold the mortgagor could:

(a)   convey the fee simple together with a covenant to repay the loan in a set period of time, with a proviso that if the loan were paid by the said date the property would be reconveyed to the mortgagor;
(b)   lease the land to the mortgagee for a term of years. If the debt had not been repaid by the end of the lease, however, the term would automatically vest in the mortgagee absolutely.

If the land were leasehold land, the mortgagor could:

(a)   sublease his term of years to the mortgagee for a period which was less than the remainder of the term subject to a proviso for redemption; or
(b)   assign the lease subject to a proviso for redemption.

After the Law of Property Act 1925, the following mortgages could be created:

(a)   legal mortgage of a fee simple;
(b)   legal mortgage of a term of years;
(c)   a legal charge;
(d)   equitable mortgages.

Law of Property Act 1925

85. Mode of mortgaging freeholds

(1) A mortgage of an estate in fee simple shall only be capable of being effected at law either by a demise for a term of years absolute, subject to a provision for cesser on redemption, or by a charge by deed expressed to be by way of legal mortgage:

Provided that a first mortgagee shall have the same right to the possession of documents as if his security included the fee simple.

(2) Any purported conveyance of an estate in fee simple by way of mortgage made after the commencement of this Act shall (to the extent of the estate of the mortgagor) operate as a demise of the land to the mortgagee for a term of years absolute, without impeachment for waste, but subject to cesser on redemption, in manner following, namely:—

(a) A first or only mortgagee shall take a term of three thousand years from the date of the mortgage;

(b) A second or subsequent mortgagee shall take a term (commencing from the date of the mortgage) one day longer than the term vested in the first or other mortgagee whose security ranks immediately before that of such second or subsequent mortgagee: and, in this subsection, any such purported conveyance as aforesaid includes an absolute conveyance with a deed of defeasance and any other assurance which, but for this subsection, would operate in effect to vest the fee simple in a mortgagee subject to redemption.

(3) This section applies whether or not the land is registered under the Land Registration Act, 1925, or the mortgage is expressed to be made by way of trust for sale or otherwise.

(4) Without prejudice to the provisions of this Act respecting legal and equitable powers, every power to mortgage or to lend money on mortgage of an estate in fee simple shall be construed as a power to mortgage the estate for a term of years absolute, without impeachment for waste, or by a charge by way of legal mortgage or to lend on such security.

86. Mode of mortgaging leaseholds

(1) A mortgage of a term of years absolute shall only be capable of being effected at law either by a subdemise for a term of years absolute, less by one day at least than the term vested in the mortgagor, and subject to a provision for cesser on redemption, or by a charge by deed expressed to be by way of legal mortgage; and where a licence to subdemise by way of mortgage is required, such licence shall not be unreasonably refused:

Provided that a first mortgagee shall have the same right to the possession of documents as if his security had been effected by assignment.

(2) Any purported assignment of a term of years absolute by way of mortgage made after the commencement of this Act shall (to the extent of the estate of the mortgagor) operate as a subdemise of the leasehold land to the mortgagee for a term of years absolute, but subject to cesser on redemption, in manner following, namely:—

(a) The term to be taken by a first or only mortgagee shall be ten days less than the term expressed to be assigned;

(b) The term to be taken by a second or subsequent mortgagee shall be one day longer than the term vested in the first or other mortgagee whose security ranks immediately before that of the second or subsequent mortgagee, if the length of the last mentioned term permits, and in any case for a term less by one day at least than the term expressed to be assigned:

and, in this subsection, any such purported assignment as aforesaid includes an absolute assignment with a deed of defeasance and any other assurance which, but for this subsection, would operate in effect to vest the term of the mortgagor in a mortgagee subject to redemption.

(3) This section applies whether or not the land is registered under the Land Registration Act, 1925, or the mortgage is made by way of sub-mortgage of a term of years absolute, or is expressed to be by way of trust for sale or otherwise.

(4) Without prejudice to the provisions of this Act respecting legal and equitable powers, every power to mortgage for or to lend money on mortgage of a term of years absolute by way of assignment shall be construed as a power to mortgage the term by subdemise for a term of years absolute or by a charge by way of legal mortgage, or to lend on such security.

87. Charges by way of legal mortgage

(1) Where a legal mortgage of land is created by a charge by deed expressed to be by way of legal mortgage, the mortgagee shall have the same protection, powers and remedies (including the right to take proceedings to obtain possession from the occupiers and the persons in receipt of rents and profits, or any of them) as if—

(a) where the mortgage is a mortgage of an estate in fee simple, a mortgage term for three thousand years without impeachment of waste had been thereby created in favour of the mortgagee; and

(b) where the mortgage is a mortgage of a term of years absolute, a sub-term less by one day than the term vested in the mortgagor had been thereby created in favour of the mortgagee.

Note
The effect of a charge was considered in the following case.

Regent Oil Co. Ltd v *J. A. Gregory (Hatch End) Ltd*
[1966] Ch 402 (CA)

HARMAN LJ: In my opinion, the new charge by way of legal mortgage created by section 87 was intended to be a substitute in all respects for a mortgage by demise, and anything which would be good in the one is good in the other. It would indeed be a trap if the rights of the mortgagee depended on whether his charge were created in one way or the other. Support for this view is to be found in *Grand Junction Co. Ltd* v *Bates* [1954] 2 QB 160; I read from the judgment of Upjohn J (at 168):

> My approach to the problem is this: A charge by way of legal mortgage, as I have already said, was introduced as a conveyancing device by the Law of Property Act, 1925, with a view to simplifying conveyancing, and it would be a pity to introduce subtle differences between one way of creating a charge and another way of creating a charge unless the words of the Act so required. It may be that there is the difference with regard to obtaining consent of the landlord to the charge, though that depends on the construction of the lease; but in any event that is no reason for making another difference between the two forms of creating a security, unless the Act so requires.

Note
A mortgage and charge are different, in that a mortgage 'involves some degree of transfer of the mortgaged property to the morgagee, with a provision for retransfer on repayment of the loan, whereas a charge merely gives the chargee

a right of recourse to the charged property as security for the loan' (Law Com No. 204, para 2.14).

The Law Commission has recommended that the two concepts be amalgamated as one (para. 2.16).

Question
What advantages are there in creating a mortgage by way of a legal charge? Are there any problems?

Equitable mortgages
There are four methods by which an equitable mortgage can be created:

(i) *Contract to create a legal mortgage* A contract to create a legal mortgage generally gives rise to an equitable mortgage based on the equitable maxim, equity regards done that which ought to be done. See *Walsh* v *Lonsdale* (1882) 21 ChD 9, chapter 4. In the case of mortgages, the following conditions must be satisfied:

(a) The mortgage money must have *actually been advanced*, since a contract to make a loan is not specifically enforceable by either party whether the contract is made under seal or otherwise (*Sichel* v *Mosenthal* (1862) 30 Beav 371);

(b) The contract must be one for which the courts will order a decree of specific performance, (*Tebb* v *Hodge* (1869) LR 5 C P 73);

(c) Prior to the Law of Property (Miscellaneous Provisions) Act 1989, the contract was not specifically enforceable unless it was evidenced by a memorandum in writing or supported by an act of part performance.

(d) Since September 1989, it is thought that the contract will only be enforced if it complies with s. 2 of the 1989 Act. Therefore the contract must be in writing.

(ii) *Informal mortgage by deposit of title deeds* Since *Russel* v *Russel* (1783) 1 Bro CC 269, an equitable mortgage can be created by the mortgagor delivering the title deeds of the land to the mortgagee, provided that it is intended that the land be used as security.

Before 1989, no memorandum was necessary, the mere deposit of the deeds was a sufficient act of part performance to give rise to a contract to execute a legal mortgage. Nevertheless a written document of some kind was desirable, first for evidential reasons and, secondly, because the deposit of title deeds by one joint tenant without the other's consent is insufficient to create an equitable charge of jointly owned land. It may create a charge of the equitable interest of the depositor, if it can be said that the deposit is tantamount to an act of severance (see *Thames Guaranty Ltd* v *Campbell* [1984] 2 All ER 585 and *First National Securities Ltd* v *Hegerty* [1984] 3 All ER 641, page 317 *et seq.*).

Since 1989, however, it is doubtful whether the deposit of title deeds can create an equitable mortgage since s. 2 of the 1989 Act says that 'A contract for the sale or other disposition of an interest in land can only be made in writing

...'. Thus, if an equitable mortgage is to be enforceable, then the *agreement* must be made in *writing*. A mere delivery of the title deeds or memorandum evidencing the intention of the parties would be insufficient.

See Law Commission, 'Transfer of Land — Land Mortgages' (Law Com No. 204).

(iii) *Equitable charge*

Matthews v Goodday
(1861) 31 LJ Ch 282

KINDERSLEY V-C: With regard to what are called equitable mortgages, my notion is this. Suppose a man signed a written contract, by which he simply agreed that he thereby charged his real estate with £500 to A, what would be the effect of it? It would be no agreement to give a legal mortgage, but a security by which he equitably charged his lands with payment of a sum of money, and the mode of enforcing it would be by coming into a court of equity to have the money raised by sale or mortgage; that would be the effect of such a simple charge. It is the same thing as if a testator devised an estate to A charged with the payment of a sum of money to B. B's right is not to foreclose A, but to have his charge raised by sale or mortgage of the lands. So in the simple case put of an agreement by a party that his lands should stand charged with the payment of a sum of money to A, the only right of the party in whose favour the agreement is made is to come into equity and ask to have the charge raised by sale or mortgage; but he has no right to come into this court for a decree that the party shall give him a legal mortgage. It is to be borne in mind that a legal mortgage may be more or less beneficial to the party than to have the sum raised by sale or mortgage. But the thing would be distinctly an equitable charge, and not a mortgage nor an agreement to give one. On the other hand the party might agree that, having borrowed a sum of money, he would give a legal mortgage whenever called upon. That agreement might be enforced according to its terms, and the Court would decree a legal mortgage to be given, and would also foreclose the mortgage, unless the money was paid.

(iv) *Mortgage of an equitable interest* A mortgage of an equitable interest in land must be equitable. In such a case the normal method of creation is to transfer the whole interest to the mortgagee together with a proviso for a retransfer on repayment of the loan. Such a transfer, if made *inter vivos* must comply with s. 53(1)(c) of the Law of Property Act 1925. The mortgagee should also give written notice to the owner of the legal estate in order to protect himself (see Law of Property Act 1925, s. 137(1), at page 473).

See Law Commission Working Paper, No. 99, 'Land Mortgages' (1986), paras 5.3, 5.4, 5.5, and Law Com No. 204, Part III.

Question
Do you think that informal mortgages should continue to be recognised by English Law?

SECTION 3: THE RIGHTS OF THE MORTGAGOR

A: THE EQUITY OF REDEMPTION

At common law, the land was conveyed to the mortgagee on condition that the loan be repaid on a date fixed by the agreement, and on fulfilment of such a

Mortgages

condition the mortgagor could re-enter the premises. If the condition was not fulfilled the mortgagee took the property absolutely and the mortgagor lost all rights to the property. The problem with the common-law rules was that they did not provide for the mortgagor to redeem the mortgage after the date set by the contract. This resulted in unfairness, and equity developed the equitable right to redeem, which gave the mortgagor the right to redeem the mortgage after the contractual right had passed provided that the loan and interest was repaid. Such a right is subject to the usual rules relating to the enforcement of equitable rights.

See Law Com No. 204, paras 6.42 to 6.43.

(a) The legal nature of the equity of redemption

In *Casborne* v *Scarfe* (1738) 1 Atk 603 (High Court of Chancery), Lord Hardwick LC said:

An equity of redemption has always been considered as an estate in the land, for it may be devised, granted, or entailed with remainders, and such entail and remainders may be barred by a fine and recovery, and therefore cannot be considered as a mere right only, but such an estate whereof there may be a seisin; the person therefore entitled to the equity of redemption is considered as the owner of the land, and a mortgage in fee is considered as personal assets.

By a devise of all lands, tenements and hereditaments, a mortgage in fee shall not pass, unless the equity of redemption be foreclosed: and if, after such devise made, a foreclosure is had, yet such estate shall not pass by those general words of lands, tenements, and hereditaments, because a foreclosure is considered as a new purchase of the land.

The interest of the land must be some where, and cannot be in abeyance; but it is not in the mortgagee, and therefore must remain in the mortgagor. A devises his estate and after makes a mortgage in fee, tho' that is a total revocation in law, yet in this court it is a revocation *pro tanto* only.

It is certain the mortgagee is not barely a trustee to the mortgagor, but to some purposes, *videlicet*, with regard to the inheritance he certainly is, till a foreclosure.

Note

Prior to 1925, the equity of redemption was the only interest in the property retained by the mortgagor. If the mortgagor wished to create a subsequent mortgage, that interest would be transferred to the mortgagee.

(b) Undue influence

It was thought in the case of *Lloyds Bank* v *Bundy* [1975] QB 326 that the relationship between a bank and a mortgagor was one that could give rise to a fiduciary duty of care by the bank towards the mortgagor, and hence one where there could be undue influence in cases where the mortgagor received no independent advice on the merits of the transaction.

The doctrine in *Lloyds Bank* v *Bundy* was severely curtailed in the case of *National Westminster Bank* v *Morgan* [1985] AC 686, where it was said that a transaction should only be set aside on the basis of undue influence if it was wrongful in that it had constituted a manifest and unfair disadvantage to the person seeking to avoid it. There must be an element of victimisation, and something more than a mere relationship between the parties. Moreover, the relationship of banker and client is not usually one that gives rise to a presumption of undue influence.

There are nevertheless two exceptions to the rule in *National Westminster Bank* v *Morgan*, as the next two cases show.

Kings North Trust Ltd v Bell [1986] 1 WLR 119 (CA)

H had a business and raised finance for its expansion by borrowing money from P. The finance was to be raised by means of two charges, one over the business and another on H's home in which his wife (W) had a beneficial interest. P's solicitors arranged for H's solicitors to have the mortgage deeds executed and also to act as their agents on completion. H's solicitors gave the mortgage deed relating to the house to H so that he could obtain W's signature. W received no independent legal advice and H deliberately misrepresented the purpose and scope of the mortgage. H fell into arrears and P sought possession. Held: when obtaining W's signature H had acted as P's agent and P were therefore bound by H's fraudulent misrepresentation to W.

Cornish v Midland Bank plc [1985] 3 All ER 513 (CA)

P was asked by her bank to sign a second mortgage in the bank's favour. The effect of that mortgage was not explained to her and she did not know that the mortgage secured a loan of £2,000 *and* unlimited further advances made to her husband. She was not advised to have independent legal advice. Held: If a bank takes it upon itself to advise a customer in relation to a mortgage then it is under a duty of care not to negligently misstate the effect of that mortgage. However, a mortgage will only be set aside on the basis of undue influence if the bank has used its influence to take unfair advantage of the customer.

See C. J. Barton and P. M. Rank, 'Undue influence — a retreat?' [1985] Conv 387.

(c) **Exclusion of the right to redeem**
Any provision which prevents or restricts the mortgagor from recovering his property after he has performed his obligation is repugnant since it transgresses the nature of the mortgage (which is merely to provide the mortgagee with security) and as such is void.

Samuel v Jarrah Timber & Wood Paving Corporation Ltd
[1904] AC 323 (HL)

A company used the security of their debenture stock to raise a mortgage advance from P. A condition of the advance was that P was to have an option to purchase the stock at 40 per cent within 12 months. The loan was to become due and payable, with interest, upon either party giving 30 days' notice. Within 12 months of the loan, and before the mortgagor gave notice of its intention to repay the loan, P sought to exercise the option to purchase the stock at the agreed price. Held: the option was void on the basis that a mortgagee cannot convert a security into a purchase by providing at the time of the loan for an event or condition upon which the equity of redemption would be discharged.

Question
How can you reconcile this case with the doctrine of freedom of contract? See P. V. Baker, (1961) 77 LQR 163.

Reeve v *Lisle* [1902] AC 461 (HL)

A granted a mortgage over a steam ship in favour of R who advanced £3000 to A and agreed to lend up to a further £2000 over the following two years. A subsequently approached R to ask for an extension of the mortage term. By an agreement entered into much later than the first mortgage transaction A and R entered into an agreement which gave R an option to purchase the mortgaged property. The effect was to deprive A of the equity of redemption. Held: the option was not void because it was separate and independent.

But see the next case.

Lewis v *Frank Love Ltd*
[1961] 1 WLR 261 (ChD)

P mortgaged property to A. A died and his personal representatives gave notice calling in the debt. They received judgment for the total amount due under the mortgage and, as P did not pay, they issued a bankruptcy notice against P. P wished to pay off A's mortgage and apply for planning permission to develop the property. He approached D who was prepared to lend him the £6,500 he required but only upon the condition that P gave D an option to purchase part of the property. A's personal representatives transferred the benefit of their legal charge to D and D paid £6,070 to them. By an agreement made at the same time, in consideration of D agreeing not to require payment of the principal sum secured by the legal charge for two years, P granted D the option to purchase the part of the property he wanted for £4,000. P was never given the balance of the proposed loan of £6,500. D served a notice in order to exercise the option, but P refused to comply. Held: the option was void and unenforceable.

PLOWMAN J: A number of cases on the principles which apply to questions of clogging the equity were cited, and the first to which I should refer to is *Reeve* v *Lisle* [1902] AC 461. I refer to this case because, to my mind, it establishes, first of all, that what has to be looked at in the case of a mortgage transaction is the substance of the matter and not the form in which the bargain is carried out.

Lord Halsbury LC said:

The view of the Court of Appeal, who had all the facts before them (and I do not propose to question the view which they have taken of these documents read together), is this, that the later transaction was entirely separate — that it was, in truth, a matter applicable to the contemplated partnership, and that the real position of the parties was this, that all the securities were already in their possession, that this further transaction altered the rate of interest, but that the real substance of the second transaction was the contemplated partnership. Under these circumstances it was a mere question of what inferences ought properly to be drawn from the nature of the instruments, and the object and purpose with which they were entered into, as well as what the documents contained in themselves.

Lord Halsbury is there stating that it is not enough merely to look at the documents themselves for the purpose of discovering what the true transaction is, but that the object and purpose with which the documents were entered into must be inquired into....

The specific question of an option to purchase as a clog on the equity was dealt with by the House of Lords in *Samuel* v *Jarrah Timber and Wood Paving Corporation Ltd* [1904] AC 323, ... Lord Lindley said:

The first question is, What is the true nature of this agreement? Is it a mortgage with an option to purchase, or is it a conditional sale? Or is it an agreement giving Samuel an option to hold the debenture stock as a mortgage or a purchase? It appears to me to be clearly a mortgage with an option to purchase. A loan of £5,000 on security was what the company wanted, and what Samuel agreed to let the company have on terms. They were not bargaining for anything else. As soon as the £5,000 was advanced and the debenture stock was placed at Samuel's disposal he was in the position of mortgagee of that stock. He had the rights of a mortgagee, and the company had the rights of a mortgagor. There was that reciprocity and mutuality of remedies which distinguish a mortgage transaction from a conditional sale and from other transactions more or less resembling a mortgage, but not really constituting a mortgage. The transaction was in my opinion a mortgage, plus, amongst other things, an option to purchase, which if exercised by the mortgagee would put an end to the mortgagor's right to redeem, i.e., would prevent him from getting back his mortgaged property. This was the view taken by Kekewich J and by all members of the Court of Appeal, and I am unable myself to view the transaction differently.

In *Lisle* v *Reeve* [1902] 1 Ch 53, 58, Buckley J suggested some instances in which he considered a mortgagee might validly stipulate for an option to buy the equity of redemption; but although his decision was affirmed first by the Court of Appeal and afterwards by this House, the affirmance proceeded entirely on the fact that the agreement to buy the equity of redemption was no part of the original mortgage transaction, but was entered into subsequently, and was an entirely separate transaction to which no objection could be taken. It is plain that the decision would not have been affirmed if the agreement to buy the equity of redemption had been one of the terms of the original mortgage. ... The doctrine 'Once a mortgage always a mortgage' means that no contract between a mortgagor and a mortgagee made at the time of the mortgage and as part of the mortgage transaction, or, in other words, as one of the terms of the loan, can be valid if it prevents the mortgagor from getting back his property on paying off what is due on his security.

Applying that last sentence to the facts of the present case, it seems to me clear that one of the terms on which the defendants were prepared to advance the sum of £6,500 was that they should obtain an option to purchase part of the plaintiff's land. If that is so, it follows from what Lord Lindley was there saying that the doctrine of clogging the equity applies to that transaction; and if the doctrine of clogging the equity does apply, it is, I should have thought, beyond argument that the option to purchase was in fact a clog on the equity because, of course, if it is exercised it will prevent the plaintiff from getting back the piece of land to which it applies.

Lord Lindley went on: 'Any bargain which has that effect is invalid, and is inconsistent with the transaction being a mortgage. This principle is fatal to the appellant's contention if the transaction under consideration is a mortgage transaction, as I am of opinion it clearly is.'

(d) Postponement of the date of redemption

A provision in a mortgage the object of which is to postpone the redemption for a considerable period is void as it interferes with the mortgagor's rights. The equitable right to redeem arises only after the legal date has passed, and therefore the question arises whether the terms of a mortgage can in effect make it irredeemable by postponing the contractual date for redemption.

The following case was affirmed in the House of Lords ([1940] AC 613) on the ground that the mortgage was a debenture within the Companies Act 1929, s. 380, and therefore not invalid by reason of postponement of the date of redemption.

Knightsbridge Estates Trust Ltd v *Byrne*
[1939] Ch 441 (CA)

A company mortgaged its various freehold properties to F. The company covenanted with F to repay the principal sum borrowed plus interest by means of 80 half-yearly instalments of principal and interest. The mortgage deed also provided that in default of payment of any one instalment the principal sum with interest to date would become payable. There was a further provision to the effect that, if the company made the payments due, upon time, and were not in breach of any covenant in the deed, then F would not require payment of the principal moneys in any other manner. The mortgage deed devised the properties to F for a long term of years with a proviso for cesser on redemption. The company found a cheaper source of finance and gave notice to F of its intention to repay the mortgage within six months. F refused to accept this. The company sought a declaration releasing them from the time clause. Held: provisions in the deed were not onerous and unreasonable, and in the circumstances there was no clog on the equity of redemption.

SIR WILFRID GREENE MR: We will deal first with the arguments originally presented on behalf of the respondents. The first argument was that the postponement of the contractual right to redeem for forty years was void in itself, in other words, that the making of such an agreement between mortgagor and mortgagee was prohibited by a rule of equity. It was not contended that a provision in a mortgage deed making the mortgage irredeemable for a period of years is necessarily void. The argument was that such a period must be a 'reasonable' one, and it was said that the period in the present case was an unreasonable one by reason merely of its length. This argument was not the one accepted by the learned judge.

Now an argument such as this requires the closest scrutiny, for, if it is correct, it means that an agreement made between two competent parties, acting under expert advice and presumably knowing their own business best, is one which the law forbids them to make upon the ground that it is not 'reasonable'. If we were satisfied that the rule of equity was what it is said to be, we should be bound to give effect to it. But in the absence of compelling authority we are not prepared to say that such an agreement cannot lawfully be made. A decision to that effect would, in our view, involve an unjustified interference with the freedom of business men to enter into agreements best suited to their interests and would impose upon them a test of 'reasonableness' laid down by the Courts without reference to the business realities of the case.

... [W]e are of opinion that the respondents have failed to establish (and the burden is on them) that there is anything unreasonable in the mere extension of the period of forty years in the circumstances of the present case.

But in our opinion the proposition that a postponement of the contractual right of redemption is only permissible for a 'reasonable' time is not well-founded. Such a postponement is not properly described as a clog on the equity of redemption, since it is concerned with the contractual right to redeem. It is indispensable that any provision which hampers redemption after the contractual date for redemption has passed will not be permitted. Further, it is undoubtedly true to say that a right of redemption is a necessary element in a mortgage transaction, and consequently that, where the contractual right of redemption is illusory, equity will grant relief by allowing redemption. This was the point in the case of *Fairclough* v *Swan Brewery Co.* [1912] AC 565 ... [In the present case] The resulting agreement was a commercial agreement between two important corporations experienced in such matters, and has none of the features of an oppressive bargain where the borrower is at the mercy of an unscrupulous lender. In transactions of this kind it is notorious that there is competition among the large insurance companies and other bodies having large funds to invest, and we are not prepared to view the agreement made as anything but a proper business transaction.

But it is said not only that the period of postponement must be a reasonable one, but that in judging the 'reasonableness' of the period the considerations which we have mentioned cannot be regarded; that the Court is bound to judge 'reasonableness' by a consideration of the terms of the mortgage deed itself and without regard to extraneous matters. In the absence of clear authority we emphatically decline to consider a question of 'reasonableness' from a standpoint so unreal. To hold that the law is to tell business men what is reasonable in such circumstances and to refuse to take into account the business considerations involved, would bring the law into disrepute. Fortunately, we do not find ourselves forced to come to any such conclusion.

Moreover, equity may give relief against contractual terms in a mortgage transaction if they are oppressive or unconscionable, and in deciding whether or not a particular transaction falls within this category the length of time for which the contractual right to redeem is postponed may well be an important consideration. In the present case no question of this kind was or could have been raised.

But equity does not reform mortgage transactions because they are unreasonable. It is concerned to see two things — one that the essential requirements of a mortgage transaction are observed, and the other that oppressive or unconscionable terms are not enforced. Subject to this, it does not, in our opinion, interfere. The question therefore arises whether, in a case where the right of redemption is real and not illusory and there is nothing oppressive or unconscionable in the transaction, there is something in a postponement of the contractual right to redeem, such as we have in the present case, that is inconsistent with the essential requirements of a mortgage transaction? Apart from authority the answer to this question would, in our opinion, be clearly in the negative. Any other answer would place an unfortunate restriction on the liberty of contract of competent parties who are at arm's length — in the present case it would have operated to prevent the respondents obtaining financial terms which for obvious reasons they themselves considered to be most desirable.

Fairclough v Swan Brewery Co. Ltd
[1912] AC 565 (PC)

A lease on the mortgaged property had 17 and a half years left to run. A provision in the mortgage deed purported to prevent the mortgagor from redeeming at any time earlier than six weeks before the lease was due to expire. Held: the covenant was void.

LORD MACNAGHTEN: Here the provision for redemption is nugatory. The incumbrance on the lease the subject of the mortgage according to the letter of the bargain falls to be discharged before the lease terminates, but at a time when it is on the very point of expiring, when redemption can be no advantage to the mortgagor even if he should be so fortunate as to get his deeds back before the actual termination of the lease. For all practical purposes this mortgage is irredeemable. It was obviously meant to be irredeemable. It was made irredeemable in and by the mortgage itself.

Note
See, however, the earlier case of *Santley* v *Wilde*.

Santley v Wilde [1899] 2 Ch 474 (CA)

Here there was a lease of a theatre and the lease had 10 years to run. The theatre was mortgaged to W and the mortgage contained a covenant that repayment was to be made by way of instalments and that the mortgagor would, during the remainder of the term, pay a sum equal to one-third of the profits from the lease. The mortgage should determine on the payment of the principal sum plus interest and all other moneys that had been covenanted to be paid. Held: the mortgagor could not redeem the mortgage except by performing all his obligations and observing the covenants. In this case there was no fetter on the equity of redemption and no hardship or oppression.

(e) Collateral advantages
A collateral advantage is an advantage which the mortgagee reserves to himself in addition to the mortgagor repaying the principal sum borrowed plus interest. For example, a mortgagor who owns a petrol station may agree that in addition to repaying the principal sum and interest borrowed he will buy all petrol to sell in the garage from the mortgagee. The courts have in fact, changed their attitude towards such clauses. The older cases restrict any attempt by the mortgagee to reserve a collateral advantage.

In *Biggs* v *Hoddinott* [1898] 2 Ch 307, the Court of Appeal said that there is nothing to prevent a mortage from providing for a collateral advantage in favour of the mortgagee provided that the stipulation does not fetter the equity of redemption and that the bargain is not unreasonable or oppressive, being made between the parties while on equal terms, without any improper pressure, unfair dealing or undue influence. Chitty LJ said:

It is contended that the covenant by the mortgagors is void in equity. The first objection I have to make is that it in no way affects the equity of redemption, for it is not stipulated that damages for breach of the covenant shall be covered by the security, and redemption takes place quite independently of the covenant; so this is not a case where the right to redeem is affected. Equity has always looked upon a mortgage as only a security for money, and here the right of the mortgagors to redeem on payment of principal, interest, and costs is maintained. It has been contended that the principle is established by the authorities that a mortgagee shall not stipulate for any collateral advantage to himself. I think the cases only establish that the mortgagee shall not impose on the mortgagor an unconscionable or oppressive bargain. The present appears to me to be a reasonable trade bargain between two business men who enter into it with their eyes open, and it would be a fanciful doctrine of equity that would set it aside.

Note
Such collateral advantages, although they can endure for the period of the mortgage (provided they are not unconscionable) will not *usually* continue once the mortgage is redeemed.

Noakes & Co. Ltd v *Rice*
[1902] AC 24 (HL)

The mortgagor was the lessee of a public house. He covenanted with the mortgagees, who were brewers, that he and all persons deriving title under him should not use any malt liquors other than those supplied by the mortgagees. The covenant was worded to charge the premises themselves throughout the term of the lease, whether or not the mortgage debt had been repaid. Held: the covenant was a 'clog' on the equity of redemption.

LORD DAVEY: My Lords, there are three doctrines of the Courts of Equity in this country which have been referred to in the course of the argument in this case. The first doctrine to which I refer is expressed in the maxim, 'Once a mortgage always a mortgage'. The second is that the mortgagee shall not reserve to himself any collateral advantage outside the mortgage contract; and the third is that a provision or stipulation which will have the effect of clogging or fettering the equity of redemption is void.

My Lords, the first maxim presents no difficulty: it is only another way of saying that a mortgage cannot be made irredeemable, and that a provision to that effect is void.

My Lords, the second doctrine to which I refer, namely, that the mortgagee shall not reserve to himself any collateral advantage outside the mortgage contract, was established long ago when the usury laws were in force. The Court of Equity went beyond the usury laws, and set its face against every transaction which tended to usury. It therefore declared void every stipulation by a mortgagee for a collateral advantage which made his total remuneration for the loan indirectly exceed the legal interest. I think it will be found that every case under this head of equity was decided either on this ground, or on the ground that the bargain was oppressive and unconscionable. The abolition of the usury laws has made an alteration in the view the Court should take on this subject, and I agree that a collateral advantage may now be stipulated for by a mortgagee, provided that no unfair advantage be taken by the mortgagee which would render it void or voidable, according to the general principles of equity, and provided that it does not offend against the third doctrine. On these grounds I think the case of *Biggs* v *Hoddinott* in the Court of Appeal was rightly decided.

The third doctrine to which I have referred is really a corollary from the first, and might be expressed in this form: Once a mortgage always a mortgage and nothing but a mortgage. The meaning of that is that the mortgagee shall not make any stipulation which will prevent a mortgagor, who has paid principal, interest, and costs, from getting back his mortgaged property in the condition in which he parted with it. I do not dissent from the opinion expressed by my noble and learned friend opposite (Lord Lindley), when Master of the Rolls, in the case of *Santley* v *Wilde* [1899] 2 Ch 474. He says: 'A clog or fetter is something which is inconsistent with the idea of security; a clog or fetter is in the nature of a repugnant condition.' But I ask, 'security' for what? I think it must be security for the principle, interest, and costs, and, I will add, for any advantages in the nature of increased interest or remuneration for the loan which the mortgagee has validly stipulated for during the continuance of the mortgage. There are two elements in the conception of a mortgage: first, security for the money advanced; and, secondly, remuneration for the use of the money. When the mortgage is paid off the security is at an end, and, as the mortgagee is no longer kept out of his money, the remuneration to him for the use of his money is also at an end. I confess I should have decided the case of *Santley* v *Wilde* differently from the way in which it was dealt with in the Court of Appeal. After the payment of principal and interest, and everything which had become payable up to the date of redemption, the property in that case remained charged with the payment to the mortgagee of one-third share of the profits, and the stipulation to that effect should, I think, have been held to be a clog or fetter on the right to redeem. The principle is this — that a mortgage must not be converted into something else; and when once you come to the conclusion that a stipulation for the benefit of the mortgagee is part of the mortgage transaction, it is but part of his security, and necessarily comes to an end on the payment off of the loan. In my opinion, every yearly or other recurring payment stipulated for by the mortgagee should be held to be in the nature of interest, and no more payable after the principal is paid off than interest would be. I apprehend a man could not stipulate for the continuance of payment of interest after the principal is paid, and I do not think he can stipulate for any other recurring payment such as a share of profits. Any stipulation to that effect would, in my opinion, be void as a clog or fetter on the equity of redemption.

LORD LINDLEY: The conclusion thus arrived at is not inconsistent with *Santley* v *Wilde*, on which the appellants so strongly rely. Some of your Lordships think that case went too far. I do not think so myself. . . . I believe the true principle applicable to these cases to be that expounded by the Court of Appeal in *Biggs* v *Hoddinott* and *Santley* v *Wilde*. That principle is perfectly consistent with a real pledge and with the maxim 'Once a mortgage always a mortgage'; but it will not render valid the covenant which your Lordships have to consider in the present case.

Bradley v *Carritt*
[1903] AC 253 (HL)

X mortgaged his shares in a tea company subject to a provision in favour of the mortgagee that X would use his best endeavours to ensure that the mortgagee would always be used by the company as its broker. X was obliged to pay an amount to the mortgagees (equivalent to the amount of commission that would have been payable to him as broker) should the company not sell their tea through him. After the mortgage was redeemed, the company changed brokers. The mortgagees sought to enforce the agreement against X. Held: (Lords Lindley and Shand dissenting), the agreement was not binding as it was a clog on the equity of redemption.

LORD DAVEY: It is, in my opinion, idle to say that the mortgagor in this case has got his property back unfettered or that he has the unrestricted enjoyment of it, if the agreements contained in the fourth clause of the contract of May 16, 1892, are held to constitute a continuing obligation. It is said that the performance of these agreements is not secured on the shares. But, my Lords, that is not necessary. The agreements which were held objectionable, both in *Browne* v *Ryan* [1901] 2 IR 653 and in *Noakes* v *Rice* [1902] AC 24, did not constitute charges on the mortgaged premises, but they fettered the mortgagor, in the one case, in the free disposition and, in the other, in the free enjoyment of his property. In the present case the agreement is that the appellant W M Bradley will, 'as a shareholder,' use his best endeavours to secure the sale of the company's teas to the respondent or his firm, and in the event of the teas being sold through another broker will pay to the respondent the amount of the commission which he or his firm might have earned. In other words, he agrees to use the voting power attached to his shares in a particular way for the respondent's benefit. Now, what is a share? It is but a bundle of rights, of which the right of voting at meetings of the company is not the least valuable. My Lords, can it be said that the mortgagee does not retain a hold upon the shares which form the mortgaged property, or that the mortgagor has full redemption of it, when the latter is not free to exercise an important right in such manner as he may think most conducive to his own interests? He may think it advantageous to the company to employ another broker, or that the change would produce a better return on his shares, but if he gives effect to his opinion he incurs what is in effect a heavy penalty. Again, the appellant could not part with or otherwise deal with his shares without losing the influence in the company's counsels which might enable him to secure the performance of the first part of the agreement, or running a serious risk of liability under the second part.

My Lords, I can see no difference in principle between this case and the case of *Browne* v *Ryan* [1901] 2 IR 653, which has already been approved in this House. The respondent can no more claim to be continuously employed as broker for the sale of the teas of the appellant's company, or to be compensated for loss of his commission if not so employed, than the land agent in *Browne* v *Ryan* could claim to be employed in the sale of the farmer's estate, or to be compensated for the loss of his commission. I am, therefore, of opinion that, even if the fourth clause of the contract bears the construction which has been put upon it by the Courts below, the agreements contained in it are such as cannot, in the circumstances, be enforced by the Courts of this country.

But, my Lords, I doubt whether we ought to put that construction on the clause in question. Prima facie a clause in a mortgage contract is limited to the duration of the mortgage relation between the contracting parties. In this clause we have the words 'always hereafter'; but I observe that in two other clauses (the third and the fifth) a similar phrase, 'at any time hereafter,' is used and is limited by the context to the duration of the mortgage. I am disposed to say that the words 'always hereafter,' having regard to the nature and purport of the agreement, in like manner mean at any time hereafter during the currency of the loan. But in the view which I take of the case it is not necessary for me to express a decided opinion on this question.

With regard to the appellant, James Bradley's, agreement, I think it was part of the same transaction and ancillary to the principal agreement, and by way of further security to the respondent and increased remuneration to him for the use of his money. And I am of opinion that it must be construed in the same way, and stand or fall with the principal agreement.

I am, therefore, of opinion that the decision of the Court of Appeal should be reversed, and instead thereof the action should be dismissed with costs, and the respondent should pay the costs in the Court of Appeal and in this House.

LORD LINDLEY: Clause 4 in no way fetters the right to redeem, nor obstructs the mortgagor in the practical exercise of that right, or of the use or enjoyment of his shares when he gets them back. He can then do what he likes with them, free from all control by the mortgagee. How it can be said that clause 4 clogs the equity of redemption or infringes the rule, once a mortgage always a mortgage, passes my comprehension. It is admitted that after redemption the mortgagor can sell the shares; but it is said that so long as he holds them he is bound to use whatever influence they give him in favour of the mortgagee, so as to enable him to retain his position of broker to the tea company. This observation, so far as it is true, applies to whatever shares Mr William Bradley might happen to hold when it became necessary to use his influence in Mr Carritt's favour. But clause 4 gives Mr Carritt no legal or equitable right to have shares, still less any particular shares held by Mr Bradley, used in any particular way. By the first part of clause 4 Mr Bradley has bound himself to use his best endeavours to secure the tea brokerage for Mr Carritt: this might or might not involve voting for him. The votes conferred by the shares might be too few to be of any use, and other endeavours than voting in respect of them might be more likely to prevail. But to say that the equitable principle under discussion is infringed, and that clause 4 is invalid simply because it might be necessary for Mr Bradley to use the influence which the mortgaged shares, if retained, would confer in order to perform his engagement to Mr Carritt, seems to me to stretch the doctrine under consideration to an extent not warranted by principle or authority.

Kreglinger v *New Patagonia Meat & Cold Storage Co. Ltd*
[1914] AC 25 (HL)

The plaintiffs (P) were wool brokers who had agreed to lend money to a meat preserving company, D, at an interest rate of 6 per cent. Provided that all interest was paid punctually in accordance with the agreement, the principal was not to be repaid until September 1915. However, D could redeem the mortgage early by giving P one month's notice. The agreement for the loan, which was secured by way of a floating charge, provided that the company should not sell sheepskins to anyone except P as long as P were willing to buy them at the best price. The arrangement was to continue for a period of five years, the approximate term of the loan. D were also to pay P a commission on all sheepskins sold by D to others. D exercised their right to pay off the loan early in January 1913. P claimed that they were entitled to exercise their right of pre-emption for the full period of five years, even though the loan had been repaid. Held: the agreement regarding the purchase of sheepskins was a collateral contract, separate from the mortgage itself, and did not amount to a clog in the equity of redemption, nor was it repugnant to the right to redeem.

VISCOUNT HALDANE LC: My Lords, the question in the present case is whether the right to redeem has been interfered with. . . . What was the true character of the transaction? Did the appellants make a bargain such that the right to redeem was cut down, or did they simply stipulate for a collateral undertaking, outside and clear of the mortgage, which would give them an exclusive option of purchase of the sheepskins of the respondents? The question is in my opinion not whether the two contracts were made at the same moment and evidenced by the same instrument, but whether they were in substance a single and undivided contract or two distinct contracts. Putting aside for the moment considerations turning on the character of the floating charge, such an option no doubt affects the freedom of the respondents in carrying on their business even after the mortgage has been paid off. But so might other arrangements which would be plainly collateral, an agreement, for example, to take permanently into the firm a new partner as a condition of obtaining fresh capital in the form of a loan. The question is one not of form but of substance, and it can be answered in each case only by looking at all the circumstances, and not by mere reliance on some abstract principle, or upon the dicta which have fallen obiter from judges in other and different cases. . . .

My Lords, if in the case before the House your Lordships arrive at the conclusion that the agreement for an option to purchase the respondents' sheepskins was not in substance a fetter on the exercise of their right to redeem, but was in the nature of a collateral bargain the entering into which was a preliminary and separable condition of the loan, the decided cases cease to present any great difficulty. In questions of this kind the binding force of previous decisions, unless the facts are indistinguishable, depends on whether they establish a principle. . . . What is vital in the appeal now under consideration is to classify accurately the transaction between the parties. What we have to do is to ascertain from scrutiny of the circumstances whether there has really been an attempt to effect a mortgage with a provision preventing redemption of what was pledged merely as security for payment of the amount of the debt and any charges besides that may legitimately be added. It is not, in my opinion, conclusive in favour of the appellants that the security assumed the form of a floating charge. A floating charge is not the less a pledge because of its floating character, and a contract which fetters the right to redeem on which equity insists as regards all contracts of loan and security ought on principle to be set aside as readily in the case of a floating security as in any other case. But it is material that such a floating charge, in the absence of bargain to the contrary effect, permits the assets to be dealt with freely by the mortgagor until the charge becomes enforceable. If it be said that the undertaking of the respondents which was charged extended to their entire business, including the right to dispose of the skins of which they might from time to time become possessed, the comment is that at least they were to be free, so long as the security remained a floating one, to make contracts in the ordinary course of business in regard to these skins. If there had been no mortgage such a contract as the one in question would have been an ordinary incident in such a business. We are considering the simple question of what is the effect on the right to redeem of having inserted into the formal instrument signed when the money was borrowed an ordinary commercial contract for the sale of skins extending over a period. It appears that it was the intention of the parties that the grant of the security should not affect the power to enter into such a contract, either with strangers or with the appellants, and if so I am unable to see how the equity of redemption is affected. No doubt it is the fact that on redemption the respondents will not get back their business as free from obligation as it was before the date of the security. But that may well be because outside the security and consistently with its terms there was a contemporaneous but collateral contract, contained in the same document as constituted the security, but in substance independent of it. If it was the intention of the parties, as I think it was, to enter into this contract as a condition of the respondents getting their advance, I know no reason either in morals or in equity which ought to prevent this intention from being left to have its effect. What was to be capable of redemption was an undertaking which was deliberately left to be freely changed in its details by ordinary business transactions with which the mortgage was not to interfere. Had the charge not been a floating one it might have been more difficult to give effect to this intention. . . .

[Viscount Haldane LC then discusses *Noakes & Co.* v *Rice* and sets out the decision in *Bradley* v *Carritt*] The decision [in *Bradley* v *Carritt*] was a striking one. It was not unanimous, for Lord Lindley dissented from the conclusions of Lord Macnaghten and Lord Davey. . . . [I]t certainly cannot, in my opinion, be taken as authoritatively laying down that the mere circumstance that after redemption the property redeemed may not, as the result of some bargain made at the time of the mortgage, be in the same condition as it was before that time, is conclusive against the validity of that bargain. To render it invalid the bargain must, when its substance is examined, turn out to have formed part of the terms of the mortgage and to have really cut down a true right of redemption. I think that the tendency of recent decisions has been to lay undue stress on the letter of the principle which limits the jurisdiction of equity in setting aside contracts. The origin and reason of the principle ought, as I have already said, to be kept steadily in view in applying it to fresh cases. There appears to me to have grown up a tendency to look to the letter rather than to the spirit of the doctrine. The true view is, I think, that judges ought in this kind of jurisdiction to proceed cautiously, and to bear in mind the real reasons which have led Courts of Equity to insist on the free right to redeem and the limits within which the purpose of the rule ought to confine its scope. I cannot but think that the validity of the bargain in such cases as *Bradley* v *Carritt* and *Santley* v *Wilde* might have been made free from serious question if the parties had chosen to seek what would have been substantially the same result in a different form. For form may be very important when the question is one of the construction of ambiguous words in which people have expressed their intentions. . . .

(f) Unconscionable or oppressive collateral advantage

Cityland & Property (Holdings) Ltd v *Dabrah*
[1968] Ch 166 (ChD)

An agreement imposed a very high premium on the mortgagor, rather than requiring interest to be repaid. The capital was repayable by monthly instalments over six years. Held: a mortgagee may generally benefit from a collateral advantage but the premium in this case was oppressive and unreasonable.

GOFF J: It follows from those authorities that the defendant cannot succeed merely because this is a collateral advantage, but he can succeed if — and only if — on the evidence, the bonus in this case was, to use the language of Lord Parker, 'unfair and unconscionable,' or, to use the language used in Halsbury's Laws of England, 'unreasonable'; and I therefore have to determine whether it was or was not. In doing that, I have to consider all the circumstances. Unlike the facts in *Kreglinger* v *New Patagonia Meat & Cold Storage Co. Ltd* [1914] AC 25, this was not a bargain between two large trading concerns. It was the case of a man who was buying his house and a man who was obviously of limited means because he was unable to find more than £600 towards the purchase, whereas, in evidence filed for another purpose, the plaintiffs have stated that all the other persons who had purchased property from them had been able themselves to finance or to arrange finance for the purchases. The premium which was added to the loan was, as I understand, no less than 57 per cent of the amount of the loan. I do not think it is really open to the plaintiffs to justify this premium as being in lieu of interest because they claim interest on the aggregate of the loan and the premium; but even if it should be, then, taking the mortgage as a six-year mortgage — and, of course, they bound themselves not to call it in within that time if the instalments were duly paid — it would still represent interest at 19 per cent, which is out of all proportion to any investment rates prevailing at the time. Moreover, it was expressly provided by the charge that, on default, the whole should immediately become due.

Note
See Granville L. Williams, 'The doctrine of repugnancy III: "clogging the equity" and miscellaneous applications' (1944) 60 LQR 190.

Multiservice Bookbinding Ltd v *Marden* [1979] Ch 84

P executed a mortgage of their premises. The loan was repayable with interest at 2 per cent per annum above bank rate. The mortgage provided that, so long as P paid the interest due by quarterly instalments and made annual capital repayments in accordance with a set scale, D would not seek to enforce the mortgage. The mortgage also provided, *inter alia*, that all sums payable under the mortgage were to be 'increased or decreased proportionally, if at the close of business on the day preceding the day on which payment is made the rate of exchange between the Swiss franc and pound sterling shall vary by more than 3 per cent from the rate of $12.07\frac{5}{8}$ francs to the pound'. Held: index-linking money obligations is not contrary to public policy.

Note
See H. W. Wilkinson, 'Index-linked mortgages' [1978] Conv 346; R. A. Bowles, 'Mortgages and interest rates: an economist's view' (1981) 131 NLJ 4. See also *Nationwide Building Society* v *Registry of Friendly Societies* [1983] 3 All ER 296, [1983] 1 WLR 1226.

(g) Extortionate credit bargains

Consumer Credit Act 1974

137. Extortionate credit bargains
(1) If the court finds a credit bargain extortionate it may reopen the credit agreement so as to do justice between the parties.
 (2) In this section and sections 138 to 140,—
  (a) 'credit agreement' means any agreement between an individual (the 'debtor') and any other person (the 'creditor') by which the creditor provides the debtor with credit of any amount, and
  (b) 'credit bargain'—
   (i) where no transaction other than the credit agreement is to be taken into account in computing the total charge for credit, means the credit agreement, or

(ii) where one or more other transactions are to be so taken into account, means the credit agreement and those other transactions, taken together.

138. When bargains are extortionate
(1) A credit bargain is extortionate if it—
   (a) requires the debtor or a relative of his to make payments (whether unconditionally, or on certain contingencies) which are grossly exorbitant, or
   (b) otherwise grossly contravenes ordinary principles of fair dealing.

(2) In determining whether a credit bargain is extortionate, regard shall be had to such evidence as is adduced concerning—
   (a) interest rates prevailing at the time it was made,
   (b) the factors mentioned in subsections (3) to (5), and
   (c) any other relevant considerations.

(3) Factors applicable under subsection (2) in relation to the debtor include—
   (a) his age, experience, business capacity and state of health; and
   (b) the degree to which, at the time of making the credit bargain, he was under financial pressure, and the nature of that pressure.

(4) Factors applicable under subsection (2) in relation to the creditor include—
   (a) the degree of risk accepted by him, having regard to the value of any security provided;
   (b) his relationship to the debtor; and
   (c) whether or not a colourable cash price was quoted for any goods or services included in the credit bargain.

(5) Factors applicable under subsection (2) in relation to a linked transaction include the question how far the transaction was reasonably required for the protection of debtor or creditor, or was in the interest of the debtor.

Notes
1. The test as to whether a bargain is extortionate is similar to that for unconscionability. In *Coldunell Ltd* v *Gallon* [1986] 1 All ER 429, it was said that as there was nothing unusual about the loan, the rate of interest was not unreasonable and the mortgagee had acted in the way that an ordinary commercial lender would have been expected to act, the mortgagee had discharged the burden of proving that the bargain was not extortionate.
2. In *A. Ketley Ltd* v *Scott* [1981] ICR 241, the rate of interest on a loan was 12 per cent for three months (equal to a rate of 48 per cent per annum). The court refused to reopen the credit agreement as the mortgagor knew precisely the nature of the transaction.
3. Sir Nicholas Browne-Wilkinson in **Woodstead Finance Ltd v Petrou** [1986] NLJ Rep 188 (CA) said:

> The claim that the rate of interest was extortionate, within the meaning of s. 137 of the Consumer Credit Act 1974, requires the court, as s. 138(2) makes clear, to have regard to 'such evidence as is adduced concerning' a number of different factors, including the prevailing interest rates, the age, experience, business capacity and state of health of the debtor, the financial pressure on the debtor and the degree of risk accepted by the creditor. It is clear that what we have to have regard to is the evidence adduced. As I have said, the evidence actually adduced at the trial all indicated that, given the

circumstances and the payment record of the husband, the loan arrangement and the rate of interest was normal for a risk of this kind. Accordingly, it was impossible for the judge to hold that this was an extortionate credit bargain within the meaning of the Act. . . .

See J. E. Adams, 'Mortgages and the Consumer Credit Act' (1975) 39 Conv 94; H. W. Wilkinson, 'Extortionate mortgages' (1980) 130 NLJ 749.

(h) Restraint of trade

A mortgage can be invalidated by the common-law doctrine of restraint of trade if the restriction is one that unreasonably restricts a person from carrying on his trade or profession.

Esso Petroleum Co. Ltd v *Harper's Garage (Stourport) Ltd*
[1968] AC 269 (HL)

D owned two garages and P was a supplier of motor fuels. P and D entered into separate agreements regarding each garage. Both involved covenants by D to sell only Esso products. The first agreement was for a period of four years and five months, whereas the second was for a period of 21 years. In return for the sales agreement, D benefited from a reduced price. Also, in relation to the second garage P agreed to lend £7,000 to D repayable in instalments of principal and interest over 21 years. In the mortgage deed, D covenanted to keep the garage open during normal working hours and to purchase all motor fuels at the mortgaged premises from P for the continuance of the mortgage. The mortgage was not to be redeemed except in accordance with the repayment terms of the deed, effectively postponing D's right of redemption for 21 years.

Held:

(1) As D was required to give up his existing right to sell other suppliers' petrol, the agreements were within the scope of the doctrine of restraint of trade.

(2) A 'tie' of five years was not unreasonable but one of 21 years went beyond any period which was reasonable (in the absence of evidence of some advantage to P for which a shorter period would not be adequate). The longer agreement was therefore void.

(3) The existence of the mortgage did not prevent the doctrine of restraint of trade from being applied.

Note
See also *Alec Lobb (Garages) Ltd* v *Total Oil (Great Britain) Ltd* [1985] 1 WLR 173, where it was said that the doctrine of restraint of trade applied where the covenantor gave up an existing freedom to trade, or where an existing tie of short duration was extended for a substantial period.

See Paul Todd, '*Alec Lobb (Garages) Ltd* v *Total Oil (Great Britain) Ltd*' [1985] Conv 141.

B: RIGHT TO GRANT LEASE

Law of Property Act 1925

99. Leasing powers of mortgagor and mortgagee in possession

(1) A mortgagor of land while in possession shall, as against every incumbrancer, have power to make from time to time any such lease of the mortgaged land, or any part thereof, as is by this section authorised.

(2) A mortgagee of land while in possession shall, as against all prior incumbrancers, if any, and as against the mortgagor, have power to make from time to time any such lease as aforesaid.

(3) The leases which this section authorises are —

(i) agricultural or occupation leases for any term not exceeding twenty-one years, or, in the case of a mortgage made after the commencement of this Act, fifty years; and

(ii) building leases for any term not exceeding ninety-nine years, or, in the case of a mortgage made after the commencement of this Act, nine hundred and ninety-nine years.

(4) ...

(5) Every such lease shall be made to take effect in possession not later than twelve months after its date.

(6) Every such lease shall reserve the best rent that can reasonably be obtained, regard being had to the circumstances of the case, but without any fine being taken.

(7) Every such lease shall contain a covenant by the lessee for payment of the rent, and a condition of re-entry on the rent not being paid within a time therein specified not exceeding thirty days.

(8) A counterpart of every such lease shall be executed by the lessee and delivered to the lessor, of which execution and delivery the execution of the lease by the lessor shall, in favour of the lessee and all persons deriving title under him, be sufficient evidence.

(9)–(10) ...

(11) In case of a lease by the mortgagor, he shall, within one month after making the lease, deliver to the mortgagee, or, where there are more than one, to the mortgagee first in priority, a counterpart of the lease duly executed by the lessee, but the lessee shall not be concerned to see that this provision is complied with.

(12) A contract to make or accept a lease under this section may be enforced by or against every person on whom the lease if granted would be binding.

(13) This section applies only if and as far as a contrary intention is not expressed by the mortgagor and mortgagee in the mortgage deed, or otherwise in writing, and has effect subject to the terms of the mortgage deed or of any such writing and to the provisions therein contained.

(14) The mortgagor and mortgagee may, by agreement in writing, whether or not contained in the mortgage deed, reserve to or confer on the mortgagor or the mortgagee, or both, any further or other powers of leasing or having reference to leasing; and any further or other powers so reserved or conferred shall be exercisable, as far as may be, as if they were conferred by this Act, and with all the like incidents, effects, and consequences:

Provided that the powers so reserved or conferred shall not prejudicially affect the rights of any mortgagee interested under any other mortgage subsisting at the date of the agreement, unless that mortgagee joins in or adopts the agreement.

(15) Nothing in this Act shall be construed to enable a mortgagor or mortgagee to make a lease for any longer term or on any other conditions than such as could have

been granted or imposed by the mortgagor, with the concurrence of all the incumbrancers, if this Act and the enactments replaced by this section had not been passed:

Provided that, in the case of a mortgage of leasehold land, a lease granted under this section shall reserve a reversion of not less than one day.

Note

If the power of leasing is excluded in the mortgage deed, or if the lease does not satisfy the provisions of the Law of Property Act 1925, the lease may be binding by estoppel (see *Church of England Building Society* v *Piskor*, chapter 6). Such a lease is void between the lessee and the mortgagee and his successors. When there is an unauthorised lease, the mortgagee can either treat the lessee as a trespasser or as his own tenant.

C: POWER TO ACCEPT SURRENDER OF LEASES

Law of Property Act 1925

100. Powers of mortgagor and mortgagee in possession to accept surrenders of leases

(1) For the purpose only of enabling a lease authorised under the last preceding section, or under any agreement made pursuant to that section, or by the mortgage deed (in this section referred to as an authorised lease) to be granted, a mortgagor of land while in possession shall, as against every incumbrancer, have, by virtue of this Act, power to accept from time to time a surrender of any lease of the mortgaged land or any part thereof comprised in the lease, with or without an exception of or in respect of all or any of the mines and minerals therein, and, on a surrender of the lease so far as it comprises part only of the land or mines and minerals leased, the rent may be apportioned.

(2) For the same purpose, a mortgagee of land while in possession shall, as against all prior or other incumbrancers, if any, and as against the mortgagor, have, by virtue of this Act, power to accept from time to time any such surrender as aforesaid.

(5) No surrender shall, by virtue of this section, be rendered valid unless:—

(a) An authorised lease is granted of the whole of the land or mines and minerals comprised in the surrender to take effect in possession immediately or within one month after the date of the surrender; and

(b) The term certain or other interest granted by the new lease is not less in duration than the unexpired term or interest which would have been subsisting under the original lease if that lease had not been surrendered; and

(c) Where the whole of the land mines and minerals originally leased has been surrendered, the rent reserved by the new lease is not less than the rent which would have been payable under the original lease if it had not been surrendered; or where part only of the land or mines and minerals has been surrendered, the aggregate rents respectively remaining payable or reserved under the original lease and new lease are not less than the rent which would have been payable under the original lease if no partial surrender has been accepted.

(7) This section applies only if and as far as a contrary intention is not expressed by the mortgagor and mortgagee in the mortgage deed, or otherwise in writing, and shall have effect subject to the terms of the mortgage deed or of any such writing and to the provisions therein contained.

D: RIGHT TO SUE

Law of Property Act 1925

98. Actions for possession by mortgagors

(1) A mortgagor for the time being entitled to the possession or receipt of the rents and profits of any land, as to which the mortgagee has not given notice of his intention to take possession or to enter into the receipt of the rents and profits thereof, may sue for such possession, or for the recovery of such rents or profits, or to prevent or recover damages in respect of any trespass or other wrong relative thereto, in his own name only, unless the cause of action arises upon a lease or other contract made by him jointly with any other person.

(2) This section does not prejudice the power of a mortgagor independently of this section to take proceedings in his own name only, either in right of any legal estate vested in him or otherwise.

(3) This section applies whether the mortgage was made before or after the commencement of this Act.

SECTION 4: THE RIGHTS OF THE LEGAL MORTGAGEE

A: RIGHT TO POSSESSION OF THE LAND

A legal mortgage or a legal charge gives the mortgagee a legal estate in the property. One of the incidents of this legal estate is the mortgagee's right of possession.

Question
The Law Commission say that 'this right is neither needed nor wanted by mortgagees and that its continued existence is an unnecessary complication in the law' (Law Com No. 204, para. 6.16). Do you agree?

Notes
1. In *Four-Maids Ltd* v *Dudley Marshall (Properties) Ltd* [1957] 1 Ch 317 (ChD), Harman J defined the right to possession as follows:

> ... the right of the mortgagee to possession in the absence of some contract has nothing to do with default on the part of the mortgagor. The mortgagee may go into possession before the ink is dry on the mortgage unless there is something in the contract, express or by implication, whereby he has contracted himself out of that right. He has the right because he has a legal term of years in the property or its statutory equivalent. If there is an attornment clause, he must give notice. If there is a provision that, so long as certain payments are made, he will not go into possession, then he has contracted himself out of his rights. Apart from that, possession is a matter of course.

2. The right of the mortgagee to take possession of the land from the moment of creation of the mortgage may be restricted by a clause in the mortgage deed.

Usually the mortgagee enters into possession only as a preliminary step to sale and not in any other situation. The reason for this is twofold:

(a) If the mortgagee decides to enter into possession he is not entitled to receive anything from the mortgage other than the repayment of the principal sum with interest and costs.

(b) He is liable to account for any sum he has actually received or might have received but for his wilful default or neglect. See *White v City of London Brewery Company* (1889) 42 ChD 237 (CA), where a brewery exercised their right to take possession and let the premises (a free house) as a tied public house selling only their beer. The mortgagees had to account for such additional rent that they would have received by letting the premises free of the tied home restriction.

3. Where a mortgagee enters into possession of the land, he may use the income from it *in lieu* of the interest payments due to him. Any surplus can be used to pay off capital if he so wishes.

See Charles Harpum, 'A mortgagee's right to possession and the mischief rule' (1977) 40 MLR 356; Stephen Tromans, 'Mortgages; possession by default' [1984] Conv 91; R. A. Pearce, 'Keeping a mortgagee out of possession' [1979] CLJ 257.

(a) Common law relief of mortgagor

At common law, the court has no jurisdiction to refuse an order for possession unless the mortgagee agrees to such an action, but it can adjourn the proceedings or allow a stay of execution to allow the mortgagor to redeem the mortgage.

Citibank Trust Ltd v Ayivor
[1987] 3 All ER 241 (ChD)

D obtained a mortgage from P. Prior to the mortgage P had arranged for a survey of the premises to be carried out but a copy of the survey report was not sent to D. The report suggested that there was rising damp and dry rot in the property. The offer of mortgage was made subject to a retention in respect of repair works and D was required to obtain a specialist report on the damp and dry rot. After the mortgage had been executed, D arranged for a specialist to inspect and report. The estimated cost of remedial work was over £9,000. D said P should have shown him their survey report and therefore refused to make repayments of the mortgage. P applied for possession. D counterclaimed.

MERVYN DAVIES J: One starts with the general rule that a legal mortgagee has a right to possession of the mortgaged property: see e.g. *Western Bank Ltd v Schindler* [1976] 2 All ER 393, [1977] Ch 1. The next question that arises in this case is whether or not the existence of the counterclaim affects the right to possession. The cases show that the existence of the counterclaim does not affect that right. In *Barclays Bank plc v Tennet* [1984] CA Transcript 242 Slade LJ said:

... and, in my opinion, the *Keller* case [*Samuel Keller (Holdings) Ltd* v *Martins Bank Ltd* [1970] 3 All ER 950, [1971] 1 WLR 43] makes it quite clear that the existence of the counterclaim cannot defeat the right to possession which the bank enjoys as mortgagee. Indeed, only recently in *Mobil Oil Co Ltd* v *Rawlinson* (in a decision given on 31 July 1981 apparently reported only in Lexis reports), which was brought to our attention, Nourse J specifically held that the existence of a counterclaim will not defeat the legal mortgagee's right to possession where he establishes his indebtedness. The correctness of that decision does not appear to be in doubt as a matter of principle.

The *Mobil* case there referred to is reported in the Solicitors' Journal (126 SJ 15).

Administration of Justice Act 1970

36. Additional powers of court in action by mortgagee for possession of dwelling-house
(1) Where the mortgagee under a mortgage of land which consists of or includes a dwelling-house brings an action in which he claims possession of the mortgaged property, not being an action for foreclosure in which a claim for possession of the mortgaged property is also made, the court may exercise any of the powers conferred on it by subsection (2) below if it appears to the court that in the event of its exercising the power the mortgagor is likely to be able within a reasonable period to pay any sums due under the mortgage or to remedy a default consisting of a breach of any other obligation arising under or by virtue of the mortgage.
(2) The court —
  (a) may adjourn the proceedings, or
  (b) on giving judgment, or making an order, for delivery of possession of the mortgaged property, or at any time before the execution of such judgment or order, may —
    (i) stay or suspend execution of the judgment or order, or
    (ii) postpone the date for delivery of possession,
for such period or periods as the court thinks reasonable.
(3) Any such adjournment, stay, suspension or postponement as is referred to in subsection (2) above may be made subject to such conditions with regard to payment by the mortgagor of any sum secured by the mortgagee or the remedying of any default as the court thinks fit.
(4) The court may from time to time vary or revoke any condition imposed by virtue of this section.
(5) This section shall have effect in relation to such an action as is referred to in subsection (1) above begun before the date on which this section comes into force unless in that action judgment has been given, or an order made, for delivery of possession of the mortgaged property and that judgment or order was executed before that date.

38A. This Part of this Act shall not apply to a mortgage securing an agreement which is a regulated agreement within the meaning of the Consumer Credit Act 1974.

Administration of Justice Act 1973

8. Extension of powers by court in action by mortgagee of dwelling-house
(1) Where by a mortgage of land which consists of or includes a dwelling-house, or by any agreement between the mortgagee under such a mortgage and the mortgagor,

the mortgagor is entitled or is to be permitted to pay the principal sum secured by instalments or otherwise to defer payment of it in whole or in part, but provision is also made for earlier payment in the event of any default by the mortgagor or of a demand by the mortgagee or otherwise, then for purposes of section 36 of the Administration of Justice Act 1970 (under which a court has power to delay giving a mortgagee possession of the mortgaged property so as to allow the mortgagor a reasonable time to pay any sums due under the mortgage) a court may treat as due under the mortgage on account of the principal sum secured and of interest on it only such amounts as the mortgagor would have expected to be required to pay if there had been no such provision for earlier payment.

(2) A court shall not exercise by virtue of subsection (1) above the powers conferred by section 36 of the Administration of Justice Act 1970 unless it appears to the court not only that the mortgagor is likely to be able within a reasonable period to pay any amounts regarded (in accordance with subsection (1) above) as due on account of the principal sum secured, together with the interest on those amounts, but also that he is likely to be able by the end of that period to pay any further amounts that he would have expected to be required to pay by then on account of that sum and of interest on it if there had been no such provision as is referred to in subsection (1) above for earlier payment.

(3) Where subsection (1) above would apply to an action in which a mortgagee only claimed possession of the mortgaged property, and the mortgagee brings an action for foreclosure (with or without also claiming possession of the property), then section 36 of the Administration of Justice Act 1970 together with subsections (1) and (2) above shall apply as they would apply if it were an action in which the mortgagee only claimed possession of the mortgaged property, except that —

(a) section 36(2)(b) shall apply only in relation to any claim for possession; and
(b) section 36(5) shall not apply.

Note
See Alison Clarke, 'Further implications of section 36 of the Administration of Justice Act 1970' [1983] Conv 293.

Citibank Trust Ltd v *Ayivor*
[1987] 3 All ER 241

The facts of this case appear at page 448.

MERVYN DAVIES J: Accordingly, since here we have a dwelling house, one goes on to consider s. 36 of the Administration of Justice Act 1970 as read with s. 8 of the Administration of Justice Act 1973. [He then reiterates s. 36 and s. 8:] Section 36 was considered in *Western Bank Ltd* v *Schindler* [1976] 2 All ER 393 at 399, [1977] Ch 1 at 13, where Buckley LJ said:

> Accordingly, in my judgment, on the true construction of the section, it applies to any case in which a mortgagee seeks possession, whether the mortgagor be in arrear or otherwise in default under the mortgage or not, but, where the mortgagor is in arrear or in default, the discretion is limited by the conditional clause.

As I understand it s. 36 modifies the rule that a mortgagee is entitled to possession by conferring a discretion on the court. The court is given certain powers which it may exercise. But, where the mortgagor is in arrear (see Buckley LJ in the passage cited above) it may exercise such powers only 'if it appears to the court that in the event of its exercising the power the mortgagor is likely to be able within a reasonable period to pay any sums due under the mortgage ... ' ...

Counsel for the defendants submitted that in exercising the s. 36 discretion the court is not in this case confined to such a calculation of time as I have set out. Counsel said account should be taken of the following considerations (among others): (a) that the second defendant is on a catering course and may from July onwards be able to add to the family income; (b) that a sale of the house before cure of the dry rot will result in a very depressed price; (c) that the principal sum owing is secured by the endowment policy; (d) that it would be right to allow time for a sale by the defendants particularly since Citibank is a bank (as opposed to an individual) and the security is not depreciating; and (e) that the defendants' counterclaim may result in a substantial sum being owed by Citibank to the defendants within, say, the next year.

As to (a) above there was no evidence. I do not feel justified in supposing that this possibility offers the likelihood of any imminent substantial reduction in the arrears. Considerations (b) and (c) do not seem to me to be considerations that can properly be taken into account in the context of s. 36. As to (d) Browne LJ said in *Royal Trust Co of Canada* v *Markham* [1975] 3 All ER 433 at 439, [1975] 1 WLR 1416 at 1423:

> I also agree with [Sir John Pennycuick] that, for the reasons he has given, it is not possible to accept counsel's submission that in a proper case the court could not stay or suspend an order to enable a property to be sold. I suppose that in all probability this would only be done where there was clear evidence that a sale was going to take place in the near future and that the price would cover all the sums due to the mortgagee for capital and interest. But in such circumstances, and if the court thought it proper, in my view there would be jurisdiction to make such an order.

However, here there is no evidence or indeed any statement by counsel that there is in prospect any sale by the defendants. Consequently I do not see that I can give any effect to consideration (d). Consideration (e) may be an inadmissible consideration. To allow weight to (e) might nullify or circumvent the rule that the existence of a counterclaim does not prevent the mortgagee from obtaining possession. The wording of s. 36 does not seem to impinge on that rule. But however that may be, in this particular case, I do not, on the evidence, find myself able to say that the existence of the counterclaim means that the defendants are likely 'to be able within a reasonable period' to pay off the arrears. Even if I assume that the defendants' prospects of success on the counterclaim are good that does not justify me in concluding that the defendants are likely soon to reduce the arrears by paying over any damages they may recover.

Counsel for Citibank very fairly said that Citibank would expect to wait for some time, perhaps up to 18 months, for the arrears. I find myself confined by the wording of s. 36. On the evidence I cannot see that the defendants are likely to be able within any reasonable period to pay off their arrears. It follows that the s. 36 discretion may not be exercised in favour of the defendants, so that the appropriate order to make is an order for possession in 28 days.

Habib Bank Ltd v *Tailor*
[1982] 1 WLR 1218 (CA)

D had an overdraft with his bank, secured on his home, repayable on demand. D exceeded his overdraft and the bank made a written demand for payment of the principal together with interest and bank charges. Payment was not made and the bank applied for possession of the house. The registrar decided against exercising his discretion to postpone possession under the Administration of Justice Act 1973. On appeal, the judge remitted the matter to the registrar to consider the exercise of the discretion. The bank appealed. Held: the words 'Where . . . the mortgagor is to be permitted . . . otherwise to defer payment' in s. 8 of the Administration of Justice Act 1973 presupposed the existence of a legal liability to pay which was deferred by the terms of the mortgage or covenant. Payment could not be deferred in this case as the principal sum only became due once a written demand was made from the bank and it became due by virtue of that demand. Therefore s. 8 did not apply to the legal charge and an immediate order for possession was made.

OLIVER J: The reasoning by which [Judge Aron Owen, on appeal] arrived at his conclusion that the section applied was that he was referred to a decision of Goulding J in *Centrax Trustees Ltd* v *Ross* [1979] 2 All ER 952. It was a case in which there was a mortgage with a fixed date for repayment six months ahead of the date of the mortgage, the classic case in effect of the old type of fixed mortgage where the legal date for redemption is fixed at six months after the date of the execution of the mortgage, but there was a clear intention from other provisions in the mortgage, notably the provision for the payment of interest (which was clearly envisaged as extending beyond the period of six months limited for the repayment of the principal) which indicated that the common intention of the parties was that the mortgage would be allowed to stay out indefinitely and that the mortgagor would be entitled to defer payment of the principal sum beyond the date fixed so long as he paid interest on that principal sum.

Goulding J, in the course of his judgment, read section 8, and said, at p. 955:

> Given a mortgage of a dwelling house, there are two provisions which, as counsel for the plaintiffs pointed out, must be present if section 8 is to apply. One is a provision that the mortgagor is entitled or is to be permitted to pay the principal by instalments or otherwise to defer payment thereof. The second is a provision for earlier payment in the event of any default by the mortgagor or of a demand by the mortgagee or otherwise. Both provisions must be terms of the contract between the parties, for they must be made either by the mortgage or by an agreement between mortgagee and mortgagor. In the present case, in my judgment, the provisions can be found only in the mortgage itself.

Then he deals with an exchange of letters.

. . . He goes on to hold that the section applied in that case.

That of course was a very different case from the instant case. It was a case where there was a fixed date for repayment of the principal sum and it was a case where it was quite clearly intended that the actual payment of the principal sum should be deferred beyond that fixed date. And it was a case also where, if default was made in payment of interest, the mortgage contained a provision for calling in the whole sum.

Note
See P. H. Kenny, '*Habib Bank Ltd* v *Tailor*' [1983] Conv 80.

(b) Relief of mortgagor in equity

Quennell v *Maltby*
[1979] 1 WLR 318 (CA)

Q mortgaged his house. It was a term of the mortgage that Q would not let the house without the bank's consent although there were already tenants at the property when the mortgage was executed. Q let the house to a succession of tenants and, eventually to M, who became a statutory tenant. The tenancy bound Q but not the bank. Q wanted to sell the house with vacant possession and asked the bank to bring an action as mortgagees for possession. The bank refused. Q's wife then paid off the mortgage and took a transfer of the mortgage from the bank. She then claimed possession against M as mortgagee. Possession was granted and M appealed. Held: the legal right to possession is to be used to protect or enforce the security but not for an ulterior motive.

LORD DENNING MR: So the objective is plain. It was not to enforce the security or to obtain repayment or anything of that kind. It was in order to get possession of the house and to overcome the protection of the Rent Acts.

Is that permissible? It seems to me that this is one of those cases where equity steps in to mitigate the rigour of the law. Long years ago it did the same when it invented the equity of redemption. As is said in *Snell's Principles of Equity*:

> The courts of equity left the legal effect of the transaction unaltered but declared it to be unreasonable and against conscience that the mortgagee should retain as owner for his own benefit what was intended as a mere security.

So here in modern times equity can step in so as to prevent a mortgagee, or a transferee from him, from getting possession of a house contrary to the justice of the case. A mortgagee will be restrained from getting possession except when it is sought bona fide and reasonably for the purpose of enforcing the security and then only subject to such conditions as the court thinks fit to impose. When the bank itself or a building society lends the money, then it may well be right to allow the mortgagee to obtain possession when the borrower is in default. But so long as the interest is paid and there is nothing outstanding, equity has ample power to restrain any unjust use of the right to possession.

It is plain that in this transaction Mr and Mrs Quennell had an ulterior motive. It was not done to enforce the security or due payment of the principal or interest. It was done for the purpose of getting possession of the house in order to resell it at a profit. It was done so as to avoid the protection which the Rent Acts afford to tenants in their occupation. If Mr Quennell himself had sought to evict the tenants, he would not be allowed to do so. He could not say the tenancies were void. He would be estopped from saying so. They certainly would be protected against him. Are they protected against his wife now that she is the transferee of the charge? In my opinion they are protected, for this simple reason: she is not seeking possession for the purpose of enforcing the loan or the interest or anything of that kind. She is doing it simply for an ulterior purpose of getting possession of the house, contrary to the intention of Parliament as expressed in the Rent Acts.

On that simple ground it seems to me that this action fails and it should be dismissed.

B: RIGHT TO SUE ON THE PERSONAL COVENANT

The mortgagee can sue on the personal covenant for the recovery of his money once the date for repayment of the principal sum and interest has passed.

The mortgagor will remain liable on the covenant even if he assigns his interest in the property, although it is usual to take out an indemnity covenant from the assignee (see *Kinnaird* v *Trollope* (1888) 39 ChD 636).

Limitation Act 1980

20. Time limit for actions to recover money secured by a mortgage or charge or to recover proceeds of the sale of land

(1) No action shall be brought to recover—
 (a) any principal sum of money secured by a mortgage or other charge on property (whether real or personal); or
 (b) proceeds of the sale of land;
after the expiration of twelve years from the date on which the right to receive the money accrued.

(5) Subject to subsections (6) and (7) below, no action to recover arrears of interest payable in respect of any sum of money secured by a mortgage or other charge or payable in respect of proceeds of the sale of land, or to recover damages in respect of such arrears shall be brought after the expiration of six years from the date on which the interest became due.

(6) Where—
 (a) a prior mortgagee or other incumbrancer has been in possession of the property charged; and
 (b) an action is brought within one year of the discontinuance of that possession by the subsequent incumbrancer;
the subsequent incumbrancer may recover by that action all the arrears of interest which fell due during the period of possession by the prior incumbrancer or damages in respect of those arrears, notwithstanding that the period exceeded six years.

(7) Where
 (a) the property subject to the mortgage or charge comprises any future interest or life insurance policy; and
 (b) it is a term of the mortgage or charge that arrears of interest shall be treated as part of the principal sum of money secured by the mortgage or charge;
interest shall not be treated as becoming due before the right to recover the principal sum of money has accrued or is treated as having accrued.

C: RIGHT TO GRANT LEASES

This right is available to a mortgagee who takes possession of the land. See s. 99(1) and 100(2) of the Law of Property Act 1925. See Law Com No. 204, paras 6.17–6.21.

D: RIGHT TO INSURE AT THE MORTGAGOR'S EXPENSE

Law of Property Act 1925

101. Powers incident to estate or interest of mortgagee

(1)(ii) A power, at any time after the date of the mortgage deed, to insure and keep insured against loss or damage by fire any building, or any effects or property of an insurable nature, whether affixed to the freehold or not, being or forming part of the property which or an estate or interest wherein is mortgaged, and the premiums paid for any such insurance shall be a charge on the mortgaged property or estate or interest, in addition to the mortgage money, and with the same priority, and with interest at the same rate, as the mortgage money; . . .

108. Amount and application of insurance money

(1) The amount of an insurance effected by a mortgagee against loss or damage by fire under the power in that behalf conferred by this Act shall not exceed the amount specified in the mortgage deed, or, if no amount is therein specified, two third parts of the amount that would be required, in case of total destruction, to restore the property insured.

(2) An insurance shall not, under the power conferred by this Act, be effected by a mortgagee in any of the following cases (namely):

(i) Where there is a declaration in the mortgage deed that no insurance is required:

(ii) Where an insurance is kept up by or on behalf of the mortgagor in accordance with the mortgage deed:

(iii) Where the mortgage deed contains no stipulation respecting insurance, and an insurance is kept up by or on behalf of the mortgagor with the consent of the mortgagee to the amount to which the mortgagee is by this Act authorised to insure.

(3) All money received on an insurance of mortgaged property against loss or damage by fire or otherwise effected under this Act, or any enactment replaced by this Act, or on an insurance for the maintenance of which the mortgagor is liable under the mortgage deed, shall, if the mortgagee so requires, be applied by the mortgagor in making good the loss or damage in respect of which the money is received.

(4) Without prejudice to any obligation to the contrary imposed by law, or by special contract, a mortgagee may require that all money received on an insurance of mortgaged property against loss or damage by fire or otherwise effected under this Act, or any enactment replaced by this Act, or on an insurance for the maintenance of which the mortgagor is liable under the mortgage deed, be applied in or towards the discharge of the mortgage money.

E: RIGHT TO TITLE DEEDS

See the Law of Property Act 1925, ss. 85(1) and 86(1). The first mortgagee is entitled to possession of the title deeds. The mortgagee can inspect the title deeds and make copies of them on reasonable notice.

F: RIGHT TO APPOINT A RECEIVER

Law of Property Act 1925

101. Powers incident to estate or interest of mortgagee

(1)(iii) A power, when the mortgage money has become due, to appoint a receiver of the income of the mortgaged property, or any part thereof; or, if the mortgaged property consists of an interest in income, or of a rentcharge or an annual or other periodical sum, a receiver of that property or any part thereof; . . .

Notes
1. Section 101 operates where the mortgage deed contains no special provisions relating to the appointment of a receiver.
2. The mortgagee can appoint a receiver even where he has gone into possession before the appointment is made (see *Refuge Assurance Co. Ltd* v *Pearlberg* [1938] Ch 687).

G: RIGHT OF SALE

See Paul Jackson, 'The mortgagee's power of sale' [1984] Conv 143.

Law of Property Act 1925

101. Powers incident to estate or interest of mortgagee
(1)(i) A power, when the mortgage money has become due, to sell, or to concur with any other person in selling, the mortgaged property, or any part thereof, either subject to prior charges or not, and either together or in lots, by public auction or by private contract, subject to such conditions respecting title, or evidence of title, or other matter, as the mortgagee thinks fit, with power to vary any contract for sale, and to buy in at an auction, or to rescind any contract for sale, and to re-sell, without being answerable for any loss occasioned thereby; . . .

Notes
1. In order for the power of sale to arise under s. 101, the mortgage must be made by deed.
2. In a mortgage where the money is payable by means of instalments, the power of sale is exercisable when an instalment of the mortgage money has become due (*Payne* v *Cardiff RDC* [1932] 1 KB 241). In other cases it becomes due as soon as the date fixed for repayment has passed.
3. The power is available only if there is no contrary intention in the deed.

Once the power of sale has *arisen* it becomes *exercisable* only when at least one of the conditions in s. 103 has been fulfilled.

Law of Property Act 1925

103. Regulation of exercise of power of sale
A mortgagee shall not exercise the power of sale conferred by this Act unless and until—
    (i) Notice requiring payment of the mortgage money has been served on the mortgagor or one of two or more mortgagors, and default has been made in payment of the mortgage money, or of part thereof, for three months after such service; or
    (ii) Some interest under the mortgage is in arrear and unpaid for two months after becoming due; or
    (iii) There has been a breach of some provision contained in the mortgage deed or in this Act, or in an enactment replaced by this Act, and on the part of the mortgagor, or of some person concurring in making the mortgage, to be observed or performed, other than and besides a covenant for payment of the mortgage money or interest thereon.

Note
The notice required in s. 103(1) must be made in writing (s. 196).

Law of Property Act 1925

101. Powers incident to estate or interest of mortgagee
(2) Where the mortgage deed is executed after the thirty-first day of December, nineteen hundred and eleven, the power of sale aforesaid includes the following powers as incident thereto (namely):—

(i) A power to impose or reserve or make binding, as far as the law permits, by covenant, condition, or otherwise, on the unsold part of the mortgaged property or any part thereof, or on the purchaser and any property sold, any restriction or reservation with respect to building on or other user of land, or with respect to mines and minerals, or for the purpose of the more beneficial working thereof, or with respect to any other thing:

(ii) A power to sell the mortgaged property, or any part thereof, or all or any mines and minerals apart from the surface:—

(a) With or without a grant or reservation of rights of way, rights of water, easements, rights, and privileges for or connected with building or other purposes in relation to the property remaining in mortgage or any part thereof, or to any property sold: and

(b) With or without an exception or reservation of all or any of the mines and minerals in or under the mortgaged property, and with or without a grant or reservation of powers or working, wayleaves, or rights of way, rights of water and drainage and other powers, easements, rights, and privileges for or connected with mining purposes in relation to the property remaining unsold or any part thereof, or to any property sold: and

(c) With or without covenants by the purchaser to expend money on the land sold.

Waring (Lord) v *London and Manchester Assurance Company Ltd*
[1935] 1 Ch 310 (ChD)

The mortgagee, in exercise of its power of sale, entered into a contract for the sale of the mortgaged property. The mortgagor wished to redeem the mortgage and sought an injunction to restrain completion on the grounds that there was no sale until conveyance. Held: where the mortgagees were acting in good faith, the court would not grant an injunction.

CROSSMAN J: After a contract has been entered into, however, it is, in my judgment, perfectly clear (subject to what has been said to me today) that the mortgagee (in the present case, the company) can be restrained from completing only on the ground that he has not acted in good faith and that the sale is therefore liable to be set aside. Counsel for the plaintiff, who has argued the case most excellently, submitted that, notwithstanding that the company exercised its power of sale by entering into the contract, the plaintiff's equity of redemption has not been extinguished, as there has been no completion by conveyance, and that, pending completion, the plaintiff is still entitled to redeem, that is, to have the property reconveyed to him on payment of principal, interest, and costs. Counsel is relying, to some extent, on the provisions of the Law of Property Act, 1925, which creates a statutory power of sale. In my judgment, s. 101 of that Act, which gives to a mortgagee power to sell the mortgaged property, is perfectly clear, and means that the mortgagee has power to sell out and out, by private contract or by auction, and subsequently to complete by conveyance; and the power to sell is, I think, a power by selling to bind the mortgagor. If that were not so, the extraordinary result would follow that every purchaser from a mortgagee would, in effect, be getting a conditional contract liable at any time to be set aside by the mortgagor's coming in and paying the principal, interest, and costs. Such a result would make it impossible for a mortgagee, in the ordinary course of events, to sell unless he was in a position to promise that completion should take place immediately or on the day after the contract, and there would have to be a rush for completion in order to defeat a possible claim by the mortgagor.

Notes
1. This case was approved in the Court of Appeal in *Property & Bloodstock Ltd* v *Emerton* [1968] Ch 94.
2. If the mortgagee attempts to sell the property before the statutory power of sale arises, the purchaser receives only those rights which the mortgagee enjoyed as mortgagee and the legal estate of the mortgagor is not transferred.
3. The effect of a conveyance by the mortgagee once the power of sale has arisen is to vest in the purchaser the mortgagor's legal estate, subject to any prior legal mortgage which has priority to the mortgagee's, and to overreach all interests that are capable of being overreached.

Duke v *Robson* [1973] 1 WLR 267 (ChD)

D1 and D2 owned a house which was subject to a charge by way of legal mortgage to D3. D1 contracted to purchase D2's beneficial interest and then, in March 1972, entered into an agreement to sell the freehold to P. D3 took possession of the property in September 1972. In October 1972, P registered their purchase contract as a C(iv) land charge. In November, D3 contracted to sell the property to D4, in exercise of their power of sale as mortgagee. Held: D's contract with P concerned only the equity of redemption and could be overreached, regardless of registration as a land charge, as it did not effect the mortgagee's rights.

Note
The purchaser will take subject to prior mortgages where the vendor is not the first mortgagee. He can then be deprived of the fee simple if the first mortgagee wishes to exercise his power of sale.

Law of Property Act 1925

104. Conveyance on sale
(1) A mortgagee exercising the power of sale conferred by this Act shall have power, by deed, to convey the property sold, for such estate and interest therein as he is by this Act authorised to sell or convey or may be the subject of the mortgage, freed from all estates, interests, and rights to which the mortgage has priority, but subject to all estates, interests, and rights which have priority to the mortgage.
(2) Where a conveyance is made in exercise of the power of sale conferred by this Act, or any enactment replaced by this Act, the title of the purchaser shall not be impeachable on the ground —
    (a) that no case had arisen to authorise the sale, or
    (b) that due notice was not given; or
    (c) where the mortgage is made after the commencement of this Act, that leave of the court, when so required, was not obtained; or
    (d) whether the mortgage was made before or after such commencement, that the power was otherwise improperly or irregularly exercised;

and a purchaser is not, either before or on conveyance, concerned to see or inquire whether a case has arisen to authorise the sale, or due notice has been given, or the power is otherwise properly and regularly exercised; but any person damnified by an unauthorised, or improper, or irregular exercise of the power shall have his remedy in damages against the person exercising the power.

(3) A conveyance on sale by a mortgagee, made after the commencement of this Act, shall be deemed to have been made in exercise of the power of sale conferred by this Act unless a contrary intention appears.

Note
The purchaser must only satisfy himself that the right to sell has arisen. He must act in good faith. If he does not, for example if he knows that no right to sell has arisen, he will not get good title (see *Bailey* v *Barnes* [1894] 1 Ch 25).

Law of Property Act 1925

89. Realisation of leasehold mortgages
(1) Where a term of years absolute has been mortgaged by the creation of another term of years absolute limited thereout or by a charge by way of legal mortgage and the mortgagee sells under his statutory or express power of sale, —

(a) the conveyance by him shall operate to convey to the purchaser not only the mortgage term, if any, but also (unless expressly excepted with the leave of the court) the leasehold reversion affected by the mortgage, subject to any legal mortgage having priority to the mortgage in right of which the sale is made and to any money thereby secured, and thereupon

(b) the mortgage term, or the charge by way of legal mortgage and any subsequent mortgage term or charge, shall merge in such leasehold reversion or be extinguished unless excepted as aforesaid;

and such conveyance may, as respects the leasehold reversion, be made in the name of the estate owner in whom it is vested.

Where a licence to assign is required on a sale by a mortgagee, such licence shall not be unreasonably refused.

Note
Proceeds of sale are to be applied in accordance with s. 105 of the Act.

Law of Property Act 1925

105. Application of proceeds of sale
The money which is received by the mortgagee, arising from the sale, after discharge of prior incumbrances to which the sale is not made subject, if any, or after payment into court under this Act of a sum to meet any prior incumbrance, shall be held by him in trust to be applied by him, first, in payment of all costs, charges, and expenses properly incurred by him as incident to the sale or any attempted sale, or otherwise; and secondly, in discharge of the mortgage money, interest, and costs, and other money, if any, due under the mortgage; and the residue of the money so received shall be paid to the person entitled to the mortgaged property, or authorised to give receipts for the proceeds of the sale thereof.

Cuckmere Brick Co. Ltd v Mutual Finance Ltd
[1971] Ch 949 (CA)

P owned certain land with the benefit of planning permission for 100 flats. The land was mortgaged to D. P subsequently applied for and obtained planning permission to build 35 houses on the land. No development had started by the time D went into possession of the land two years later. D, in exercise of their power of sale, instructed auctioneers to sell the land. When the land was advertised, only the planning permission for 35 houses was referred to, not that in respect of the flats. P asked to postpone the sale and to re-advertise the land, together with the benefit of all planning permissions. D refused and the land was sold for £44,000. P claimed it was worth £75,000. Held:

(1) A mortgagee owes a duty to the mortgagor to take reasonable care to obtain a proper price (or the true market value, per Salmon LJ) when selling property under a power of sale.

(2) D was in breach of his duty in these circumstances. (Cross LJ dissenting.)

Note
The decision in *Cuckmere Brick Co.* v *Mutual Finance* was referred to in **Standard Chartered Bank Ltd v Walker** [1982] 1 WLR 1410 (CA), where Lord Denning MR said:

We have had much discussion on the law. So far as mortgages are concerned the law is set out in *Cuckmere Brick Co. Ltd* v *Mutual Finance Ltd* [1971] Ch 949. If a mortgagee enters into possession and realises a mortgaged property, it is his duty to use reasonable care to obtain the best possible price which the circumstances of the case permit. He owes this duty not only to himself, to clear off as much of the debt as he can, but also to the mortgagor so as to reduce the balance owing as much as possible, and also the guarantor so that he is made liable for as little as possible on the guarantee. This duty is only a particular application of the general duty of care to your neighbour which was stated by Lord Atkin in *Donoghue* v *Stevenson* [1932] AC 562 and applied in many cases since: see *Dorset Yacht Co. Ltd* v *Home Office* [1970] AC 1004 and *Anns* v *Merton London Borough Council* [1978] AC 728. The mortgagor and the guarantor are clearly in very close 'proximity' to those who conduct the sale. The duty of care is owing to them — if not to the general body of creditors of the mortgagor. There are several dicta to the effect that the mortgagee can choose his own time for the sale, but I do not think this means that he can sell at the worst possible time. It is at least arguable that, in choosing the time, he must exercise a reasonable degree of care.

Building Societies Act 1986

SCHEDULE 4   ADVANCES: SUPPLEMENTARY PROVISIONS

Provisions as to sale of mortgaged property

1. — (1) Where any land has been mortgaged to a building society as security for an advance and a person sells the land in the exercise of a power (whether statutory or express) exercisable by virtue of the mortgage, it shall be his duty —
 (a) in exercising that power to take reasonable care to ensure that the price at which the land is sold is the best price that can reasonably be obtained, and
 (b) within 28 days from the completion of the sale, to send to the mortgagor at his last-known address by the recorded delivery service a notice containing the prescribed particulars of the sale.
 (2) In so far as any agreement relieves, or may have the effect of relieving, a building society or any other person from the obligation imposed by sub-paragraph (1)(a) above, the agreement shall be void.

Note
The following case considered the question whether the mortgagee owes a duty to third parties.

Parker-Tweedale v *Dunbar Bank plc (No. 1)* [1990] 2 All ER 577 (CA)

H and W purchased a 50 acre farm with the aid of a mortgage from D which charged the property with all borrowings made by H or W. The property was transferred into W's sole name. H occupied as licensee and agreed that he would make no claim against the mortgagee. The mortgage fell into arrears and the bank obtained possession of the property and placed the property with an estate agent to sell it by auction. The agents valued the property at between £380,000 and £450,000. Before the proposed auction a development company, X, offered £575,000 for the property. The bank accepted the offer with W's approval. A week later X sold the property to Y for £700,000. H alleged he had an equitable interest in the property and brought an action against the bank alleging that it had not obtained a proper price for the property and was thereby in breach of a duty of care owed to him. Held: the duty owed by the mortgagee to the mortgagor to take reasonable care when exercising his power of sale arose from the relationship between them under the rule of equity. It was not part of the tort of negligence and there was no such duty owed to a beneficiary under a trust of mortgaged property of which the mortgagor was trustee, regardless of notice.

Note
The sale must be a genuine sale and a mortgagee is not allowed to sell to himself even if the purchase price is the full value of the property. In *Farrar* v *Farrars Ltd* (1888) 40 ChD 395 (CA), Lindley LJ said:

> It is perfectly well settled that a mortgagee with a power of sale cannot sell to himself either alone or with others, nor to a trustee for himself: *Downes* v

Grazebrook 3 Mer 200; *Robertson* v *Norris* 1 Giff 421; nor to any one employed by him to conduct the sale: *Whitcomb* v *Minchin* 5 Madd 91; *Martinson* v *Clowes* 21 ChD 857. A sale by a person to himself is no sale at all, and a power of sale does not authorize the donee of the power to take the property subject it at a price fixed by himself, even although such price be the full value of the property. Such a transaction is not an exercise of the power, and the interposition of a trustee, although it gets over the difficulty so far as form is concerned, does not affect the substance of the transaction.

A sale by a person to a corporation of which he is a member is not, either in form or in substance, a sale by a person to himself. To hold that it is, would be to ignore that principle which lies at the root of the legal idea of a corporate body, and that idea is that the corporate body is distinct from the persons composing it. A sale by a member of a corporation to the corporation itself is in every sense a sale valid in equity as well as at law. . . .

See also *Tse Kwong Lam* v *Wong Chit Sen* [1983] 1 WLR 1349 (PC), where it was held that if a mortgagee, in exercise of his power of sale, sold property to a company in which he has an interest, then the onus is upon the mortgagee to show that he made the sale in good faith and took reasonable precautions to obtain the best price reasonably obtainable at the time.

See Paul Jackson, 'The mortgagee's power of sale' [1984] Conv 143; Law Com No. 204, paras 7.5–7.25; M. P. Thompson, 'Negligent sales by mortgagees' [1986] Conv 442.

H: RIGHT TO FORECLOSURE

This right is tantamount to confiscation of the mortgagor's interest in the property. The court in such an action extinguishes the mortgagor's equitable right to redeem and the mortgagee becomes the legal and equitable owner of the property, subject only to any prior legal mortgages having priority to him. A foreclosure order cannot be obtained unless the legal date of redemption has passed *and* an action is brought in the Chancery Division asking that the mortgagor pay the moneys due or be foreclosured.

If the court decides to grant a foreclosure order it must first order a foreclosure *nisi*, which directs that if the mortgagor does not pay upon a certain date specified the mortgagor will lose his property. A motion can then be made for a foreclosure absolute if on the due date the sum outstanding is not paid.

Law of Property Act 1925

88. Realisation of freehold mortgages

(2) Where any such mortgagee obtains an order for foreclosure absolute, the order shall operate to vest the fee simple in him (subject to any legal mortgage having priority to the mortgage in right of which the foreclosure is obtained and to any money thereby accrued), and thereupon the mortgage term, if any, shall thereby be merged in the fee simple, and any subsequent mortgage term or charge by way of legal mortgage bound by the order shall thereupon be extinguished.

89. Realisation of leasehold mortgages

(2) Where any such mortgagee obtains an order for foreclosure absolute, the order shall, unless it otherwise provides, operate (without giving rise to a forfeiture for want of a licence to assign) to vest the leasehold reversion affected by the mortgage and any subsequent mortgage term in him, subject to any legal mortgage having priority to the mortgage in right of which the foreclosure is obtained and to any money thereby secured, and thereupon the mortgage term and any subsequent mortgage term or charge by way of legal mortgage bound by the order shall, subject to any express provision to the contrary contained in the order, merge in such leasehold reversion or be extinguished.

Note

Even after the foreclosure order has been made absolute, the action can be re-opened. See **Campbell v Holyland** (1877) 7 ChD 166 (ChD), where Jessel MR said:

> In that foreclosure suit the Court made various orders — interim orders fixing a time for payment of the money — and at last there came the final order which was called foreclosure absolute, that is, in form, that the mortgagor should not be allowed to redeem at all; but it was form only, just as the original deed was form only; for the Courts of Equity soon decided that, notwithstanding the form of that order, they would after that order allow the mortgagor to redeem. That is, although the order of foreclosure absolute appeared to be a final order of the Court, it was not so, but the mortgagee still remained liable to be treated as mortgagee and the mortgagor still retained a claim to be treated as mortgagor, subject to the discretion of the Court. Therefore everybody who took an order for foreclosure absolute knew that there was still a discretion in the Court to allow the mortgagor to redeem.
>
> Under what circumstances that discretion should be exercised is quite another matter. The mortgagee had a right to deal with an estate acquired under foreclosure absolute the day after he acquired it; but he knew perfectly well that there might be circumstances to entitle the mortgagor to redeem, and everybody buying the estate from a mortgagee who merely acquired a title under such an order was considered to have the same knowledge, namely, that the estate might be taken away from him by the exercise, not of a capricious discretion, but of a judicial discretion by the Court of Equity which had made the order.
>
> That being so, on what terms is that judicial discretion to be exercised? It has been said by the highest authority that it is impossible to say *a priori* what are the terms. They must depend upon the circumstances of each case.

See Law Com No. 204, paras 7.26–7.27.

I: OTHER RIGHTS

The right to tack is treated at page 480 *et seq*.

SECTION 5: RIGHTS OF AN EQUITABLE MORTGAGEE

The rights available where the mortgage is equitable depend on whether the mortgage is made by a charge on the property or otherwise, i.e. a deposit of title deeds, a contract to create a legal mortgage, or is a mortgage of an equitable interest in the land.

A: RIGHTS OF EQUITABLE MORTGAGEE

(a) Right to sue for debt
An equitable mortgagee can sue the mortgagor personally on the debt.

(b) Right to retain title deeds
If an equitable mortgage is created by the deposit of title deeds, there is an implied contract that the mortgagee may retain the deeds until he is paid.

(c) Right of sale
The statutory power of sale only applies to mortgages made by deed, and therefore if the mortgage is not made by deed there is no automatic right of sale. Therefore, either an express power of sale may be inserted into the mortgage, or else the equitable mortgage may be executed as a memorandum under seal.

Re White Rose Cottage [1965] Ch 940 (CA)

In order to obtain bank advances, a company (C) deposited the land certificate of some land and executed a memorandum of deposit under seal. C undertook to execute a legal charge when required to do so by the bank. C gave the bank an irrevocable power of attorney to vest the legal estate in a purchaser in exercise of the mortgagee's statutory powers, free of all rights of redemption. Notice of the deposit was entered on the register in May 1962. On June 20 and August 9 1962, a firm of contractors obtained charging orders on the property and subsequently lodged cautions with the land registry the last of which was lodged on the 14th August 1962. On 31 August 1962, the bank applied to enter a notice on the register of an equitable charge created by the memorandum. Notice was given to the contractors who objected, claiming priority. On 26 October 1962 the bank used their power of attorney from C to transfer the land to a purchaser, released from the moneys secured by the memorandum. The purchaser executed a legal charge in favour of a building society dated contemporaneously with the transfer. Application was made by P to register the transactions. The contractors objected to registration free from their charging orders. Held:

(1) The effect of the transfer by the bank under a power of attorney was the same as a sale by C themselves with the concurrence of bank as mortgagee. It could not be construed as an exercise by the bank of their

Mortgages

power of sale. The purchaser took the same title the company had, free from the bank's mortgage, but subject to the equitable charges in favour of the contractors conferred by the charging orders.

(2) The bank's notice of deposit of the land certificate had the same effect as a caution. Thus the contractors could not object to the registration of the bank's charge as the notice of deposit preceded the contractors' cautions in relation to the charging orders. An equitable mortgagee under a deed in the terms of the memorandum of deposit can, by virtue of the power of attorney contained in it, convey to a purchaser the legal estate in the mortgaged property without first going through the form of calling for the execution by the mortgagor of a legal mortgage.

(d) Appointment of a receiver

The statutory right is available to an equitable mortgagee only where the mortgage is made by deed.

(e) Right of possession

Unless a right to possession has been expressly reserved, an equitable mortgagee has no automatic right to possession (*Barclays Bank v Bird* [1954] Ch 274). An equitable mortgagee can enter into possession if the court grants an order to that effect. But see H. W. R. Wade, 'An equitable mortgagee's right to possession' (1955) 71 LQR 204.

(f) Right to foreclosure

This is the equitable mortgagee's main remedy.

B: RIGHTS OF EQUITABLE CHARGEE

A charge on the land does not involve the transfer of any interest, legal or equitable, to the chargee. In such a case the chargee has a debt which can be discharged out of the land. The only remedies that are available to him are to have the charge satisfied out of the sale of the land and the right to have a receiver appointed by the court.

If, however, the charge is by deed by way of legal mortgage, the chargee has the same remedies as if he held a term of years absolute.

Question

There is at present no statutory provision relating to repair of the mortgaged property. Do you think it is desirable that the law be changed to allow for one?
See Law Com No. 204, paras 6.13–6.15.

C: RIGHT TO CONSOLIDATE

See Law Com No. 204, para 6.44, which recommends the right to consolidate be abolished.

Where a person is entitled to two mortgages on different properties which have been made by the same mortgagor, he can consolidate them and refuse to allow the mortgagor to redeem one without redeeming the other. This right applies whether the mortgages are legal or equitable. For example, X mortgages Blackacre and Whiteacre to Y by separate transactions. X can be made to redeem both mortgages even if he wishes to redeem only one. The reason for this is that the value of Blackacre may have depreciated, whereas that of Whiteacre has appreciated. It is unfair to Y to allow X merely to redeem Blackacre leaving Y with a bad security while the good one has been redeemed.

The doctrine in its simplest form applies where the mortgagees are the same, but it has been developed to cases where the original mortgages were made to different mortgagees (see *Pledge* v *White* [1890] AC 187). For example, X mortgages Blackacre to A and then mortgages Whiteacre to B. A and B transfer their mortgages to C. X can be prevented by C from redeeming one property without redeeming the other.

In order for there to be a right to consolidate, four conditions must be fulfilled:

(a) The legal date for redemption must have passed.

Cummins v *Fletcher*
(1879) 14 ChD 699 (CA)

Trustees of a building society were mortgagees of two separate properties with a common mortgagor. Each property was held in respect of separate advances. The building society refused to allow the redemption of the first mortgage without the other. All moneys due had been paid under the first mortgage, but not the second. Held: consolidation applies only where default has been made on all the securities in respect of which it is claimed.

JAMES LJ: But it seems to me that where a man has a legal right in property A, and an equity of redemption in property B which is an insufficient security, and has no occasion, and never will have any occasions, to come to a Court of Equity with respect to property A, the fact of the two properties being subject to two mortgages gives the Court no more power to take from him property A, than it has to take any other property belonging to him, for the purpose of satisfying the debt for which there is insufficient security.

(b) Both mortgages must be made by the same mortgagor.

Cummins v *Fletcher*
(1879) 14 ChD 699 (CA)

JAMES LJ: With regard to *Beevor* v *Luck* LR 4 Eq 537, where it was decided that you could consolidate a security given by a partner for his own private debt with a security given by two or more partners for a partnership debt, I am bound to say I am unable to see myself upon what principle that could be done. It is admitted here, for instance, that *Vaughan's* partner *Neesham* could not be made a party properly in respect of the redemption of the 1871 mortgage, and I cannot conceive any mode in which any action could be instituted bringing those two properties into one action for the purpose of

Mortgages

redemption, whether it was by the mortgagee or whether it was by *Vaughan*, which *Neesham* could not have demurred to as being a person improperly brought in to deal with an estate with which he had nothing whatever to do, either as to the property or as to the debt. The language of the order under appeal saying his right is to be reserved seems to me to shew how utterly impossible it is to work out anything which makes a security of two or more persons a security of one person only for his own debt. That is a point as to which I think it necessary to express the opinion I have stated which I entertain very strongly . . .

(c) Where a mortgage is made after 1881, then a mortgagee only has the right to consolidate if such a right is expressed in the mortgage deeds.

Law of Property Act 1925

93. Restriction on consolidation of mortgages

(1) A mortgagor seeking to redeem any one mortgage is entitled to do so without paying any money due under any separate mortgage made by him, or by any person through whom he claims, solely on property other than that comprised in the mortgage which he seeks to redeem.

This subsection applies only if and as far as a contrary intention is not expressed in the mortgage deeds or one of them.

(d) There must be or have been a time when both (or all) mortgages were vested in one person and simultaneously both (or all) equities of redemption vested in another.

Pledge v *White*
[1896] AC 187 (HL)

B was the original owner and mortgagor of seven properties. He mortgaged properties 1 and 2 to J on 26 May and 26 August 1863. He mortgaged property 3 to S on 12 October 1865, and then properties 4, 5, 6 and 7 to other mortgagees at various dates between 18 October 1865 and 24 November 1866. He then made a second mortgage of 4, 5, 6 and 7 to K on 27 November 1866. He then made a second mortgage of 1, 2 and 3 and a third mortgage of 4, 5, 6, 7 to K and H in one deed dated 20 August 1868, i.e. he assigned the equity of redemption on all seven properties to K and H. At that stage K and H could have redeemed 1, 2 or 3 without redeeming the other properties, but they could not redeem 4, 5, 6 or 7 without redeeming all four of those properties. P became the transferee from K and H of their equity of redemption of all the seven properties on 1st April 1885. K became the transferee of the first mortgage on Nos 1, 2, 4 and 5 during 1871–73. K died in 1877 and D were his executors. On 27 December 1980, they became the transferees of the first mortgage of No. 3. From that date the equity of redemption on all seven properties was vested in P, subject to mortgages on the several properties all vested in D. P sought a declaration that he was entitled to redeem No. 2 alone on payment of money due on the first mortgage. D claimed to consolidate their mortgages on all seven properties. Held: D could consolidate.

LORD DAVEY: Originally it may have been a right of a mortgagee holding two separate mortgages on estates of the same mortgagor which have become absolute estates at law against the mortgagor and debtor personally to refuse to be redeemed as regards one estate without having his other debt also paid. But it has long been settled that the right of consolidation may be exercised by the transferee of the mortgages as well as by the original mortgagee, and may be exercised in respect of equitable mortgages as well as by a mortgagee holding the legal estate absolute at law; and on the other hand, that it may be asserted against the assignee of an equity of redemption from the mortgagor as well as against the mortgagor himself.

Notes
1. *Pledge* v *White* illustrates the position where one person acquires all the equities. In such a situation the mortgages can be consolidated even where, against the mortgagor, the mortgages did not vest in the mortgagee until after the time the person seeking redemption obtained the equities.
2. Consolidation is clearly available if at the date redemption is sought all the mortgages, having originally been made by one mortgagor, are vested in one mortgagee and all the equities of redemption vested in another. But the doctrine also applies if after this has occurred the equities of redemption have become separated — such a transferee of the equity cannot stand in a better position than the transferor.
3. An assignee of an equity, however, does not become subject to the doctrine of consolidation in respect of mortgages created after the assignment to him.
4. Where two mortgages, made by the same mortgagor to different mortgagees on different pieces of land, become united for the first time in one person after the mortgagor has assigned the equity of redemption in one of them, the owner of the two mortgages cannot consolidate them as against the assignee of the equity, even though both mortgages were created before the assignment (*Harter* v *Colman* (1882) 19 ChD 630).

SECTION 6: DISCHARGE OF MORTGAGES

Law of Property Act 1925

115. Reconveyances of mortgages by endorsed receipts
(1) A receipt endorsed on, written at the foot of, or annexed to, a mortgage for all money thereby secured, which states the name of the person who pays the money and is executed by the chargee by way of legal mortgage or the person in whom the mortgaged property is vested and who is legally entitled to give a receipt for the mortgage money shall operate, without any reconveyance, surrender, or release—

(a) Where a mortgage takes effect by demise or subdemise, as a surrender of the term, so as to determine the term or merge the same in the reversion immediately expectant thereon;

(b) Where the mortgage does not take effect by demise or subdemise, as a reconveyance thereof to the extent of the interest which is the subject matter of the mortgage, to the person who immediately before the execution of the receipt was entitled to the equity of redemption;

and in either case, as a discharge of the mortgaged property from all principal money and interest secured by, and from all claims under the mortgage, but without prejudice to any term or other interest which is paramount to the estate or interest of the mortgagee or other person in whom the mortgaged property was vested.

(2) Provided that, where by the receipt the money appears to have been paid by a person who is not entitled to the immediate equity of redemption, the receipts shall operate as if the benefit of the mortgage had by deed been transferred to him; unless—
    (a) it is otherwise expressly provided; or
    (b) the mortgage is paid off out of capital money, or other money in the hands of a personal representative or trustee properly applicable for the discharge of the mortgage, and it is not expressly provided that the receipt is to operate as a transfer.

(3) Nothing in this section confers on a mortgagor a right to keep alive a mortgage paid off by him, so as to affect prejudicially any subsequent incumbrancer; and where there is no right to keep the mortgage alive, the receipt does not operate as a transfer.

(4) This section does not affect the right of any person to require a reassignment, surrender, release, or transfer to be executed in lieu of a receipt.

(5) A receipt may be given in the form contained in the Third Schedule to this Act, with such variations and additions, if any, as may be deemed expedient. . . .

(6) In a receipt given under this section the same covenants shall be implied as if the person who executes the receipt had by deed been expressed to convey the property as mortgagee, subject to any interest which is paramount to the mortgage.

(7) Where the mortgage consists of a mortgage and a further charge or of more than one deed, it shall be sufficient for the purposes of this section, if the receipt refers either to all the deeds whereby the mortgage money is secured or to the aggregate amount of the mortgage money thereby secured and for the time being owing, and is endorsed on, written at the foot of, or annexed to, one of the mortgage deeds.

(8) This section applies to the discharge of a charge by way of legal mortgage, and to the discharge of a mortgage, whether made by way of statutory mortgage or not, executed before or after the commencement of this Act, but only as respects discharges effected after such commencement.

(9) The provisions of this section relating to the operation of a receipt shall (in substitution for the like statutory provisions relating to receipts given by or on behalf of a building . . . society) apply to the discharge of a mortgage made to any such society, provided that the receipt is executed in the manner required by the statute relating to the society . . .

(10) This section does not apply to the discharge of a charge or incumbrance registered under the Land Registration Act, 1925.

SECTION 7: PRIORITY OF MORTGAGES

See W. A. Lee, 'An insoluble problem of mortgagees', (1968) 32 Conv 325; R. E. Megarry, 'Priority after 1925 of mortgages of a legal estate in land' 7 CLJ 243.

A: THE LEGAL MORTGAGEE'S POSITION PRIOR TO 1925 WHERE THE LAND WAS LEGAL

Prior to 1926, there could only be one legal mortgagee of land, who would have the fee simple of the legal estate conveyed to him. All other mortgages were equitable. The priority of mortgages before 1926 was governed by three principles: 'legal interests are valid against the whole world'; 'equitable interests are valid against anyone except a bona fide purchaser for value of the legal estate without notice'; and 'where the equities are equal the law prevails'. Therefore, a legal mortgagee ranked above prior and subsequent equitable mortgagees.

The general rule giving pre-eminence to the legal mortgagee did *not* apply where, by reason of some act or omission on his part, or for any other reason, the equitable mortgagee had a better *moral* claim to priority, i.e. the equities were not equal. This would be so, for example, where:

(a) the legal mortgagee had actual or constructive notice of an earlier mortgage (see *Berwick & Co.* v *Price* [1905] 1 Ch 632); or
(b) where the legal mortgagee was negligent in regard to the title deeds.

If the title deeds are not produced by the mortgagor this should alert the mortgagee to the possibility that they may already be with some other person. If they are produced to the mortgagee, then he should take proper care of them and retain possession of them.

Walker v *Linom* [1907] 2 Ch 104 (ChD)

W conveyed his real estate to trustees of a marriage settlement under the trusts of which he took a life interest determinable on alienation. The solicitors acting were holding a bundle of deeds and were not aware that W still held the deed by which the property was conveyed to him. W used that deed to obtain a mortgage and then absconded. The mortgagee later sold the land. Neither the mortgagee nor the subsequent purchaser had notice of the settlement. Held: the trustees had been guilty of negligence and therefore their legal estate must be postponed to the subsequent equitable interest of the purchaser.

Oliver v *Hinton*
[1899] 2 Ch 264 (CA)

LINDLEY MR: In my opinion this case does not present any serious difficulty when once the facts are understood. The defendant has been cheated by Hill, but she has not been in any way cheated by the plaintiff. In 1888 Hill gave the plaintiff a mortgage of the three houses in question and two others. It was not a legal mortgage, but an equitable mortgage by deposit of title-deeds, accompanied by a memorandum of deposit, by which Hill agreed to execute a legal mortgage when requested by the plaintiff to do so. The plaintiff had a good equitable mortgage, and she cannot be charged with any neglect or breach of duty in not obtaining a legal mortgage. She ran, however, the risk of losing her priority in case the legal estate should be conveyed to a subsequent purchaser for value without notice of her charge. Who is it that now claims to override her charge? The only person who can do so, if he has acquired his title subsequently to hers, is a bona fide purchaser for value without notice of her charge. But this does not include a purchaser for value who is so grossly negligent as to take none of the ordinary precautions which ought to be taken in such a matter — who, in fact, takes no precautions whatever. He may be a bona fide purchaser for value without notice of a prior charge, but he is not entitled to the protection of the Court. I do not base my judgment upon constructive notice of the plaintiff's charge, nor do I mean to suggest that there was any fraud or any complicity in fraud on the part of either the defendant or her agent, Price. Price gave his evidence with perfect candour. The defendant left the arrangement of the purchase entirely to him. He inquired about the title-deeds, and was told by Hill that they were in his possession, but that they would not be delivered up to the purchaser because they related also to other property. No abstract of title was asked for or delivered, and no further inquiry was made. Price in his evidence admitted that he made a mistake in not asking to see the deeds, but said that he relied upon Hill. Can a person whose agent acted in this way be regarded as a bona fide purchaser for value without notice who is entitled to the protection of the legal estate? To allow a purchaser who acts with such gross carelessness to deprive a prior innocent mortgagee of her priority would be the greatest injustice. None of the cases which have been cited really assist the defendant, with the exception of *Ratcliffe* v *Barnard* LR 6 Ch 652. The actual decision in that case was, I think, perfectly right. But I think that James LJ went too far in the language which he used. He said [ibid., 654]: 'Turner LJ has, in *Hunt* v *Elmes* (1860) 2 DF & J 578, expressed the only principle upon which in this Court a man will have his legal security taken away. He must have been guilty of fraud or of that wilful negligence which leads the Court to conclude that he is an accomplice in the fraud. If a man abstains from inquiry under such circumstances that the Court will infer that he abstained in order to deprive himself of knowledge, then he will not be allowed to hold the property merely because he did not inquire.' I am not prepared to go to that length, and I do not think that what James LJ said is justified by the case of *Hunt* v *Elmes*, to which he referred. In that case, and also in *Hewitt* v *Loosemore* 9 Hare 449, it was said that to deprive a man of the protection of the legal estate he must have been guilty of either fraud or gross and wilful negligence. To deprive a purchaser for value without notice of a prior incumbrance of the protection of the legal estate it is not, in my opinion, essential that he should have been guilty of fraud; it is sufficient that he has been guilty of such gross negligence as would render it unjust to deprive the prior incumbrancer of his priority.

The appeal must be dismissed.

Notes

1. The result would have been the same if the 'purchaser' had been a mortgagee acquiring the legal estate in land.
2. A legal mortgagee/purchaser must be 'grossly negligent' before his interest will be postponed to the prior equitable interest. See *Hewitt* v *Loosemore* (1851) 9 Hare 449, where it was said that a legal mortgagee is not to be postponed to a prior equitable one, on the ground of his not having obtained the title deeds, unless there is fraud or gross or wilful negligence on his part.
3. Failure to obtain the title deeds through fraud or gross negligence may also postpone the legal mortgagee to a later equitable interest. See **Grierson v National Provincial Bank of England, Ltd** [1913] 2 Ch 18 (ChD), where A charged leasehold premises to Bank B and deposited the lease as security. A then created a legal mortgage by sub-demise to C, expressly subject to the bank's charge. C failed to give the bank notice of his mortgage. A redeemed the mortgage with Bank B and took back the lease. C did not know that B's mortgage had been repaid or that A had the lease. A deposited the lease with bank D, who had no knowledge of the legal mortgage. Held: the legal

mortgagee retained his priority in the absence of any misconduct, negligence or want of caution for which he could be held directly or indirectly responsible.

Northern Counties of England Fire Insurance Company v Whipp (1884) 26 ChD 482 (CA)

C executed a legal mortgage of his own freehold estate to a company of which he was himself the manager. The title deeds were given to the company and put in the company safe. C held keys to the safe and later removed the deeds (except the mortgage) and used them to obtain a further mortgage. C executed a mortgage deed in favour of W, to whom he gave the deeds. W had no notice of the company's mortgage. Held: the court will postpone a legal mortgage to a subsequent equitable mortgage:

(a) where the legal mortgagee has assisted in or connived in the fraud which led to the creation of the subsequent equitable estate (in this regard the care of the legal mortgagee in inquiring after or keeping the title deeds may amount to evidence of assistance or connivance if his conduct cannot otherwise be explained); or

(b) where the mortgagor is given authority by the legal mortgagee to use the title deeds in order to raise money and the mortgagor, acting as the agent of the mortgagee, has not disclosed the existence of the prior mortgage

Mere carelessness or want of prudence on the part of the legal mortgagee as in this case, is not sufficient to lead to the court postponing a legal mortgagee to a subsequent equitable mortgagee.

Perry Herrick v Attwood (1857) 2 De G & J 21 (CA in Chancery)

The sisters of A had a mortgage in respect of a debt but let A keep the title deeds to enable him to obtain another mortgage in priority to their own. The deeds were deposited with B, as mortgagee. A later, and without B's concurrence, took back the deeds and used them to obtain a mortgage from P. A delivered the deeds to P, who had no notice of the mortgage to the sisters. Held: the mortgage to the sisters was postponed to that of P as they had allowed A to keep the deeds and put him in a position where he could hold himself out as being the unincumbered owner. P had relied on A's possession of the deeds before advancing moneys.

B: THE EQUITABLE MORTGAGEE'S POSITION PRIOR TO 1925 WHERE THE LAND WAS LEGAL

The general rule for priority between equitable mortgages on a legal estate of land was that the first in time had priority — *qui prior est tempore potior est jure*. There were, however, two exceptions to this rule:

(a) For the rule to apply the equities had to be equal. Negligence on the part of the earlier equitable mortgagee would therefore cause him to lose his priority. It could amount to negligence if the mortgagee failed to obtain or retain the title deeds (see *Farrand* v *Yorkshire Banking Co.* (1888) 40 ChD 182, and *Waldron* v *Sloper* (1852) 1 Drew 193).

(b) Where the doctrine of tacking applied the rule would not apply. Before 1926 there were two ways in which tacking would arise:

(i) Where an equitable mortgagee acquired a legal estate in the land, for example—
1 July, legal mortgage of Blackacre to A.
2 July, equitable mortgage of Blackacre to B.
3 July, equitable mortgage of Blackacre to C.
30 July, C pays off A and takes a conveyance of Blackacre.

C would gain priority over B in respect of the amount advanced by A and his mortgage on 3 July, provided that B and C had equal equities. This would not be so, however, if he had notice of B's earlier mortgage at the time he made his mortgage (3 July), but his state of knowledge at the time he acquired the legal estate is not relevant.

(ii) Where further advances are made by a legal mortgagee, for example—
1 July, A advances money by way of legal mortgage to X on Blackacre.
2 July, B advances money by way of equitable mortgage to X on Blackacre.
3 July, C advances money by way of equitable mortgage to X on Blackacre.
10 July, A makes a further advance to X on security of Blackacre.

If A has no notice of the equitable mortgages created after his legal mortgage he could tack his second advance onto the first and recover the whole amount in priority to B and C. Again, the equities between A, B and C must be equal.

C: THE EQUITABLE MORTGAGEE'S POSITION POST 1925 WHERE THE LAND IS EQUITABLE

Law of Property Act 1925

137. Dealings with life interests, reversions and other equitable interests

(1) The law applicable to dealings with equitable things in action which regulates the priority of competing interest therein, shall, as respects dealings with equitable interests in land, capital money, and securities representing capital money effected after the commencement of this Act, apply to and regulate the priority of competing interests therein.

This subsection applies whether or not the money or securities are in court.

Dearle v *Hall*
(1823–8) 3 Russ 1 (High Court of Chancery)

X had a beneficial interest under a trust which he assigned to A for valuable consideration. A failed to serve a notice of assignment on the trustees. X fraudulently offered to sell the same interest to B. B made inquiry of the trustees as to the property before completing the purchase and was told by them that X's title was free from incumbrances. B completed the purchase and gave notice to the trustees of this. Held: the sale to B took priority.

SIR THOMAS PLUMBER: . . . It is observable in the first place, that the right, which *Zachariah Brown* had under the will of his father, was simply a right to a chose in action. The legal interest in the residue was vested in the executrix and executors; . . . wherever it is intended to complete the transfer of a chose in action, there is a mode of dealing with it which a court of equity considers tantamount to possession, namely, notice given to the legal depositary of the fund. Where a contract, respecting property in the hands of other persons, who have a legal right to the possession, is made behind the back of those in whom the legal interest is thus vested, it is necessary, if the security is intended to attach on the thing itself, to lay hold of that thing in the manner in which its nature permits it to be laid hold of — that is, by giving notice of the contract to those in whom the legal interest is. By such notice, the legal holders are converted into trustees for the new purchaser, and are charged with responsibility towards him; and the *cestui que trust* is deprived of the power of carrying the same security repeatedly into the market, and of inducing third persons to advance money upon it, under the erroneous belief that it continues to belong to him absolutely, free from incumbrance, and that the trustees are still trustees for him and for no one else. That precaution is always taken by diligent purchasers and incumbrancers: if it is not taken, there is neglect; and it is fit that it should be understood, that the solicitor, who conducts the business for the party advancing the money, is responsible for that neglect. The consequence of such neglect is, that the trustee of the fund remains ignorant of any alteration having taken place in the equitable rights affecting it: he considers himself to be a trustee for the same individual as before, and no other person is known to him as his *cestui que trust*. The original *cestui que trust*, though he has in fact parted with his interest, appears to the world to be the complete equitable owner, and remains in the order, management, and disposition of the property as absolutely as ever; so that he has it in his power to obtain, by means of it, a false and delusive credit. He may come into the market to dispose of that which he has previously sold; and how can those, who may chance to deal with him, protect themselves from his fraud? Whatever diligence may be used by a *puisne* incumbrancer or purchaser — whatever inquiries he may make in order to investigate the title, and to ascertain the exact state of the original right of the vendor, and his continuing right, — the trustees, who are the persons to whom application for information would naturally be made, will truly and unhesitatingly represent to all who put questions to them, that the fund remains the sole absolute property of the proposed vendor. These inconveniences and mischiefs are the natural consequences of omitting to give notice to trustees; and they must be considered as foreseen by those who, in transactions of that kind, omit to give notice; for they are the consequences which, in the experience of mankind, usually follow such omissions. To give notice is a matter of no difficulty: and whenever persons, treating for a chose in action, do not give notice to the trustee or executor, who is the legal holder of the fund, they do not perfect their title; they do not do all that is necessary in order to make the thing belong to them in preference to all other persons; and they become responsible, in some respects, for the easily foreseen consequences of their negligence. . . .

The ground of this claim is priority of time. They rely upon the known maxim, borrowed from the civil law, which in many cases regulates equities — '*qui prior est in tempore, potior est in jure*'. If, by the first contract, all the thing is given, there remains nothing to be the subject of the second contract, and priority must decide. But it cannot be contended that priority in time must decide, where the legal estate is outstanding.

For the maxim, as an equitable rule, admits of exception, and gives way, when the question does not lie between bare and equal equities. If there appears to be, in respect of any circumstance independent of priority of time, a better title in the *puisne* purchaser to call for the legal estate, than in the purchaser who precedes him in date, the case ceases to be a balance of equal equities, and the preference, which priority of date might otherwise have given, is done away with and counteracted. The question here is, — not which assignment is first in date, — but whether there is not, on the part of *Hall*, a better title to call for the legal estate than *Dearle* or *Sherring* can set up? or rather, the question is, Shall these Plaintiffs now have equitable relief to the injury of *Hall*?

What title have they shown to call on a court of justice to interpose on their behalf, in order to obviate the consequences of their own misconduct? All that has happened is owing to their negligence (a negligence not accounted for) in forbearing to do what they ought to have done, what would have been attended with no difficulty, and what would have effectually prevented all the mischief which has followed. Is a Plaintiff to be heard in a court of equity, who asks its interposition in his behoof, to indemnify him against the effects of his own negligence at the expense of another who has used all due diligence, and who, if he is to suffer loss, will suffer it by reason of the negligence of the very person who prays relief against him? The question here is not, as in *Evans* v *Bicknell*, whether a court of equity is to deprive the Plaintiffs of any right — whether it is to take from them, for instance, a legal estate, or to impose any charge upon them. It is simply, whether they are entitled to relief against their own negligence. They did not perfect their securities; a third party has innocently advanced his money, and has perfected his security as far as the nature of the subject permitted him; is this Court to interfere to postpone him to them?

They say, that they were not bound to give notice to the trustees; for that notice does not form part of the necessary conveyance of an equitable interest. I admit, that, if you mean to rely on contract with the individual, you do not need to give notice; from the moment of the contract, he, with whom you are dealing, is personally bound. But if you mean to go further, and to make your right attach upon the thing which is the subject of the contract, it is necessary to give notice; and, unless notice is given, you do not do that which is essential in all cases of transfer of personal property. The law of *England* has always been, that personal property passes by delivery of possession; and it is possession which determines the apparent ownership. If, therefore, an individual, who in the way of purchase or mortgage contracts with another for the transfer of his interest, does not divest the vendor or mortgagor of possession, but permits him to remain the ostensible owner as before, he must taken the consequences which may ensue from such a mode of dealing. That doctrine was explained in *Ryall* v *Rowles* (1 Ves Sen 348; 1 Atk 165), before Lord *Hardwicke* and three of the Judges. If you, having the right of possession, do not exercise that right, but leave another in actual possession, you enable that person to gain a false and delusive credit, and put it in his power to obtain money from innocent parties on the hypothesis of his being the owner of that which in fact belongs to you. The principle has been long recognised, even in courts of law. In *Twyne's* case (3 Rep. 80), one of the badges of fraud was that the possession had remained in the vendor. Possession must follow right; and if you, who have the right, do not take possession, you do not follow up the title, and are responsible for the consequences.

Notes

1. The effect of s. 137 was to extend *Dearle* v *Hall* (which pre-1926 applied only when successive mortgages and assignments were made of an equitable

interest in pure personalty, be it legal or equitable) to successive mortgages and assignments of equitable interests over equitable freeholds and leaseholds.
2. In order to gain priority the mortgagee must give notice.

Law of Property Act 1925

137. Dealings with life interests, reversions and other equitable interests

(2)(i) In the case of a dealing with an equitable interest in settled land, capital money or securities representing capital money, the persons to be served with notice of the dealing shall be the trustees of the settlement; and where the equitable interest is created by a derivative or subsidiary settlement, the persons to be served with notice shall be the trustees of that settlement.

(ii) In the case of a dealing with an equitable interest in the proceeds of sale of land or in the rents and profits until sale the persons to be served with notice shall, as heretofore, be the trustees for sale.

(iii) In any other case the person to be served with notice of a dealing with an equitable interest in land shall be the estate owner of the land affected.

The persons on whom notice is served pursuant to this subsection shall be affected thereby in the same manner as if they had been trustees of personal property out of which the equitable interest was created or arose.

This subsection does not apply where the money or securities are in court.

(3) A notice, otherwise than in writing, given to, or received by, a trustee after the commencement of this Act as respects any dealing with an equitable interest in real or personal property, shall not affect the priority of competing claims of purchasers in that equitable interest.

Notes

1. In respect of equitable interests in settled land or capital money, notice must be given to the trustees of the settlement. Similarly, when dealing with interests in a derivative settlement, notice must be given to the trustees of the derivative settlement.
2. In the case of equitable interests in a trust for sale, notice must be given to the trustees for sale.
3. Where dealings take place with other forms of equitable interests, notice should be given to the estate owner.
4. If the notice is not given to all the trustees this may result in postponement to a later mortgagee. See *Smith* v *Smith* (1833) 2 C & M 231, in which a distinction was drawn between notice given to one of several trustees and notice given to all trustees in office for the time being. The former is only effective against later mortgages created whilst that trustee is in office. A notice to all trustees would continue to be valid after they have all left office.
5. Where land was registered, the priority of mortgages of the beneficial interest at one time depended on what was known as entry in the Index of Minor Interests. The Land Registration Act 1986, s. 5 abolished the index as it was not used, and now *Dearle* v *Hall* applies to registered and unregistered land.

D: THE MORTAGEE'S POSITION POST 1925 WHERE THE LAND IS LEGAL

See R. E. Megarry, 'Priority after 1925 of mortgages of a legal estate in land' [1940] CLJ 243.

The 1925 legislation introduced a scheme by which, in theory at least, priority of mortgages should depend upon the order of registration, and introduced a method for creating more than one legal mortgage of the same legal estate.

Law of Property Act 1925

97. Priorities as between puisne mortgages
Every mortgage affecting a legal estate in land made after the commencement of this Act, whether legal or equitable (not being a mortgage protected by the deposit of documents relating to the legal estate affected) shall rank according to its date of registration as a land charge pursuant to the Land Charges Act, 1925.

This subsection does not apply to mortgages or charges to which the Land Charges Act 1972 does not apply by virtue of section 14(3) of that Act (which excludes certain land charges created by instruments necessitating registration under the Land Registration Act 1925), or to mortgages or charges of registered land.

Note
See also the Law of Property Act 1925, s. 198(1) and the Land Charges Act 1925, ss. 2(4), 4(5) and 17(1).

If the mortgagee obtains the title deeds to the property, whether the mortgage is legal or equitable, then it is specifically provided that the mortgage cannot be registered. This appears to have been enacted to enable short-term lending, using deeds as security, to continue without the hindrance of registration.

(a) No mortgagee obtains title deeds
Where there is a series of mortgages none of which is accompanied by the delivery of title deeds, priority is governed by s. 97 of the Law of Property Act 1925 and s. 4(5) of the Land Charges Act 1972. There may be a problem with the interpretation of these two sections in the following situation:

(i) A creates a mortgage without taking title deeds.
(ii) B creates a mortgage without taking title deeds.
(iii) Mortgage A is registered.
(iv) Mortgage B is registered.
(v) C creates a mortgage without taking the title deeds.

The problem is that if one applies s. 4(5) of the Land Charges Act 1972, the latter mortgage has priority since the earlier mortgage was not registered when B mortgage was *created*. If one applies s. 97 of the Law of Property Act 1925, the former takes priority because it was registered as a land charge before B was *registered*.

See, however, A. D. Hargreaves (1939–41) 13 MLR 534; R. E. Megarry, 'Priority after 1925 of mortgages of a legal estate in land' (1940) 7 CLJ 253–257. The aim of the system is to allow a mortgagee to examine the mortgagor's title and see if it is encumbered in any way. The subsequent mortgagee will therefore take subject to prior mortgages registered before the subsequent charge is created, regardless of the order of registration.

Question
What is meant by the doctrine of subrogation and what is its use in priority of mortgages?

(b) Mortgagee obtains title deeds

Where the first mortgagee obtains title deeds there are four situations that require consideration:

(i) The first mortgage is legal, the second is equitable. Applying the pre-1926 rule here, the first mortgagee would have priority unless there was negligence on his part with regard to the deeds. Post–1925:

Law of Property Act 1925

13. Effect of possession of documents
This Act shall not prejudicially affect the right or interest of any person arising out of or consequent on the possession by him of any documents relating to a legal estate in land, nor affect any question arising out of or consequent upon any omission to obtain or any other absence of possession by any person of any documents relating to a legal estate in land.

Note
See also s. 97 of the Land Charges Act 1925.
The effect of such provisions would indicate that the position is the same as pre-1926.

(ii) Both mortgages are legal. Here it would appear that the first mortgagee would have priority since he has the earlier legal estate and possession of the deeds, although that priority may be lost if he is negligent in relation to the deeds.

(iii) The first mortgage is equitable, the second is legal. Pre-1926 the second mortgagee had priority unless he had failed to make enquiries as to the deeds, failed to insist on their production, or had notice of the first equitable mortgage at the time of his mortgage.

The question of what constitutes notice to the second mortgagee is answered by the legislation for these purposes.

Law of Property Act 1925

199. Restrictions on constructive notice

(1) A purchaser [including a mortgagee] shall not be prejudicially affected by notice of —

(i) any instrument or matter capable of registration under the provisions of the Land Charges Act, 1925, or any enactment which it replaces, which is void or not enforceable as against him under that Act or enactment, by reason of the non-registration thereof;

(ii) any other instrument or matter or any fact or thing unless —

(a) it is within his own knowledge, or would have come to his knowledge if such inquiries and inspections had been made as ought reasonably to have been made by him, or

(b) in the same transaction with respect to which a question of notice to the purchaser arises, it has come to the knowledge of his counsel, as such, or of his solicitor or other agent, as such, or would have come to the knowledge of his solicitor or other agent, as such, if such inquiries and inspections had been made as ought reasonably to have been made by the solicitor or other agent.

(2) Paragraph (ii) of the last subsection shall not exempt a purchaser from any liability under, or any obligation to perform or observe, any covenant, condition, provisions, or restriction contained in any instrument under which his title is derived, mediately or immediately; and such liability or obligation may be enforced in the same manner and to the same extent as if that paragraph had not been enacted.

(3) A purchaser shall not by reason of anything in this section be affected by notice in any case where he would not have been so affected if this section had not been enacted.

(4) This section applies to purchases made either before or after the commencement of this Act.

(iv) The first and second mortgages are equitable. Pre-1926 this was governed by the maxim *qui prior est tempore potior est jure*, and this presumably is still the case in the absence of fraud.

According to s. 97 of the Law of Property Act 1925, the first mortgagee will have priority over the second mortgage, with either a legal or equitable mortgage, if the first mortgagee registers his mortgage before the second mortgage is completed. Such a registration constitutes notice to all persons and for all purposes (s. 198). If the first mortgagee failed to obtain the title deeds due to gross negligence, then it is arguable that, despite registration, he may by virtue of s. 13 of the Law of Property Act 1925 be postponed to the second mortgagee on the principles of pre-1926 law.

The first mortgagee must register his mortgage before the second mortgage is completed, otherwise he will be postponed to the later mortgage under s. 4(5) of the Land Charges Act 1972. Although s. 13 of the Law of Property Act 1925 may preserve the right of the first mortgagee to plead that he has made inquiry about the deeds and accepted a reasonable excuse for their non-delivery, still post-1926 any subsequent mortgagee could reply that the first has been negligent in failing to register.

It should also be noted that successive mortgages of the same property can alter the priorities of the mortgages, without the mortgagor's consent, because usually the priority of mortgages affects merely the rights of mortgagees inter se — see *Cheah Theam Swee* v *Equiticorp Finance Group Ltd* [1991] 4 All ER 989.

(c) Tacking post-1925

Law of Property Act 1925

94. Tacking and further advances

(1) After the commencement of this Act, a prior mortgagee shall have a right to make further advances to rank in priority to subsequent mortgages (whether legal or equitable) —

    (a) if an arrangement has been made to that effect with the subsequent mortgagees; or

    (b) if he had no notice of such subsequent mortgages at the time when the further advance was made by him; or

    (c) whether or not he had such notice as aforesaid, where the mortgage imposes an obligation on him to make such further advances.

This subsection applies whether or not the prior mortgage was made expressly for securing further advances.

(2) In relation to the making of further advances after the commencement of this Act a mortgagee shall not be deemed to have notice of a mortgage merely by reason that it was registered as a land charge [. . .], if it was not so registered at the [time when the original mortgage was created] or when the last search (if any) by or on behalf of the mortgagee was made, whichever last happened.

This subsection only applies where the prior mortgage was made expressly for securing a current account or other further advances.

(3) Save in regard to the making of further advances as aforesaid, the right to tack is hereby abolished:

Provided that nothing in this Act shall affect any priority acquired before the commencement of this Act by tacking, or in respect of further advances made without notice of a subsequent incumbrance or by arrangement with the subsequent incumbrancer.

(4) This section applies to mortgages of land made before or after the commencement of this Act, but not to charges registered under the Land Registration Act, 1925, or any enactment replaced by that Act.

Notes

1. A later mortgagee can no longer gain priority over an earlier one by buying the legal estate (but see *McCarthy & Stone Ltd* v *Julian S. Hodge & Co. Ltd* [1971] 1 WLR 1547).

2. The right to tack under s. 94 is given to the first mortgagee, the legal mortgagee or any prior mortgagee, legal or equitable, against every later mortgagee, but it can only be used:

    (a) when the later mortgagees agree; or

    (b) when a mortgagee has no notice of subsequent mortgagees when making a further advance; or

(c) when the mortgage imposes an obligation on the mortgagee to make further advances.

For the purpose of (b) above, the registration of a later mortgage as a land charge is deemed to constitute actual notice (Law of Property Act 1925, s. 198(1).

See R. Geoffrey Rowley, 'Tacking further advances' (1958) 22 Conv 44.

Questions
1. Are there any problems with the relationship between s. 97 Law of Property Act 1925 and s. 4(5) Land Charges Act 1972?
2. On 1 July 1992 Arthur grants a legal mortgage of Blackacre to Brian, the mortgage having been protected by the deposit of title deeds. On 12 July 1992 Arthur grants a second legal mortgage of Blackacre to Colin. This mortgage was not protected by a deposit of title deeds. On 14 July 1992 Arthur grants a third legal mortgage to Derek. This again has not been protected by the deposit of title deeds. On 16 July 1992 Colin registers his intent on the land charges register and on 30 July Derek also registers his interest. What is the priority of the mortgages?

SECTION 8: MORTGAGES OF REGISTERED LAND

A mortgage of registered land may be created in one of three ways:

(a) a registered charge;
(b) an unregistered mortgage;
(c) deposit of the land or charge certificate.

(a) Registered charge

Land Registration Act 1925

25. Proprietor's power to create charges
(1) The proprietor of any registered land may by deed —
(a) charge the registered land with the payment at an appointed time of any principal sum of money either with or without interest;
(b) charge the registered land in favour of a building society [(within the meaning of the Building Societies Act 1986), in accordance with] the rules of that society.
(2) A charge may be in any form provided that —
(a) the registered land comprised in the charge is described by reference to the register or in any other manner sufficient to enable the registrar to identify the same without reference to any other document;
(b) the charge does not refer to any other interest or charge affecting the land which —
(i) would have priority over the same and is not registered or protected on the register,
(ii) is not an overriding interest.
(3) Any provision contained in a charge which purports to —

(i) take away from the proprietor thereof the power of transferring it by registered disposition or of requiring the cessation thereof to be noted on the register; or

(ii) affect any registered land or charge other than that in respect of which the charge is to be expressly registered,
shall be void.

26. Registration of charges

(1) The charge shall be completed by the registrar entering on the register the person in whose favour the charge is made as the proprietor of such charge, and the particulars of the charge.

(2) A charge may be registered notwithstanding that it contains any trust, power to appoint new trustees, or other provisions for giving effect to the security.

(3) Where the land, in respect of which a charge is registered, is registered with a good leasehold, qualified or possessory title, the charge shall take effect subject to the provisions of this Act with respect to land registered with such a title.

27. Terms of years implied in or granted by charges

(1) A registered charge shall, unless made or taking effect by demise or subdemise, and subject to any provision to the contrary contained in the charge, take effect as a charge by way of legal mortgage.

(2) Subject to the provisions of the Law of Property Act 1925, a registered charge may contain in the case of freehold land, an express demise, and in the case of leasehold land an express subdemise of the land to the creditor for a term of years absolute, subject to a proviso for cesser on redemption.

(3) Any such demise or subdemise or charge by way of legal mortgage shall take effect from the date of the delivery of the deed containing the same, but subject to the estate or interest of any person (other than the proprietor of the land) whose estate or interest (whenever created) is registered or noted on the register before the date of registration of the charge.

(4) Any charge registered before the commencement of this Act shall take effect as a demise or subdemise of the land in accordance with the provisions of the Law of Property Act 1925, and the registered estate shall (without prejudice to any registered charge or any term or subterm created by a charge or by this Act) vest in the person appearing by the register to be entitled to the ultimate equity of redemption.

Notes
1. A registered charge is a legal interest created by deed and may be a charge by way of legal mortgage, or express demise (if the land is freehold), or express sub-demise (if the land is leasehold).
2. An equitable charge is not registrable under s. 25 (see *Re White Rose Cottages* [1965] Ch 940).
3. A legal estate does not arise until the charge is registered (see *Grace Rymer Investments Ltd* v *Waite* [1958] Ch 831).
4. The registered proprietor of a charge has all the powers conferred by law on the owner of a legal mortgage, subject to any entry on the register or provision in the charge to the contrary (see s. 34 of the Land Registration Act 1925).
5. If a mortgagee forecloses he will be registered as proprietor of the land, free of all incumbrances inferior to his charge.

6. If a mortgagee sells the land, on registration the sale is completed and the legal estate is vested in the purchaser, free of the cancelled charge and all inferior incumbrances and entries on the register.

7. A registered charge can only be discharged by that discharge being entered on the register.

Land Registration Act 1925

29. Priorities of registered charges
Subject to any entry to the contrary on the register, registered charges on the same land shall as between themselves rank according to the order in which they are entered on the register, and not according to the order in which they are created.

30. Protection of charges for securing further advances
(1) When a registered charge is made for securing further advances, the registrar shall, before making any entry on the register which would prejudicially affect the priority of any further advance thereunder, give to the proprietor of the charge at his registered address, notice by registered post of the intended entry, and the proprietor of the charge shall not, in respect of any further advance, be affected by such entry, unless the advance is made after the date when the notice ought to have been received in due course of post.

(2) If, by reason of any failure on the part of the registrar or the post office in reference to the notice, the proprietor of the charge suffers loss in relation to a further advance, he shall be entitled to be indemnified under this Act in like manner as if a mistake had occurred in the register; but if the loss arises by reason of an omission to register or amend the address for service, no indemnity shall be payable under this Act.

(3) Where the proprietor of a charge is under an obligation, noted on the register, to make a further advance, a subsequent registered charge shall take effect subject to any further advance made pursuant to the obligation.

Note
In the case of registered land, tacking can arise only if the registered proprietor is under an obligation to make further advances, or if a registered charge is made for securing future advances. The Law of Property Act 1925, s. 94 does not apply.

(b) Unregistered mortgage of registered land
Registered land may be mortgaged in the same way as if it were unregistered, provided there is no entry to the contrary on the register. Such a mortgage takes effect in equity and must be protected by means of notice or caution, as a minor interest — see *The Mortgage Corporation Ltd* v *Nationwide Credit Corporation Ltd, The Times*, 27 July 1992.

(c) Deposit of land or charge certificate

Land Registration Act 1925

66. Creation of liens by deposit of certificates
The proprietor of any registered land or charge may, subject to the overriding interests, if any, to any entry to the contrary on the register, and to any estates, interests, charges,

or rights registered or protected on the register at the date of the deposit, create a lien on the registered land or charge by deposit of the land certificate or charge certificate; and such lien shall, subject as aforesaid, be equivalent to a lien created in the case of unregistered land by the deposit of documents of title or of the mortgage deed by an owner entitled for his own benefit to the registered estate, or a mortgagee beneficially entitled to the mortgage, as the case may be.

Notes
The holder of the lien is bound by overriding interests, registered interests and any entries on the register.

Question
On 1 September 1991 Ann grants Betty a registrable mortgage of Whiteacre. On 15 September 1991 Ann grants Claudia a registrable mortgage on the same property. Betty registers her interest on 30 September 1991 and on 3 October Ann grants a registrable mortgage to Doris. What is the order of priority?

INDEX

Acquisition of land
  adverse possession *see* Adverse possession
  options to purchase   119–25
    nature of   120–4
    pre-emption rights   124–5
  see also Contract; Conveyance
Actual occupation   72–6
  act of   76–7
  date of occupation   81–5
  date of registration   84
  extent   80–1
  overreaching   65–7
  through agent   78–80
Adverse possession   126–53
  abandonment of possession
    not taken by another   148
    succession of squatters   148
    taken up by different squatter   148
  animus possidendi   129–31
  death of squatter   147–8
  foreclosure action   126–7
  interest acquired
    dispossession of lease   144–7
    third party rights   143–4
    title of former owner   142–3
    title of squatter   143
  registered land   148–52
  running of time   127–42
    breach of condition   133
    concealment   140–1
    disability   139–40
    forfeiture   133
    fraud   140–1
    future interests   133–4
    land held on trust   133–5
    mistake   140–1

Adverse possession – *continued*
  mortgages   138–9
  non-payment of rent   137
  periodic tenancies   137–8
  postponement of period   139–41
  present interests   127–32
  reversioner on lease   135
  rights of entry   137
  settled land   133–4
  starting time running afresh   141–2
  tenant   135–7
  squatting   128–30, 147–8
  successive squatters   147–8
  time limit for actions   126
  unregistered land   152
Animus possidendi   129–31
Annuities, register of   29
Assignment by original lessee   200–3
Attornment clause   447
Austerberry rules   397–401

Bankruptcy
  co-ownership   319–31
    interests of family   321–31
    petitions for sale by trustee in
      bankruptcy   321–2
    rights of occupation
      bankrupt   323
      spouse   322
    setting aside transactions   319–21
  see also Insolvency
Bargains, extortionate   442–4
Bona fide purchaser *see* Good faith purchaser
British Coal search   103

Charge Certificate   54, 55

Charges *see* Charge certificate; Charges register; Legal interests
Charges register 54
Chattels, real and personal 1
Children
  matrimonial home and 312–15
  trusts 250, 256
Co-ownership 294–341
  bankruptcy and s.30 319–31
    interests of family 321–31
    petitions for sale by trustee in bankruptcy 321–2
    rights of occupation
      bankrupt 323
      spouse 322
    setting aside transactions 319–21
  insolvency 316–19
  Law of Property Act 1925 s.30 311–16
  matrimonial property *see* Matrimonial property
  position in law and equity 297–300
  termination
    partition 310
    sale of legal estate 310
    union in sole ownership 311
  trust for sale 297–8
  underlying purpose test 312–16
  undivided share 295–6
  see also Joint tenancies; Tenancy in common
Collateral contracts 111–12
Collateral contractual rights 72
Commonholds 215
Concealment 140–1
Concessi 201
Conditions, breach of 133
Consideration 4, 46–7
  money or money's worth 47
  valuable 47, 92
Consolidation right 465–8
Constructive notice doctrine *see* Notice doctrine
Constructive trusts 91, 92–3
  contractual licences and 229, 232–6
Contract 103–4
  collateral contracts 72, 111–12
  effect of 112–13
  fraud 106
  made before 27 September 1989 104–8
    part performance doctrine 104–8
  made on or after 27 September 1989 108–12
    joinder of documents doctrine 109
  part performance 112
  pre-contract procedure 102–3
    British Coal search 103
    inquiries of vendor 103

Contract – *continued*
  local authority searches 102–3
  Public Index Map search 103
  register of commons search 103
  survey of property 103
  signature 110
  subject to contract 109, 110
  vendor dies before completion 112–13
  waiver doctrine 111
  in writing 104, 108–9
Contractual licences *see* Licences
Conversion doctrine 285, 298
Conveyance 113–16
  by deed 113–14, 115
  conveyancer meaning 110
  delivery 115–16
  incomplete transfers or creations 117–19
  parol of leases 114
  to self 116–17
Covenants
  breach *see* Leases, breach of covenants
  freehold *see* Freehold covenants
  leasehold *see* Leasehold covenants
  repairing covenant 28

Dearle v *Hall* rule 5, 473–6
Dedi 201
Deeds
  conveyancing 113–14, 115
  delivery 115–16
Deeds of arrangement 29
Delivery 115–16
Demisi 201
Detriment *see* Licences, estoppel and
Disclaimer 191
Discontinuance 127
Dispossession 127
Distress 197
Doctrine of conversion 285, 298
Doctrine of estates 14
Doctrine of joinder of documents 109
Doctrine of notice *see* Notice doctrine
Doctrine of part performance 104–8
Doctrine of tenures 14
Doctrine of waiver 111

Easements 245
  acquisition 354–90
    by prescription or presumed grant 369–86
      continuous user 373–4
      lost modern grant 376–81
      Prescription Act 1832 381–6
      prescription at common law 376
      prescription or long user method 369–70
      user in fee simple 374–6

Index

Easements – *continued*
    user as of right   370–3
    user without concealment   373
    express grant or reservation   354–62
        express grant   356–7
        Law of Property Act s.62   357–62
        reservation   357
        words implied in conveyances   357
    implied grant or reservation   362–9
        common intention   364–6
        easements of necessity   362–4
        implied grant   366–9
        implied reservation   362–6
        Wheeldon v *Burrows*   367–9
    dominant and servient land   343, 345
    dominant and servient owners different   343, 346
    dominant tenement accommodation   343, 346
    enjoyment beyond living memory   376, 380–1
    equitable easements   40, 63–4, 284
    extent of rights   386–90
        acquired by express grant   387–90
        acquired by prescription   386–7
        dominant tenement alteration   388–9
        servient tenement alteration   389–90
    extinguishing
        release   390
        statute   390
        unity of seisin   390–1
    legal   22, 63
    light and air   385
    must lie in grant   343, 346–9
        capable grantee   346–7
        capable grantor   347
        certainty of description   347–8
    nature of   342
    necessity   362–4
    negating factors   349–54
        exclusive or joint user   352–4
        expenditure of money by servient owner   349–50
        negative nature of right   350–2
        negative   350–2
        positive   350
    time immemorial   376, 380–1
    valid   342–9, 354
    wind and air   351
Encouragement   242
Enlargement   191–3
Entry rights
    legal interest   23 23
    running of time   137
Equitable charge, registration   29
Equitable easements   40, 63–4, 284

Equitable interests
    creation and disposition   17
    legal estates and   18
    notice doctrine   23
    overreaching   23, 41
    protection   23–41
    registrable interests
        annuities   29
        class D land charges   31–4
        class F land charges   34–6
        deeds of arrangement   29
        estate contract   29–31
        general equitable charge   29
        land charges *see* Registration of land charges
        pending actions registration   26–9
        puisne mortgage   29
        register of land charges   24–6
        section 2   29–36
        writs and orders affection land   29
    registration of land charges   23
    registration of title   23
    root title   24
    third-party rights   24
    transfer   117
    unregistered land   24
    unregistrable interests   37–41
        charging order on undivided share of land   41
        contractual licences   39
        estoppel-based   40–1
        resulting or implied trust beneficial interests   37–9
Equity
    development   2
    doctrine of notice   3–4
    land law and   2–3
    licences and *see* Licences, equity and
    licences coupled with   225–6
Equity of redemption *see* Mortgages
Estate contract registration   29–31
Estate per autre vie   16
Estates
    doctrine of estates   14
    legal *see* Legal Estates
    privity of estate   200, 202
Estoppel
    assignees of leasehold covenants and   214
    equitable interests based on   40–1
    licences and   234, 236–47
        detriment   237–41
            expenditure   237–8
            other than expenditure   238–41
        encouragement   242
        expectation or belief   241–2
        no bar to equity   242
        satisfaction of equity   242–4

Estoppel – *continued*
  tests for 236–7
Extortionate credit bargains 442–4

Facchini v *Bryson* test 171–2
Fee simple 15, 16
  absolute in possession 17–18
Fee tail 15, 16, 17
Fees *see* Fee simple; Fee tail; Modified fees
Feoffment 201
Foreclosure 126, 462–3
Forfeiture
  adverse possession 133
  joint tenancy severance 307
  leasehold covenants 208
  leases 190, 193–7
Fraud
  contract and 106
  limitation period postponement 140–1
Freehold covenants 392–423
  annexation
    delayed annexation by assignment 410
    express 405–7
    implied 407–9
    statutory 409–15
  assignment 397
  Austerberry rules 397–401
    chain of indemnity covenants 399
    circumvention 398–401
    Crow v *Wood* 400–1
    estate rentcharges 400
    Halsall v *Brizell* 399–400
    Law of Property Act s.79 401
    Law of Property Act s.153 399
    lease instead of sale 398
    re-entry rights 400
  common law
    benefits 394–7
    burden 397–8
    enforcement 394–401
  creation of restrictive covenants 423
  discharge of restrictive covenants 421–3, 423
  enforcement
    at common law 394–401
    between original parties 392–3
    in equity 401–21
  in equity
    benefit
      assignment 415–18
      see also annexation
    building scheme 418–21
    burden 403–4
    scheme of development 418–21
    Tulk v *Moxhay* 398, 402–3, 404–5
  notices of restrictive covenants 423
  registered land 423

Good faith purchaser 45
  notice doctrine 12–13
    with notice from purchaser without notice 13

Hereditaments
  corporeal 1–2
  incorporeal 1–2
  overriding interest registration 63–5
Hostel accommodation 179–81

Indemnity, registration of title 98–9
Infants
  matrimonial home and 312–15
  trusts 250, 256
Insolvency
  co-ownership 316–19
    charging orders 316
    property that may be charged 316–17
  see also Bankruptcy
Interesse termini 158
Interests
  creation by parol 114
  definition 110
  minor *see* Minor interests
  see also Equitable *and* Legal interests

Joinder of documents doctrine 109
Joint tenancies 294, 295, 296–7
  creation 300–2
  equitable presumption 301
  severance 302–10
    acquisition of larger interest 307
    alienation of interest 307
    course of dealing 309–10
    forfeiture 307
    mutual agreement 307–9
    notice in writing 302–7
  see also Co-ownership
Jus spatiandi 348

Land, meaning 2
Land Certificate 54, 55
Land charges
  class D 31–4
    equitable easements 31
    restrictive covenants 31
    unpaid inheritance tax 31
  class F 34–6
  register *see* Land Charges Register
  registration *see* Registration of land charges
Land Charges Act 1925 15
Land Charges Register 24–6, 54
  search *see* Search of land charges register
Law of Property Act 1925 14, 15

Index

Leasehold covenants
  assignment
    breaches before   205–7
    by original lessee   200–3
    by original lessor   203–8
  breach *see* Leases, breach of covenants
  burden of   202, 207–8
  in conveyance   203
  enforceability   198–209
  enforcement
    in agreement for lease   209–15
    benefit of covenant   211–14
    by and against sub-tenants   208–9
      forfeiture   208
    equitable lease   209
    estoppel application to assignees   214
    liabilities
      assignee of reversion to original tenant   210
      assignees   210–15
      original tenant to assignee   209–10
    Tulk v *Moxhay*   208
  feoffment   201
  implied covenants   203
  privity of estate   200, 202
  quodammodo annexed   201
  reversioner   203–4, 208
  touching and concerning land   199–200
Leases
  acceptance of surrender by mortgagor   446
  breach of covenants
    landlord's remedies
      action for arrears of rent   198
      damages for breach   198
      damages for waste   198
      distress   197
      ejectment proceedings   194
      forfeiture of lease   193–7
      injunction   198
      re-entry right enforcement   193
      waiver of breach   197
    tenant's remedies
      appointment of receiver   198
      damages for breach   198
      injunction   198
      self-help   198
      specific performance   198
  conditions required   154–70
    commencement date certain   155–62
    exclusive possession   163–70
    rent payment   162
    term certain   155–62
    term determinable by special notice   157
  covenants *see* breach of covenants; Leasehold covenants

Leases – *continued*
  creation of interests by parol   114
  discontinuous period   155
  dispossession of   144–7
  equitable lease   183–4
  fixed term lease   185
  forfeiture   208
  form   183–4
  future leases   158
  grant by legal mortgagee   454
  grant by mortgagor   445–6
  hostel accommodation   179–81
  interesse termini   158
  licences compared
    acts of friendship or generosity   171–2
    descriptive labels   173–4
    exclusive possession   164–70, 170–9
    Facchini v *Bryson* test   171–2
    intention   172
    joint occupation   174–9
    local authorities and   179–81
    non-residential tenancies   181–3
    rent payment   179
    service occupation   179
    services provision   172–3
    sham agreements   173–4
  licensees   164–70
  lifetime leases   158–9
  periodic tenancy   137–8, 161–2, 183, 185
  perpetually renewable   159–61
  rent   162
  reversioner   203–4, 208
    running of time   135
  running of time
    non-payment of rent   137
    periodic tenancies   137–8
    reversioner   135
    rights of entry   137
  service occupation   164, 166, 179
  Street v *Mountford*   163–70, 181–3
  surrender, acceptance by mortgagor   446
  tenancy at sufferance   186
  tenancy at will   186
  tenancy by estoppel
    covenants in leases   188–9
    determination of landlord's title   189
    'feeding the estoppel'   186–7
  term of years absolute   154, 156
  termination
    disclaimer   191
    enlargement   191–3
    expiry   189–90
    forfeiture   190, 193–7
    frustration   193
    merger   191
    notice to quit   190
    surrender   190–1

Leases – *continued*
  terms of years absolute 18–19
  until marriage 159
Legal estates 16–17
  equitable interests and 18
  fees
    modified 19–22
    subject to re-entry right 21
    see also Fee simple; Fee tail
  notice doctrine
    actual notice 9
    constructive notice 9–10
    equitable interests 8
    imputed notice 10–12
    mere equities 8
    priority of competing interests 4–5
    subsequent acquisition 5–8
  reduction in number 16
  terms of years absolute *see* Leases
  see also Matrimonial home and property
Legal interests
  charges created by statute 23
  easements *see* Easements
  mortgage *see* Mortgages, legal
  rentcharges 22–3, 400
  rights of entry 23
Legal mortgages *see* Mortgages, legal
Legislation
  purpose 15
  reduction in legal estates and interests in land 16
Licences
  bare licences 216
  contractual licences 71, 217–36
    equity and 225–6
    inferred 221–3
    revocability 217, 218–19
    specific performance 223
    third parties and
      binding on third parties 225–32
      traditional view 223–5
    unregistrable equitable interests 39
  coupled with grant or interest 217
  created by contract 219–20
  equity and 225–6
    dismissal of action 243
    easement 245
    equitable lien 243
    injunction 243
    lease 244
    licence for as long as encourager wishes 246
    licence until loan paid 246
    no bar to equity 242
    perpetual licence 245–6
    satisfaction of equity 242–4
    title 243

Licences – *continued*
  estoppel and 234, 236–47
    detriment 237–41
      expenditure 237–8
      other than expenditure 238–41
    encouragement 242
    expectation or belief 241–2
    satisfaction of equity 242–4
    tests for 236–7
    see also equity and
  leases compared
    acts of friendship or generosity 171–2
    descriptive labels 173–4
    exclusive possession 164–70, 170–9
    Facchini v *Bryson* test 171–2
    intention 172
    joint occupation 174–9
    local authorities and 179–81
    non-residential tenancies 181–3
    rent payment 179
    service occupation 179
    services provision 172–3
    sham agreements 173–4
  nature of 216
Licensees exclusive possession 164–70
Life estates 16, 17
Local authorities, lease licence distinction 179–81

Marriage consideration 4
Matrimonial home and property 322–31
  actual occupation *see* Actual occupation
  children 312–13, 314–15
  class F land charges 34–6
  conduct of female partner 340
  current view 337–41
  legal estate
    vested in both parties 332–3
    vested in one party alone 333–7
  occupation rights 68–71
  unmarried partners 322, 323, 337–9
Merger of leases 191
Minor interests
  donees 89
  failure to enter on register 88–95
  knowledge of unprotected interest 90–5
  meaning 87
  protection
    caution 88
    inhibition 88
    notice 87
  purchaser and 89
  registration 87–95
  trusts for sale 289
  see also Registration of title
Mirror principle 61

Index

Mistake, limitation period postponement 140–1
Modified fees 19–22
  conditional fees 20–1
  determinable fees 19, 20–1
  enlargement 22
  repugnant clauses 21–2
Mortgagees *see* Mortgages, rights of legal *and* equitable mortgagee
Mortgages 424–84
  acknowledgment or part payment 139
  charges by way of legal mortgage 426–7
  consolidation 465–8
  creation 424–8
    equitable mortgages 427–8
    freeholds 425
    leaseholds 425–6
  discharge 468–9
  equity of redemption 428–44
    collateral advantages 435–41
      unconscionable or oppressive 441–2
    exclusion of right to redeem 430–3
    extortionate credit bargains 442–3
    legal nature 428
    postponement of date 433–5
    restraint of trade 444
    undue influence 429–30
  priority 469–81
    behaviour 471, 472, 477–8
    Dearle v *Hall* rule 473–6
    equitable mortgagee
      post 1925 473–6
      prior to 1925 472–3
    legal mortgagee
      post 1925 477–81
      prior to 1925 469–72
    tacking post 1925 480–1
  puisne mortgages 477
  redemption *see* equity of redemption
  registered land 481–4
    deposit of land or charge certificate 483–4
    registered charge 481–3
    unregistered mortgage 483
  right to consolidate 465–8
  rights of equitable chargee 465
  rights of equitable mortgagee 464–8
    possession 465
    receiver appointment 465
    sale 464–5
    sue for debt 464
    title deeds 464
  rights of legal mortgagee
    common law relief of mortgagor 448–52
    equitable relief of mortgagor 452–3
    foreclosure 462–3

Mortgages – *continued*
  grant of leases 454
  insure at mortgagor's expense 454–5
  possession of land 447–553
  realisation of freehold mortgages 462
  receiver appointment 455
  sale *see* Sale, rights of legal mortgagee
  sue on personal covenant 453–4
  tacking 463
  title deeds 455
  rights of mortgagor
    acceptance of surrender of leases 446
    grant of lease 445–6
    sue 447
    see also equity of redemption
  running of time 138–9
  tacking 6, 480–1
  time limit for redemption actions 138
  title deeds
    mortgagee obtains 478–80
    mortgagee right to 455, 464
    no mortgagee obtains 477–8
Mortgagor *see* Mortgages, rights of mortgagor

National Conveyancing Protocol 103
Notice doctrine 3–4
  constructive notice 37, 38
  equitable interest 23
  good faith purchaser 12–13
    with notice from purchaser without notice 13
  legal estate
    equitable interests 8
    mere equities 8
    priority of interests 4–5
    subsequent acquisition 5–8
  minor interests 87
  purchaser for value 4
  without notice
    actual notice 9
    constructive notice 9–10
    imputed notice 10–12

Occupation of matrimonial home 68–71
  see also Actual occupation
Option right 30
Options to purchase 119–25
  nature of 120–4
  pre-emption rights 124–5
Overreaching 23, 32
  ad hoc settlements or trusts for sale 285–6
  equitable interests 41
  registration of overriding interests 85–7
  strict settlements 282–3
  trusts for sale 283–6

Overriding interests
  rectification of register and 96–7
  see also Registration of title, overriding interests
Ownership, co-ownership see Co-ownership

Parol of leases 114
Part performance doctrine 104–8, 112
Pending action registration 26–9
Periodic tenancies 137–8, 161–2, 183, 185
Perpetual licence 245–6
Perpetuities, rule against 119
Possession
  acquisition of title by 148–52
  adverse see Adverse possession
  definition 18
  fee simple absolute in possession 17–18
  leases and exclusive possession 163–70
  rights of equitable mortgagee 465
  rights of legal mortgagee 447–553
Power of sale see Sale, rights of legal mortgagee
Pre-emption rights 29–31, 124–5
Priorities
  Dearle v Hall rule 5
  legal estate competing interests 4–5
  mortgages see Mortgages
  registration of land charge 51–2
  registration of title 99–101
Privity of estate 200, 202
Profits a prendre 63, 391
Property
  chattels 1
  classification 1–2
  hereditaments 1–2
  personal 1
  real 1
  trust property 3
Property adjustment order 26–8
Property register 54
Proprietary estoppel see Estoppel, licences and
Proprietary register 54
Public Index Map search 103
Puisne mortgages 477
  registration 29
Purchaser
  for value 4, 46
  meaning 42, 44, 45, 46, 47
  see also Good faith purchaser

Quasi-matrimonial property see Matrimonial home and property

Re-entry
  fees subject to 21
  freehold covenants 400

Re-entry – *continued*
  landlord's right 193
  repugnant clauses 21–2
Receiver appointment
  by equitable mortgagee 465
  by legal mortgagee 455
Redemption see Mortgages, equity of redemption
Register of annuities 29
Register of land charges 24–6
  entry 48
Registered land
  adverse possession 148–52
  freehold covenants 423
  mortgages 481–4
    deposit of land or charge certificate 483–4
    registered charge 481–3
    unregistered mortgage 483
  settlements 271
  trusts for sale 281–2
Registration of land charges
  effect of 41–52
  entry on register 48
  failure to register 42–8
  priority notices 51–2
  purchaser 42, 44, 45, 46, 47
  searches 48–51
    land charges discovered
      after completion 50–1
      after contracts exchanged 49–50
      after lease grant 51
    Search Certificate 49
Registration of title 53–101
  actual occupation, date of registration 84
  charge certificate 54, 55
  charges register 54
  fraud and 93–5
  indemnity 98–9
  land certificate 54, 55
  Land Charges Acts 1925 and 1972 53–4
  Land Registration Act 1925 53–4
  minor interests 87–95
  overriding interests 61–87
    actual occupation
      act of 76–7
      date of occupation 81–5
      extent 80–1
      through agent 78–80
    incorporeal hereditaments 63–5
    leases for terms not exceeding 21 years 65
    liability of registered land to 61–2
    Limitation Acts 65
    meaning 61
    overreaching 85–7
    receipt of rent and profits 72–85

Index

Registration of title – *continued*
   section 70(1)(g)   65–87
      actual occupation   72–85
      conditions   66
      objects of section   65–6
      rights not within section   67–72
      rights within section   66–7
   priorities   99–101
   property register   54
   proprietorship register   54
   rectification   95–8
      contribution by registered proprietor to error   97
      effect   97–8
      effective date   98
      statutory circumstances   96–7
      unjust so to do   97
   register of title   54–5
   registered interests   55–61
      first registration   56–7
      grades of title
         absolute freehold title   57
         absolute leasehold title   58–9
         conversion of title   58
         good leasehold title   59
         possessory freehold title   57–8
         possessory leasehold title   59
         qualified freehold title   58
         qualified leasehold title   59–60
      registration of leaseholds   60
      subsequent transfers of registered land   61
      upgrading of titles   60
   settled land   68
Rent   162
Rentcharges   22–3, 400
Repair duty   349–50
Repairing covenants   28
Repugnant clauses   21–2
Restraint of trade   444
Restrictive covenants
   creation   423
   discharge   421–3, 423
   notices of   423
   registered land   423
Reversioner on lease   203–4, 208
   running of time   135
Reverter right   21
Right of option   30
Right of pre-emption   29–31, 124–5
Right of reverter   21
Rights of entry *see* Entry rights
Root title   24

Sale
   rights of equitable mortgagee   464–5
   rights of legal mortgagee   456–62

Sale – *continued*
   application of proceeds   459
   conveyance on sale   458–9
   duty to third parties   461
   genuine sale   461–2
   realisation of leasehold mortgages   459, 463
   taken subject to prior mortgage   458
   true market value   460
Search of land charges register   48–51
   land charges discovered
      after completion   50–1
      after contracts exchanged   49–50
      after lease grant   51
   Search Certificate   49
Searches
   pre-contract   102–3
   pre-contract procedure
      British Coal   103
      Commons Register   103
      Public Index Map search   103
   see also Search of land charges register
Seisin, unity of   390–1
Self-help remedy   198
Service occupation   164, 179
Settled land
   adverse possession   133–4
   registration   68, 271
Settled Land Act 1925   15
Settlements *see* Strict settlements; Trustees; Trusts; Trusts for sale
Signature   110
Specific performance
   contractual licences   223
   tenant's remedy   198
Squatters *see* Adverse possession
Statutory trusts   295
Strict settlements   248, 249–71
   creation
      by will   253
      inter vivos   252
      vesting deeds   252
   definition   249–51
   duration   270–1
   family arrangements   251
   incompletely constituted settlements   253–4
   infants   250, 256
   limitation subject to gift over   250
   overreaching   282–3, 295–6
   ownership change   262–5
   protection of purchasers   265–70
      good faith purchaser   268–70
      restriction on dispositions   265–6
      trustees' receipts   266
   registered land   271
   'springing interest'   250–1

Strict settlements – *continued*
  tenant for life
    meaning 254–5
    no tenant for life 256
    powers 258–60
      exercisable with consent 259
      exercisable on giving notice 259
      fiduciary nature of 261–2
      non-assignability of powers 260–1
    termination 270–1
    trustees 256–8
      appointment 257
      compound settlements 257
      functions 257
'Subject to contract' 109, 110

Tacking 463, 480–1
  mortgages 6
Tenancy in common 294, 297
  exists in equity 297
  future dispositions 294–5
  resulting from trusts 298–9
  see also Co-ownership
Tenant for life *see* Strict settlements, tenant for life
Tenants; Tenancy *see also* Leases
Tenures doctrine 14
Testator's estate 16
Title
  absolute freehold 57
  absolute leasehold 58–9
  conversion of 58
  good leasehold 59
  possessory freehold 57–8
  possessory leasehold 59
  qualified freehold 58
  qualified leasehold 59–60
  rectification
    contribution by registered proprietor to error 97
    effect 97–8
    effective date 98
    of register 95–8
    statutory circumstances 96–7
    unjust so to do 97
  registration *see* Registration of title
  root title 24
  unregistered land 24
  upgrading 60
Title deeds
  mortgagee obtains 478–80
  no mortgagee obtains 477–8
  retention

Title deeds – *continued*
  by equitable mortgagee 464
  by legal mortgagee to 455
Transfers
  equitable interests 117
  incomplete 117–19
  see also Conveyance
Trust land
  adverse possession 133–4
  time limit for actions 134–5
Trust property 3
Trustee Act 1925 15
Trustees 3
  in bankruptcy 321–2
  constructive 91, 92–3
  numbers of 300
  see also Strict settlements; Trusts; Trusts for sale
Trusts 2–3
  beneficial interests under 37–9
  constructive trusts 229, 232–6
  statutory 295
  see also Strict settlements: Trusts for sale
Trusts for sale 248–9, 271–82
  beneficial interest 286–93
  binding, meaning 273–6
  co-ownership and 297–8
  creation 276–7
  definitions 271–6
  immediate sale 273
  minor interests 289
  numbers of trustees 281–2, 300
  overreaching 282, 283–6
  postponement of sale 272, 277–8
  powers of trustees
    consent and consultations 279
    delegation 280–1
    Settled Land Act powers 279–80
    to postpone sale 277–8
  re-investment in land 281
  registered land 281–2
  undivided shares to take effect behind 295–6

Undue influence 429–30
Unregistered land
  adverse possession 152
  root title 24
  title evidenced by deeds 24

Vendor, pre-contract inquiries of 103

Waiver doctrine 111